/ENGERS VS. X-MEN. Contains material originally published in magazine form as AVENGERS VS. X-MEN #0-12 and POINT ONE #1. First printing 2013. ISBN# 978-0-7851-6318-3. Published by MARVEL ORLDWIDE, INC., a subsidiary of MARVEL ENTERTAINMENT, LLC. OFFICE OF PUBLICATION: 135 West 50th Street, New York, NY 10020. Copyright © 2012 and 2013 Marvel Characters, Inc. All rights reserved. # characters featured in this issue and the distinctive names and likenesses thereof, and all related indicia are trademarks of Marvel Characters, Inc. No similarity between any of the names, characters, ersons, and/or institutions in this magazine with those of any living or dead person or institution is intended, and any such similarity which may exist is purely coincidental. Printed in the U.S.A. ALAN FINE, /P - Office of the President, Marvel Worldwide, Inc. and EVP & CMO Marvel Characters B.V.; DAN BUCKLEY, Publisher & President - Print, Animation & Digital Divisions; JOE QUESADA, Chief Creative Officer;)M BREVOORT, SVP of Publishing; DAVID BOGART, SVP of Operations & Procurement, Publishing; RUWAN JAYATILLEKE, SVP & Associate Publisher, Publishing; C.B. CEBULSKI, SVP of Creator & Content evelopment; DAVID GABRIEL, SVP of Print & Digital Publishing Sales; JIM O'KEEFE, VP of Operations & Logistics; DAN CARR, Executive Director of Publishing Technology; SUSAN CRESPI, Editorial Operations anager; ALEX MORALES, Publishing Operations Manager; STAN LEE, Chairman Emeritus. For information regarding advertising in Marvel Comics or on Marvel.com, please contact Niza Disla, Director of arvel Partnerships, at ndisla@marvel.com. For Marvel subscription inquiries, please call 800-217-9158. Manufactured between 2/7/2013 and 3/2/2013 by QUAD/GRAPHICS, VERSAILLES, KY, USA.

)987654321

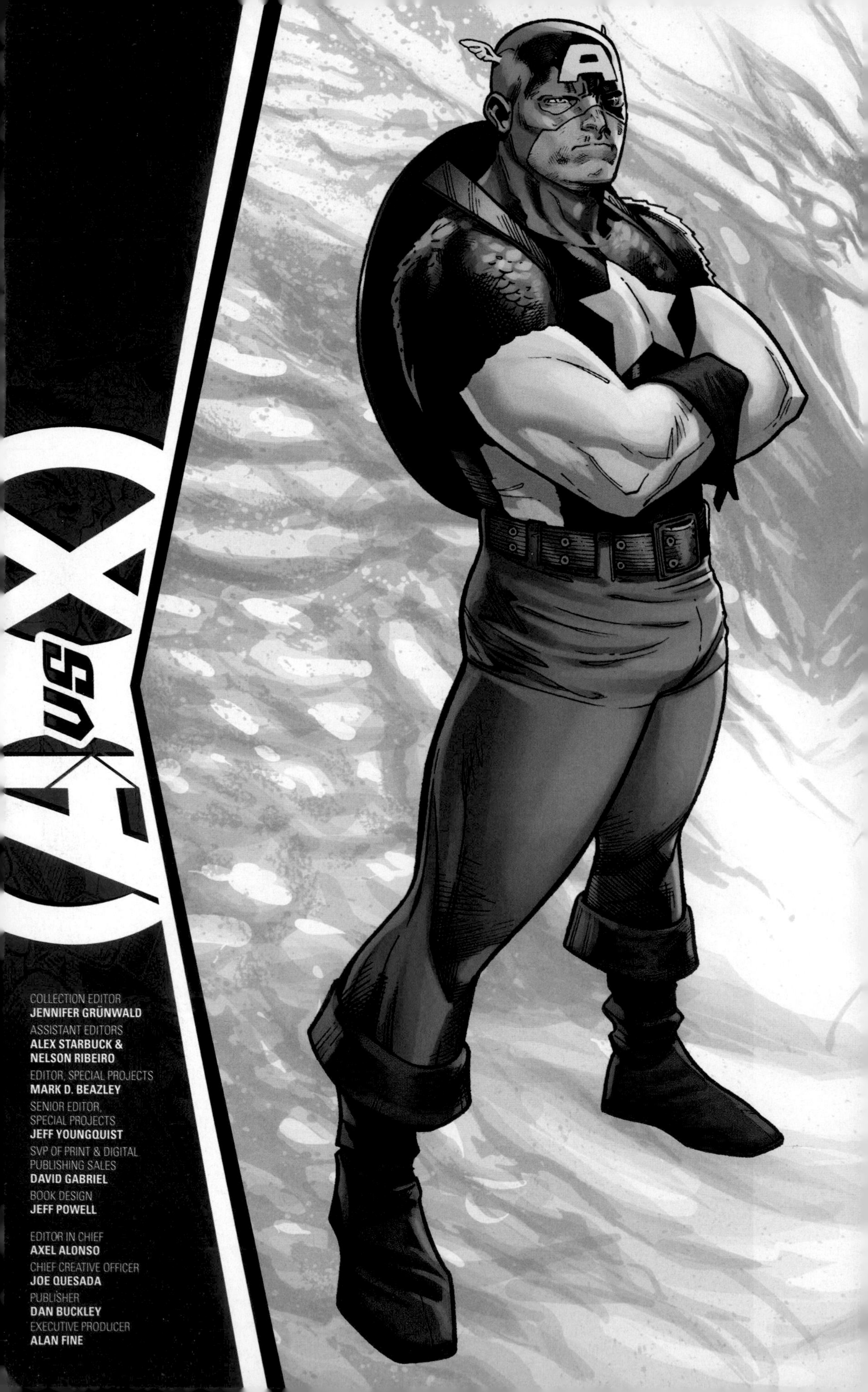

COLLECTION EDITOR
JENNIFER GRÜNWALD
ASSISTANT EDITORS
ALEX STARBUCK & NELSON RIBEIRO
EDITOR, SPECIAL PROJECTS
MARK D. BEAZLEY
SENIOR EDITOR, SPECIAL PROJECTS
JEFF YOUNGQUIST
SVP OF PRINT & DIGITAL PUBLISHING SALES
DAVID GABRIEL
BOOK DESIGN
JEFF POWELL

EDITOR IN CHIEF
AXEL ALONSO
CHIEF CREATIVE OFFICER
JOE QUESADA
PUBLISHER
DAN BUCKLEY
EXECUTIVE PRODUCER
ALAN FINE

STORY
JASON AARON, BRIAN MICHAEL BENDIS, ED BRUBAKER, MATT FRACTION & JONATHAN HICKMAN

POINT ONE #1
WRITER: **JEPH LOEB**
PENCILER: **ED McGUINNESS**
INKER: **DEXTER VINES**
COLORS: **MORRY HOLLOWELL**
COVER ART: **ADAM KUBERT & MORRY HOLLOWELL**

AVENGERS VS. X-MEN #0
WRITERS: **BRIAN MICHAEL BENDIS** (SCARLET WITCH) **& JASON AARON** (HOPE)
ARTIST: **FRANK CHO**
COLOR ART: **JASON KEITH**
COVER ART: **FRANK CHO & JASON KEITH**

AVENGERS VS. X-MEN #1
SCRIPT: **BRIAN MICHAEL BENDIS**
PENCILS: **JOHN ROMITA JR.**
INKS: **SCOTT HANNA**
COLORS: **LAURA MARTIN**
COVER ART: **JIM CHEUNG & JUSTIN PONSOR**

AVENGERS VS. X-MEN #2
SCRIPT: **JASON AARON**
PENCILS: **JOHN ROMITA JR.**
INKS: **SCOTT HANNA**
COLORS: **LAURA MARTIN**
COVER ART: **JIM CHEUNG & LAURA MARTIN**

AVENGERS VS. X-MEN #3
SCRIPT: **ED BRUBAKER**
PENCILS: **JOHN ROMITA JR.**
INKS: **SCOTT HANNA**
COLORS: **LAURA MARTIN**
COVER ART: **JIM CHEUNG & LAURA MARTIN**

AVENGERS VS. X-MEN #4
SCRIPT: **JONATHAN HICKMAN**
PENCILS: **JOHN ROMITA JR.**
INKS: **SCOTT HANNA**
COLORS: **LAURA MARTIN**
COVER ART: **JIM CHEUNG & LAURA MARTIN**

AVENGERS VS. X-MEN #5
SCRIPT: **MATT FRACTION**
PENCILS: **JOHN ROMITA JR.**
INKS: **SCOTT HANNA**
COLORS: **LAURA MARTIN**
COVER ART: **JIM CHEUNG & JUSTIN PONSOR**

AVENGERS VS. X-MEN #6
SCRIPT: **JONATHAN HICKMAN**
PENCILS: **OLIVIER COIPEL**
INKS: **MARK MORALES**
COLORS: **LAURA MARTIN**
COVER ART: **JIM CHEUNG & JUSTIN PONSOR**

AVENGERS VS. X-MEN #7
SCRIPT: **MATT FRACTION**
PENCILS: **OLIVIER COIPEL**
INKS: **MARK MORALES**
COLORS: **LAURA MARTIN**
COVER ART: **JIM CHEUNG & JUSTIN PONSOR**

AVENGERS VS. X-MEN #8
SCRIPT: **BRIAN MICHAEL BENDIS**
PENCILS: **ADAM KUBERT**
INKS: **JOHN DELL**
COLORS: **LAURA MARTIN** WITH **LARRY MOLINAR**
COVER ART: **JIM CHEUNG & JUSTIN PONSOR**

AVENGERS VS. X-MEN #9
SCRIPT: **JASON AARON**
PENCILS: **ADAM KUBERT**
INKS: **JOHN DELL**
COLORS: **LAURA MARTIN** WITH **LARRY MOLINAR**
COVER ART: **JIM CHEUNG, MARK MORALES & JUSTIN PONSOR**

AVENGERS VS. X-MEN #10
SCRIPT: **ED BRUBAKER**
PENCILS: **ADAM KUBERT**
INKS: **JOHN DELL**
COLORS: **LAURA MARTIN** WITH **LARRY MOLINAR**
COVER ART: **JIM CHEUNG & JUSTIN PONSOR**

AVENGERS VS. X-MEN #11
SCRIPT: **BRIAN MICHAEL BENDIS**
PENCILS: **OLIVIER COIPEL**
INKS: **MARK MORALES**
COLORS: **LAURA MARTIN**
COVER ART: **JIM CHEUNG & JUSTIN PONSOR**

AVENGERS VS. X-MEN #12
SCRIPT: **JASON AARON**
PENCILS: **ADAM KUBERT**
INKS: **JOHN DELL** WITH **MARK MORALES & ADAM KUBERT**
COLORS: **LAURA MARTIN** WITH **JUSTIN PONSOR**
COVER ART: **JIM CHEUNG & JUSTIN PONSOR**

LETTERS: **CHRIS ELIOPOULOS**
WITH **COMICRAFT'S ALBERT DESCHESNE** (POINT ONE)
ASSISTANT EDITORS: **JOHN DENNING & JAKE THOMAS**
ASSOCIATE EDITOR: **LAUREN SANKOVITCH**
CONSULTING EDITOR: **NICK LOWE** EDITOR: **TOM BREVOORT**

AVSX

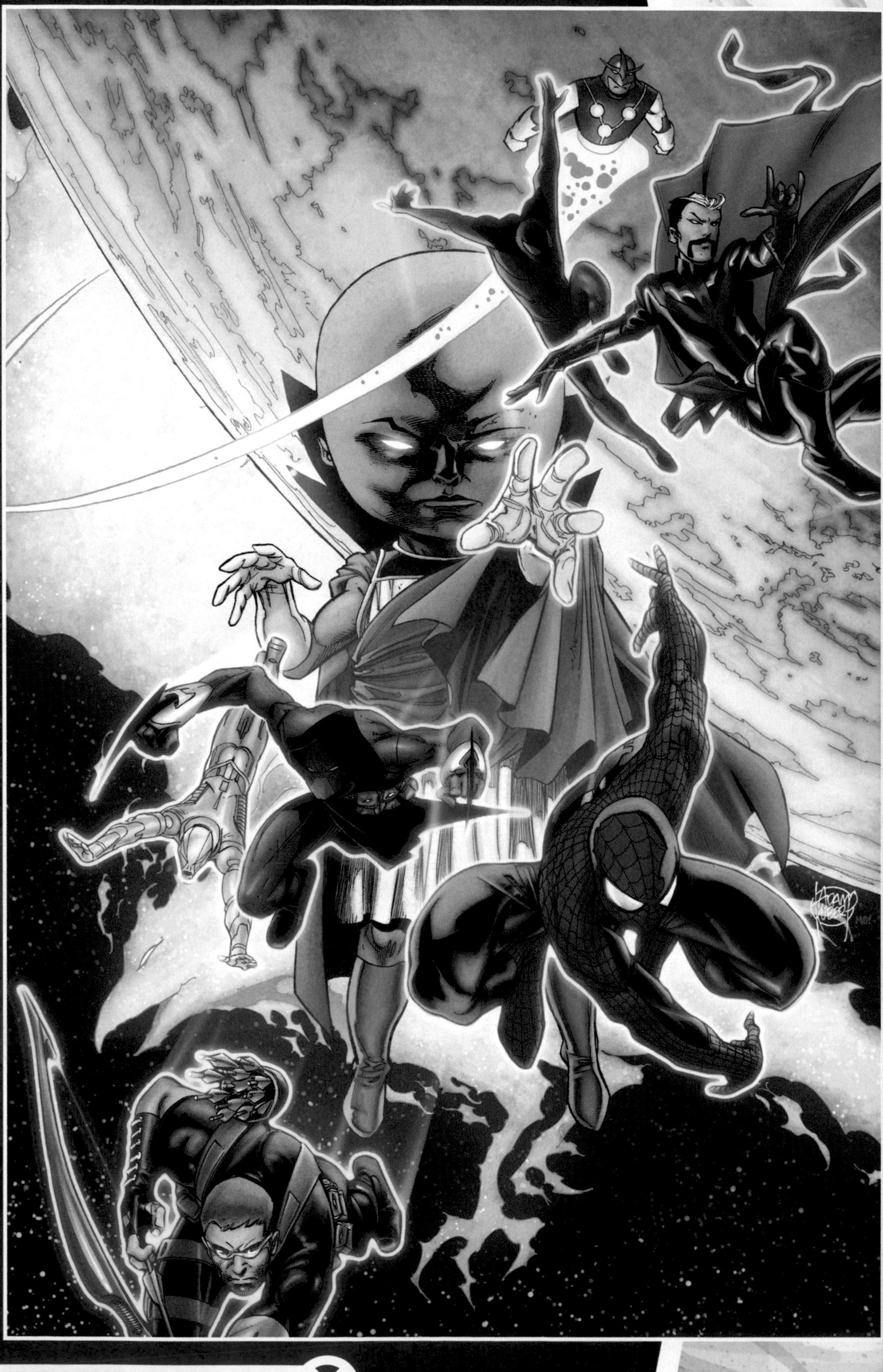

POINT ONE #1

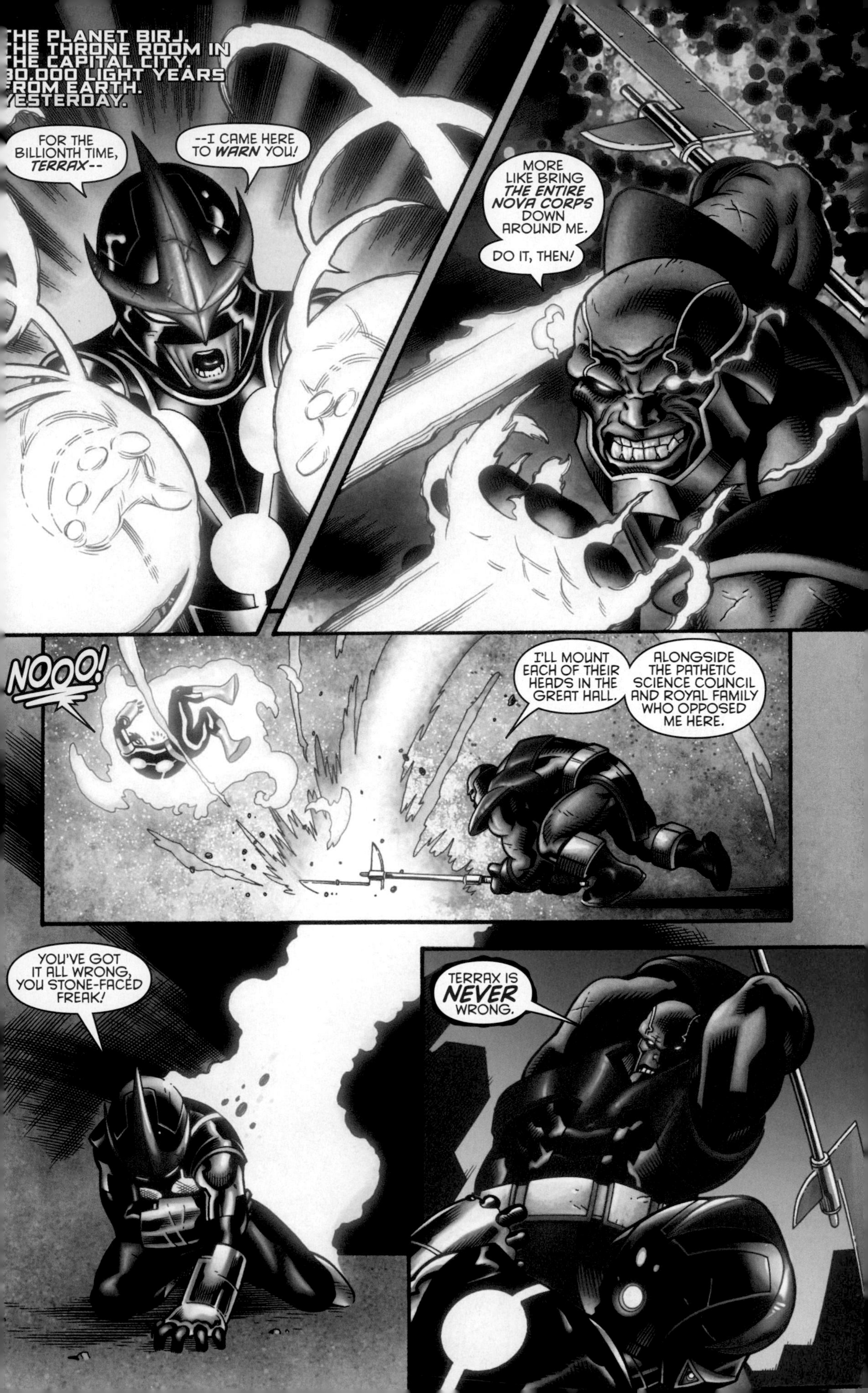
THE PLANET BIRJ. THE THRONE ROOM IN THE CAPITAL CITY. 30,000 LIGHT YEARS FROM EARTH. YESTERDAY.
FOR THE BILLIONTH TIME, TERRAX--
--I CAME HERE TO WARN YOU!
MORE LIKE BRING THE ENTIRE NOVA CORPS DOWN AROUND ME.
DO IT, THEN!
NOOO!
I'LL MOUNT EACH OF THEIR HEADS IN THE GREAT HALL.
ALONGSIDE THE PATHETIC SCIENCE COUNCIL AND ROYAL FAMILY WHO OPPOSED ME HERE.
YOU'VE GOT IT ALL WRONG, YOU STONE-FACED FREAK!
TERRAX IS NEVER WRONG.

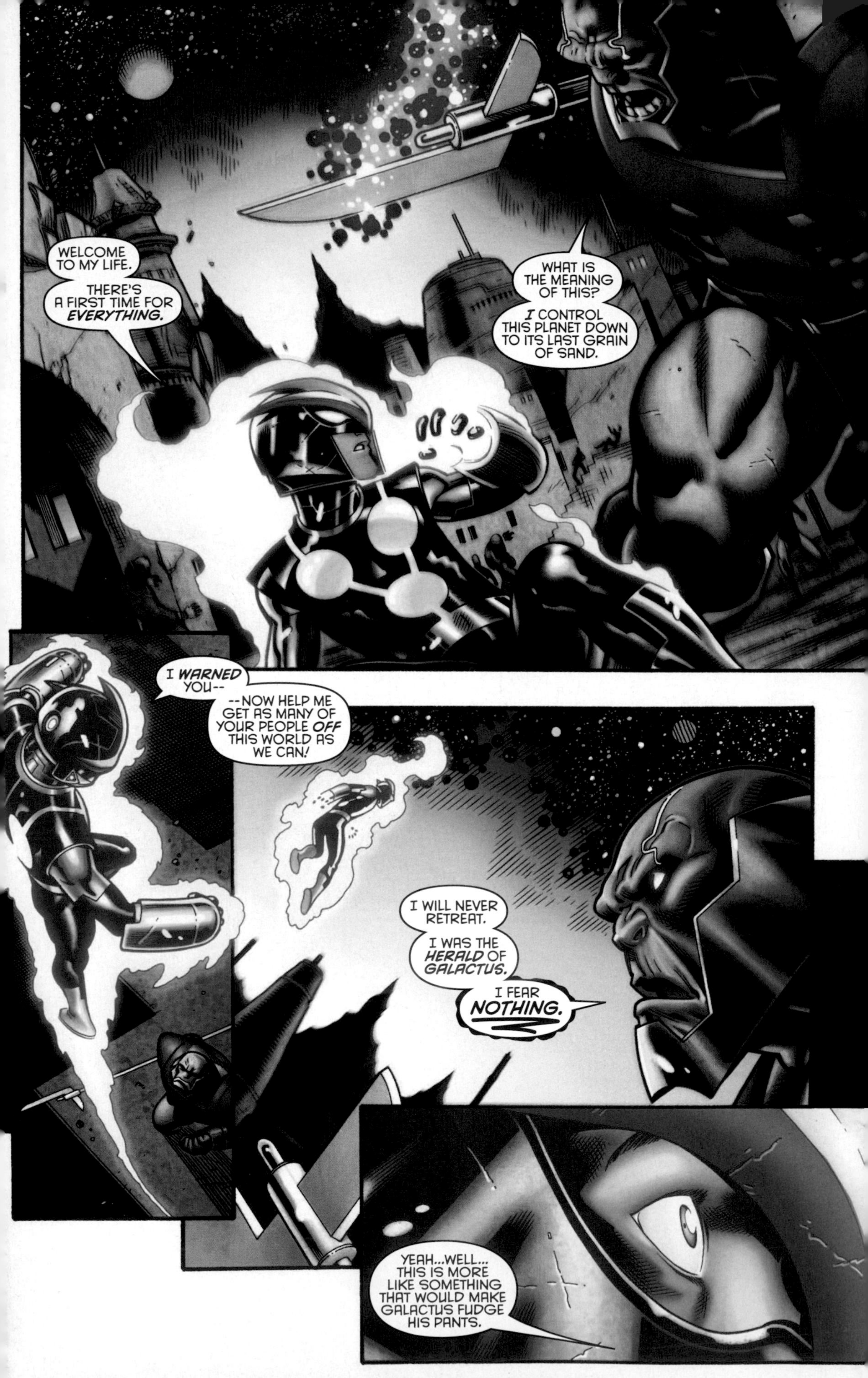
WELCOME TO MY LIFE.
THERE'S A FIRST TIME FOR EVERYTHING.
WHAT IS THE MEANING OF THIS?
I CONTROL THIS PLANET DOWN TO ITS LAST GRAIN OF SAND.
I WARNED YOU--
--NOW HELP ME GET AS MANY OF YOUR PEOPLE OFF THIS WORLD AS WE CAN!
I WILL NEVER RETREAT.
I WAS THE HERALD OF GALACTUS.
I FEAR NOTHING.
YEAH...WELL... THIS IS MORE LIKE SOMETHING THAT WOULD MAKE GALACTUS FUDGE HIS PANTS.

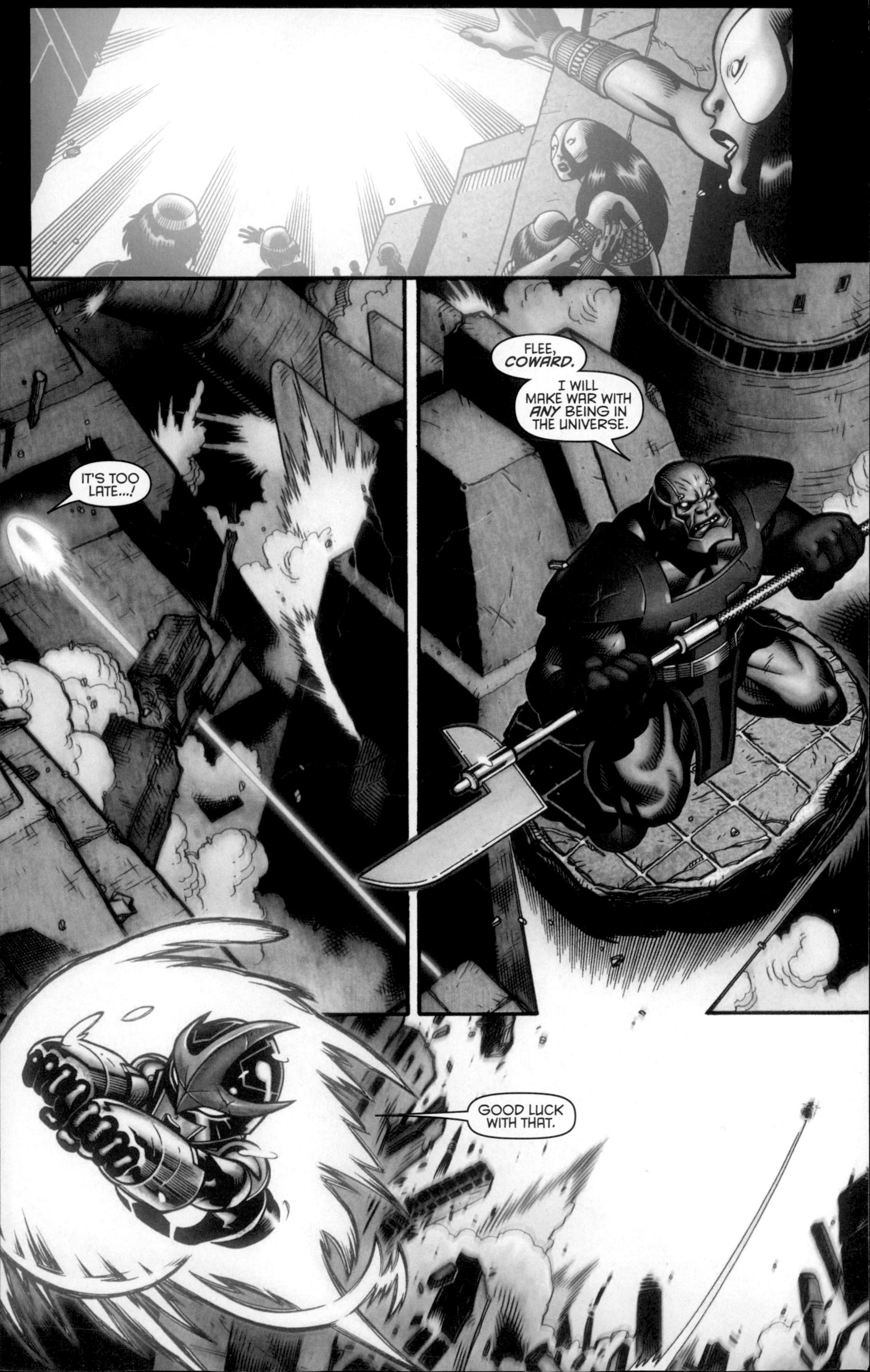
IT'S TOO LATE...!
FLEE, COWARD.
I WILL MAKE WAR WITH ANY BEING IN THE UNIVERSE.
GOOD LUCK WITH THAT.

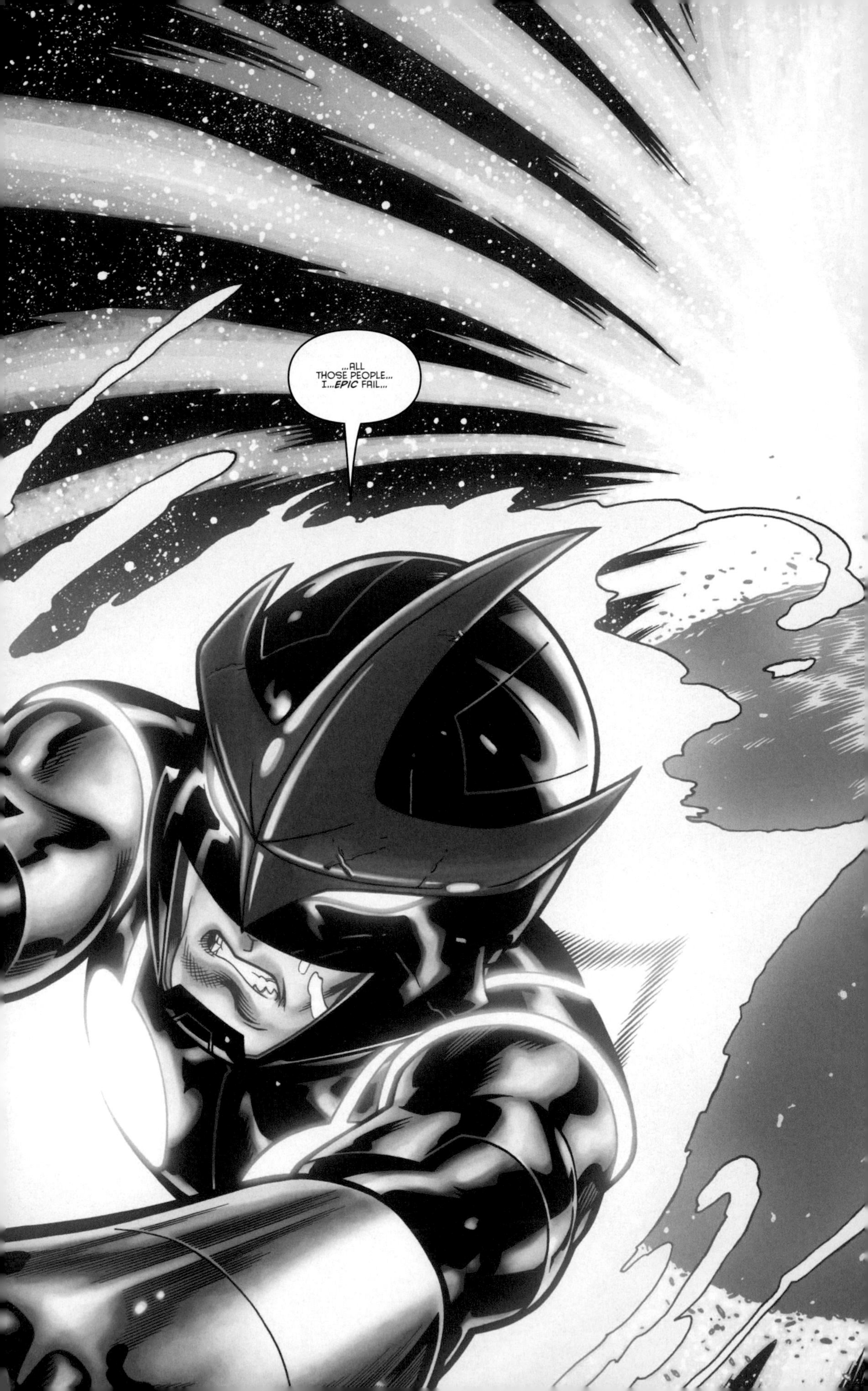
...ALL THOSE PEOPLE... I...EPIC FAIL...

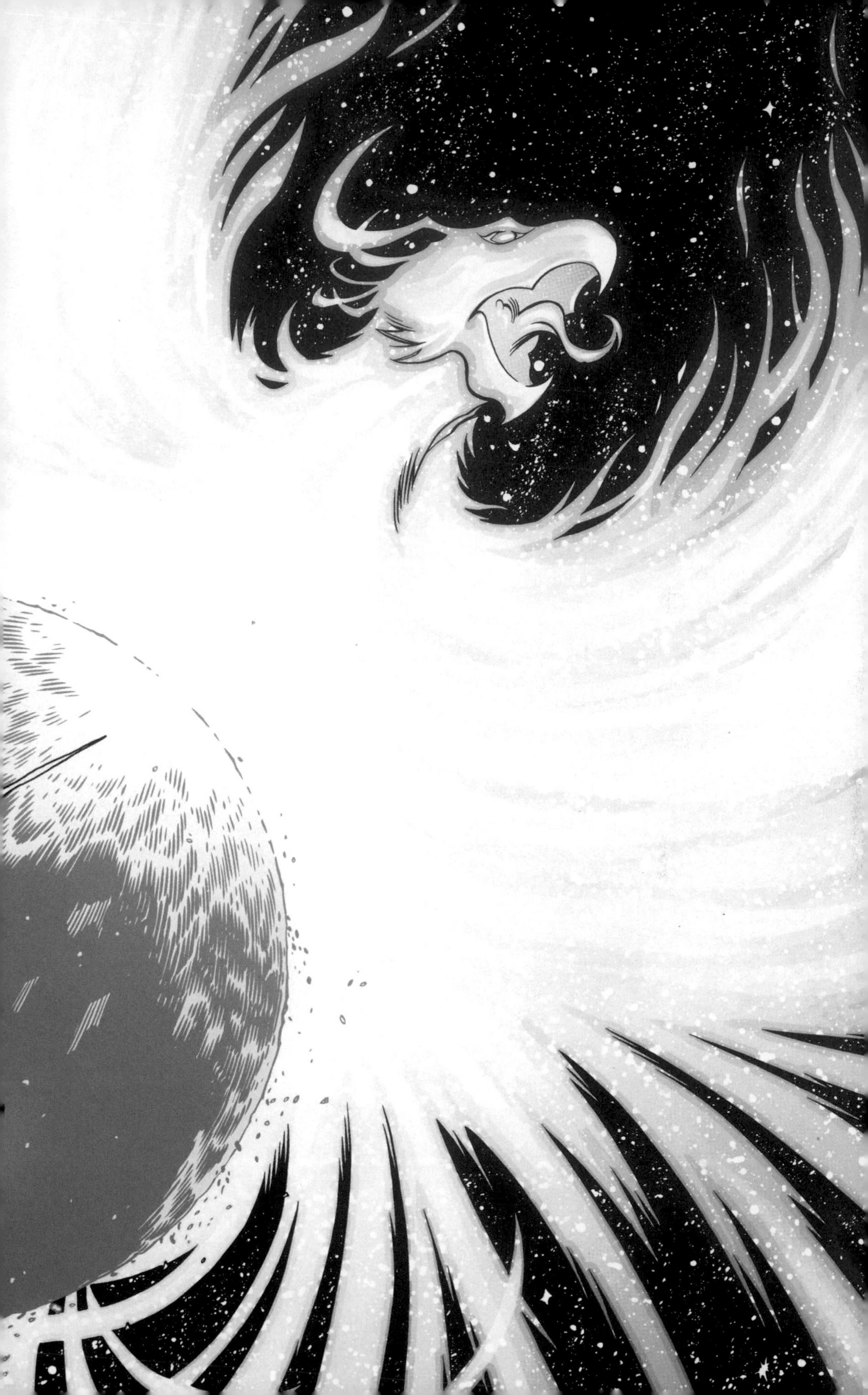

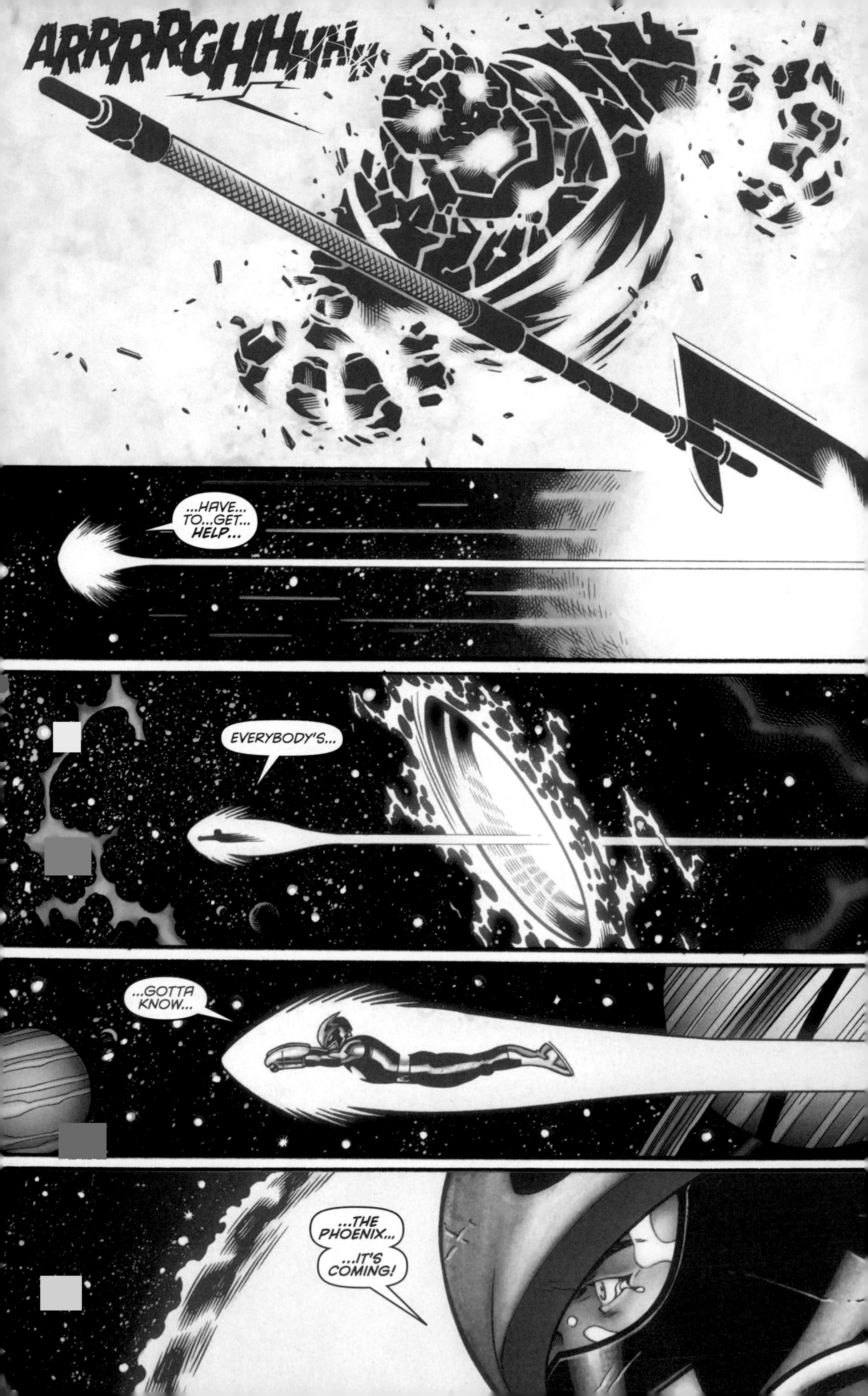
ARRRRGHHHH!!
...HAVE... TO...GET... HELP...
EVERYBODY'S...
...GOTTA KNOW...
...THE PHOENIX...
...IT'S COMING!

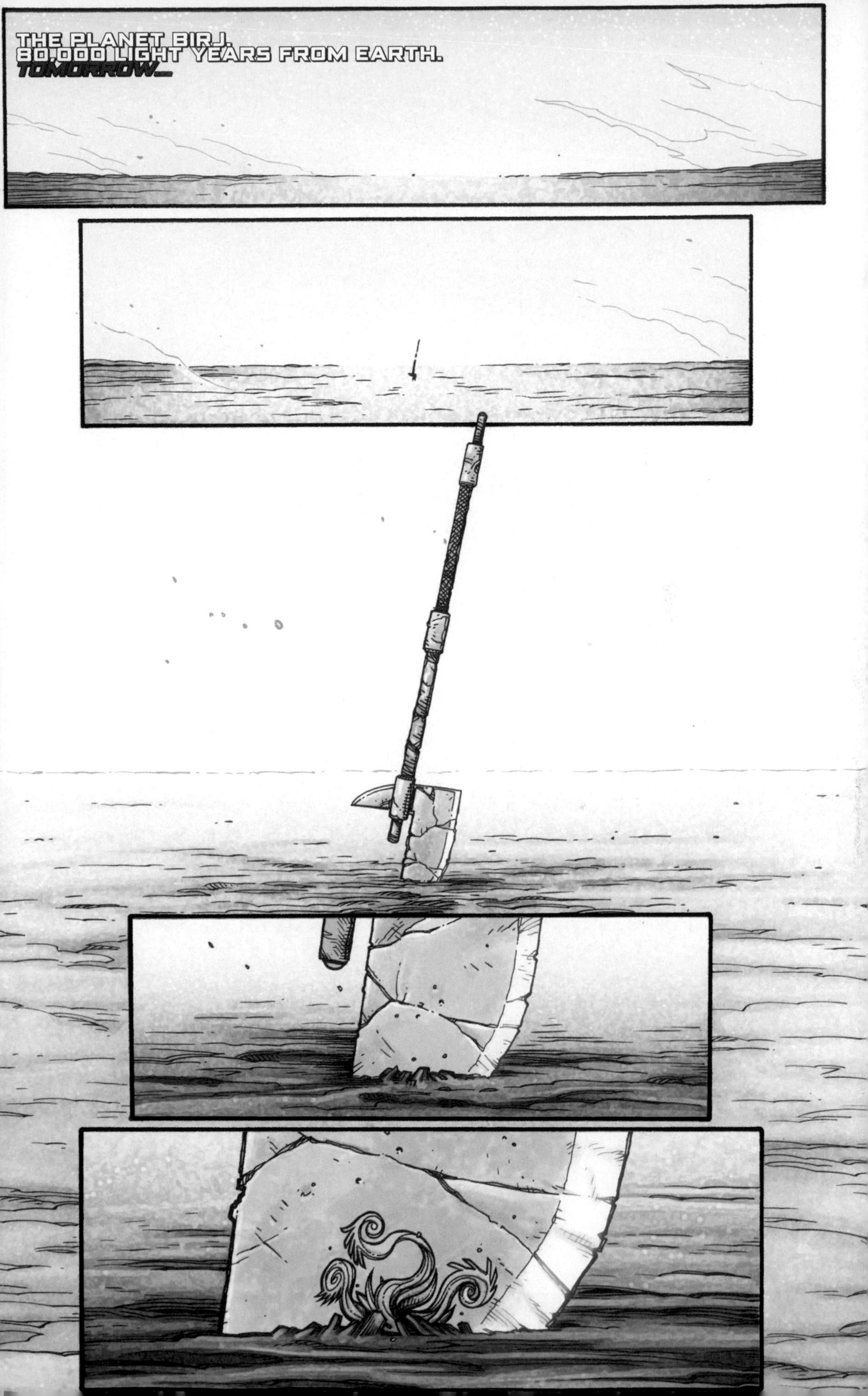
THE PLANET BIRJ.
80,000 LIGHT YEARS FROM EARTH.
TOMORROW...

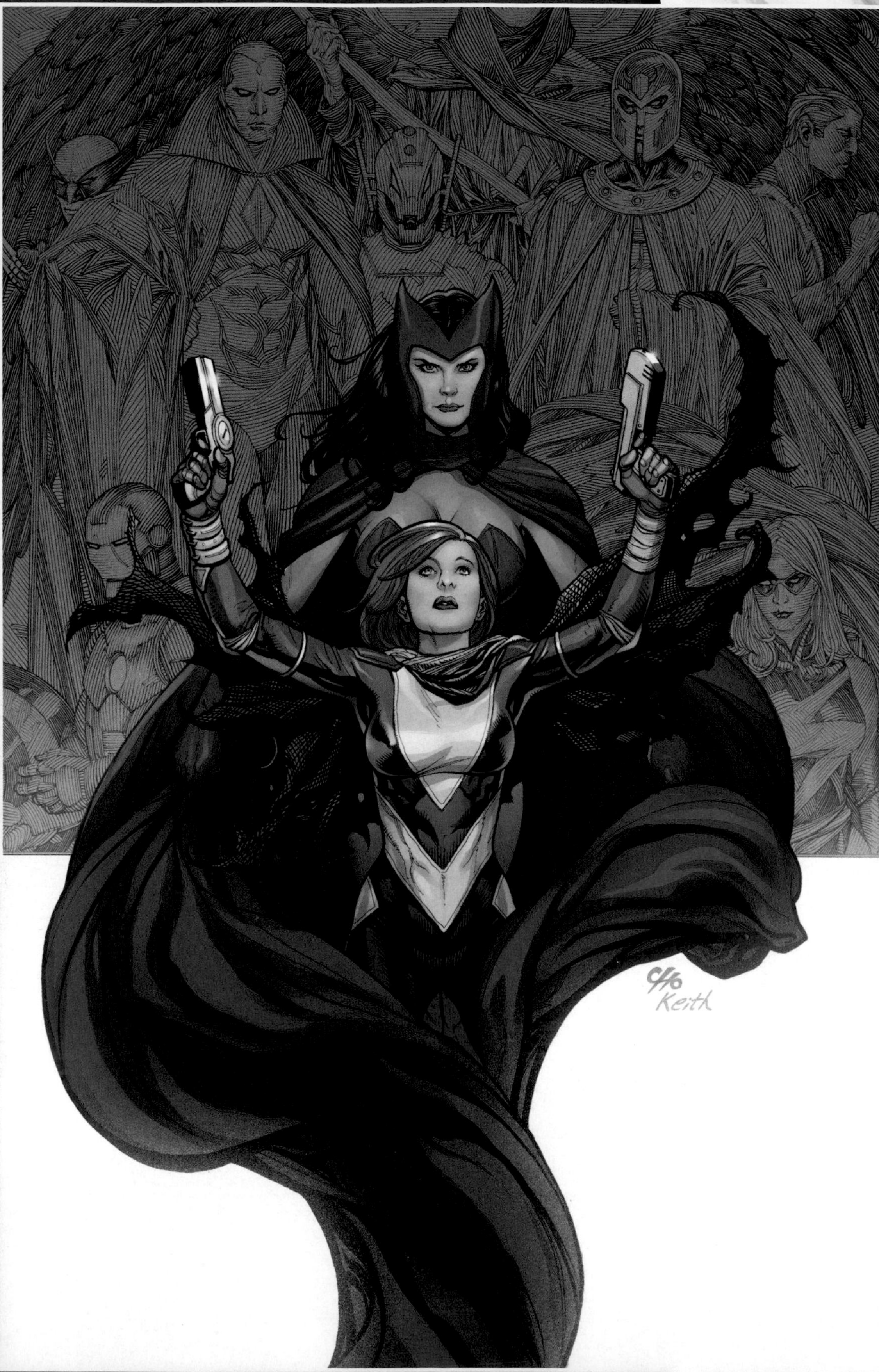
Keith

AVENGERS VS. X-MEN #0

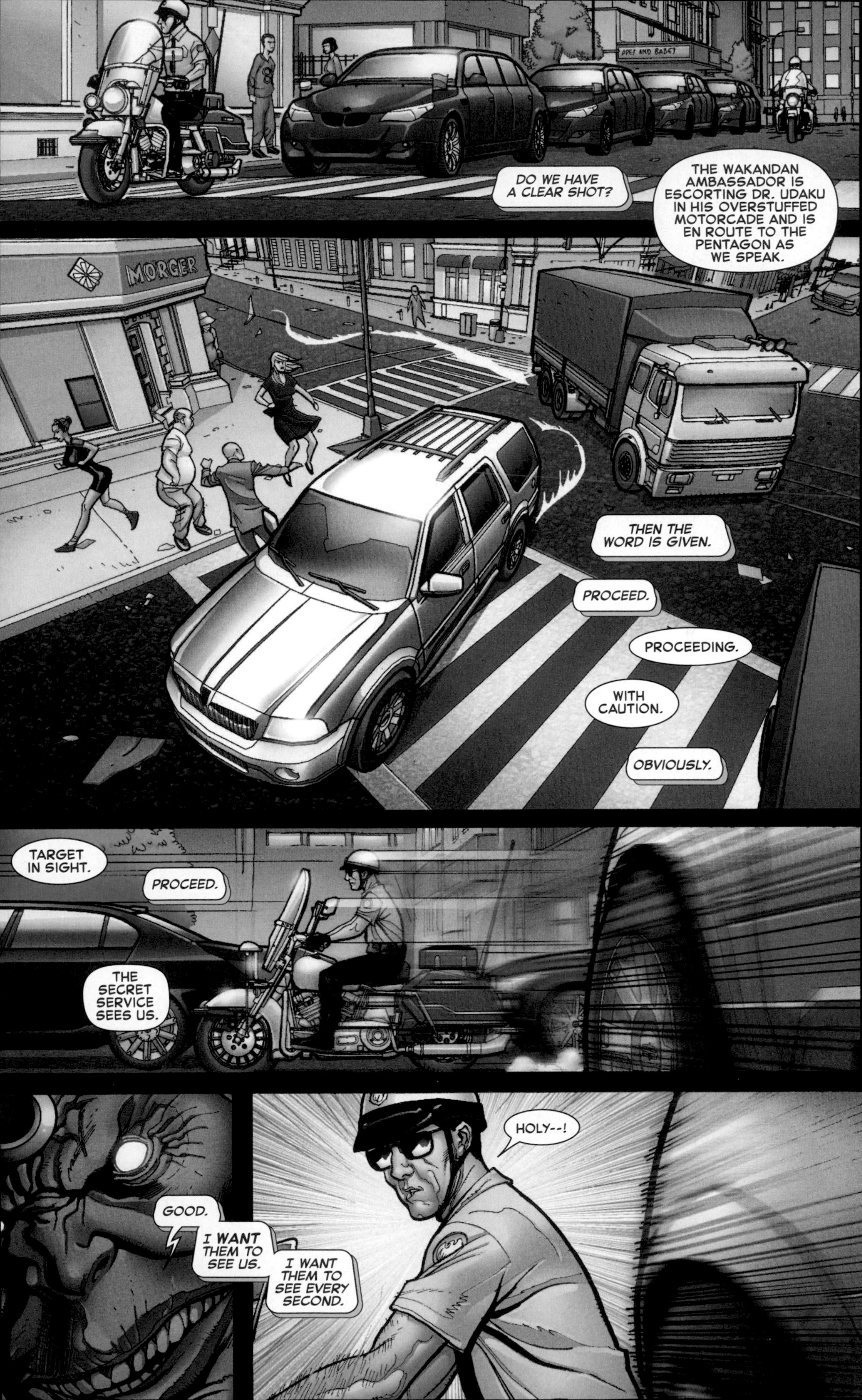
APES AND BABES
DO WE HAVE A CLEAR SHOT?
THE WAKANDAN AMBASSADOR IS ESCORTING DR. UDAKU IN HIS OVERSTUFFED MOTORCADE AND IS EN ROUTE TO THE PENTAGON AS WE SPEAK.
MORGER
THEN THE WORD IS GIVEN.
PROCEED.
PROCEEDING.
WITH CAUTION.
OBVIOUSLY.
TARGET IN SIGHT.
PROCEED.
THE SECRET SERVICE SEES US.
HOLY--!
GOOD.
I WANT THEM TO SEE US.
I WANT THEM TO SEE EVERY SECOND.

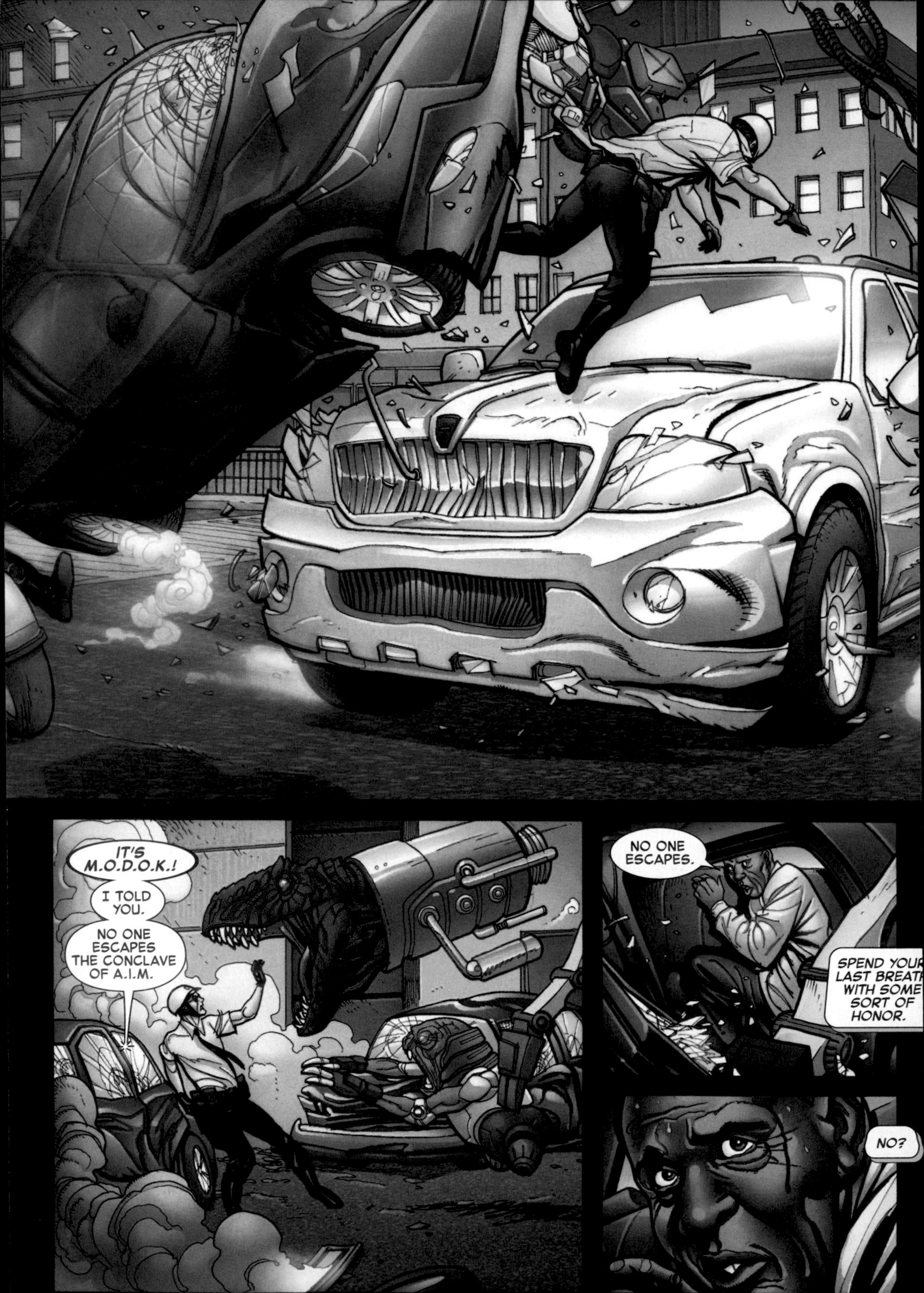
IT'S M.O.D.O.K.!
I TOLD YOU.
NO ONE ESCAPES THE CONCLAVE OF A.I.M.
NO ONE ESCAPES.
SPEND YOUR LAST BREATH WITH SOME SORT OF HONOR.
NO?

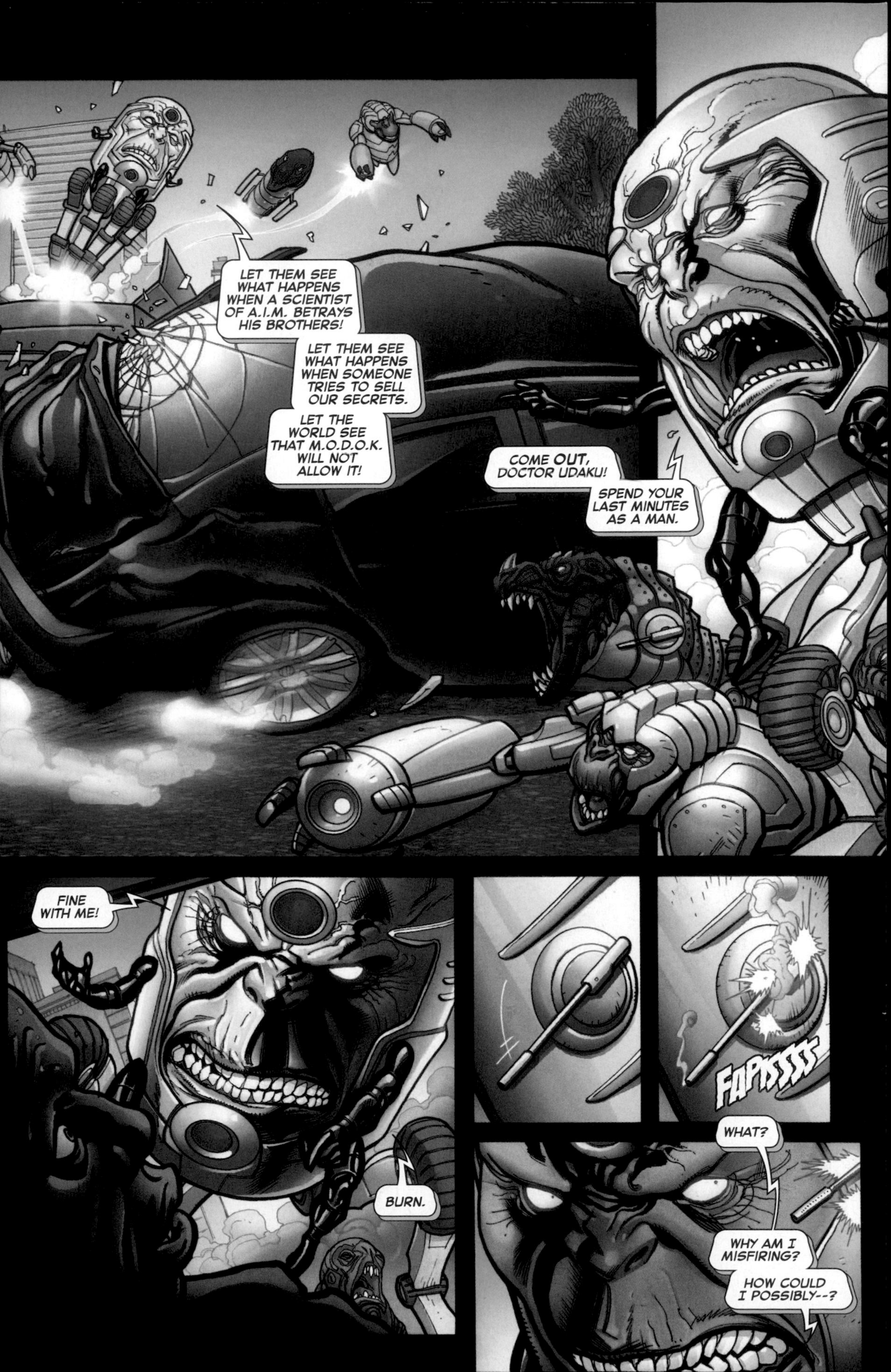
LET THEM SEE WHAT HAPPENS WHEN A SCIENTIST OF A.I.M. BETRAYS HIS BROTHERS!
LET THEM SEE WHAT HAPPENS WHEN SOMEONE TRIES TO SELL OUR SECRETS.
LET THE WORLD SEE THAT M.O.D.O.K. WILL NOT ALLOW IT!
COME OUT, DOCTOR UDAKU!
SPEND YOUR LAST MINUTES AS A MAN.
FINE WITH ME!
BURN.
FOPISSSSS
WHAT?
WHY AM I MISFIRING?
HOW COULD I POSSIBLY--?

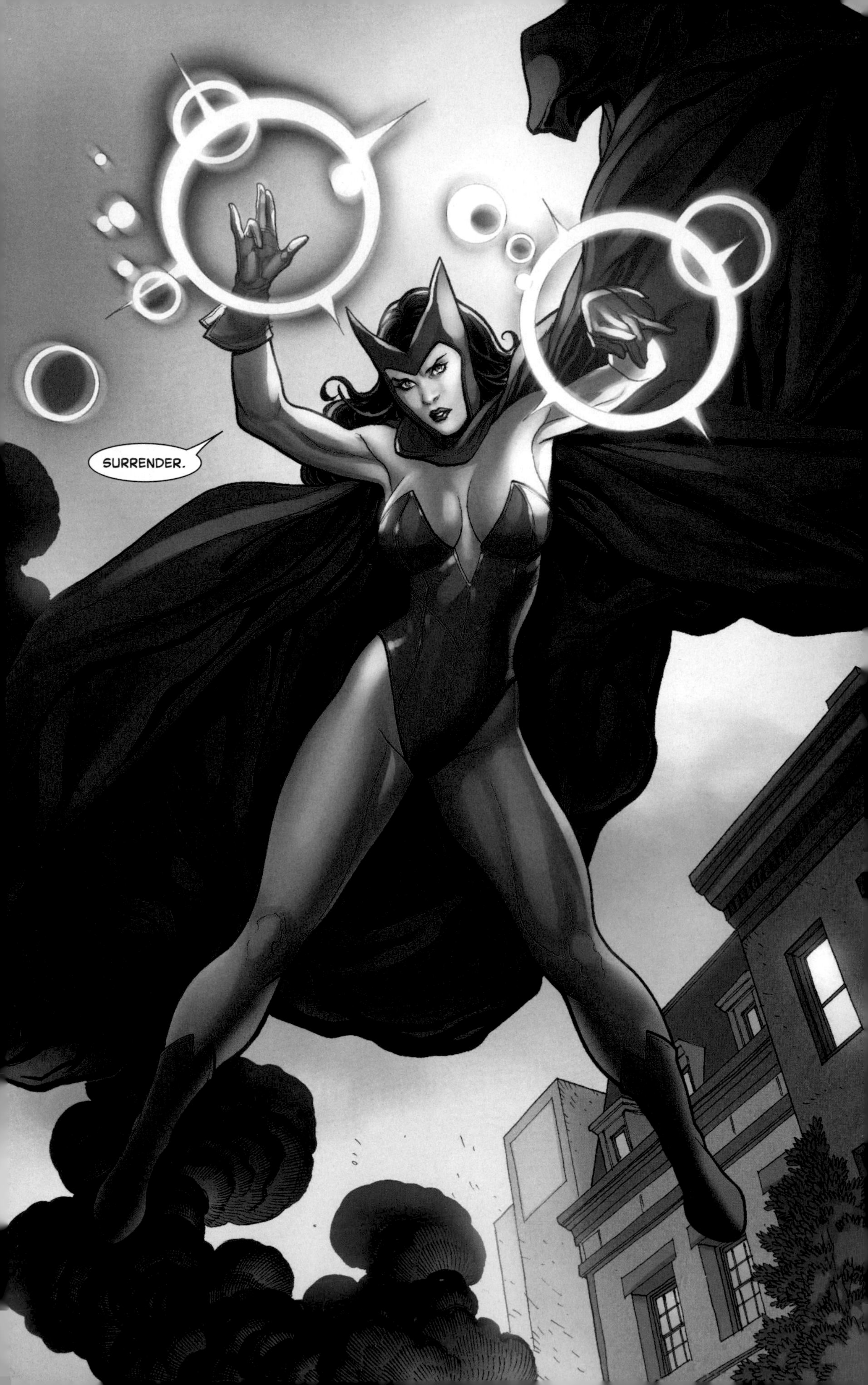
SURRENDER.

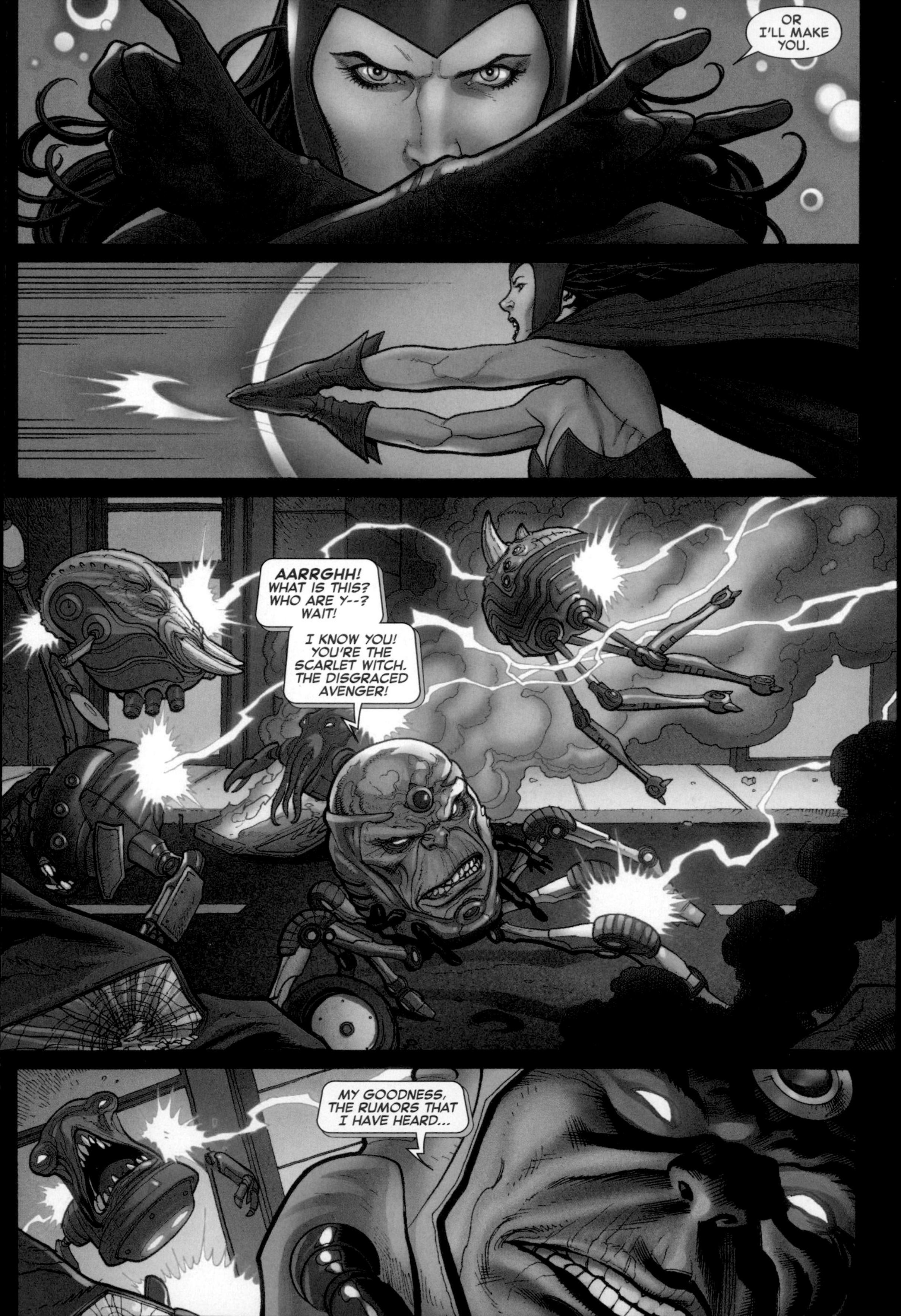
OR I'LL MAKE YOU.
AARRGHH! WHAT IS THIS? WHO ARE Y--? WAIT!
I KNOW YOU! YOU'RE THE SCARLET WITCH. THE DISGRACED AVENGER!
MY GOODNESS, THE RUMORS THAT I HAVE HEARD...

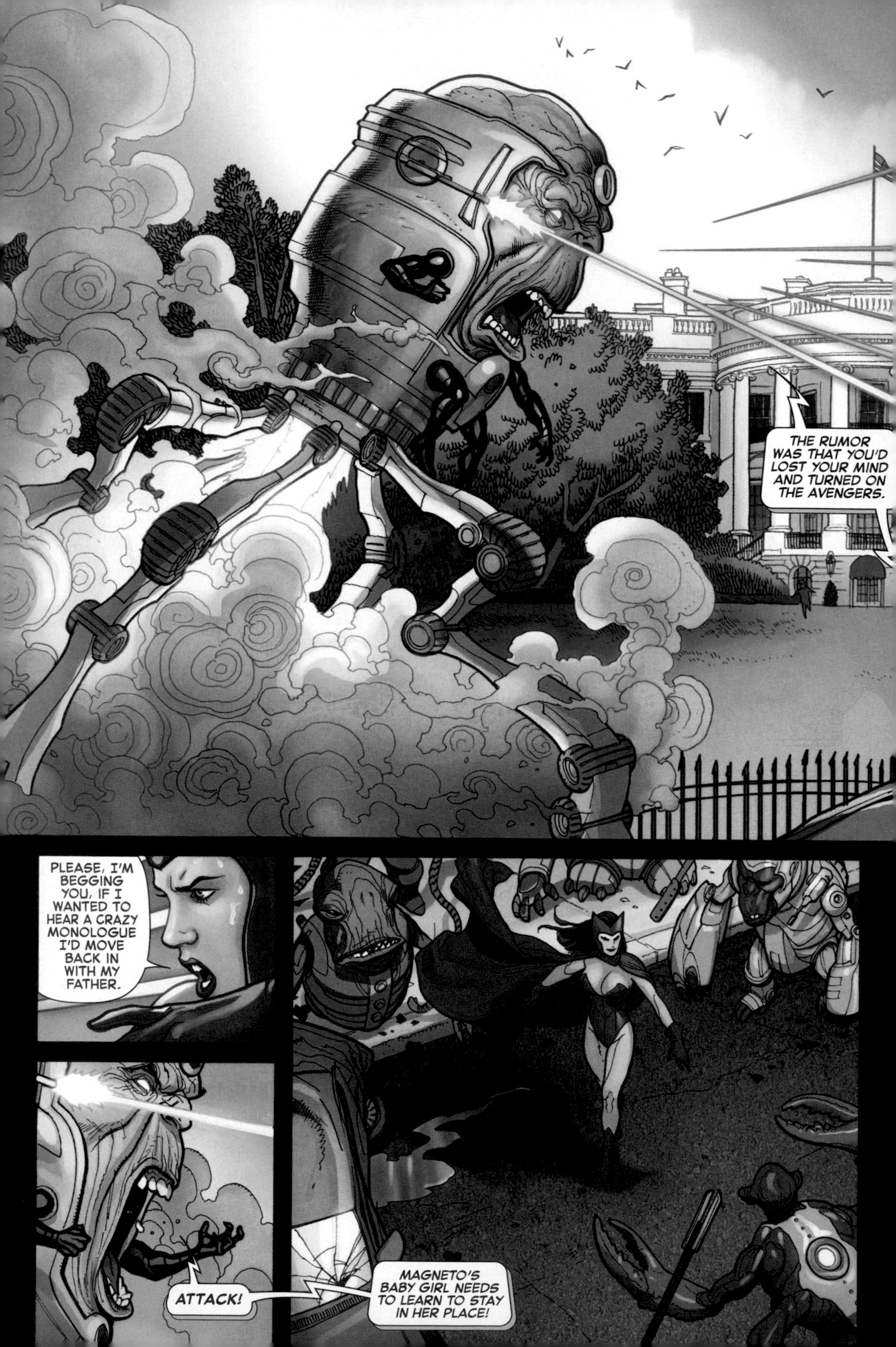
THE RUMOR WAS THAT YOU'D LOST YOUR MIND AND TURNED ON THE AVENGERS.
PLEASE, I'M BEGGING YOU, IF I WANTED TO HEAR A CRAZY MONOLOGUE I'D MOVE BACK IN WITH MY FATHER.
ATTACK!
MAGNETO'S BABY GIRL NEEDS TO LEARN TO STAY IN HER PLACE!

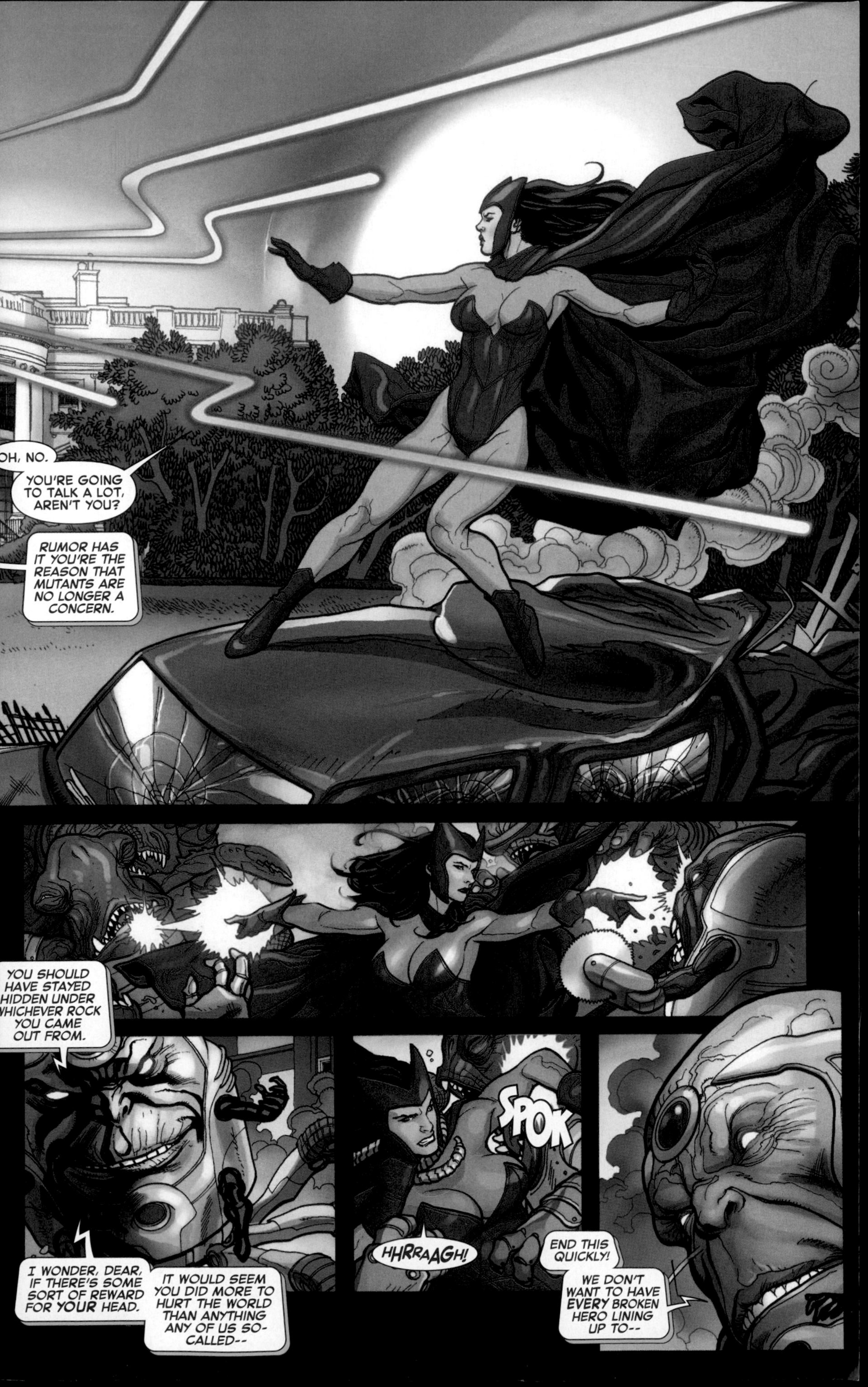

OH, NO.
YOU'RE GOING TO TALK A LOT, AREN'T YOU?
RUMOR HAS IT YOU'RE THE REASON THAT MUTANTS ARE NO LONGER A CONCERN.
YOU SHOULD HAVE STAYED HIDDEN UNDER WHICHEVER ROCK YOU CAME OUT FROM.
I WONDER, DEAR, IF THERE'S SOME SORT OF REWARD FOR YOUR HEAD.
IT WOULD SEEM YOU DID MORE TO HURT THE WORLD THAN ANYTHING ANY OF US SO-CALLED--
SPOK
HHRRAAGH!
END THIS QUICKLY!
WE DON'T WANT TO HAVE EVERY BROKEN HERO LINING UP TO--

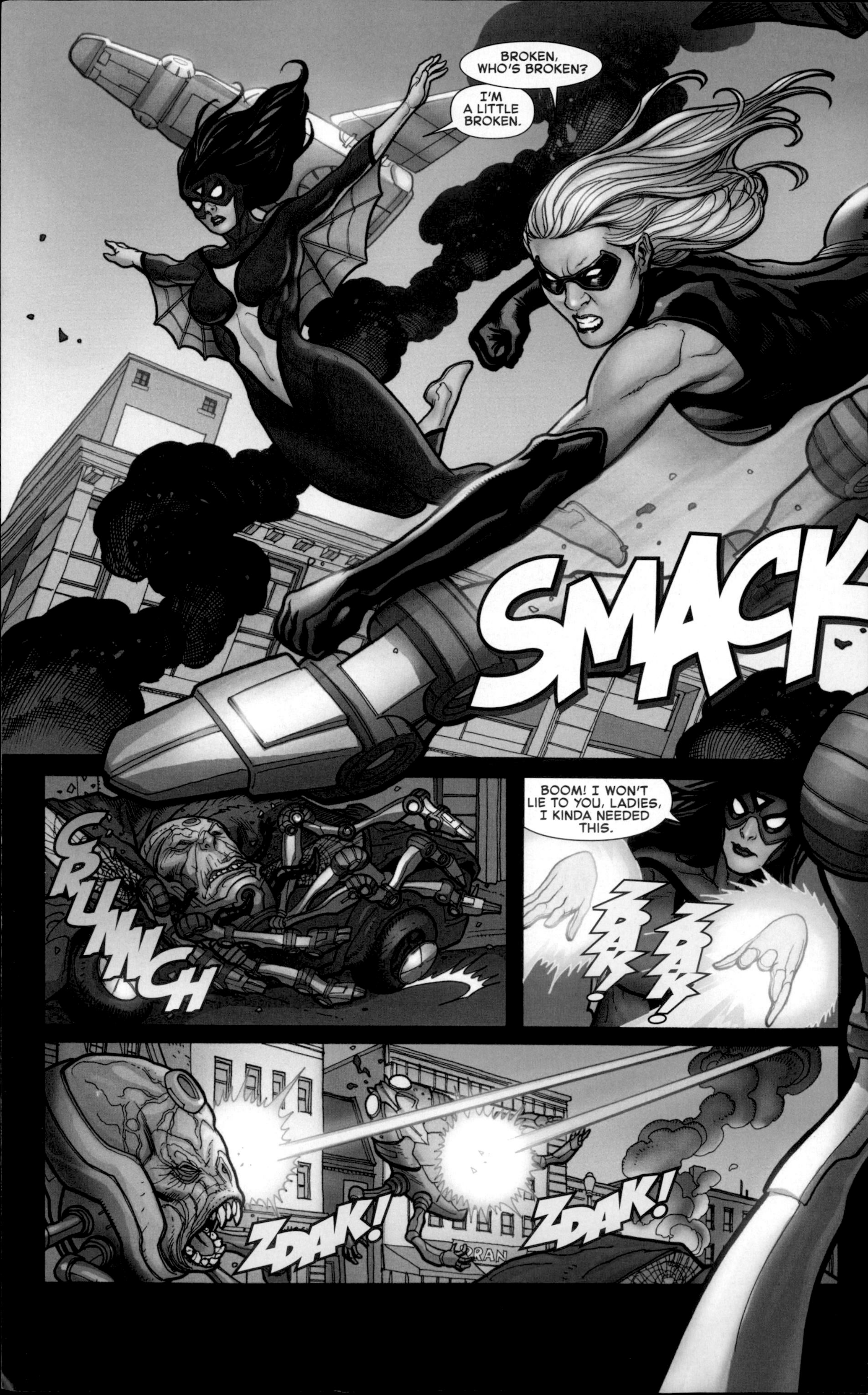
BROKEN, WHO'S BROKEN?
I'M A LITTLE BROKEN.
SMACK
CRUNNCH
BOOM! I WON'T LIE TO YOU, LADIES, I KINDA NEEDED THIS.
ZDAK!
ZDAK!
ZDAK!
ZDAK!

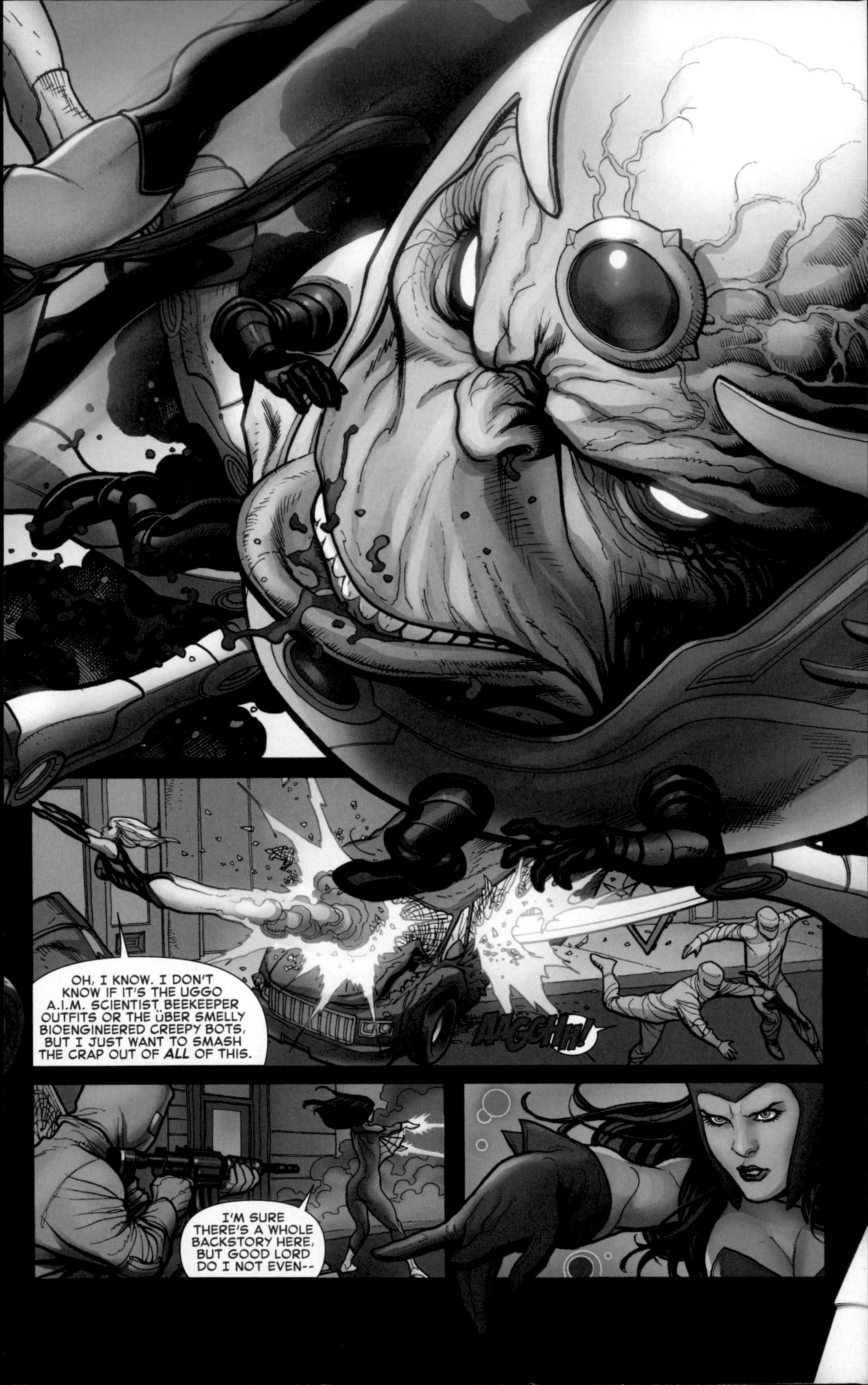
OH, I KNOW. I DON'T KNOW IF IT'S THE UGGO A.I.M. SCIENTIST BEEKEEPER OUTFITS OR THE ÜBER SMELLY BIOENGINEERED CREEPY BOTS, BUT I JUST WANT TO SMASH THE CRAP OUT OF ALL OF THIS.
AAGGHH!
I'M SURE THERE'S A WHOLE BACKSTORY HERE, BUT GOOD LORD DO I NOT EVEN--

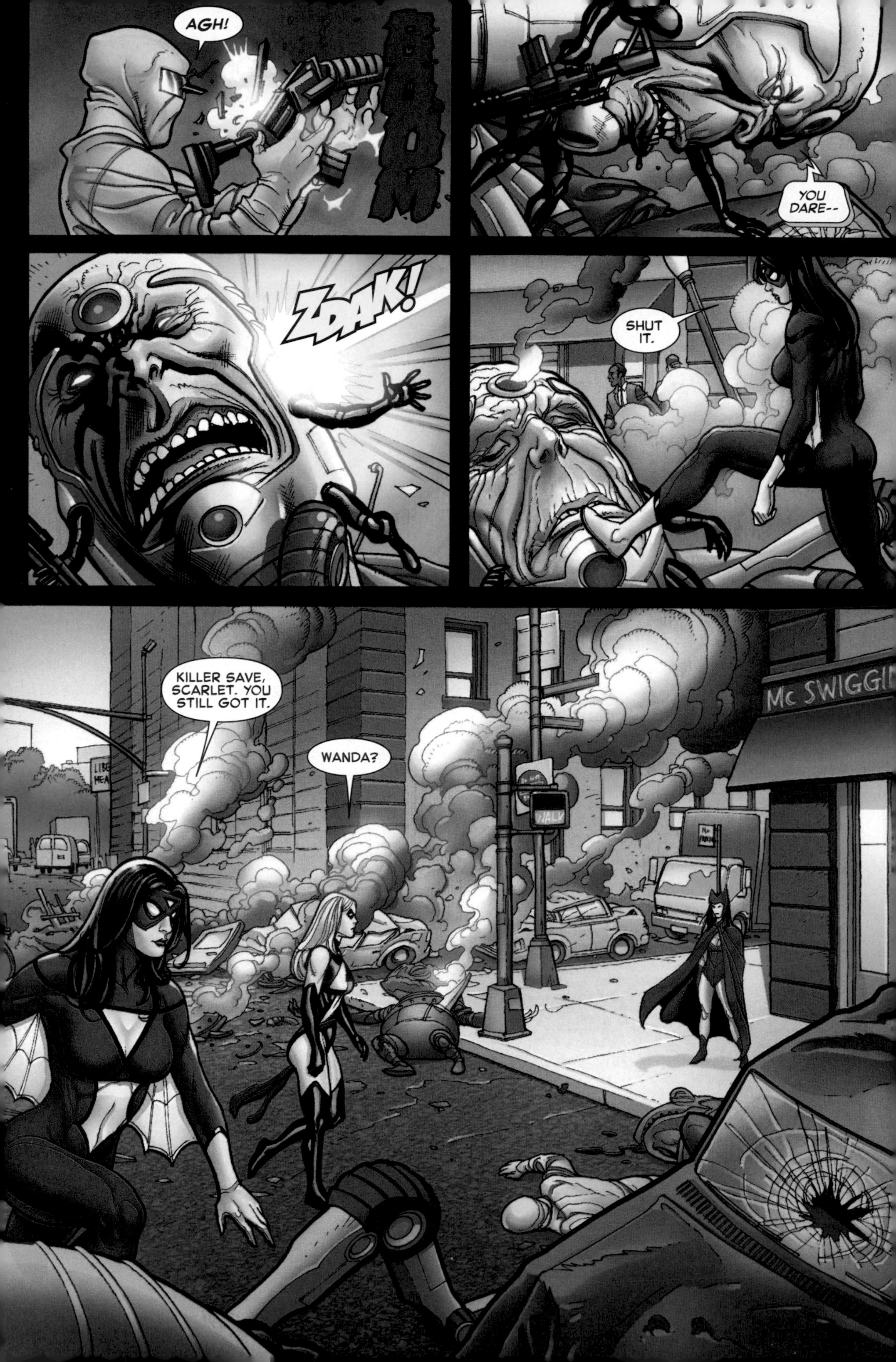
AGH!
YOU DARE--
ZDAK!
SHUT IT.
KILLER SAVE, SCARLET. YOU STILL GOT IT.
WANDA?
Mc SWIGGI

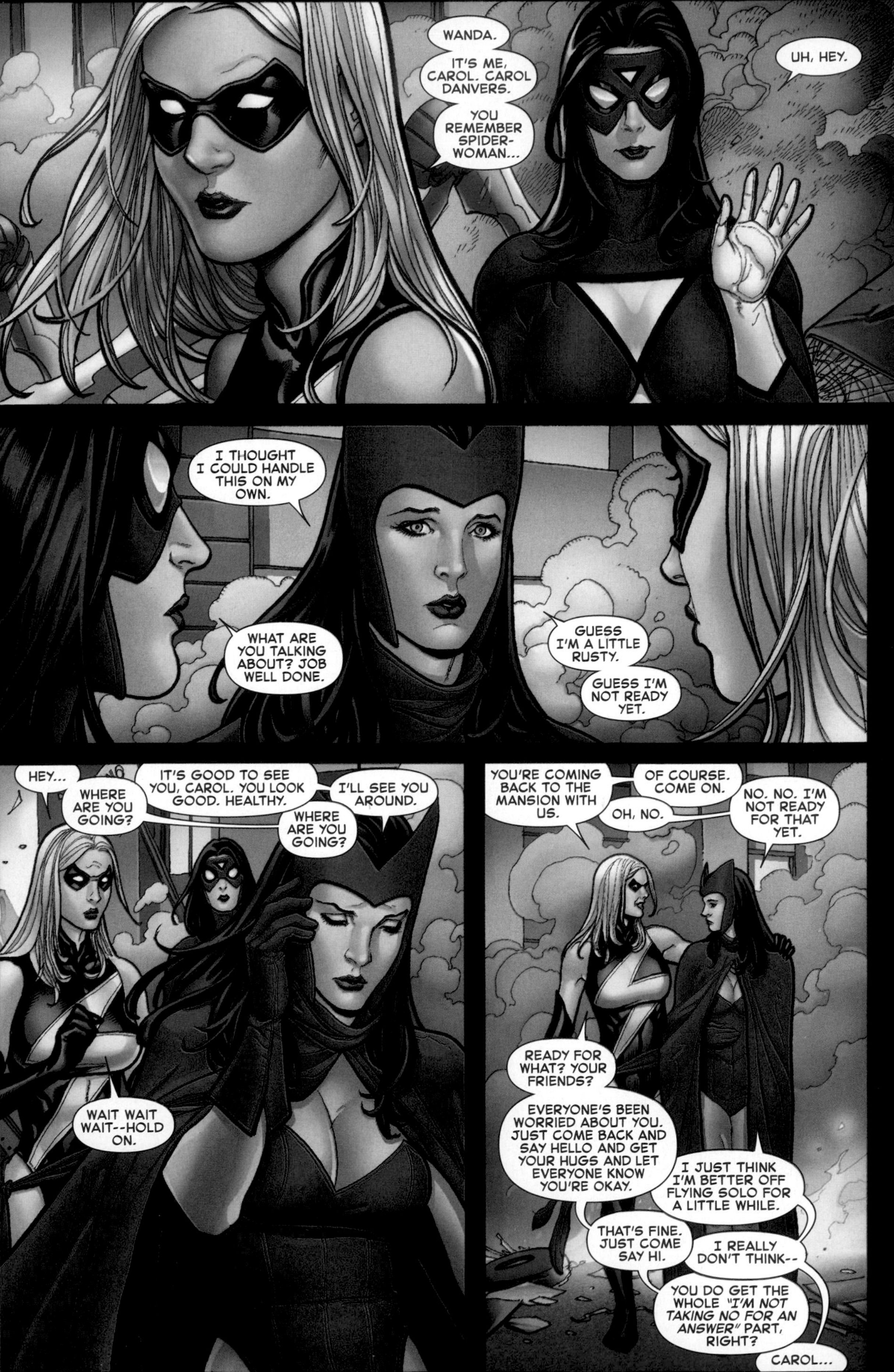
WANDA.
IT'S ME, CAROL. CAROL DANVERS.
YOU REMEMBER SPIDER-WOMAN...
UH, HEY.
I THOUGHT I COULD HANDLE THIS ON MY OWN.
WHAT ARE YOU TALKING ABOUT? JOB WELL DONE.
GUESS I'M A LITTLE RUSTY.
GUESS I'M NOT READY YET.
IT'S GOOD TO SEE YOU, CAROL. YOU LOOK GOOD. HEALTHY.
I'LL SEE YOU AROUND.
HEY...
WHERE ARE YOU GOING?
WHERE ARE YOU GOING?
WAIT WAIT WAIT--HOLD ON.
YOU'RE COMING BACK TO THE MANSION WITH US.
OF COURSE. COME ON.
OH, NO.
NO. NO. I'M NOT READY FOR THAT YET.
READY FOR WHAT? YOUR FRIENDS?
EVERYONE'S BEEN WORRIED ABOUT YOU. JUST COME BACK AND SAY HELLO AND GET YOUR HUGS AND LET EVERYONE KNOW YOU'RE OKAY.
I JUST THINK I'M BETTER OFF FLYING SOLO FOR A LITTLE WHILE.
THAT'S FINE. JUST COME SAY HI.
I REALLY DON'T THINK--
YOU DO GET THE WHOLE *"I'M NOT TAKING NO FOR AN ANSWER"* PART, RIGHT?
CAROL...

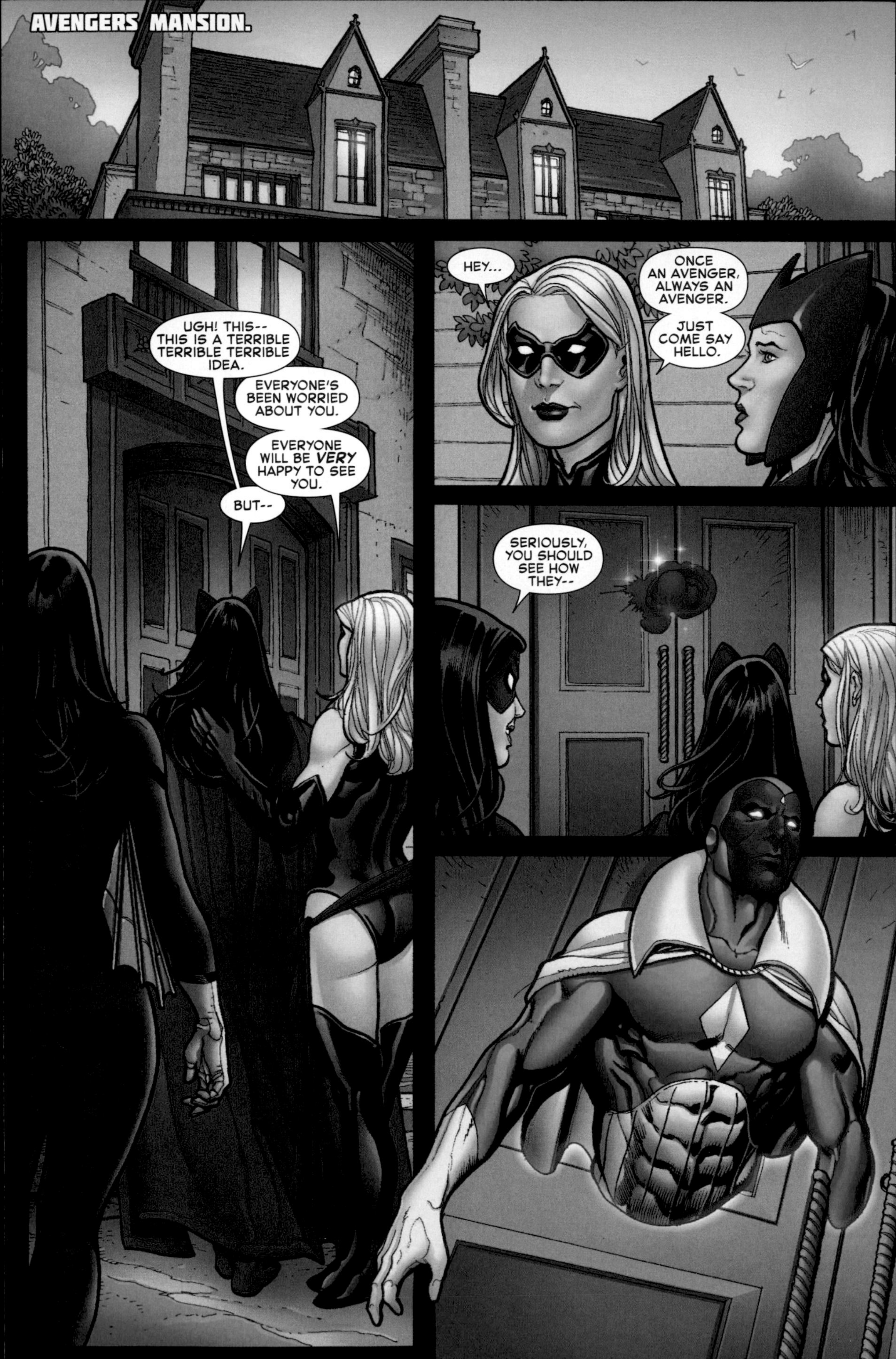

AVENGERS MANSION.
UGH! THIS-- THIS IS A TERRIBLE TERRIBLE TERRIBLE IDEA.
EVERYONE'S BEEN WORRIED ABOUT YOU.
EVERYONE WILL BE *VERY* HAPPY TO SEE YOU.
BUT--
HEY...
ONCE AN AVENGER, ALWAYS AN AVENGER.
JUST COME SAY HELLO.
SERIOUSLY, YOU SHOULD SEE HOW THEY--

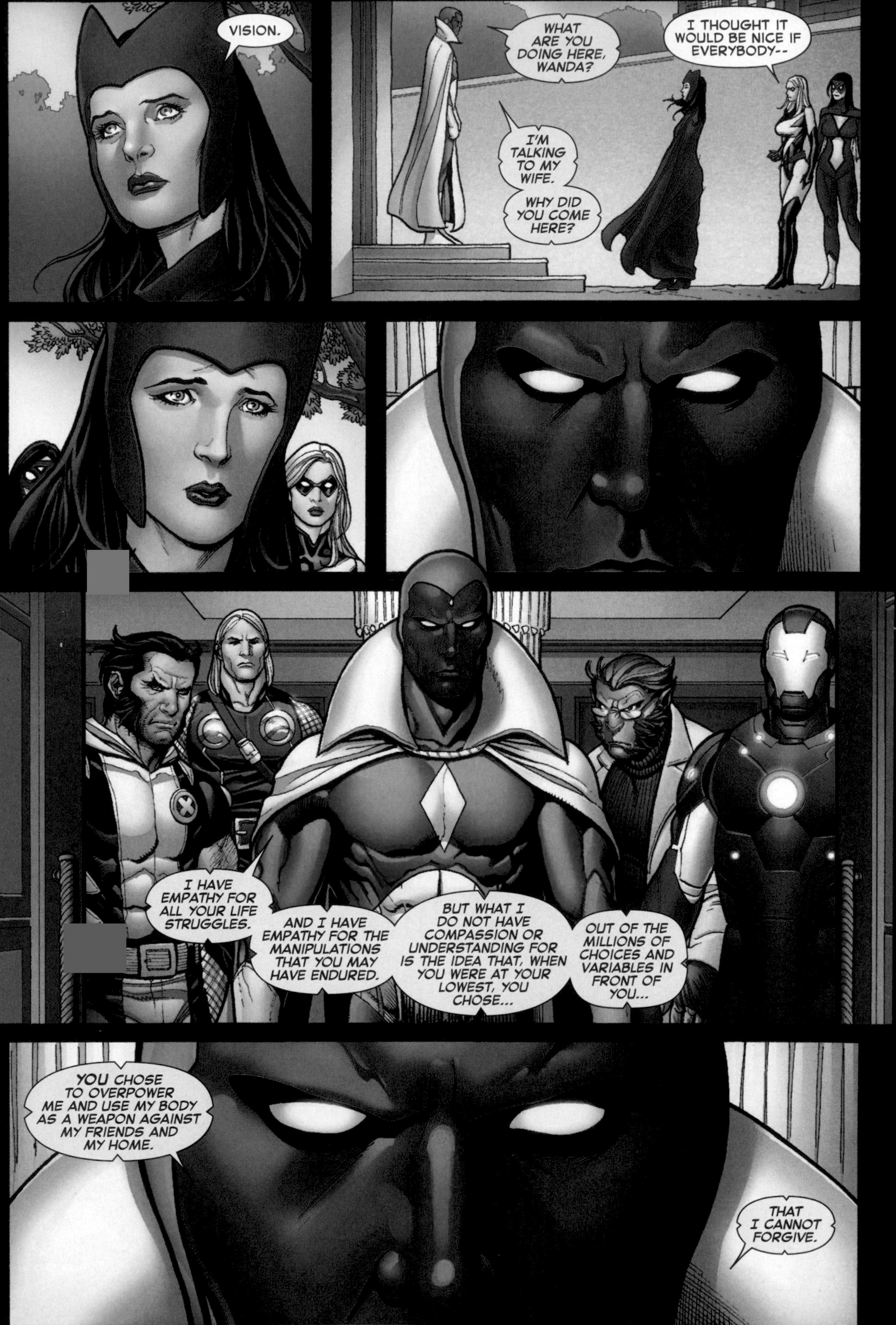
VISION.
WHAT ARE YOU DOING HERE, WANDA?
I THOUGHT IT WOULD BE NICE IF EVERYBODY--
I'M TALKING TO MY WIFE.
WHY DID YOU COME HERE?
I HAVE EMPATHY FOR ALL YOUR LIFE STRUGGLES.
AND I HAVE EMPATHY FOR THE MANIPULATIONS THAT YOU MAY HAVE ENDURED.
BUT WHAT I DO NOT HAVE COMPASSION OR UNDERSTANDING FOR IS THE IDEA THAT, WHEN YOU WERE AT YOUR LOWEST, YOU CHOSE...
OUT OF THE MILLIONS OF CHOICES AND VARIABLES IN FRONT OF YOU...
YOU CHOSE TO OVERPOWER ME AND USE MY BODY AS A WEAPON AGAINST MY FRIENDS AND MY HOME.
THAT I CANNOT FORGIVE.

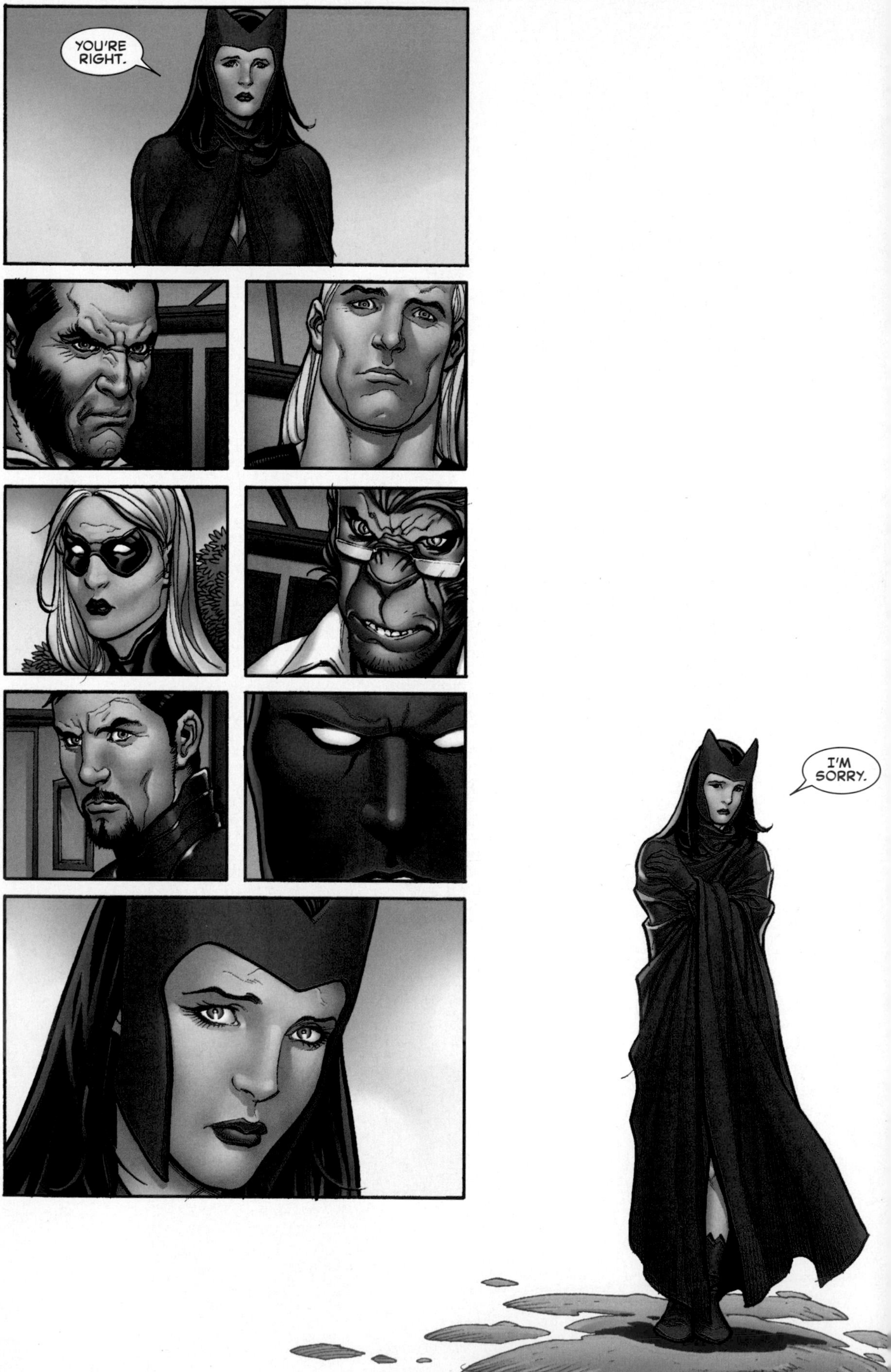
YOU'RE RIGHT.
I'M SORRY.

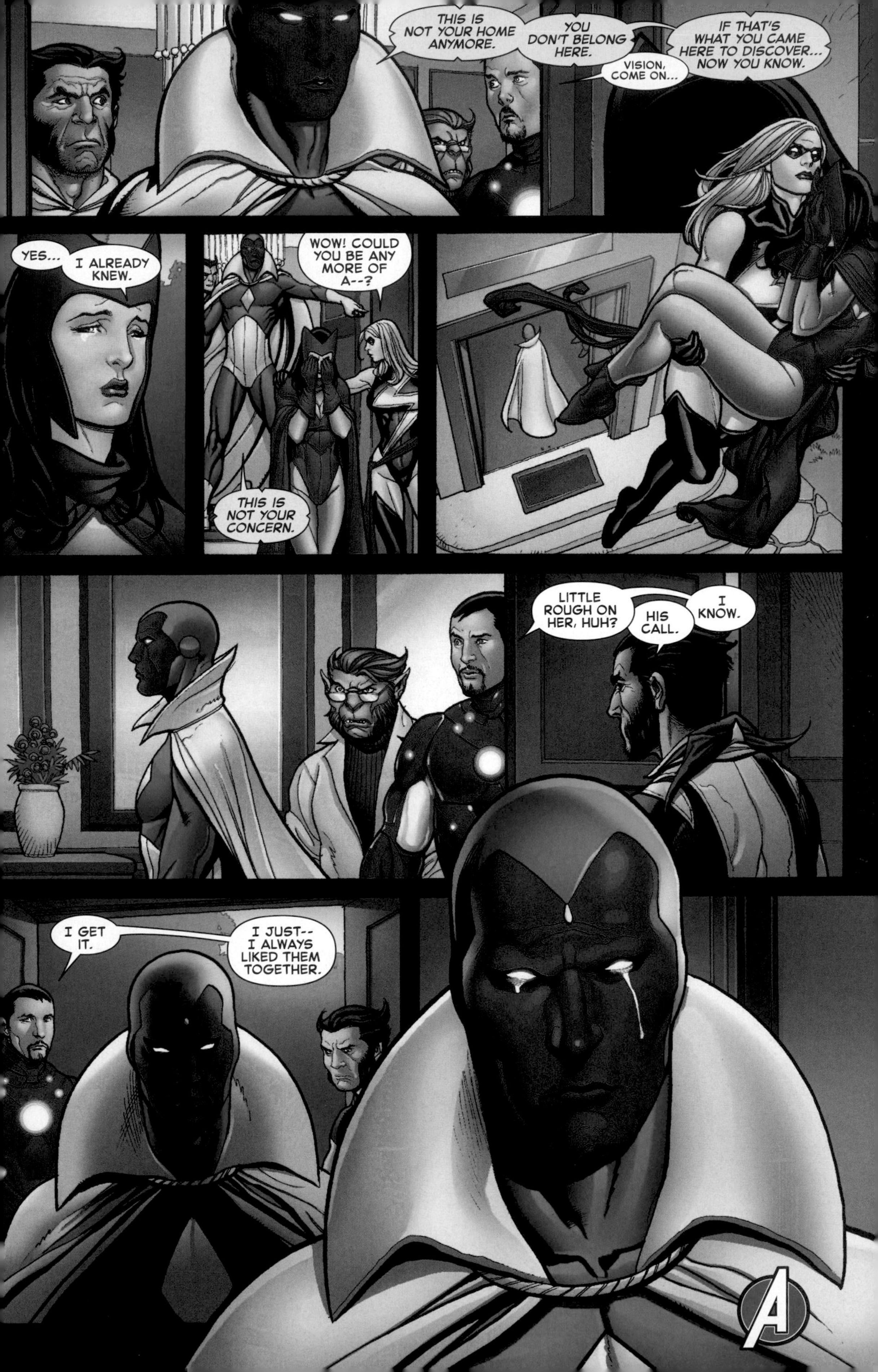
THIS IS NOT YOUR HOME ANYMORE.
YOU DON'T BELONG HERE.
IF THAT'S WHAT YOU CAME HERE TO DISCOVER... NOW YOU KNOW.
VISION, COME ON...
YES...
I ALREADY KNEW.
WOW! COULD YOU BE ANY MORE OF A--?
THIS IS NOT YOUR CONCERN.
LITTLE ROUGH ON HER, HUH?
HIS CALL.
I KNOW.
I GET IT.
I JUST-- I ALWAYS LIKED THEM TOGETHER.

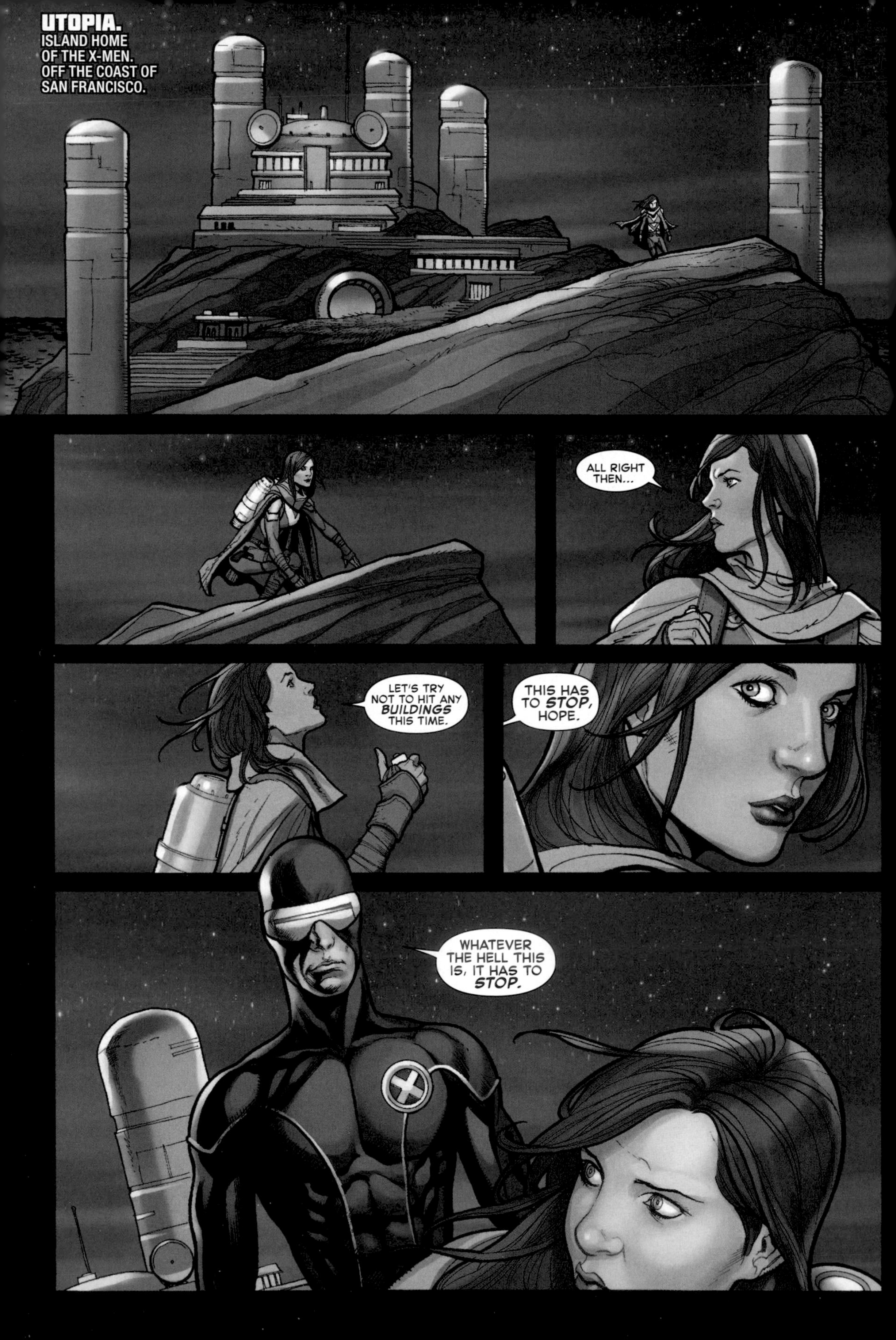
UTOPIA.
ISLAND HOME OF THE X-MEN. OFF THE COAST OF SAN FRANCISCO.
ALL RIGHT THEN...
LET'S TRY NOT TO HIT ANY BUILDINGS THIS TIME.
THIS HAS TO STOP, HOPE.
WHATEVER THE HELL THIS IS, IT HAS TO STOP.

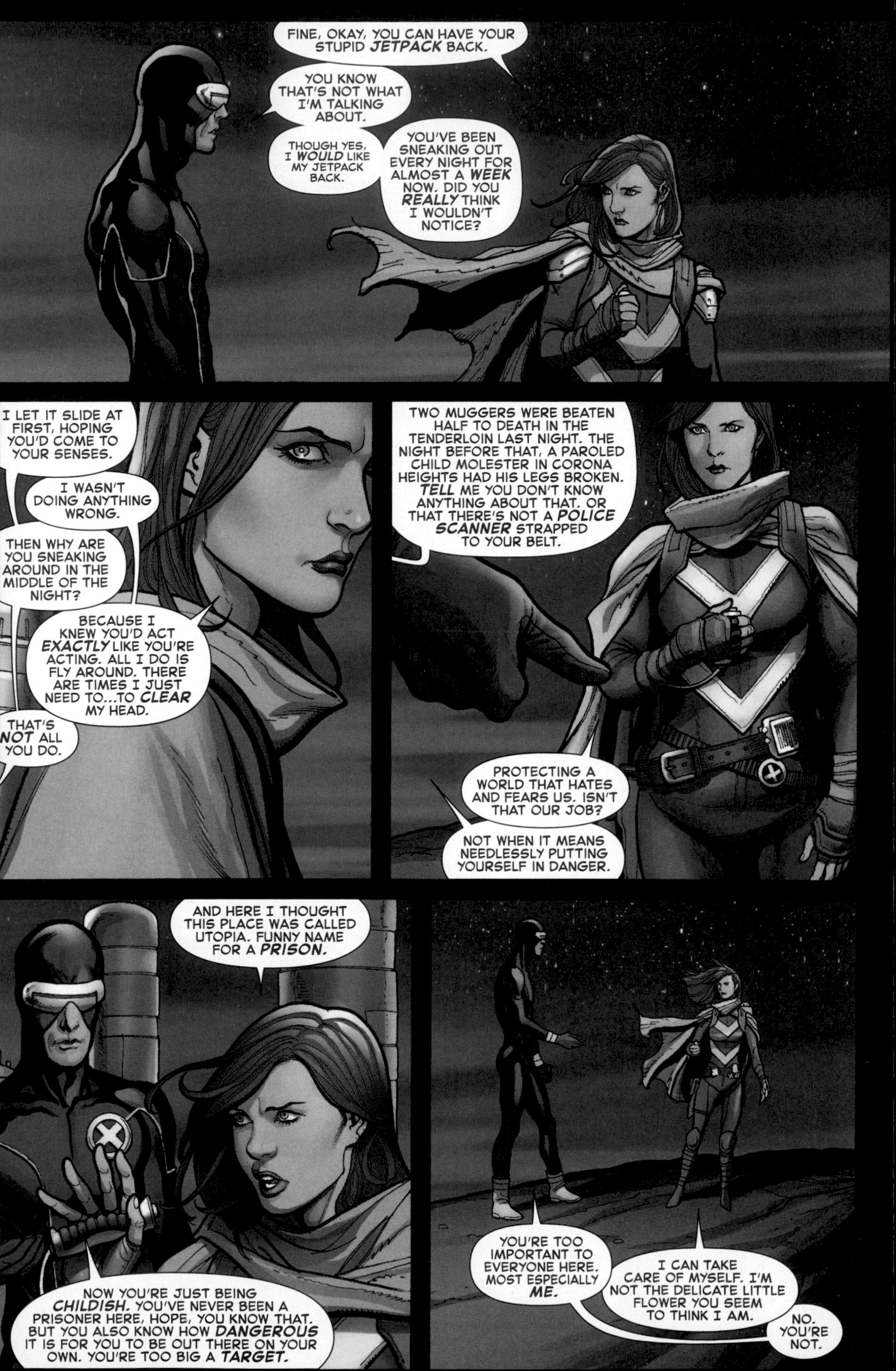
FINE, OKAY, YOU CAN HAVE YOUR STUPID JETPACK BACK.
YOU KNOW THAT'S NOT WHAT I'M TALKING ABOUT.
THOUGH YES, I WOULD LIKE MY JETPACK BACK.
YOU'VE BEEN SNEAKING OUT EVERY NIGHT FOR ALMOST A WEEK NOW. DID YOU REALLY THINK I WOULDN'T NOTICE?
I LET IT SLIDE AT FIRST, HOPING YOU'D COME TO YOUR SENSES.
I WASN'T DOING ANYTHING WRONG.
THEN WHY ARE YOU SNEAKING AROUND IN THE MIDDLE OF THE NIGHT?
BECAUSE I KNEW YOU'D ACT EXACTLY LIKE YOU'RE ACTING. ALL I DO IS FLY AROUND. THERE ARE TIMES I JUST NEED TO...TO CLEAR MY HEAD.
THAT'S NOT ALL YOU DO.
TWO MUGGERS WERE BEATEN HALF TO DEATH IN THE TENDERLOIN LAST NIGHT. THE NIGHT BEFORE THAT, A PAROLED CHILD MOLESTER IN CORONA HEIGHTS HAD HIS LEGS BROKEN. TELL ME YOU DON'T KNOW ANYTHING ABOUT THAT. OR THAT THERE'S NOT A POLICE SCANNER STRAPPED TO YOUR BELT.
PROTECTING A WORLD THAT HATES AND FEARS US. ISN'T THAT OUR JOB?
NOT WHEN IT MEANS NEEDLESSLY PUTTING YOURSELF IN DANGER.
AND HERE I THOUGHT THIS PLACE WAS CALLED UTOPIA. FUNNY NAME FOR A PRISON.
NOW YOU'RE JUST BEING CHILDISH. YOU'VE NEVER BEEN A PRISONER HERE, HOPE, YOU KNOW THAT. BUT YOU ALSO KNOW HOW DANGEROUS IT IS FOR YOU TO BE OUT THERE ON YOUR OWN. YOU'RE TOO BIG A TARGET.
YOU'RE TOO IMPORTANT TO EVERYONE HERE. MOST ESPECIALLY ME.
I CAN TAKE CARE OF MYSELF. I'M NOT THE DELICATE LITTLE FLOWER YOU SEEM TO THINK I AM.
NO. YOU'RE NOT.

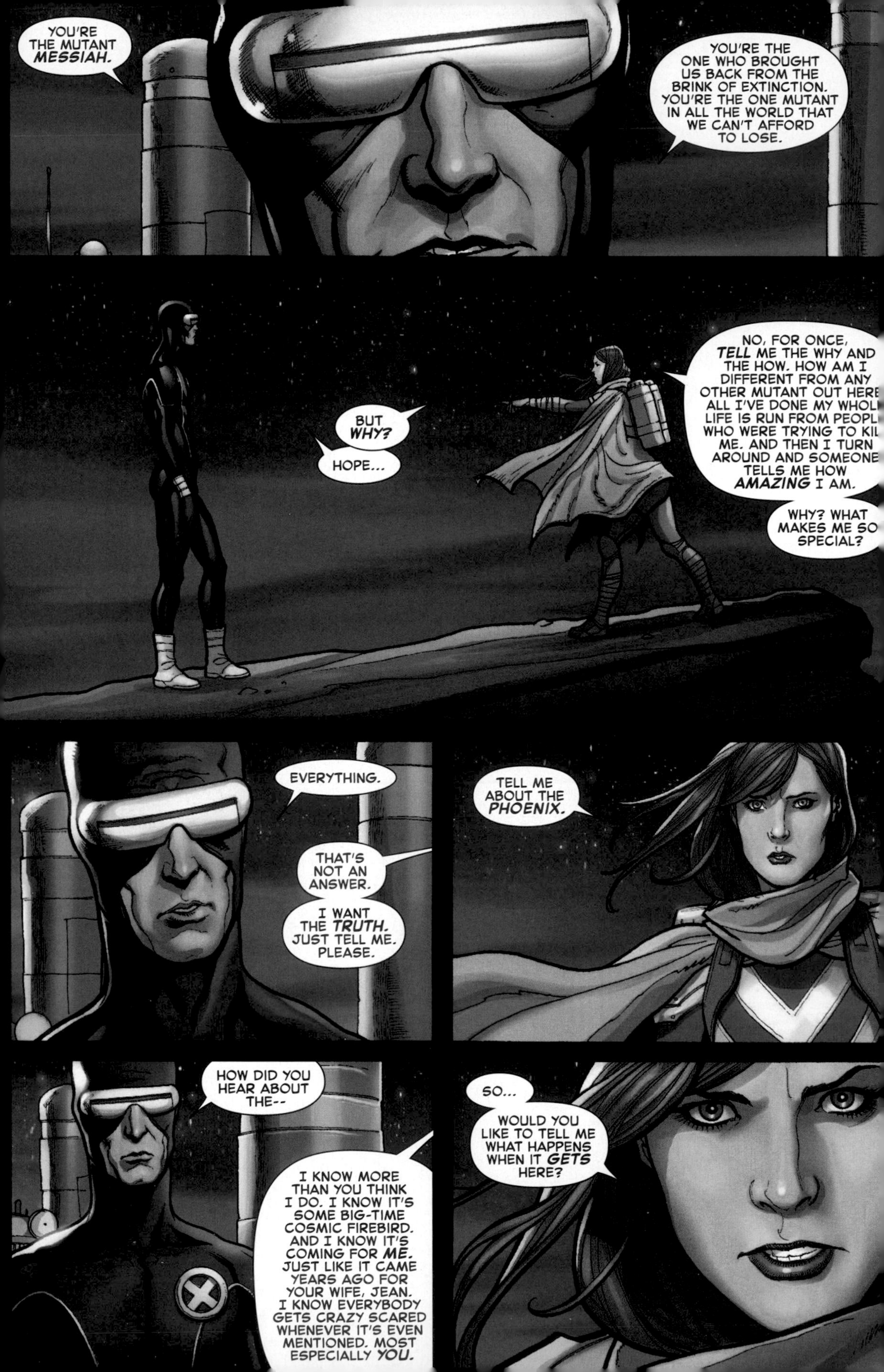
YOU'RE THE MUTANT MESSIAH.
YOU'RE THE ONE WHO BROUGHT US BACK FROM THE BRINK OF EXTINCTION. YOU'RE THE ONE MUTANT IN ALL THE WORLD THAT WE CAN'T AFFORD TO LOSE.
BUT WHY?
HOPE...
NO, FOR ONCE, TELL ME THE WHY AND THE HOW. HOW AM I DIFFERENT FROM ANY OTHER MUTANT OUT HERE? ALL I'VE DONE MY WHOLE LIFE IS RUN FROM PEOPLE WHO WERE TRYING TO KILL ME. AND THEN I TURN AROUND AND SOMEONE TELLS ME HOW AMAZING I AM.
WHY? WHAT MAKES ME SO SPECIAL?
EVERYTHING.
THAT'S NOT AN ANSWER.
I WANT THE TRUTH. JUST TELL ME. PLEASE.
TELL ME ABOUT THE PHOENIX.
HOW DID YOU HEAR ABOUT THE--
I KNOW MORE THAN YOU THINK I DO. I KNOW IT'S SOME BIG-TIME COSMIC FIREBIRD. AND I KNOW IT'S COMING FOR ME. JUST LIKE IT CAME YEARS AGO FOR YOUR WIFE, JEAN. I KNOW EVERYBODY GETS CRAZY SCARED WHENEVER IT'S EVEN MENTIONED. MOST ESPECIALLY YOU.
SO...
WOULD YOU LIKE TO TELL ME WHAT HAPPENS WHEN IT GETS HERE?

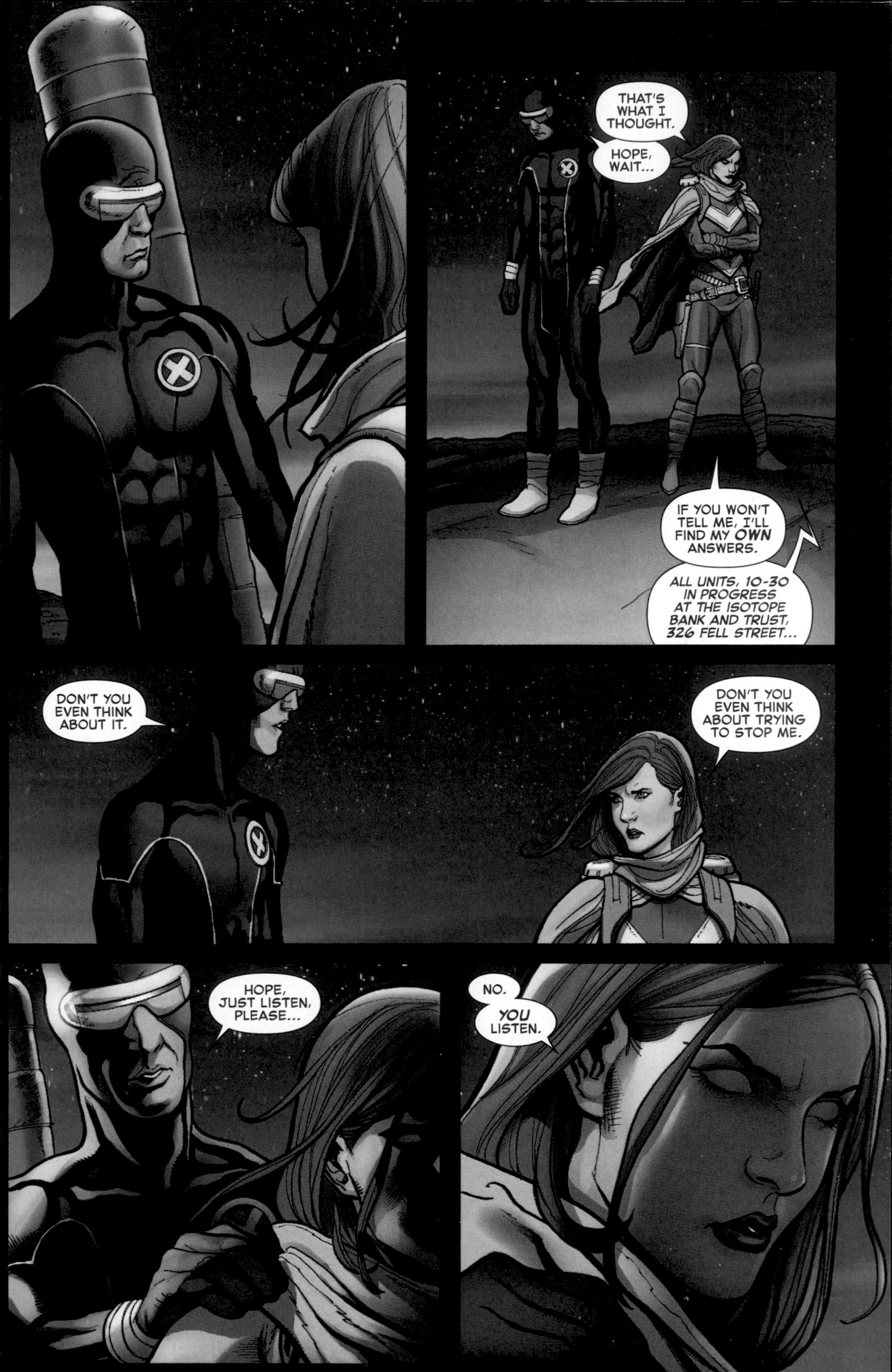

THAT'S WHAT I THOUGHT.
HOPE, WAIT...
IF YOU WON'T TELL ME, I'LL FIND MY OWN ANSWERS.
ALL UNITS, 10-30 IN PROGRESS AT THE ISOTOPE BANK AND TRUST, 326 FELL STREET...
DON'T YOU EVEN THINK ABOUT IT.
DON'T YOU EVEN THINK ABOUT TRYING TO STOP ME.
HOPE, JUST LISTEN, PLEASE...
NO.
YOU LISTEN.

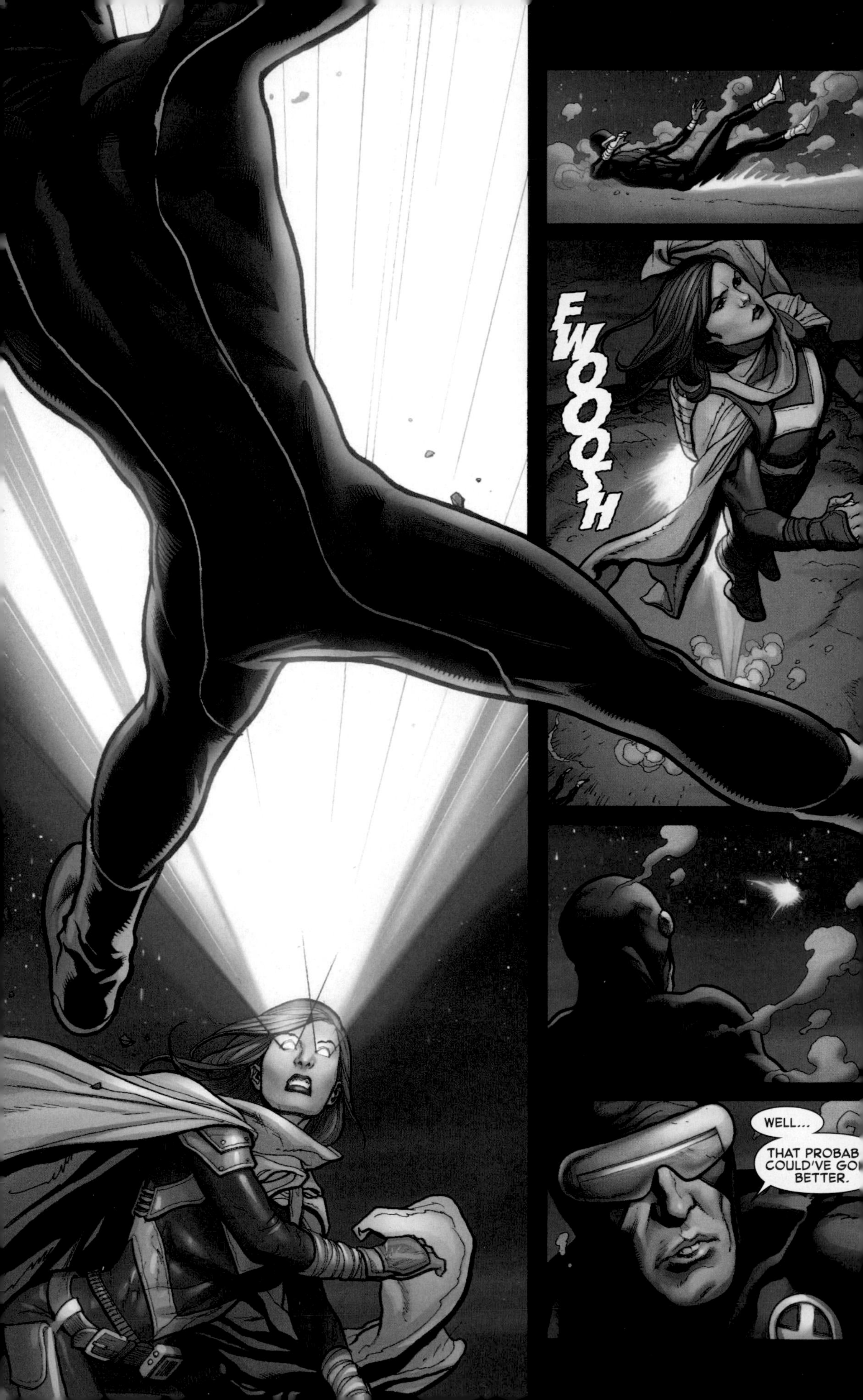
FWOOOSH
WELL...
THAT PROBAB
COULD'VE GO
BETTER.

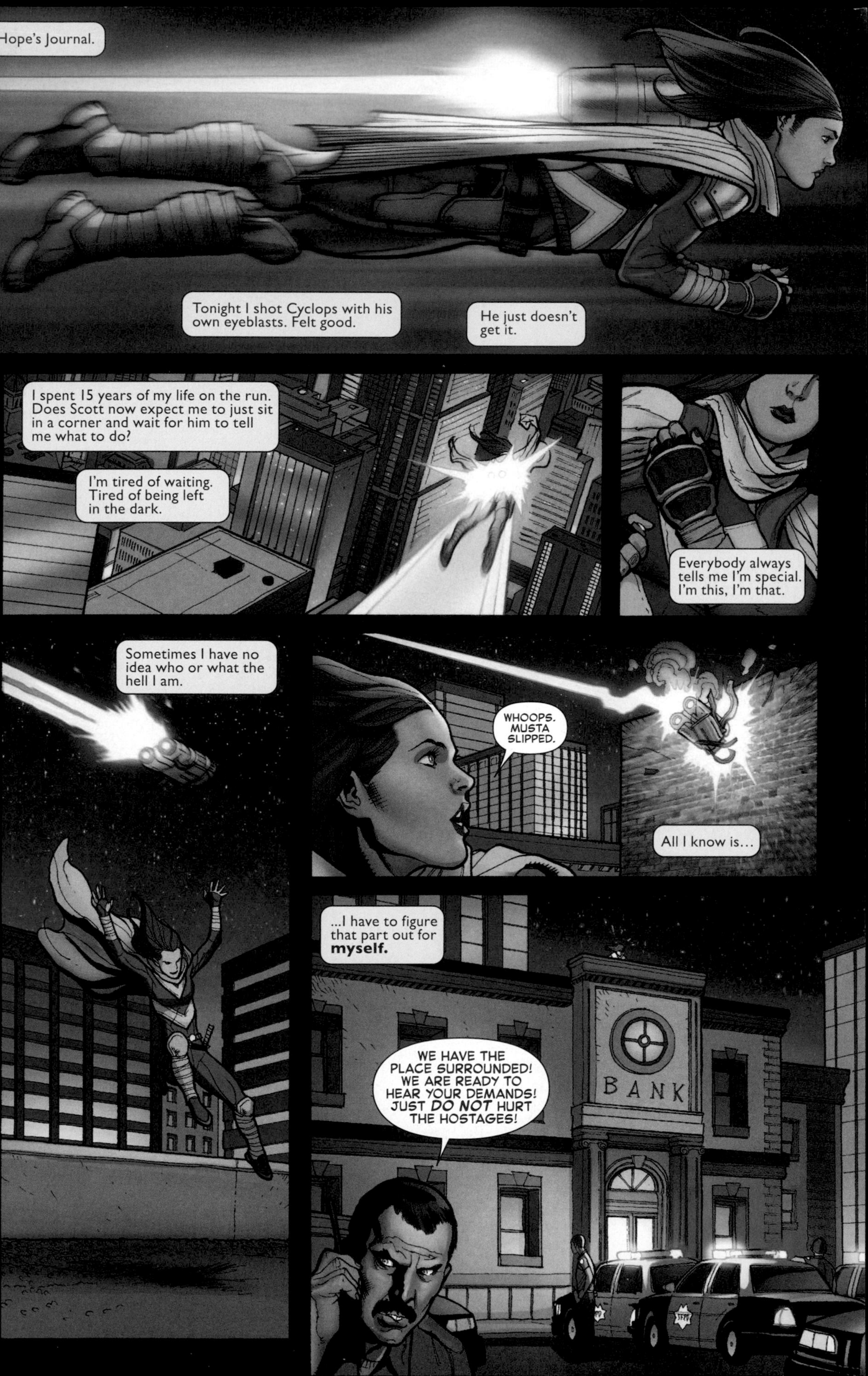
Hope's Journal.
Tonight I shot Cyclops with his own eyeblasts. Felt good.
He just doesn't get it.
I spent 15 years of my life on the run. Does Scott now expect me to just sit in a corner and wait for him to tell me what to do?
I'm tired of waiting. Tired of being left in the dark.
Everybody always tells me I'm special. I'm this, I'm that.
Sometimes I have no idea who or what the hell I am.
WHOOPS. MUSTA SLIPPED.
All I know is…
...I have to figure that part out for **myself.**
WE HAVE THE PLACE SURROUNDED! WE ARE READY TO HEAR YOUR DEMANDS! JUST ***DO NOT*** HURT THE HOSTAGES!
BANK

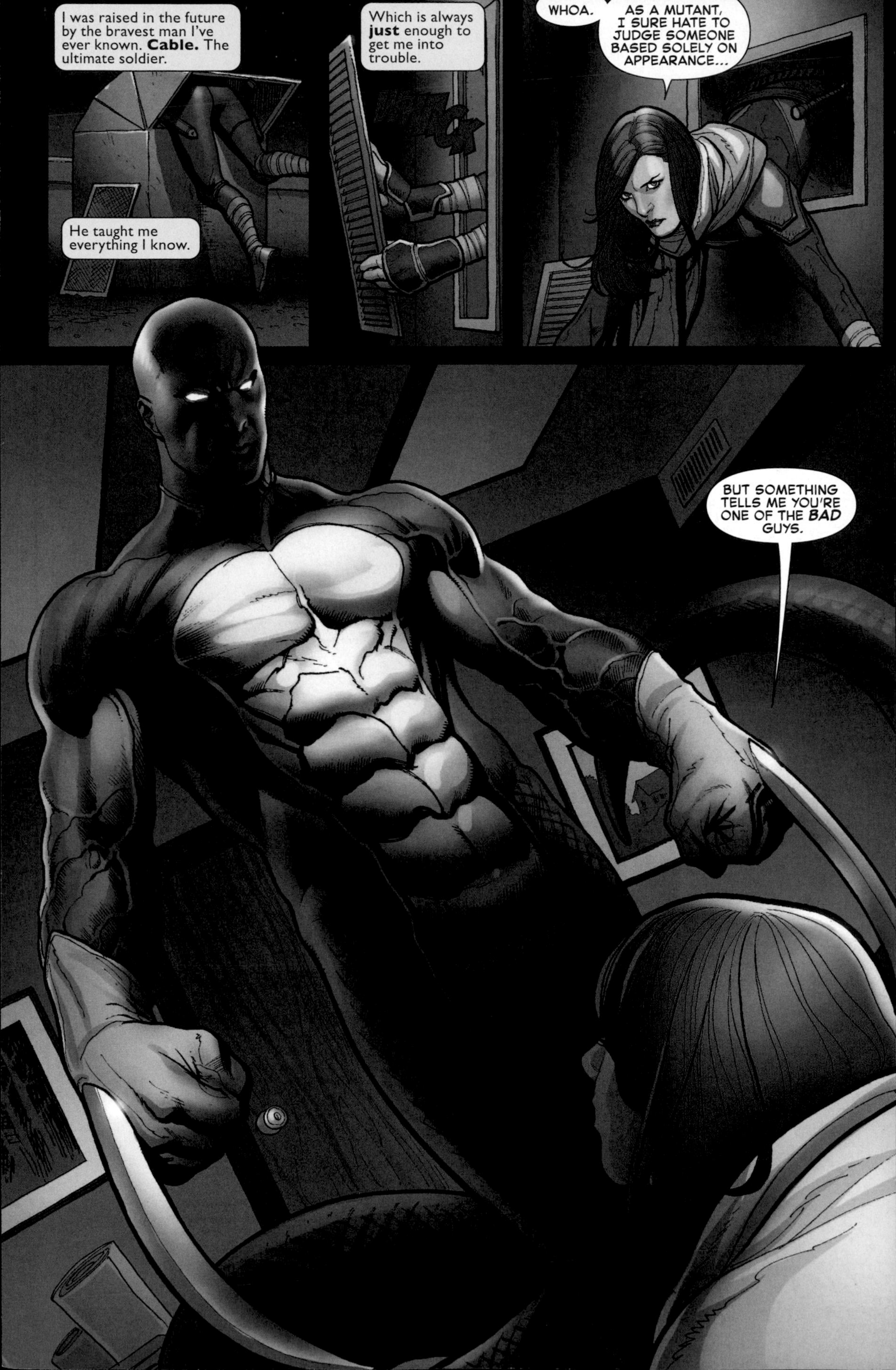
I was raised in the future by the bravest man I've ever known. **Cable.** The ultimate soldier.
He taught me everything I know.
Which is always **just** enough to get me into trouble.
WHOA.
AS A MUTANT, I SURE HATE TO JUDGE SOMEONE BASED SOLELY ON APPEARANCE...
BUT SOMETHING TELLS ME YOU'RE ONE OF THE *BAD* GUYS.

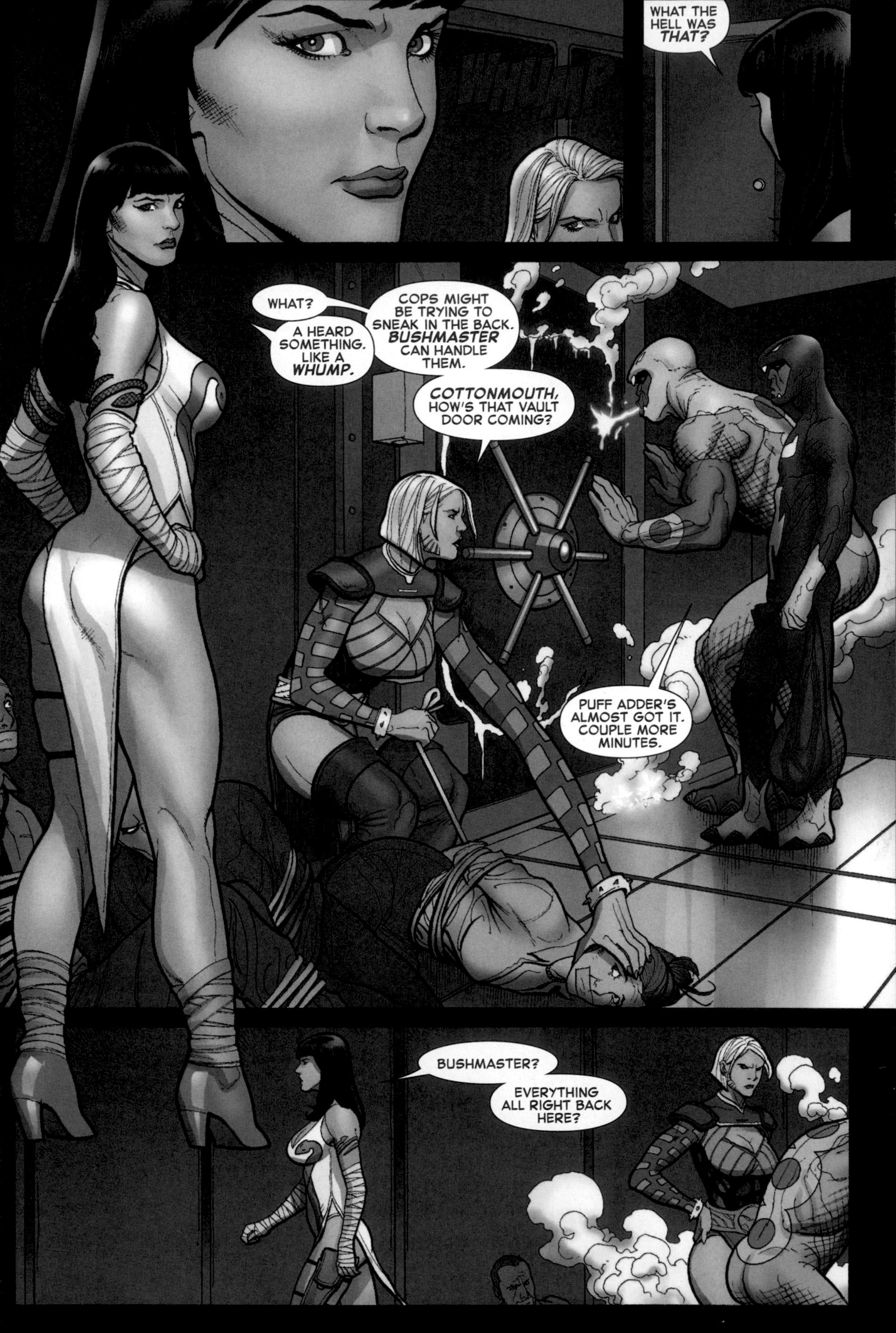
WHAT THE HELL WAS THAT?
WHAT?
A HEARD SOMETHING. LIKE A WHUMP.
COPS MIGHT BE TRYING TO SNEAK IN THE BACK. BUSHMASTER CAN HANDLE THEM.
COTTONMOUTH, HOW'S THAT VAULT DOOR COMING?
PUFF ADDER'S ALMOST GOT IT. COUPLE MORE MINUTES.
BUSHMASTER?
EVERYTHING ALL RIGHT BACK HERE?

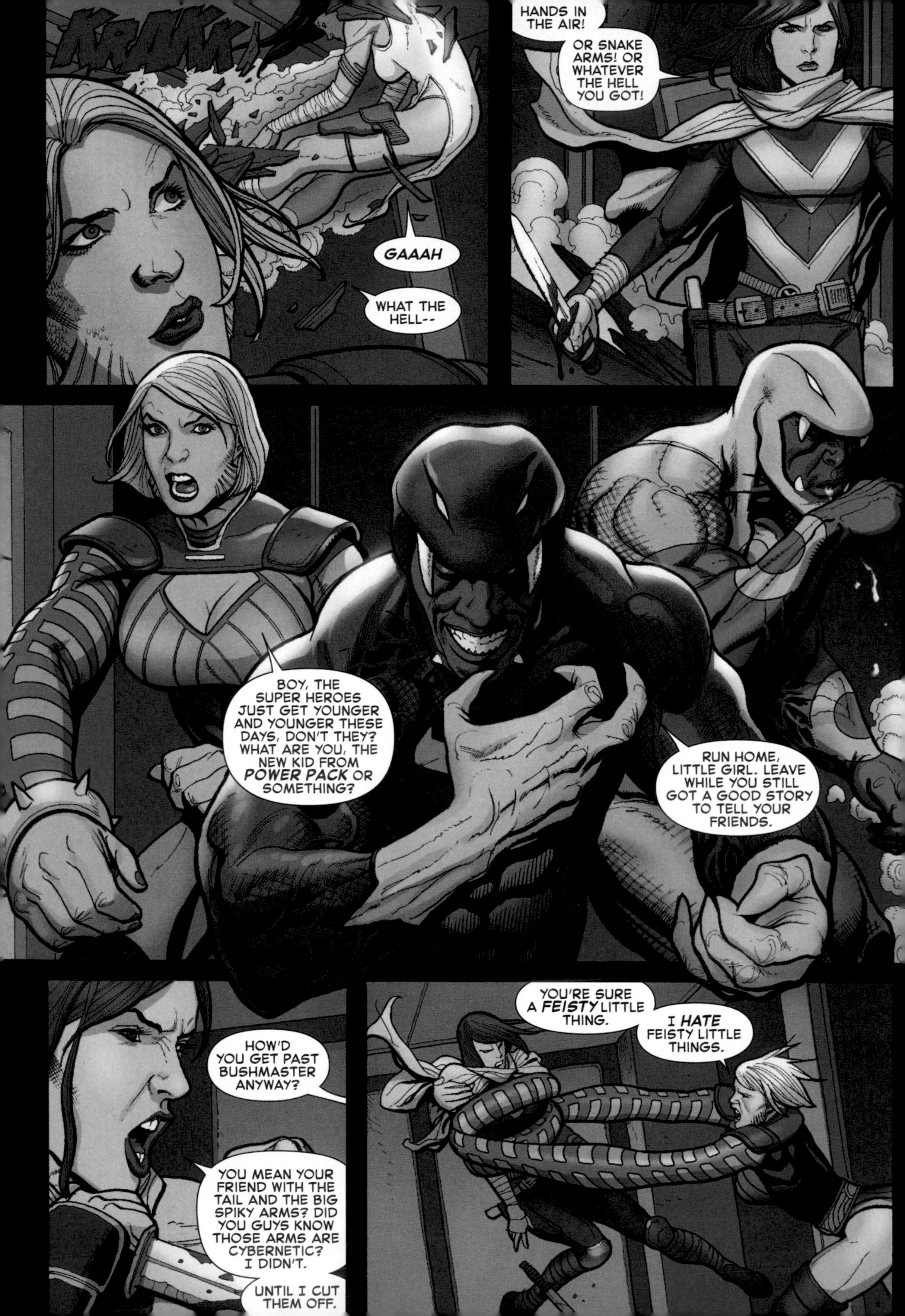
KRUNK
GAAAH
WHAT THE HELL--
HANDS IN THE AIR!
OR SNAKE ARMS! OR WHATEVER THE HELL YOU GOT!
BOY, THE SUPER HEROES JUST GET YOUNGER AND YOUNGER THESE DAYS, DON'T THEY? WHAT ARE YOU, THE NEW KID FROM POWER PACK OR SOMETHING?
RUN HOME, LITTLE GIRL. LEAVE WHILE YOU STILL GOT A GOOD STORY TO TELL YOUR FRIENDS.
HOW'D YOU GET PAST BUSHMASTER ANYWAY?
YOU MEAN YOUR FRIEND WITH THE TAIL AND THE BIG SPIKY ARMS? DID YOU GUYS KNOW THOSE ARMS ARE CYBERNETIC? I DIDN'T.
UNTIL I CUT THEM OFF.
YOU'RE SURE A FEISTY LITTLE THING.
I HATE FEISTY LITTLE THINGS.

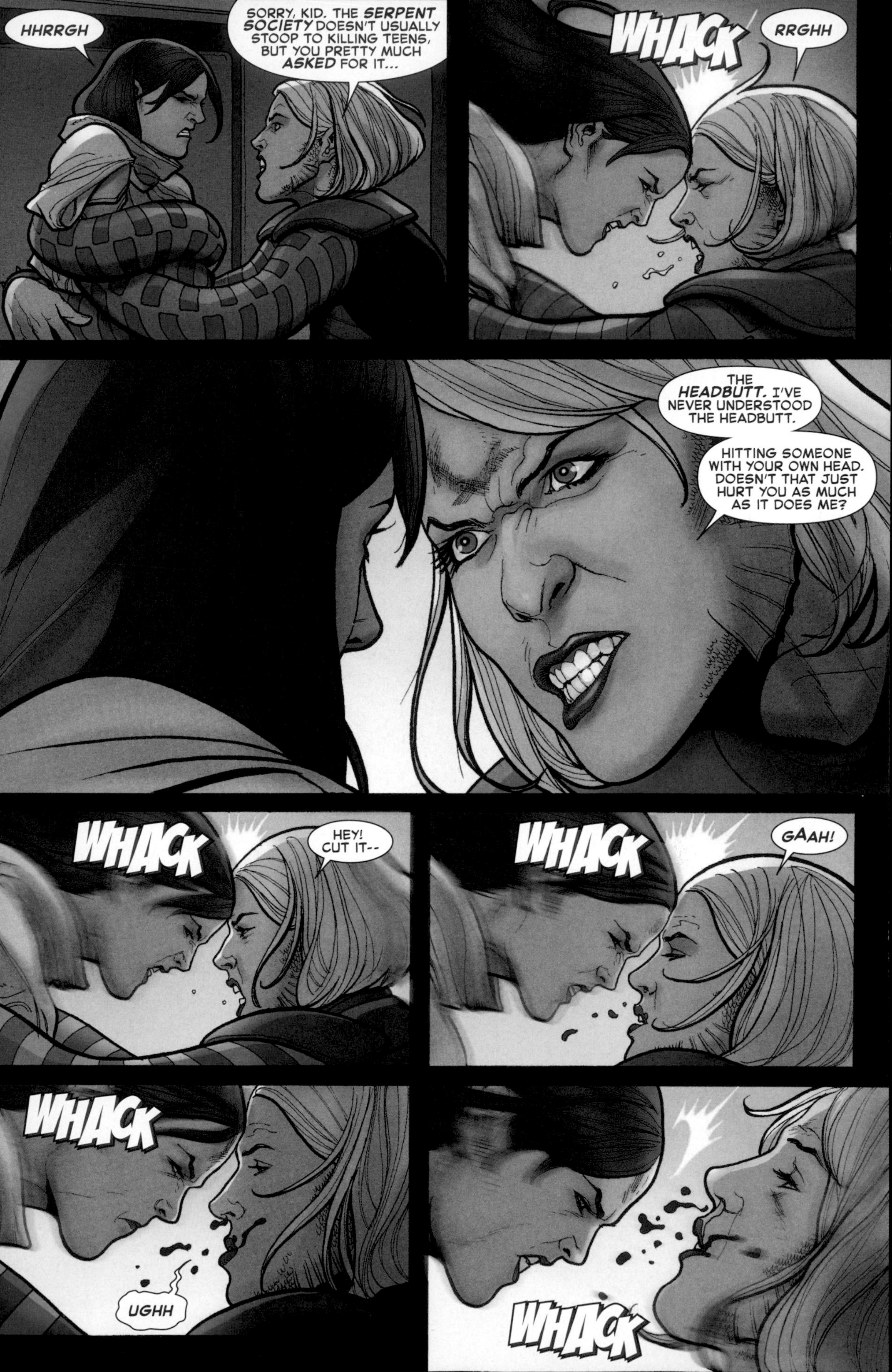
HHRRGH
SORRY, KID. THE SERPENT SOCIETY DOESN'T USUALLY STOOP TO KILLING TEENS, BUT YOU PRETTY MUCH ASKED FOR IT...
WHACK
RRGHH
THE HEADBUTT. I'VE NEVER UNDERSTOOD THE HEADBUTT.
HITTING SOMEONE WITH YOUR OWN HEAD. DOESN'T THAT JUST HURT YOU AS MUCH AS IT DOES ME?
WHACK
HEY! CUT IT--
WHACK
GAAH!
WHACK
UGHH
WHACK

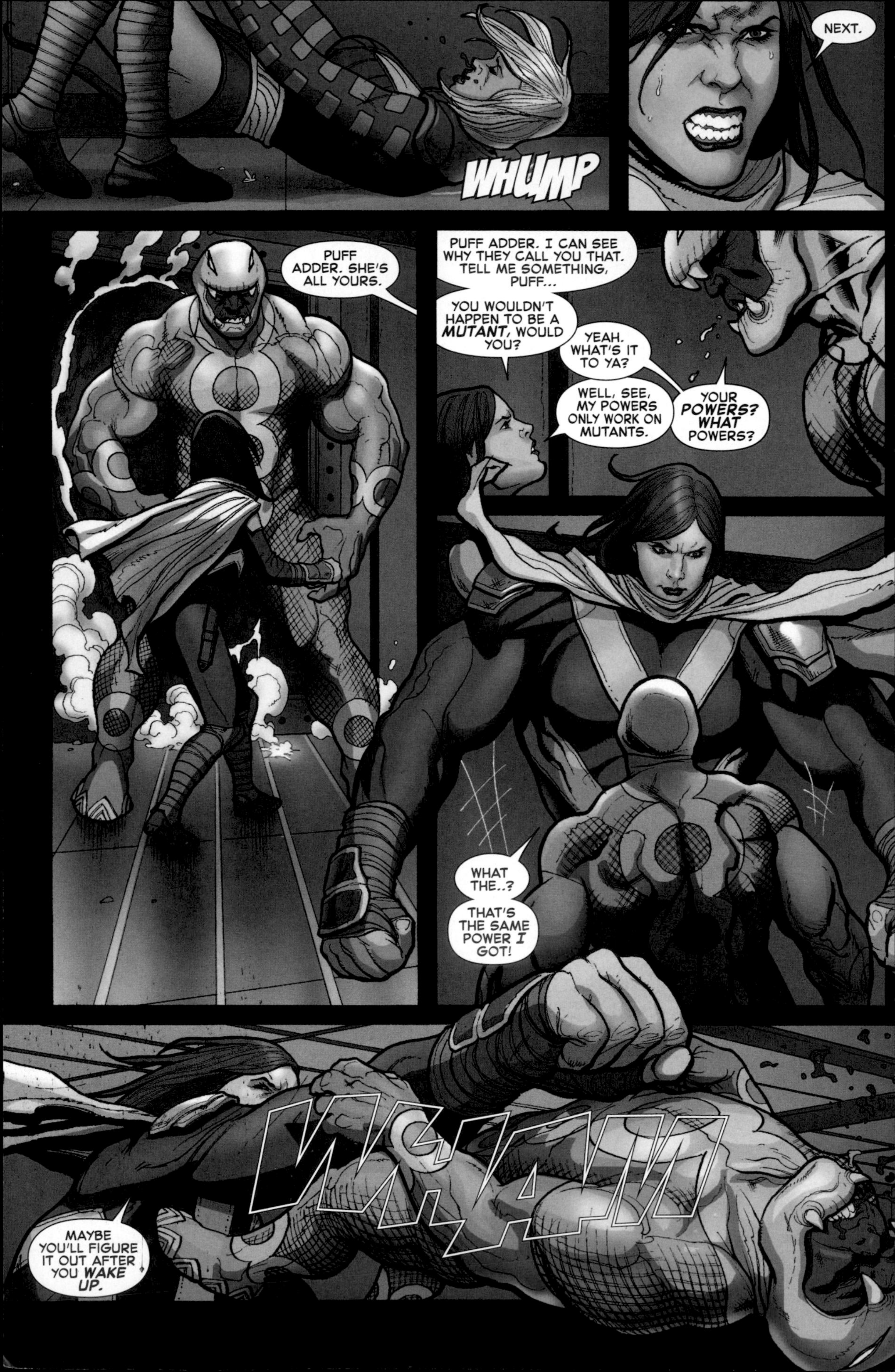
WHUMP
NEXT.
PUFF ADDER. SHE'S ALL YOURS.
PUFF ADDER. I CAN SEE WHY THEY CALL YOU THAT. TELL ME SOMETHING, PUFF...
YOU WOULDN'T HAPPEN TO BE A MUTANT, WOULD YOU?
YEAH. WHAT'S IT TO YA?
WELL, SEE, MY POWERS ONLY WORK ON MUTANTS.
YOUR POWERS? WHAT POWERS?
WHAT THE..?
THAT'S THE SAME POWER I GOT!
WHAM
MAYBE YOU'LL FIGURE IT OUT AFTER YOU WAKE UP.

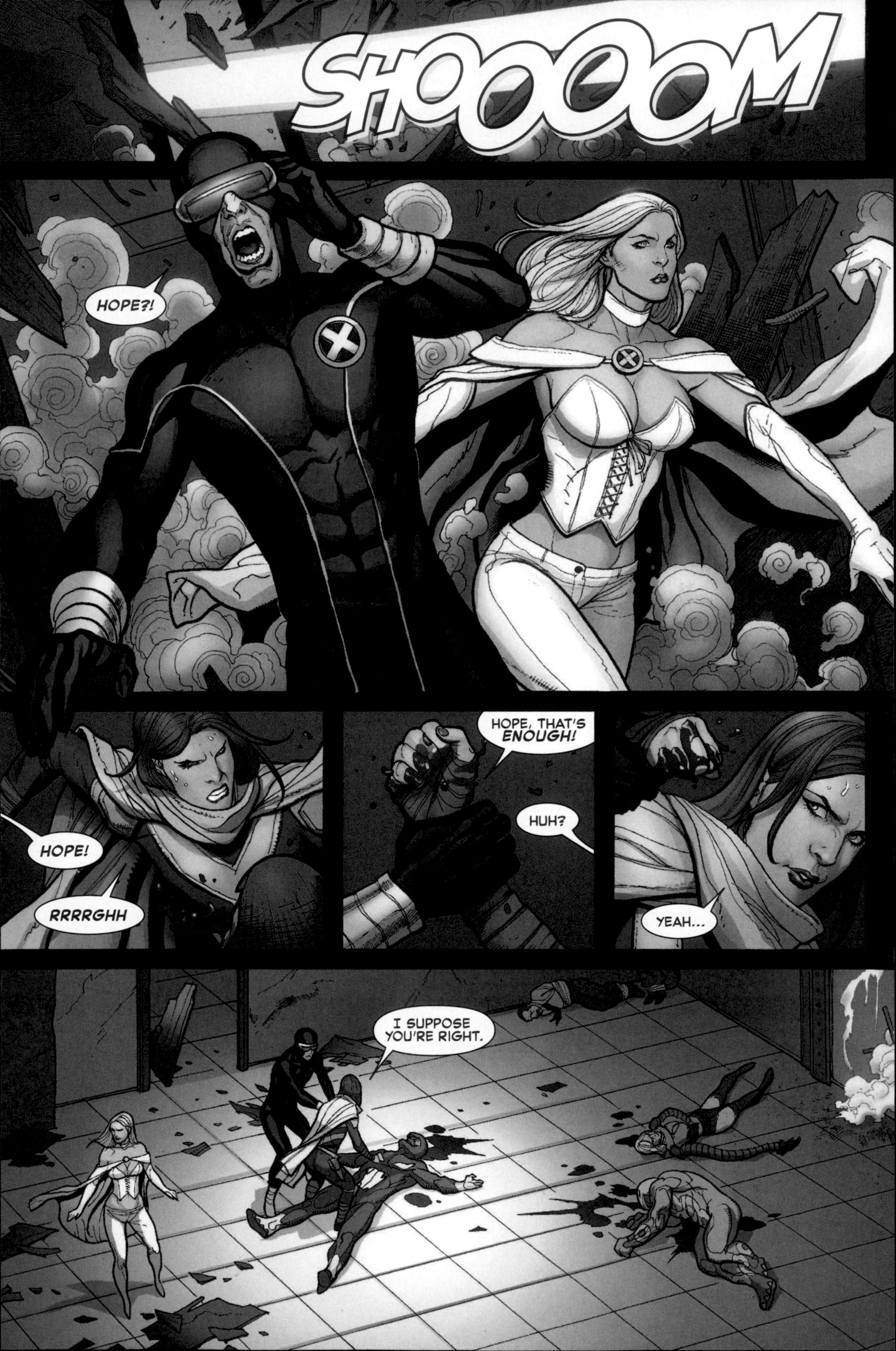
SHOOOOM
HOPE?!
HOPE!
RRRRGHH
HOPE, THAT'S *ENOUGH!*
HUH?
YEAH...
I SUPPOSE YOU'RE RIGHT.

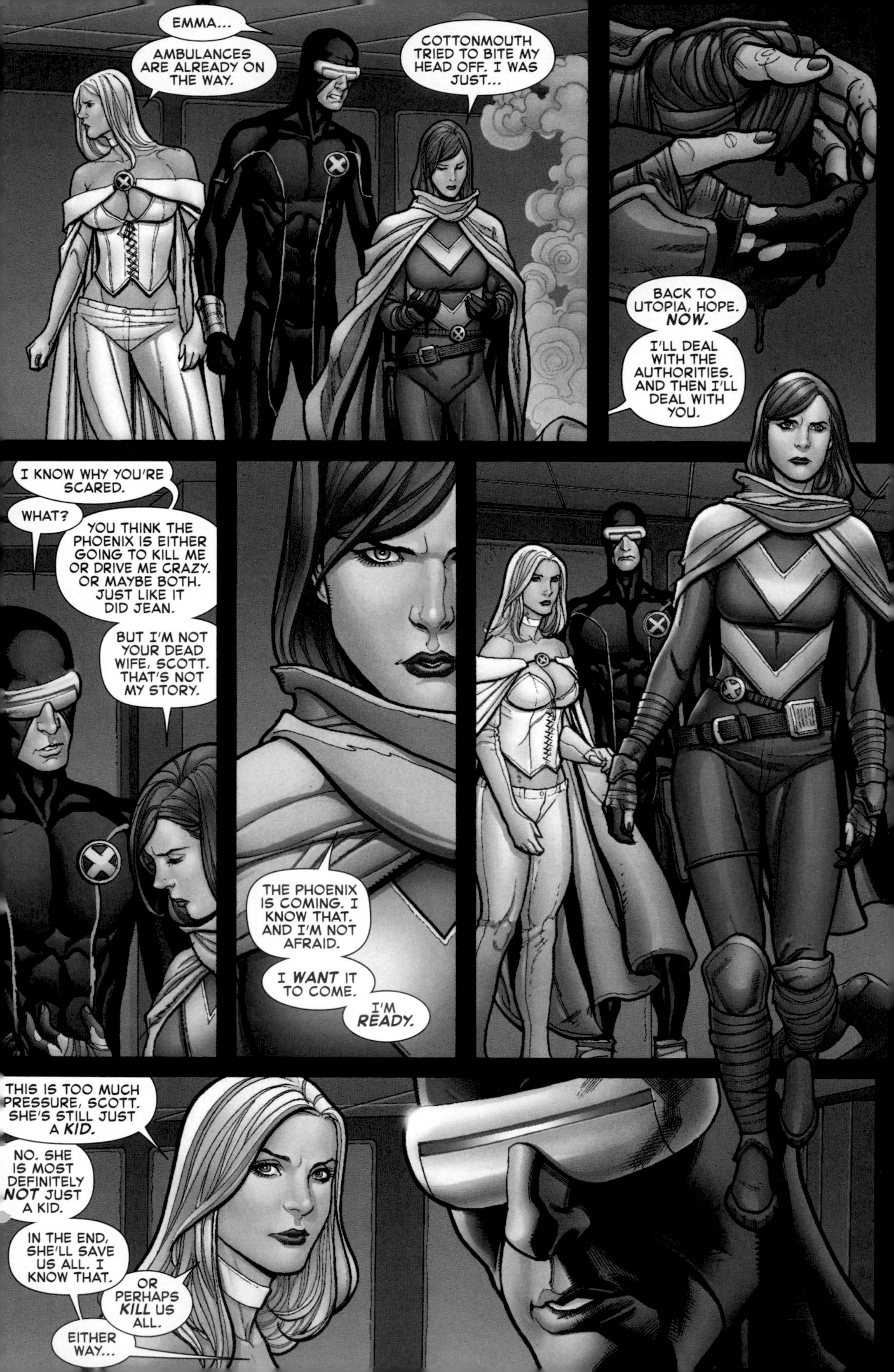

EMMA...
AMBULANCES ARE ALREADY ON THE WAY.
COTTONMOUTH TRIED TO BITE MY HEAD OFF. I WAS JUST...
BACK TO UTOPIA, HOPE. NOW.
I'LL DEAL WITH THE AUTHORITIES. AND THEN I'LL DEAL WITH YOU.
I KNOW WHY YOU'RE SCARED.
WHAT?
YOU THINK THE PHOENIX IS EITHER GOING TO KILL ME OR DRIVE ME CRAZY. OR MAYBE BOTH. JUST LIKE IT DID JEAN.
BUT I'M NOT YOUR DEAD WIFE, SCOTT. THAT'S NOT MY STORY.
THE PHOENIX IS COMING. I KNOW THAT. AND I'M NOT AFRAID.
I WANT IT TO COME.
I'M READY.
THIS IS TOO MUCH PRESSURE, SCOTT. SHE'S STILL JUST A KID.
NO. SHE IS MOST DEFINITELY NOT JUST A KID.
IN THE END, SHE'LL SAVE US ALL. I KNOW THAT.
OR PERHAPS KILL US ALL.
EITHER WAY...

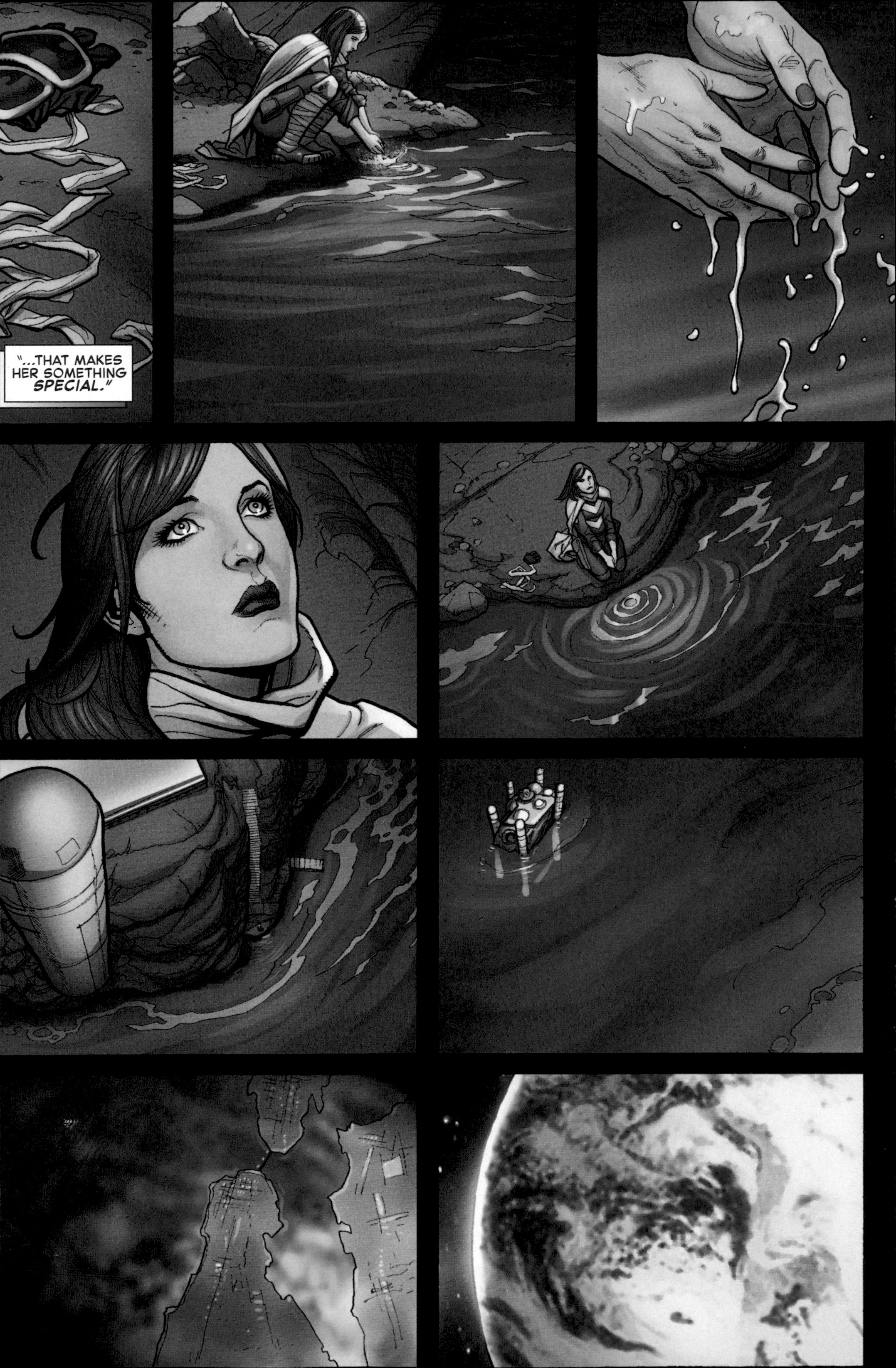
"...THAT MAKES HER SOMETHING SPECIAL."

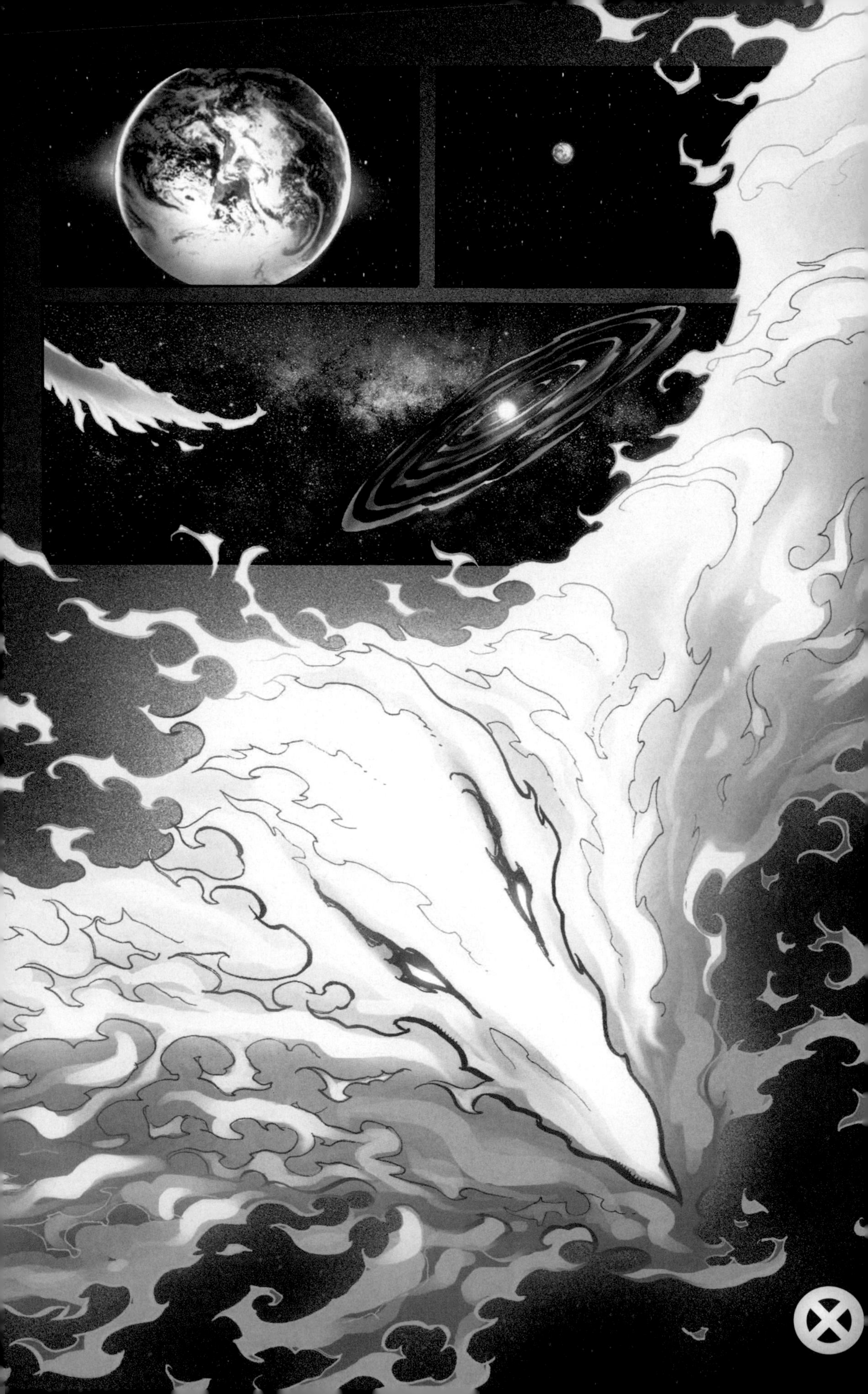

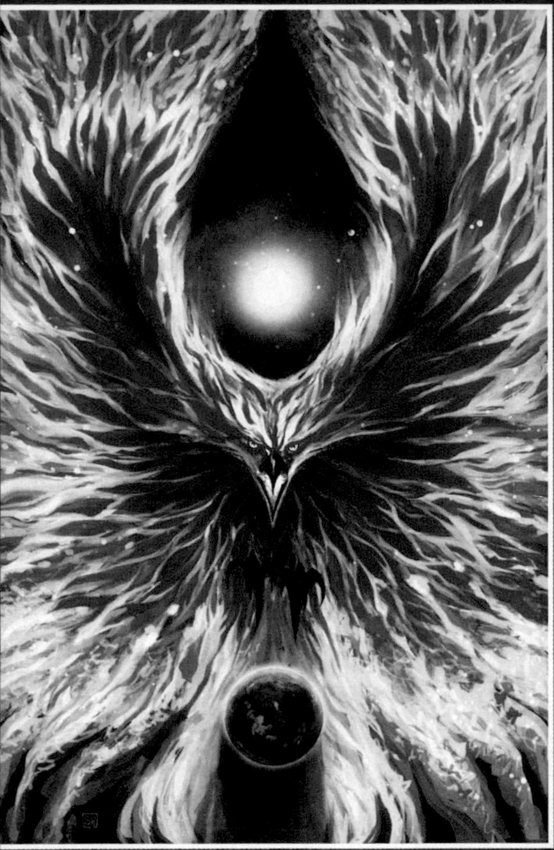

AVX #0 VARIANT
BY **STEPHANIE HANS**

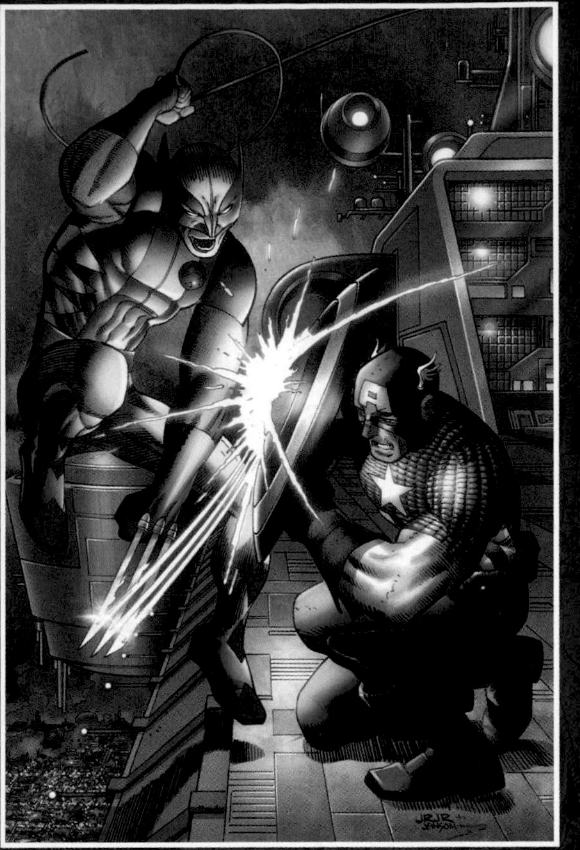

AVX #1 VARIANT
BY **JOHN ROMITA JR., KLAUS JANSON & PAUL MOUNTS**

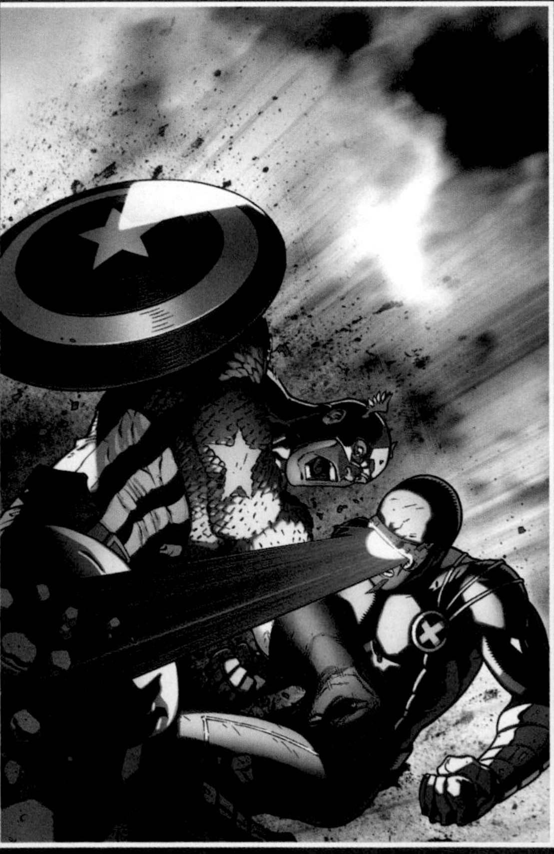

AVX #1 VARIANT
BY **RYAN STEGMAN, MICHAEL BABINSKI & MARTE GRACIA**

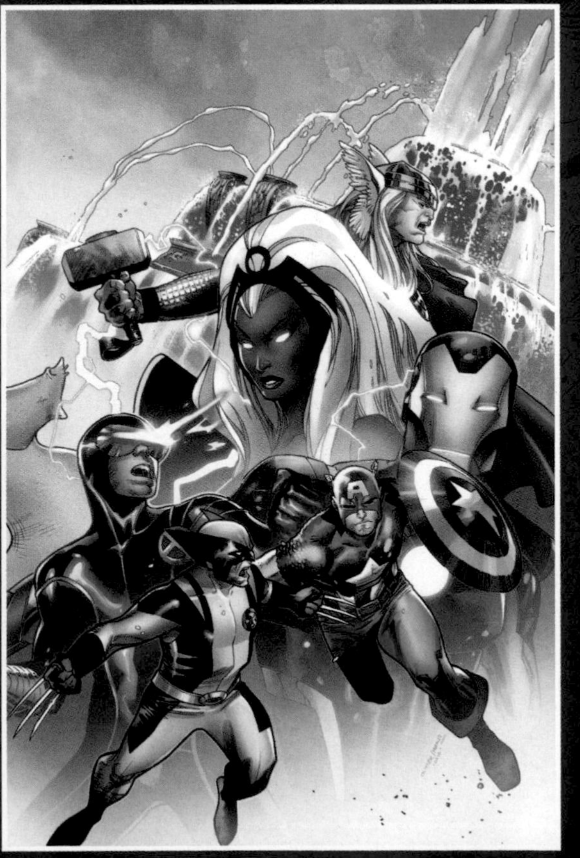

AVX #1 C2E2 VARIANT
BY **OLIVIER COIPEL**

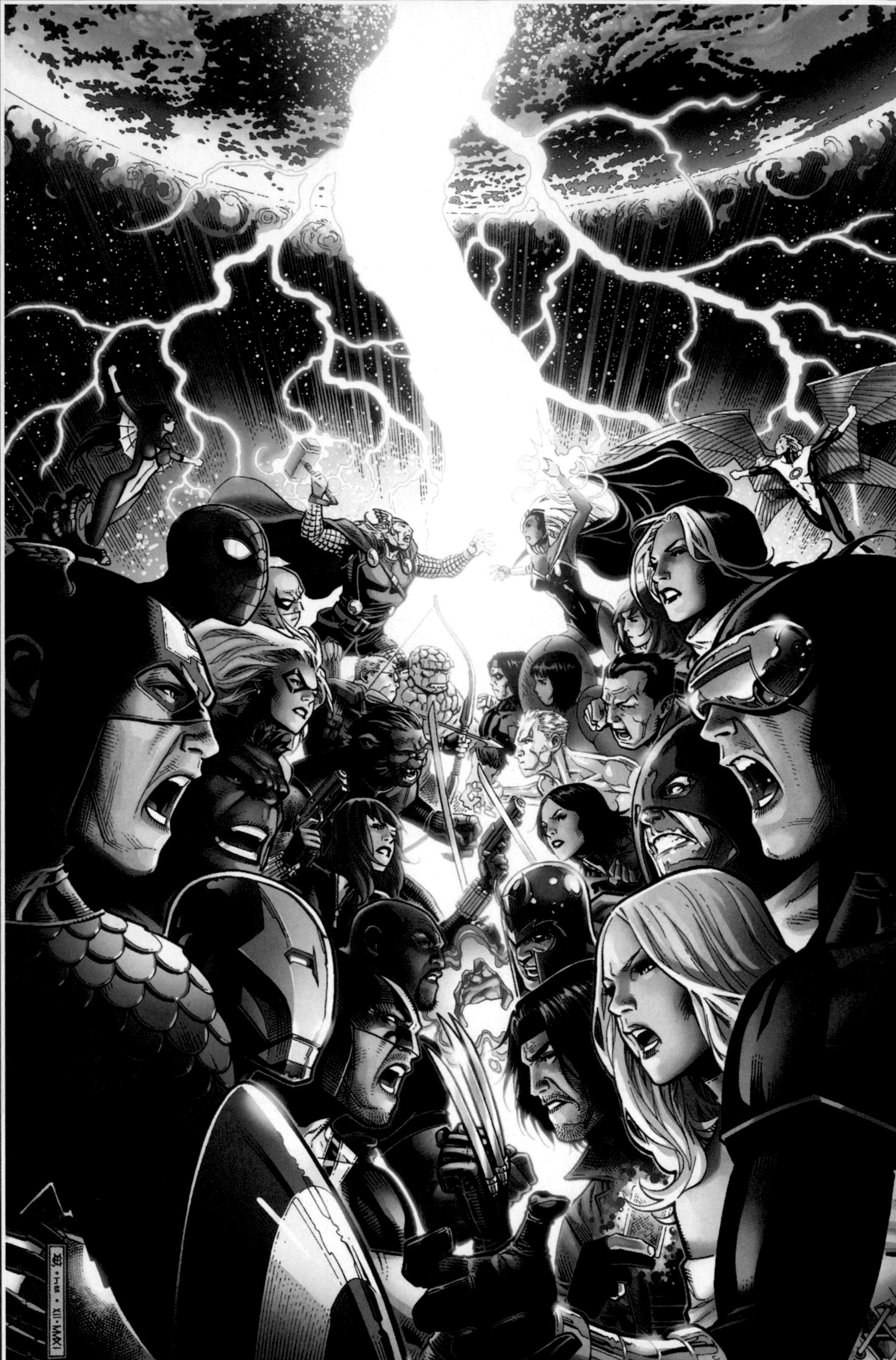

ROUND 1

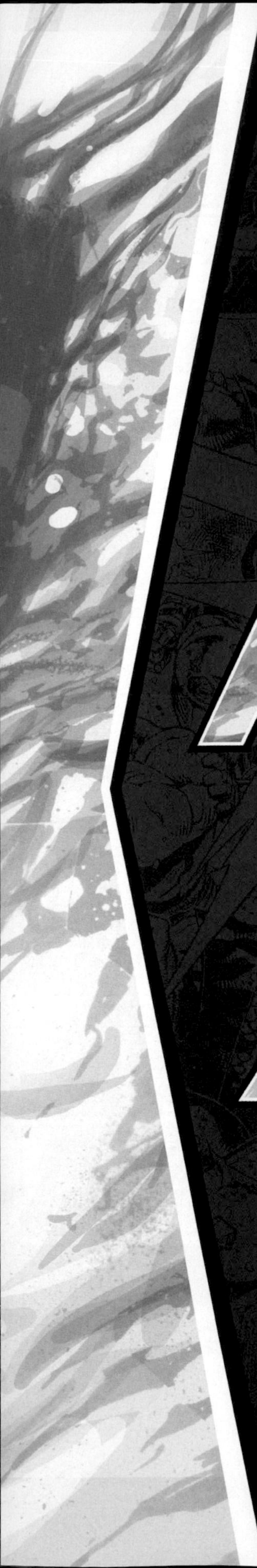

AND THERE CAME A DAY, A DAY UNLIKE ANY OTHER, WHEN EARTH'S MIGHTIEST HEROES FOUND THEMSELVES UNITED AGAINST A COMMON THREAT! ON THAT DAY THE AVENGERS WERE BORN, TO FIGHT THE FOES NO SINGLE SUPER HERO COULD WITHSTAND!

AVENGERS VS. X-MEN

CHILDREN OF THE ATOM. MUTANTS — FEARED AND HATED BY THE WORLD THEY HAVE SWORN TO PROTECT. THESE ARE THE STRANGEST HEROES OF ALL!

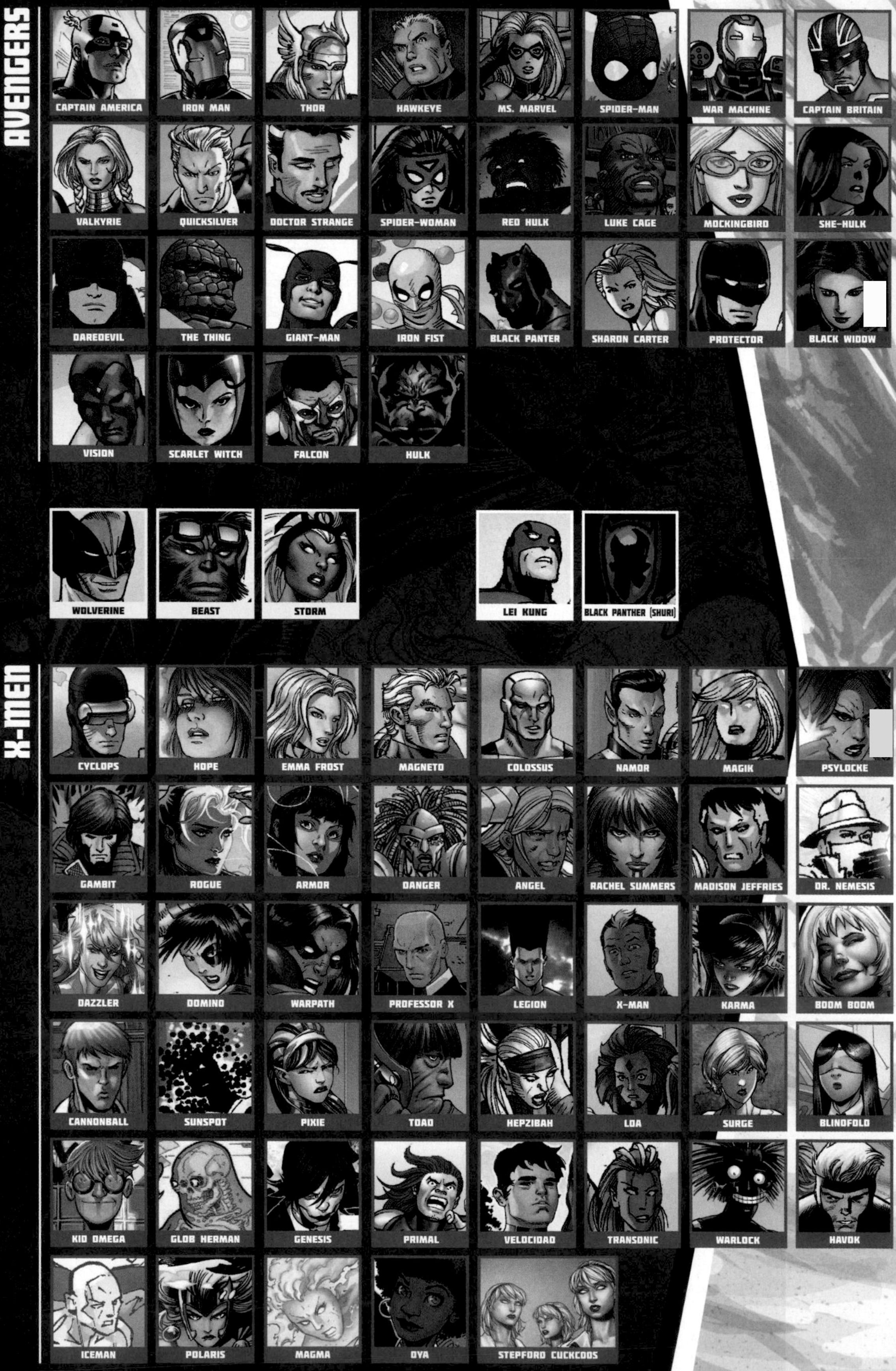

AVENGERS
CAPTAIN AMERICA
IRON MAN
THOR
HAWKEYE
MS. MARVEL
SPIDER-MAN
WAR MACHINE
CAPTAIN BRITAIN
VALKYRIE
QUICKSILVER
DOCTOR STRANGE
SPIDER-WOMAN
RED HULK
LUKE CAGE
MOCKINGBIRD
SHE-HULK
DAREDEVIL
THE THING
GIANT-MAN
IRON FIST
BLACK PANTER
SHARON CARTER
PROTECTOR
BLACK WIDOW
VISION
SCARLET WITCH
FALCON
HULK
WOLVERINE
BEAST
STORM
LEI KUNG
BLACK PANTHER (SHURI)
X-MEN
CYCLOPS
HOPE
EMMA FROST
MAGNETO
COLOSSUS
NAMOR
MAGIK
PSYLOCKE
GAMBIT
ROGUE
ARMOR
DANGER
ANGEL
RACHEL SUMMERS
MADISON JEFFRIES
DR. NEMESIS
DAZZLER
DOMINO
WARPATH
PROFESSOR X
LEGION
X-MAN
KARMA
BOOM BOOM
CANNONBALL
SUNSPOT
PIXIE
TOAD
HEPZIBAH
LOA
SURGE
BLINDFOLD
KID OMEGA
GLOB HERMAN
GENESIS
PRIMAL
VELOCIDAD
TRANSONIC
WARLOCK
HAVOK
ICEMAN
POLARIS
MAGMA
OYA
STEPFORD CUCKCOOS

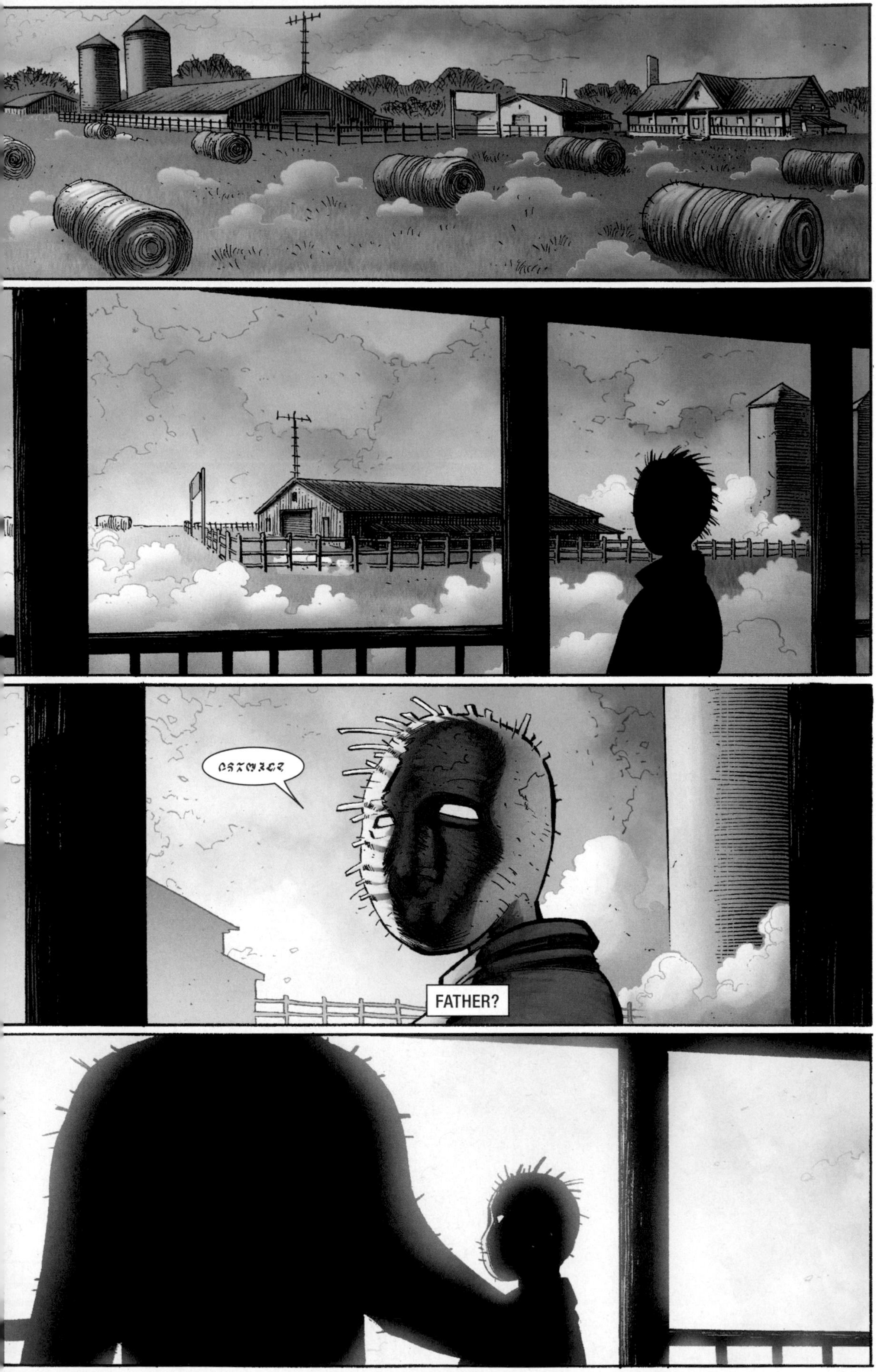
FATHER?

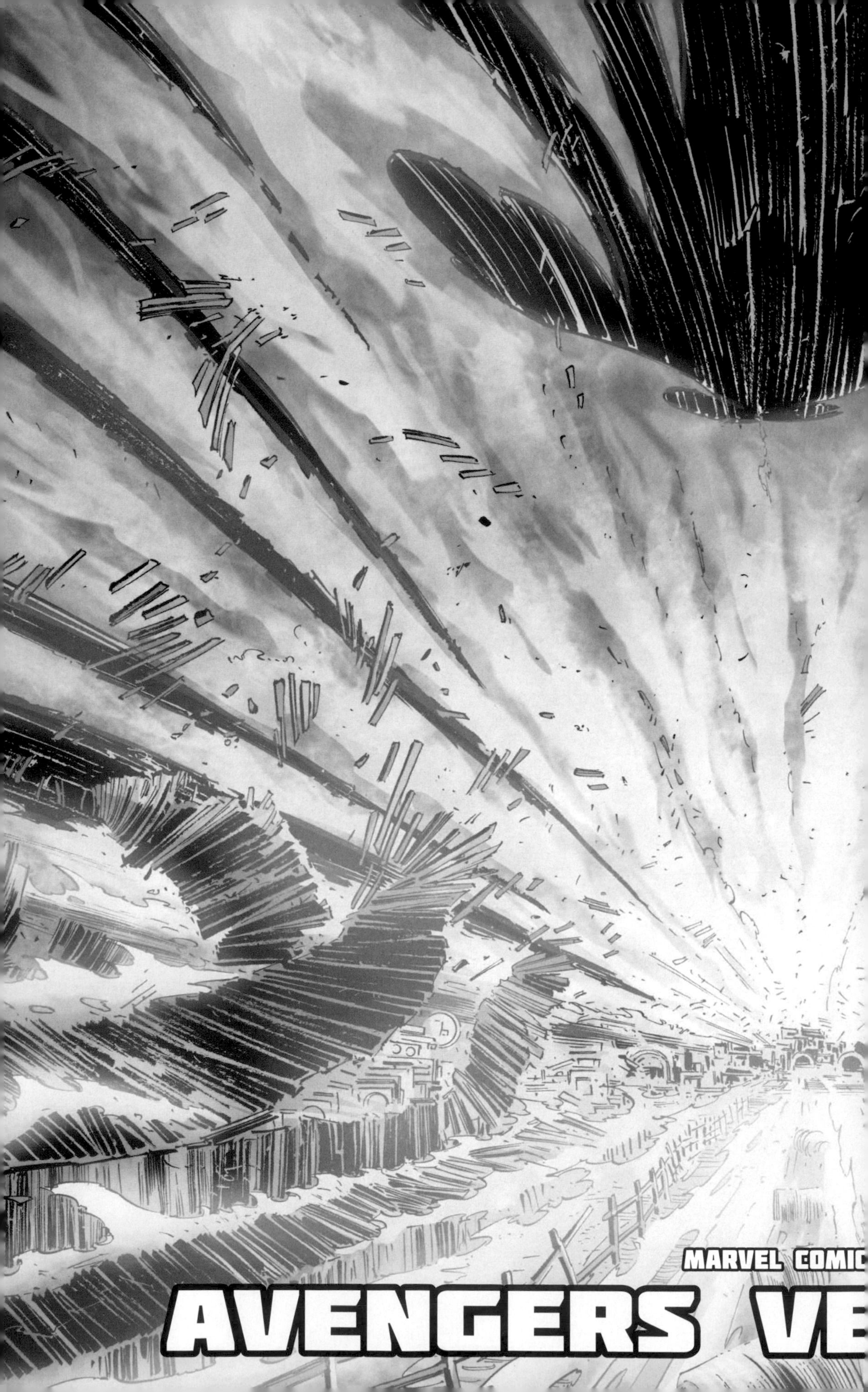
MARVEL COMIC
AVENGERS VE

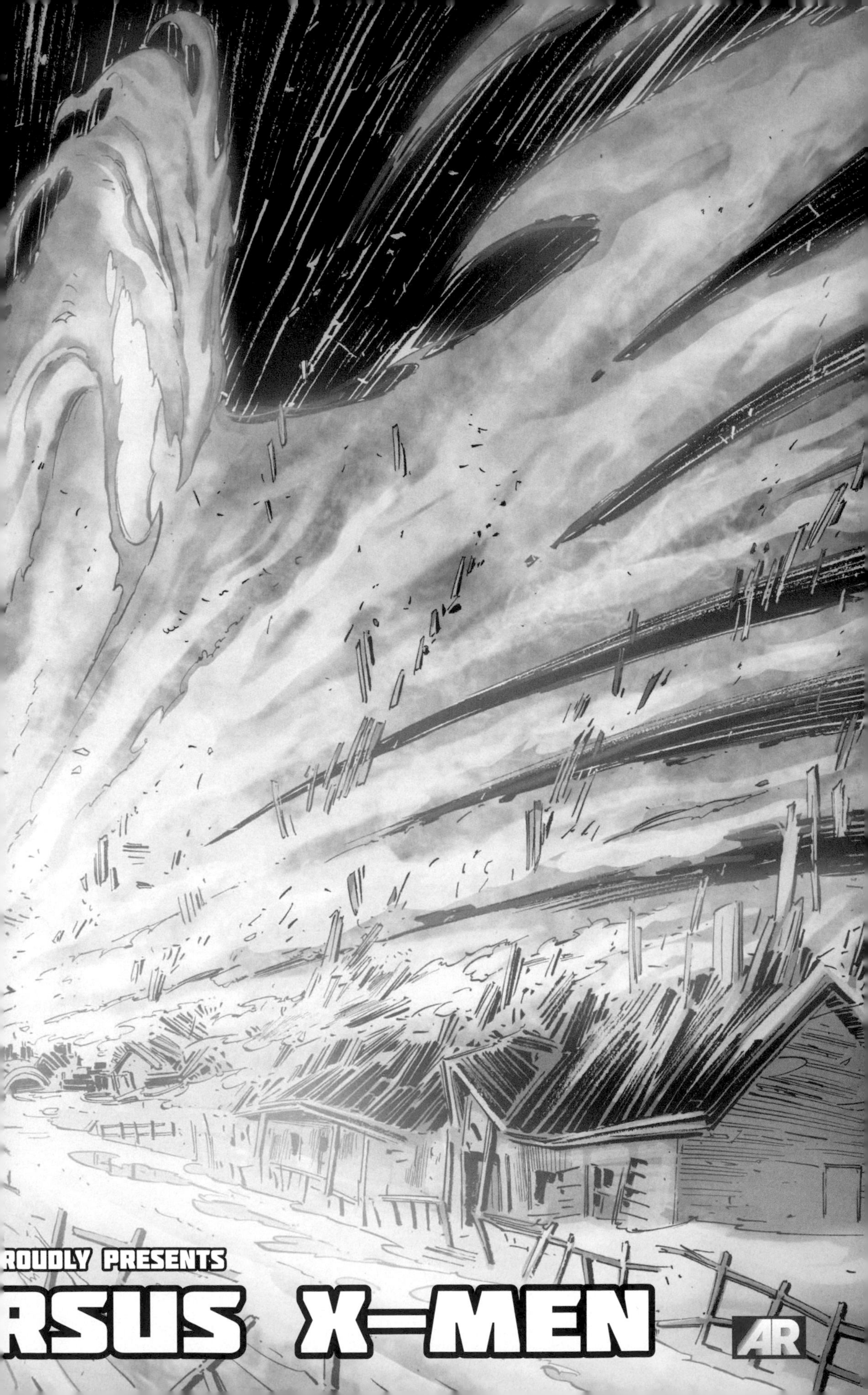
ROUDLY PRESENTS
RSUS X-MEN
AR

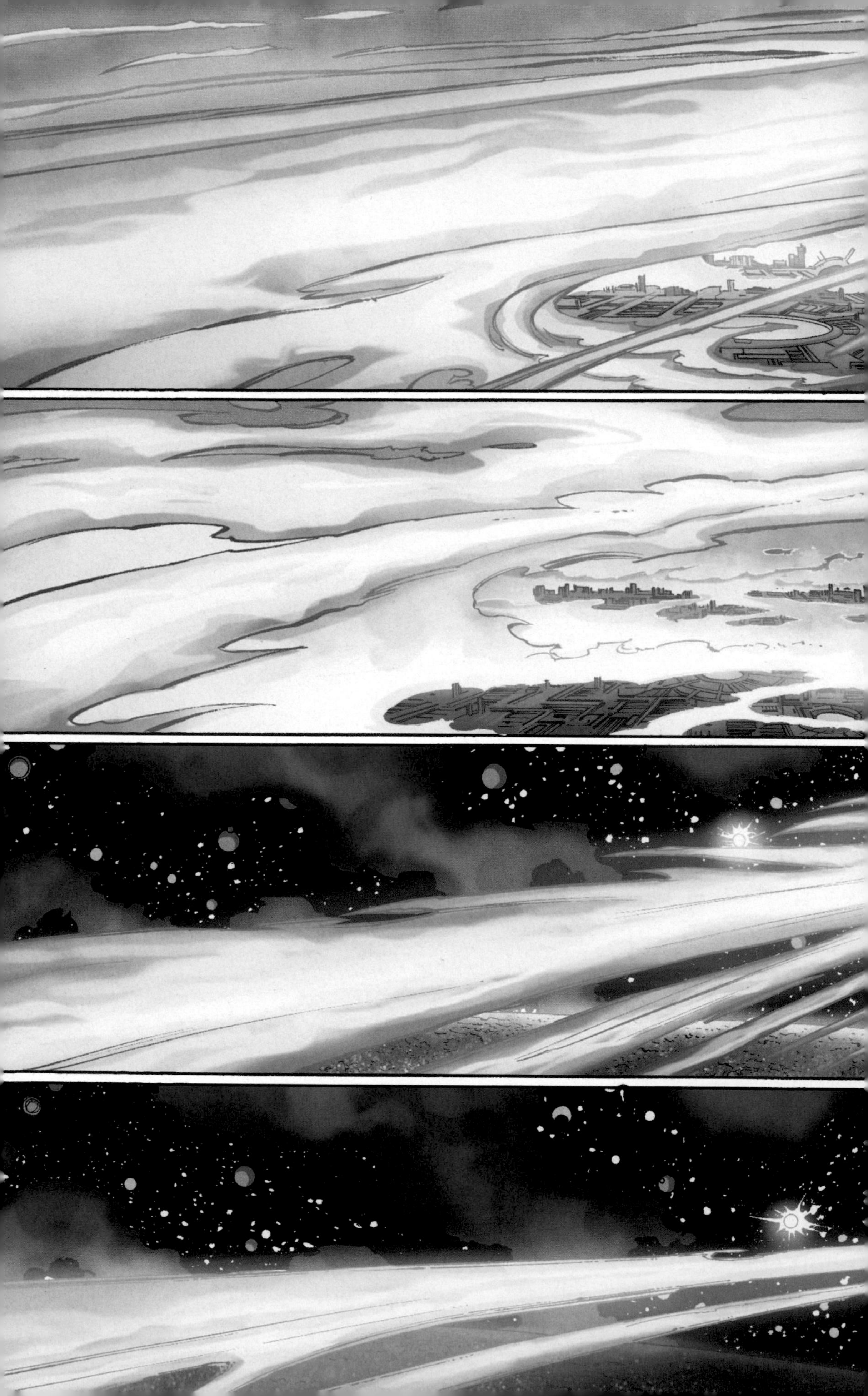

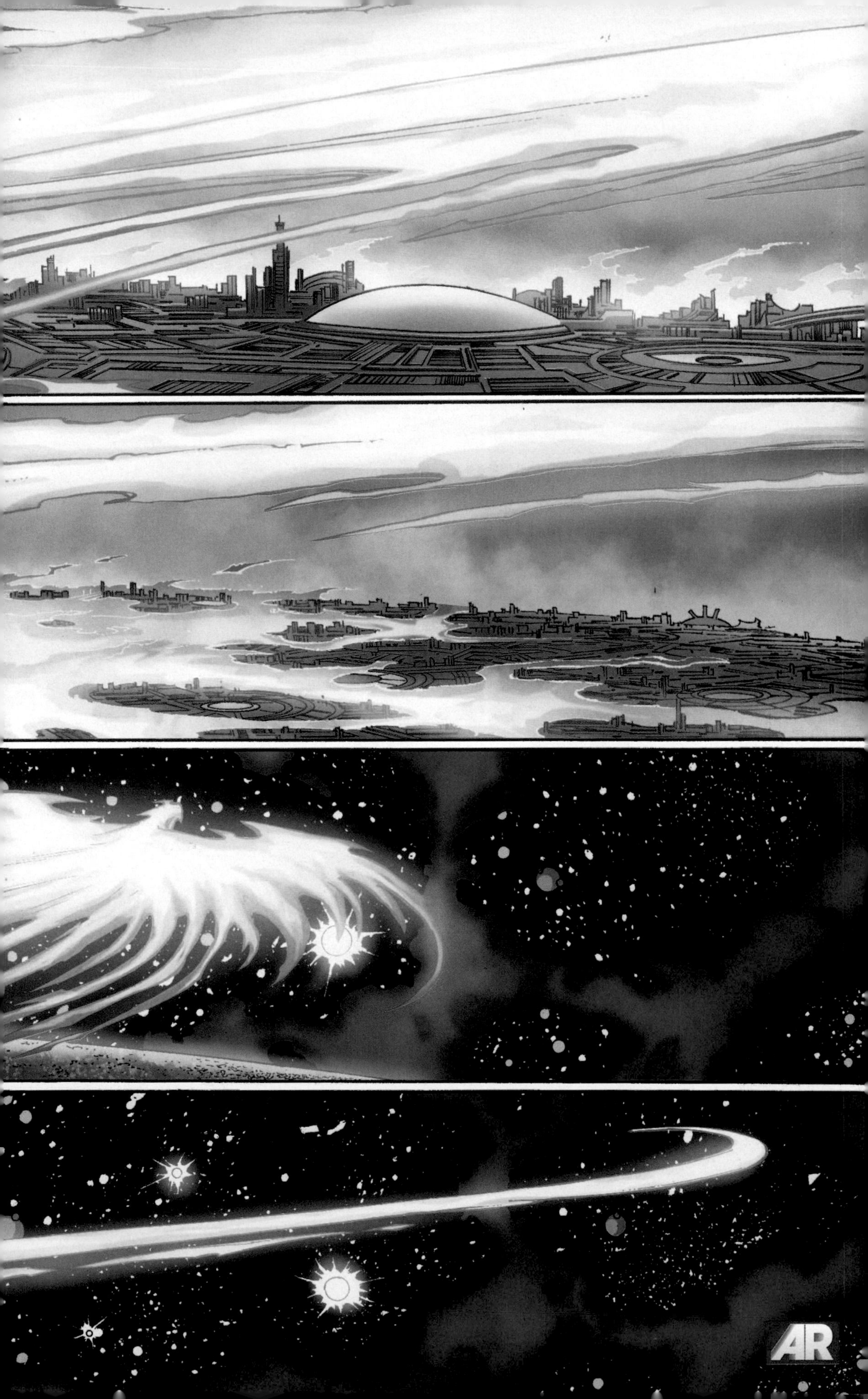

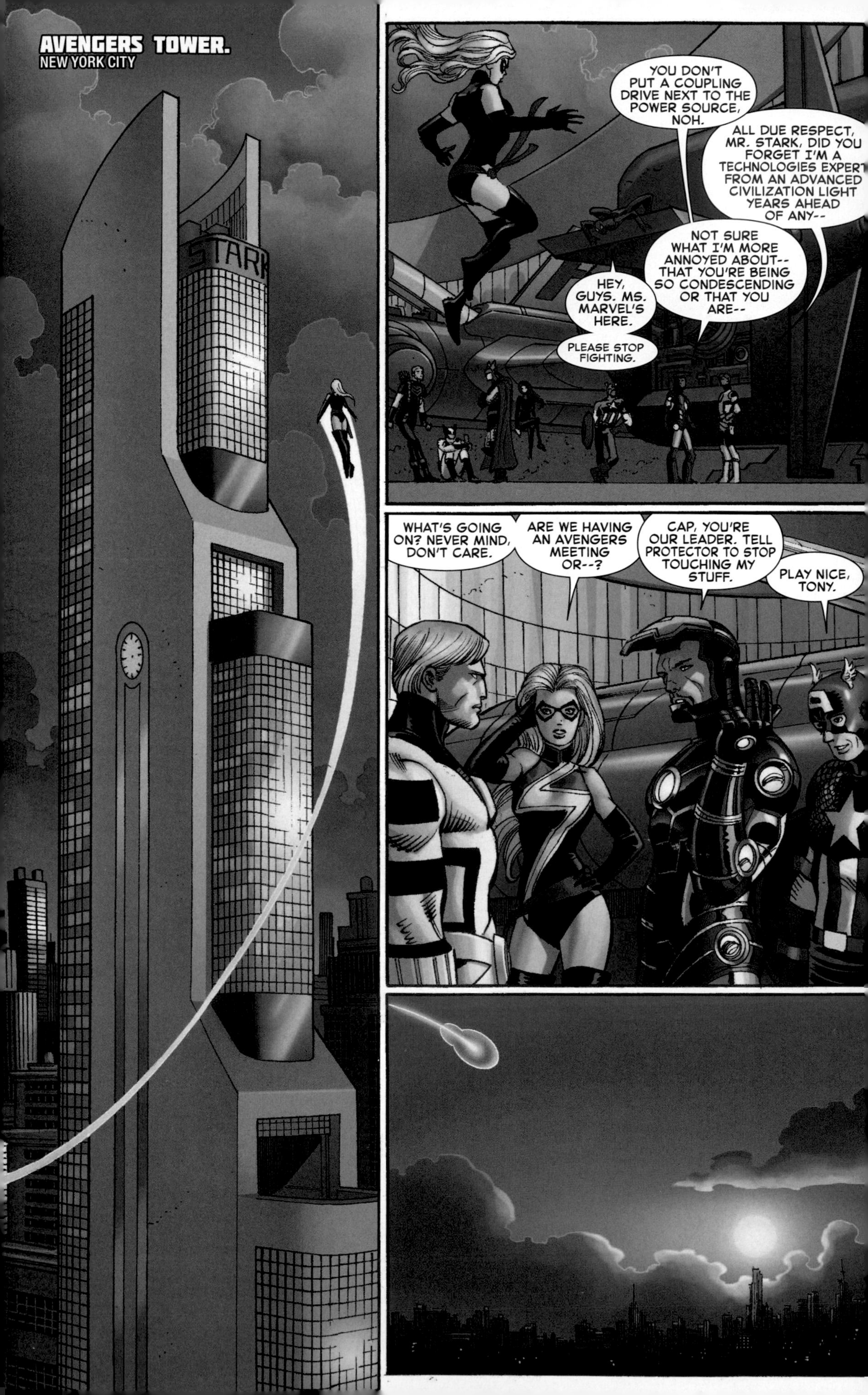
AVENGERS TOWER.
NEW YORK CITY
STARK
YOU DON'T PUT A COUPLING DRIVE NEXT TO THE POWER SOURCE, NOH.
ALL DUE RESPECT, MR. STARK, DID YOU FORGET I'M A TECHNOLOGIES EXPERT FROM AN ADVANCED CIVILIZATION LIGHT YEARS AHEAD OF ANY--
NOT SURE WHAT I'M MORE ANNOYED ABOUT-- THAT YOU'RE BEING SO CONDESCENDING OR THAT YOU ARE--
HEY, GUYS. MS. MARVEL'S HERE.
PLEASE STOP FIGHTING.
WHAT'S GOING ON? NEVER MIND, DON'T CARE.
ARE WE HAVING AN AVENGERS MEETING OR--?
CAP, YOU'RE OUR LEADER. TELL PROTECTOR TO STOP TOUCHING MY STUFF.
PLAY NICE, TONY.

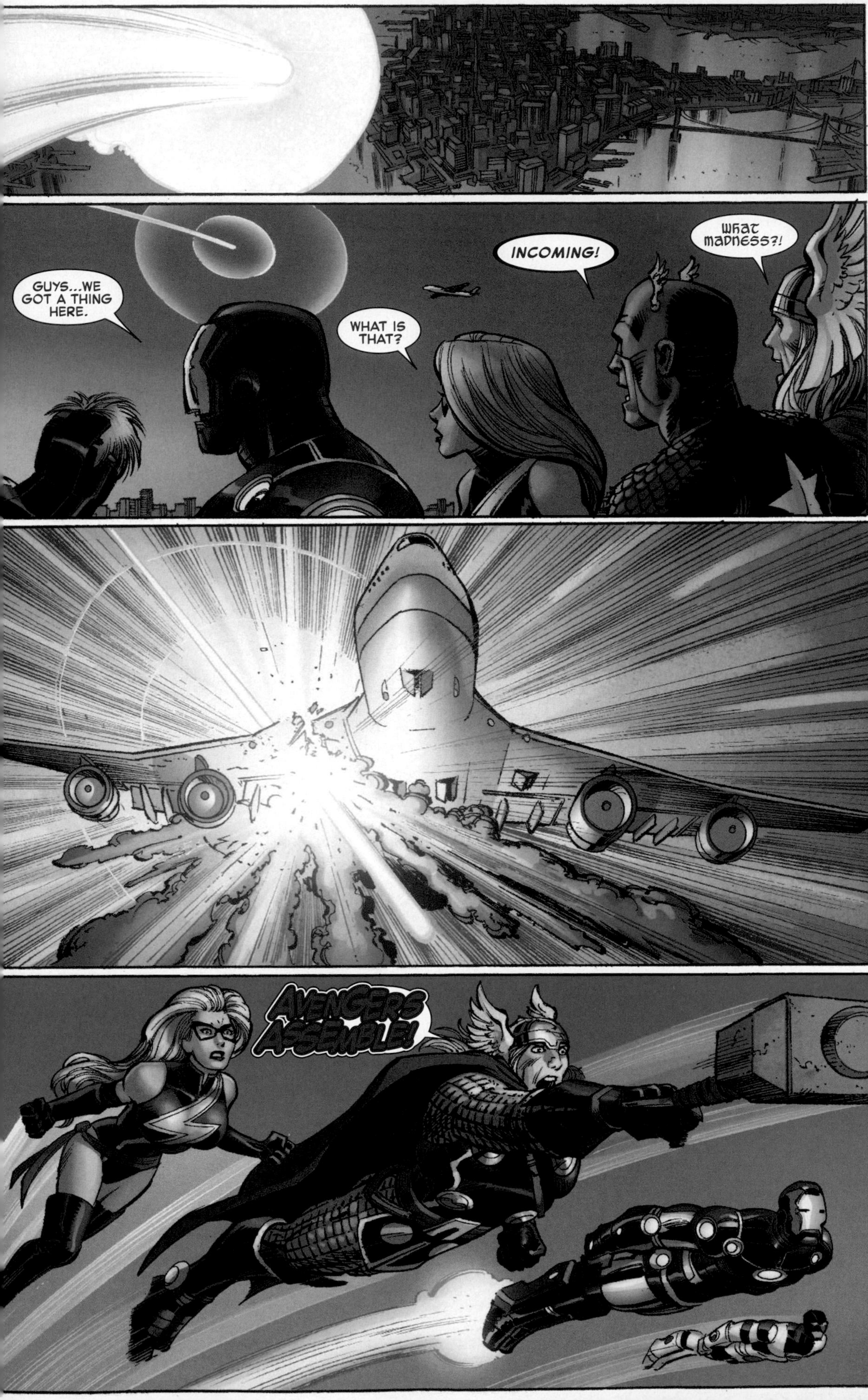

GUYS...WE GOT A THING HERE.
WHAT IS THAT?
INCOMING!
WHAT MADNESS?!
AVENGERS ASSEMBLE!

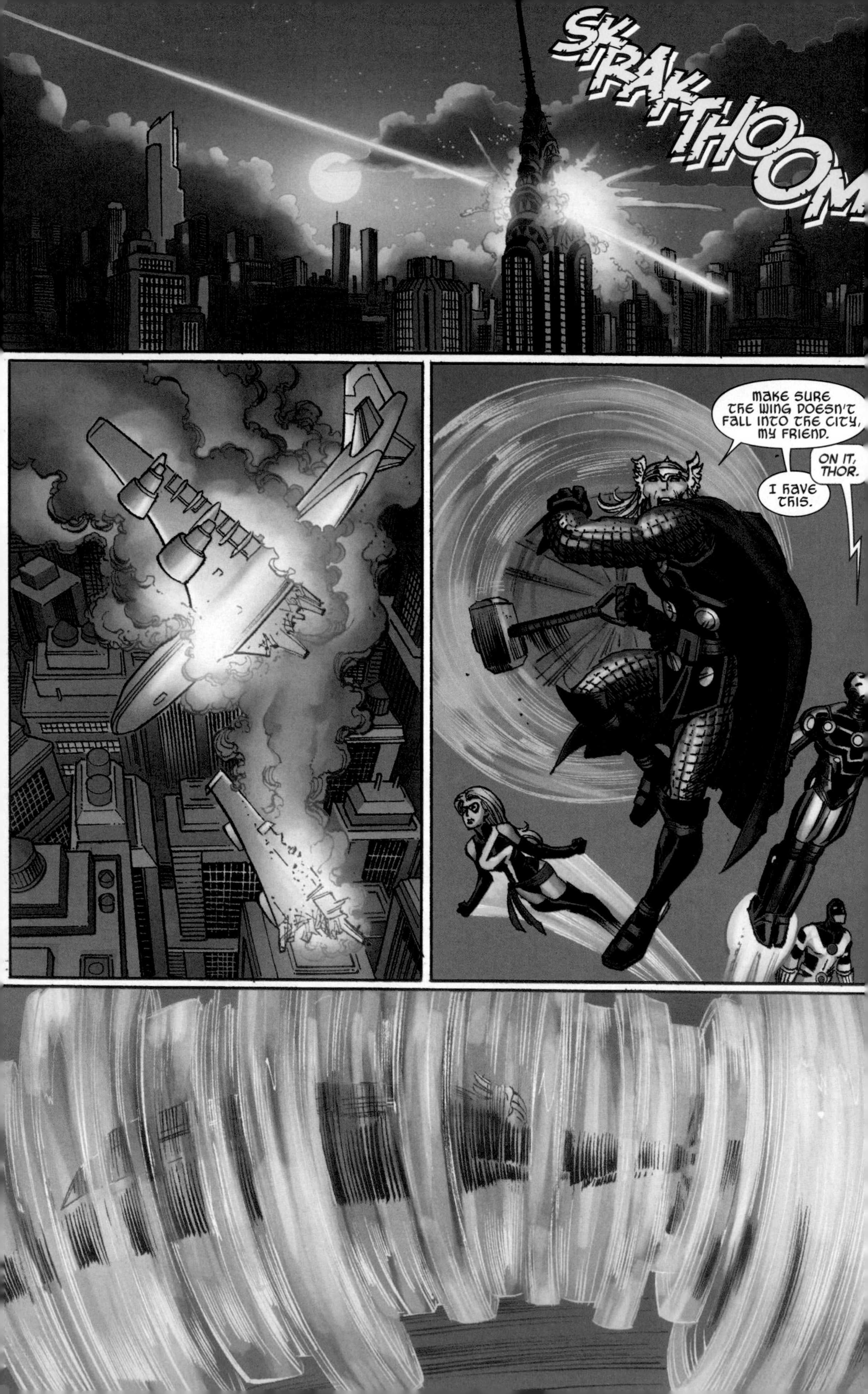
SKRAKTHOOM
MAKE SURE THE WING DOESN'T FALL INTO THE CITY, MY FRIEND.
ON IT, THOR.
I HAVE THIS.

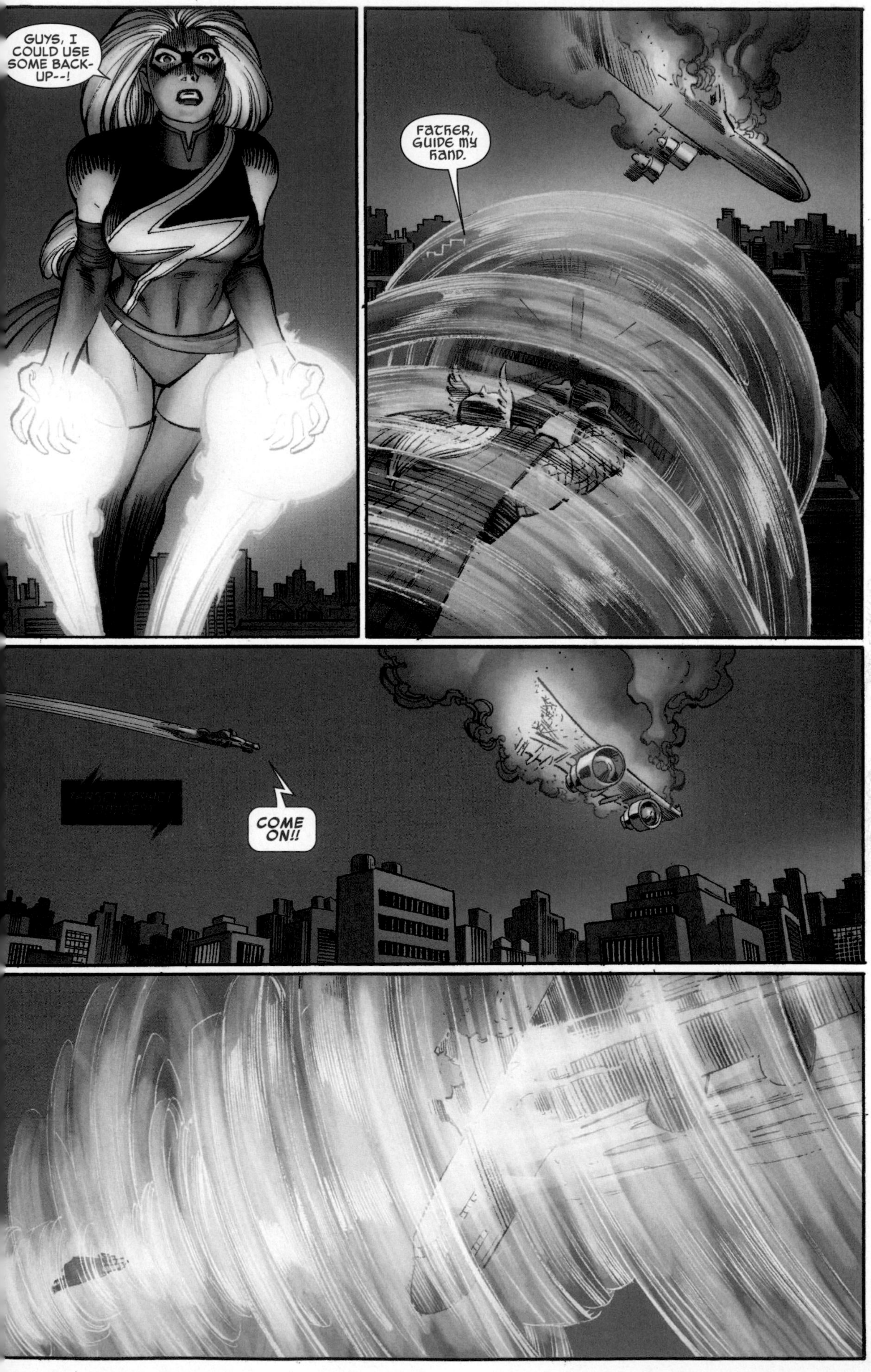
GUYS, I COULD USE SOME BACK-UP--!
FATHER, GUIDE MY HAND.
COME ON!!

FAWOOOSHHH
AAAAAAAAAAAAAGH!
FOOM
GOT IT!
AAAAND YOU'RE WELCOME.
THOSE ARE OFFICIAL SPIDER-MAN SPIDER-WEBS, BY THE WAY.
NOT SOLD IN STORES.
WOW. THAT'S IT.
I'M MOVING. I'M DONE.

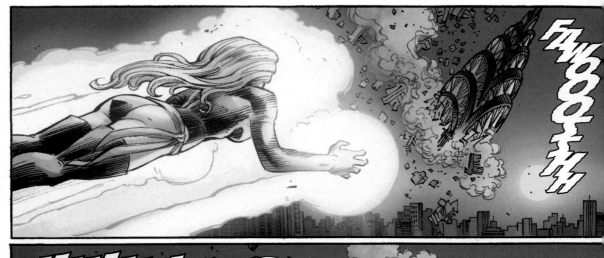

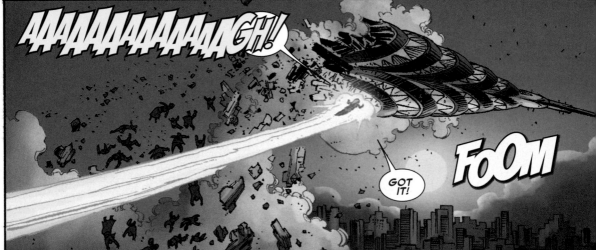

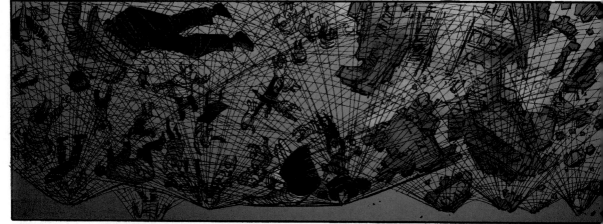

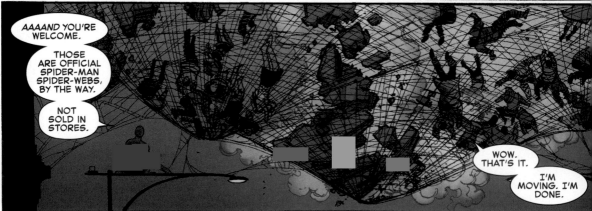

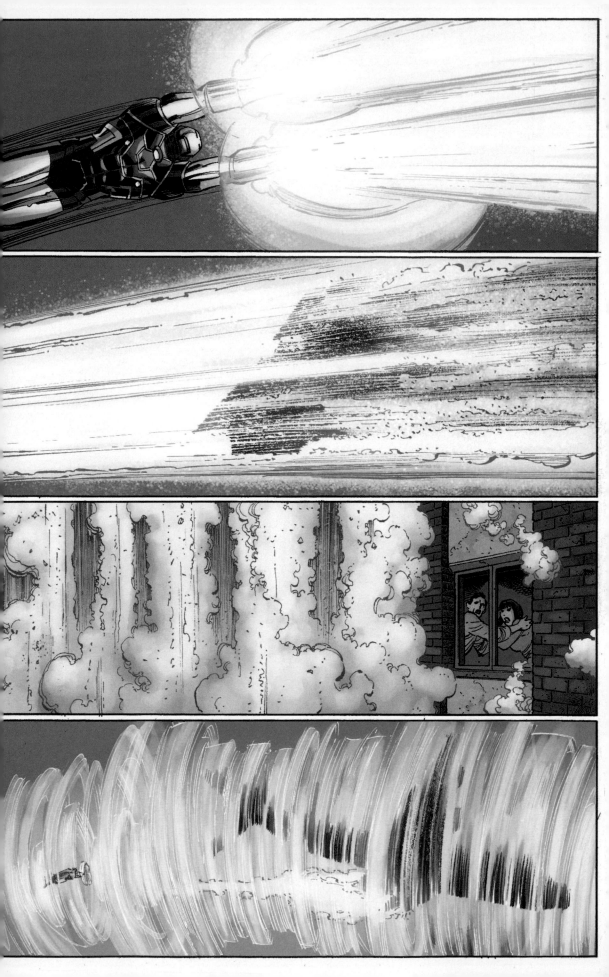

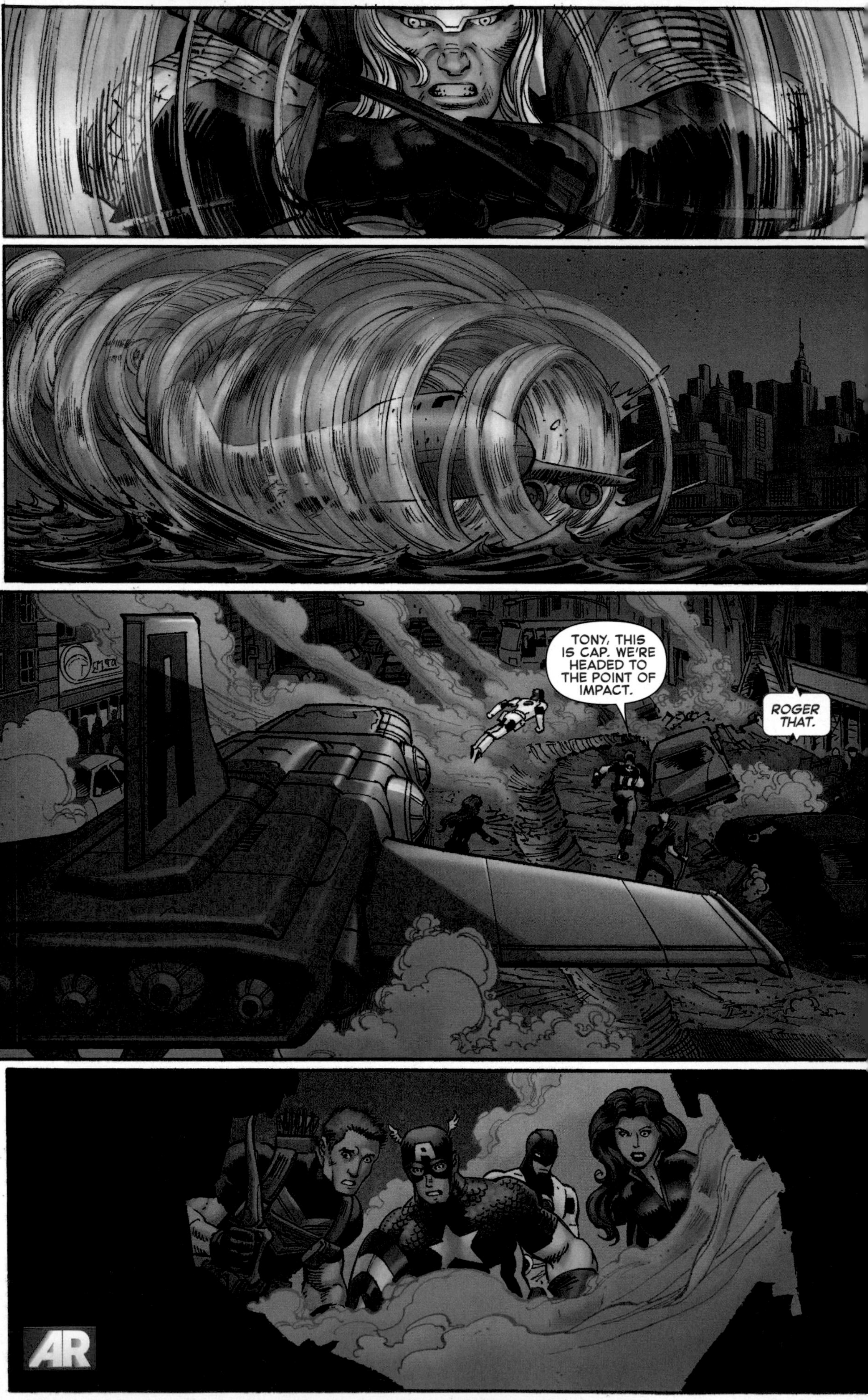
TONY, THIS IS CAP. WE'RE HEADED TO THE POINT OF IMPACT.
ROGER THAT.

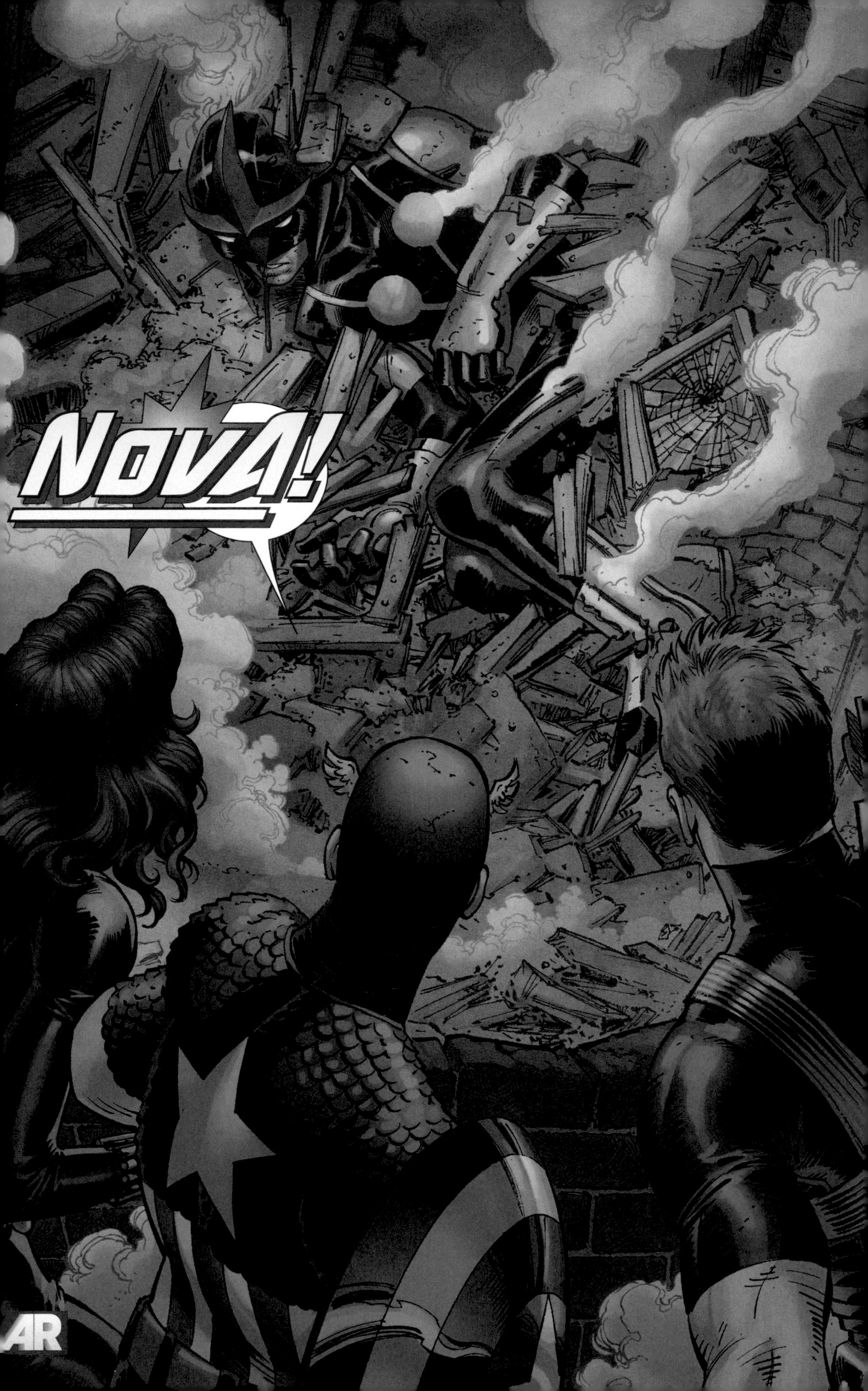
NOVA!

GET A MEDICAL CREW OVER HERE NOW!
I THOUGHT HE DIED.
NOVA!
NOVA, IT'S STEVE ROGERS! CAN YOU HEAR ME?!
IT'S--
IT'S COMING.
"IT" WHAT?
THOR, COULD YOU DO US A FAVOR AND SEE IF ANYTHING IS FOLLOWING HIM?
NOTHING ON THE INTERSTELLAR RADAR.

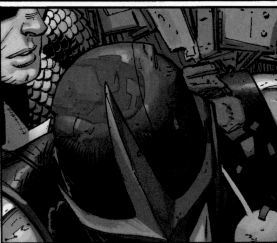

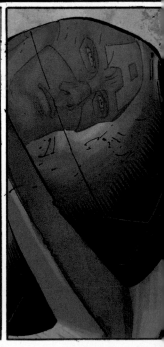

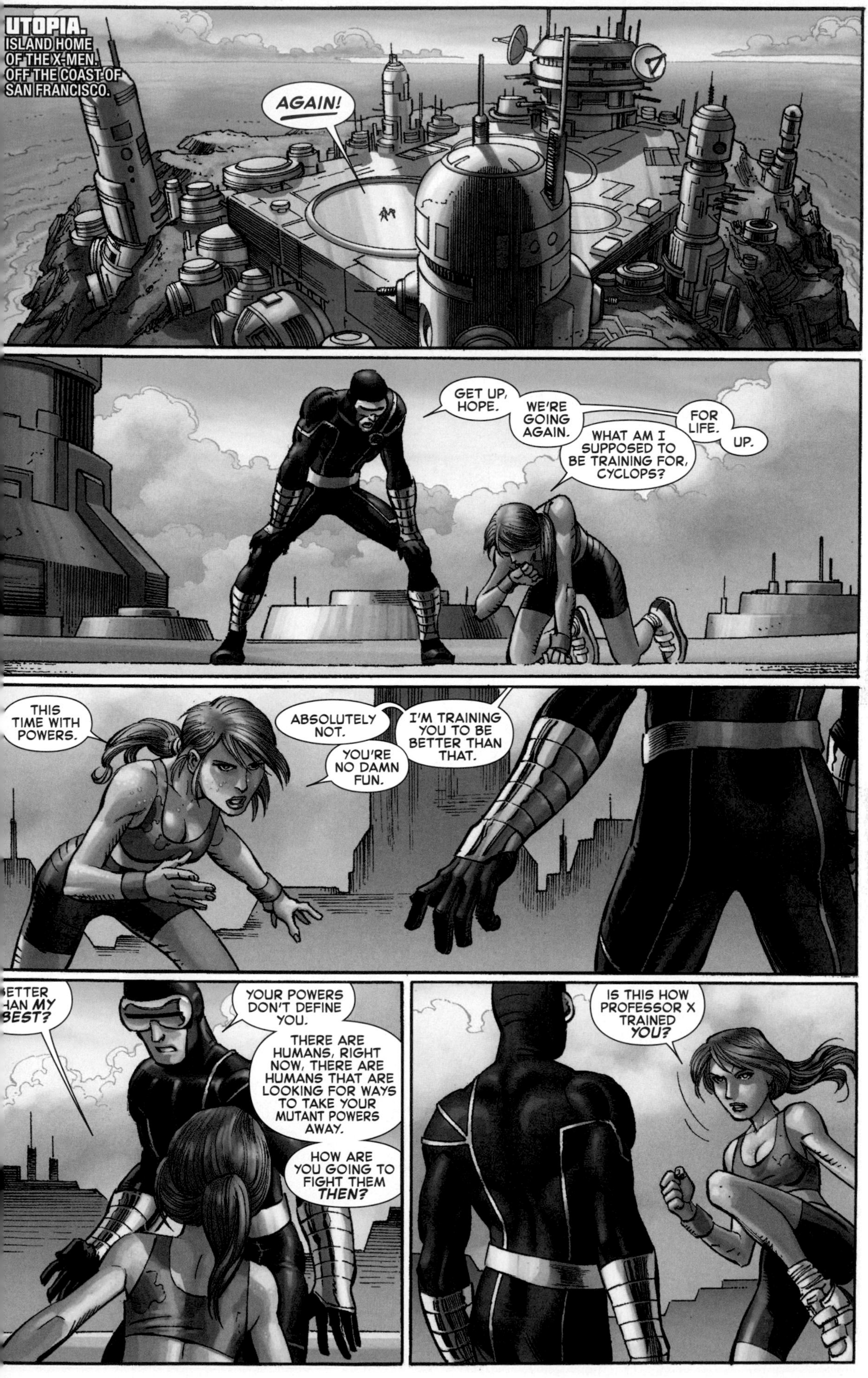
UTOPIA.
ISLAND HOME OF THE X-MEN. OFF THE COAST OF SAN FRANCISCO.
AGAIN!
GET UP, HOPE.
WE'RE GOING AGAIN.
WHAT AM I SUPPOSED TO BE TRAINING FOR, CYCLOPS?
FOR LIFE.
UP.
THIS TIME WITH POWERS.
ABSOLUTELY NOT.
YOU'RE NO DAMN FUN.
I'M TRAINING YOU TO BE BETTER THAN THAT.
ETTER HAN MY BEST?
YOUR POWERS DON'T DEFINE YOU.
THERE ARE HUMANS, RIGHT NOW, THERE ARE HUMANS THAT ARE LOOKING FOR WAYS TO TAKE YOUR MUTANT POWERS AWAY.
HOW ARE YOU GOING TO FIGHT THEM THEN?
IS THIS HOW PROFESSOR X TRAINED YOU?

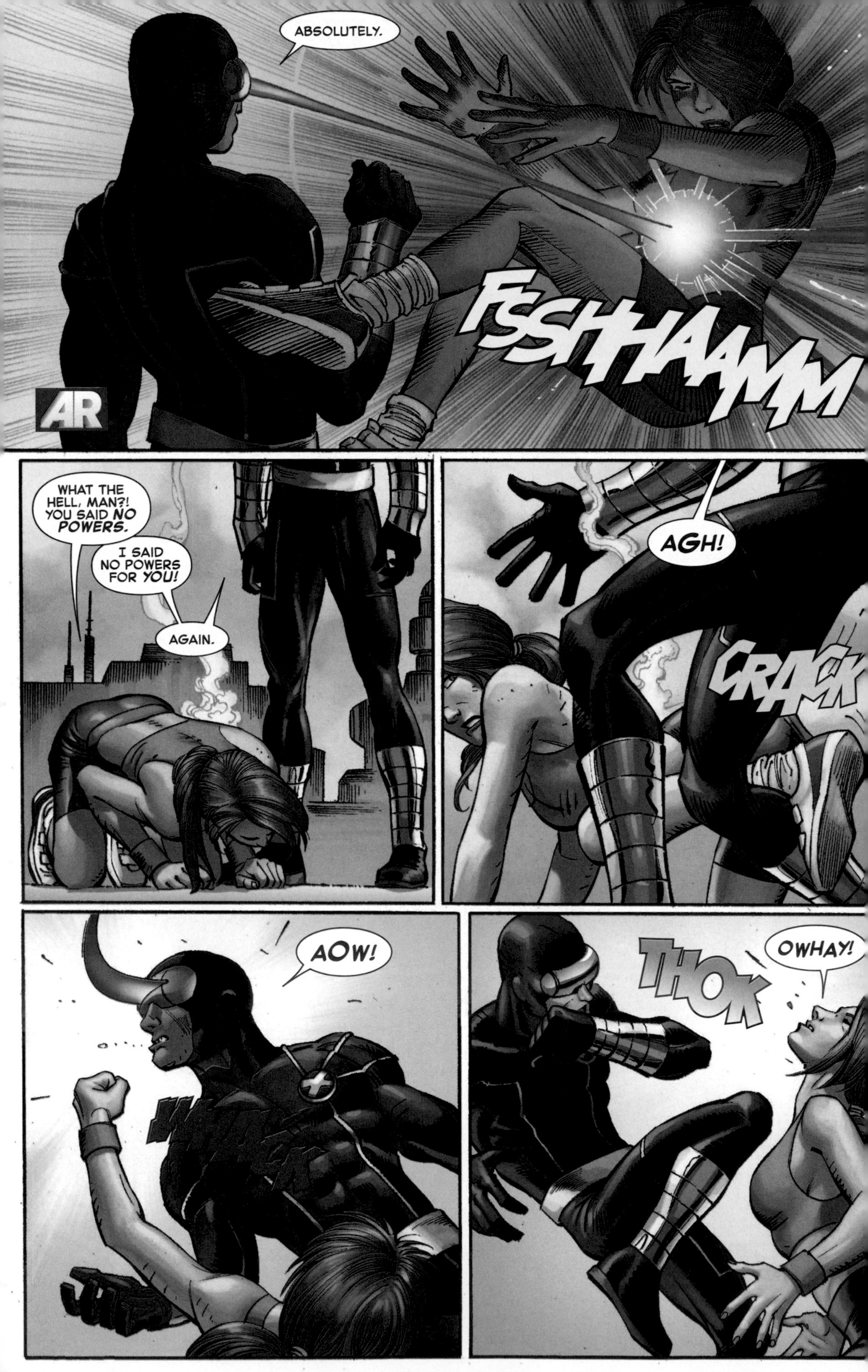
ABSOLUTELY.
FSSHAAMM
AR
WHAT THE HELL, MAN?! YOU SAID NO POWERS.
I SAID NO POWERS FOR YOU!
AGAIN.
AGH!
CRACK
AOW!
THOK
OWHAY!

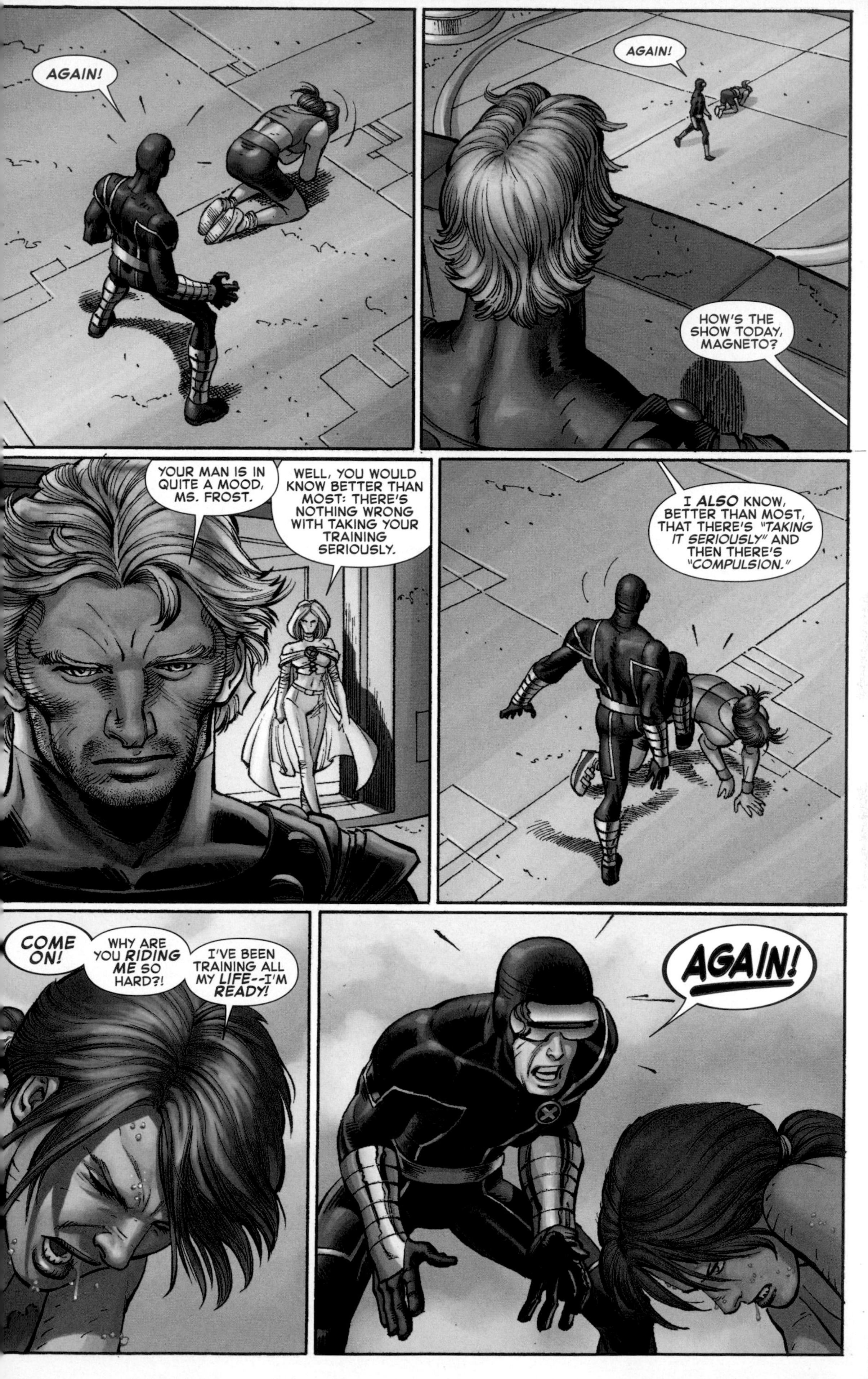
AGAIN!
AGAIN!
HOW'S THE SHOW TODAY, MAGNETO?
YOUR MAN IS IN QUITE A MOOD, MS. FROST.
WELL, YOU WOULD KNOW BETTER THAN MOST: THERE'S NOTHING WRONG WITH TAKING YOUR TRAINING SERIOUSLY.
I ALSO KNOW, BETTER THAN MOST, THAT THERE'S "TAKING IT SERIOUSLY" AND THEN THERE'S "COMPULSION."
COME ON!
WHY ARE YOU RIDING ME SO HARD?!
I'VE BEEN TRAINING ALL MY LIFE--I'M READY!
AGAIN!

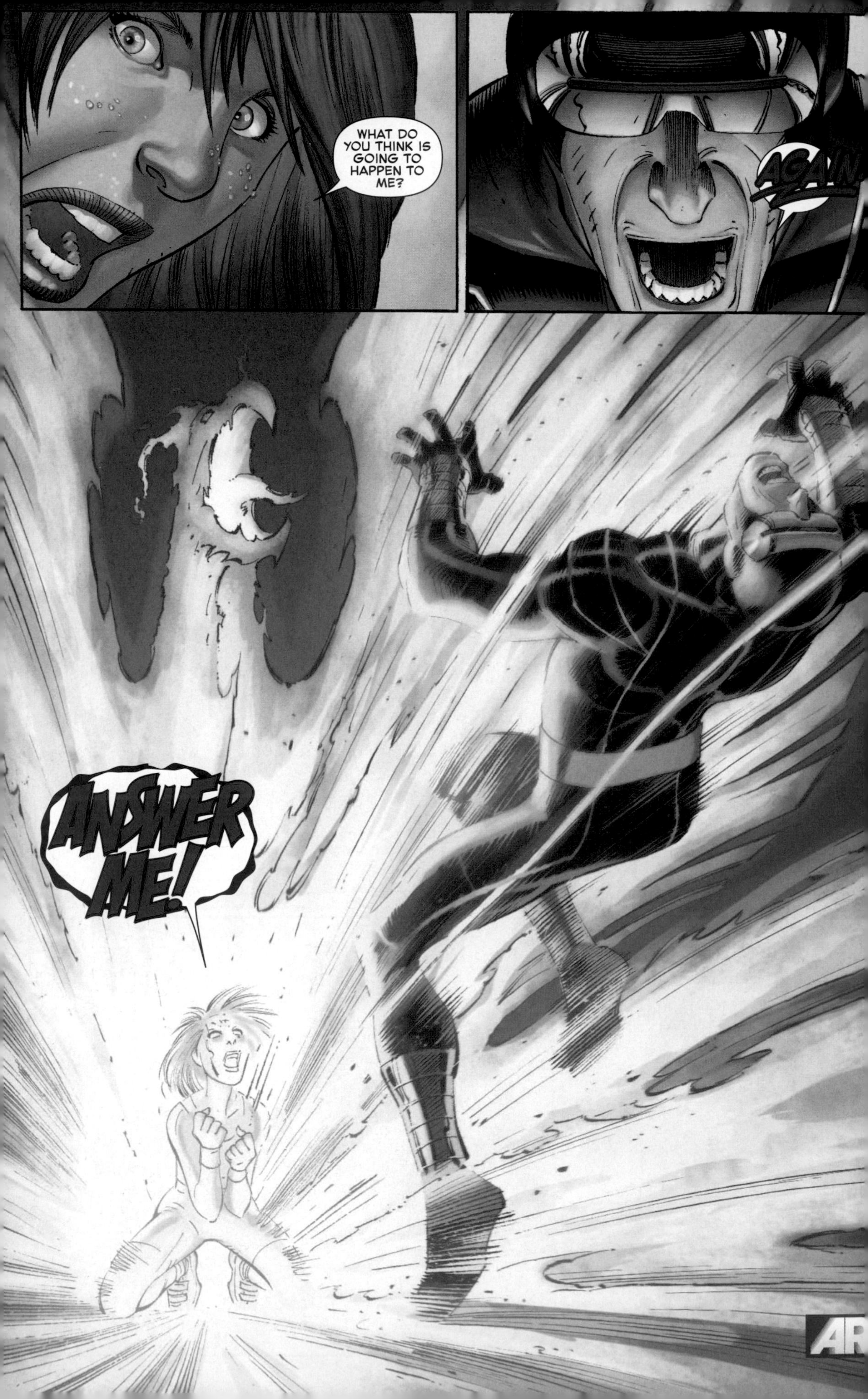
WHAT DO YOU THINK IS GOING TO HAPPEN TO ME?
AGAIN
ANSWER ME!

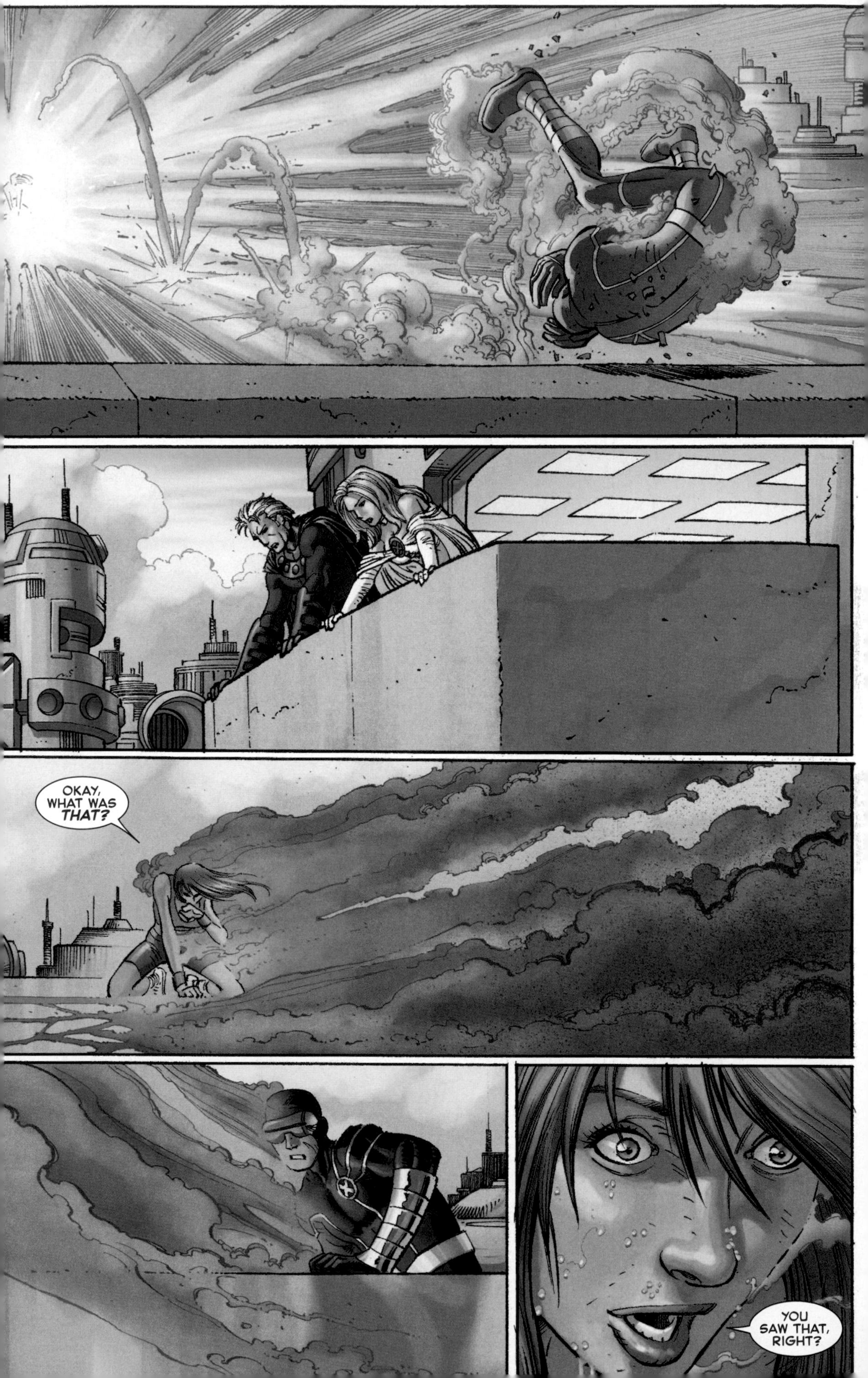
OKAY, WHAT WAS THAT?
YOU SAW THAT, RIGHT?

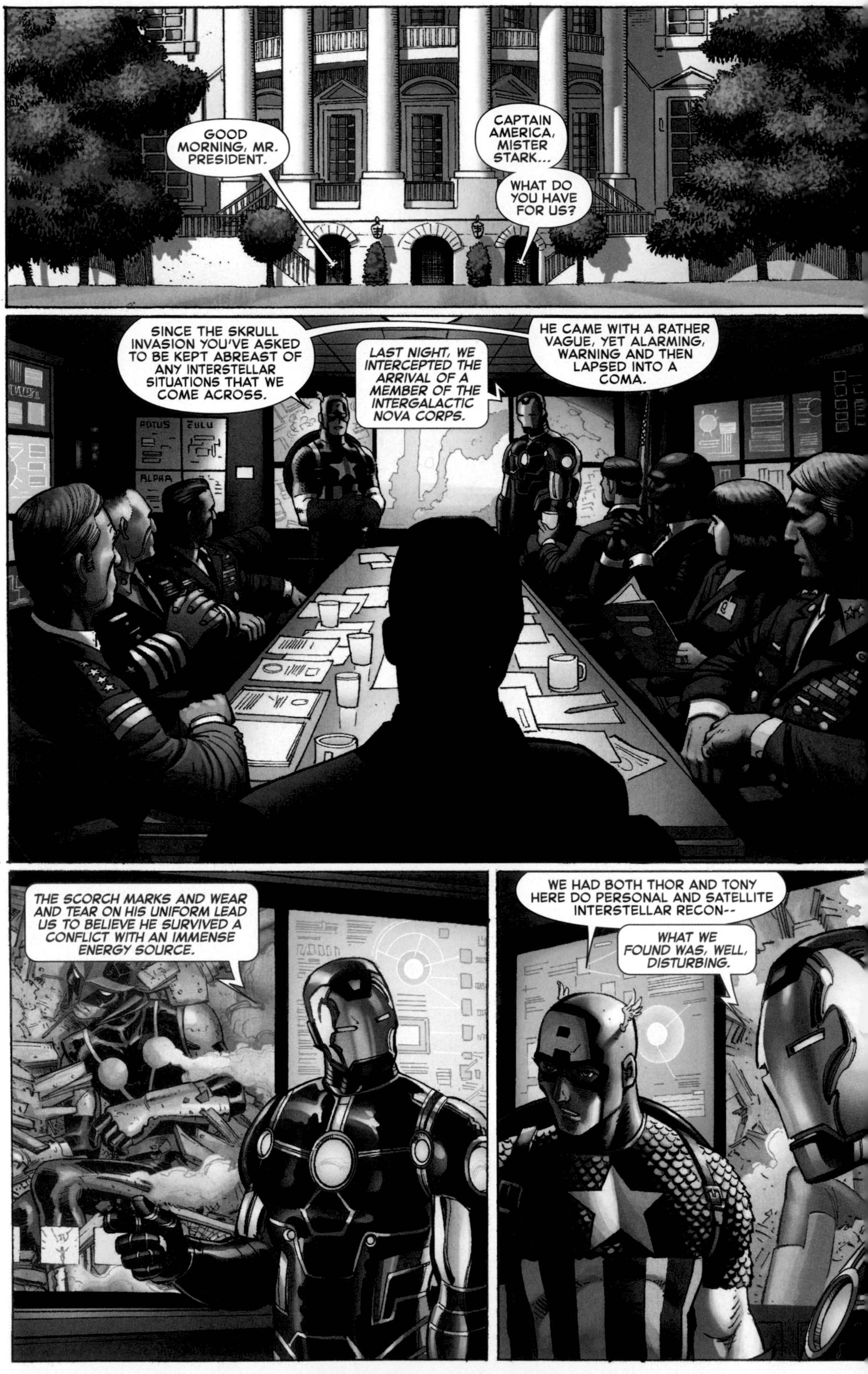
GOOD MORNING, MR. PRESIDENT.
CAPTAIN AMERICA, MISTER STARK...
WHAT DO YOU HAVE FOR US?
SINCE THE SKRULL INVASION YOU'VE ASKED TO BE KEPT ABREAST OF ANY INTERSTELLAR SITUATIONS THAT WE COME ACROSS.
LAST NIGHT, WE INTERCEPTED THE ARRIVAL OF A MEMBER OF THE INTERGALACTIC NOVA CORPS.
HE CAME WITH A RATHER VAGUE, YET ALARMING, WARNING AND THEN LAPSED INTO A COMA.
POTUS
ALPHA
THE SCORCH MARKS AND WEAR AND TEAR ON HIS UNIFORM LEAD US TO BELIEVE HE SURVIVED A CONFLICT WITH AN IMMENSE ENERGY SOURCE.
WE HAD BOTH THOR AND TONY HERE DO PERSONAL AND SATELLITE INTERSTELLAR RECON--
WHAT WE FOUND WAS, WELL, DISTURBING.

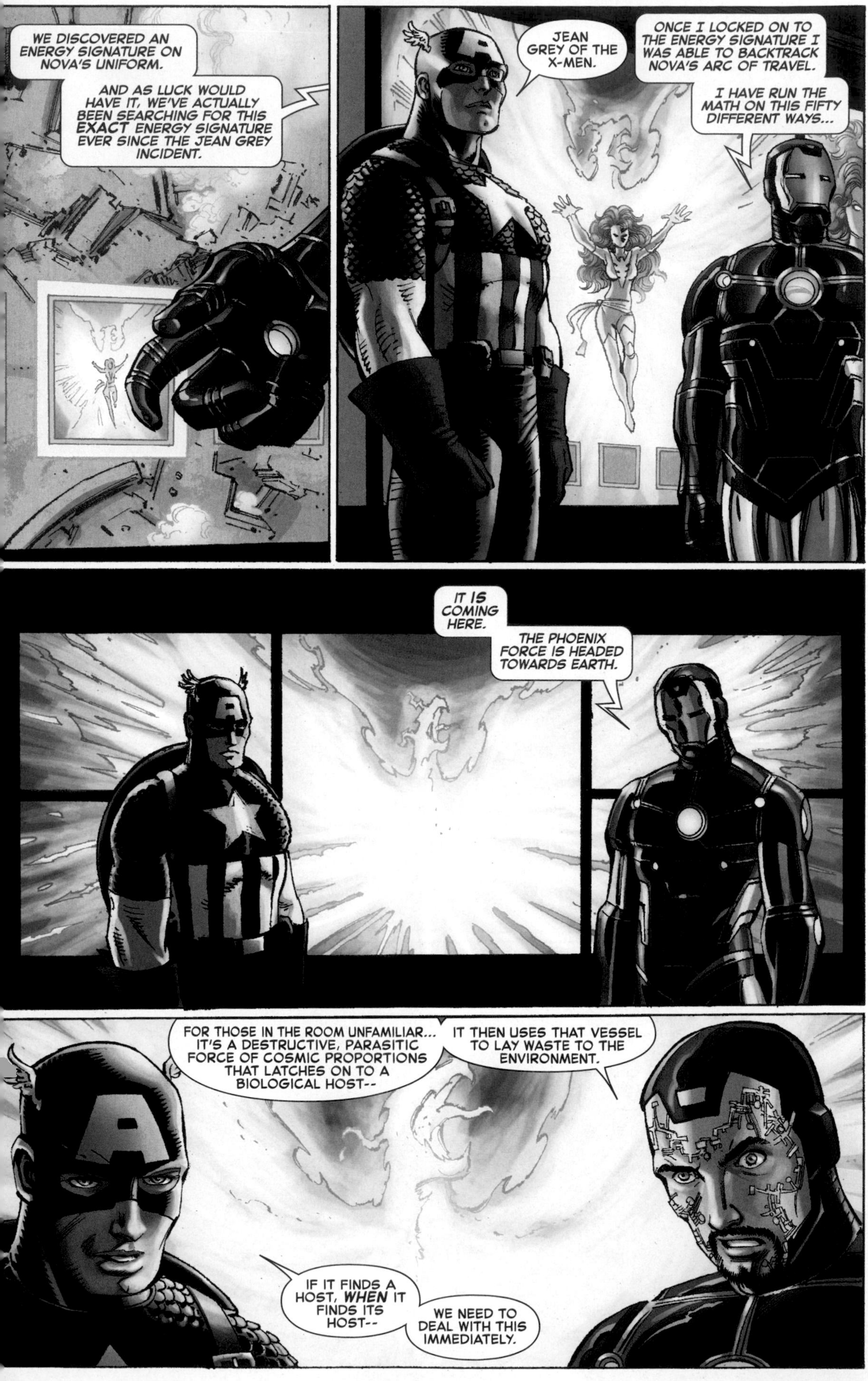

WE DISCOVERED AN ENERGY SIGNATURE ON NOVA'S UNIFORM.
AND AS LUCK WOULD HAVE IT, WE'VE ACTUALLY BEEN SEARCHING FOR THIS EXACT ENERGY SIGNATURE EVER SINCE THE JEAN GREY INCIDENT.
JEAN GREY OF THE X-MEN.
ONCE I LOCKED ON TO THE ENERGY SIGNATURE I WAS ABLE TO BACKTRACK NOVA'S ARC OF TRAVEL.
I HAVE RUN THE MATH ON THIS FIFTY DIFFERENT WAYS...
IT IS COMING HERE.
THE PHOENIX FORCE IS HEADED TOWARDS EARTH.
FOR THOSE IN THE ROOM UNFAMILIAR... IT'S A DESTRUCTIVE, PARASITIC FORCE OF COSMIC PROPORTIONS THAT LATCHES ON TO A BIOLOGICAL HOST--
IT THEN USES THAT VESSEL TO LAY WASTE TO THE ENVIRONMENT.
IF IT FINDS A HOST, WHEN IT FINDS ITS HOST--
WE NEED TO DEAL WITH THIS IMMEDIATELY.

WE ARE SENDING A TEAM OF AVENGERS TO TRY TO INTERCEPT AND DESTROY THE PHOENIX BEFORE IT GETS HERE.

WHILE IT'S TRUE THAT THERE IS A--

WE SHOULD BE CLEAR, THOUGH, IT'S A SUICIDE MISSION.

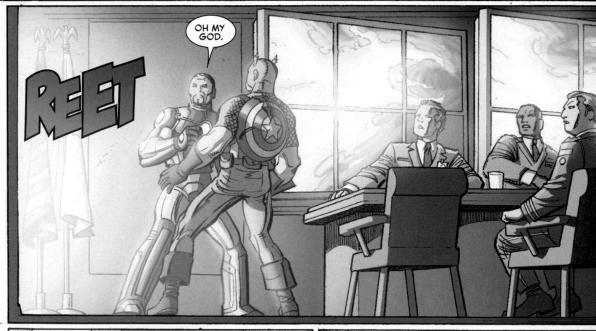

OH MY GOD.

REET

WHAT WAS THAT?

I SET PROGRAMS TO ALERT ME IF AN ENERGY SIGNATURE SIMILAR TO THE PHOENIX FORCE FLARES UP ANYWHERE ON THE GLOBE.

AND IT JUST DID.

YES.

DO YOU KNOW WHERE?

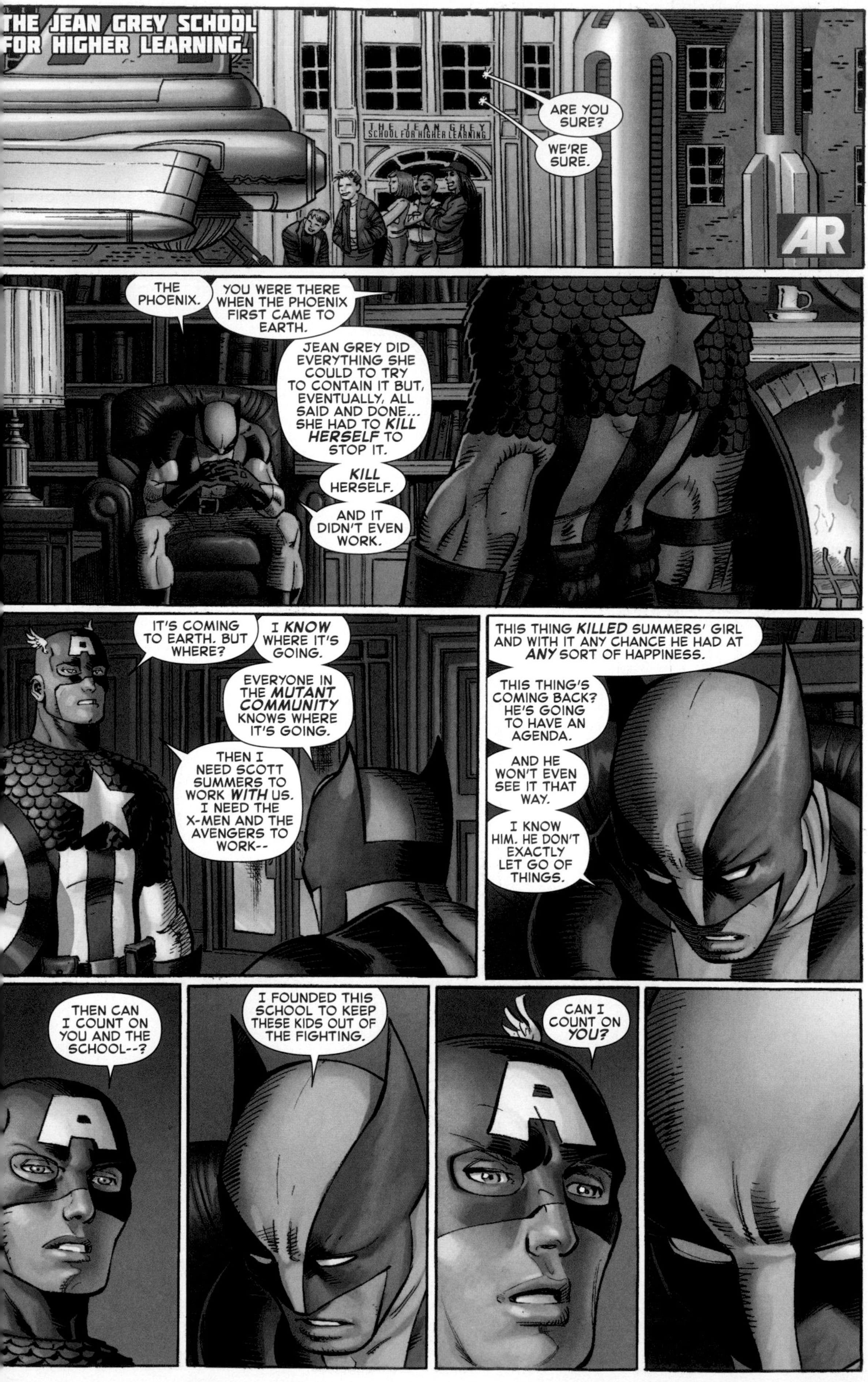
THE JEAN GREY SCHOOL FOR HIGHER LEARNING.
THE JEAN GREY SCHOOL FOR HIGHER LEARNING
ARE YOU SURE?
WE'RE SURE.
AR
THE PHOENIX.
YOU WERE THERE WHEN THE PHOENIX FIRST CAME TO EARTH.
JEAN GREY DID EVERYTHING SHE COULD TO TRY TO CONTAIN IT BUT, EVENTUALLY, ALL SAID AND DONE... SHE HAD TO KILL HERSELF TO STOP IT.
KILL HERSELF.
AND IT DIDN'T EVEN WORK.
IT'S COMING TO EARTH. BUT WHERE?
I KNOW WHERE IT'S GOING.
EVERYONE IN THE MUTANT COMMUNITY KNOWS WHERE IT'S GOING.
THEN I NEED SCOTT SUMMERS TO WORK WITH US. I NEED THE X-MEN AND THE AVENGERS TO WORK--
THIS THING KILLED SUMMERS' GIRL AND WITH IT ANY CHANCE HE HAD AT ANY SORT OF HAPPINESS.
THIS THING'S COMING BACK? HE'S GOING TO HAVE AN AGENDA.
AND HE WON'T EVEN SEE IT THAT WAY.
I KNOW HIM. HE DON'T EXACTLY LET GO OF THINGS.
THEN CAN I COUNT ON YOU AND THE SCHOOL--?
I FOUNDED THIS SCHOOL TO KEEP THESE KIDS OUT OF THE FIGHTING.
CAN I COUNT ON YOU?

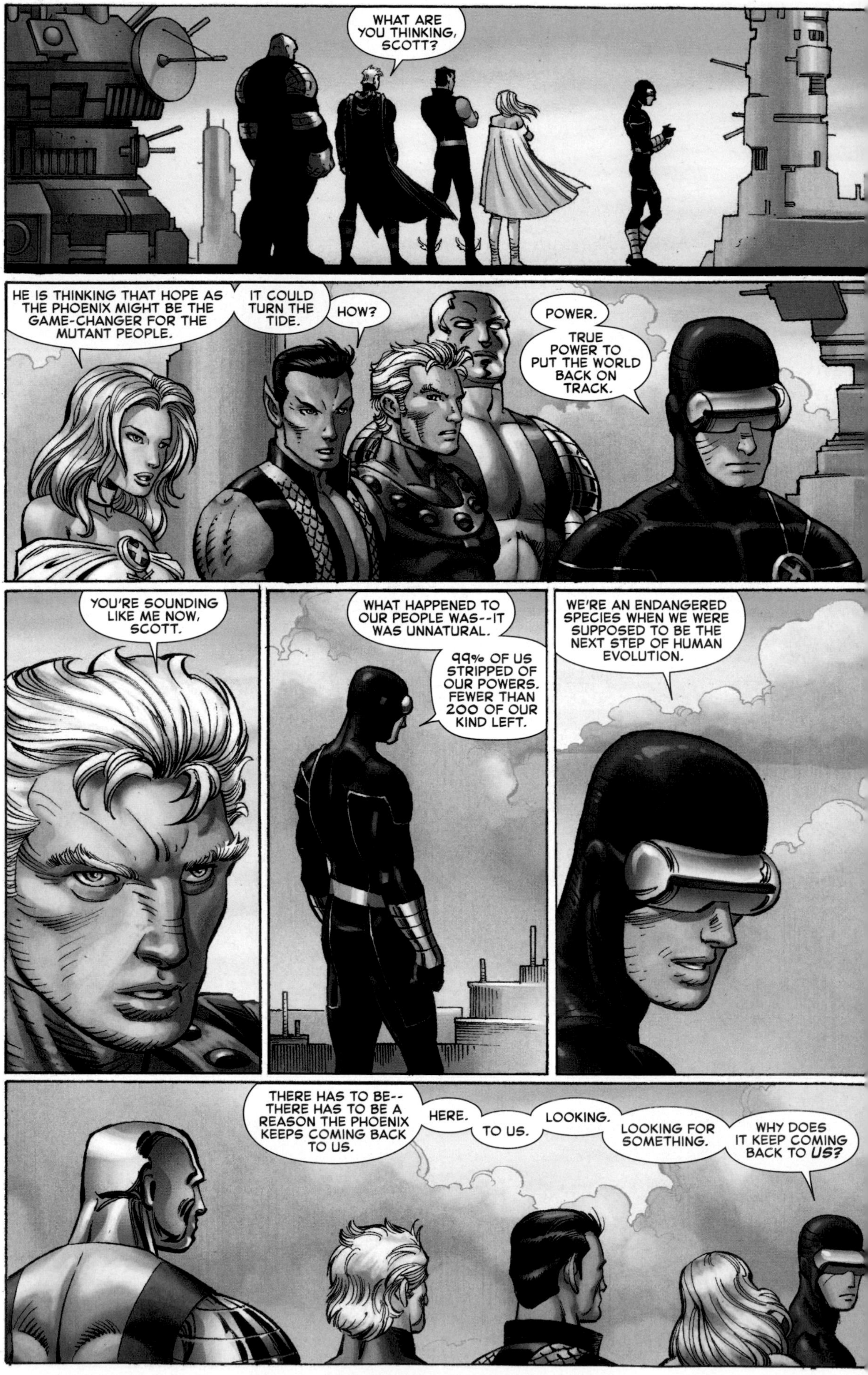
WHAT ARE YOU THINKING, SCOTT?
HE IS THINKING THAT HOPE AS THE PHOENIX MIGHT BE THE GAME-CHANGER FOR THE MUTANT PEOPLE.
IT COULD TURN THE TIDE.
HOW?
POWER.
TRUE POWER TO PUT THE WORLD BACK ON TRACK.
YOU'RE SOUNDING LIKE ME NOW, SCOTT.
WHAT HAPPENED TO OUR PEOPLE WAS--IT WAS UNNATURAL.
99% OF US STRIPPED OF OUR POWERS. FEWER THAN 200 OF OUR KIND LEFT.
WE'RE AN ENDANGERED SPECIES WHEN WE WERE SUPPOSED TO BE THE NEXT STEP OF HUMAN EVOLUTION.
THERE HAS TO BE-- THERE HAS TO BE A REASON THE PHOENIX KEEPS COMING BACK TO US.
HERE.
TO US.
LOOKING.
LOOKING FOR SOMETHING.
WHY DOES IT KEEP COMING BACK TO *US?*

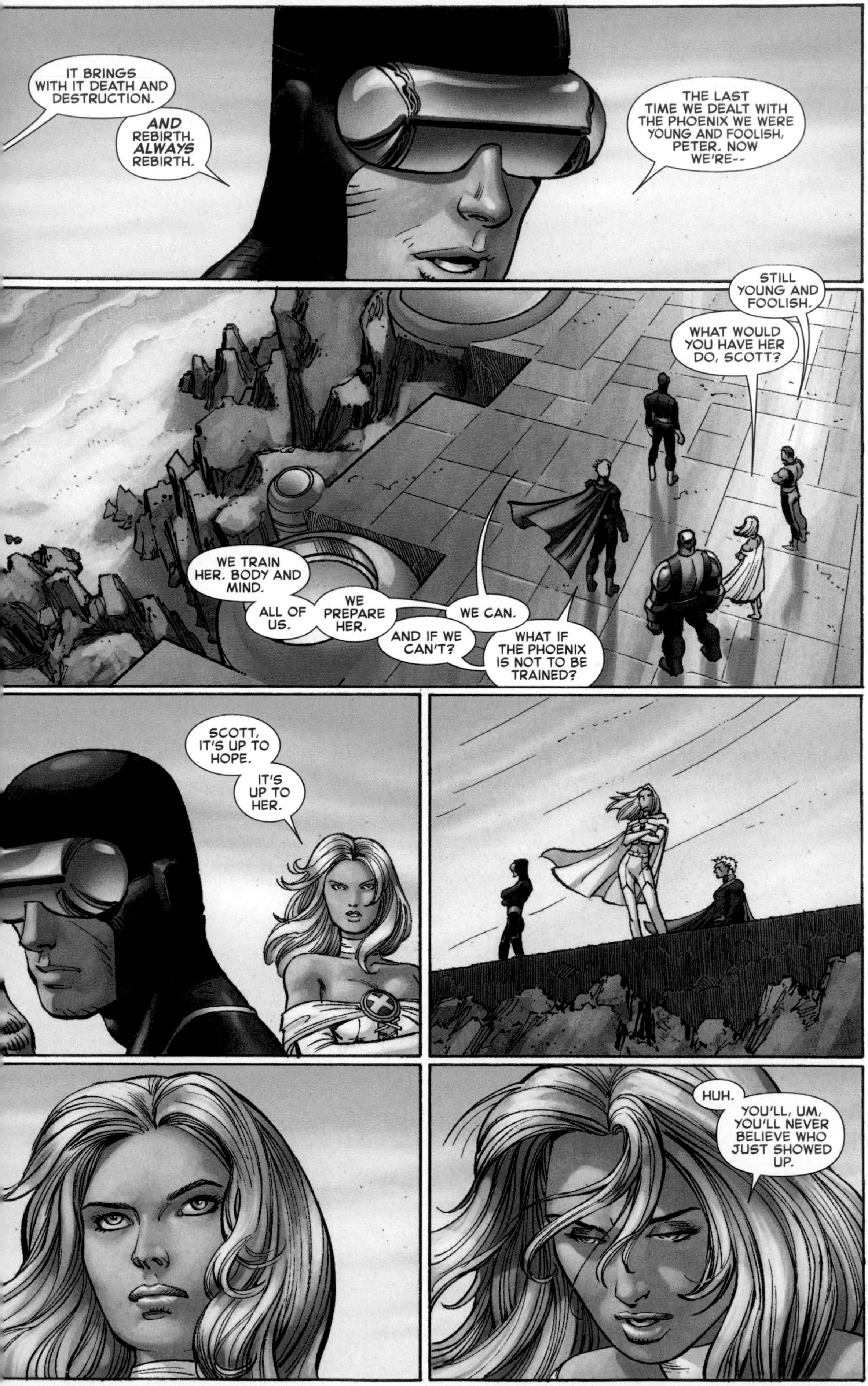
IT BRINGS WITH IT DEATH AND DESTRUCTION.
AND REBIRTH. ALWAYS REBIRTH.
THE LAST TIME WE DEALT WITH THE PHOENIX WE WERE YOUNG AND FOOLISH, PETER. NOW WE'RE--
STILL YOUNG AND FOOLISH.
WHAT WOULD YOU HAVE HER DO, SCOTT?
WE TRAIN HER. BODY AND MIND.
ALL OF US.
WE PREPARE HER.
WE CAN.
AND IF WE CAN'T?
WHAT IF THE PHOENIX IS NOT TO BE TRAINED?
SCOTT, IT'S UP TO HOPE.
IT'S UP TO HER.
HUH.
YOU'LL, UM, YOU'LL NEVER BELIEVE WHO JUST SHOWED UP.

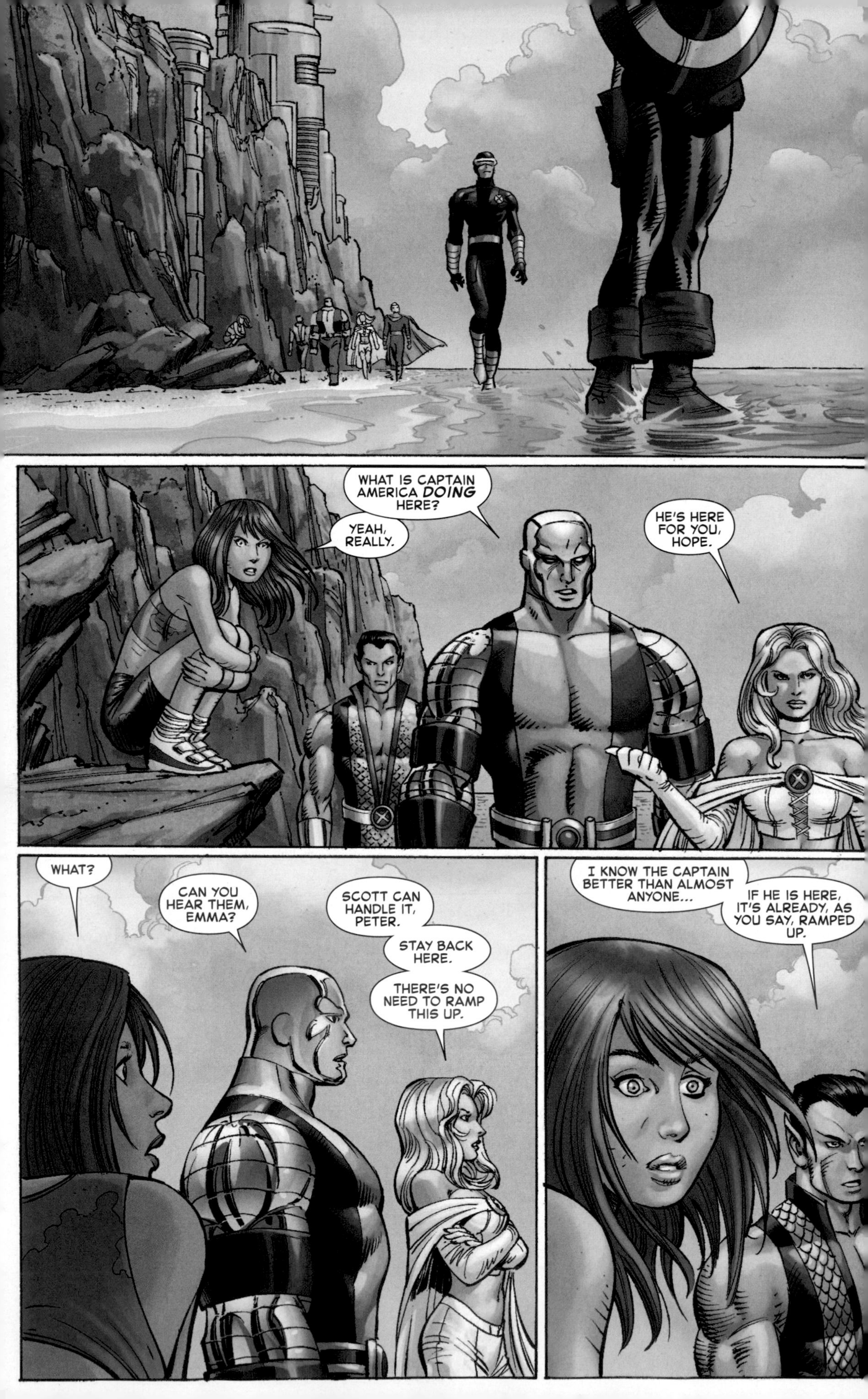
WHAT IS CAPTAIN AMERICA DOING HERE?
YEAH, REALLY.
HE'S HERE FOR YOU, HOPE.
WHAT?
CAN YOU HEAR THEM, EMMA?
SCOTT CAN HANDLE IT, PETER.
STAY BACK HERE.
THERE'S NO NEED TO RAMP THIS UP.
I KNOW THE CAPTAIN BETTER THAN ALMOST ANYONE...
IF HE IS HERE, IT'S ALREADY, AS YOU SAY, RAMPED UP.

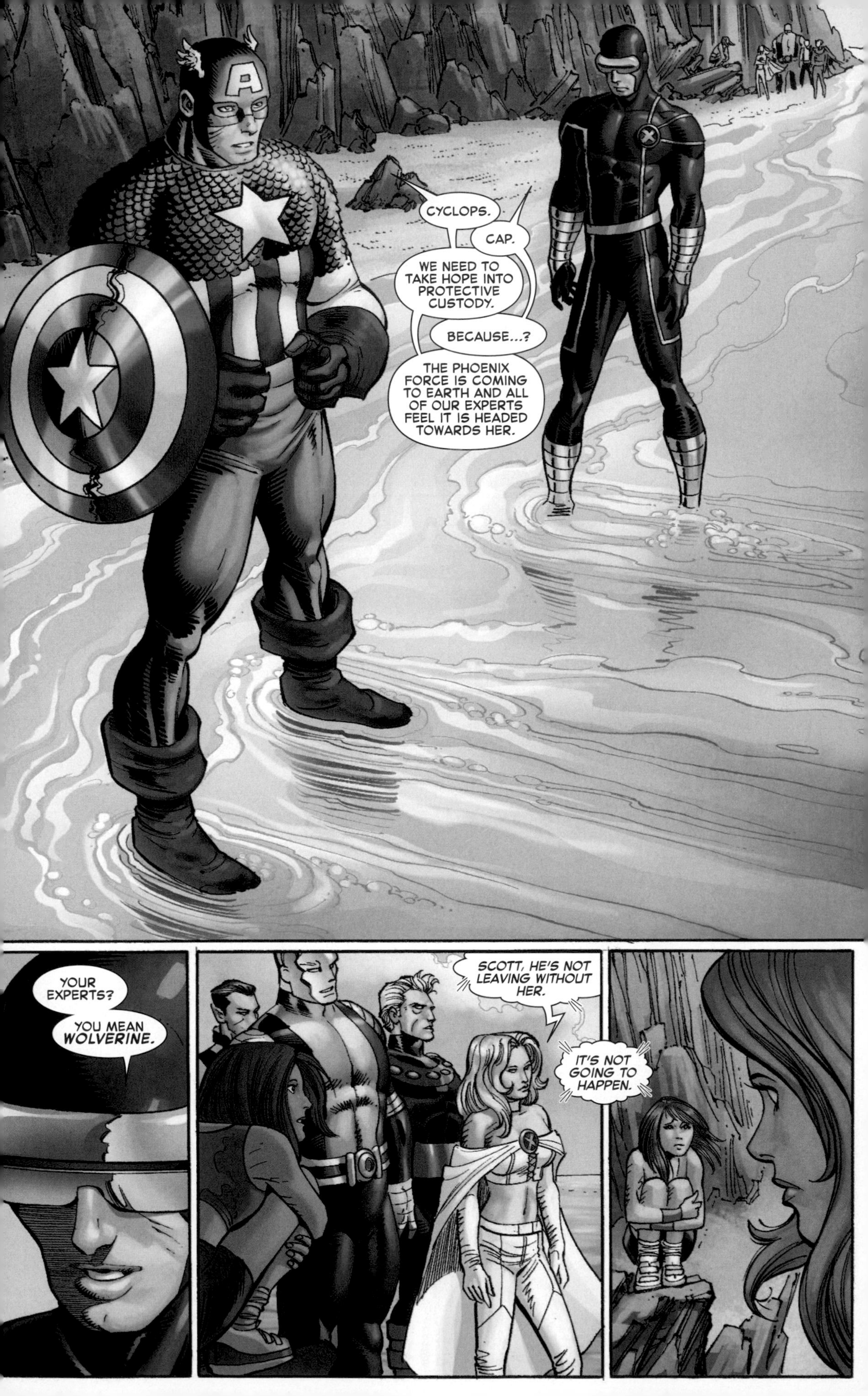
CYCLOPS.
CAP.
WE NEED TO TAKE HOPE INTO PROTECTIVE CUSTODY.
BECAUSE...?
THE PHOENIX FORCE IS COMING TO EARTH AND ALL OF OUR EXPERTS FEEL IT IS HEADED TOWARDS HER.
YOUR EXPERTS?
YOU MEAN *WOLVERINE.*
SCOTT, HE'S NOT LEAVING WITHOUT HER.
IT'S NOT GOING TO HAPPEN.

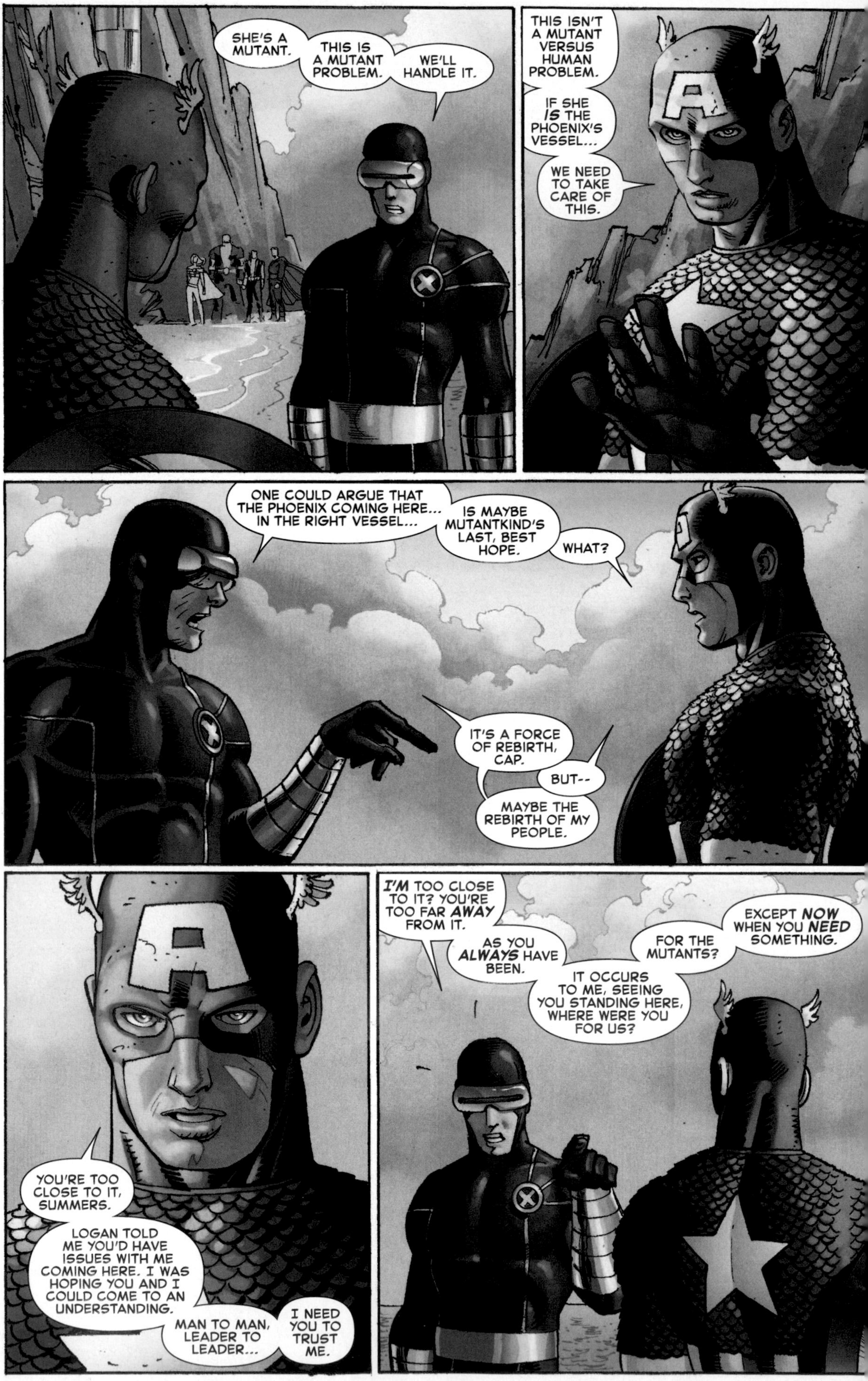

SHE'S A MUTANT.
THIS IS A MUTANT PROBLEM.
WE'LL HANDLE IT.
THIS ISN'T A MUTANT VERSUS HUMAN PROBLEM.
IF SHE *IS* THE PHOENIX'S VESSEL...
WE NEED TO TAKE CARE OF THIS.
ONE COULD ARGUE THAT THE PHOENIX COMING HERE... IN THE RIGHT VESSEL...
IS MAYBE MUTANTKIND'S LAST, BEST HOPE.
WHAT?
IT'S A FORCE OF REBIRTH, CAP.
BUT--
MAYBE THE REBIRTH OF MY PEOPLE.
YOU'RE TOO CLOSE TO IT, SUMMERS.
LOGAN TOLD ME YOU'D HAVE ISSUES WITH ME COMING HERE. I WAS HOPING YOU AND I COULD COME TO AN UNDERSTANDING.
MAN TO MAN, LEADER TO LEADER...
I NEED YOU TO TRUST ME.
I'M TOO CLOSE TO IT? YOU'RE TOO FAR *AWAY* FROM IT.
AS YOU *ALWAYS* HAVE BEEN.
IT OCCURS TO ME, SEEING YOU STANDING HERE, WHERE WERE YOU FOR US?
FOR THE MUTANTS?
EXCEPT *NOW* WHEN YOU *NEED* SOMETHING.

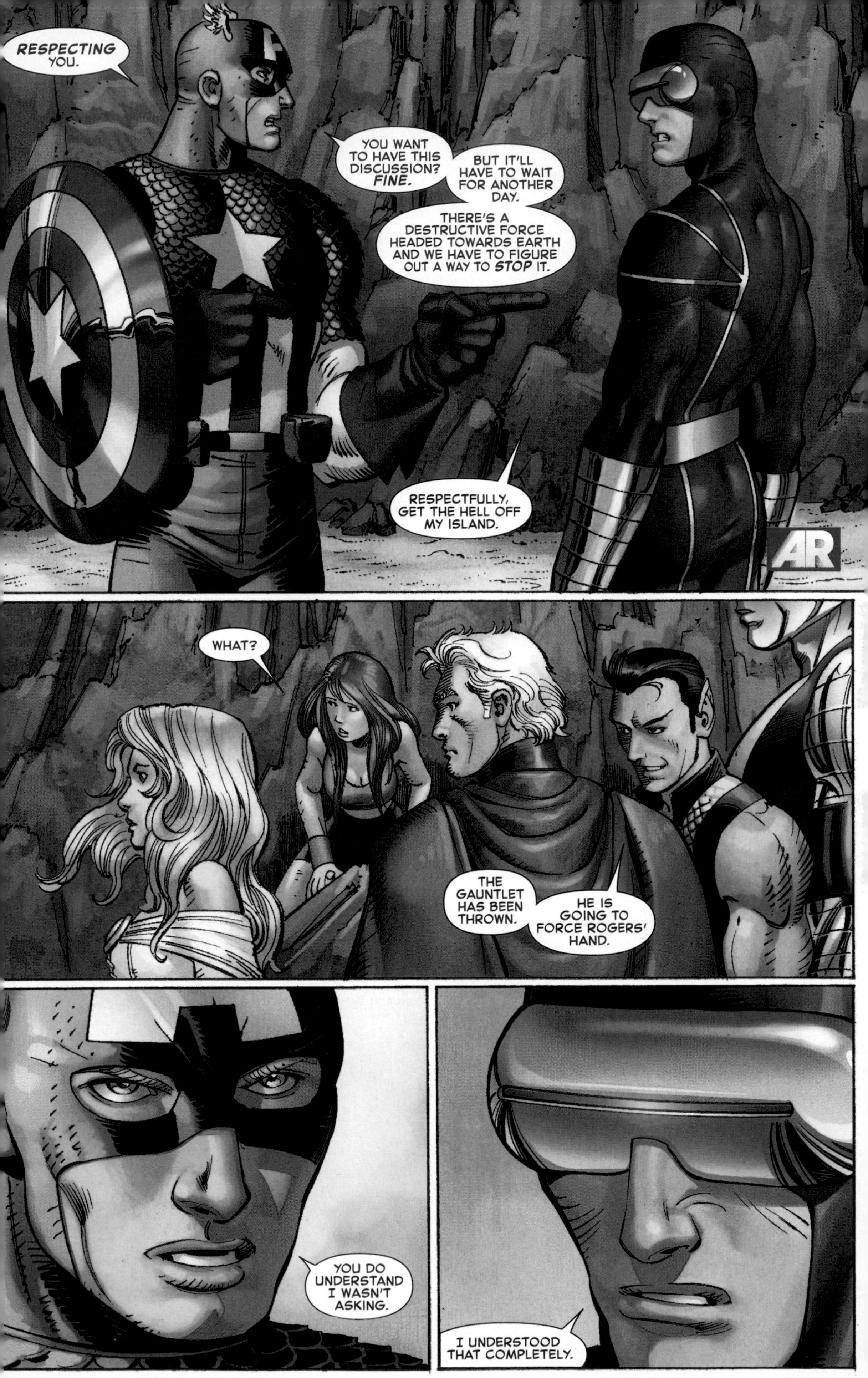
RESPECTING YOU.
YOU WANT TO HAVE THIS DISCUSSION? FINE.
BUT IT'LL HAVE TO WAIT FOR ANOTHER DAY.
THERE'S A DESTRUCTIVE FORCE HEADED TOWARDS EARTH AND WE HAVE TO FIGURE OUT A WAY TO STOP IT.
RESPECTFULLY, GET THE HELL OFF MY ISLAND.
WHAT?
THE GAUNTLET HAS BEEN THROWN.
HE IS GOING TO FORCE ROGERS' HAND.
YOU DO UNDERSTAND I WASN'T ASKING.
I UNDERSTOOD THAT COMPLETELY.

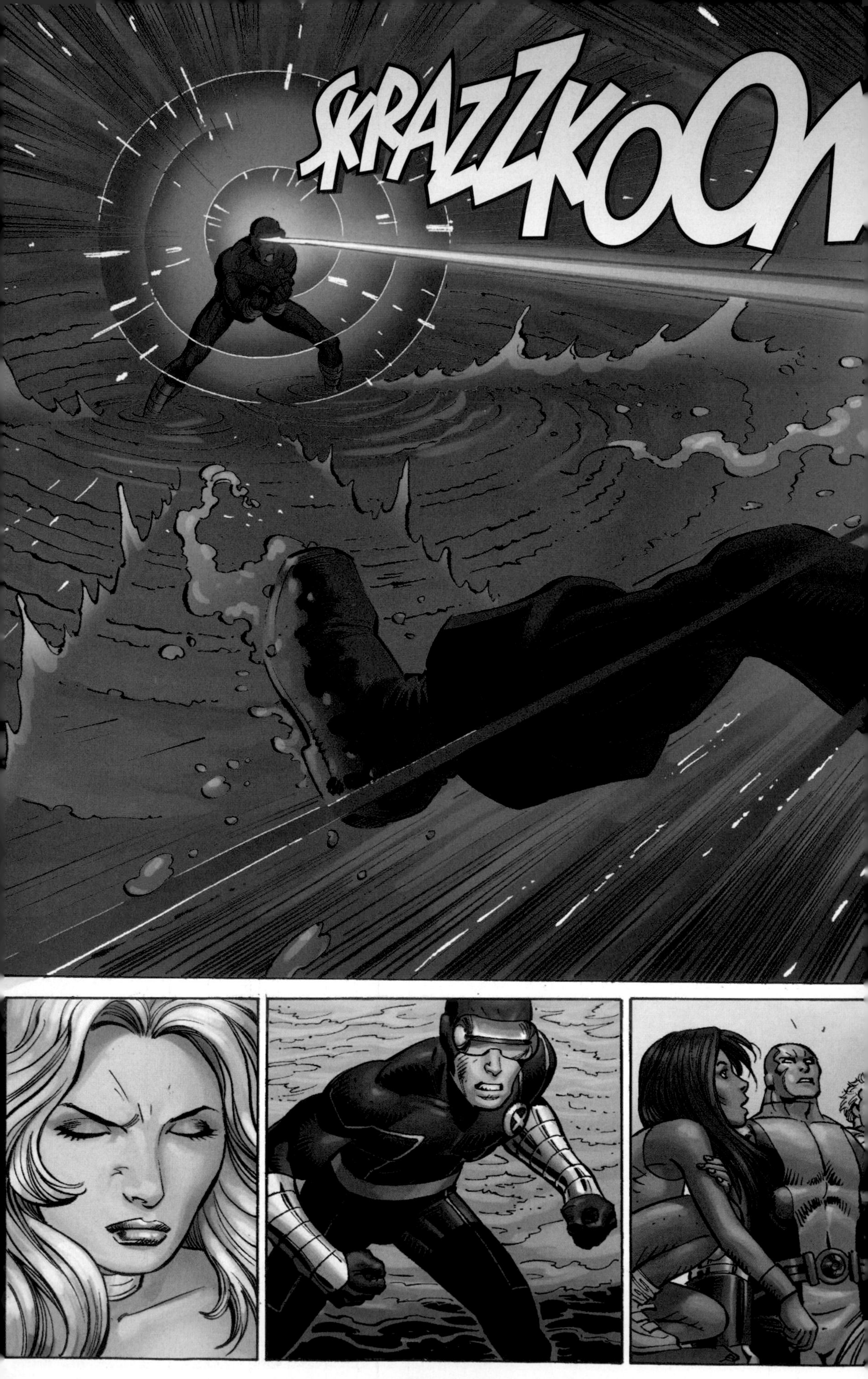
SKRAZZKOOM

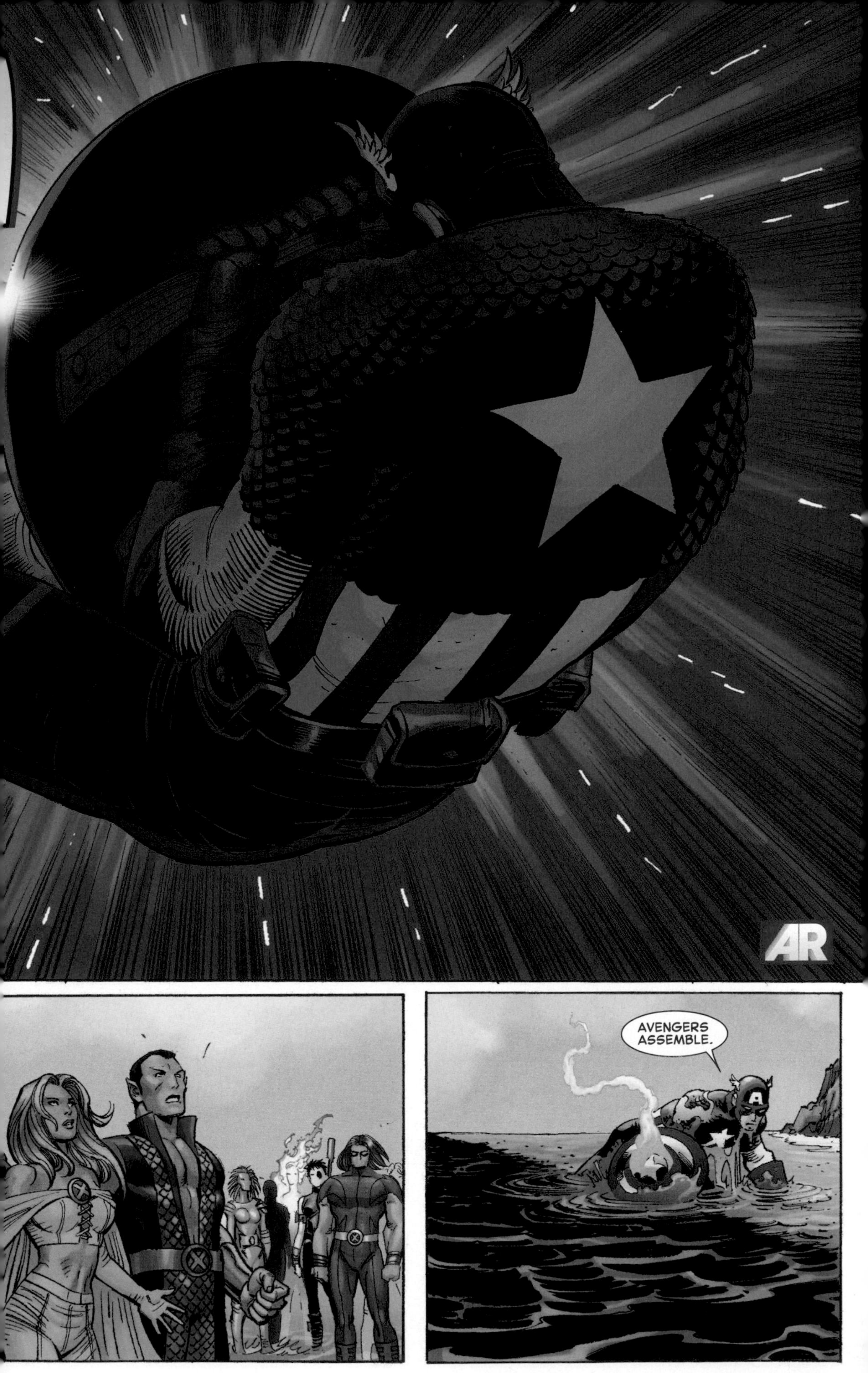
AVENGERS ASSEMBLE.

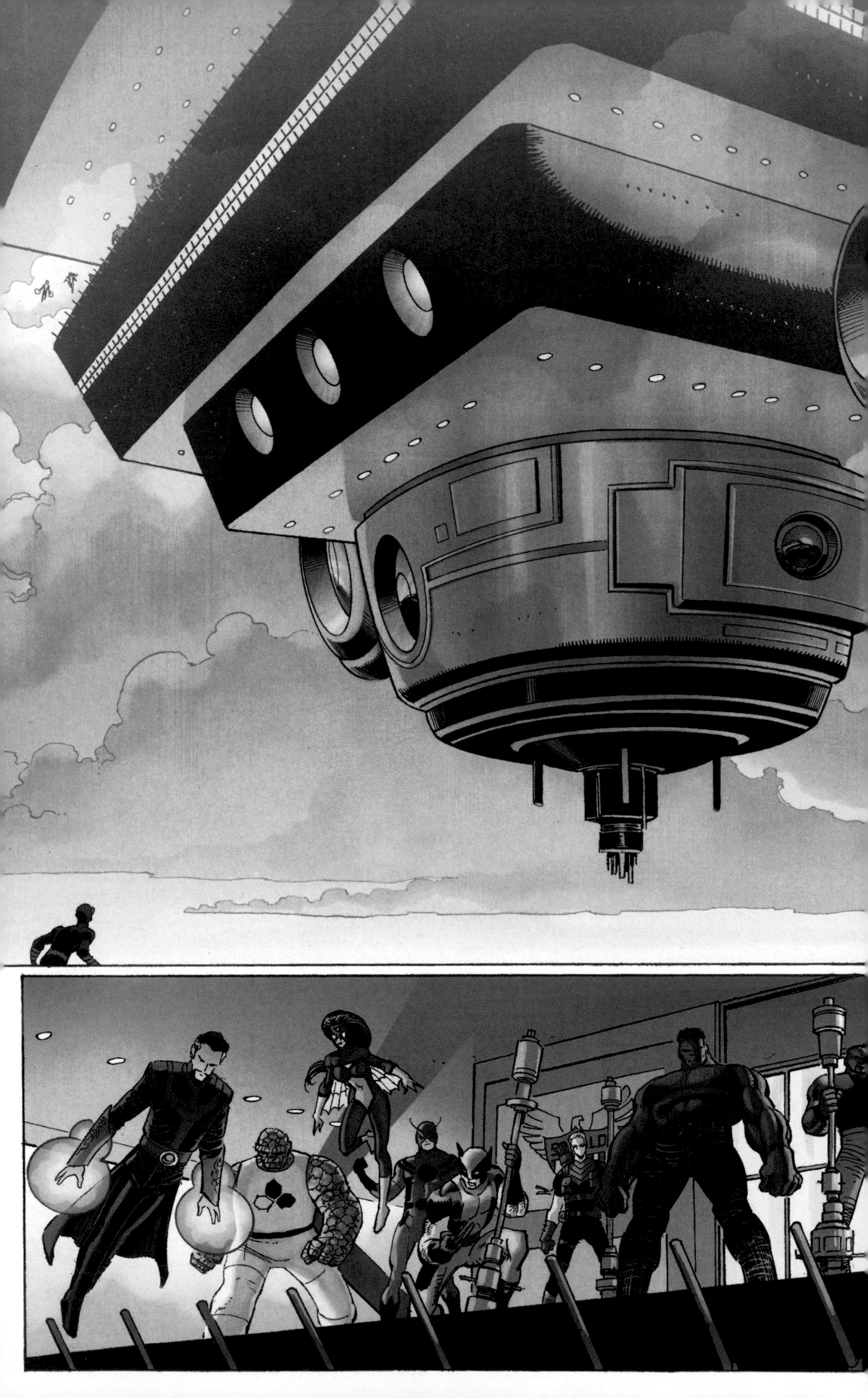

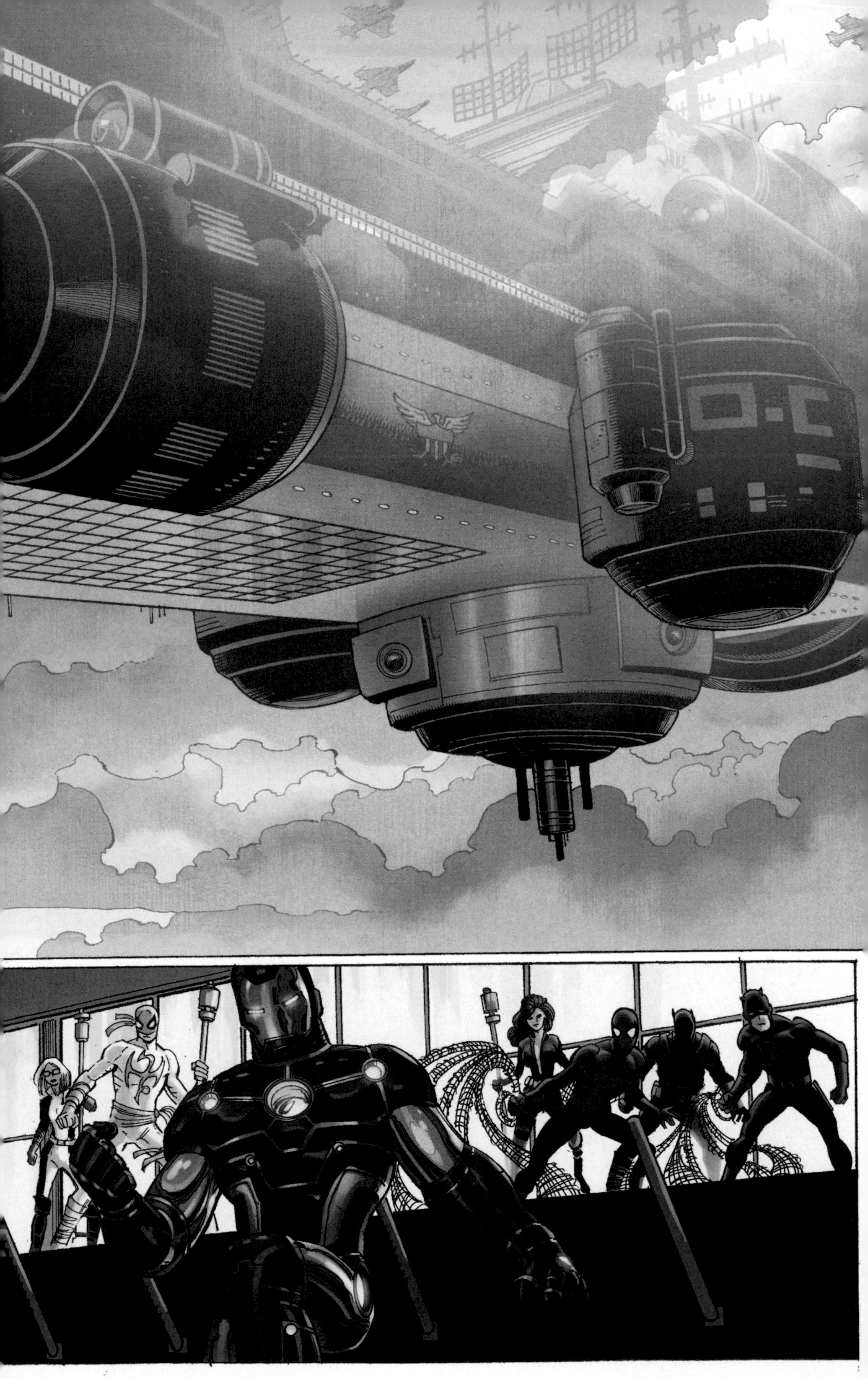

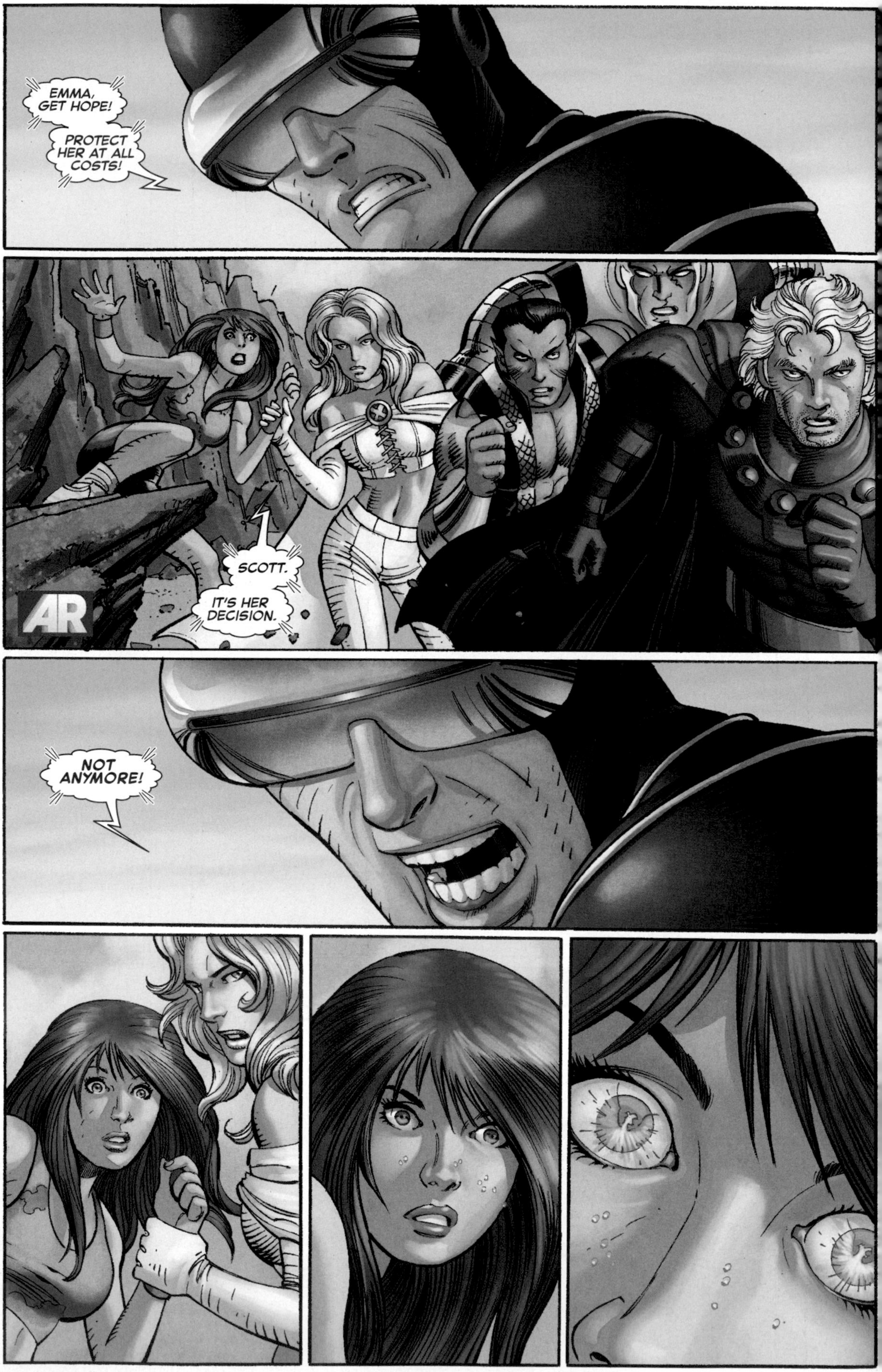
EMMA, GET HOPE!
PROTECT HER AT ALL COSTS!
SCOTT.
IT'S HER DECISION.
AR
NOT ANYMORE!

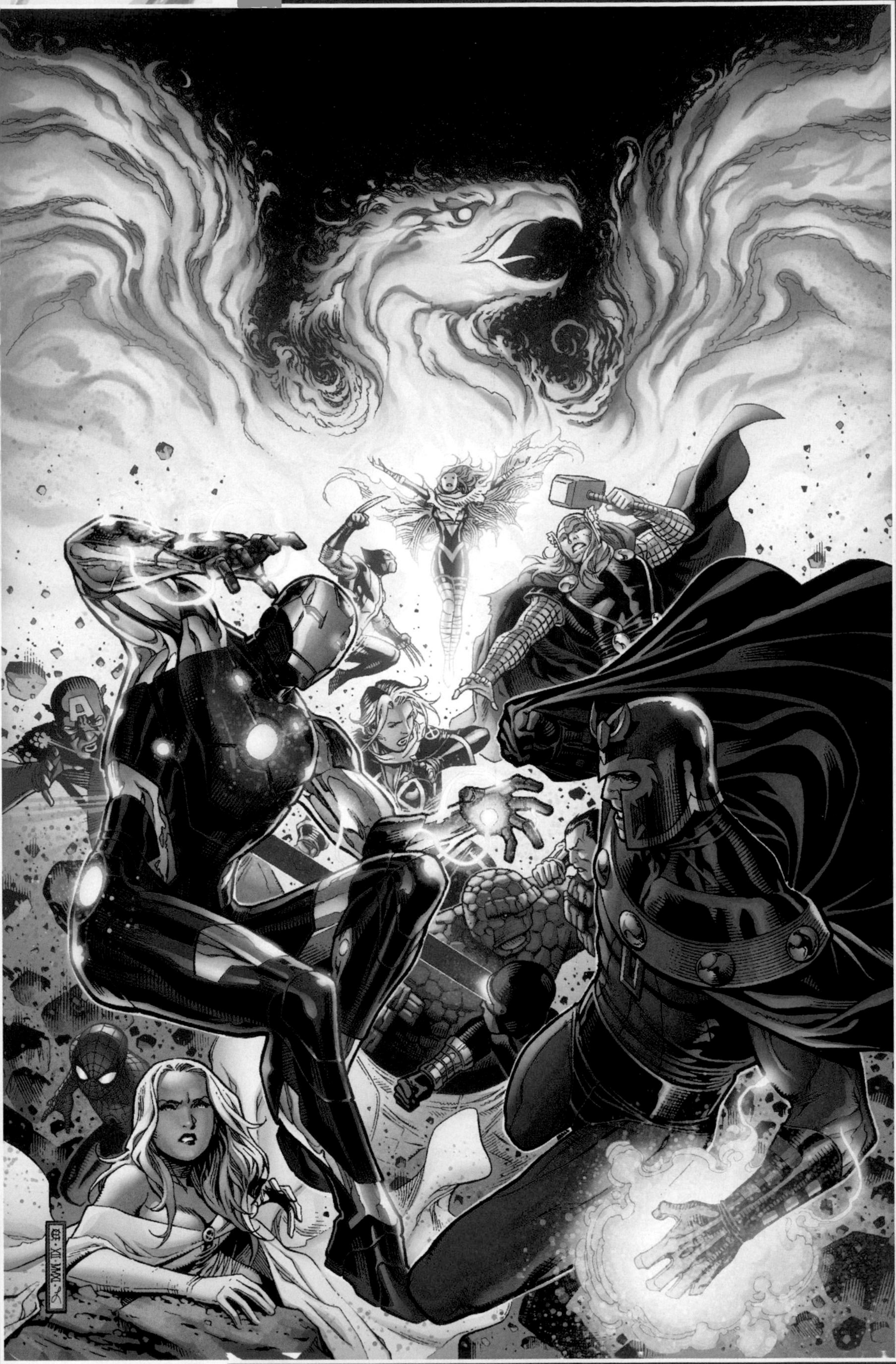

ROUND 2

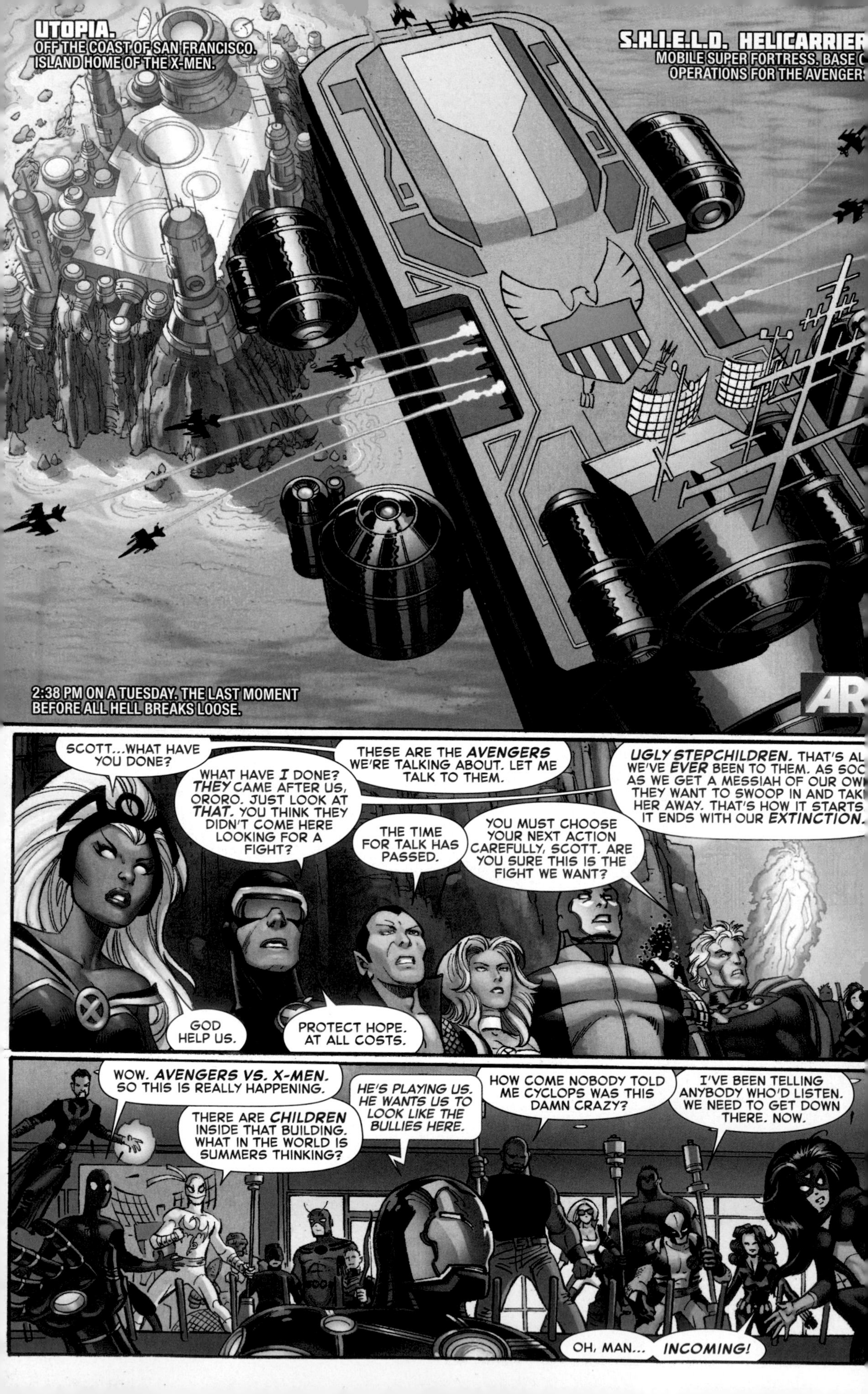
UTOPIA.
OFF THE COAST OF SAN FRANCISCO. ISLAND HOME OF THE X-MEN.
S.H.I.E.L.D. HELICARRIER
MOBILE SUPER FORTRESS. BASE O OPERATIONS FOR THE AVENGERS
2:38 PM ON A TUESDAY. THE LAST MOMENT BEFORE ALL HELL BREAKS LOOSE.
SCOTT...WHAT HAVE YOU DONE?
WHAT HAVE I DONE? THEY CAME AFTER US, ORORO. JUST LOOK AT THAT. YOU THINK THEY DIDN'T COME HERE LOOKING FOR A FIGHT?
THESE ARE THE AVENGERS WE'RE TALKING ABOUT. LET ME TALK TO THEM.
THE TIME FOR TALK HAS PASSED.
YOU MUST CHOOSE YOUR NEXT ACTION CAREFULLY, SCOTT. ARE YOU SURE THIS IS THE FIGHT WE WANT?
UGLY STEPCHILDREN. THAT'S AL WE'VE EVER BEEN TO THEM. AS SOO AS WE GET A MESSIAH OF OUR OW THEY WANT TO SWOOP IN AND TAK HER AWAY. THAT'S HOW IT STARTS IT ENDS WITH OUR EXTINCTION.
GOD HELP US.
PROTECT HOPE. AT ALL COSTS.
WOW. AVENGERS VS. X-MEN. SO THIS IS REALLY HAPPENING.
THERE ARE CHILDREN INSIDE THAT BUILDING. WHAT IN THE WORLD IS SUMMERS THINKING?
HE'S PLAYING US. HE WANTS US TO LOOK LIKE THE BULLIES HERE.
HOW COME NOBODY TOLD ME CYCLOPS WAS THIS DAMN CRAZY?
I'VE BEEN TELLING ANYBODY WHO'D LISTEN. WE NEED TO GET DOWN THERE. NOW.
OH, MAN...
INCOMING!

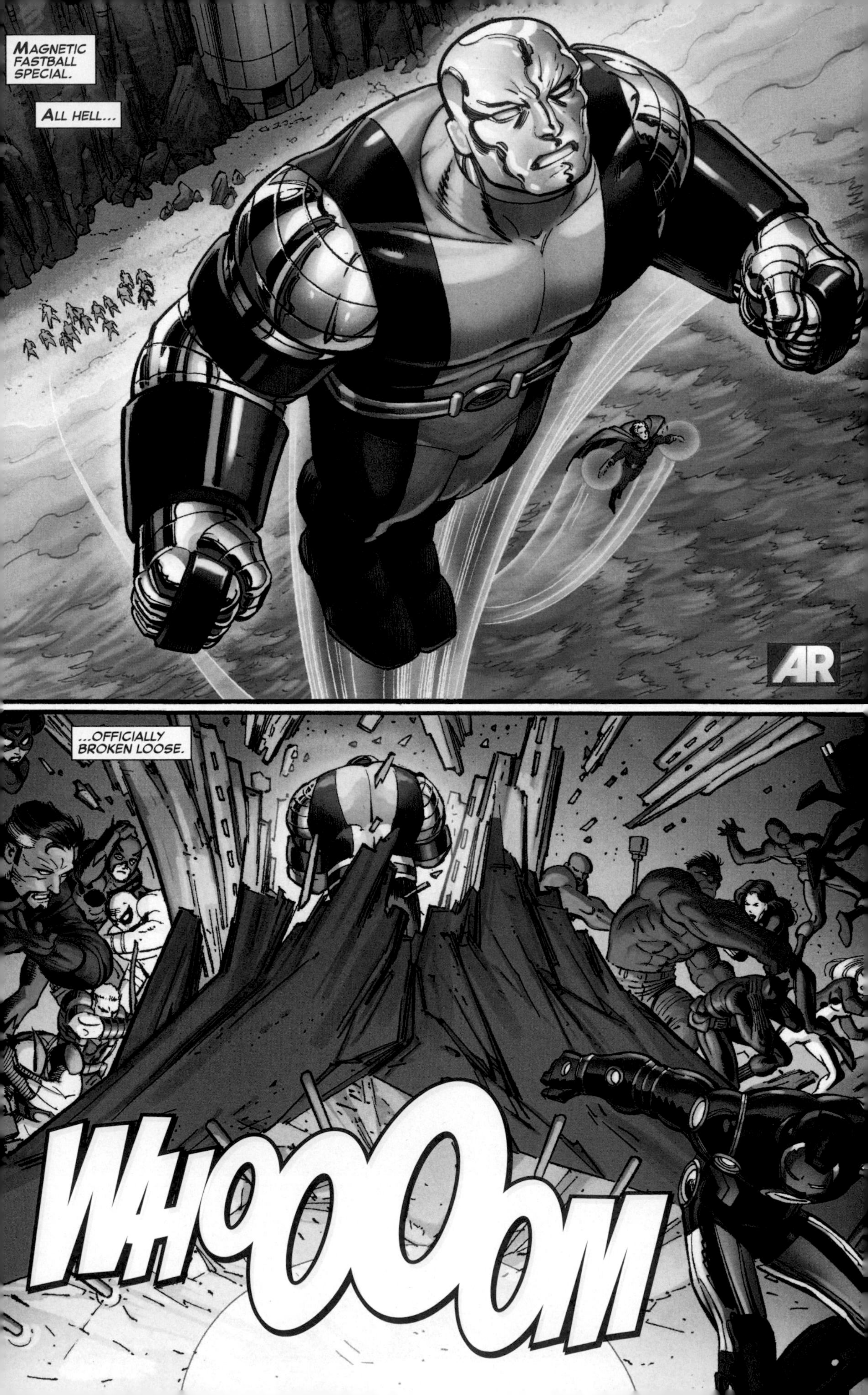
MAGNETIC FASTBALL SPECIAL.
ALL HELL...
...OFFICIALLY BROKEN LOOSE.
WHOOOOM

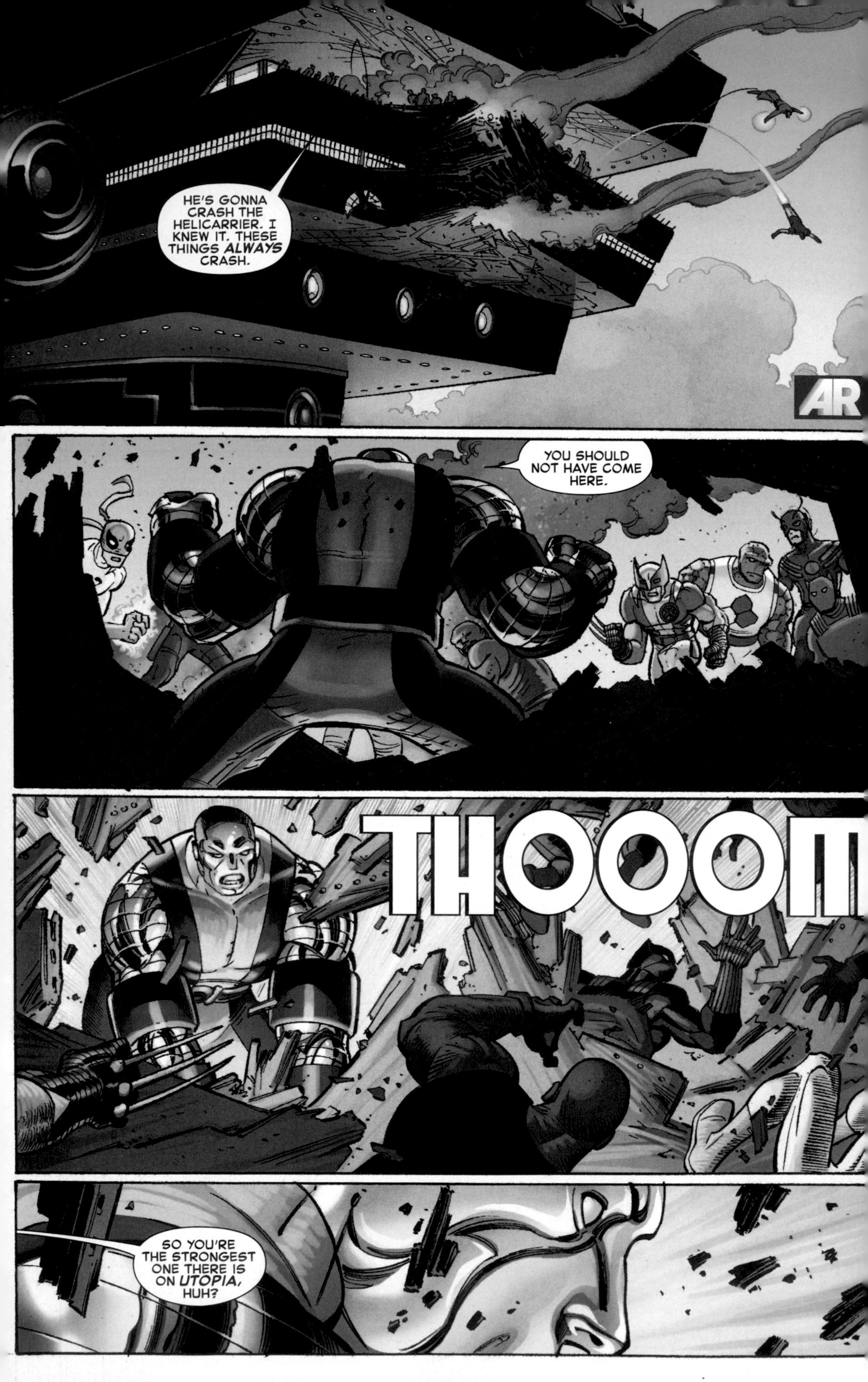
HE'S GONNA CRASH THE HELICARRIER. I KNEW IT. THESE THINGS ALWAYS CRASH.
AR
YOU SHOULD NOT HAVE COME HERE.
THOOOM
SO YOU'RE THE STRONGEST ONE THERE IS ON UTOPIA, HUH?

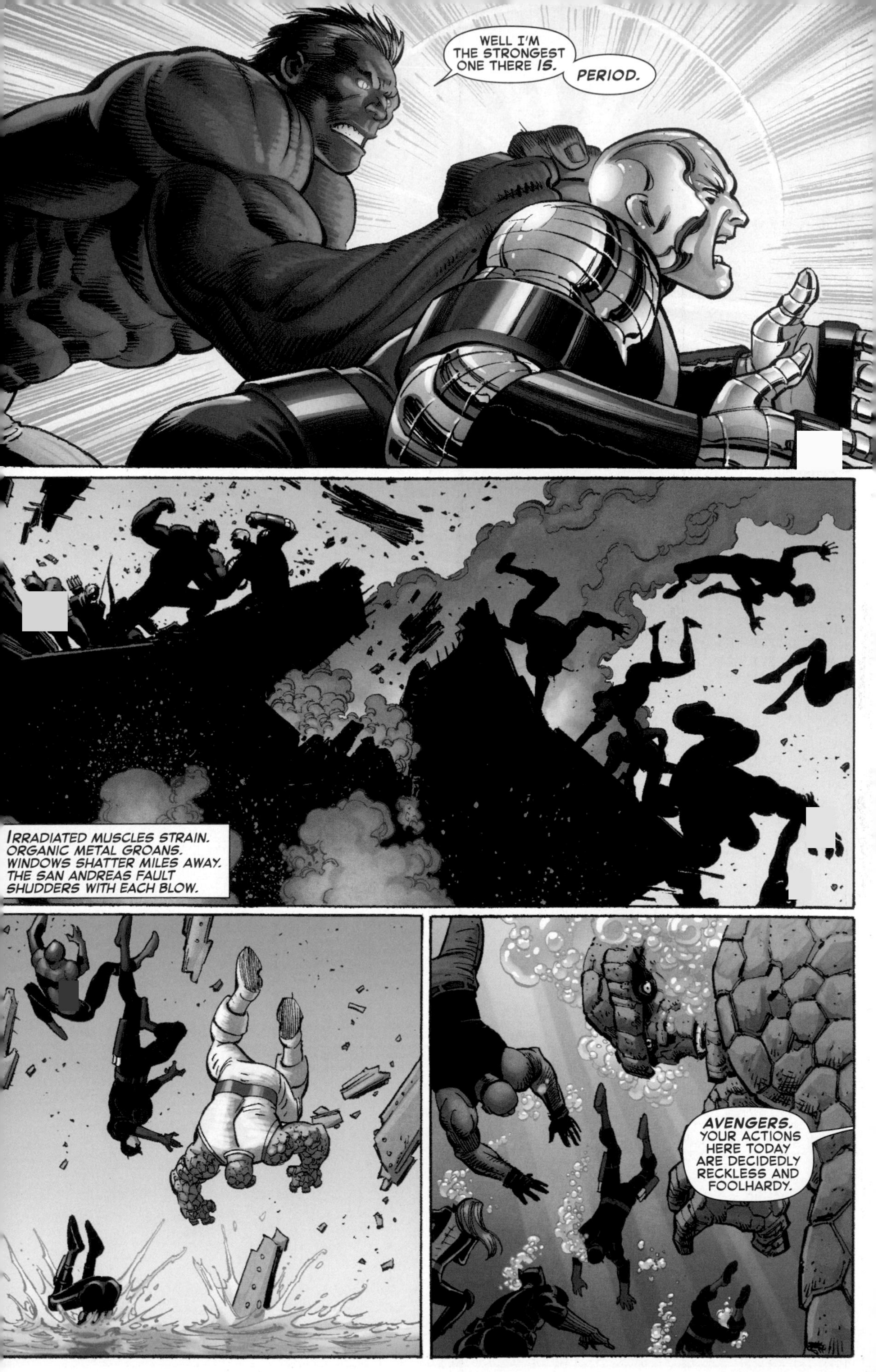
WELL I'M THE STRONGEST ONE THERE IS.
PERIOD.
IRRADIATED MUSCLES STRAIN. ORGANIC METAL GROANS. WINDOWS SHATTER MILES AWAY. THE SAN ANDREAS FAULT SHUDDERS WITH EACH BLOW.
AVENGERS. YOUR ACTIONS HERE TODAY ARE DECIDEDLY RECKLESS AND FOOLHARDY.

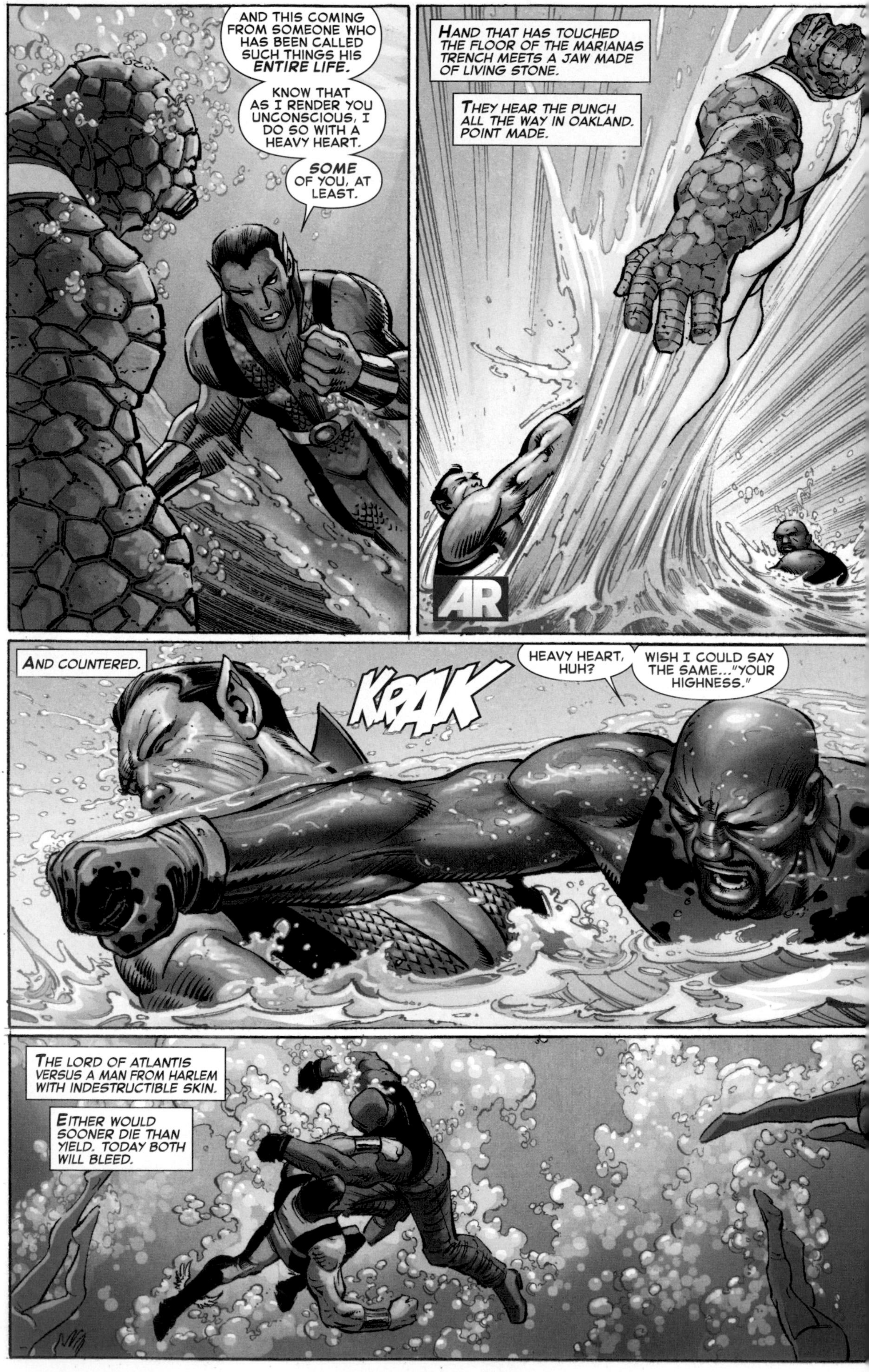

AND THIS COMING FROM SOMEONE WHO HAS BEEN CALLED SUCH THINGS HIS ENTIRE LIFE.
KNOW THAT AS I RENDER YOU UNCONSCIOUS, I DO SO WITH A HEAVY HEART.
SOME OF YOU, AT LEAST.
HAND THAT HAS TOUCHED THE FLOOR OF THE MARIANAS TRENCH MEETS A JAW MADE OF LIVING STONE.
THEY HEAR THE PUNCH ALL THE WAY IN OAKLAND. POINT MADE.
AND COUNTERED.
KRAK
HEAVY HEART, HUH?
WISH I COULD SAY THE SAME..."YOUR HIGHNESS."
THE LORD OF ATLANTIS VERSUS A MAN FROM HARLEM WITH INDESTRUCTIBLE SKIN.
EITHER WOULD SOONER DIE THAN YIELD. TODAY BOTH WILL BLEED.

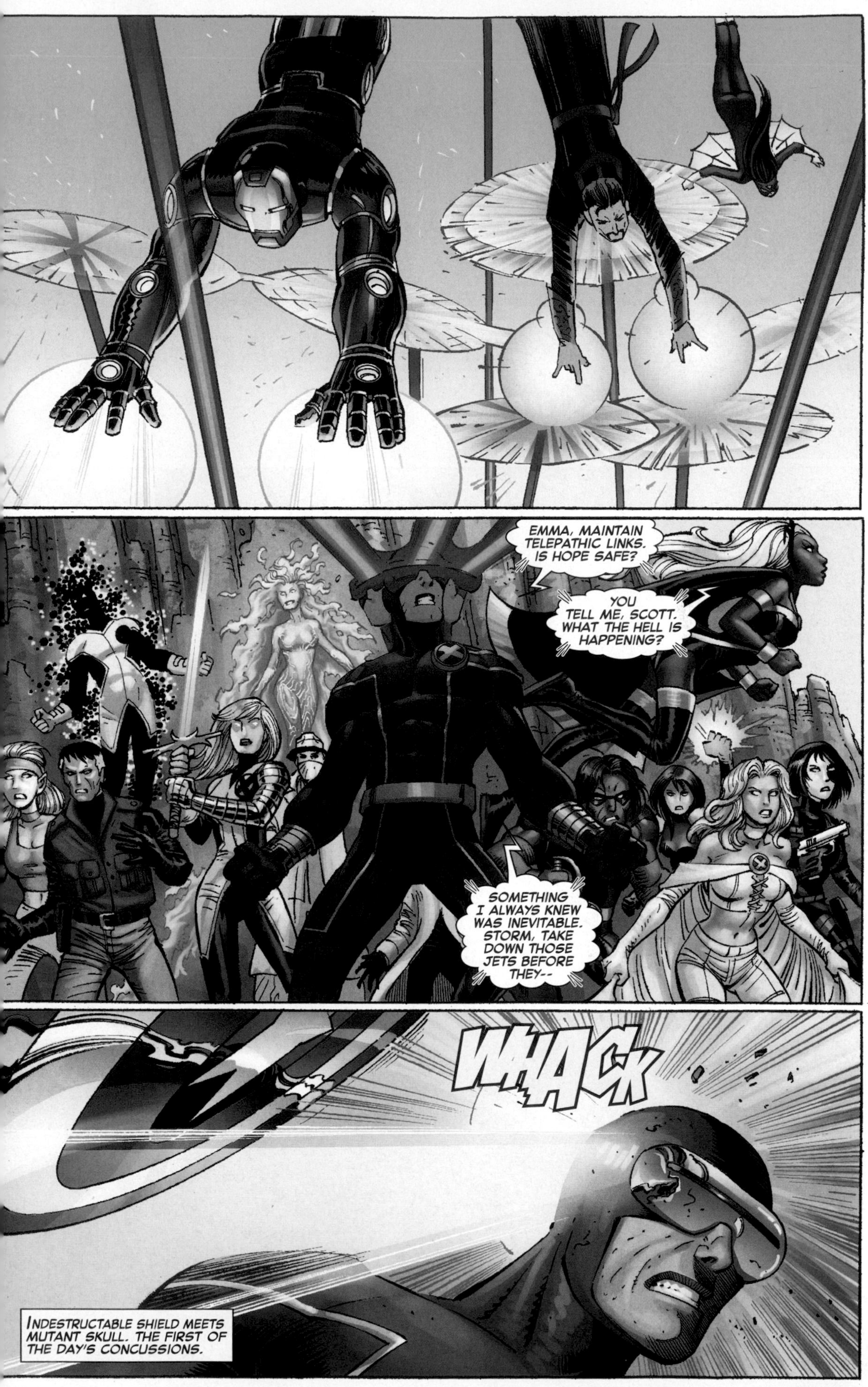
EMMA, MAINTAIN TELEPATHIC LINKS. IS HOPE SAFE?
YOU TELL ME, SCOTT. WHAT THE HELL IS HAPPENING?
SOMETHING I ALWAYS KNEW WAS INEVITABLE. STORM, TAKE DOWN THOSE JETS BEFORE THEY--
WHACK
INDESTRUCTABLE SHIELD MEETS MUTANT SKULL. THE FIRST OF THE DAY'S CONCUSSIONS.

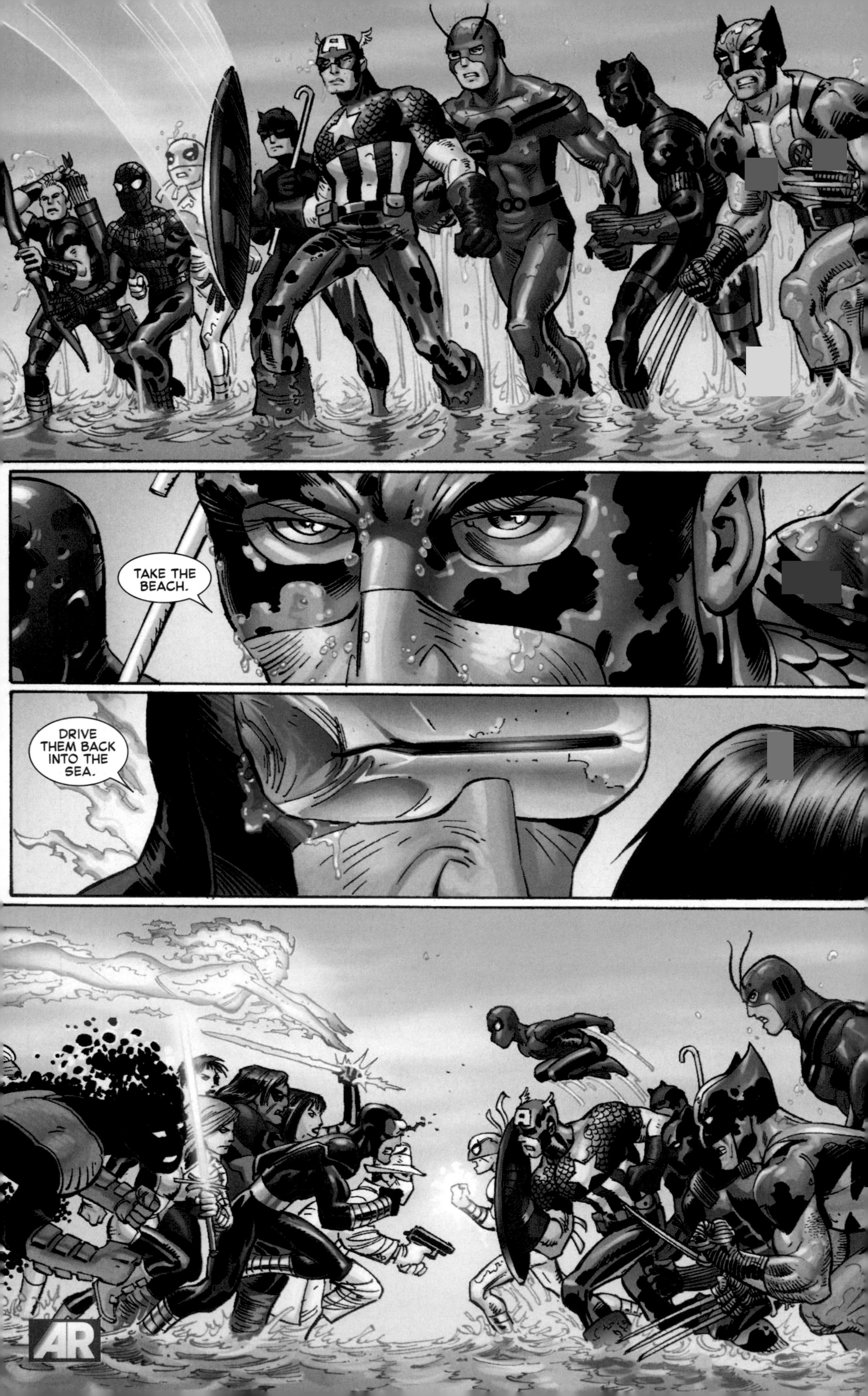
TAKE THE BEACH.
DRIVE THEM BACK INTO THE SEA.

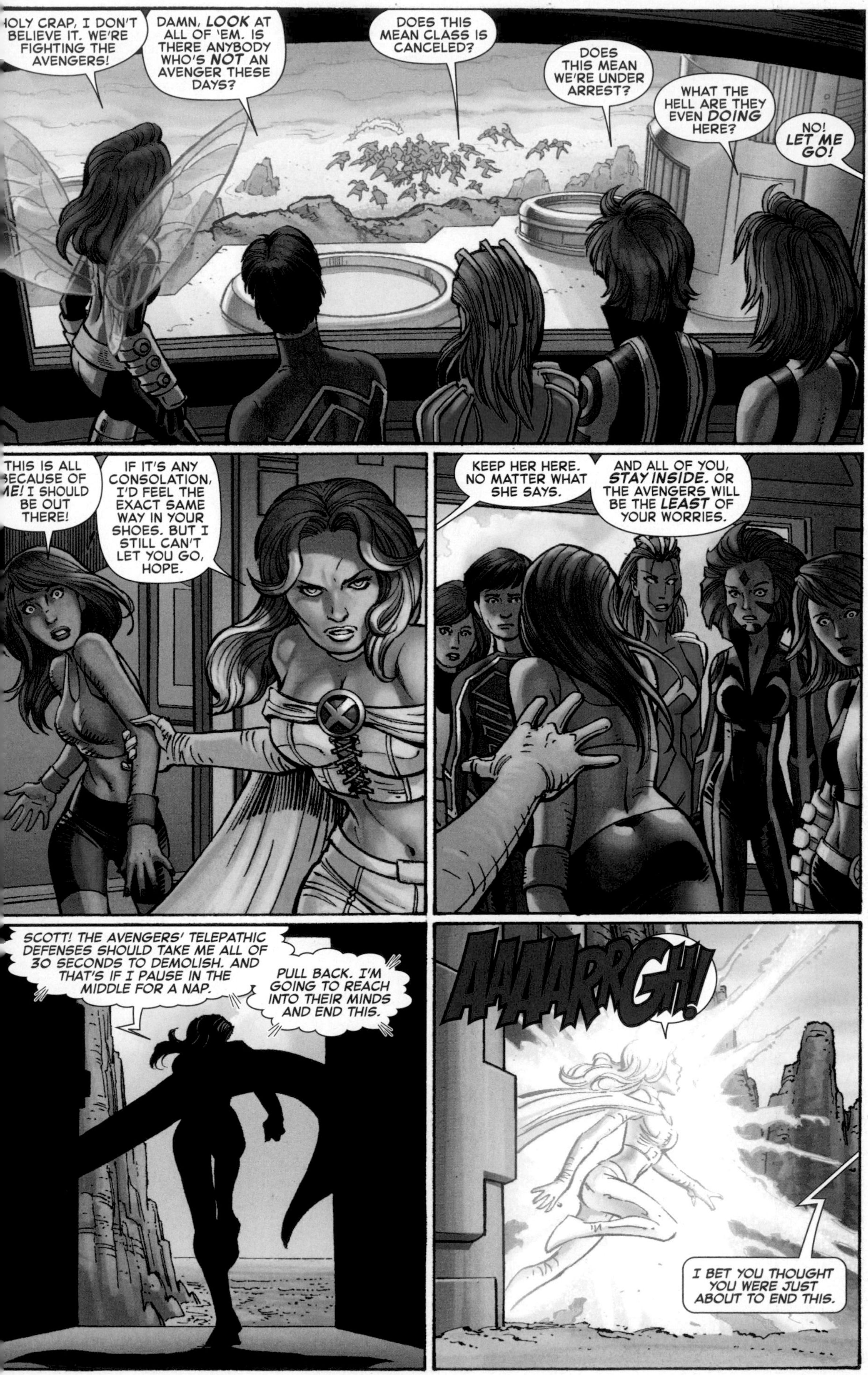
HOLY CRAP, I DON'T BELIEVE IT. WE'RE FIGHTING THE AVENGERS!
DAMN, LOOK AT ALL OF 'EM. IS THERE ANYBODY WHO'S NOT AN AVENGER THESE DAYS?
DOES THIS MEAN CLASS IS CANCELED?
DOES THIS MEAN WE'RE UNDER ARREST?
WHAT THE HELL ARE THEY EVEN DOING HERE?
NO! LET ME GO!
THIS IS ALL BECAUSE OF ME! I SHOULD BE OUT THERE!
IF IT'S ANY CONSOLATION, I'D FEEL THE EXACT SAME WAY IN YOUR SHOES. BUT I STILL CAN'T LET YOU GO, HOPE.
KEEP HER HERE. NO MATTER WHAT SHE SAYS.
AND ALL OF YOU, STAY INSIDE. OR THE AVENGERS WILL BE THE LEAST OF YOUR WORRIES.
SCOTT! THE AVENGERS' TELEPATHIC DEFENSES SHOULD TAKE ME ALL OF 30 SECONDS TO DEMOLISH. AND THAT'S IF I PAUSE IN THE MIDDLE FOR A NAP.
PULL BACK. I'M GOING TO REACH INTO THEIR MINDS AND END THIS.
AAAARRGH!
I BET YOU THOUGHT YOU WERE JUST ABOUT TO END THIS.

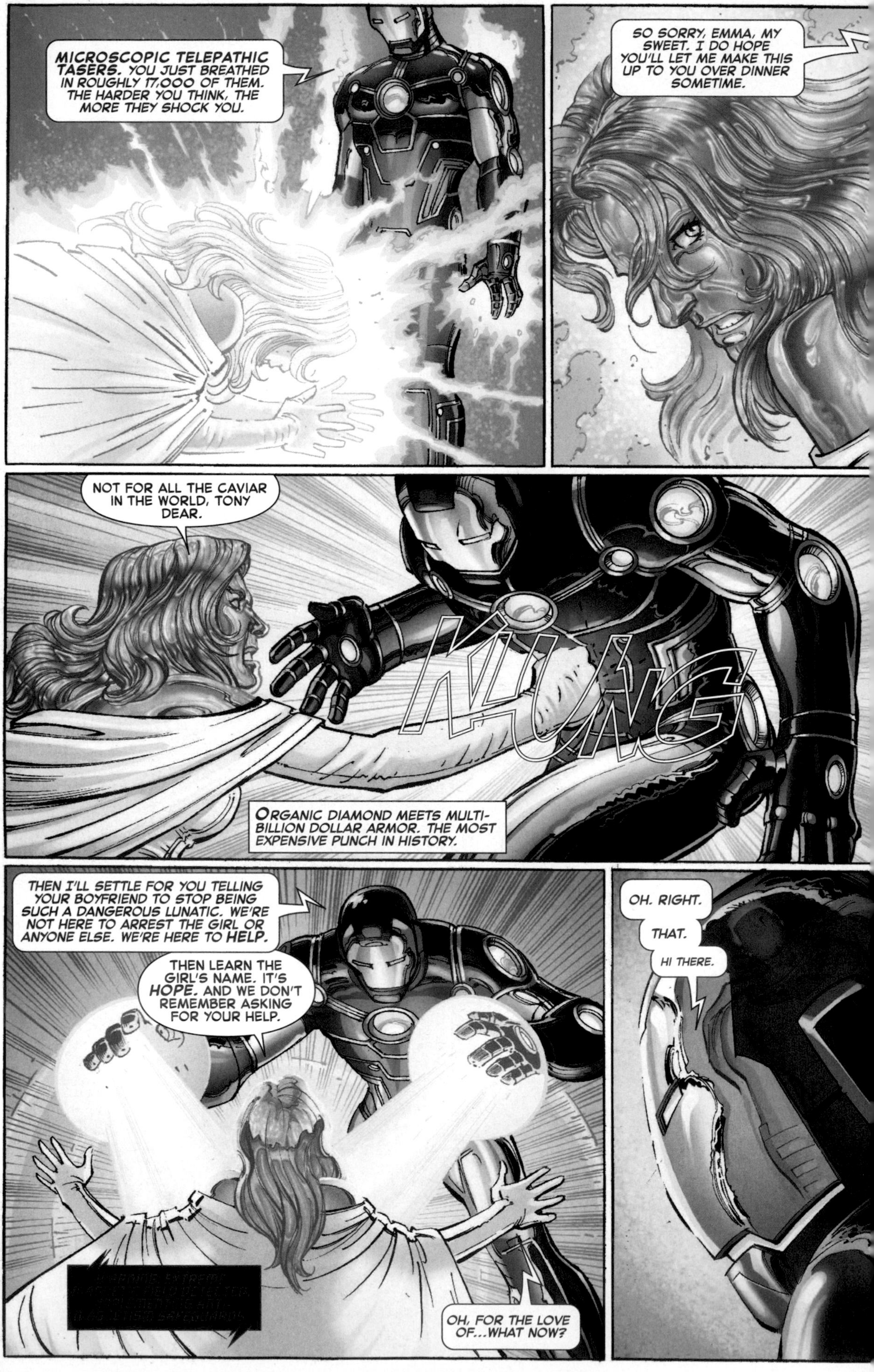
MICROSCOPIC TELEPATHIC TASERS. YOU JUST BREATHED IN ROUGHLY 17,000 OF THEM. THE HARDER YOU THINK, THE MORE THEY SHOCK YOU.
SO SORRY, EMMA, MY SWEET. I DO HOPE YOU'LL LET ME MAKE THIS UP TO YOU OVER DINNER SOMETIME.
NOT FOR ALL THE CAVIAR IN THE WORLD, TONY DEAR.
ORGANIC DIAMOND MEETS MULTI-BILLION DOLLAR ARMOR. THE MOST EXPENSIVE PUNCH IN HISTORY.
THEN I'LL SETTLE FOR YOU TELLING YOUR BOYFRIEND TO STOP BEING SUCH A DANGEROUS LUNATIC. WE'RE NOT HERE TO ARREST THE GIRL OR ANYONE ELSE. WE'RE HERE TO HELP.
THEN LEARN THE GIRL'S NAME. IT'S HOPE. AND WE DON'T REMEMBER ASKING FOR YOUR HELP.
[redacted]
OH, FOR THE LOVE OF...WHAT NOW?
OH. RIGHT.
THAT.
HI THERE.

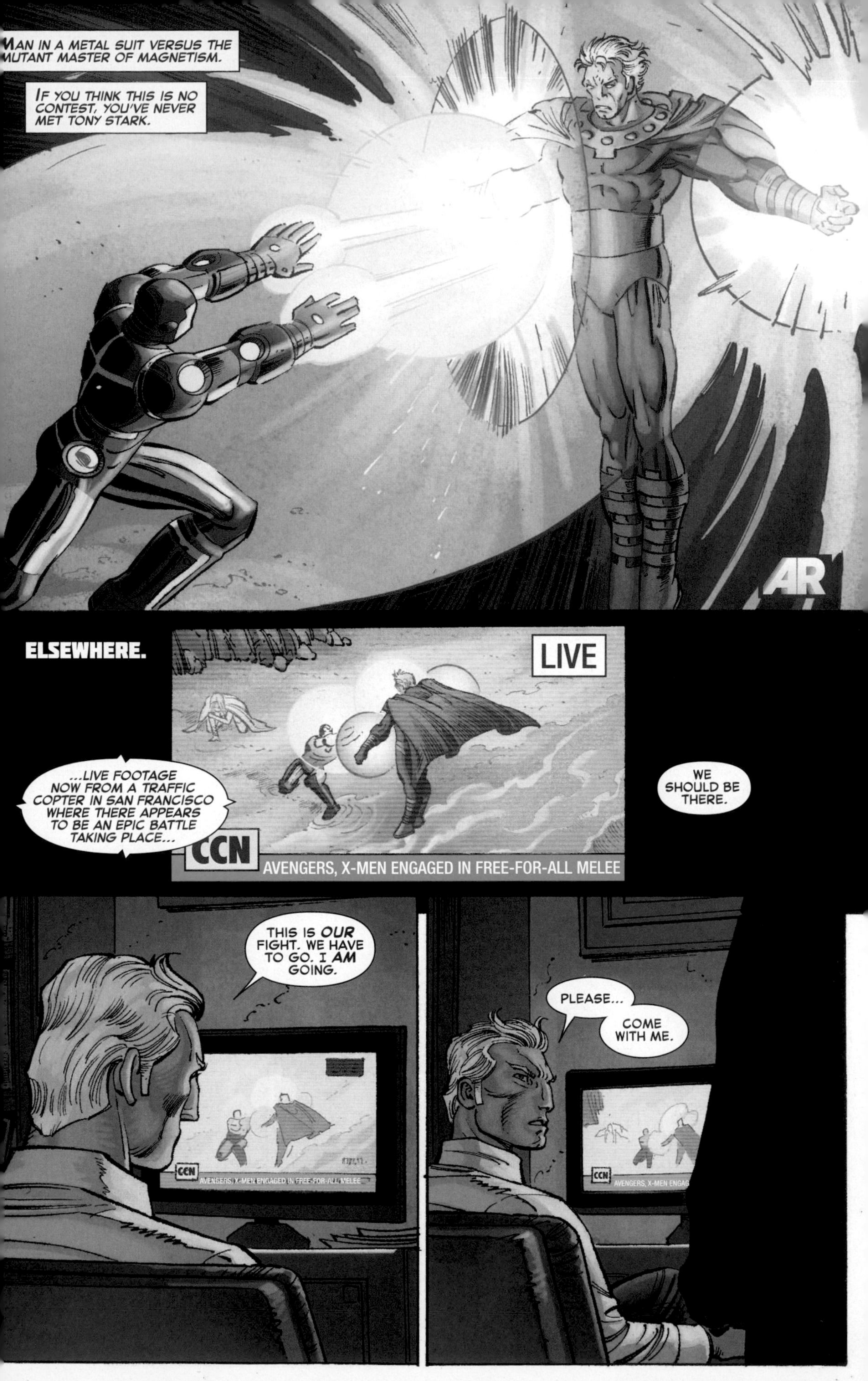

MAN IN A METAL SUIT VERSUS THE MUTANT MASTER OF MAGNETISM.
IF YOU THINK THIS IS NO CONTEST, YOU'VE NEVER MET TONY STARK.
AR
ELSEWHERE.
LIVE
...LIVE FOOTAGE NOW FROM A TRAFFIC COPTER IN SAN FRANCISCO WHERE THERE APPEARS TO BE AN EPIC BATTLE TAKING PLACE...
CCN
AVENGERS, X-MEN ENGAGED IN FREE-FOR-ALL MELEE
WE SHOULD BE THERE.
THIS IS OUR FIGHT. WE HAVE TO GO. I AM GOING.
CCN
AVENGERS, X-MEN ENGAGED IN FREE-FOR-ALL MELEE
PLEASE...
COME WITH ME.
CCN
AVENGERS, X-MEN ENGAG

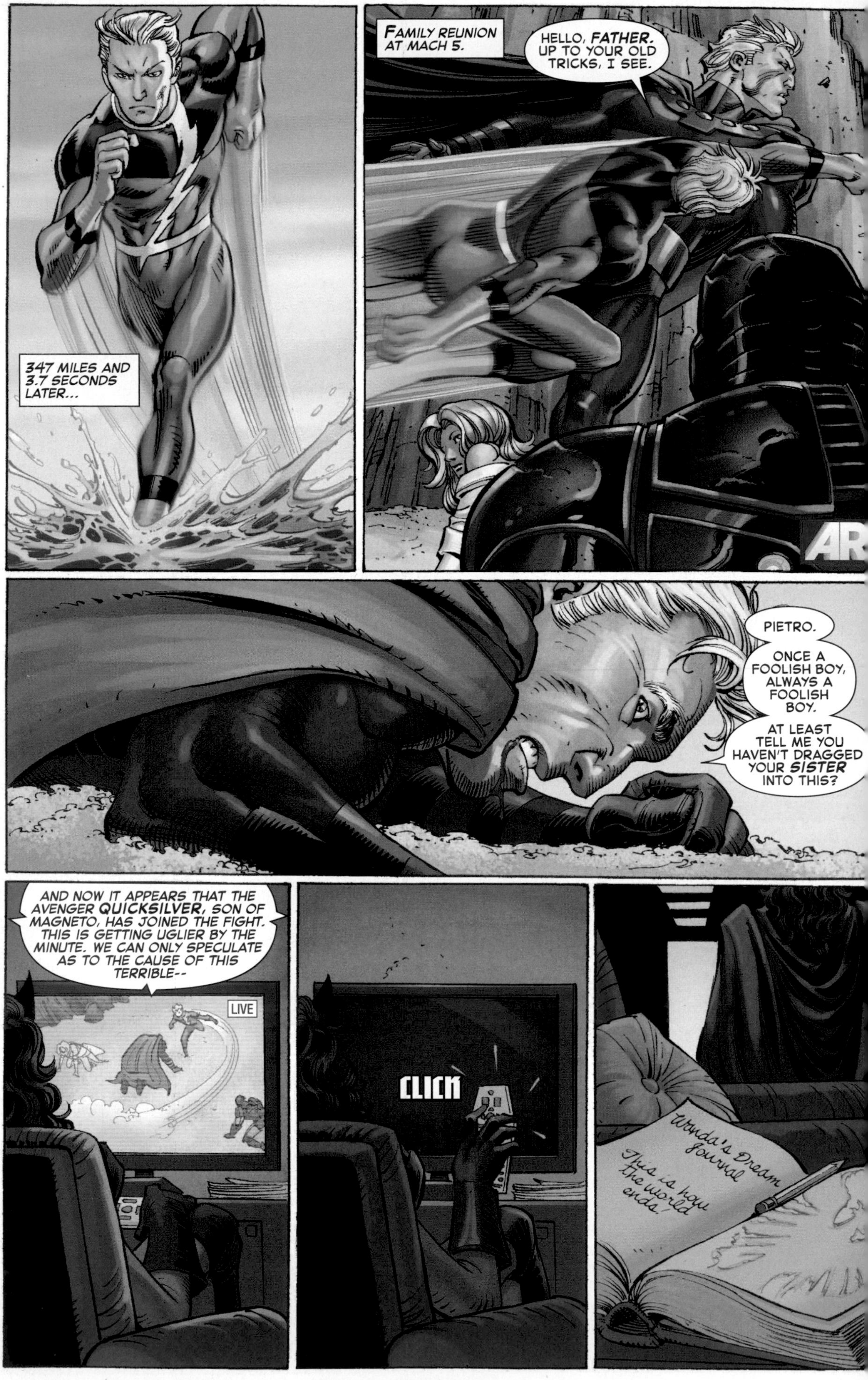

347 MILES AND 3.7 SECONDS LATER...
FAMILY REUNION AT MACH 5.
HELLO, FATHER. UP TO YOUR OLD TRICKS, I SEE.
PIETRO.
ONCE A FOOLISH BOY, ALWAYS A FOOLISH BOY.
AT LEAST TELL ME YOU HAVEN'T DRAGGED YOUR SISTER INTO THIS?
AND NOW IT APPEARS THAT THE AVENGER QUICKSILVER, SON OF MAGNETO, HAS JOINED THE FIGHT. THIS IS GETTING UGLIER BY THE MINUTE. WE CAN ONLY SPECULATE AS TO THE CAUSE OF THIS TERRIBLE--
LIVE
CLICK
Wanda's Dream Journal
This is how the world ends!

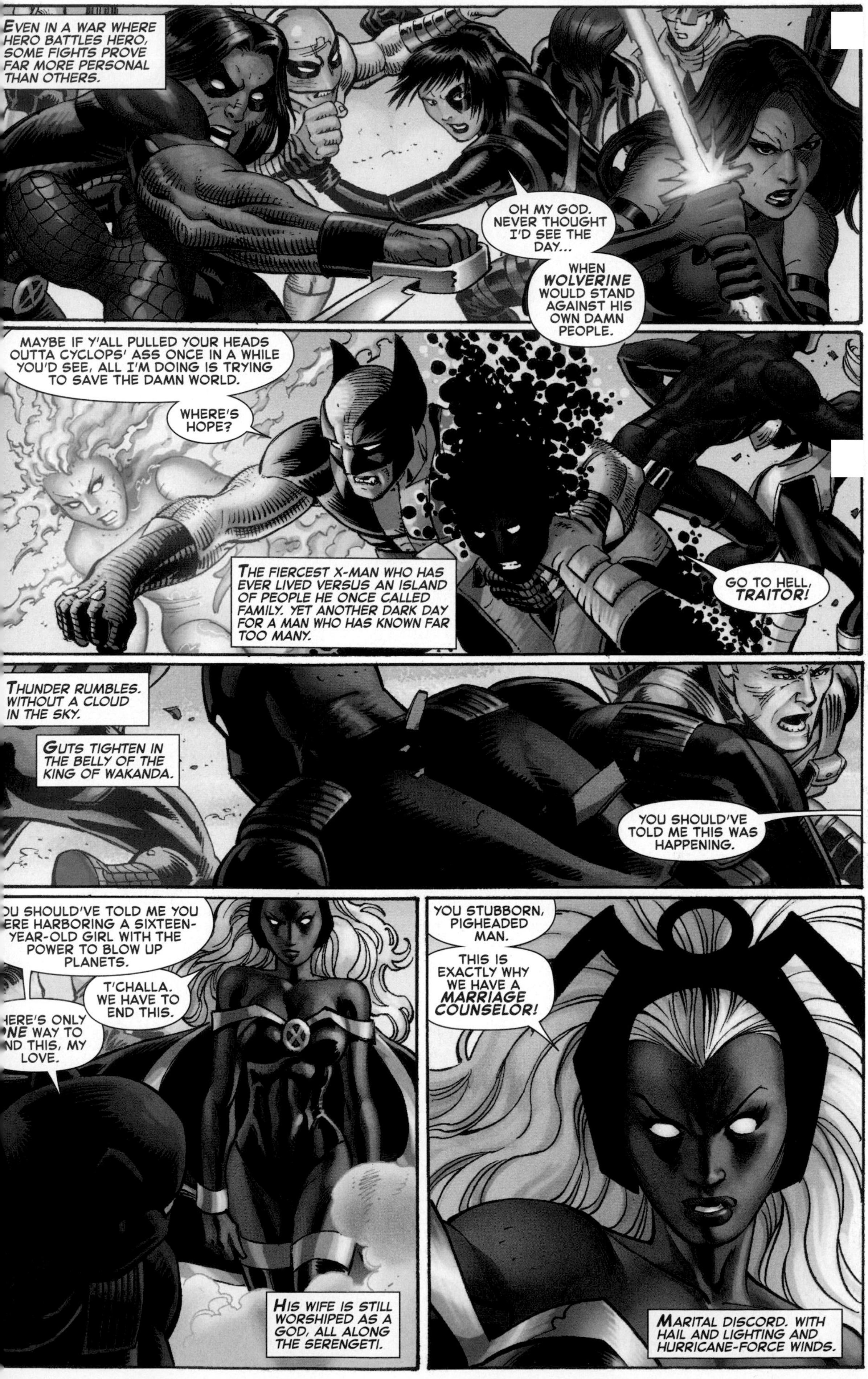
EVEN IN A WAR WHERE HERO BATTLES HERO, SOME FIGHTS PROVE FAR MORE PERSONAL THAN OTHERS.
OH MY GOD. NEVER THOUGHT I'D SEE THE DAY...
WHEN WOLVERINE WOULD STAND AGAINST HIS OWN DAMN PEOPLE.
MAYBE IF Y'ALL PULLED YOUR HEADS OUTTA CYCLOPS' ASS ONCE IN A WHILE YOU'D SEE, ALL I'M DOING IS TRYING TO SAVE THE DAMN WORLD.
WHERE'S HOPE?
THE FIERCEST X-MAN WHO HAS EVER LIVED VERSUS AN ISLAND OF PEOPLE HE ONCE CALLED FAMILY. YET ANOTHER DARK DAY FOR A MAN WHO HAS KNOWN FAR TOO MANY.
GO TO HELL, TRAITOR!
THUNDER RUMBLES. WITHOUT A CLOUD IN THE SKY.
GUTS TIGHTEN IN THE BELLY OF THE KING OF WAKANDA.
YOU SHOULD'VE TOLD ME THIS WAS HAPPENING.
OU SHOULD'VE TOLD ME YOU ERE HARBORING A SIXTEEN-YEAR-OLD GIRL WITH THE POWER TO BLOW UP PLANETS.
T'CHALLA. WE HAVE TO END THIS.
HERE'S ONLY NE WAY TO ND THIS, MY LOVE.
HIS WIFE IS STILL WORSHIPED AS A GOD, ALL ALONG THE SERENGETI.
YOU STUBBORN, PIGHEADED MAN.
THIS IS EXACTLY WHY WE HAVE A MARRIAGE COUNSELOR!
MARITAL DISCORD. WITH HAIL AND LIGHTING AND HURRICANE-FORCE WINDS.

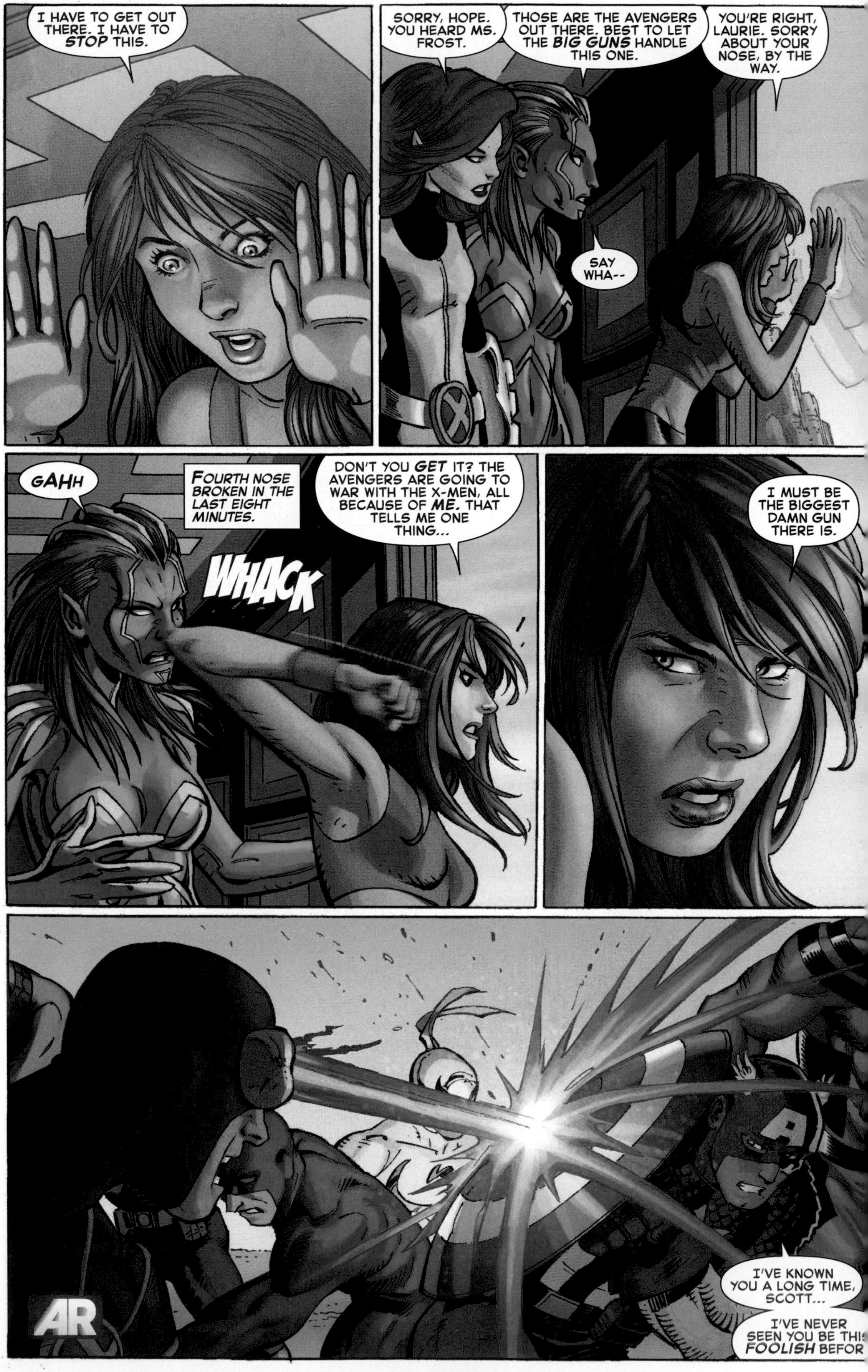
I HAVE TO GET OUT THERE. I HAVE TO STOP THIS.
SORRY, HOPE. YOU HEARD MS. FROST.
THOSE ARE THE AVENGERS OUT THERE. BEST TO LET THE BIG GUNS HANDLE THIS ONE.
YOU'RE RIGHT, LAURIE. SORRY ABOUT YOUR NOSE, BY THE WAY.
SAY WHA--
GAHH
FOURTH NOSE BROKEN IN THE LAST EIGHT MINUTES.
DON'T YOU GET IT? THE AVENGERS ARE GOING TO WAR WITH THE X-MEN, ALL BECAUSE OF ME. THAT TELLS ME ONE THING...
WHACK
I MUST BE THE BIGGEST DAMN GUN THERE IS.
I'VE KNOWN YOU A LONG TIME, SCOTT...
I'VE NEVER SEEN YOU BE THIS FOOLISH BEFOR

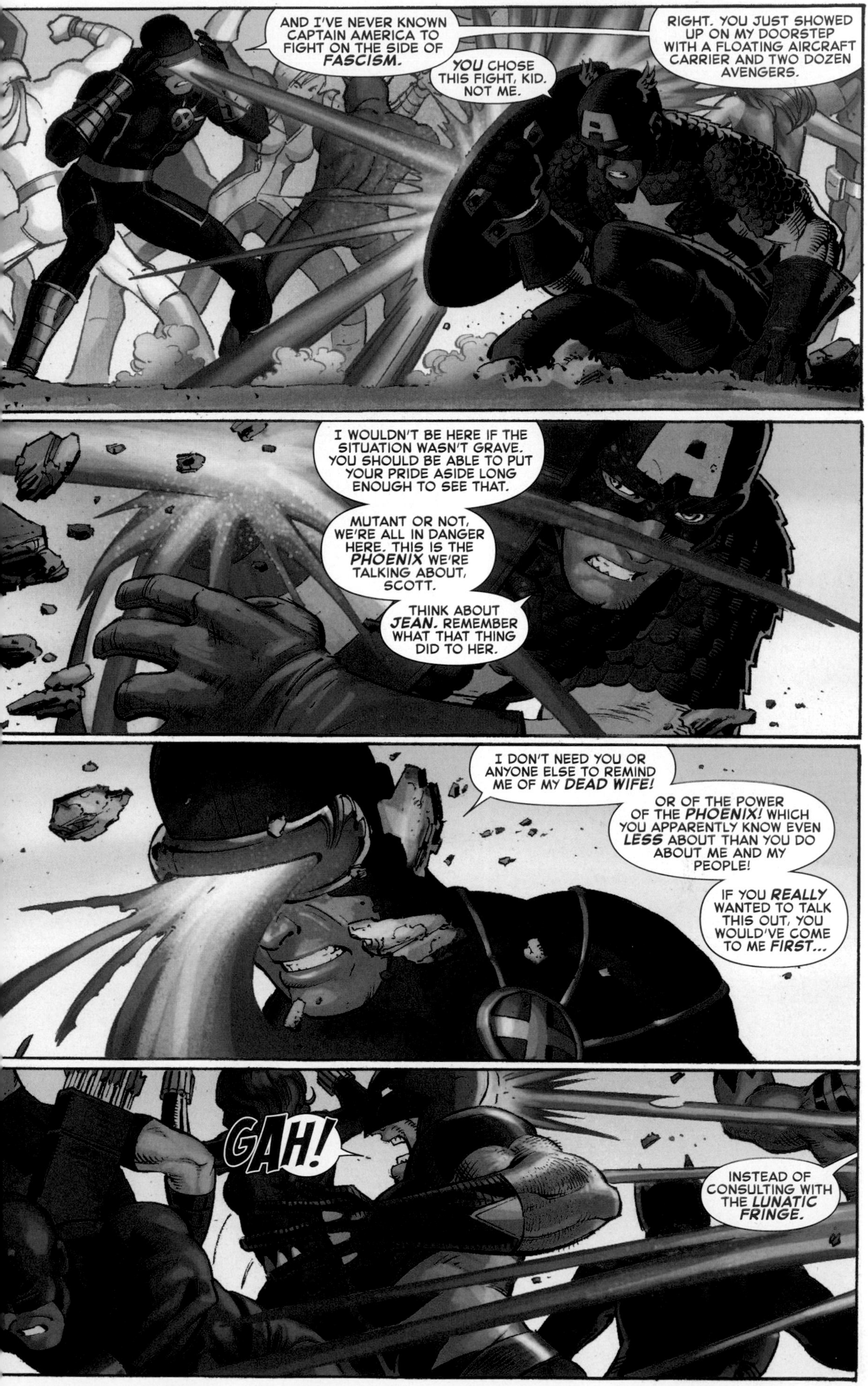
AND I'VE NEVER KNOWN CAPTAIN AMERICA TO FIGHT ON THE SIDE OF FASCISM.
RIGHT. YOU JUST SHOWED UP ON MY DOORSTEP WITH A FLOATING AIRCRAFT CARRIER AND TWO DOZEN AVENGERS.
YOU CHOSE THIS FIGHT, KID. NOT ME.
I WOULDN'T BE HERE IF THE SITUATION WASN'T GRAVE. YOU SHOULD BE ABLE TO PUT YOUR PRIDE ASIDE LONG ENOUGH TO SEE THAT.
MUTANT OR NOT, WE'RE ALL IN DANGER HERE. THIS IS THE PHOENIX WE'RE TALKING ABOUT, SCOTT.
THINK ABOUT JEAN. REMEMBER WHAT THAT THING DID TO HER.
I DON'T NEED YOU OR ANYONE ELSE TO REMIND ME OF MY DEAD WIFE!
OR OF THE POWER OF THE PHOENIX! WHICH YOU APPARENTLY KNOW EVEN LESS ABOUT THAN YOU DO ABOUT ME AND MY PEOPLE!
IF YOU REALLY WANTED TO TALK THIS OUT, YOU WOULD'VE COME TO ME FIRST...
GAH!
INSTEAD OF CONSULTING WITH THE LUNATIC FRINGE.

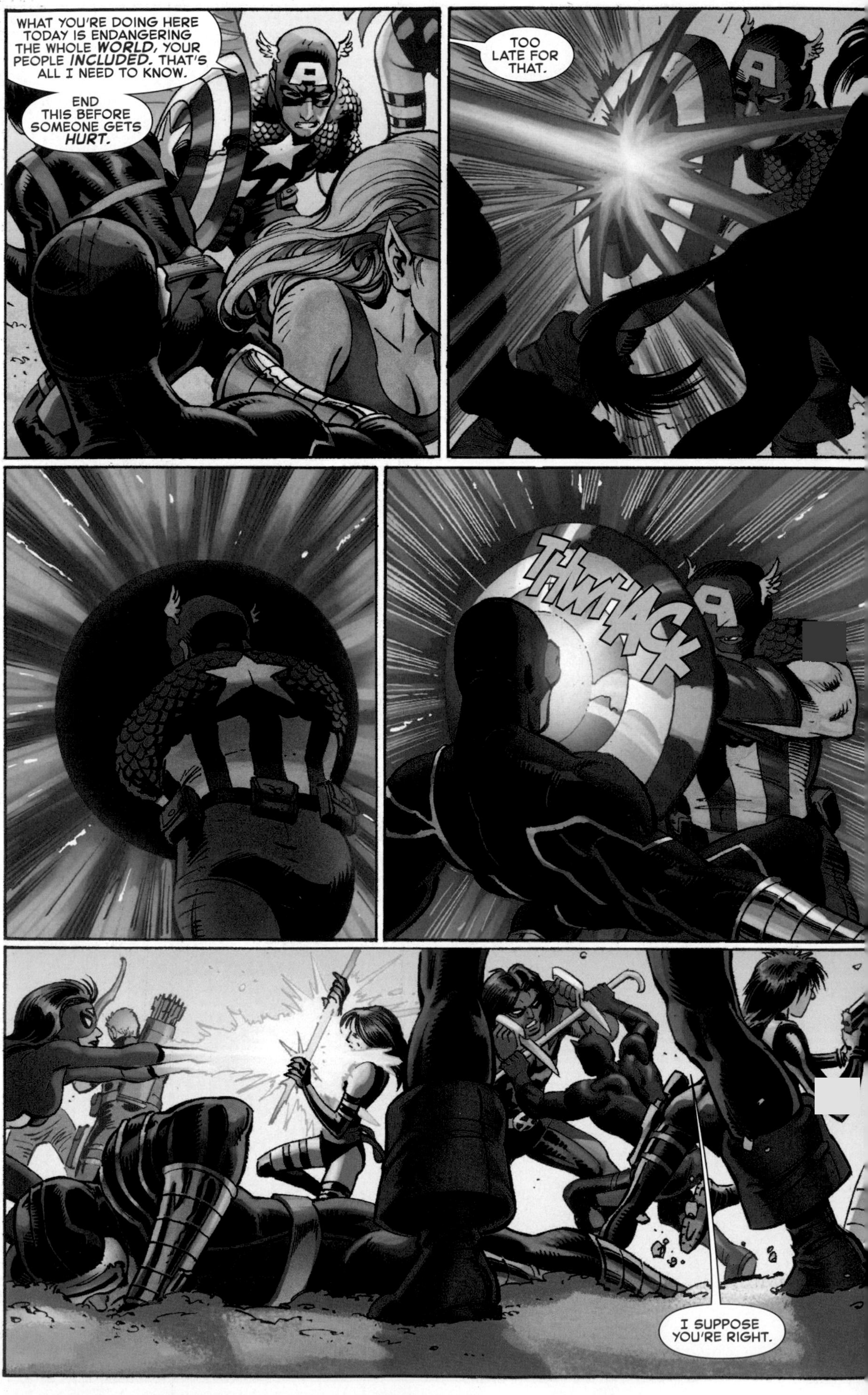
WHAT YOU'RE DOING HERE TODAY IS ENDANGERING THE WHOLE WORLD, YOUR PEOPLE INCLUDED. THAT'S ALL I NEED TO KNOW.
END THIS BEFORE SOMEONE GETS HURT.
TOO LATE FOR THAT.
THWHACK
I SUPPOSE YOU'RE RIGHT.

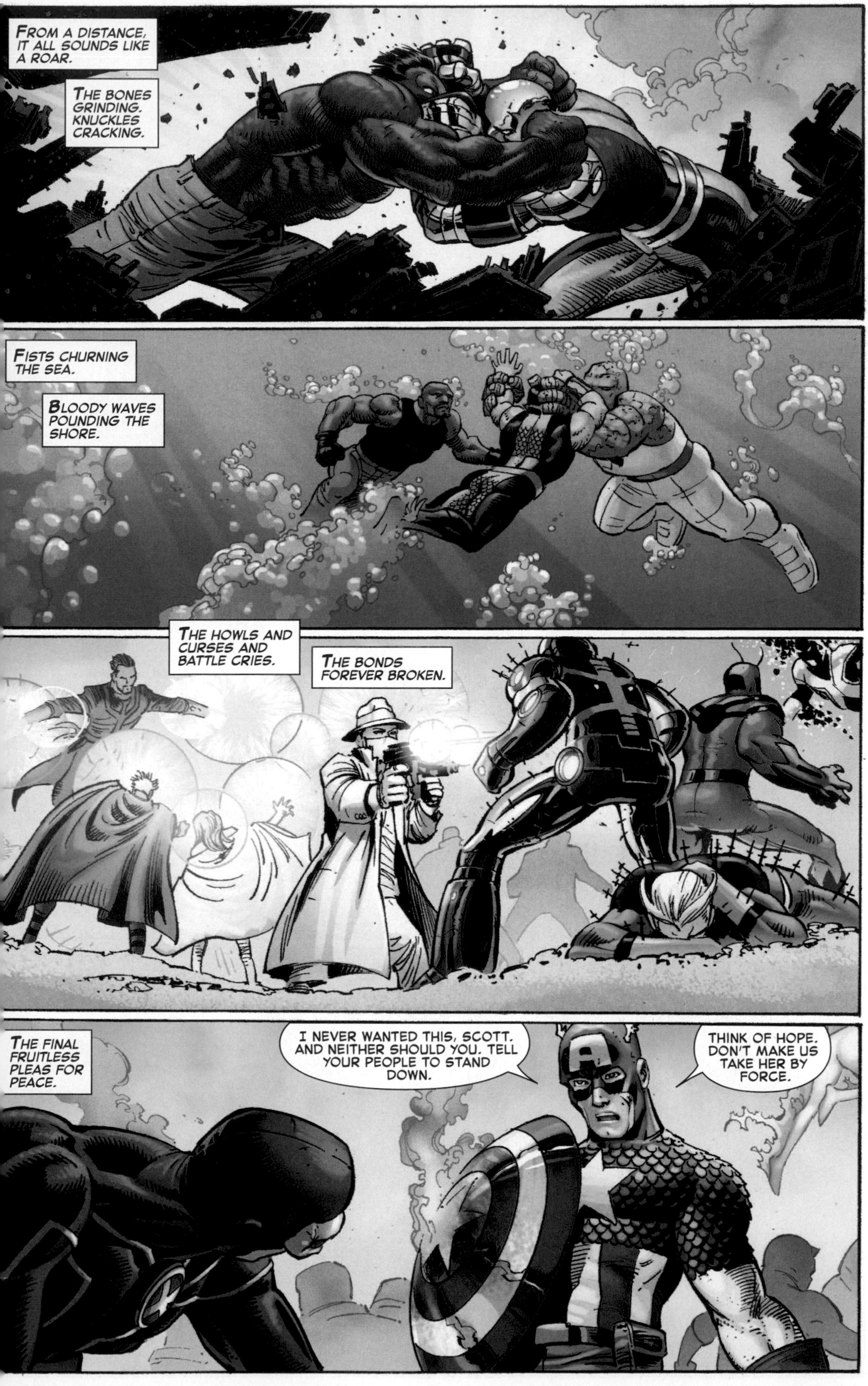
FROM A DISTANCE, IT ALL SOUNDS LIKE A ROAR.
THE BONES GRINDING. KNUCKLES CRACKING.
FISTS CHURNING THE SEA.
BLOODY WAVES POUNDING THE SHORE.
THE HOWLS AND CURSES AND BATTLE CRIES.
THE BONDS FOREVER BROKEN.
THE FINAL FRUITLESS PLEAS FOR PEACE.
I NEVER WANTED THIS, SCOTT. AND NEITHER SHOULD YOU. TELL YOUR PEOPLE TO STAND DOWN.
THINK OF HOPE. DON'T MAKE US TAKE HER BY FORCE.

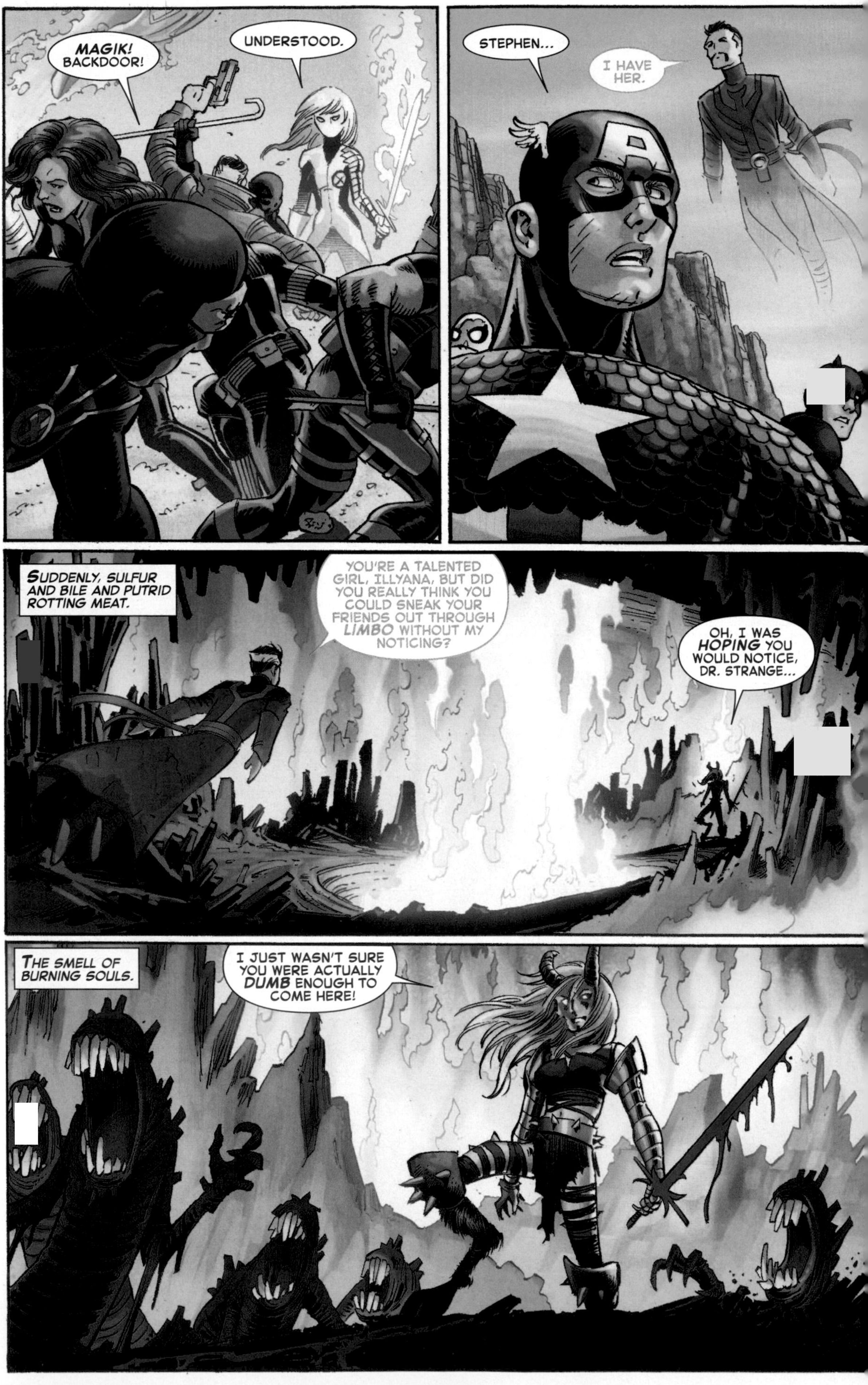
MAGIK! BACKDOOR!
UNDERSTOOD.
STEPHEN...
I HAVE HER.
SUDDENLY, SULFUR AND BILE AND PUTRID ROTTING MEAT.
YOU'RE A TALENTED GIRL, ILLYANA, BUT DID YOU REALLY THINK YOU COULD SNEAK YOUR FRIENDS OUT THROUGH LIMBO WITHOUT MY NOTICING?
OH, I WAS HOPING YOU WOULD NOTICE, DR. STRANGE...
THE SMELL OF BURNING SOULS.
I JUST WASN'T SURE YOU WERE ACTUALLY DUMB ENOUGH TO COME HERE!

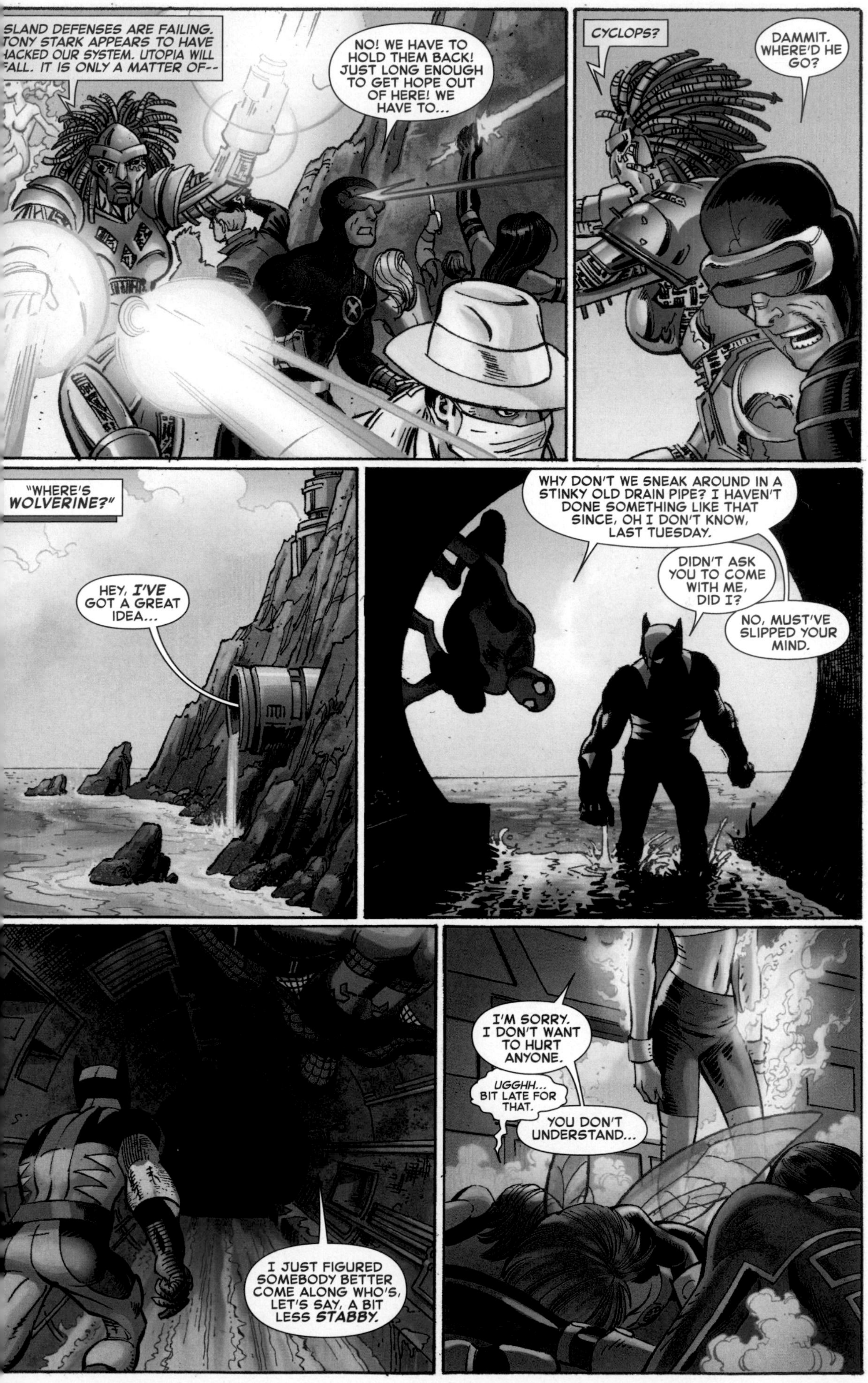

SLAND DEFENSES ARE FAILING. TONY STARK APPEARS TO HAVE HACKED OUR SYSTEM. UTOPIA WILL FALL. IT IS ONLY A MATTER OF--
NO! WE HAVE TO HOLD THEM BACK! JUST LONG ENOUGH TO GET HOPE OUT OF HERE! WE HAVE TO...
CYCLOPS?
DAMMIT. WHERE'D HE GO?
"WHERE'S WOLVERINE?"
HEY, I'VE GOT A GREAT IDEA...
WHY DON'T WE SNEAK AROUND IN A STINKY OLD DRAIN PIPE? I HAVEN'T DONE SOMETHING LIKE THAT SINCE, OH I DON'T KNOW, LAST TUESDAY.
DIDN'T ASK YOU TO COME WITH ME, DID I?
NO, MUST'VE SLIPPED YOUR MIND.
I JUST FIGURED SOMEBODY BETTER COME ALONG WHO'S, LET'S SAY, A BIT LESS STABBY.
I'M SORRY. I DON'T WANT TO HURT ANYONE.
UGGHH... BIT LATE FOR THAT.
YOU DON'T UNDERSTAND...

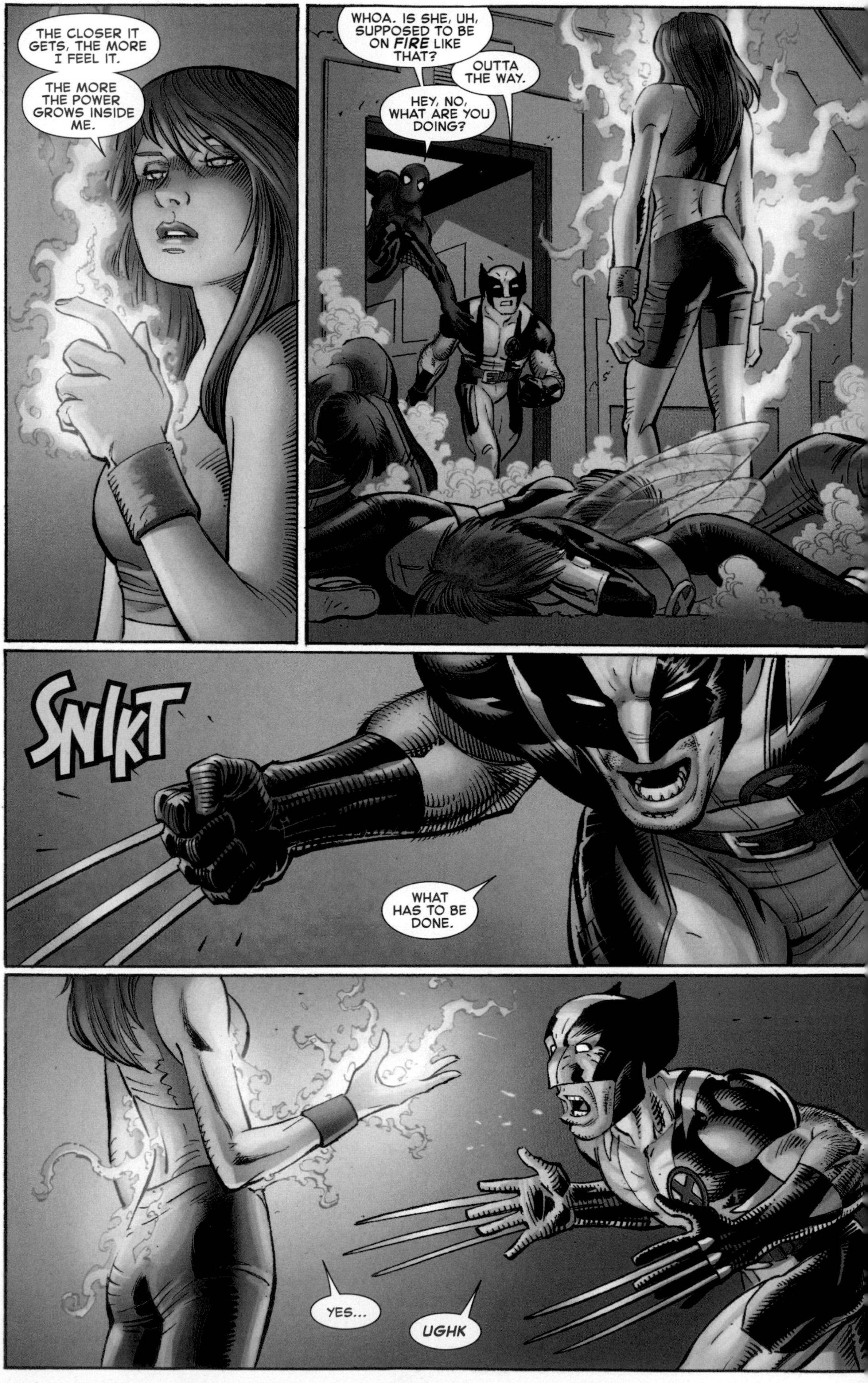
THE CLOSER IT GETS, THE MORE I FEEL IT.
THE MORE THE POWER GROWS INSIDE ME.
WHOA. IS SHE, UH, SUPPOSED TO BE ON *FIRE* LIKE THAT?
OUTTA THE WAY.
HEY, NO, WHAT ARE YOU DOING?
SNIKT
WHAT HAS TO BE DONE.
YES...
UGHK

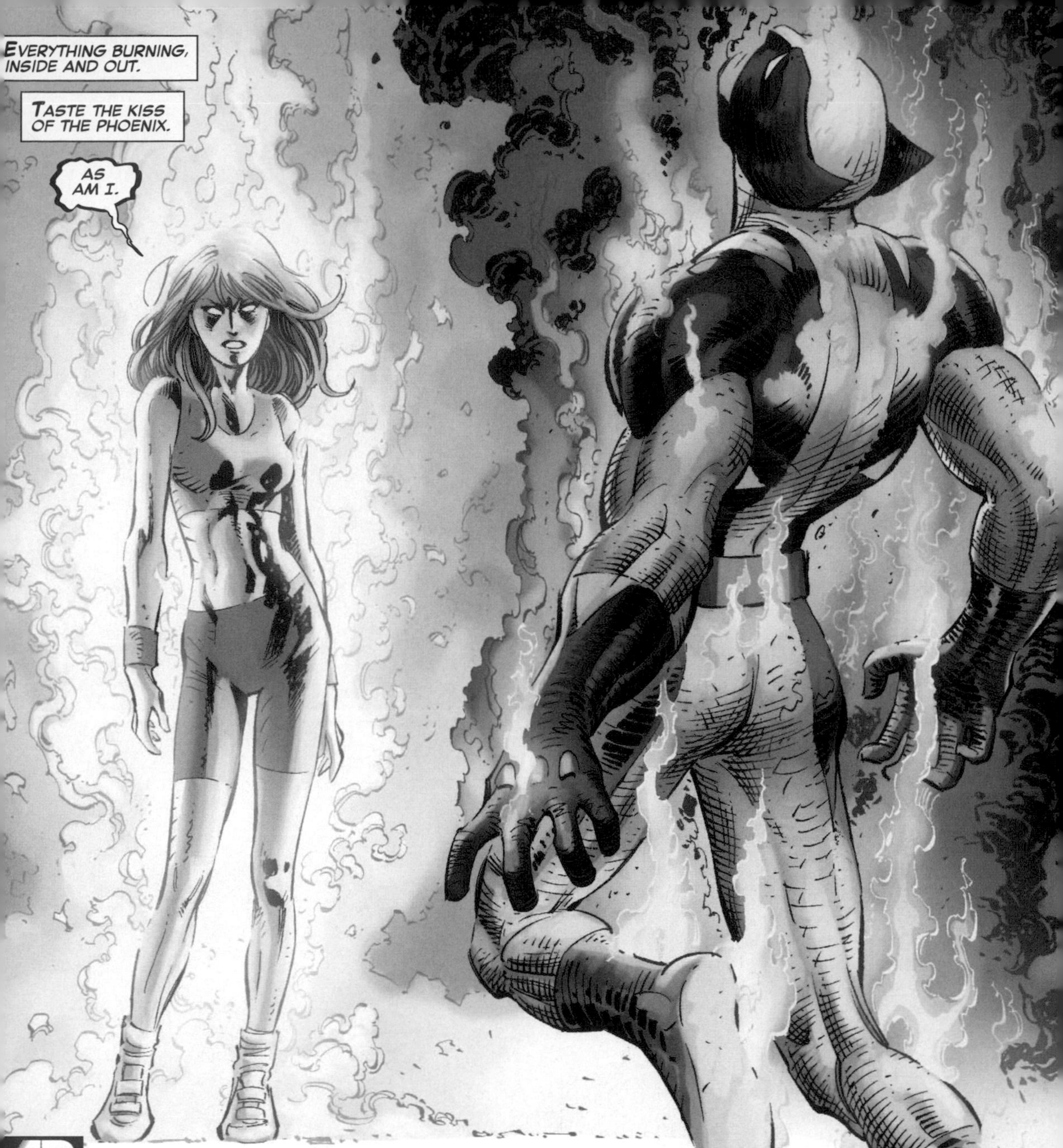
EVERYTHING BURNING, INSIDE AND OUT.
TASTE THE KISS OF THE PHOENIX.
AS AM I.

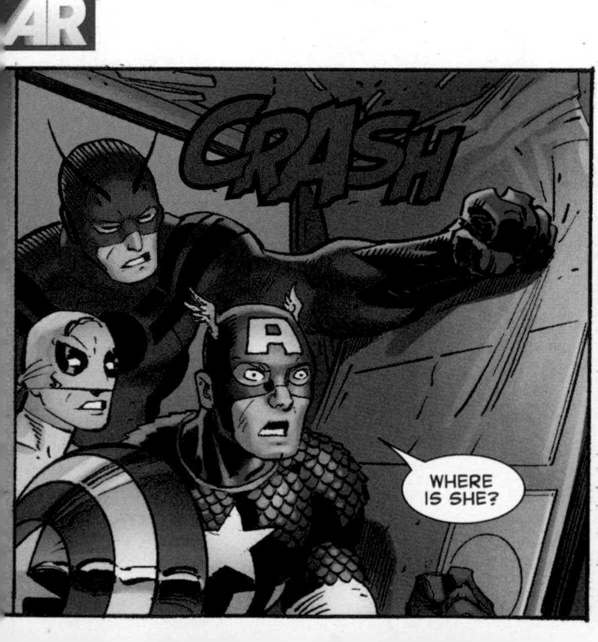
CRASH
WHERE IS SHE?

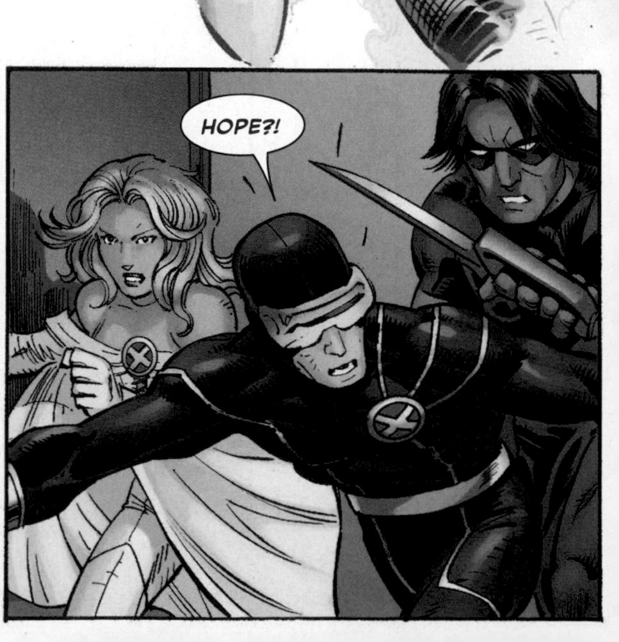
HOPE?!

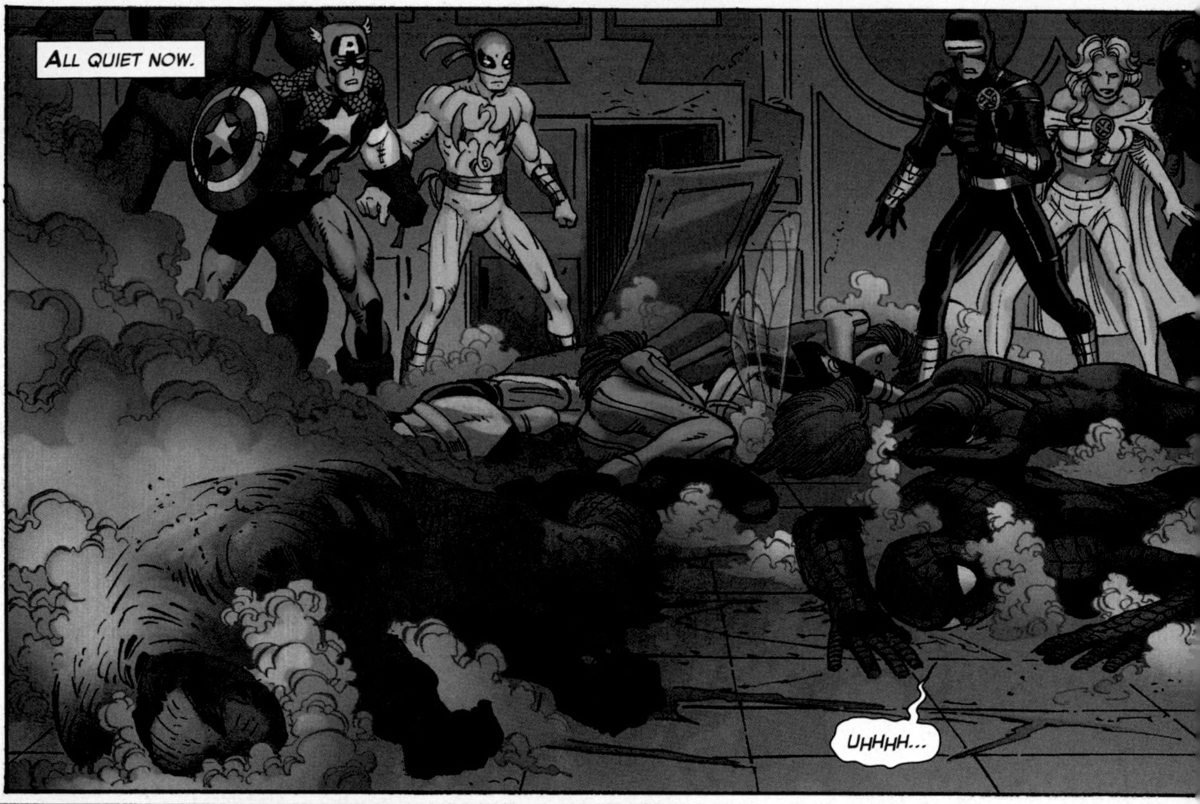
ALL QUIET NOW.
UHHHH...

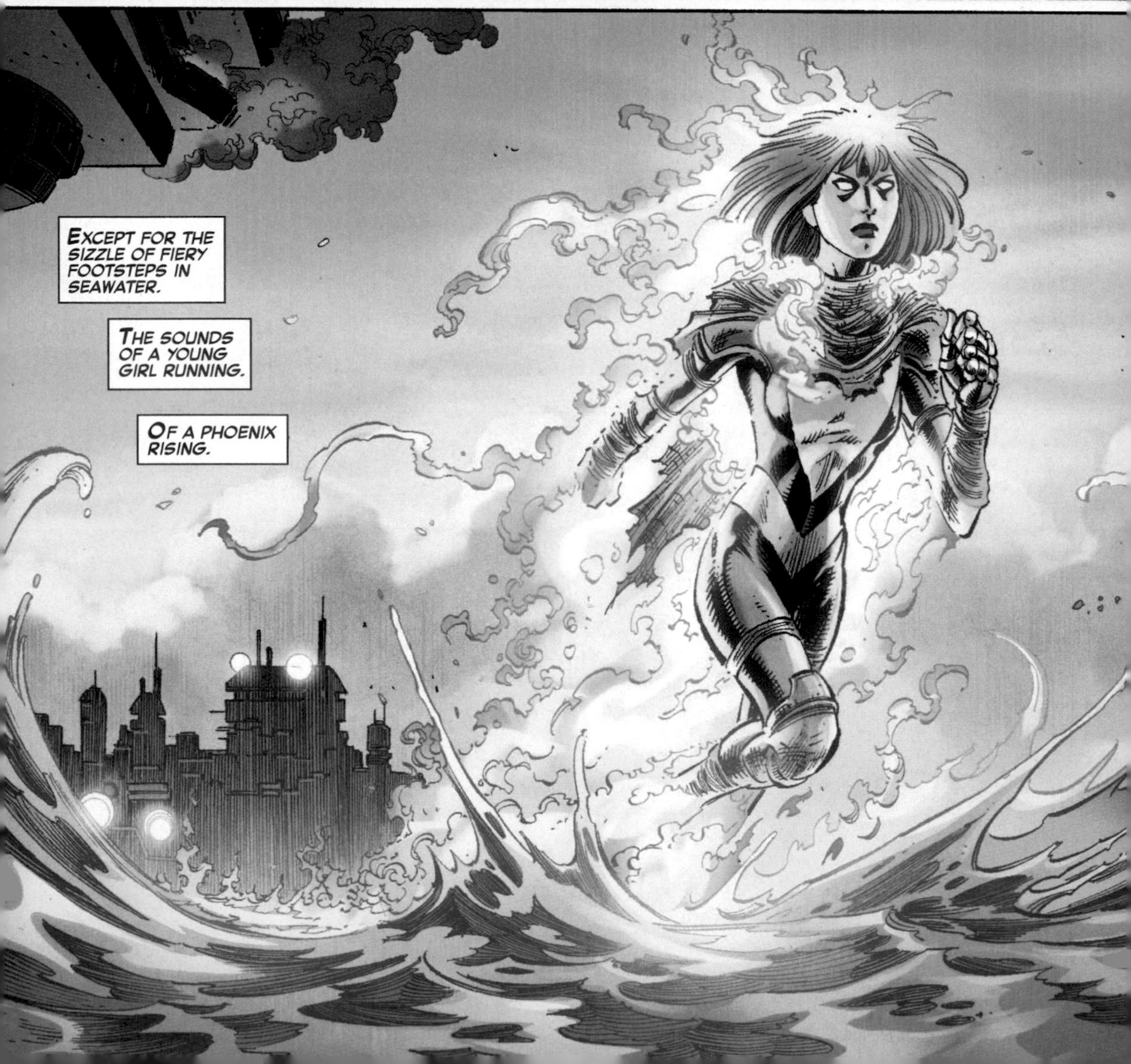
EXCEPT FOR THE SIZZLE OF FIERY FOOTSTEPS IN SEAWATER.
THE SOUNDS OF A YOUNG GIRL RUNNING.
OF A PHOENIX RISING.

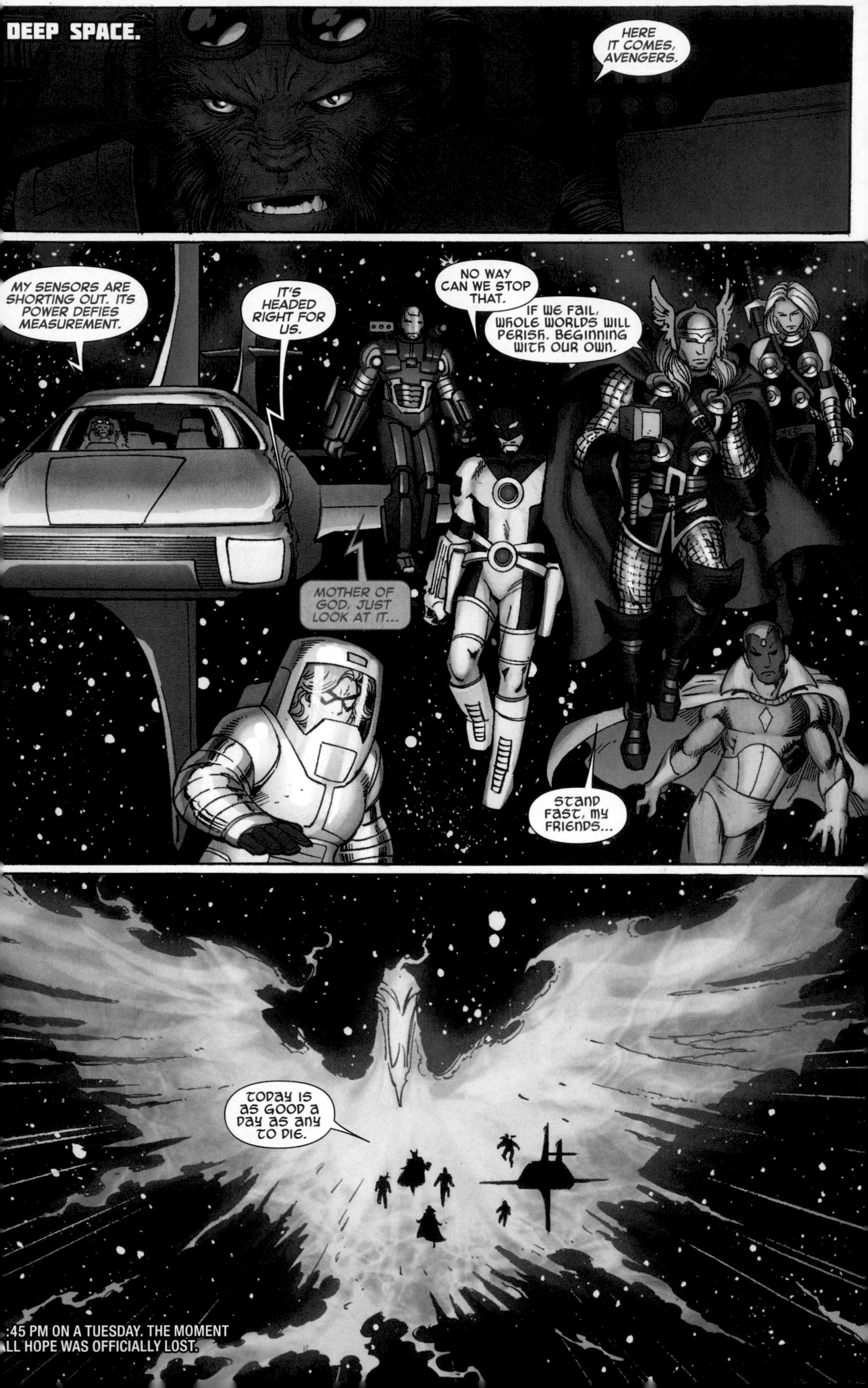
DEEP SPACE.
HERE IT COMES, AVENGERS.
MY SENSORS ARE SHORTING OUT. ITS POWER DEFIES MEASUREMENT.
IT'S HEADED RIGHT FOR US.
NO WAY CAN WE STOP THAT.
IF WE FAIL, WHOLE WORLDS WILL PERISH. BEGINNING WITH OUR OWN.
MOTHER OF GOD, JUST LOOK AT IT...
STAND FAST, MY FRIENDS...
TODAY IS AS GOOD A DAY AS ANY TO DIE.
:45 PM ON A TUESDAY. THE MOMENT
LL HOPE WAS OFFICIALLY LOST.

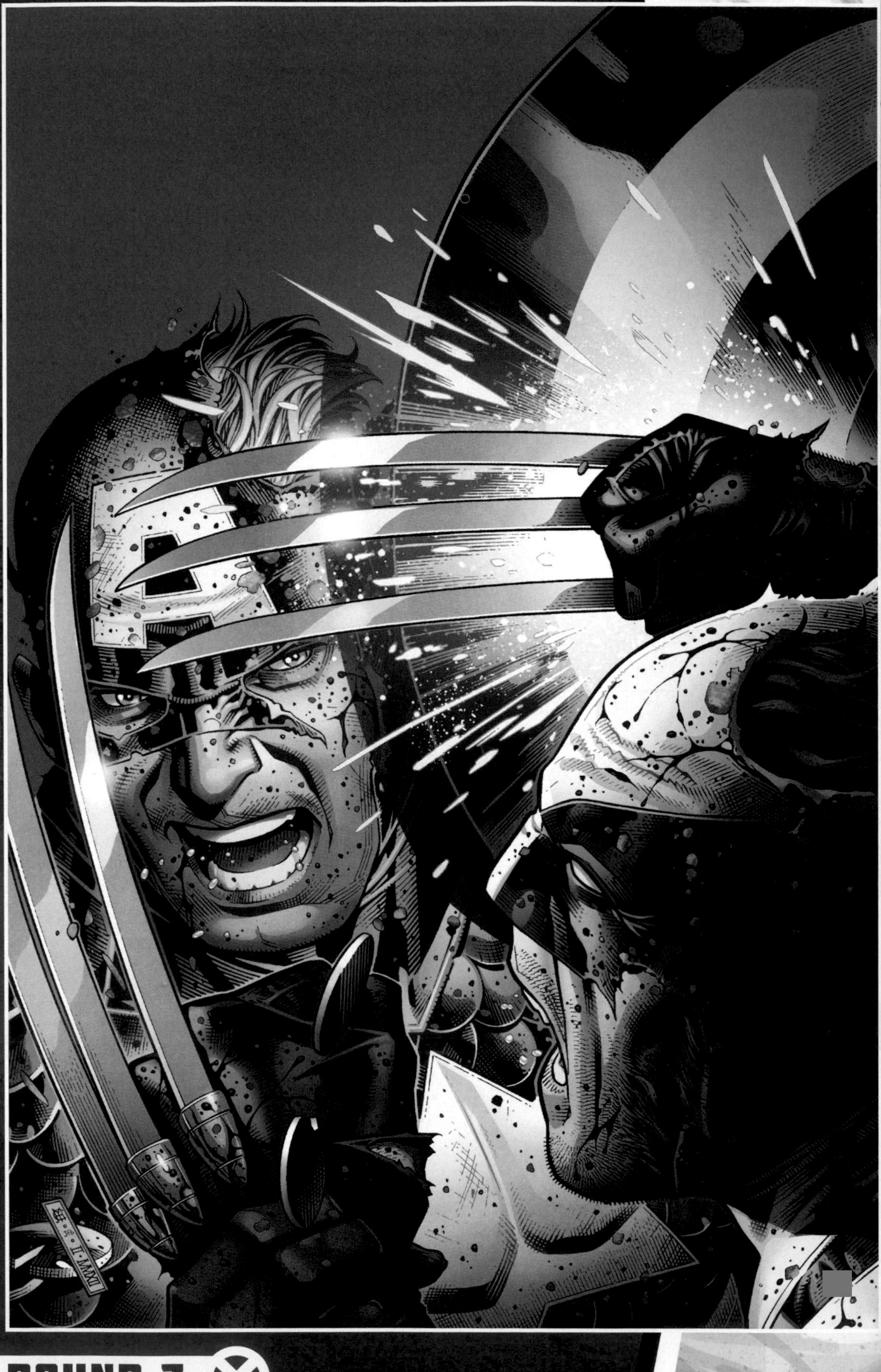

ROUND 3

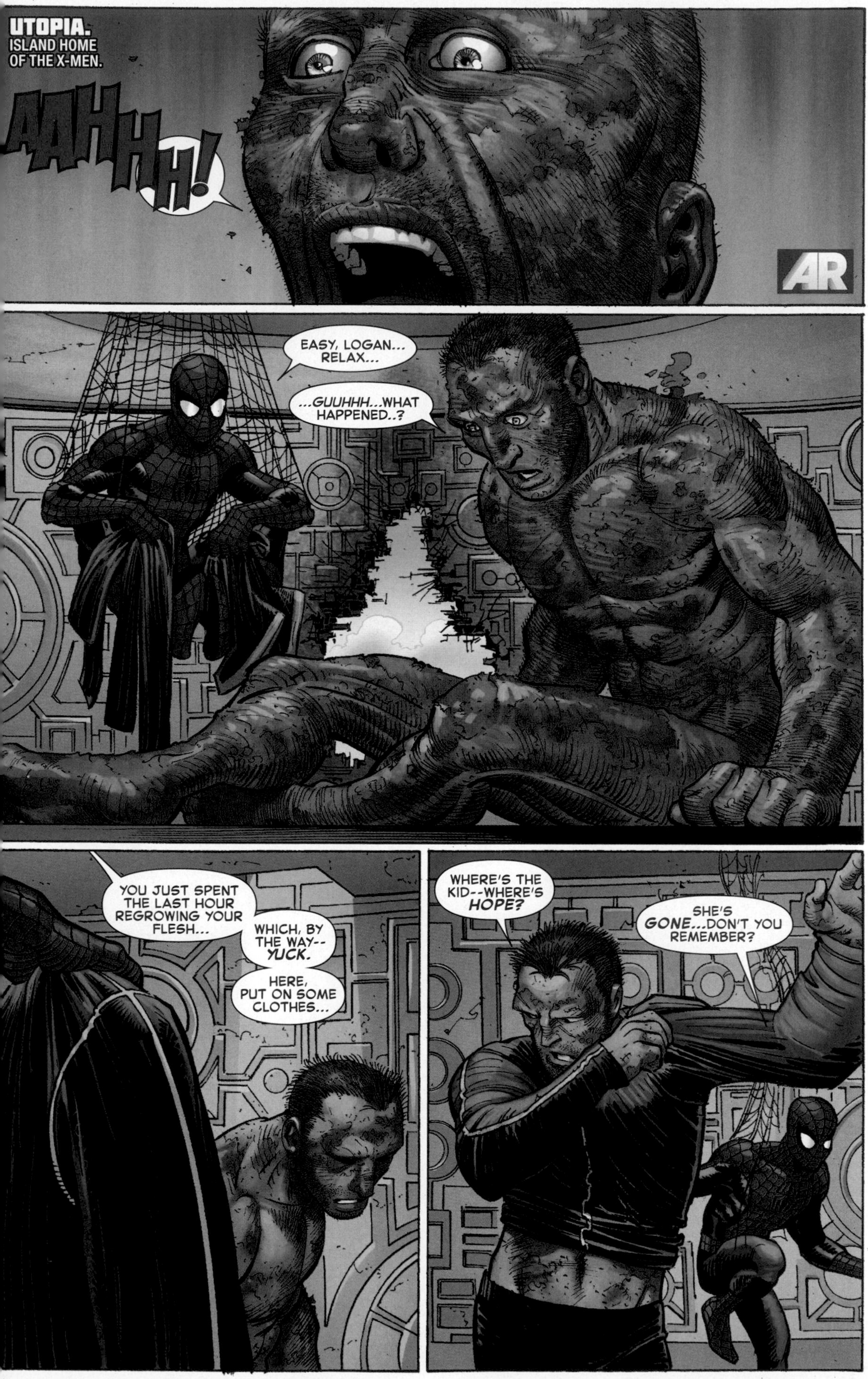
UTOPIA.
ISLAND HOME OF THE X-MEN.
AAHHHH!
EASY, LOGAN... RELAX...
...GUUHHH...WHAT HAPPENED..?
YOU JUST SPENT THE LAST HOUR REGROWING YOUR FLESH...
WHICH, BY THE WAY-- YUCK.
HERE, PUT ON SOME CLOTHES...
WHERE'S THE KID--WHERE'S HOPE?
SHE'S GONE...DON'T YOU REMEMBER?

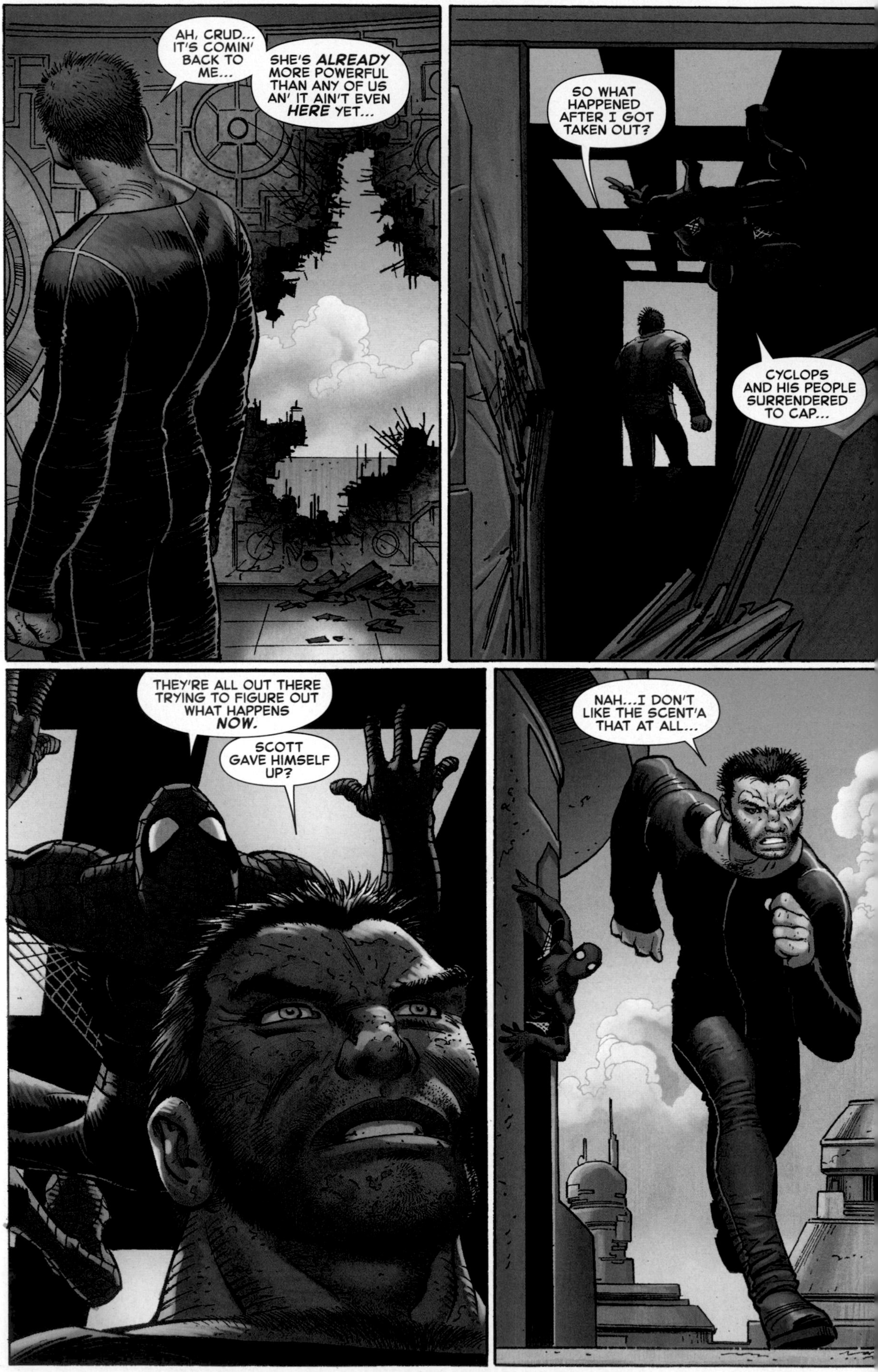
AH, CRUD... IT'S COMIN' BACK TO ME...
SHE'S ALREADY MORE POWERFUL THAN ANY OF US AN' IT AIN'T EVEN HERE YET...
SO WHAT HAPPENED AFTER I GOT TAKEN OUT?
CYCLOPS AND HIS PEOPLE SURRENDERED TO CAP...
THEY'RE ALL OUT THERE TRYING TO FIGURE OUT WHAT HAPPENS NOW.
SCOTT GAVE HIMSELF UP?
NAH...I DON'T LIKE THE SCENT'A THAT AT ALL...

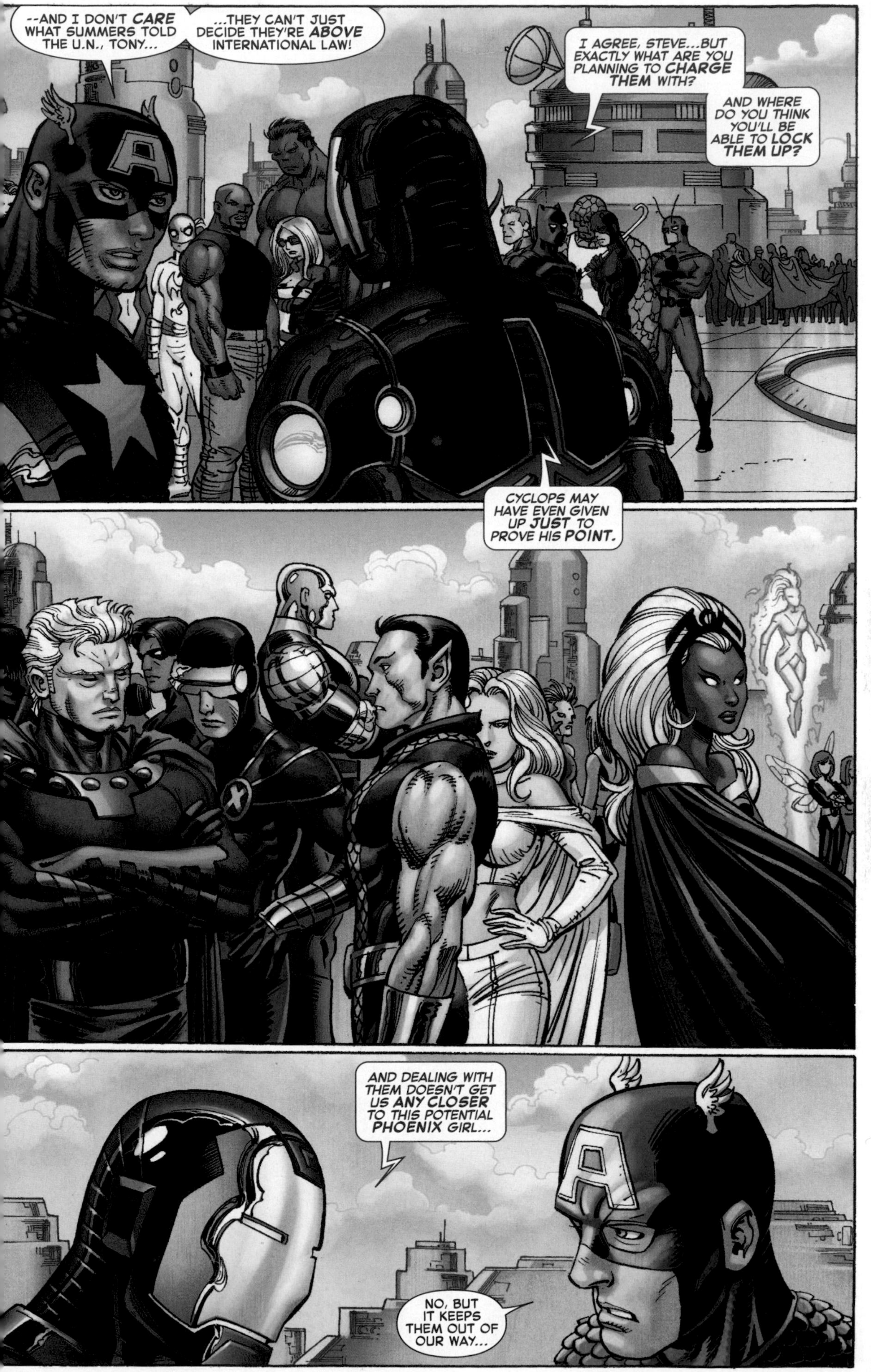
--AND I DON'T CARE WHAT SUMMERS TOLD THE U.N., TONY...
...THEY CAN'T JUST DECIDE THEY'RE ABOVE INTERNATIONAL LAW!
I AGREE, STEVE...BUT EXACTLY WHAT ARE YOU PLANNING TO CHARGE THEM WITH?
AND WHERE DO YOU THINK YOU'LL BE ABLE TO LOCK THEM UP?
CYCLOPS MAY HAVE EVEN GIVEN UP JUST TO PROVE HIS POINT.
AND DEALING WITH THEM DOESN'T GET US ANY CLOSER TO THIS POTENTIAL PHOENIX GIRL...
NO, BUT IT KEEPS THEM OUT OF OUR WAY...

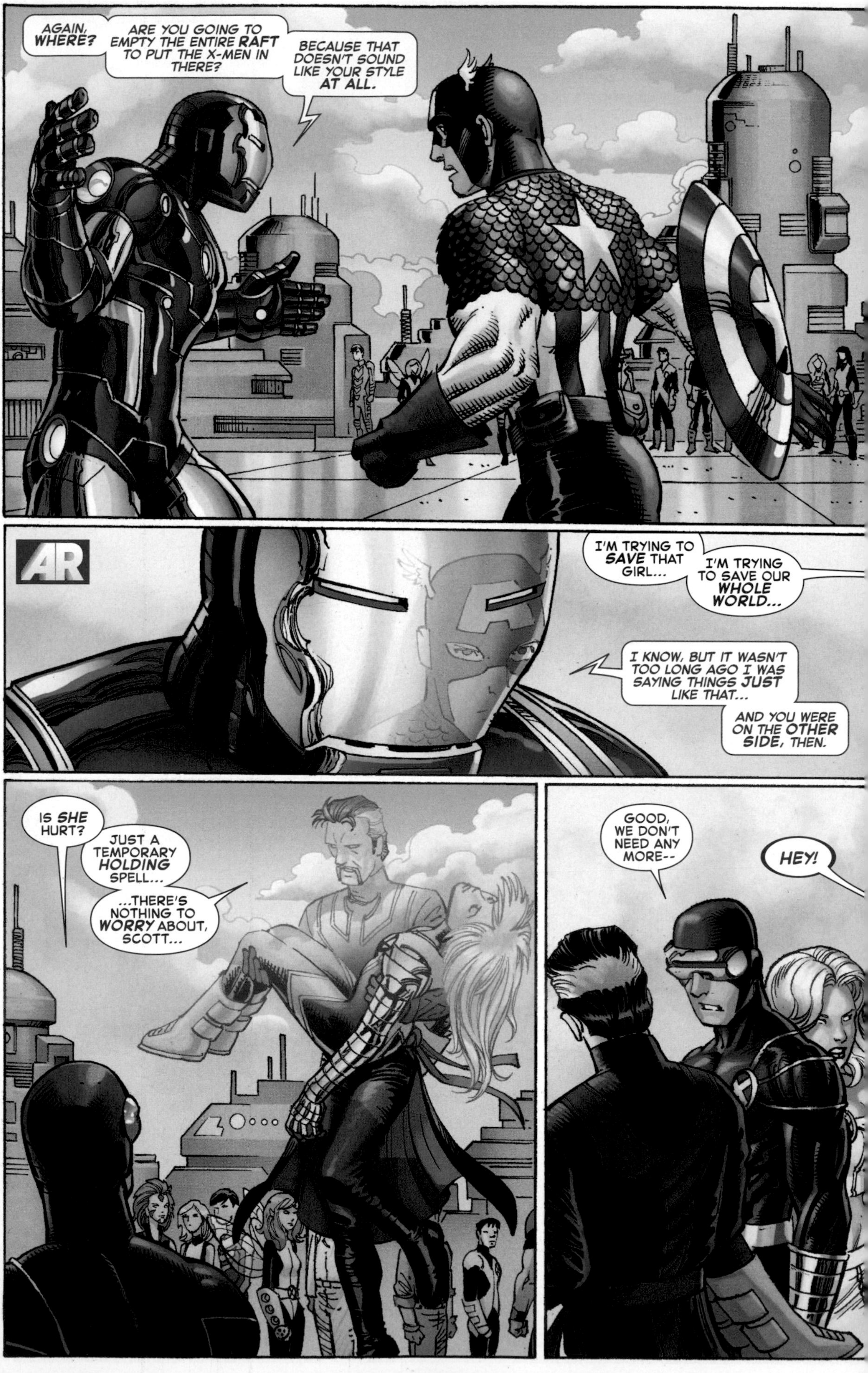
AGAIN, WHERE?
ARE YOU GOING TO EMPTY THE ENTIRE RAFT TO PUT THE X-MEN IN THERE?
BECAUSE THAT DOESN'T SOUND LIKE YOUR STYLE AT ALL.
AR
I'M TRYING TO SAVE THAT GIRL...
I'M TRYING TO SAVE OUR WHOLE WORLD...
I KNOW, BUT IT WASN'T TOO LONG AGO I WAS SAYING THINGS JUST LIKE THAT...
AND YOU WERE ON THE OTHER SIDE, THEN.
IS SHE HURT?
JUST A TEMPORARY HOLDING SPELL...
...THERE'S NOTHING TO WORRY ABOUT, SCOTT...
GOOD, WE DON'T NEED ANY MORE--
HEY!

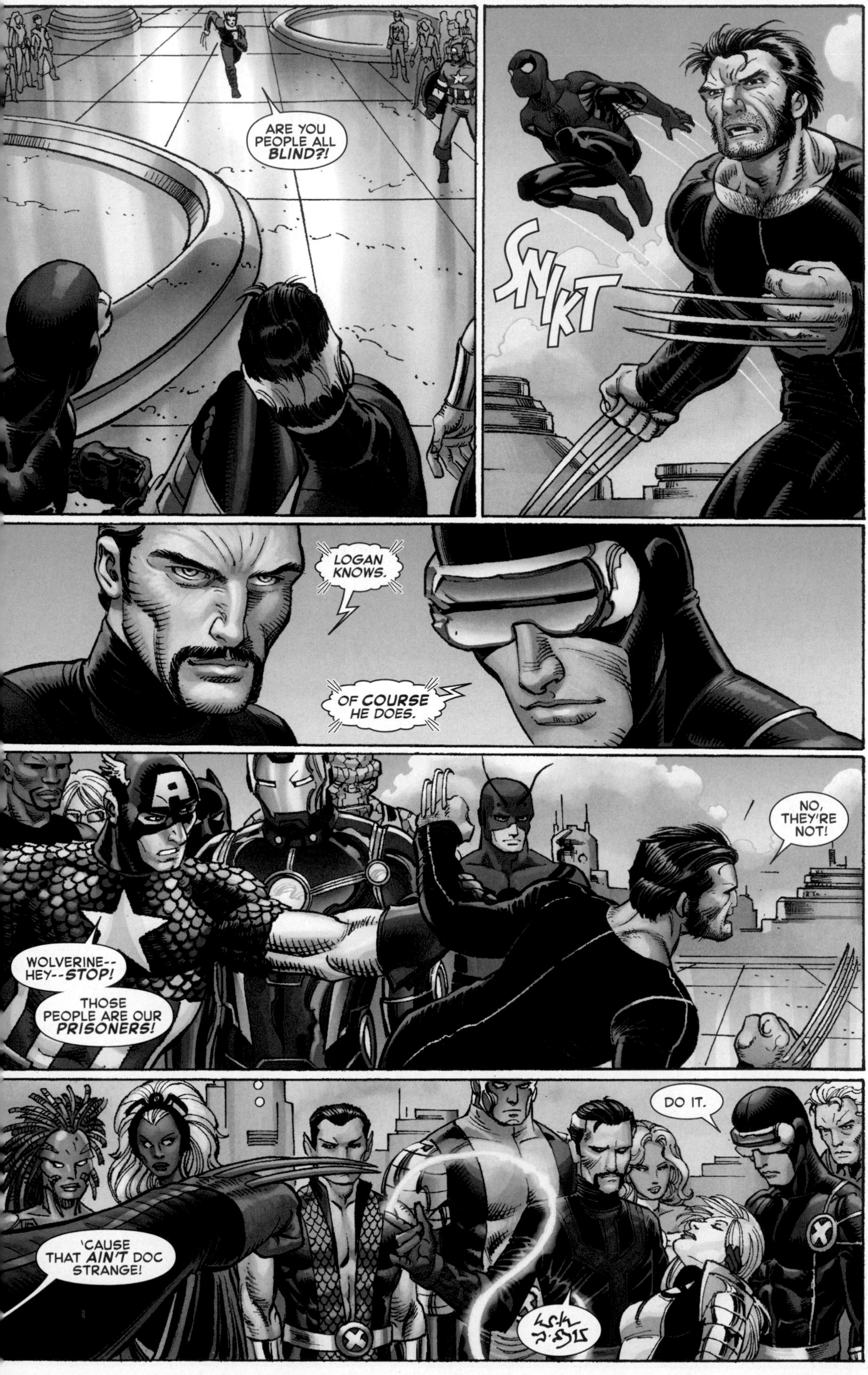
ARE YOU PEOPLE ALL *BLIND?!*
SNIKT
LOGAN KNOWS.
OF *COURSE* HE DOES.
WOLVERINE-- HEY--*STOP!*
THOSE PEOPLE ARE OUR *PRISONERS!*
NO, THEY'RE NOT!
DO IT.
'CAUSE THAT *AIN'T* DOC STRANGE!

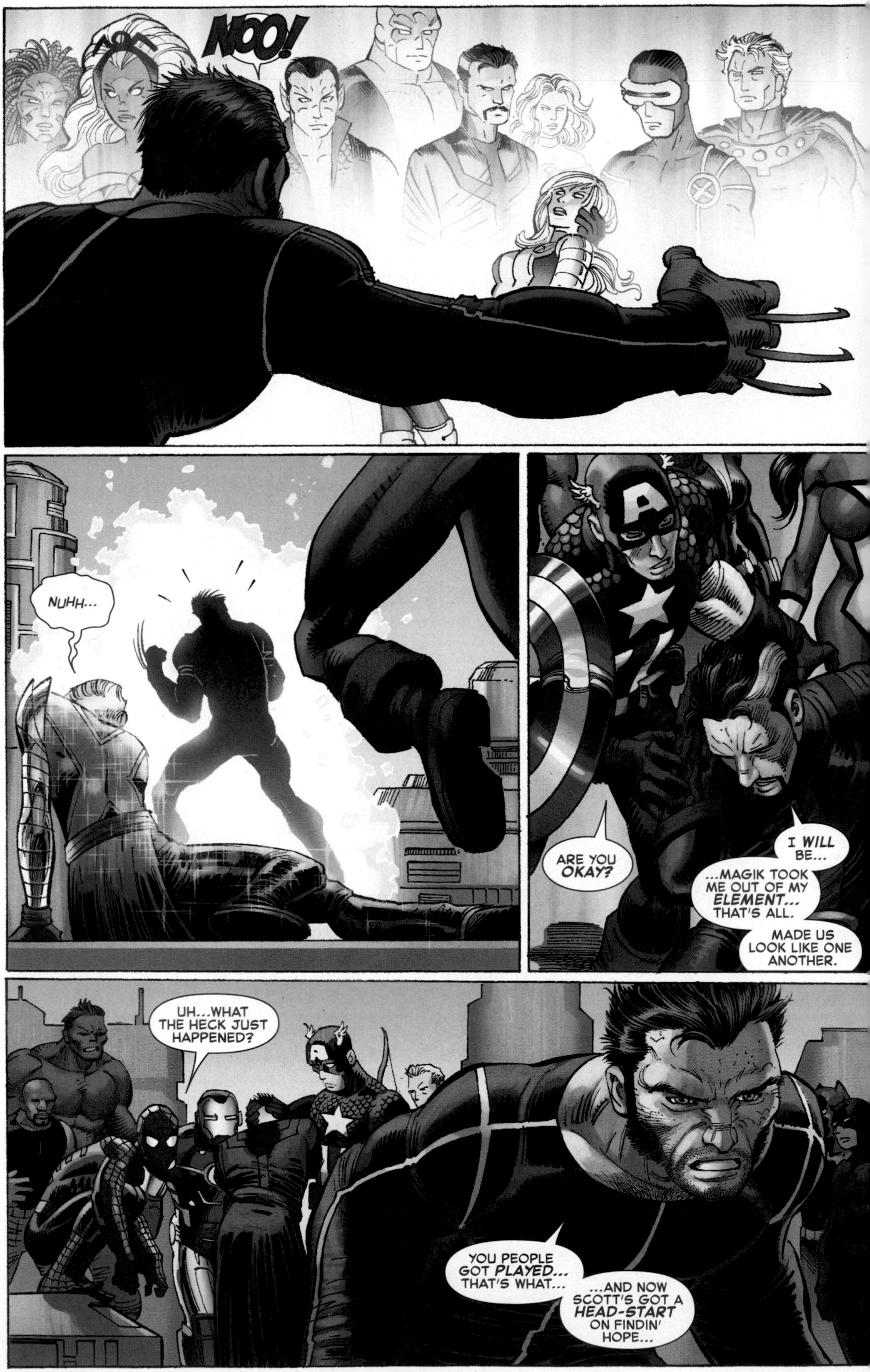
NOO!
NUHH...
ARE YOU OKAY?
I WILL BE...
...MAGIK TOOK ME OUT OF MY ELEMENT... THAT'S ALL.
MADE US LOOK LIKE ONE ANOTHER.
UH...WHAT THE HECK JUST HAPPENED?
YOU PEOPLE GOT PLAYED... THAT'S WHAT...
...AND NOW SCOTT'S GOT A HEAD-START ON FINDIN' HOPE...

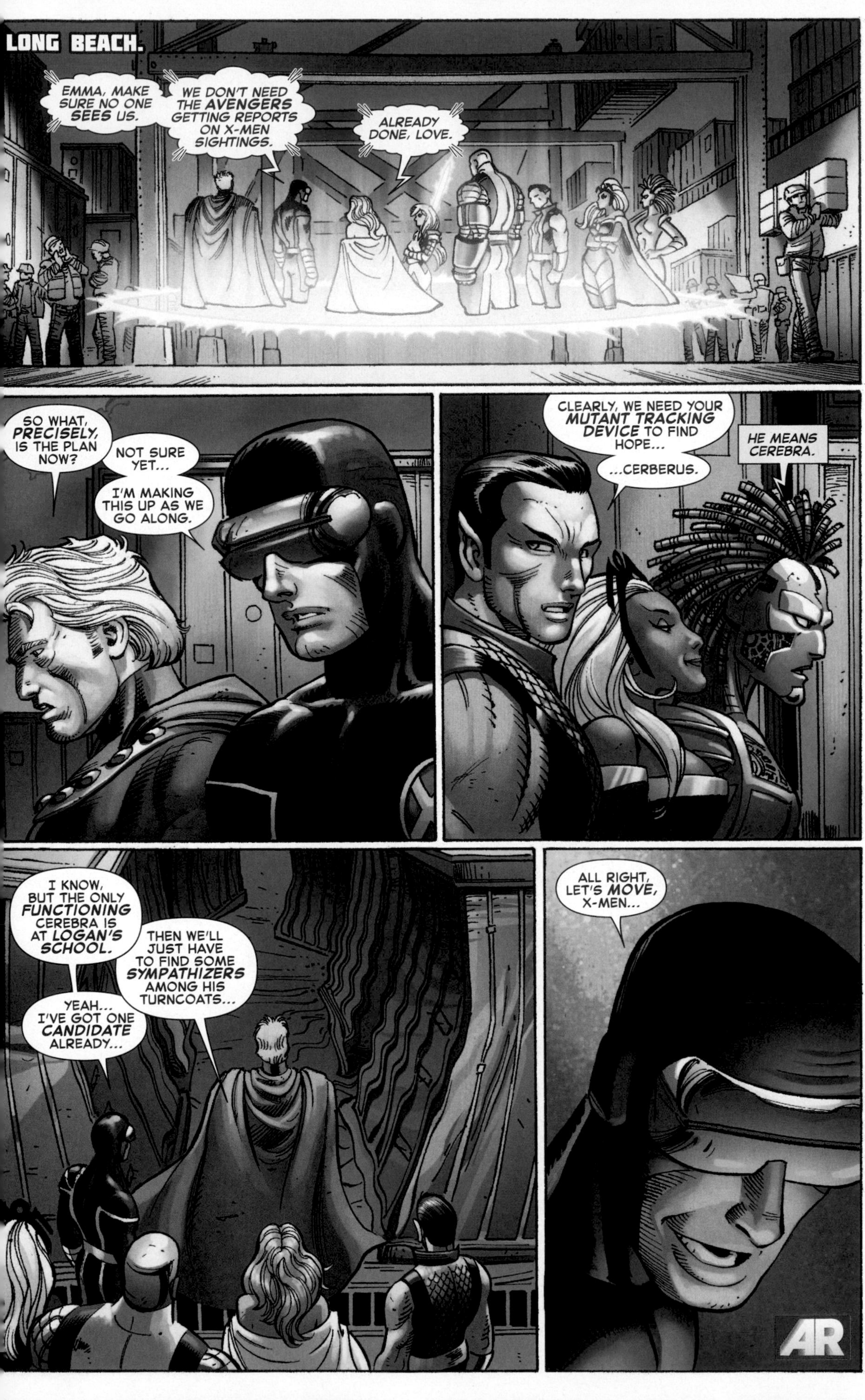
LONG BEACH.
EMMA, MAKE SURE NO ONE SEES US.
WE DON'T NEED THE AVENGERS GETTING REPORTS ON X-MEN SIGHTINGS.
ALREADY DONE, LOVE.
SO WHAT, PRECISELY, IS THE PLAN NOW?
NOT SURE YET...
I'M MAKING THIS UP AS WE GO ALONG.
CLEARLY, WE NEED YOUR MUTANT TRACKING DEVICE TO FIND HOPE...
...CERBERUS.
HE MEANS CEREBRA.
I KNOW, BUT THE ONLY FUNCTIONING CEREBRA IS AT LOGAN'S SCHOOL.
THEN WE'LL JUST HAVE TO FIND SOME SYMPATHIZERS AMONG HIS TURNCOATS...
YEAH... I'VE GOT ONE CANDIDATE ALREADY...
ALL RIGHT, LET'S MOVE, X-MEN...
AR

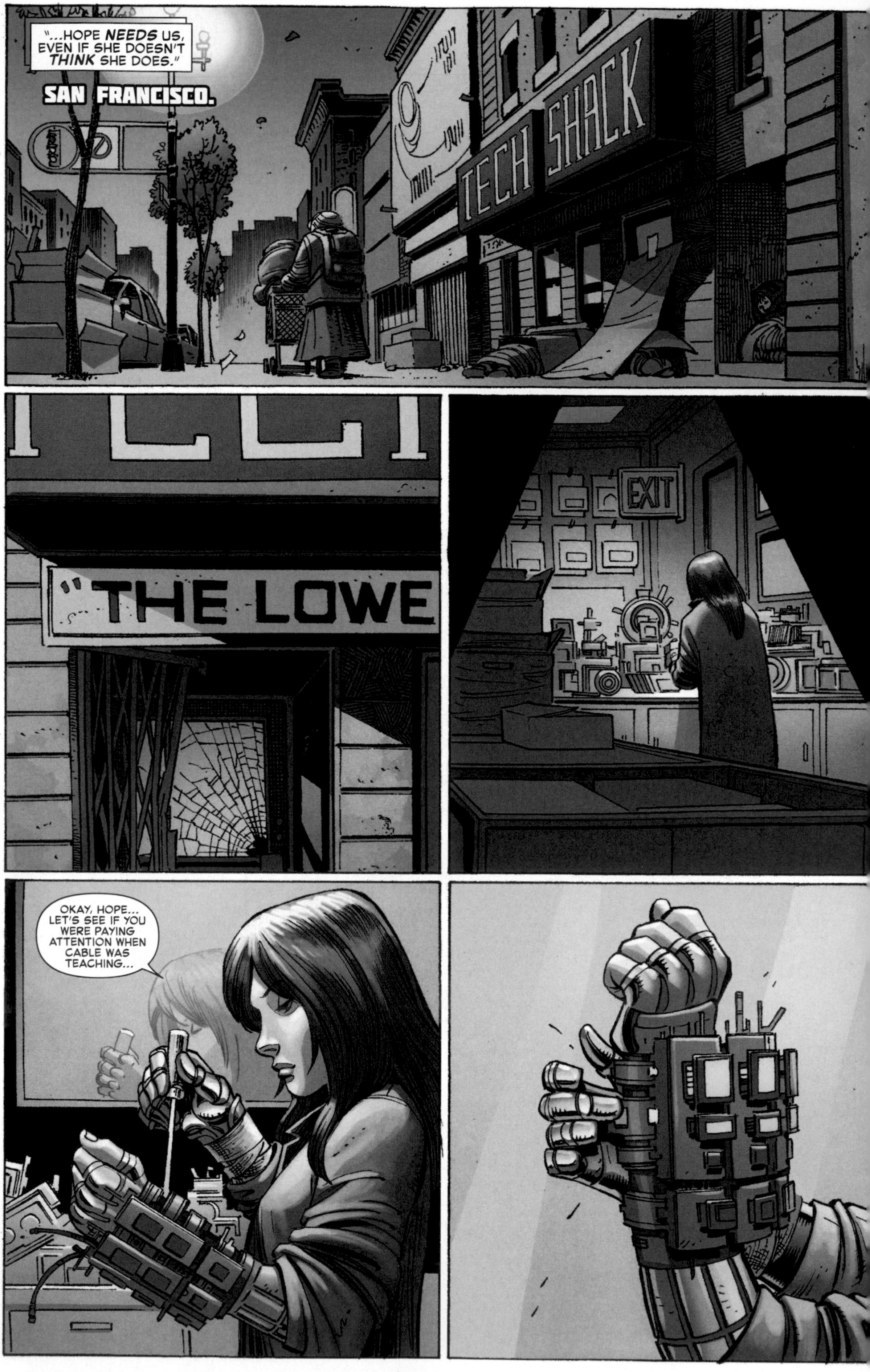
"...HOPE NEEDS US, EVEN IF SHE DOESN'T THINK SHE DOES."
SAN FRANCISCO.
TECH SHACK
"THE LOWE
EXIT
OKAY, HOPE... LET'S SEE IF YOU WERE PAYING ATTENTION WHEN CABLE WAS TEACHING...

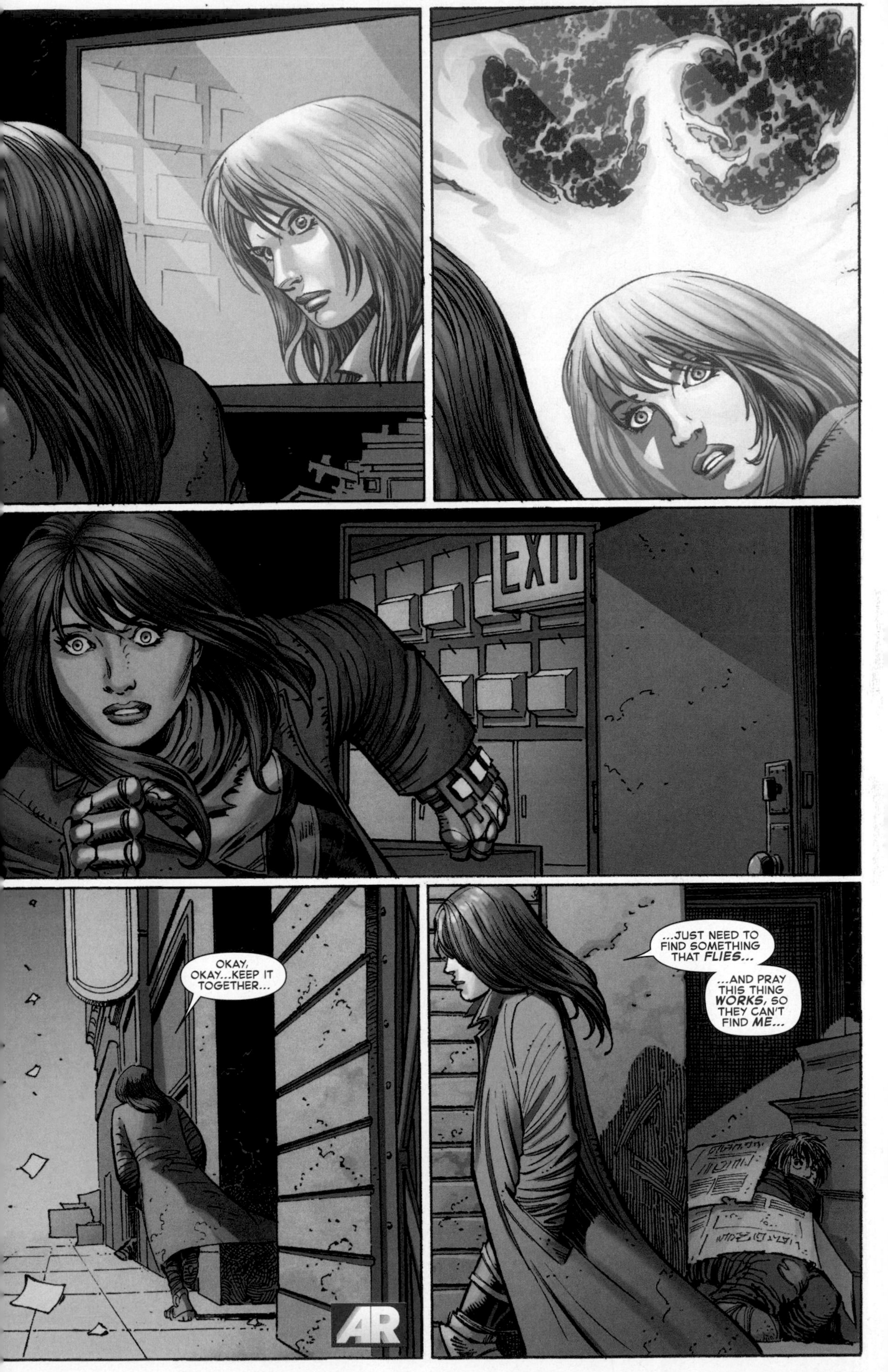
OKAY, OKAY...KEEP IT TOGETHER...
...JUST NEED TO FIND SOMETHING THAT FLIES...
...AND PRAY THIS THING WORKS, SO THEY CAN'T FIND ME...
AR

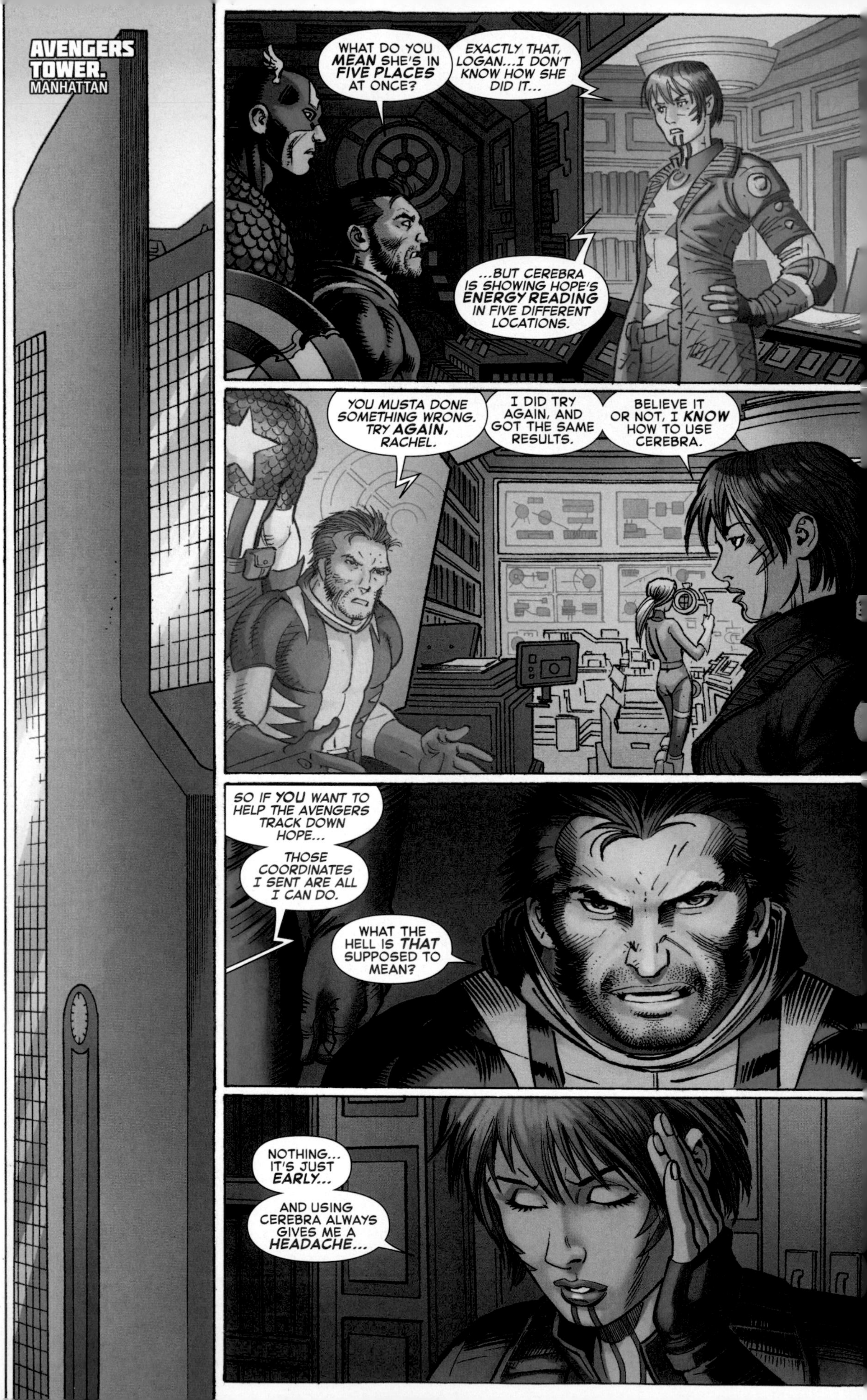
AVENGERS TOWER. MANHATTAN
WHAT DO YOU MEAN SHE'S IN FIVE PLACES AT ONCE?
EXACTLY THAT, LOGAN...I DON'T KNOW HOW SHE DID IT...
...BUT CEREBRA IS SHOWING HOPE'S ENERGY READING IN FIVE DIFFERENT LOCATIONS.
YOU MUSTA DONE SOMETHING WRONG. TRY AGAIN, RACHEL.
I DID TRY AGAIN, AND GOT THE SAME RESULTS.
BELIEVE IT OR NOT, I KNOW HOW TO USE CEREBRA.
SO IF YOU WANT TO HELP THE AVENGERS TRACK DOWN HOPE...
THOSE COORDINATES I SENT ARE ALL I CAN DO.
WHAT THE HELL IS THAT SUPPOSED TO MEAN?
NOTHING... IT'S JUST EARLY...
AND USING CEREBRA ALWAYS GIVES ME A HEADACHE...

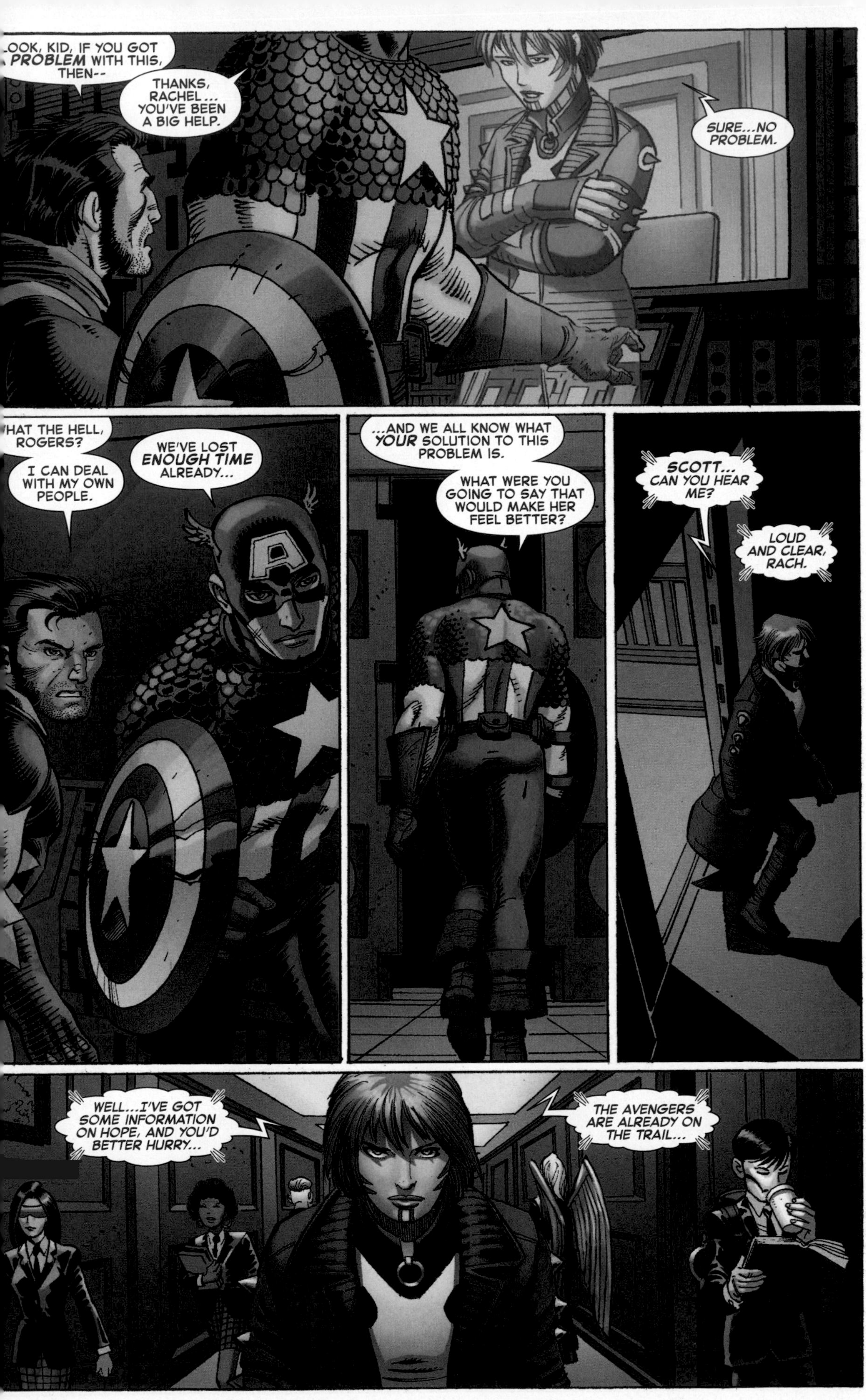
OOK, KID, IF YOU GOT PROBLEM WITH THIS, THEN--
THANKS, RACHEL... YOU'VE BEEN A BIG HELP.
SURE...NO PROBLEM.
HAT THE HELL, ROGERS?
I CAN DEAL WITH MY OWN PEOPLE.
WE'VE LOST ENOUGH TIME ALREADY...
...AND WE ALL KNOW WHAT YOUR SOLUTION TO THIS PROBLEM IS.
WHAT WERE YOU GOING TO SAY THAT WOULD MAKE HER FEEL BETTER?
SCOTT... CAN YOU HEAR ME?
LOUD AND CLEAR, RACH.
WELL...I'VE GOT SOME INFORMATION ON HOPE, AND YOU'D BETTER HURRY...
THE AVENGERS ARE ALREADY ON THE TRAIL...

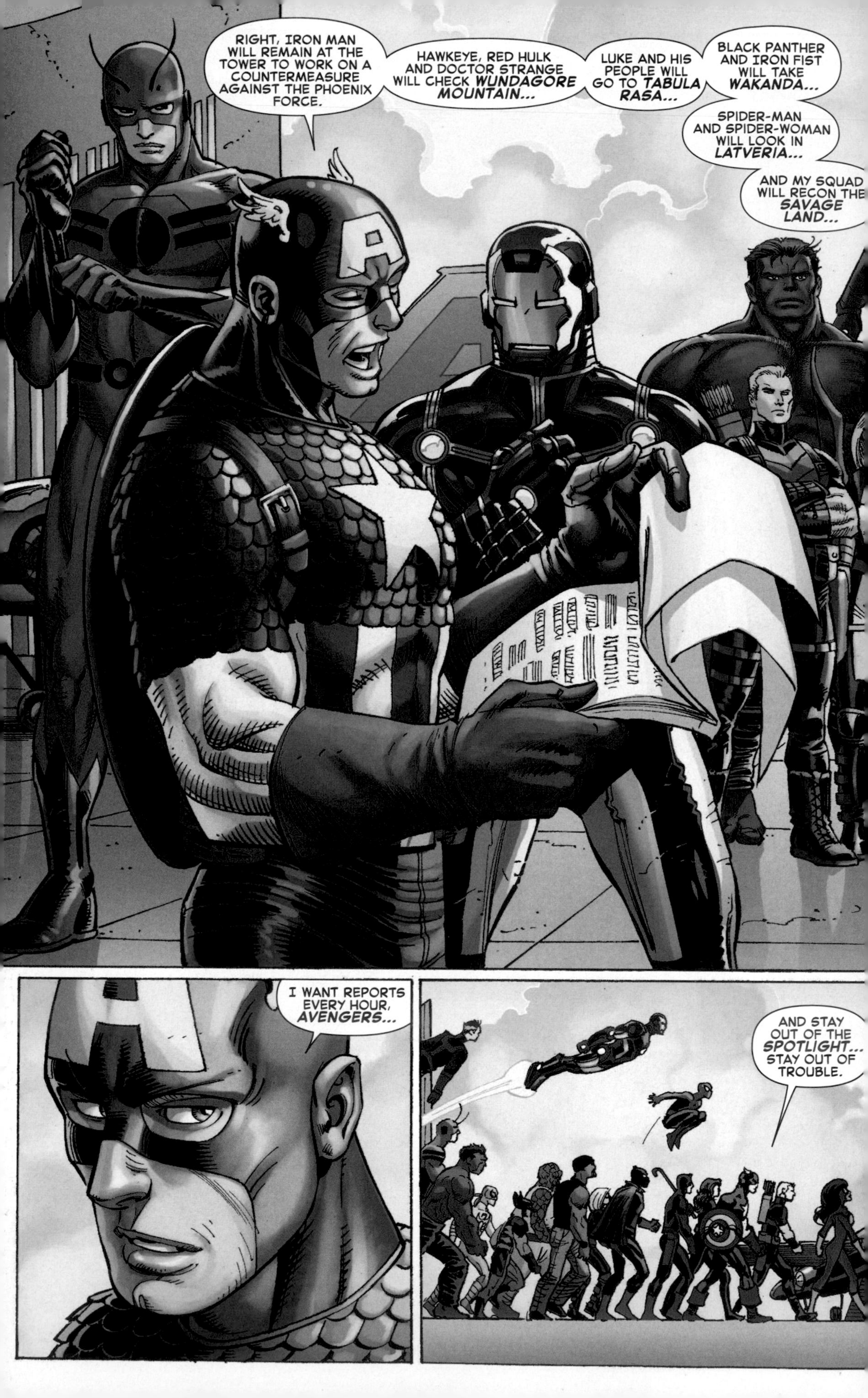
RIGHT, IRON MAN WILL REMAIN AT THE TOWER TO WORK ON A COUNTERMEASURE AGAINST THE PHOENIX FORCE.
HAWKEYE, RED HULK AND DOCTOR STRANGE WILL CHECK WUNDAGORE MOUNTAIN...
LUKE AND HIS PEOPLE WILL GO TO TABULA RASA...
BLACK PANTHER AND IRON FIST WILL TAKE WAKANDA...
SPIDER-MAN AND SPIDER-WOMAN WILL LOOK IN LATVERIA...
AND MY SQUAD WILL RECON THE SAVAGE LAND...
I WANT REPORTS EVERY HOUR, AVENGERS...
AND STAY OUT OF THE SPOTLIGHT... STAY OUT OF TROUBLE.

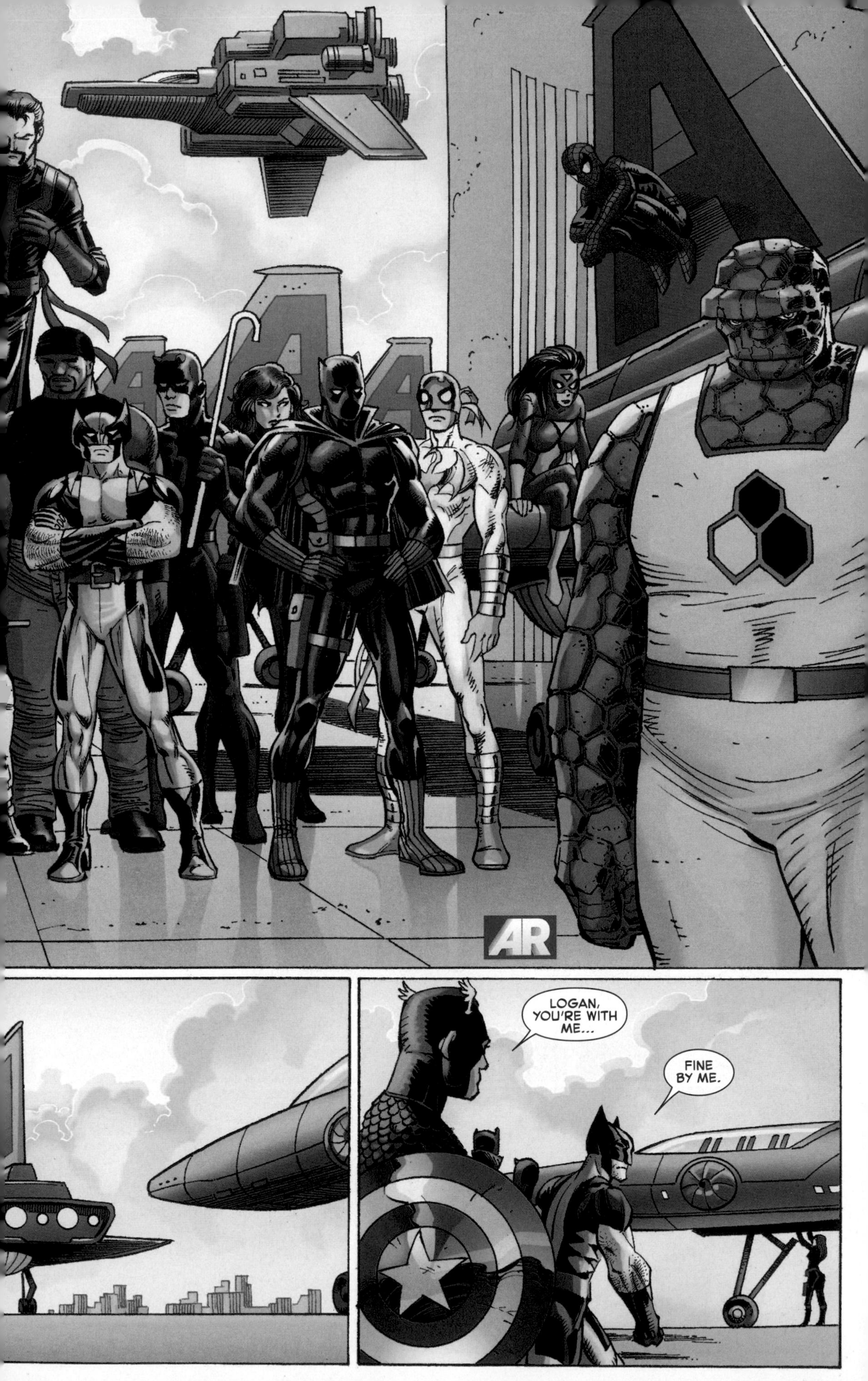
LOGAN, YOU'RE WITH ME...
FINE BY ME.

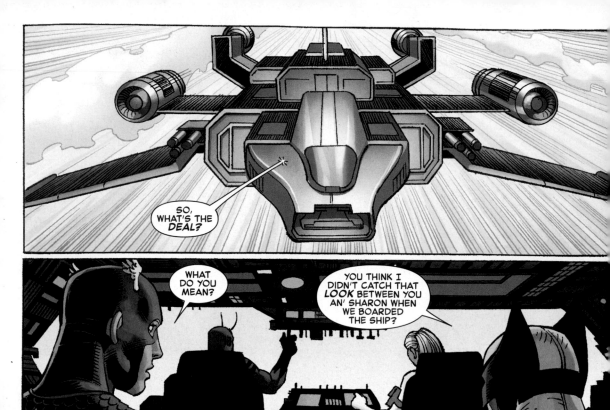

SO, WHAT'S THE DEAL?

WHAT DO YOU MEAN?

YOU THINK I DIDN'T CATCH THAT *LOOK* BETWEEN YOU AN' SHARON WHEN WE BOARDED THE SHIP?

WALK WITH ME...

YOU WENT OFF ON *YOUR OWN* IN UTOPIA...

AND YOU SCARED HOPE INTO *JACK-RABBITING.*

AW, *C'MON*... YOU THINK THAT KID WASN'T SCARED OUTTA HER MIND ALREADY?

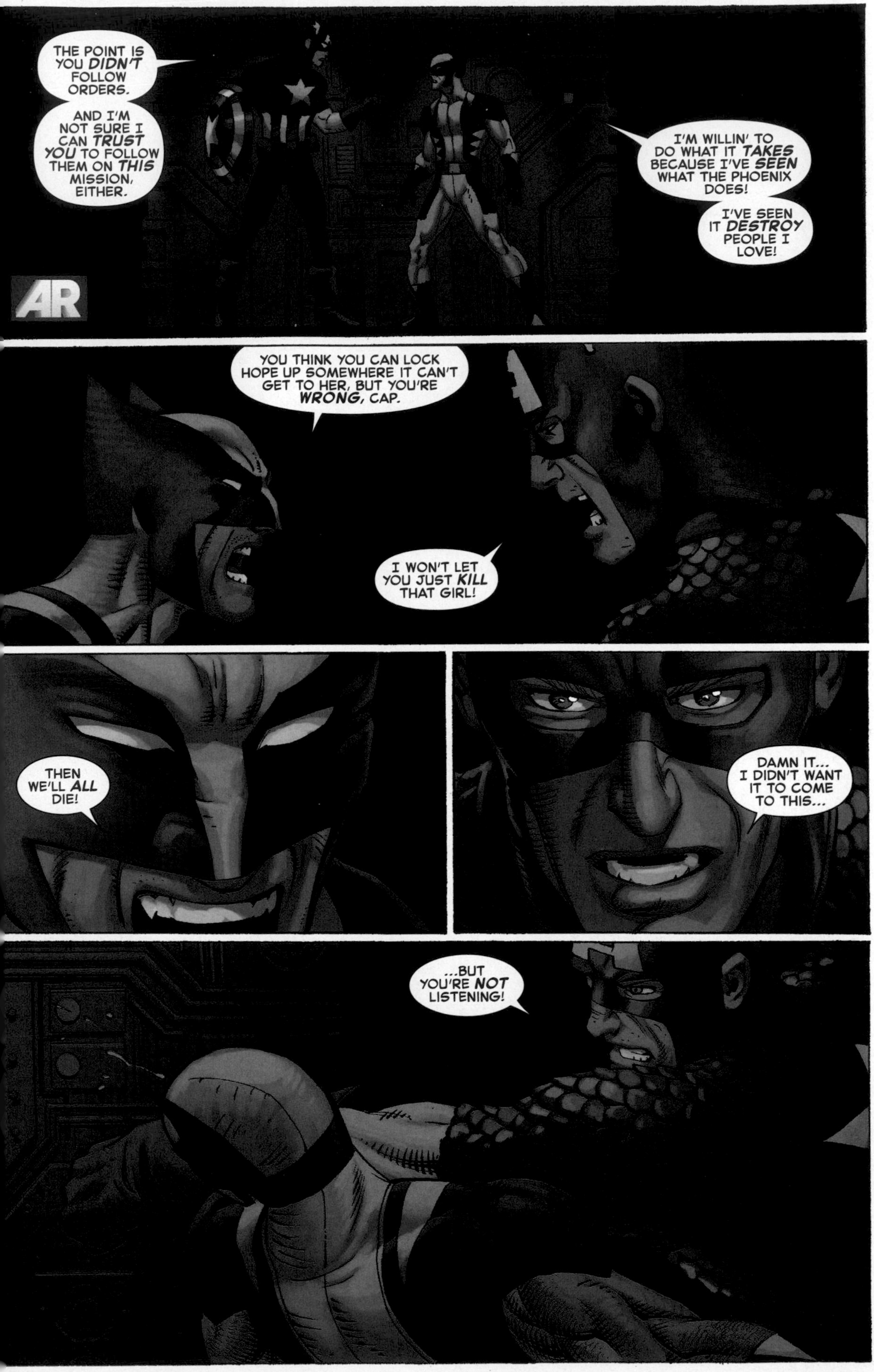
THE POINT IS YOU *DIDN'T* FOLLOW ORDERS.
AND I'M NOT SURE I CAN *TRUST YOU* TO FOLLOW THEM ON *THIS* MISSION, EITHER.
I'M WILLIN' TO DO WHAT IT *TAKES* BECAUSE I'VE *SEEN* WHAT THE PHOENIX DOES!
I'VE SEEN IT *DESTROY* PEOPLE I LOVE!
AR
YOU THINK YOU CAN LOCK HOPE UP SOMEWHERE IT CAN'T GET TO HER, BUT YOU'RE *WRONG*, CAP.
I WON'T LET YOU JUST *KILL* THAT GIRL!
THEN WE'LL *ALL* DIE!
DAMN IT... I DIDN'T WANT IT TO COME TO THIS...
...BUT YOU'RE *NOT* LISTENING!

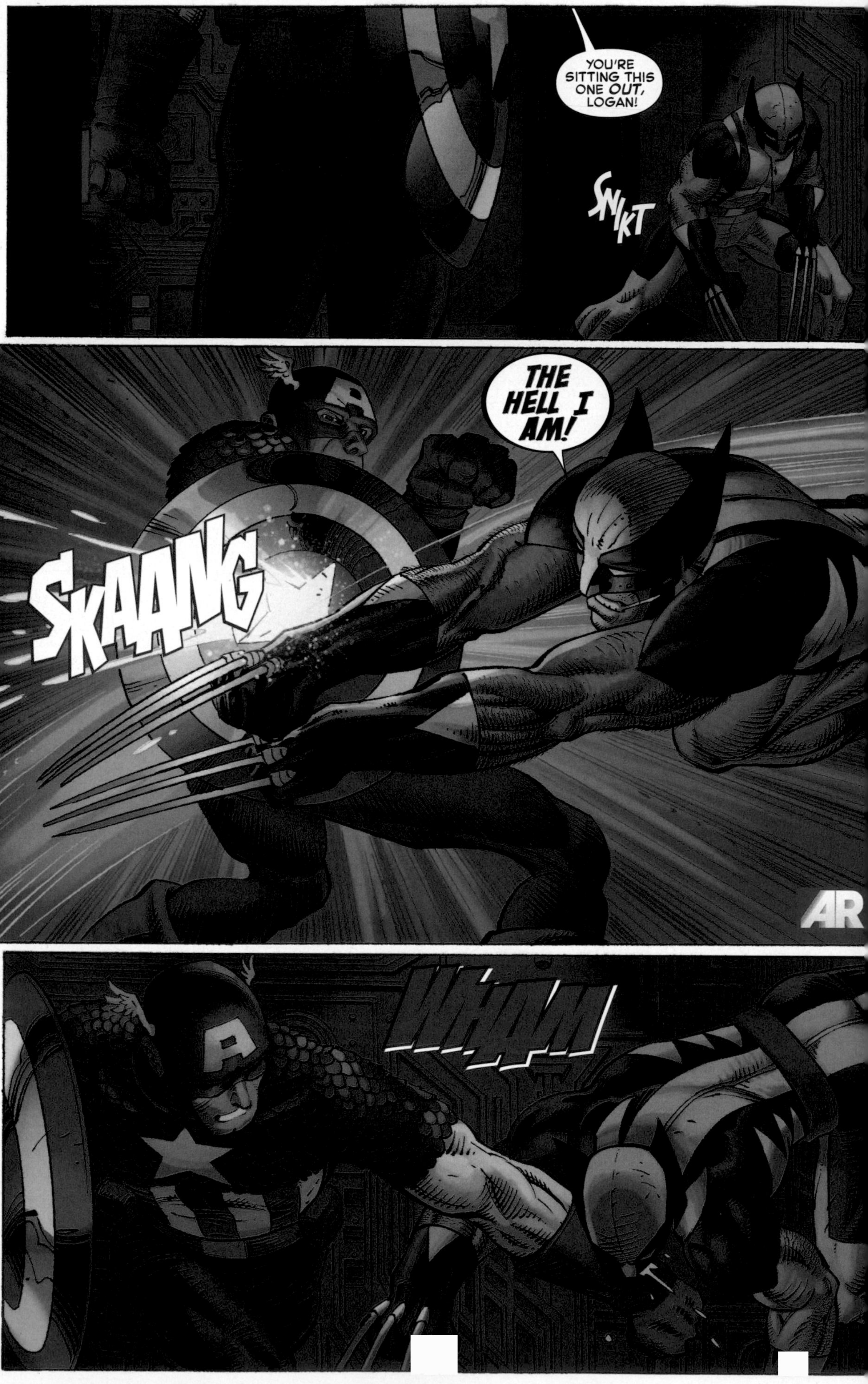
YOU'RE SITTING THIS ONE OUT, LOGAN!
SNIKT
THE HELL I AM!
SKAANG
WHAM

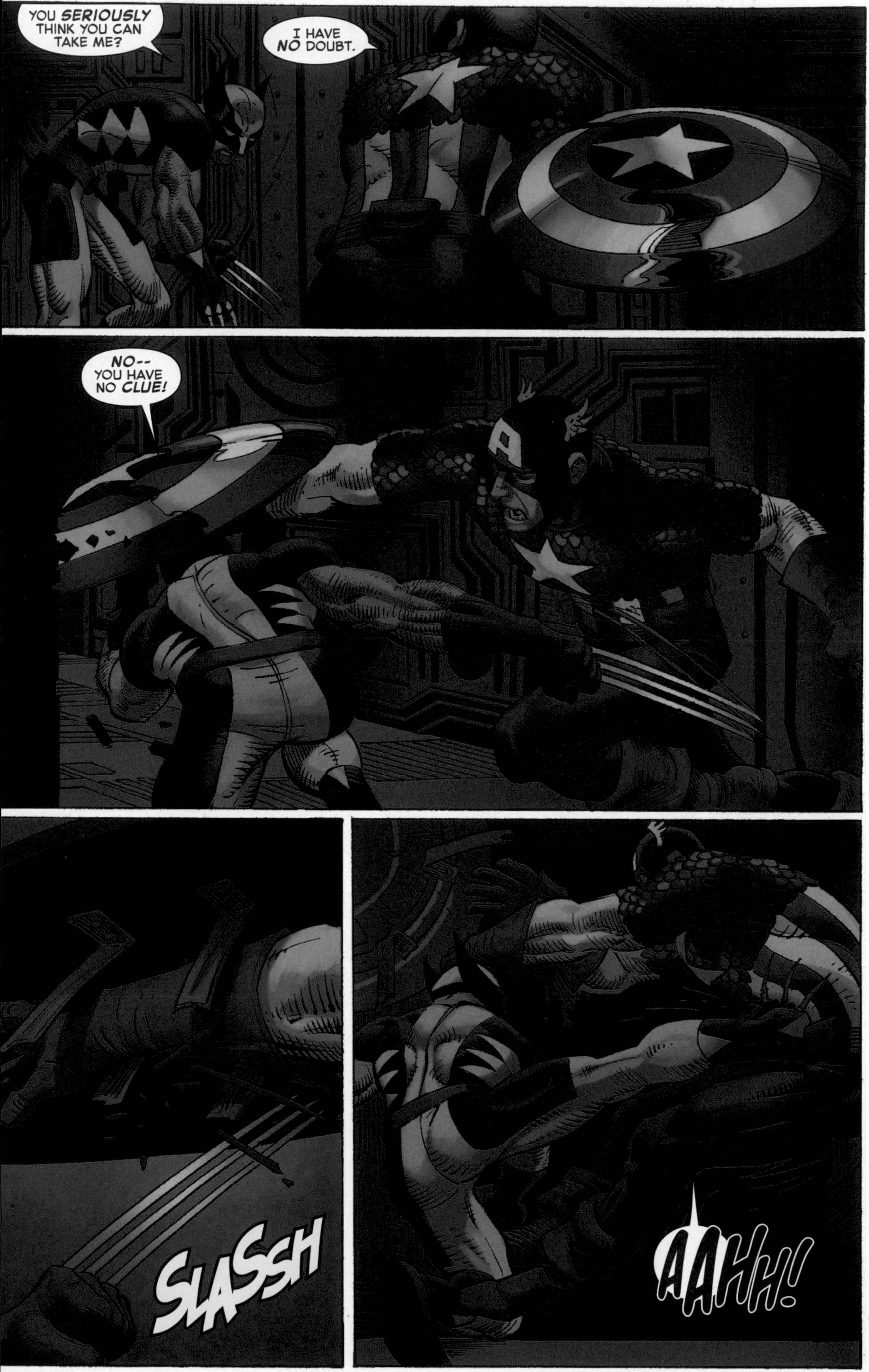
YOU SERIOUSLY THINK YOU CAN TAKE ME?
I HAVE NO DOUBT.
NO-- YOU HAVE NO CLUE!
SLASSH
AAHH!

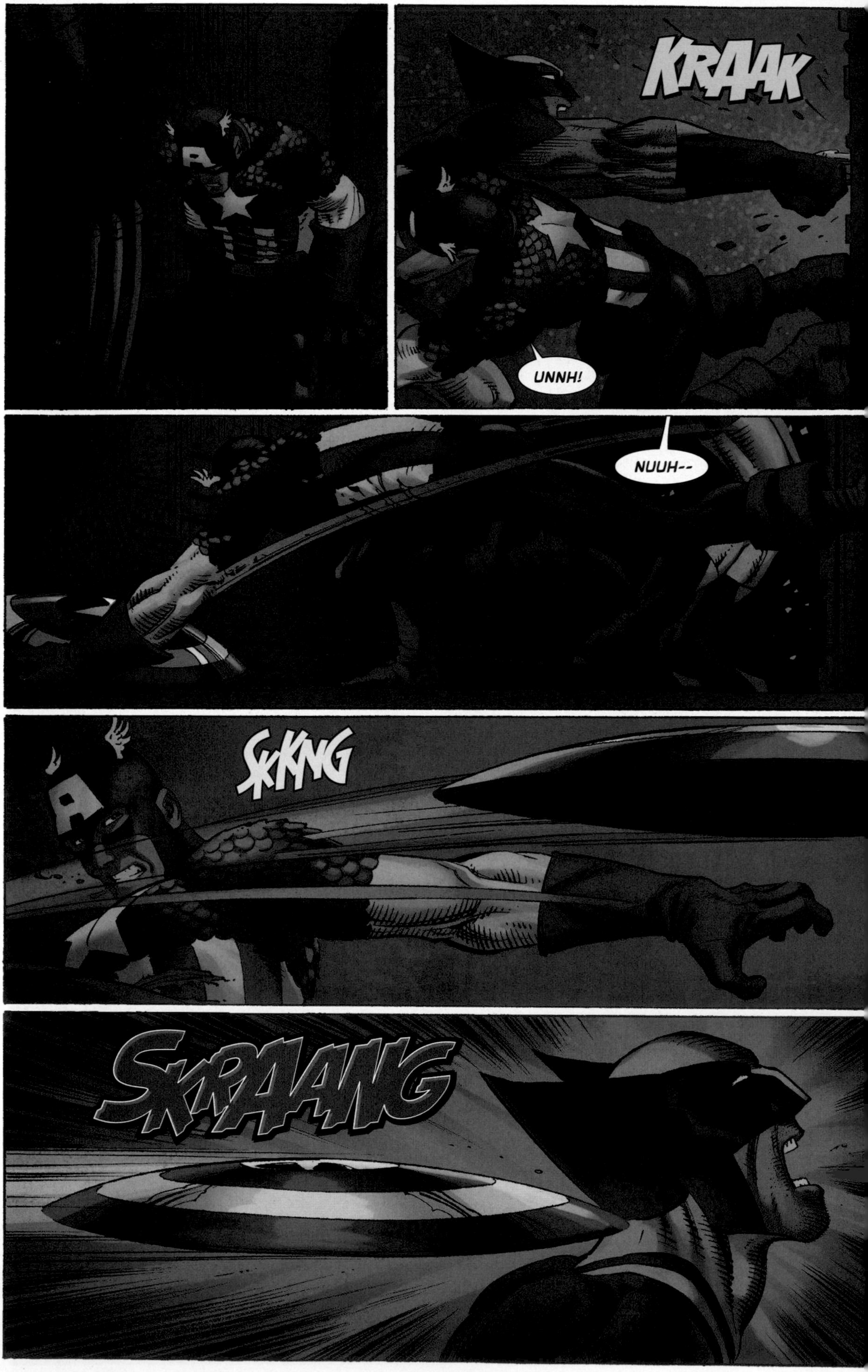
KRAAK
UNNH!
NUUH--
SKKNG
SKRAANG

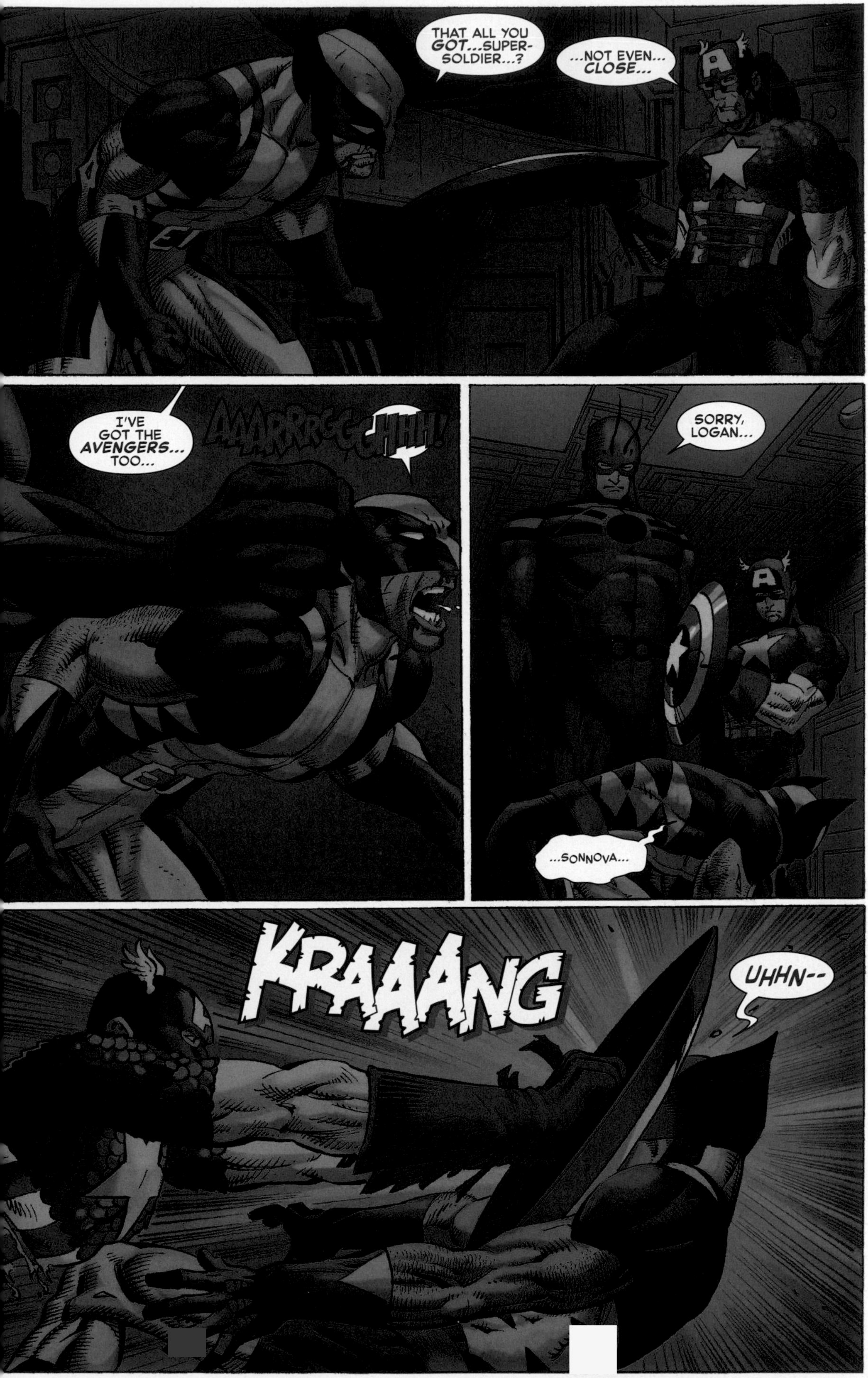
THAT ALL YOU GOT...SUPER-SOLDIER...?
...NOT EVEN... CLOSE...
I'VE GOT THE AVENGERS... TOO...
AAARRRGGHHH!
SORRY, LOGAN...
...SONNOVA...
KRAAANG
UHHN--

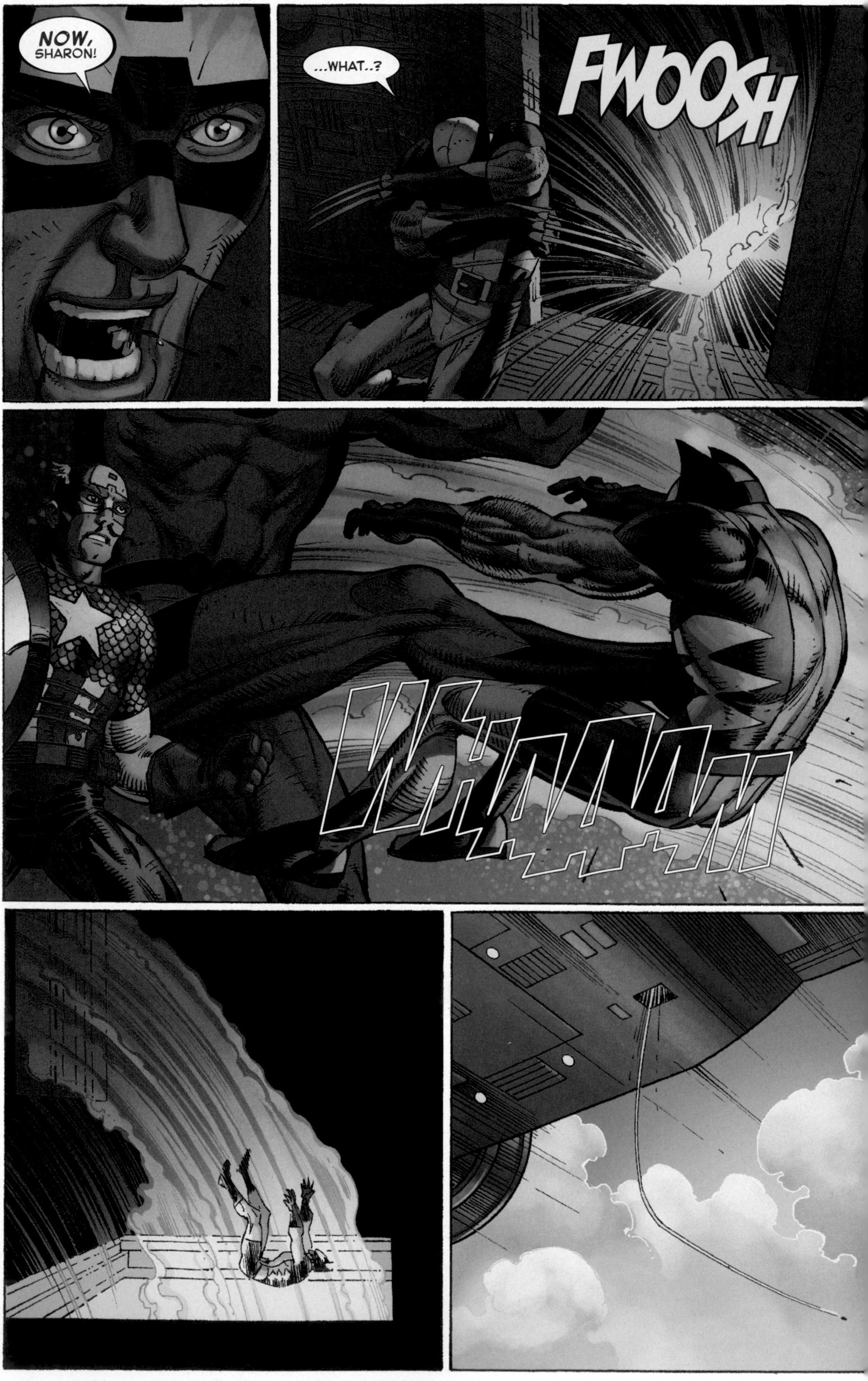
NOW, SHARON!
...WHAT..?
FWOOSH
WHAAAM

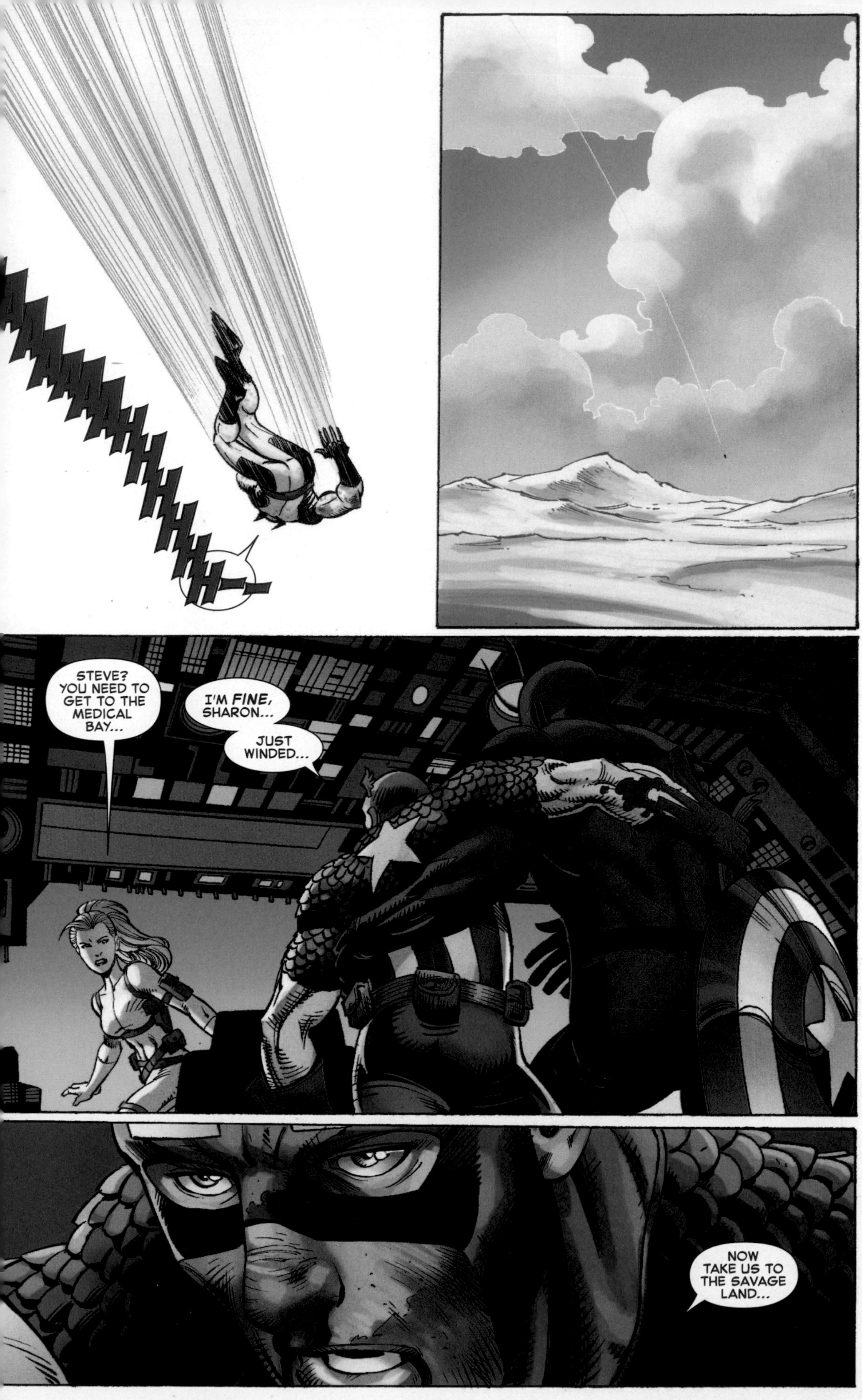
AAAAAAHHHHHHHH—
STEVE? YOU NEED TO GET TO THE MEDICAL BAY...
I'M *FINE,* SHARON...
JUST WINDED...
NOW TAKE US TO THE SAVAGE LAND...

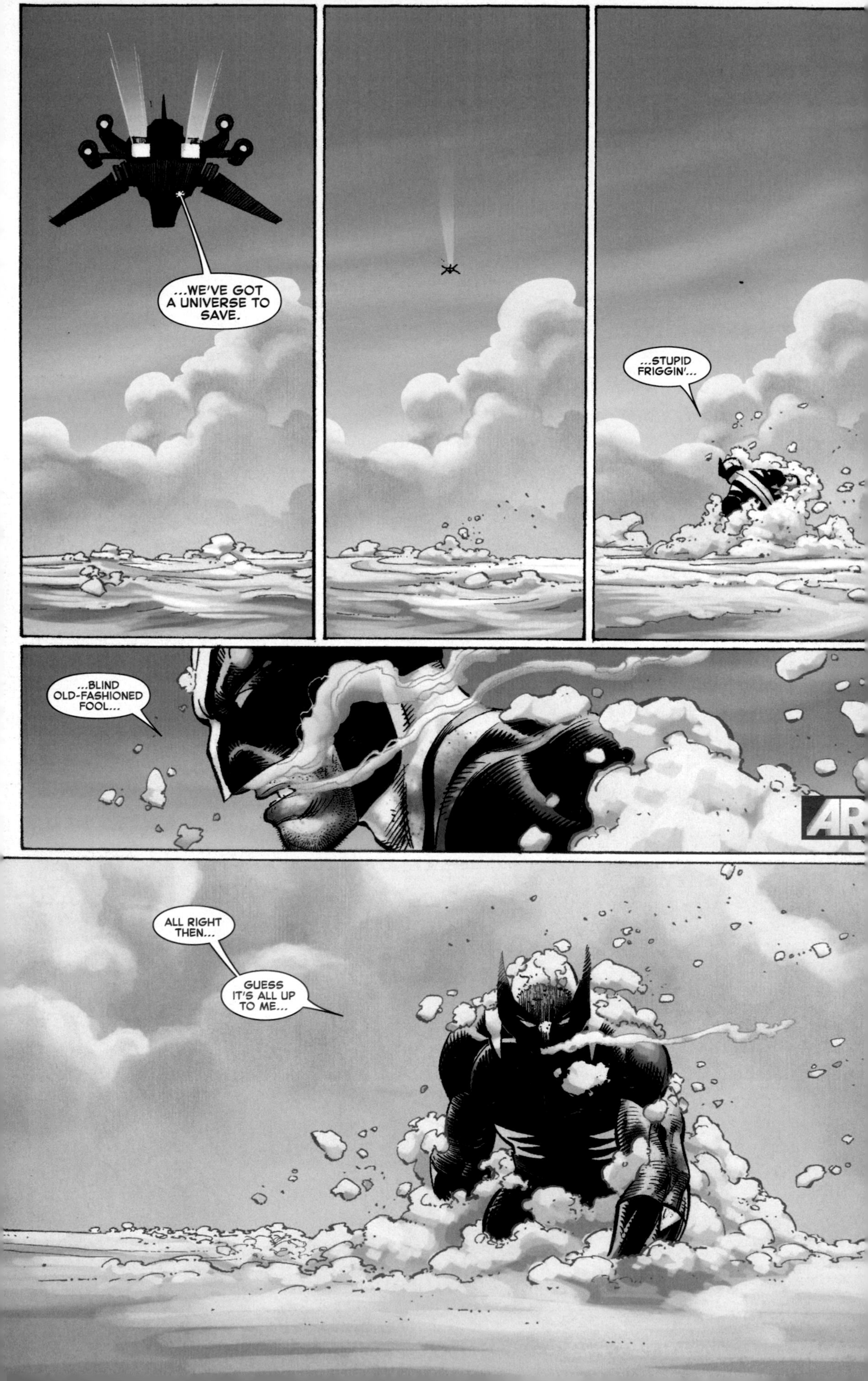
...WE'VE GOT A UNIVERSE TO SAVE.
...STUPID FRIGGIN'...
...BLIND OLD-FASHIONED FOOL...
ALL RIGHT THEN...
GUESS IT'S ALL UP TO ME...

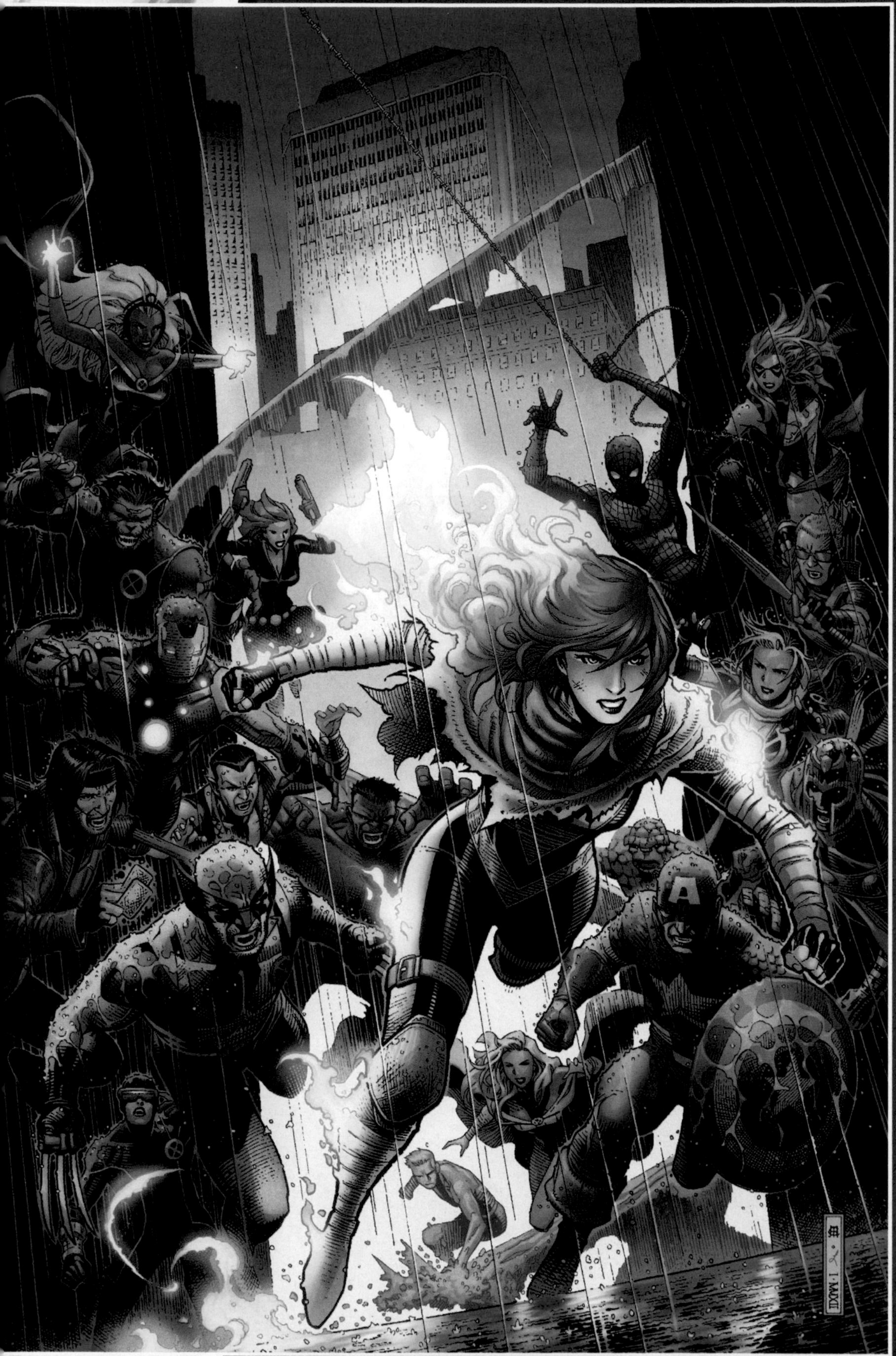

ROUND 4

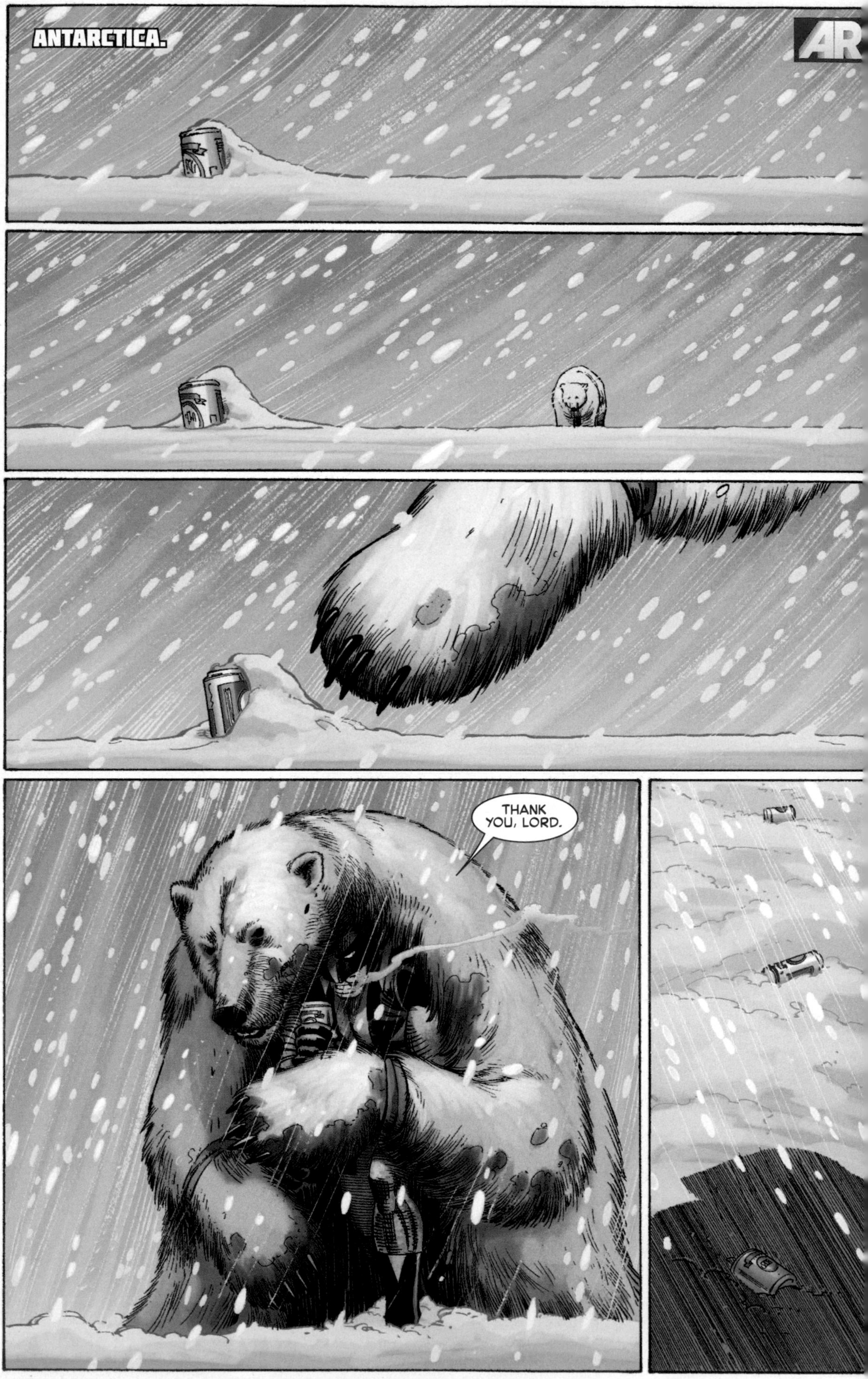
ANTARCTICA.
AR
THANK YOU, LORD.

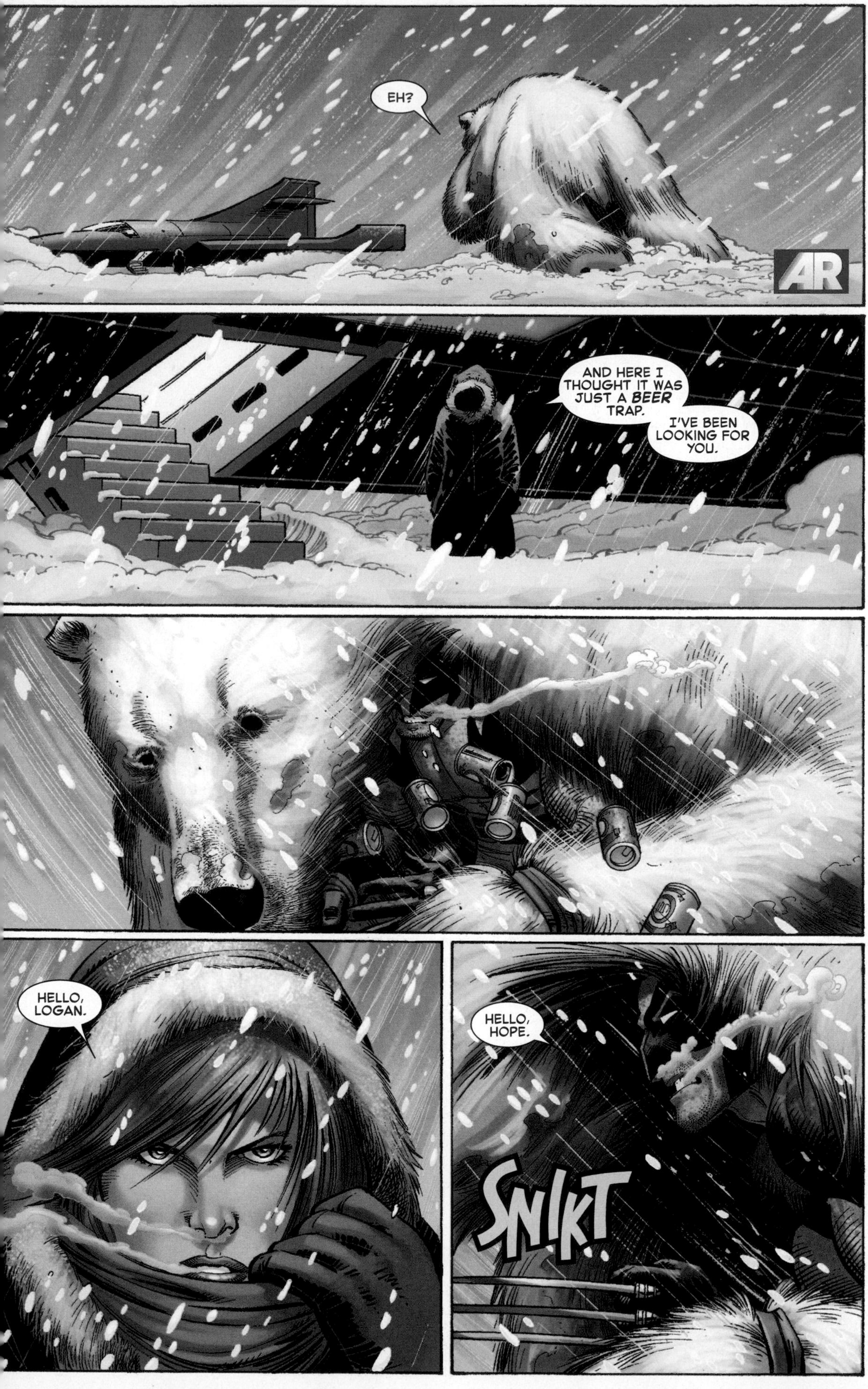
EH?
AR
AND HERE I THOUGHT IT WAS JUST A BEER TRAP.
I'VE BEEN LOOKING FOR YOU.
HELLO, LOGAN.
HELLO, HOPE.
SNIKT

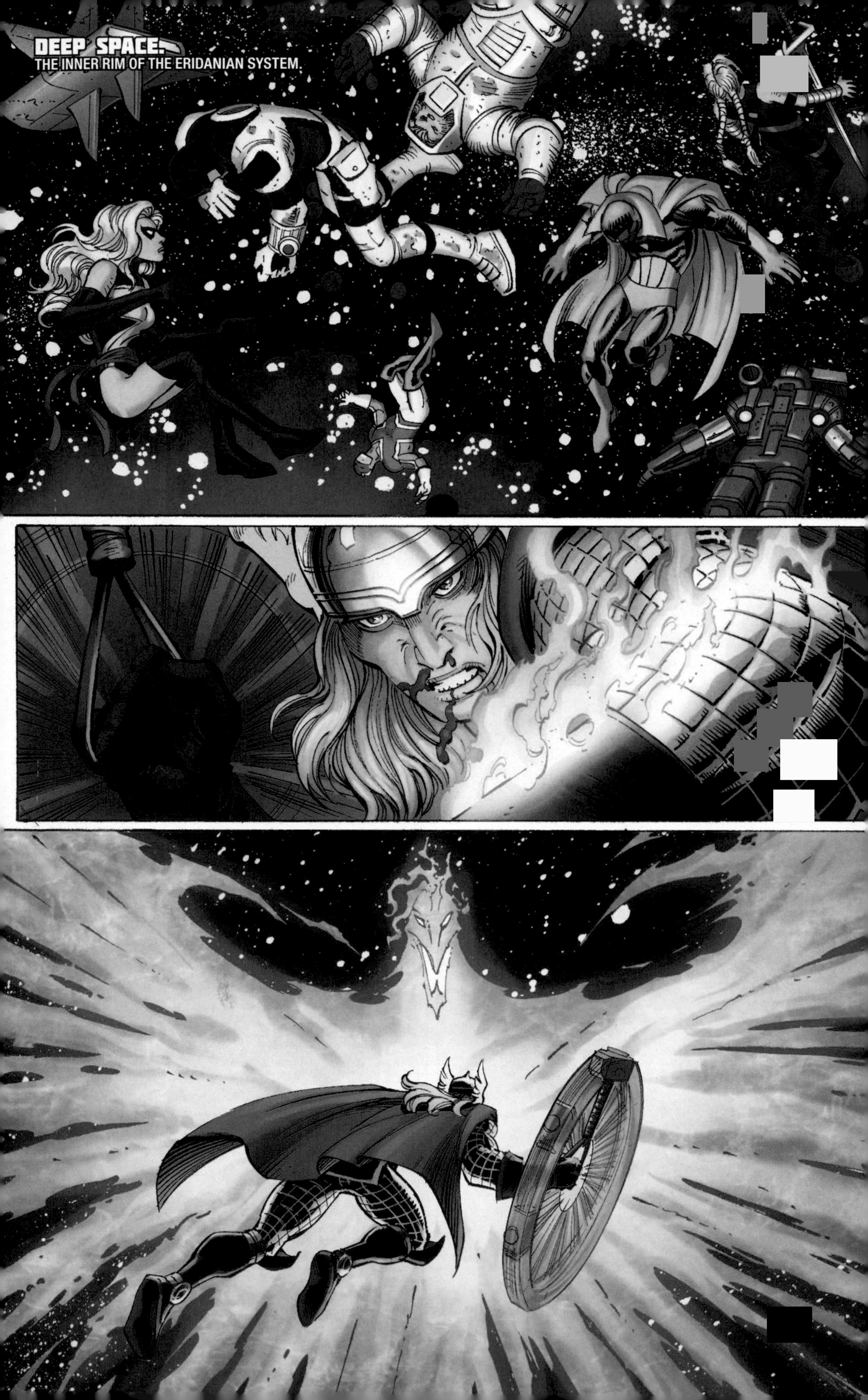
DEEP SPACE:
THE INNER RIM OF THE ERIDANIAN SYSTEM.

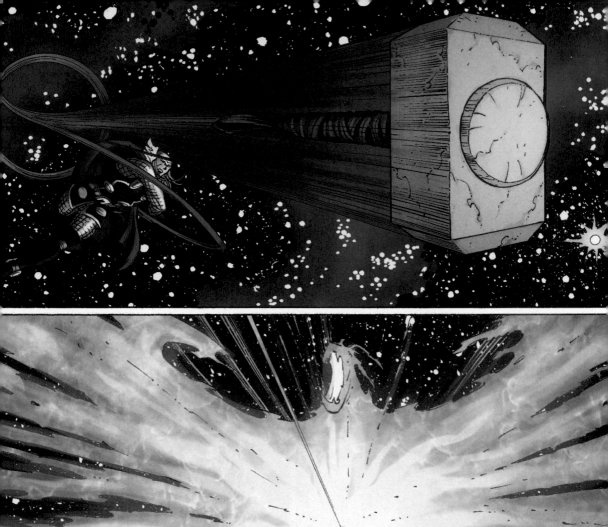

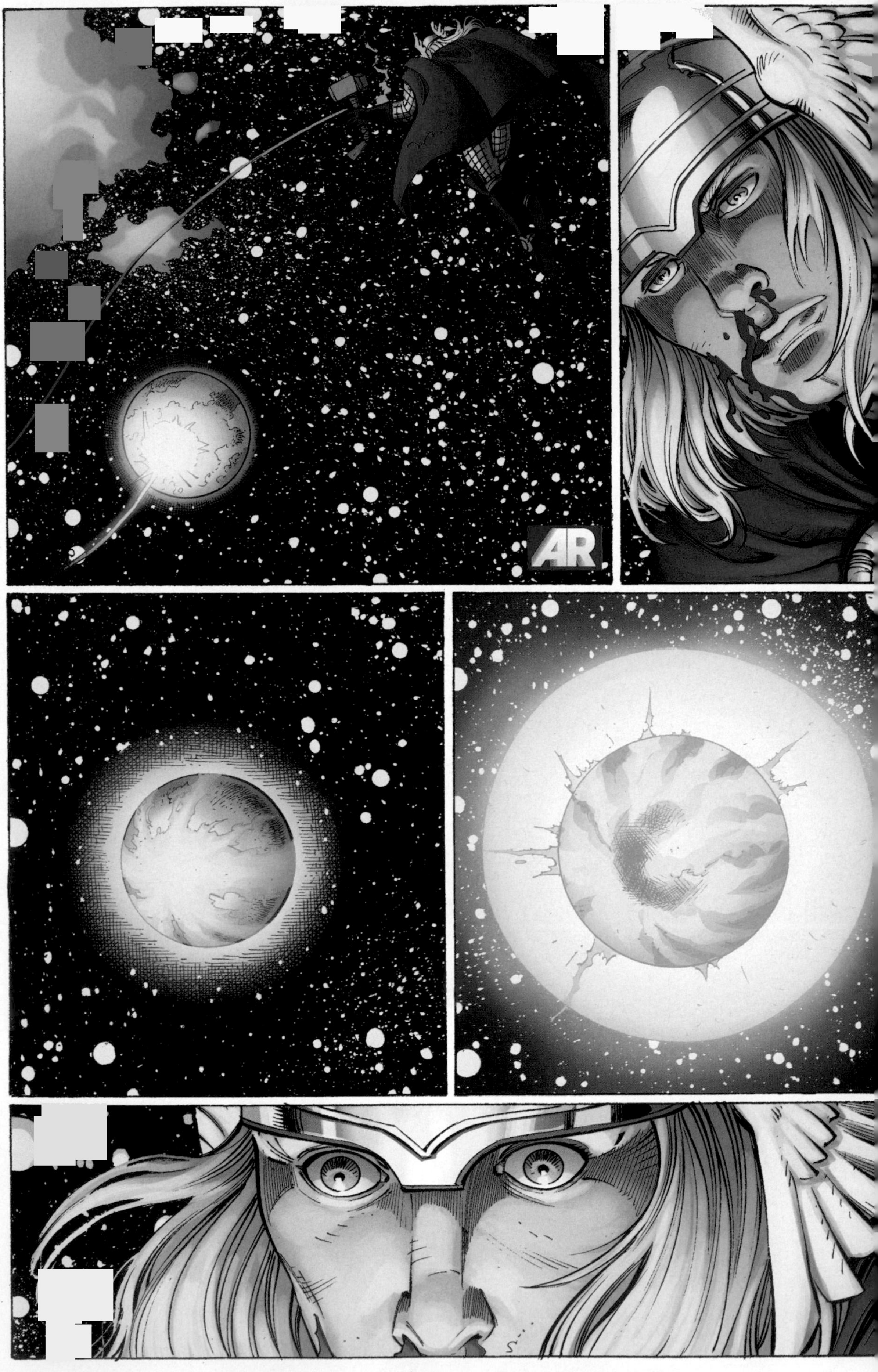

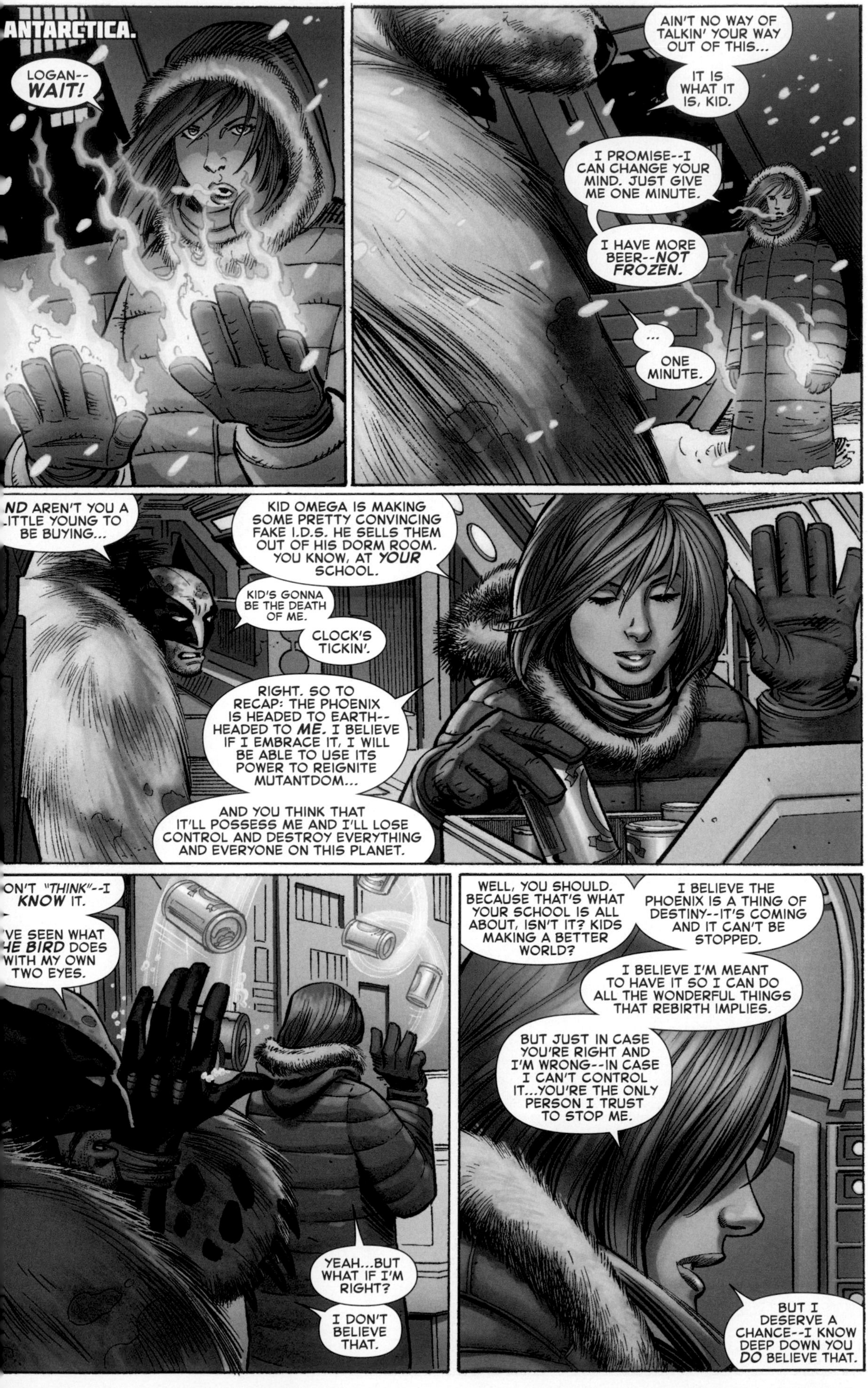
ANTARCTICA.
LOGAN-- WAIT!
AIN'T NO WAY OF TALKIN' YOUR WAY OUT OF THIS...
IT IS WHAT IT IS, KID.
I PROMISE--I CAN CHANGE YOUR MIND. JUST GIVE ME ONE MINUTE.
I HAVE MORE BEER--NOT FROZEN.
...
ONE MINUTE.
ND AREN'T YOU A ITTLE YOUNG TO BE BUYING...
KID OMEGA IS MAKING SOME PRETTY CONVINCING FAKE I.D.S. HE SELLS THEM OUT OF HIS DORM ROOM. YOU KNOW, AT YOUR SCHOOL.
KID'S GONNA BE THE DEATH OF ME.
CLOCK'S TICKIN'.
RIGHT. SO TO RECAP: THE PHOENIX IS HEADED TO EARTH-- HEADED TO ME. I BELIEVE IF I EMBRACE IT, I WILL BE ABLE TO USE ITS POWER TO REIGNITE MUTANTDOM...
AND YOU THINK THAT IT'LL POSSESS ME AND I'LL LOSE CONTROL AND DESTROY EVERYTHING AND EVERYONE ON THIS PLANET.
ON'T "THINK"--I KNOW IT.
'VE SEEN WHAT HE BIRD DOES WITH MY OWN TWO EYES.
YEAH...BUT WHAT IF I'M RIGHT?
I DON'T BELIEVE THAT.
WELL, YOU SHOULD. BECAUSE THAT'S WHAT YOUR SCHOOL IS ALL ABOUT, ISN'T IT? KIDS MAKING A BETTER WORLD?
I BELIEVE THE PHOENIX IS A THING OF DESTINY--IT'S COMING AND IT CAN'T BE STOPPED.
I BELIEVE I'M MEANT TO HAVE IT SO I CAN DO ALL THE WONDERFUL THINGS THAT REBIRTH IMPLIES.
BUT JUST IN CASE YOU'RE RIGHT AND I'M WRONG--IN CASE I CAN'T CONTROL IT...YOU'RE THE ONLY PERSON I TRUST TO STOP ME.
BUT I DESERVE A CHANCE--I KNOW DEEP DOWN YOU DO BELIEVE THAT.

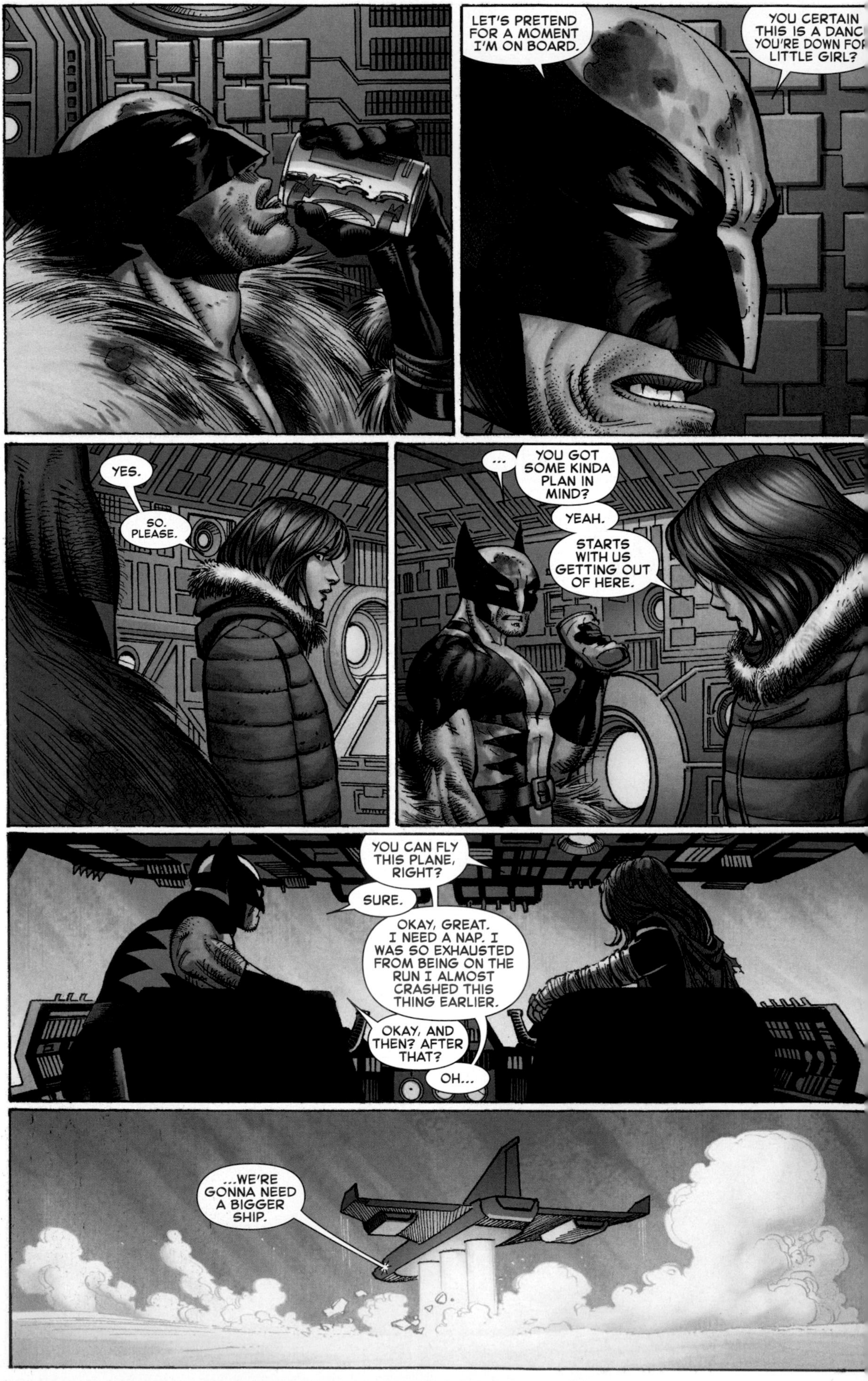
LET'S PRETEND FOR A MOMENT I'M ON BOARD.
YOU CERTAIN THIS IS A DANC YOU'RE DOWN FO LITTLE GIRL?
YES.
SO. PLEASE.
...
YOU GOT SOME KINDA PLAN IN MIND?
YEAH.
STARTS WITH US GETTING OUT OF HERE.
YOU CAN FLY THIS PLANE, RIGHT?
SURE.
OKAY, GREAT. I NEED A NAP. I WAS SO EXHAUSTED FROM BEING ON THE RUN I ALMOST CRASHED THIS THING EARLIER.
OKAY, AND THEN? AFTER THAT?
OH...
...WE'RE GONNA NEED A BIGGER SHIP.

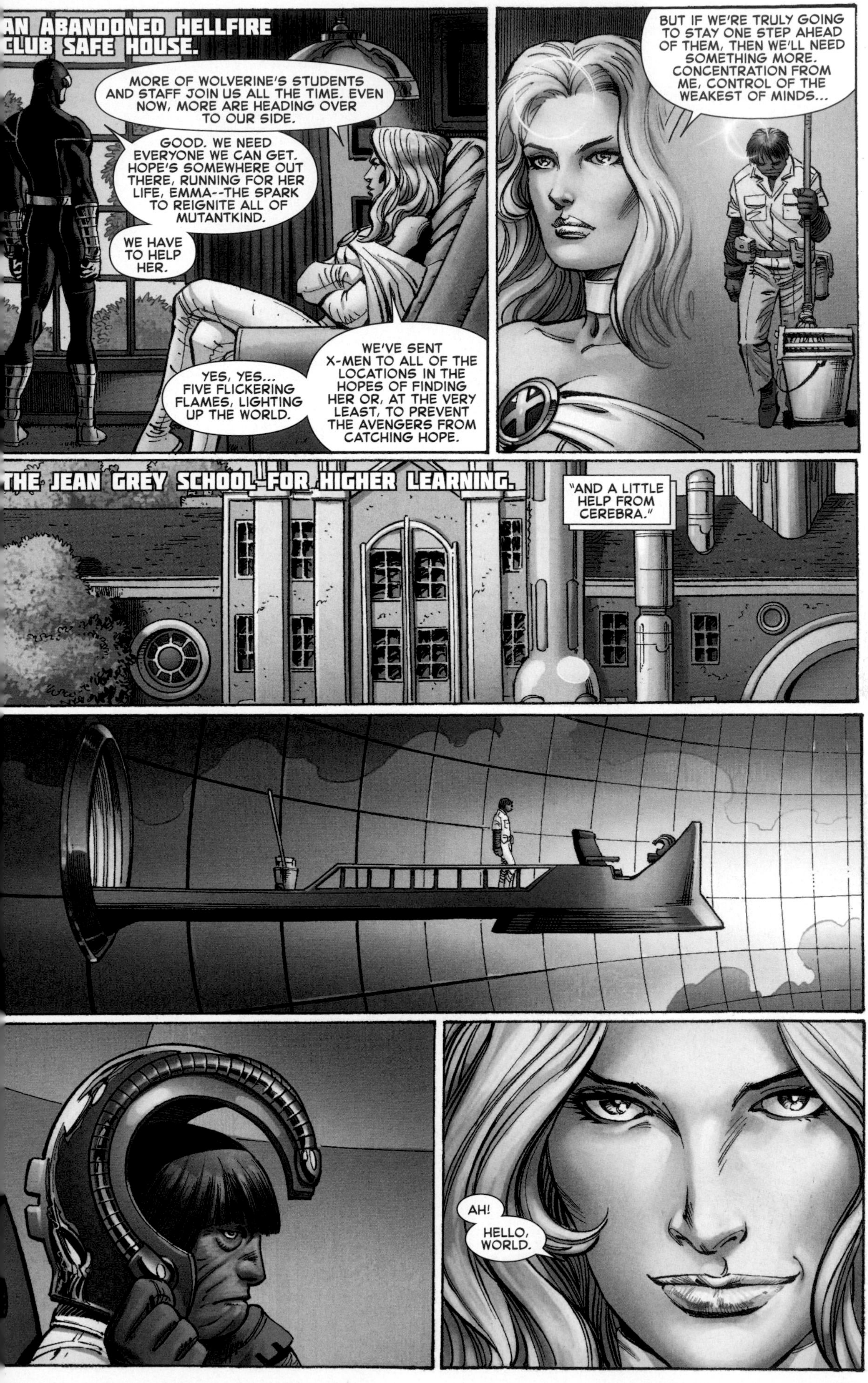
AN ABANDONED HELLFIRE CLUB SAFE HOUSE.
MORE OF WOLVERINE'S STUDENTS AND STAFF JOIN US ALL THE TIME. EVEN NOW, MORE ARE HEADING OVER TO OUR SIDE.
GOOD. WE NEED EVERYONE WE CAN GET. HOPE'S SOMEWHERE OUT THERE, RUNNING FOR HER LIFE, EMMA--THE SPARK TO REIGNITE ALL OF MUTANTKIND.
WE HAVE TO HELP HER.
WE'VE SENT X-MEN TO ALL OF THE LOCATIONS IN THE HOPES OF FINDING HER OR, AT THE VERY LEAST, TO PREVENT THE AVENGERS FROM CATCHING HOPE.
YES, YES... FIVE FLICKERING FLAMES, LIGHTING UP THE WORLD.
BUT IF WE'RE TRULY GOING TO STAY ONE STEP AHEAD OF THEM, THEN WE'LL NEED SOMETHING MORE. CONCENTRATION FROM ME, CONTROL OF THE WEAKEST OF MINDS...
THE JEAN GREY SCHOOL FOR HIGHER LEARNING.
"AND A LITTLE HELP FROM CEREBRA."
AH!
HELLO, WORLD.

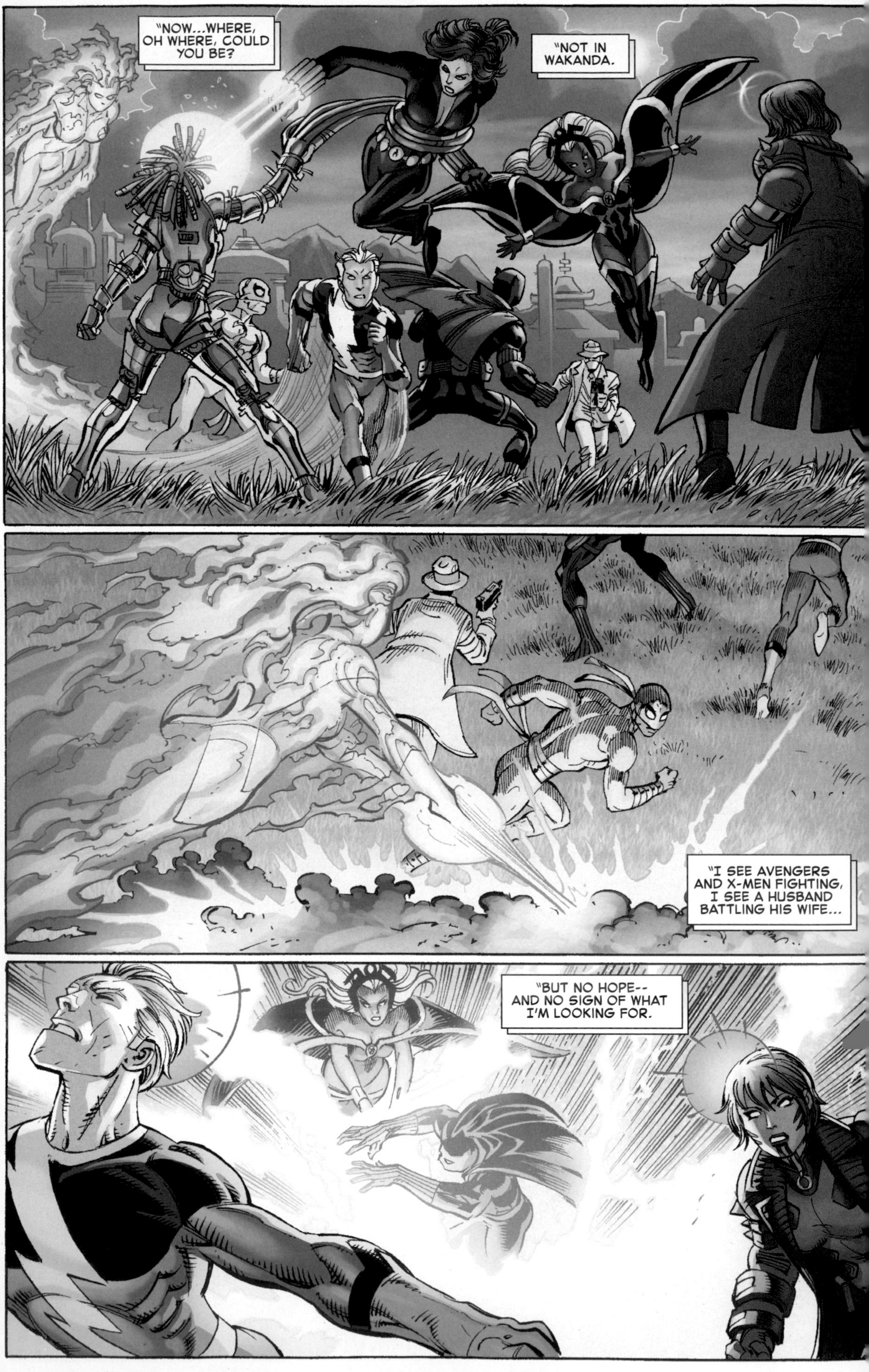

"NOW...WHERE, OH WHERE, COULD YOU BE?
"NOT IN WAKANDA.
"I SEE AVENGERS AND X-MEN FIGHTING, I SEE A HUSBAND BATTLING HIS WIFE...
"BUT NO HOPE-- AND NO SIGN OF WHAT I'M LOOKING FOR.

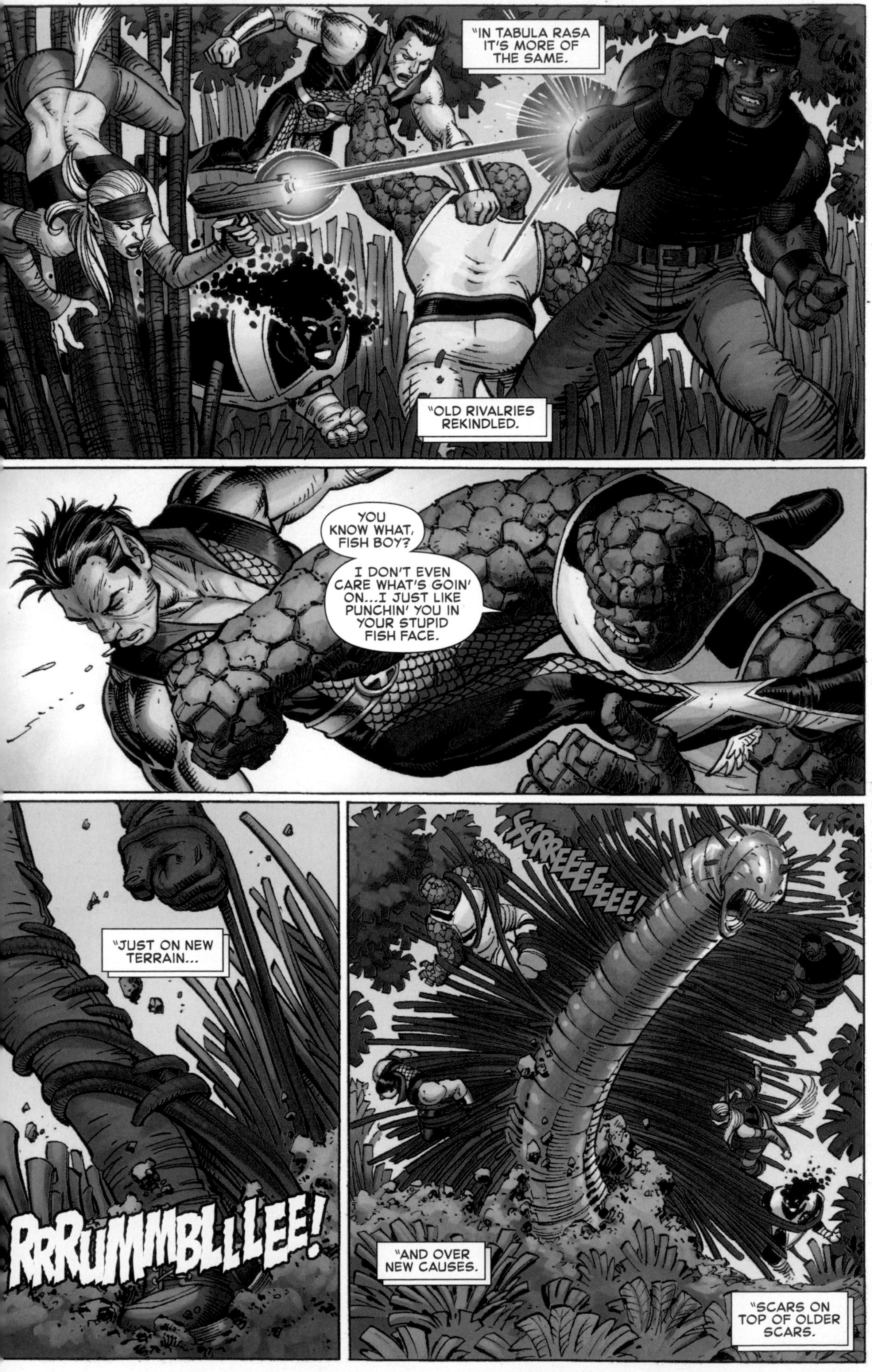
"IN TABULA RASA IT'S MORE OF THE SAME.
"OLD RIVALRIES REKINDLED.
YOU KNOW WHAT, FISH BOY?
I DON'T EVEN CARE WHAT'S GOIN' ON...I JUST LIKE PUNCHIN' YOU IN YOUR STUPID FISH FACE.
"JUST ON NEW TERRAIN...
RRRUMMBLLLEE!
SCRREEEEEEEEE!
"AND OVER NEW CAUSES.
"SCARS ON TOP OF OLDER SCARS.

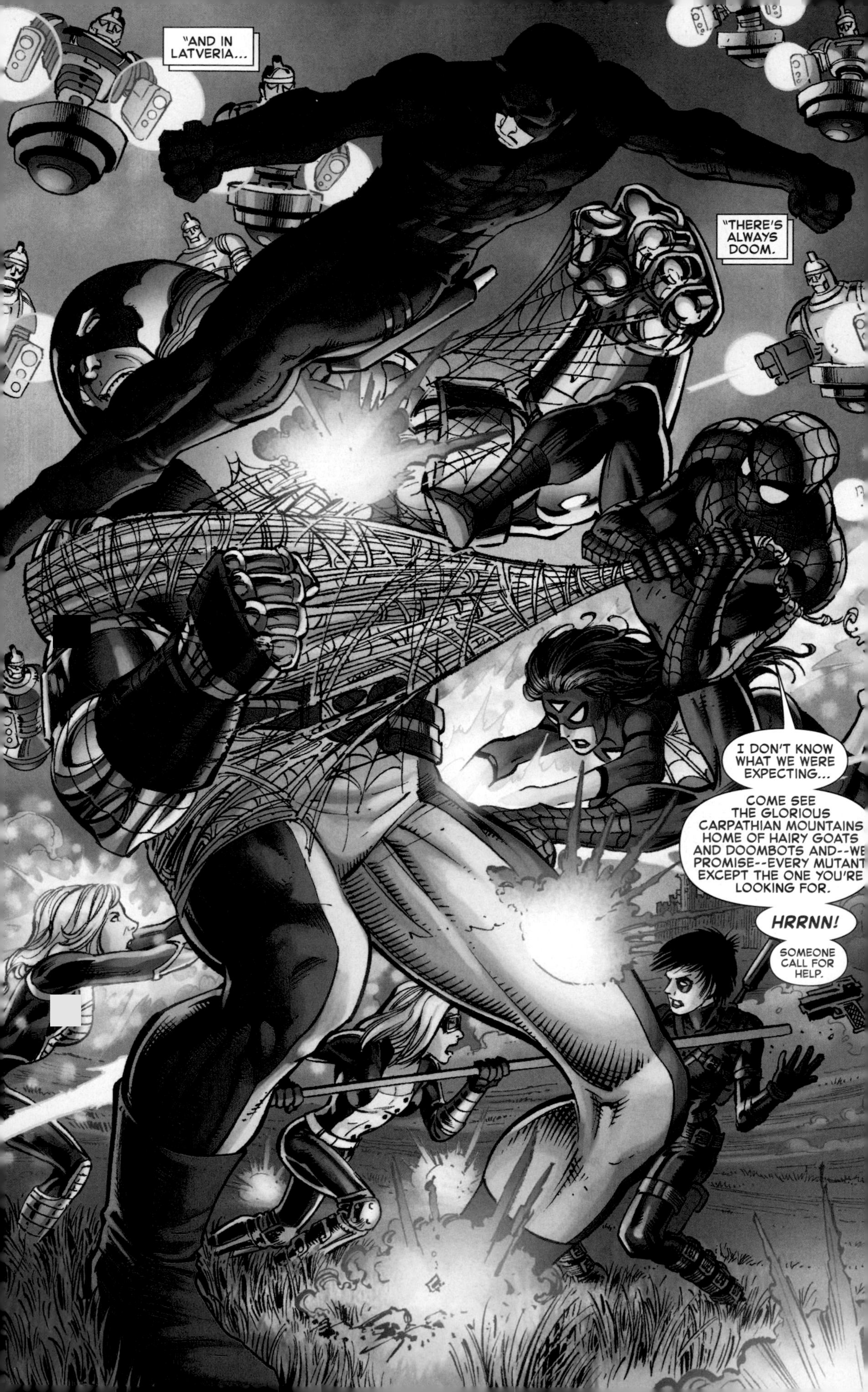
"AND IN LATVERIA...
"THERE'S ALWAYS DOOM.
I DON'T KNOW WHAT WE WERE EXPECTING...
COME SEE THE GLORIOUS CARPATHIAN MOUNTAINS HOME OF HAIRY GOATS AND DOOMBOTS AND--WE PROMISE--EVERY MUTANT EXCEPT THE ONE YOU'RE LOOKING FOR.
HRRNN!
SOMEONE CALL FOR HELP.

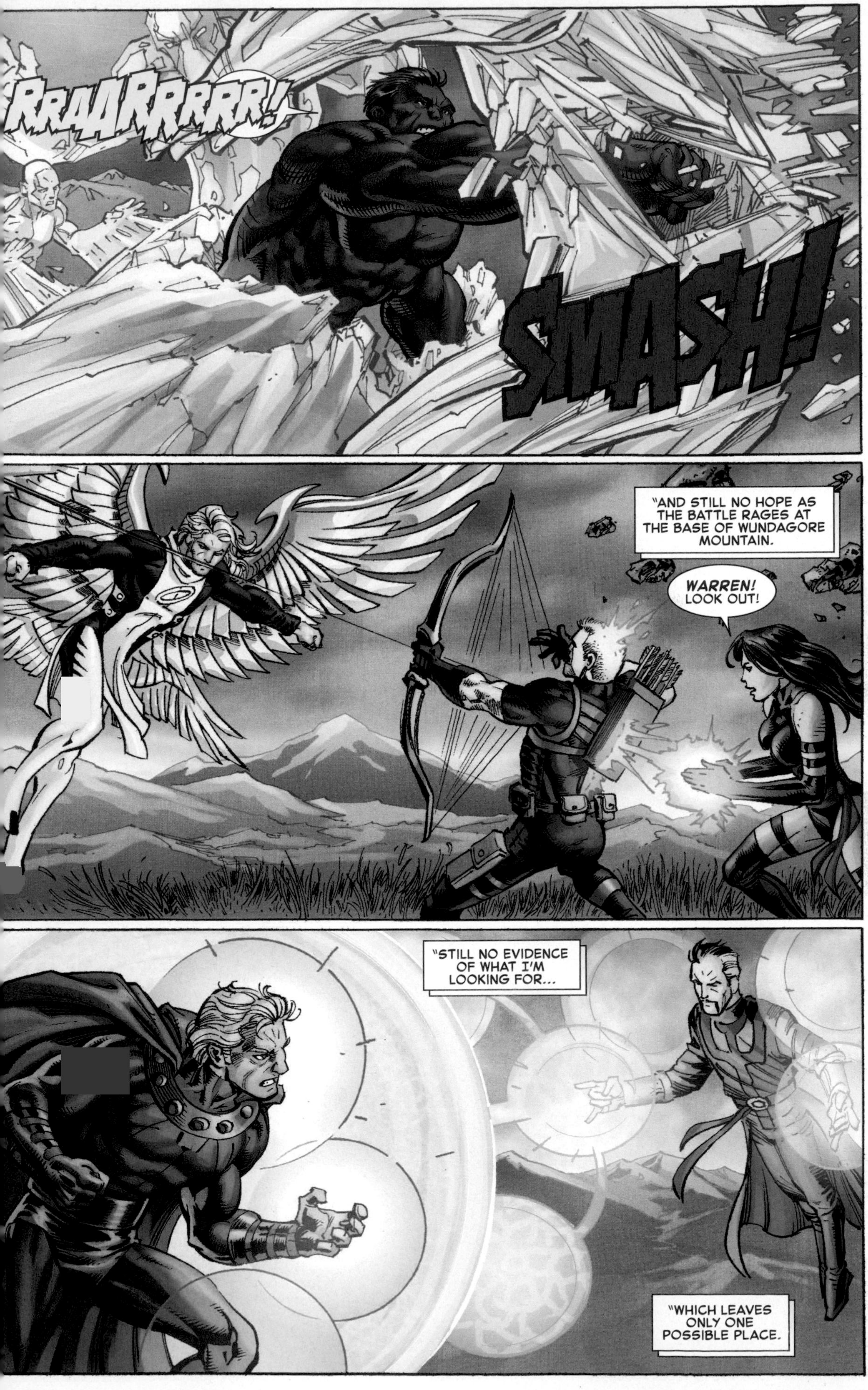
RRAAARRRRRR!
SMASH!
"AND STILL NO HOPE AS THE BATTLE RAGES AT THE BASE OF WUNDAGORE MOUNTAIN.
WARREN! LOOK OUT!
"STILL NO EVIDENCE OF WHAT I'M LOOKING FOR...
"WHICH LEAVES ONLY ONE POSSIBLE PLACE.

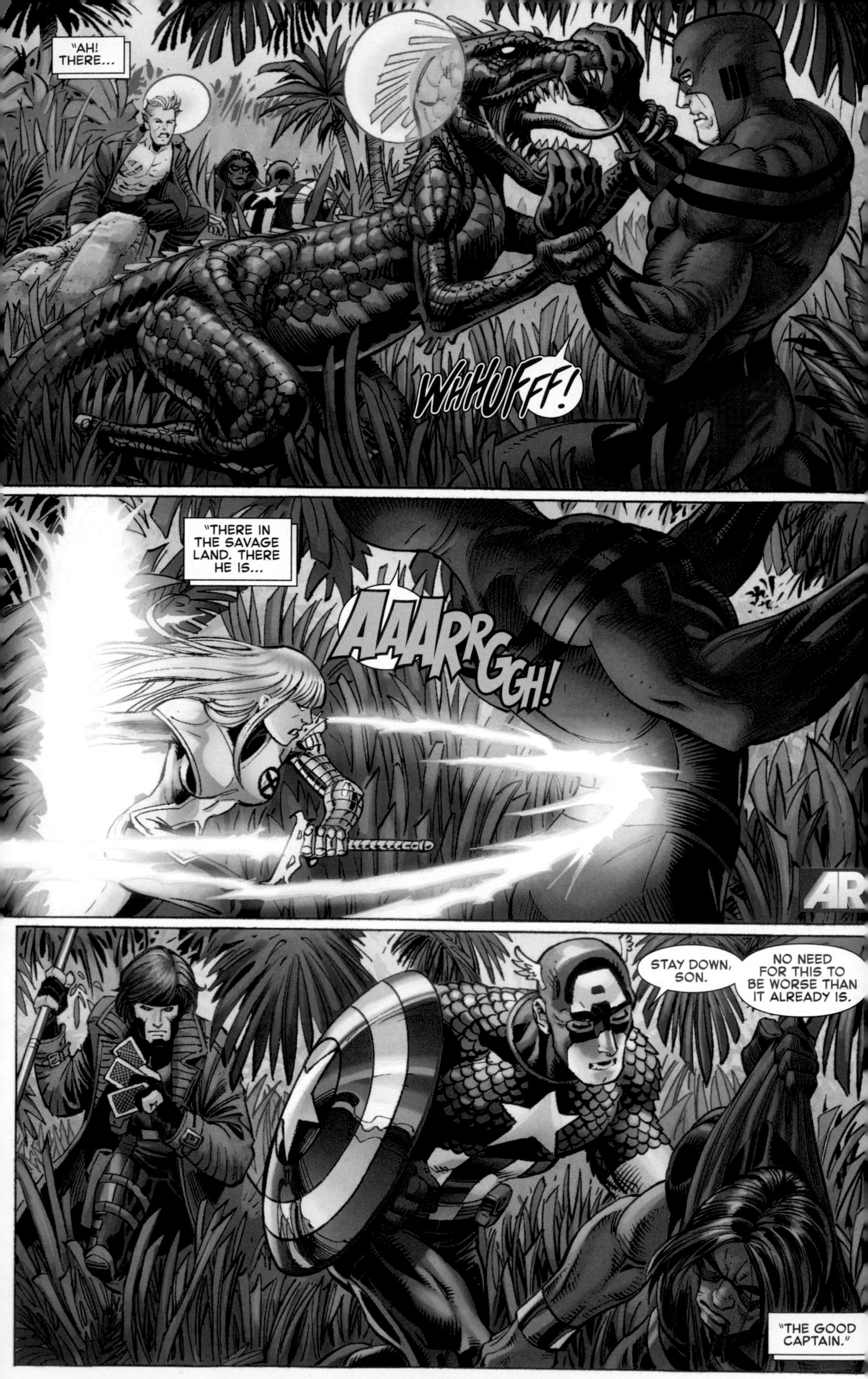

"AH! THERE...
WHHUFFF!
"THERE IN THE SAVAGE LAND. THERE HE IS...
AAARRGGH!
AR
STAY DOWN, SON.
NO NEED FOR THIS TO BE WORSE THAN IT ALREADY IS.
"THE GOOD CAPTAIN."

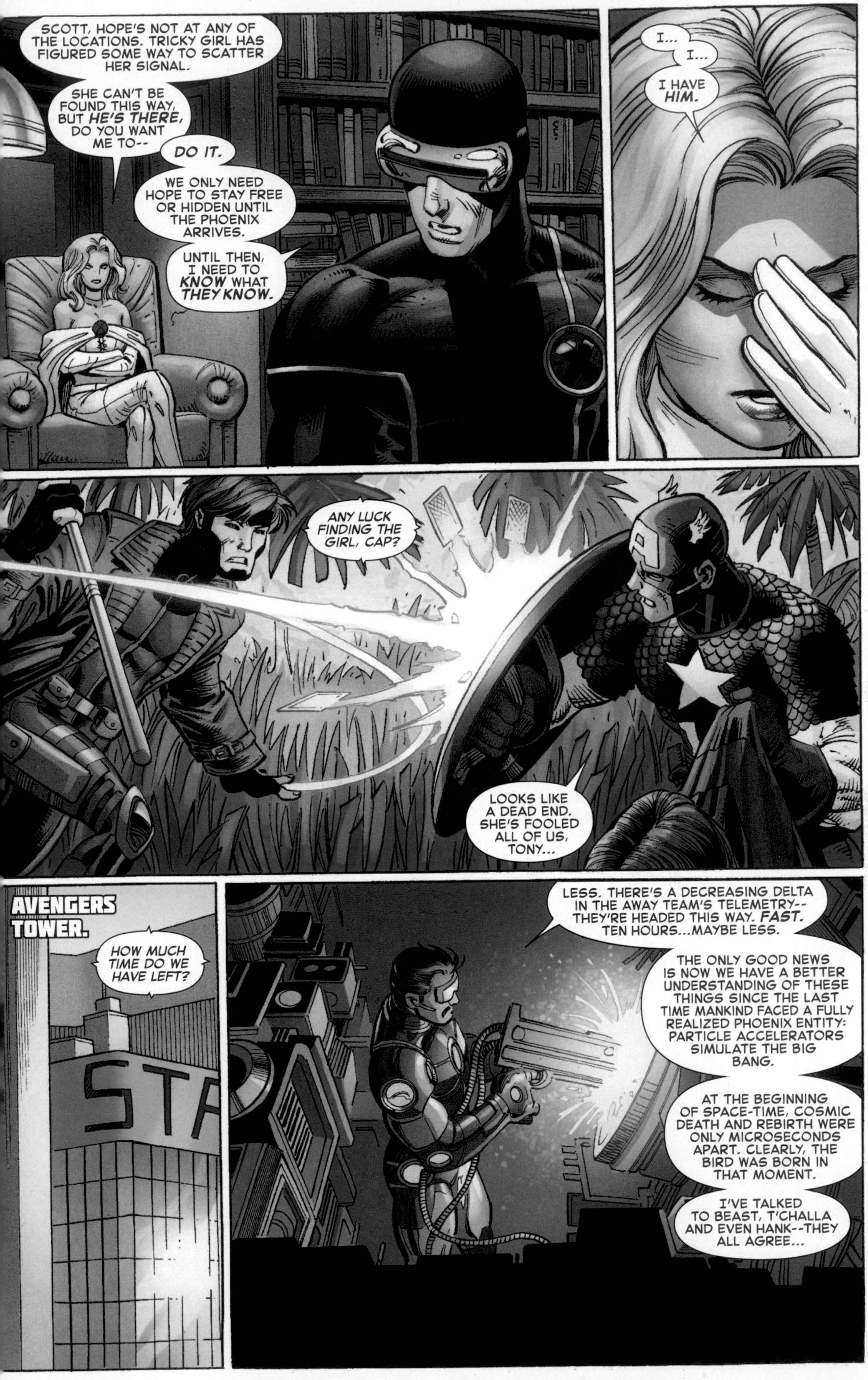
SCOTT, HOPE'S NOT AT ANY OF THE LOCATIONS. TRICKY GIRL HAS FIGURED SOME WAY TO SCATTER HER SIGNAL.
SHE CAN'T BE FOUND THIS WAY, BUT HE'S THERE, DO YOU WANT ME TO--
DO IT.
WE ONLY NEED HOPE TO STAY FREE OR HIDDEN UNTIL THE PHOENIX ARRIVES.
UNTIL THEN, I NEED TO KNOW WHAT THEY KNOW.
I...
I...
I HAVE HIM.
ANY LUCK FINDING THE GIRL, CAP?
LOOKS LIKE A DEAD END. SHE'S FOOLED ALL OF US, TONY...
AVENGERS TOWER.
HOW MUCH TIME DO WE HAVE LEFT?
LESS. THERE'S A DECREASING DELTA IN THE AWAY TEAM'S TELEMETRY--THEY'RE HEADED THIS WAY. FAST. TEN HOURS...MAYBE LESS.
THE ONLY GOOD NEWS IS NOW WE HAVE A BETTER UNDERSTANDING OF THESE THINGS SINCE THE LAST TIME MANKIND FACED A FULLY REALIZED PHOENIX ENTITY: PARTICLE ACCELERATORS SIMULATE THE BIG BANG.
AT THE BEGINNING OF SPACE-TIME, COSMIC DEATH AND REBIRTH WERE ONLY MICROSECONDS APART. CLEARLY, THE BIRD WAS BORN IN THAT MOMENT.
I'VE TALKED TO BEAST, T'CHALLA AND EVEN HANK--THEY ALL AGREE...
STA

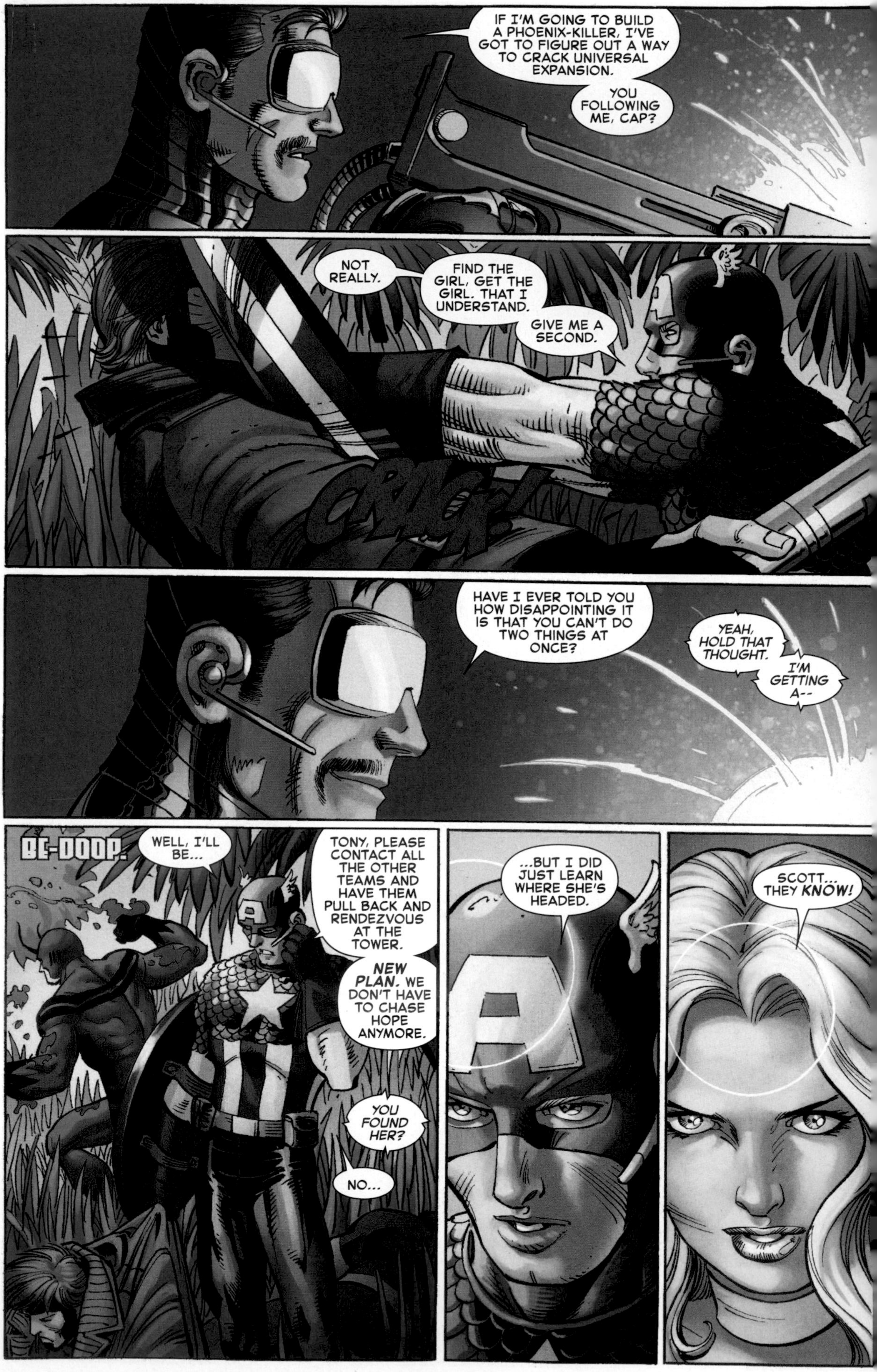
IF I'M GOING TO BUILD A PHOENIX-KILLER, I'VE GOT TO FIGURE OUT A WAY TO CRACK UNIVERSAL EXPANSION.
YOU FOLLOWING ME, CAP?
NOT REALLY.
FIND THE GIRL, GET THE GIRL. THAT I UNDERSTAND.
GIVE ME A SECOND.
CRACK!
HAVE I EVER TOLD YOU HOW DISAPPOINTING IT IS THAT YOU CAN'T DO TWO THINGS AT ONCE?
YEAH, HOLD THAT THOUGHT.
I'M GETTING A--
BE-DOOP.
WELL, I'LL BE...
TONY, PLEASE CONTACT ALL THE OTHER TEAMS AND HAVE THEM PULL BACK AND RENDEZVOUS AT THE TOWER.
NEW PLAN. WE DON'T HAVE TO CHASE HOPE ANYMORE.
YOU FOUND HER?
NO...
...BUT I DID JUST LEARN WHERE SHE'S HEADED.
SCOTT... THEY KNOW!

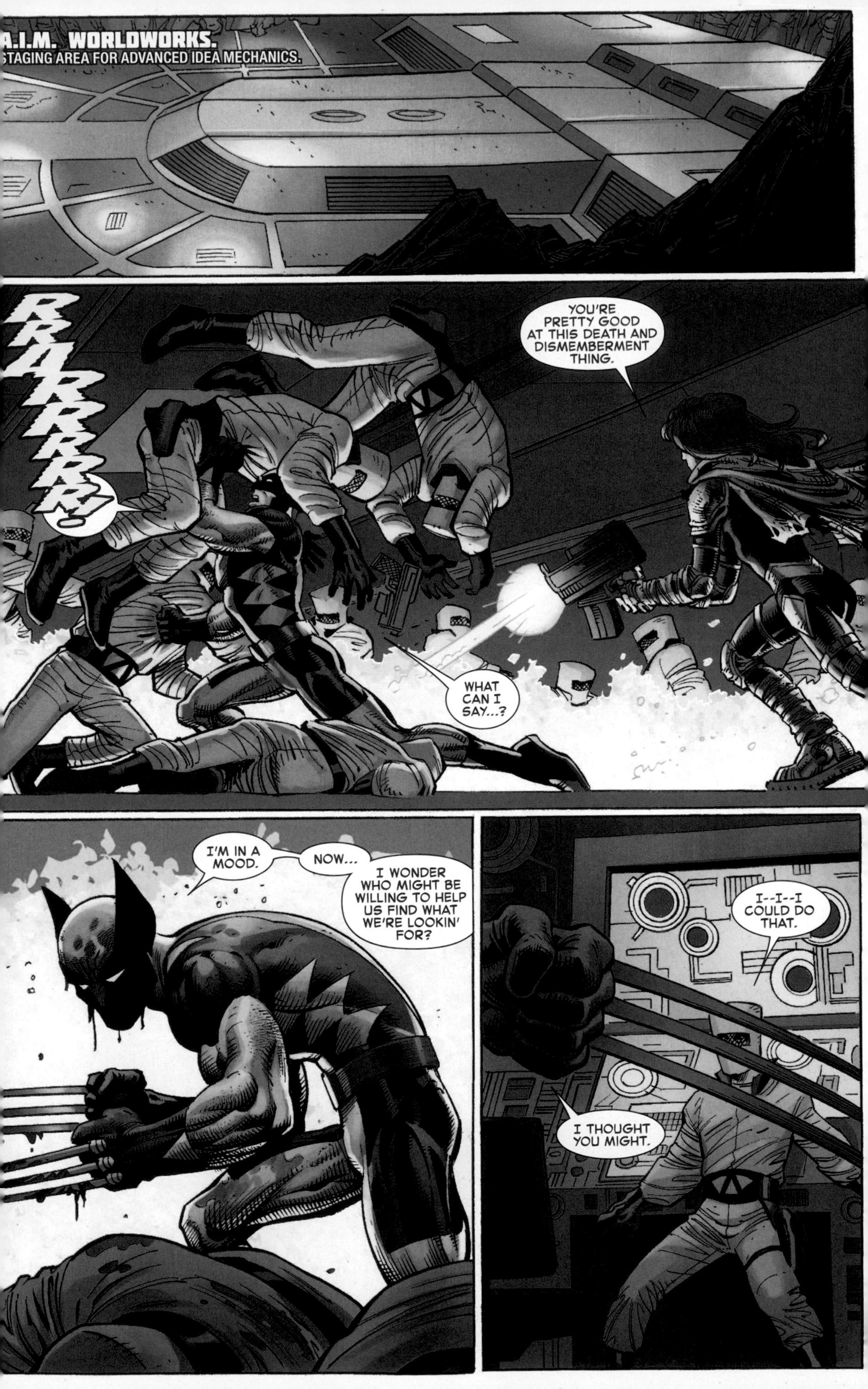
A.I.M. WORLDWORKS.
STAGING AREA FOR ADVANCED IDEA MECHANICS.
RRARRRRR!
YOU'RE PRETTY GOOD AT THIS DEATH AND DISMEMBERMENT THING.
WHAT CAN I SAY...?
I'M IN A MOOD.
NOW...
I WONDER WHO MIGHT BE WILLING TO HELP US FIND WHAT WE'RE LOOKIN' FOR?
I--I--I COULD DO THAT.
I THOUGHT YOU MIGHT.

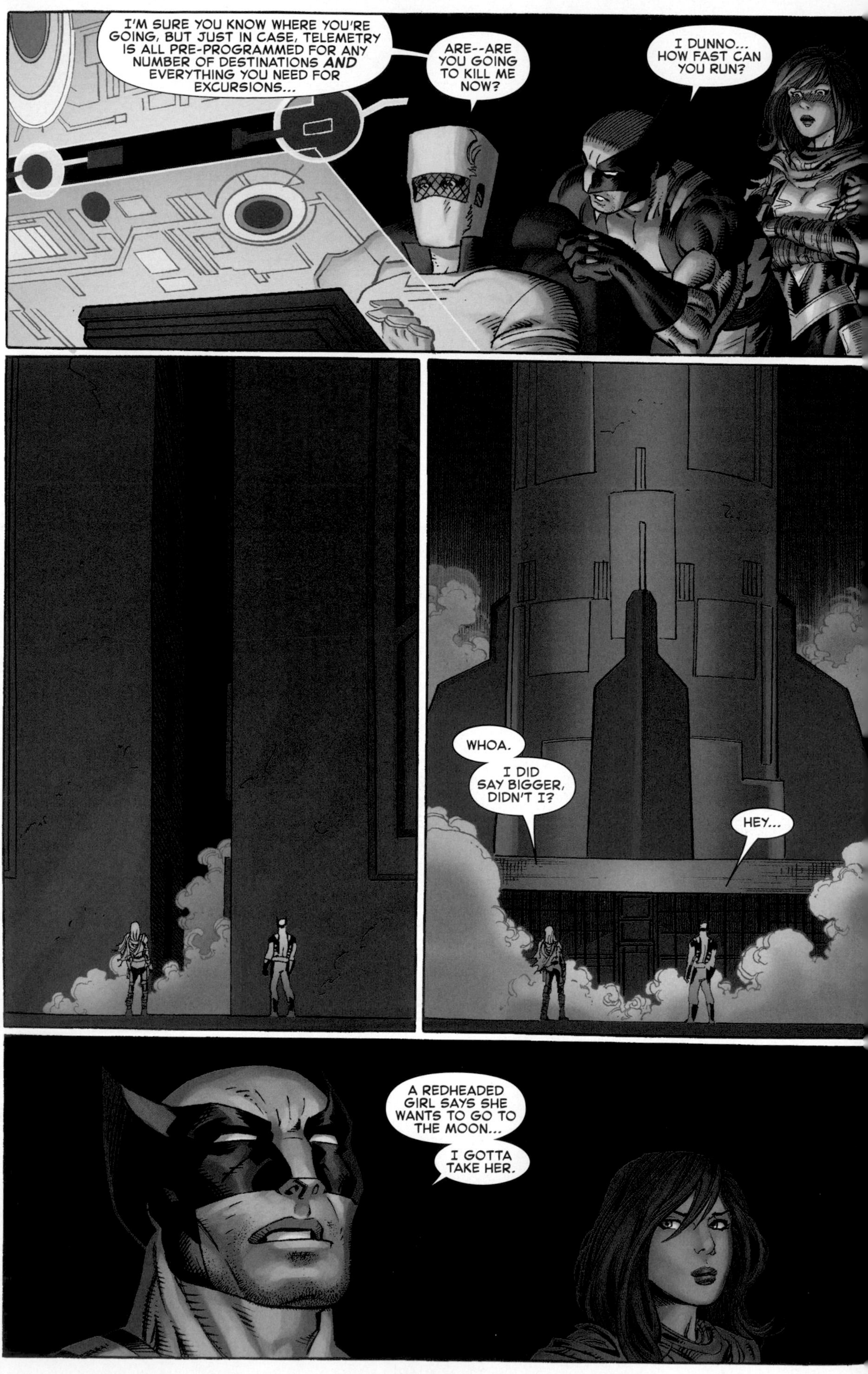
I'M SURE YOU KNOW WHERE YOU'RE GOING, BUT JUST IN CASE, TELEMETRY IS ALL PRE-PROGRAMMED FOR ANY NUMBER OF DESTINATIONS AND EVERYTHING YOU NEED FOR EXCURSIONS...
ARE--ARE YOU GOING TO KILL ME NOW?
I DUNNO... HOW FAST CAN YOU RUN?
WHOA.
I DID SAY BIGGER, DIDN'T I?
HEY...
A REDHEADED GIRL SAYS SHE WANTS TO GO TO THE MOON...
I GOTTA TAKE HER.

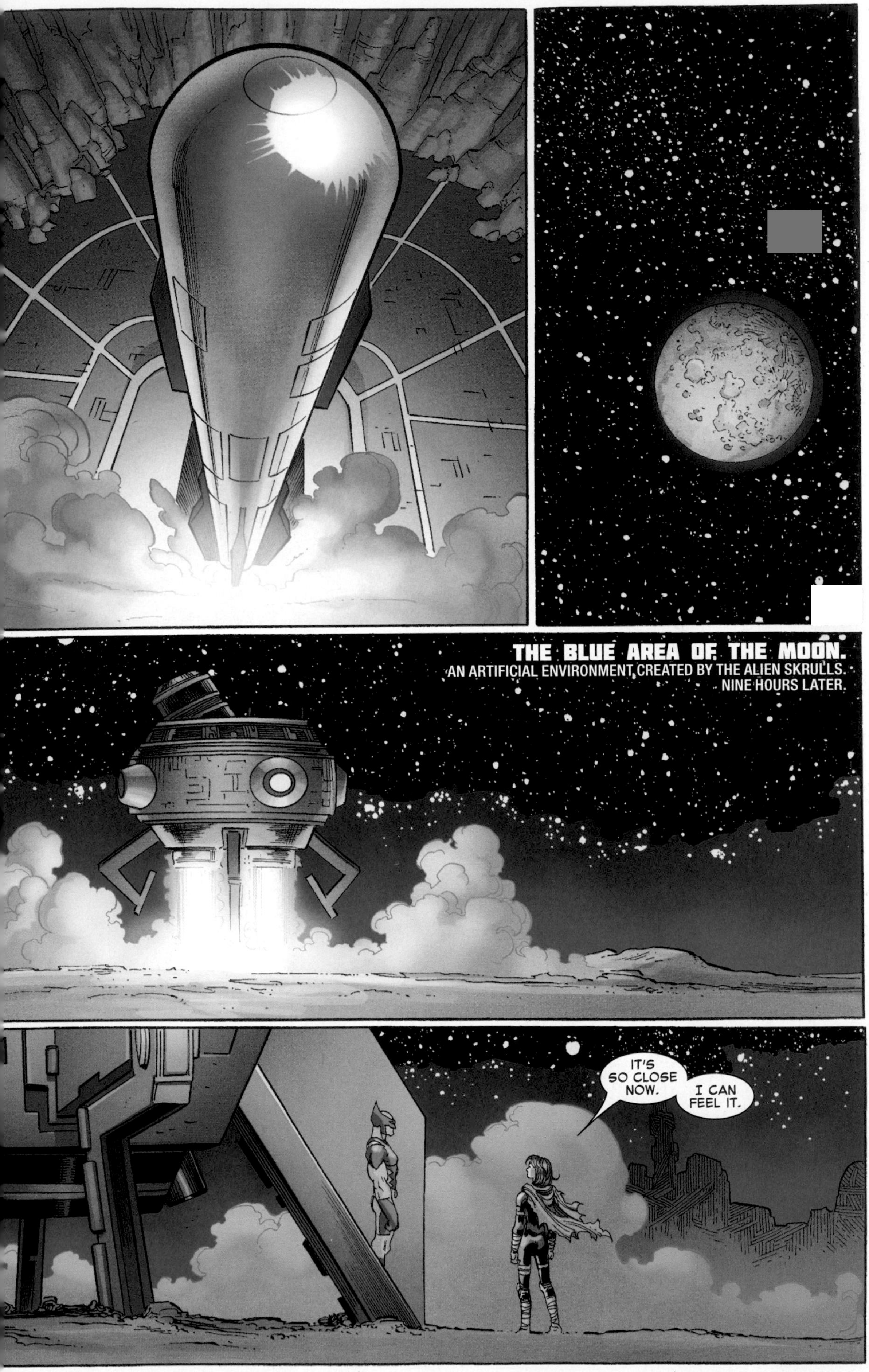
THE BLUE AREA OF THE MOON.
AN ARTIFICIAL ENVIRONMENT, CREATED BY THE ALIEN SKRULLS.
NINE HOURS LATER.
IT'S SO CLOSE NOW.
I CAN FEEL IT.

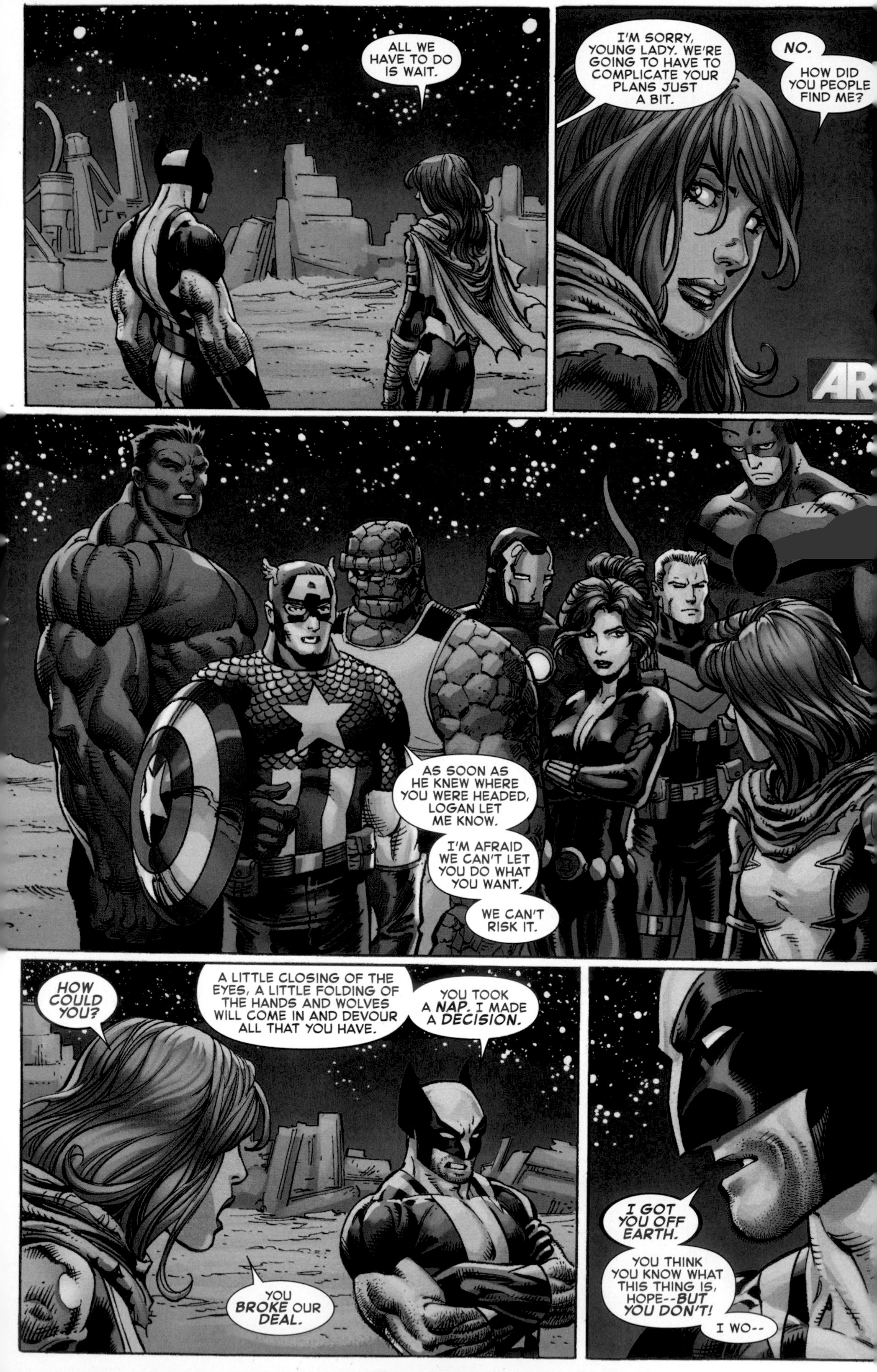
ALL WE HAVE TO DO IS WAIT.
I'M SORRY, YOUNG LADY. WE'RE GOING TO HAVE TO COMPLICATE YOUR PLANS JUST A BIT.
NO.
HOW DID YOU PEOPLE FIND ME?
AS SOON AS HE KNEW WHERE YOU WERE HEADED, LOGAN LET ME KNOW.
I'M AFRAID WE CAN'T LET YOU DO WHAT YOU WANT.
WE CAN'T RISK IT.
HOW COULD YOU?
A LITTLE CLOSING OF THE EYES, A LITTLE FOLDING OF THE HANDS AND WOLVES WILL COME IN AND DEVOUR ALL THAT YOU HAVE.
YOU TOOK A NAP. I MADE A DECISION.
YOU BROKE OUR DEAL.
I GOT YOU OFF EARTH.
YOU THINK YOU KNOW WHAT THIS THING IS, HOPE--BUT YOU DON'T!
I WO--

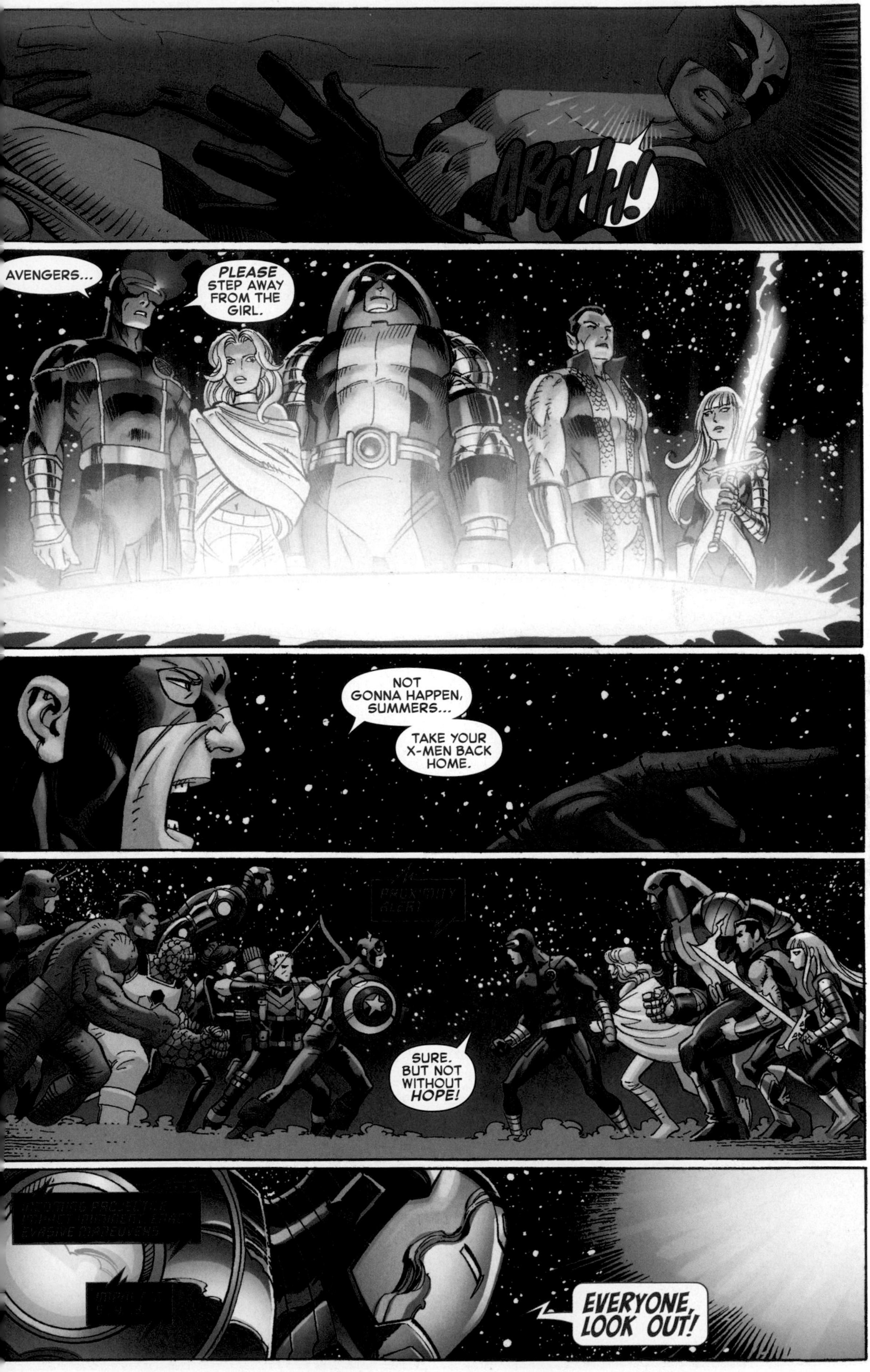
ARGHH!
AVENGERS...
PLEASE STEP AWAY FROM THE GIRL.
NOT GONNA HAPPEN, SUMMERS...
TAKE YOUR X-MEN BACK HOME.
SURE. BUT NOT WITHOUT HOPE!
EVERYONE, LOOK OUT!

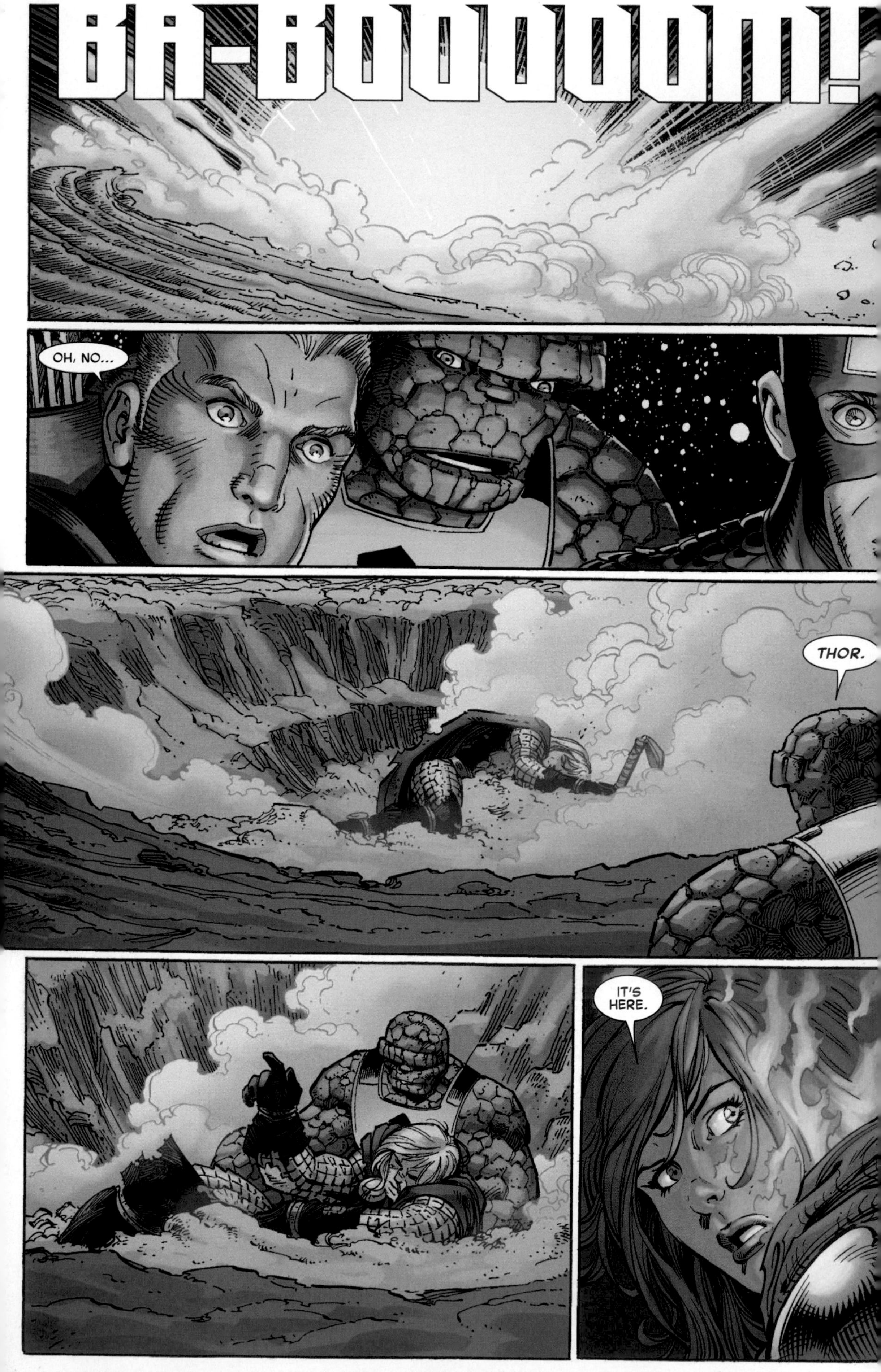
BA-BOOOOOM!
OH, NO...
THOR.
IT'S HERE.

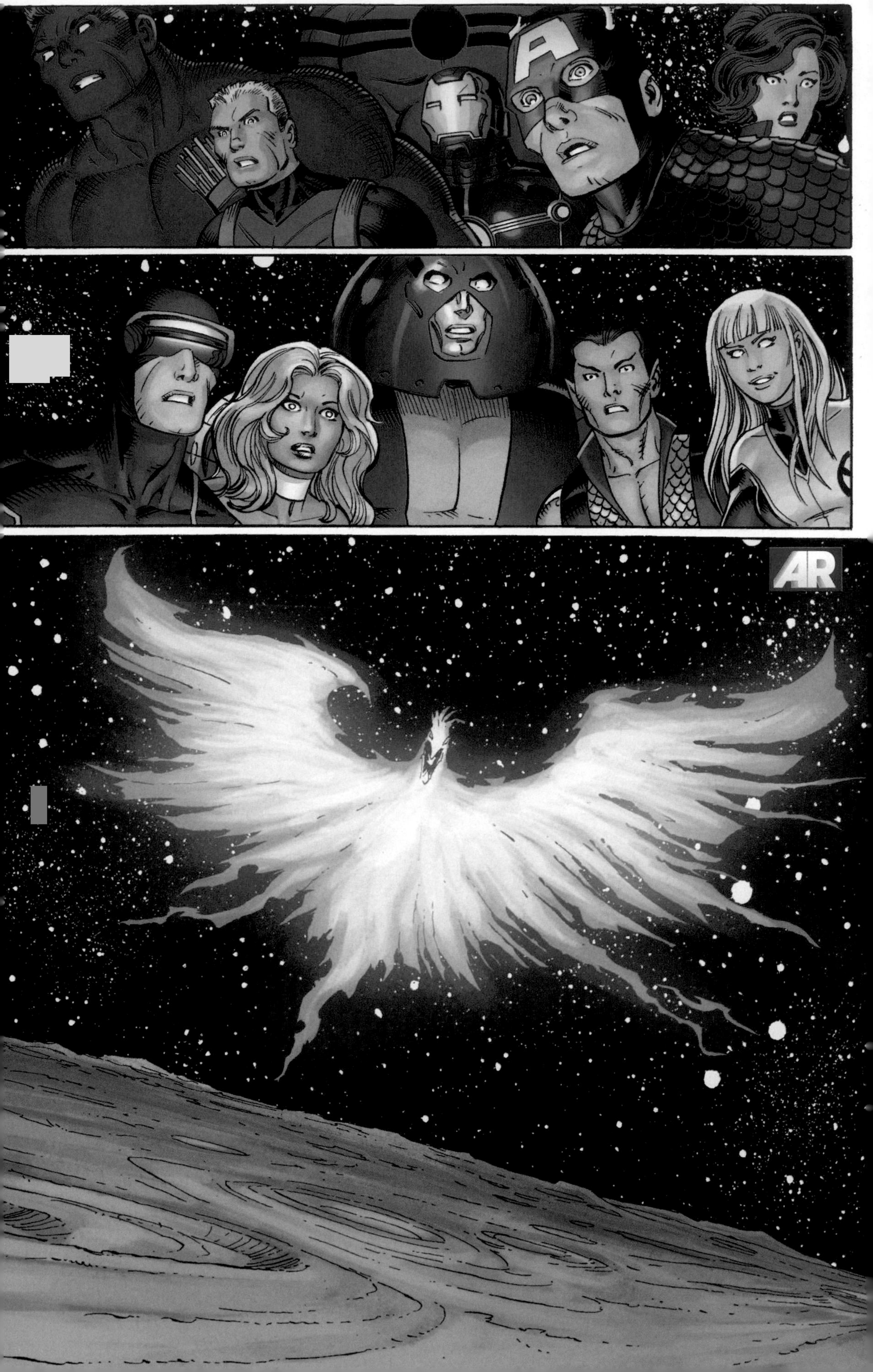

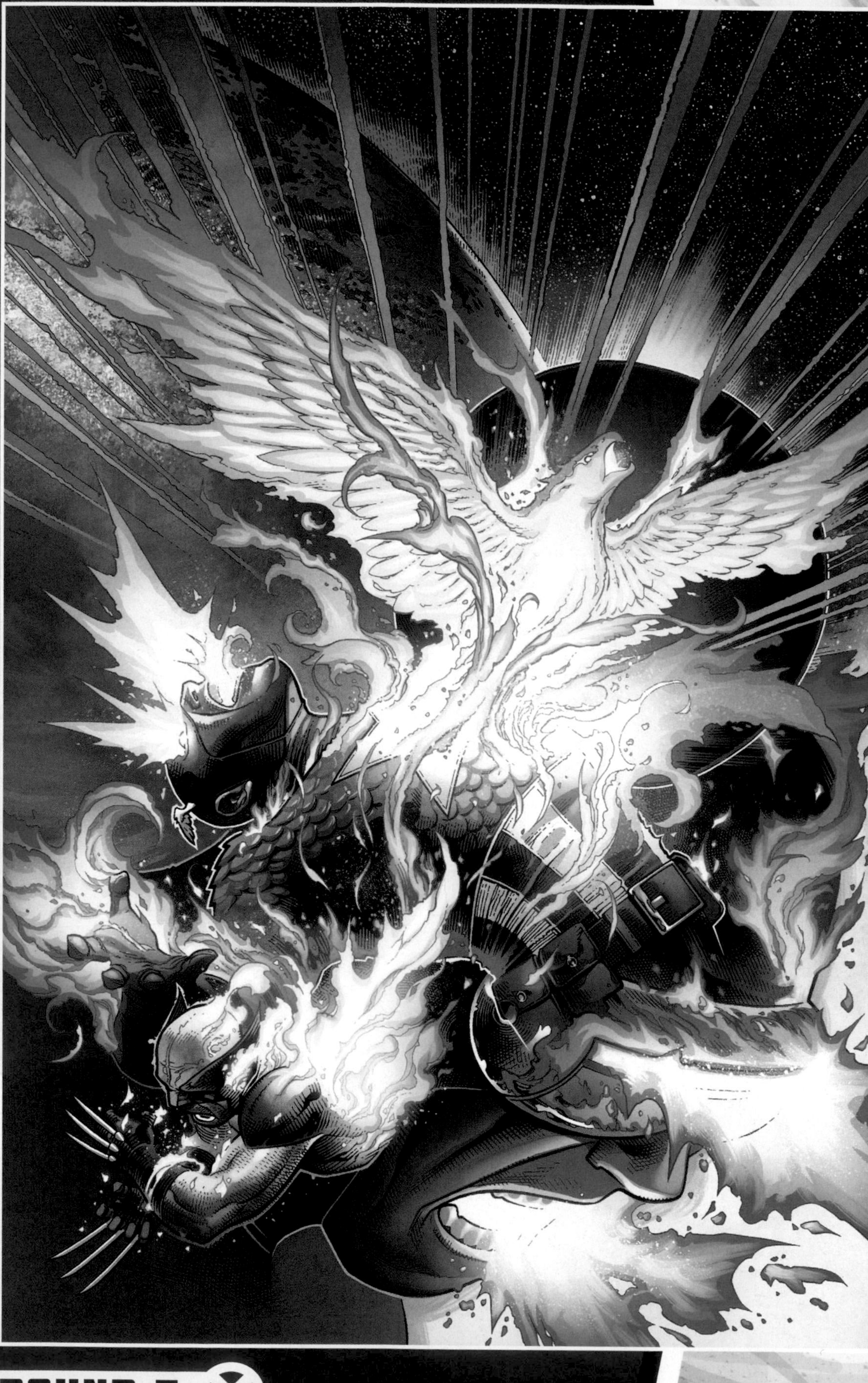

ROUND 5

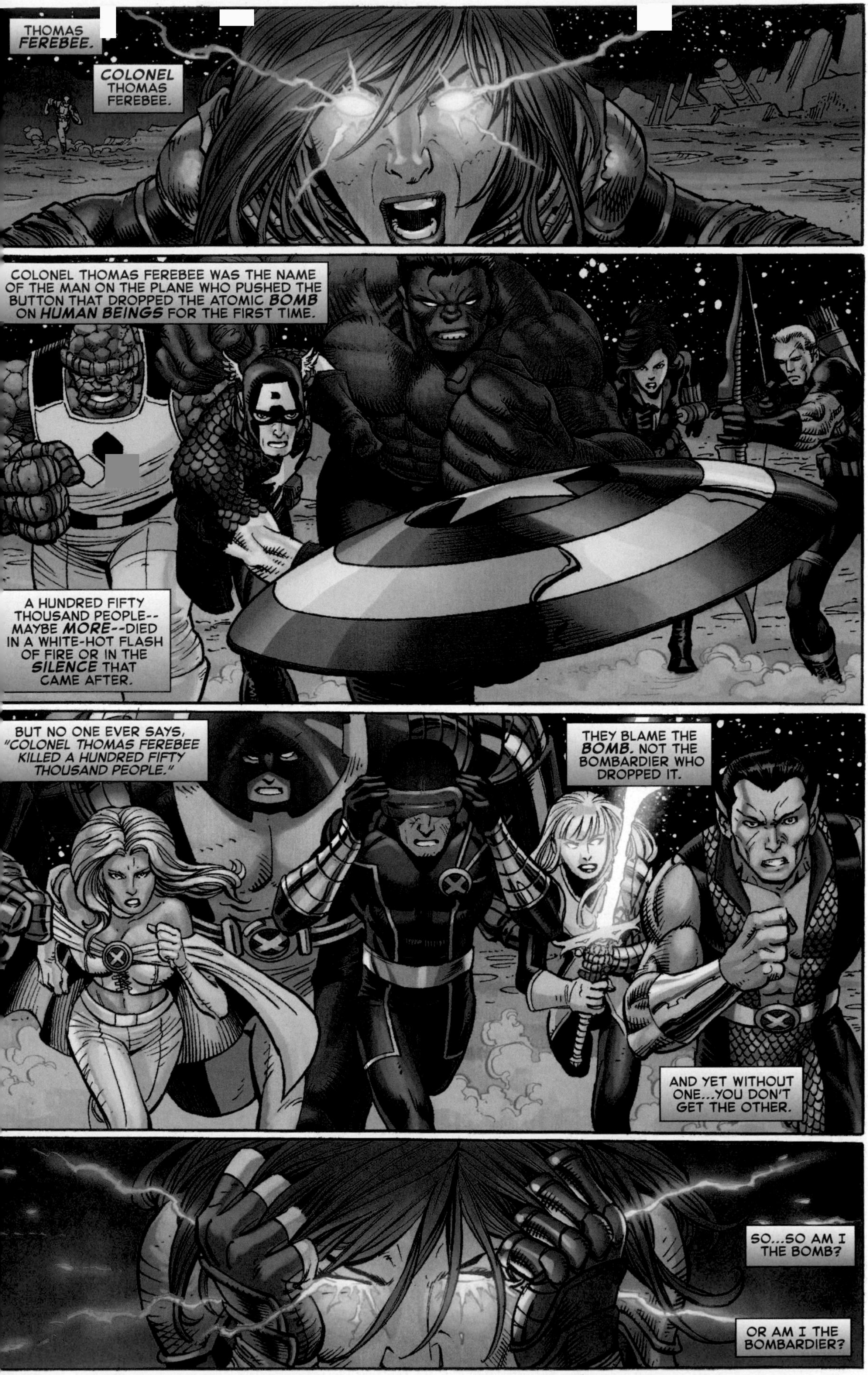
THOMAS FEREBEE.
COLONEL THOMAS FEREBEE.
COLONEL THOMAS FEREBEE WAS THE NAME OF THE MAN ON THE PLANE WHO PUSHED THE BUTTON THAT DROPPED THE ATOMIC BOMB ON HUMAN BEINGS FOR THE FIRST TIME.
A HUNDRED FIFTY THOUSAND PEOPLE--MAYBE MORE--DIED IN A WHITE-HOT FLASH OF FIRE OR IN THE SILENCE THAT CAME AFTER.
BUT NO ONE EVER SAYS, "COLONEL THOMAS FEREBEE KILLED A HUNDRED FIFTY THOUSAND PEOPLE."
THEY BLAME THE BOMB. NOT THE BOMBARDIER WHO DROPPED IT.
AND YET WITHOUT ONE...YOU DON'T GET THE OTHER.
SO...SO AM I THE BOMB?
OR AM I THE BOMBARDIER?

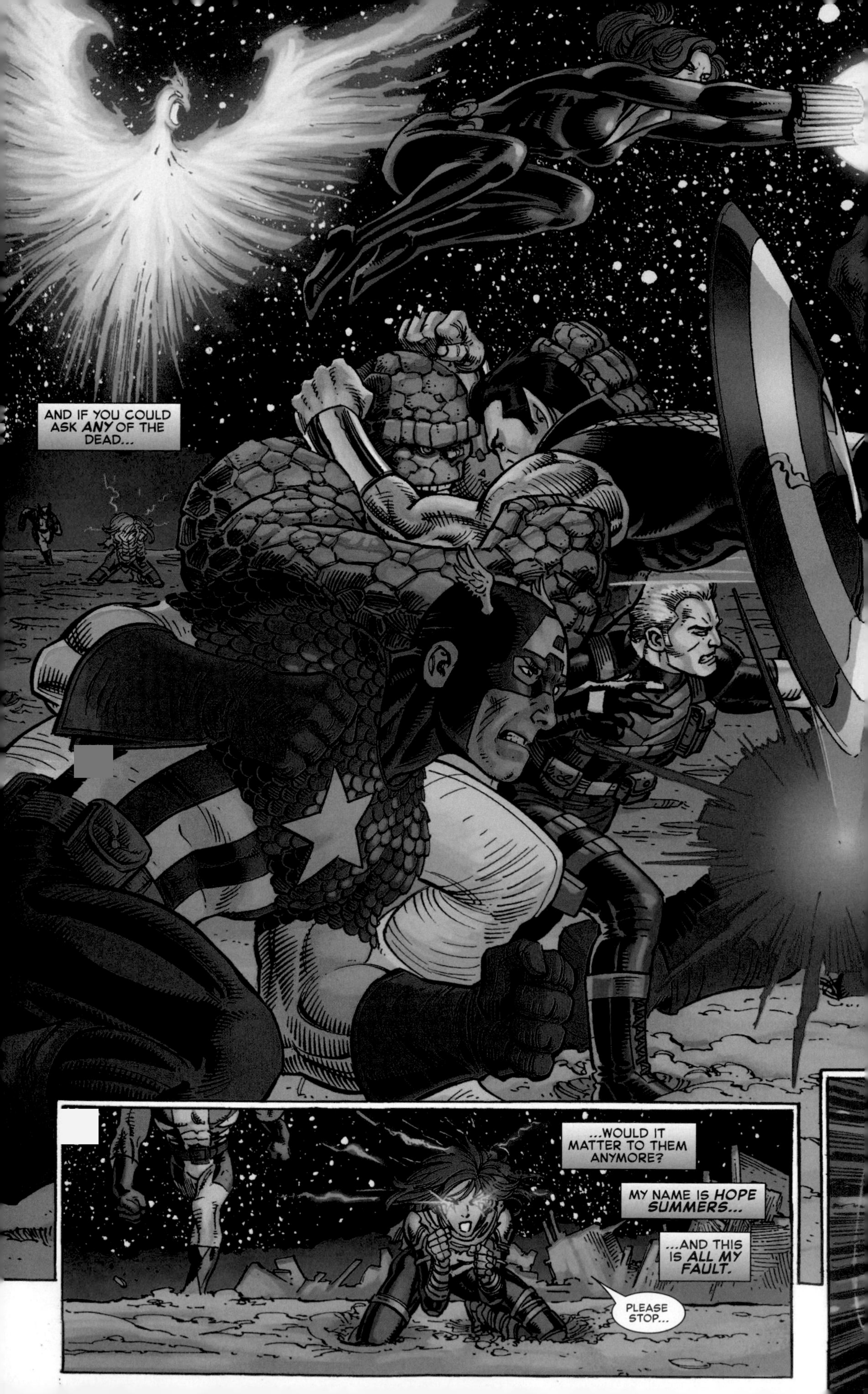
AND IF YOU COULD ASK ANY OF THE DEAD...
...WOULD IT MATTER TO THEM ANYMORE?
MY NAME IS HOPE SUMMERS...
...AND THIS IS ALL MY FAULT.
PLEASE STOP...

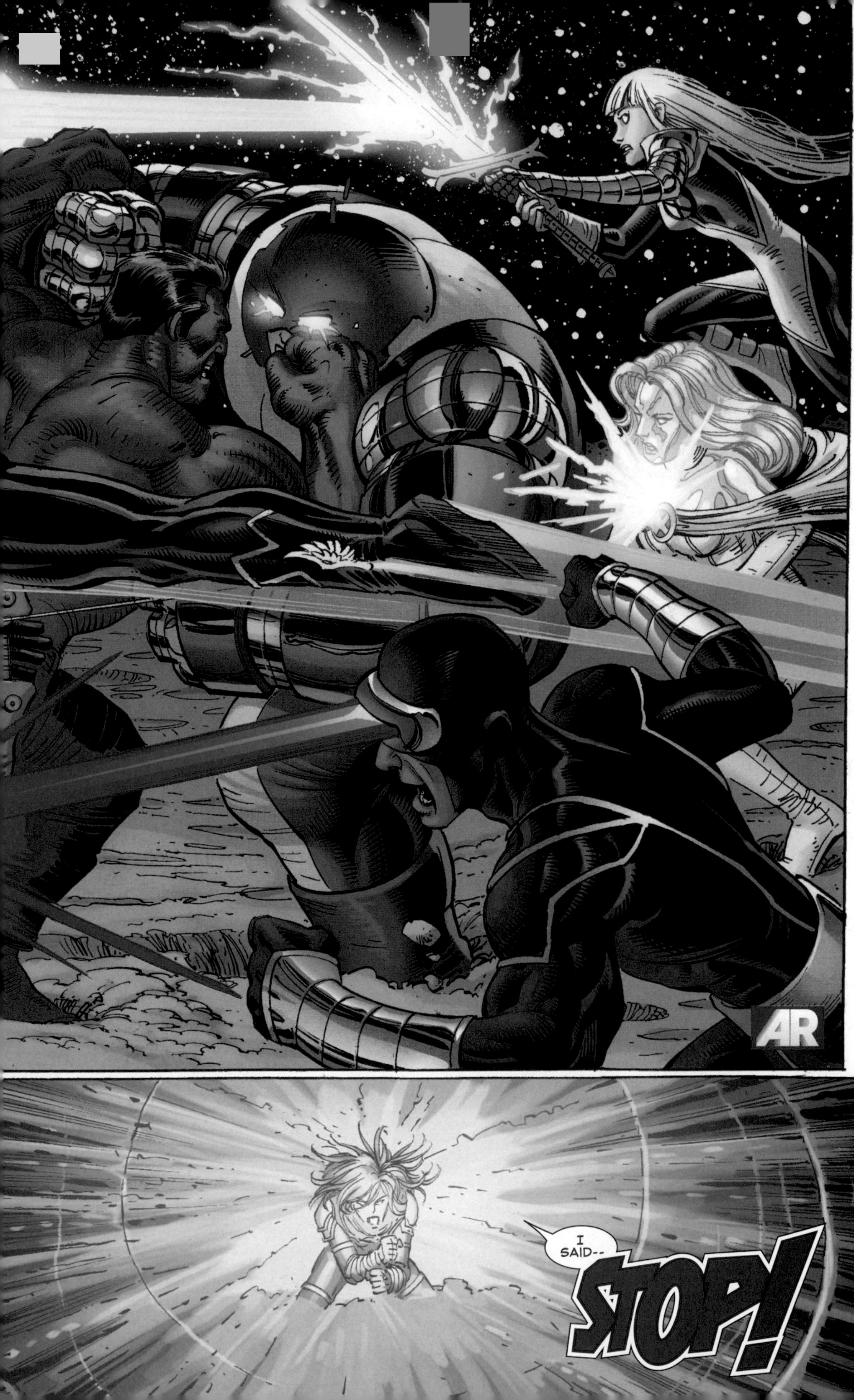
I SAID--
STOP!

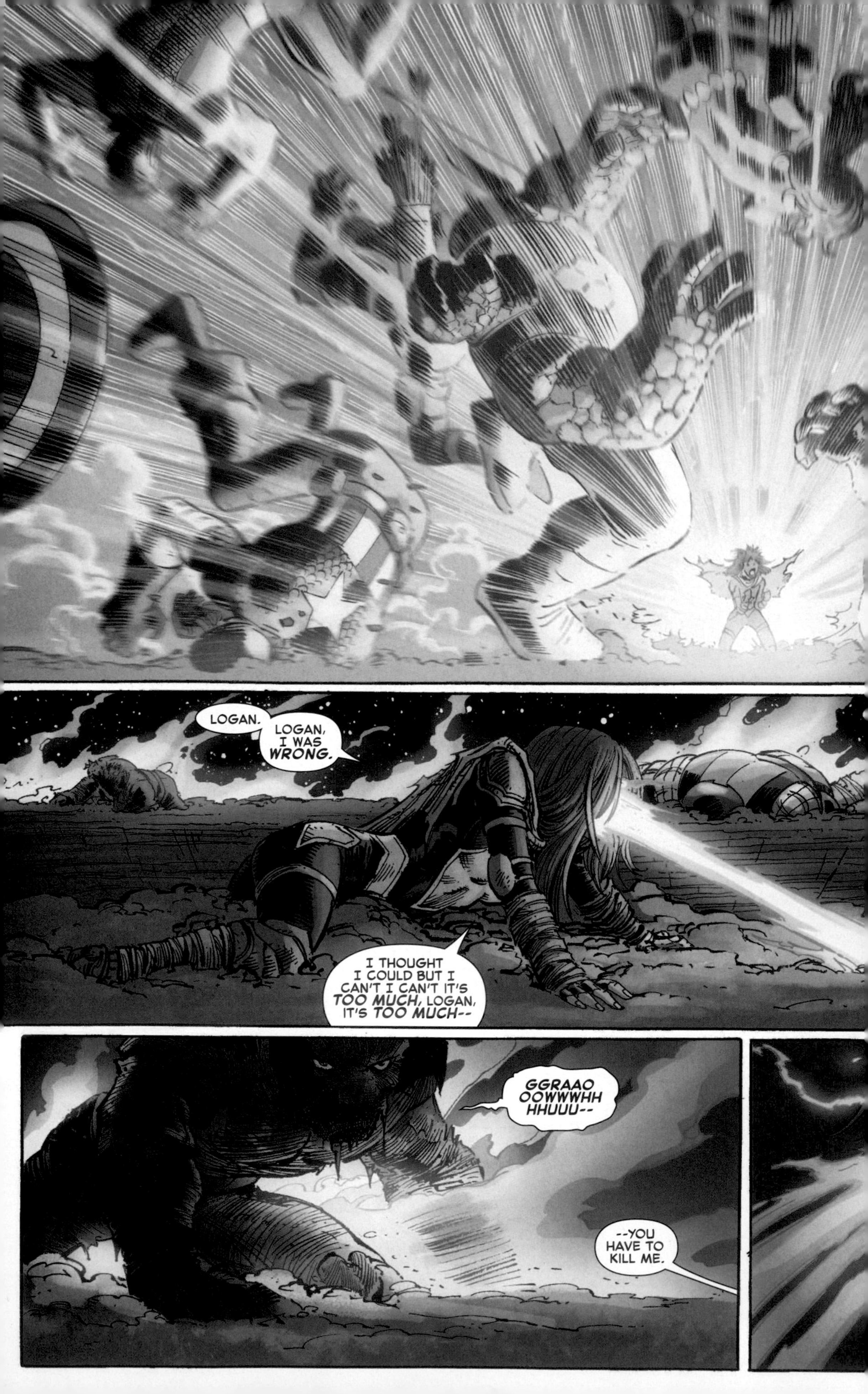
LOGAN.
LOGAN, I WAS WRONG.
I THOUGHT I COULD BUT I CAN'T I CAN'T IT'S TOO MUCH, LOGAN, IT'S TOO MUCH--
GGRAAO OOWWWHH HHUUU--
--YOU HAVE TO KILL ME.

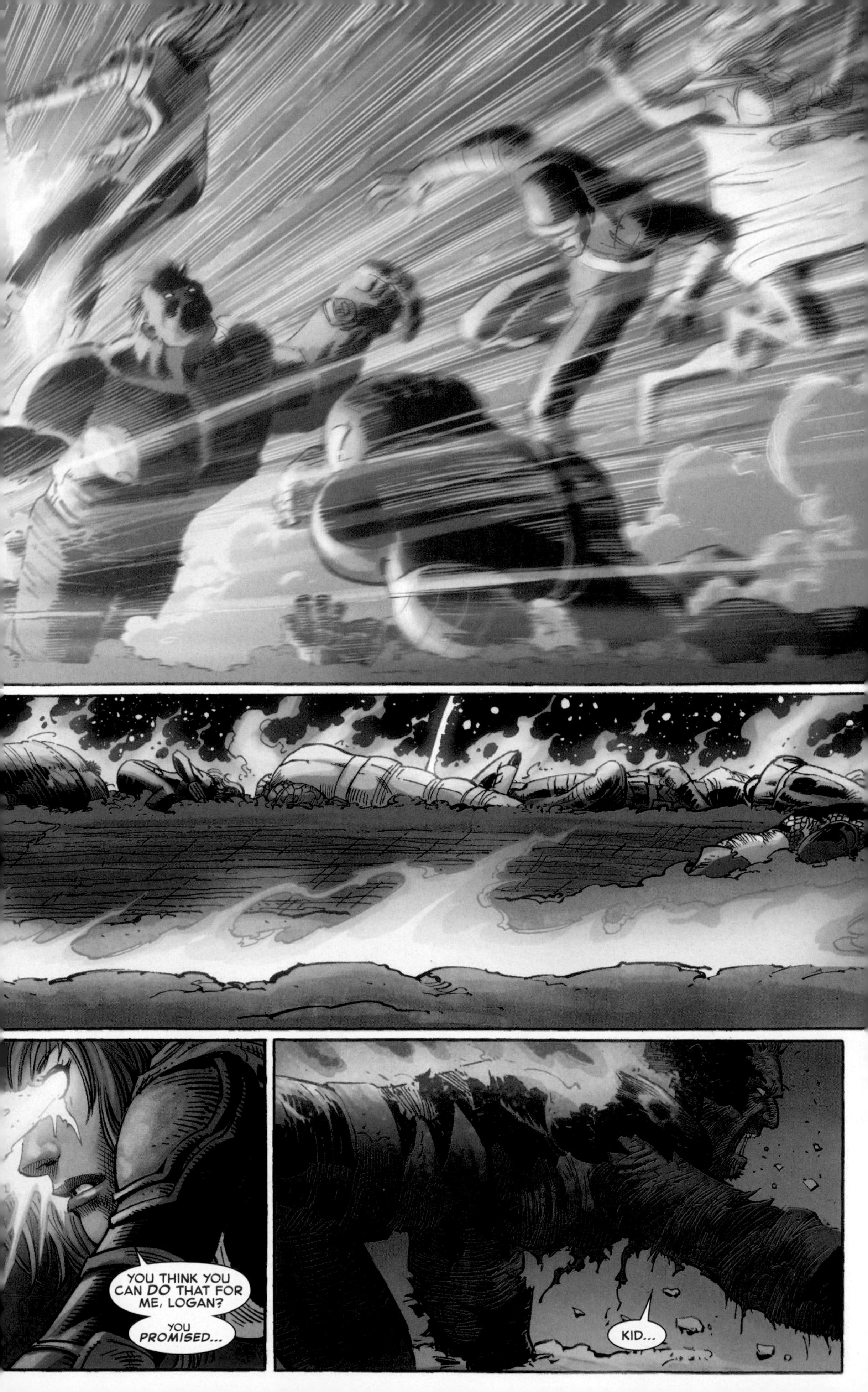
YOU THINK YOU CAN DO THAT FOR ME, LOGAN?
YOU PROMISED...
KID...

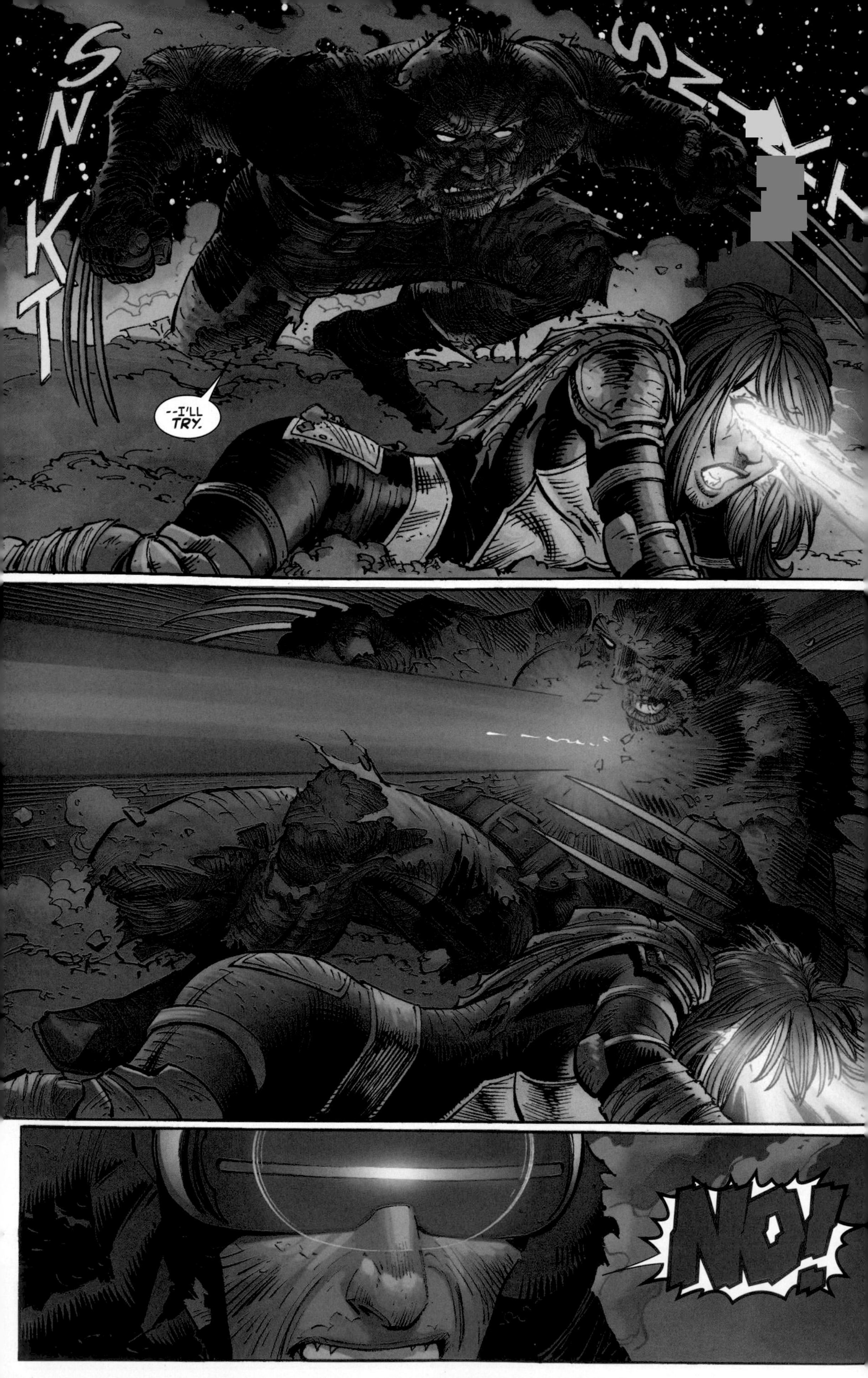
SNIKT
--I'LL TRY.
NO!

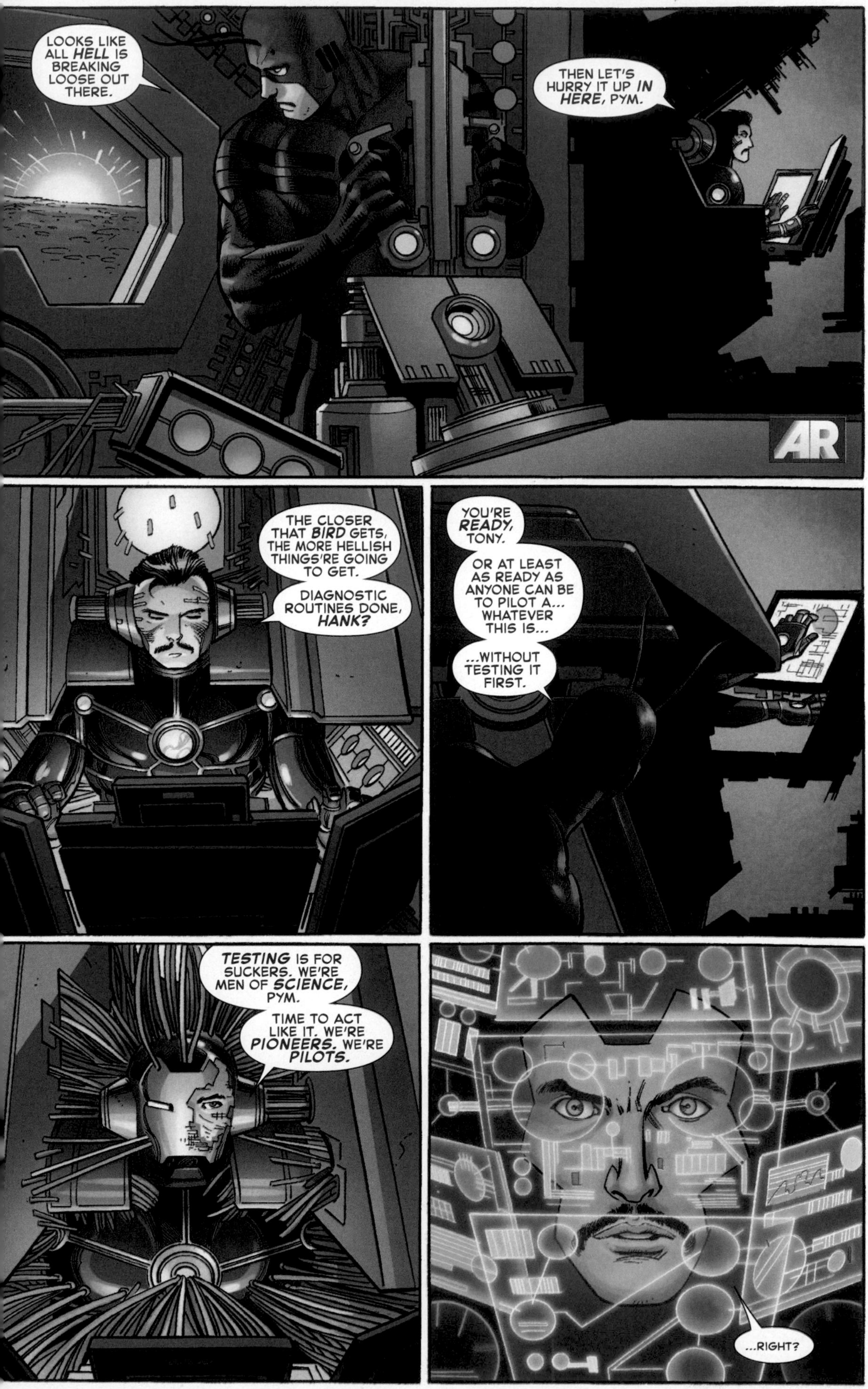
LOOKS LIKE ALL HELL IS BREAKING LOOSE OUT THERE.
THEN LET'S HURRY IT UP IN HERE, PYM.
AR
THE CLOSER THAT BIRD GETS, THE MORE HELLISH THINGS'RE GOING TO GET.
DIAGNOSTIC ROUTINES DONE, HANK?
YOU'RE READY, TONY.
OR AT LEAST AS READY AS ANYONE CAN BE TO PILOT A... WHATEVER THIS IS...
...WITHOUT TESTING IT FIRST.
TESTING IS FOR SUCKERS. WE'RE MEN OF SCIENCE, PYM.
TIME TO ACT LIKE IT. WE'RE PIONEERS. WE'RE PILOTS.
...RIGHT?

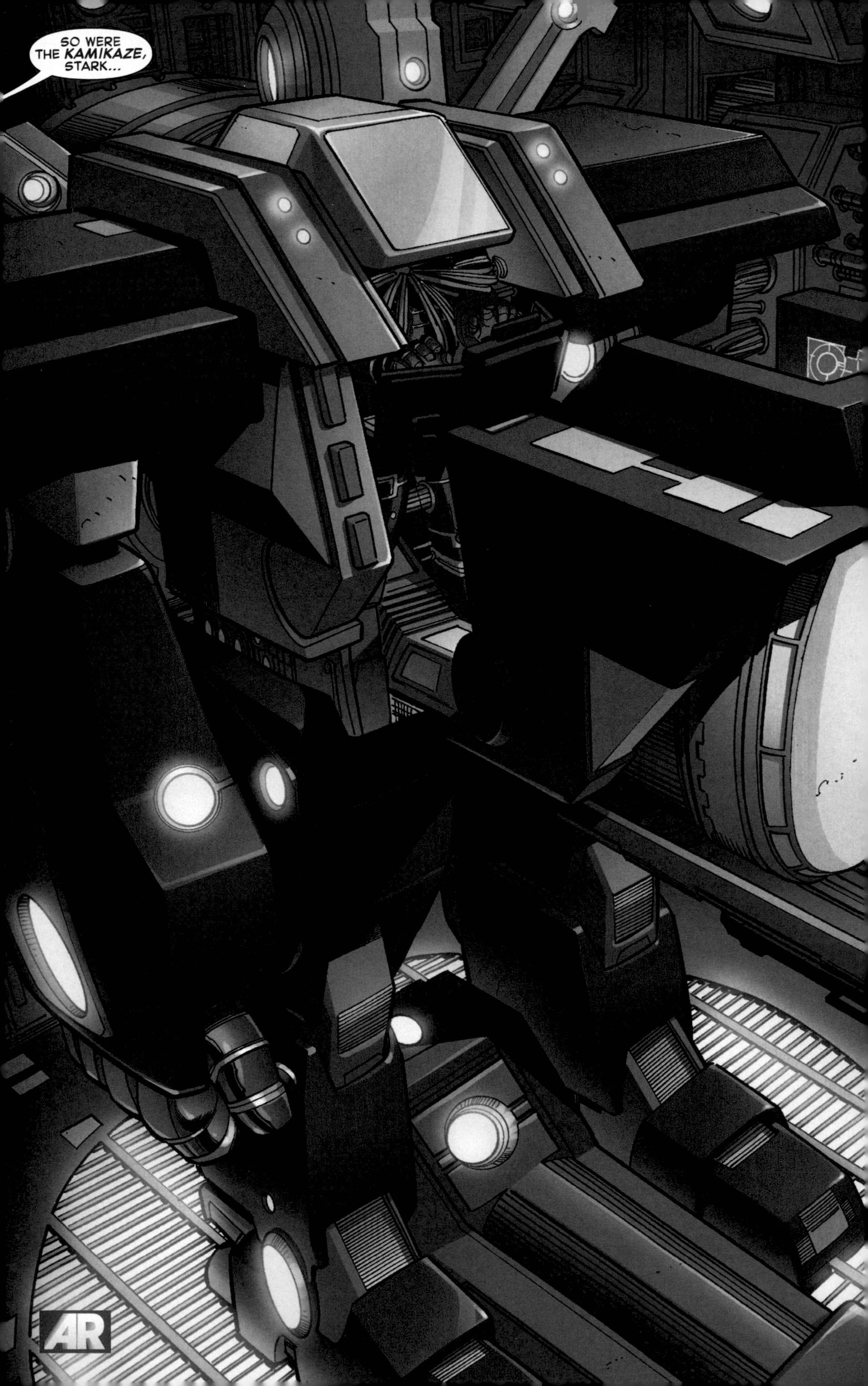
SO WERE THE KAMIKAZE, STARK...

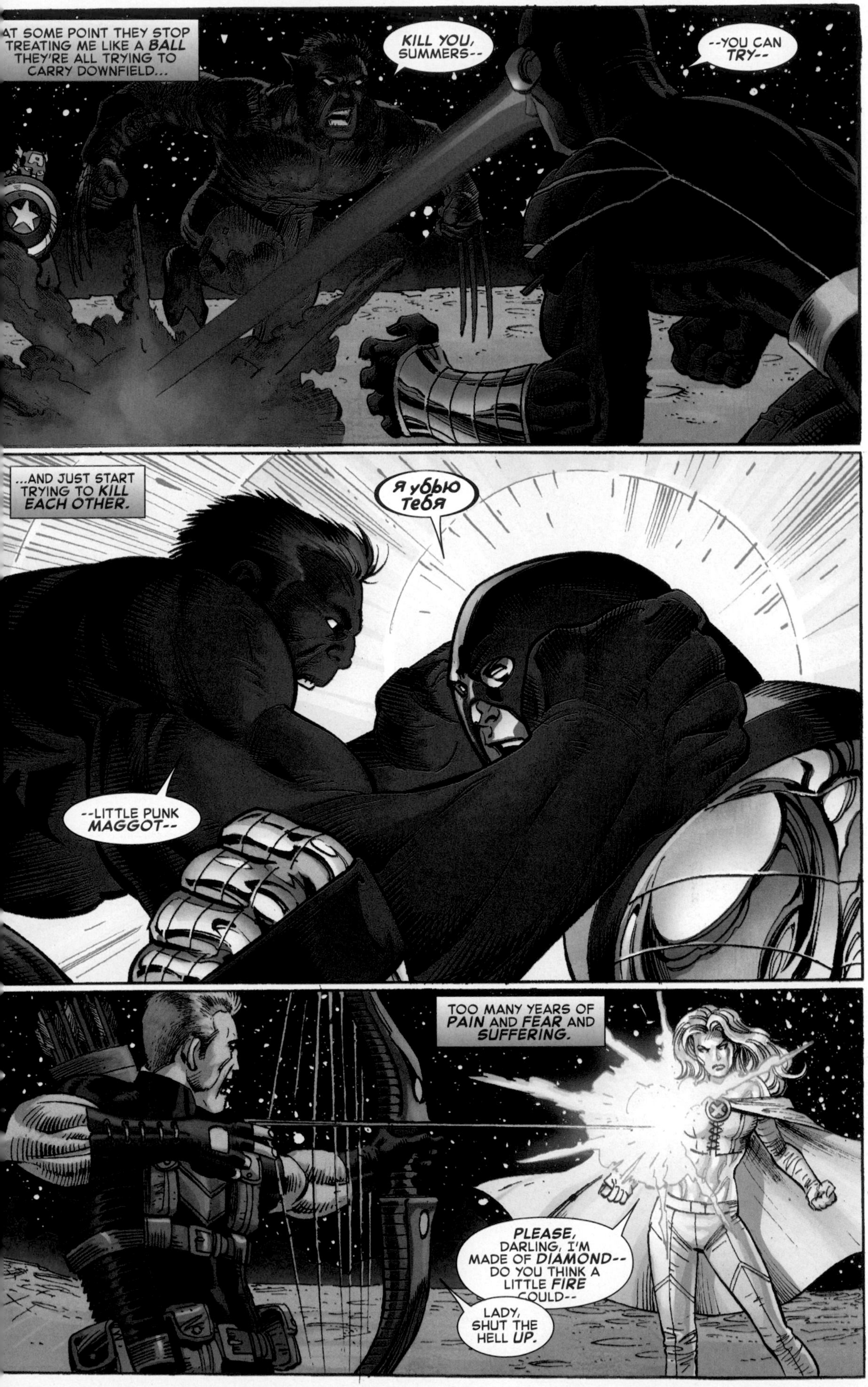
AT SOME POINT THEY STOP TREATING ME LIKE A BALL THEY'RE ALL TRYING TO CARRY DOWNFIELD...
KILL YOU, SUMMERS--
--YOU CAN TRY--
...AND JUST START TRYING TO KILL EACH OTHER.
Я убью тебя
--LITTLE PUNK MAGGOT--
TOO MANY YEARS OF PAIN AND FEAR AND SUFFERING.
PLEASE, DARLING, I'M MADE OF DIAMOND-- DO YOU THINK A LITTLE FIRE COULD--
LADY, SHUT THE HELL UP.

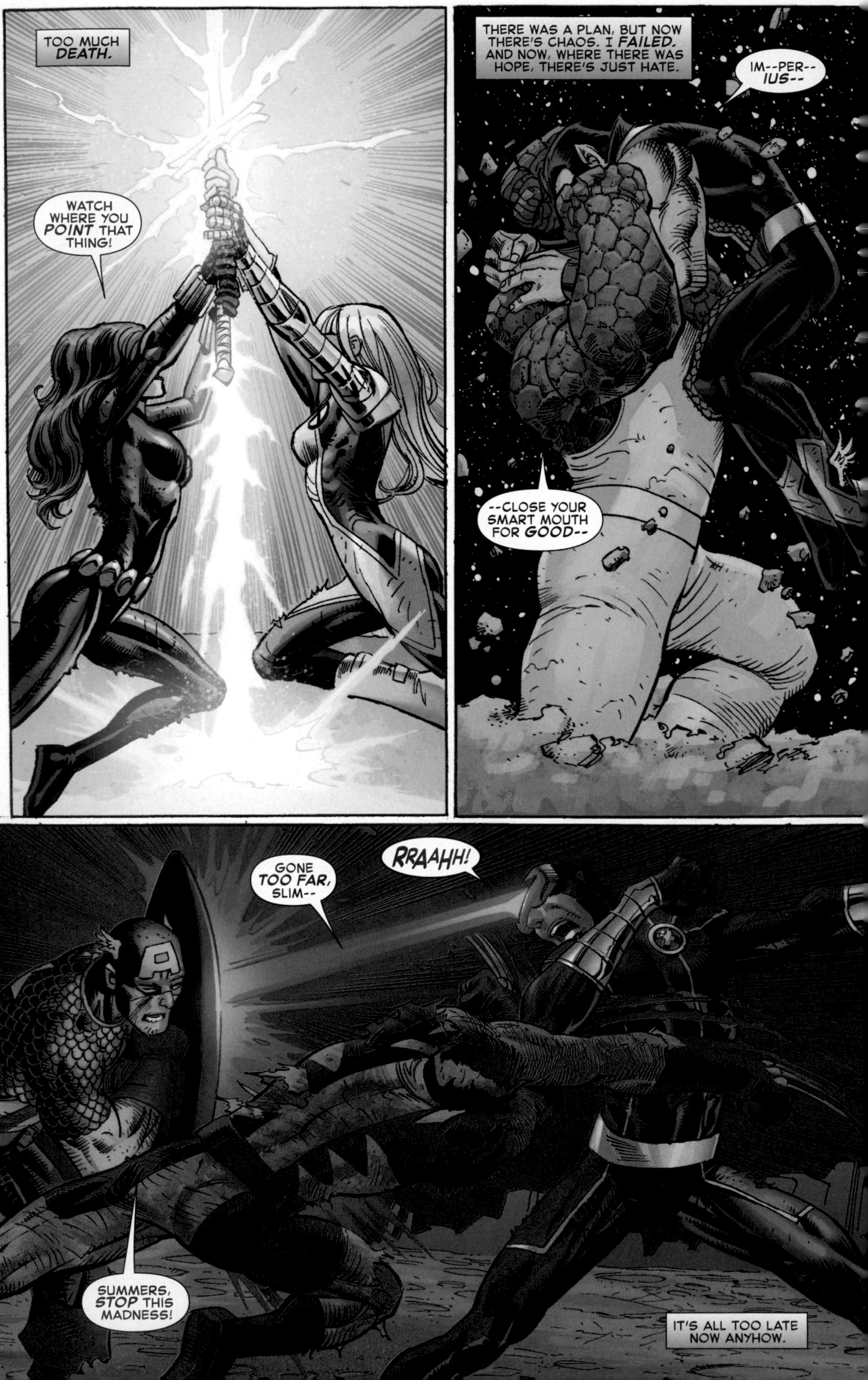
TOO MUCH DEATH.
WATCH WHERE YOU POINT THAT THING!
THERE WAS A PLAN, BUT NOW THERE'S CHAOS. I FAILED. AND NOW, WHERE THERE WAS HOPE, THERE'S JUST HATE.
IM--PER--IUS--
--CLOSE YOUR SMART MOUTH FOR GOOD--
GONE TOO FAR, SLIM--
RRAAHH!
SUMMERS, STOP THIS MADNESS!
IT'S ALL TOO LATE NOW ANYHOW.

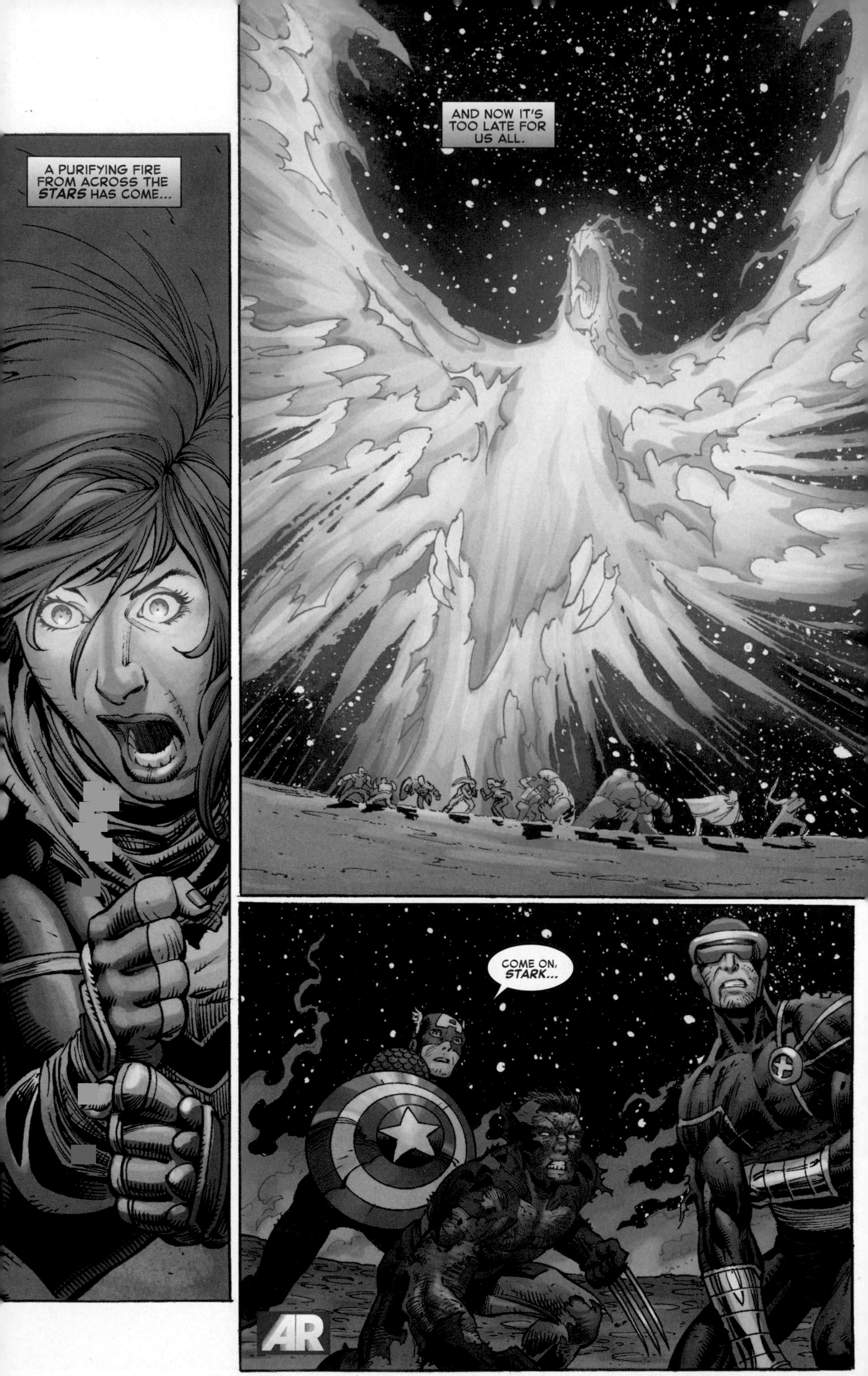
A PURIFYING FIRE FROM ACROSS THE STARS HAS COME...
AND NOW IT'S TOO LATE FOR US ALL.
COME ON, STARK...

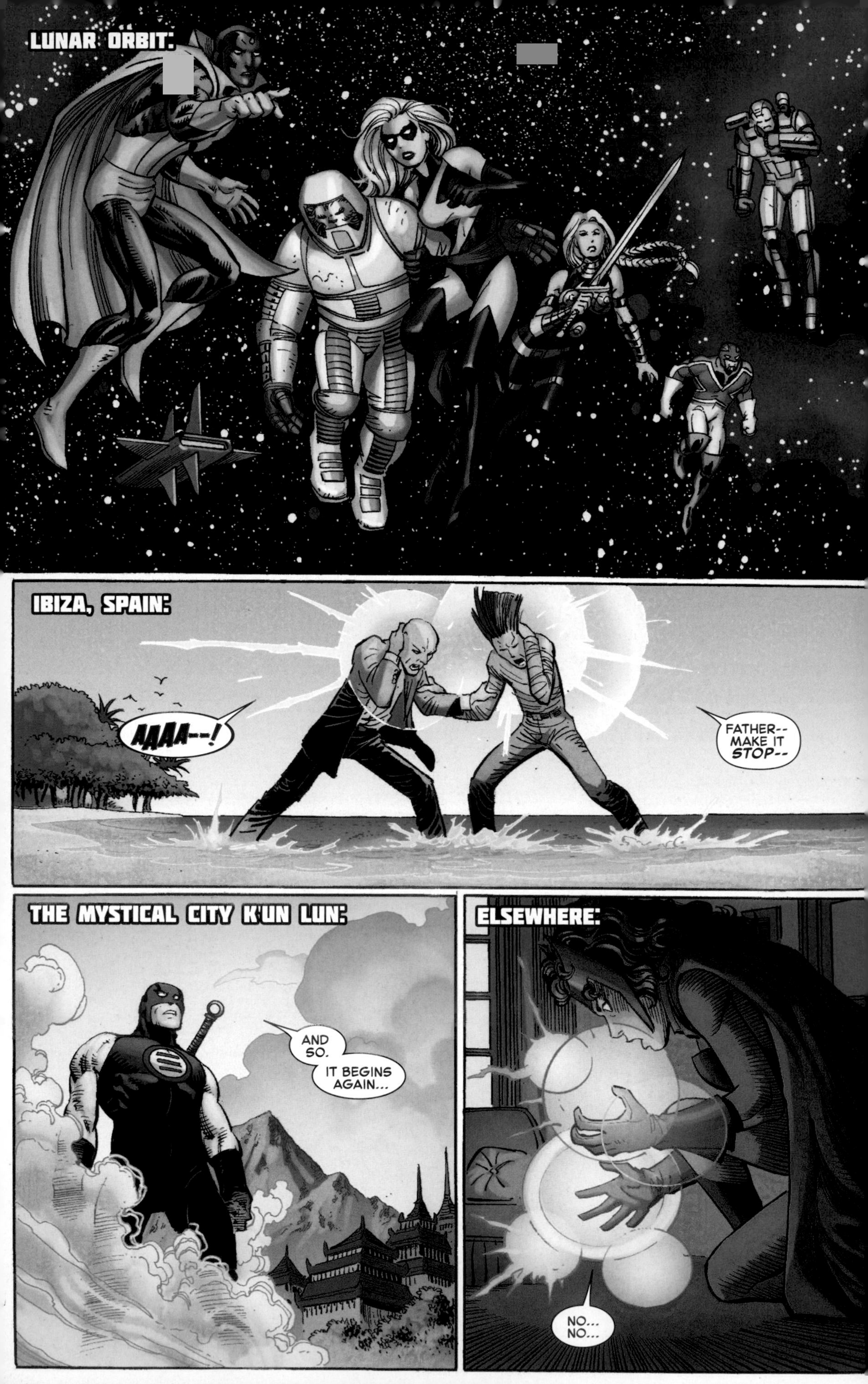
LUNAR ORBIT:
IBIZA, SPAIN:
AAAA--!
FATHER-- MAKE IT STOP--
THE MYSTICAL CITY K'UN LUN:
AND SO.
IT BEGINS AGAIN...
ELSEWHERE:
NO... NO...

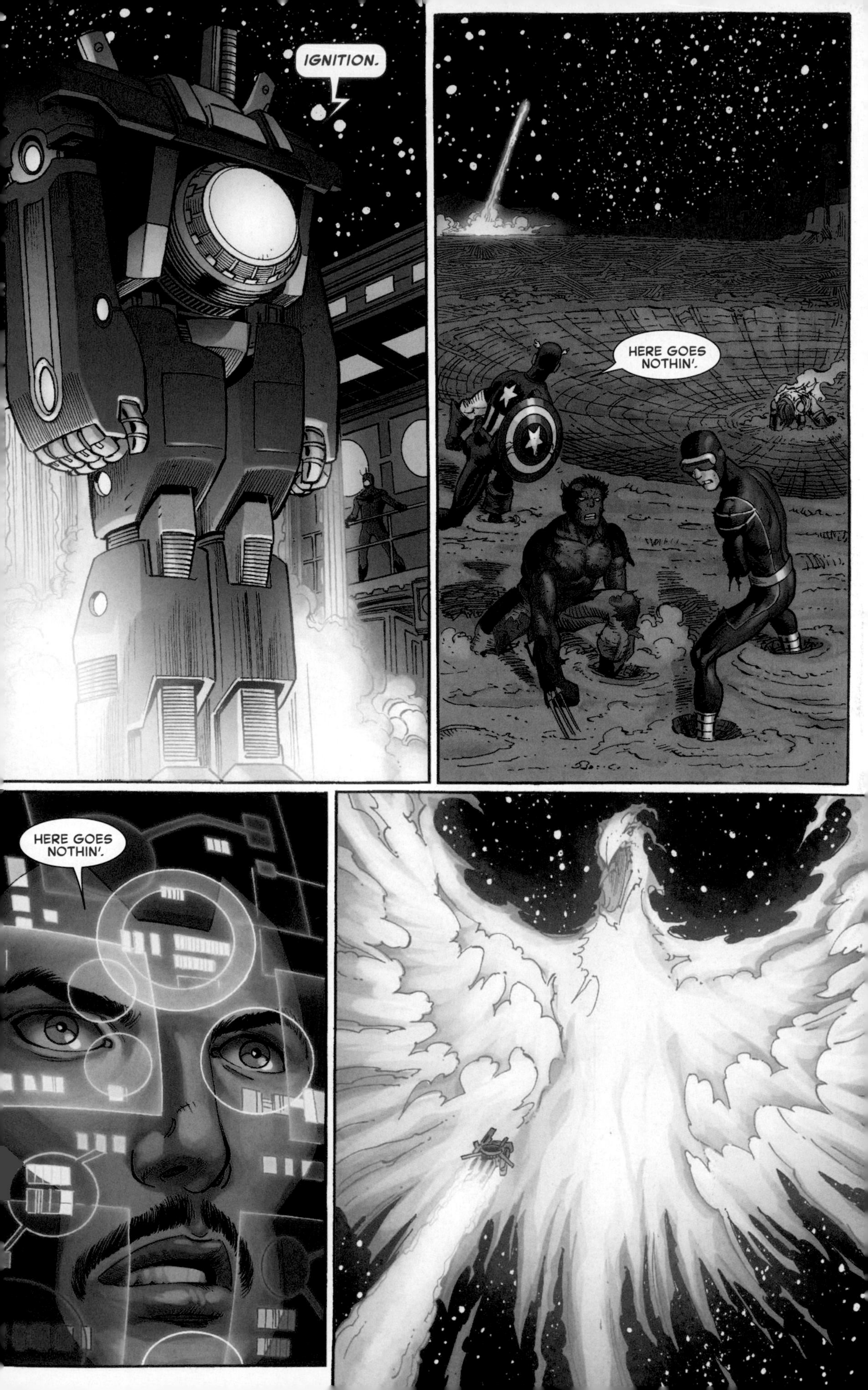

IGNITION.
HERE GOES NOTHIN'.
HERE GOES NOTHIN'.

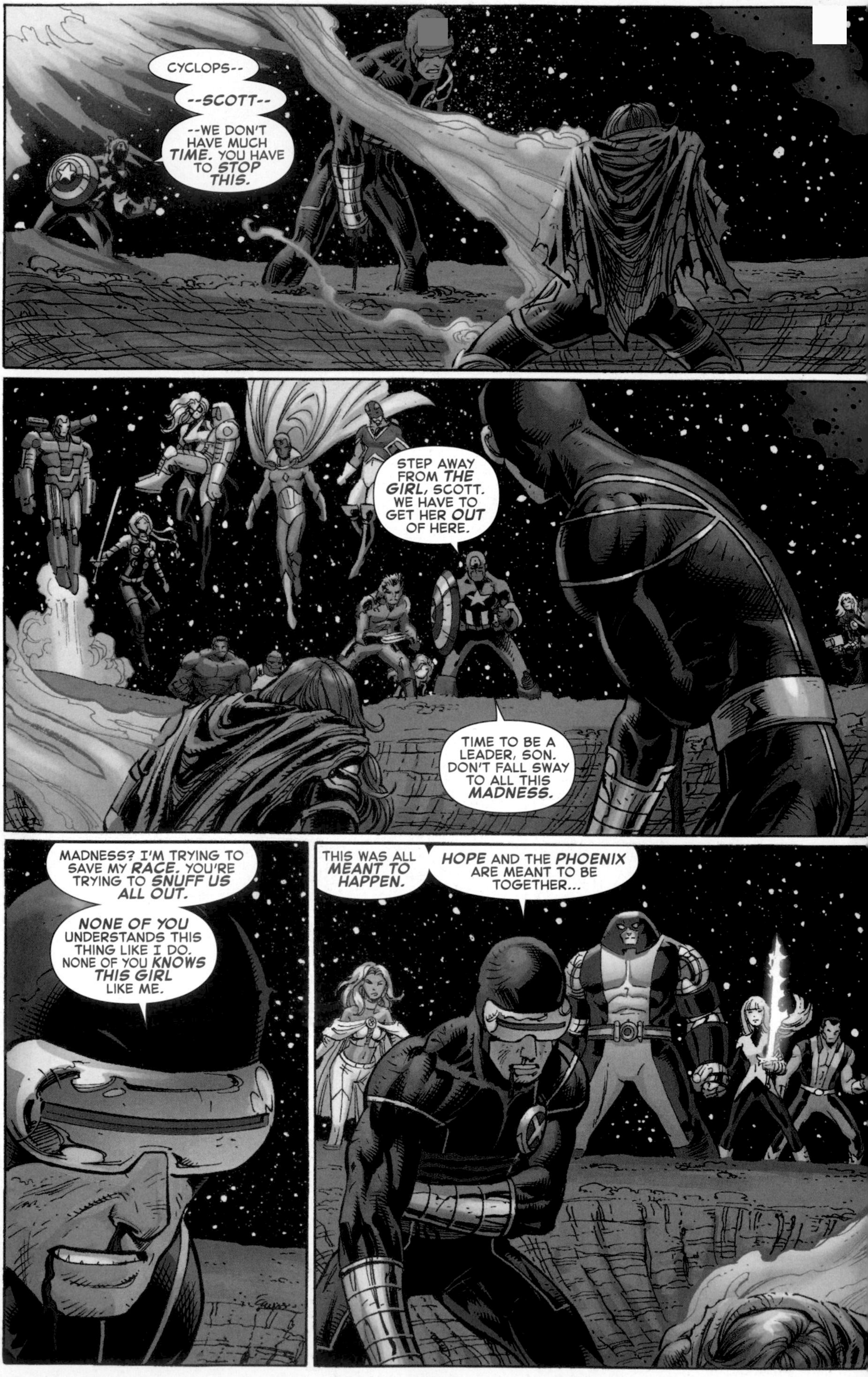
CYCLOPS--
--SCOTT--
--WE DON'T HAVE MUCH TIME. YOU HAVE TO STOP THIS.
STEP AWAY FROM THE GIRL, SCOTT. WE HAVE TO GET HER OUT OF HERE.
TIME TO BE A LEADER, SON. DON'T FALL SWAY TO ALL THIS MADNESS.
MADNESS? I'M TRYING TO SAVE MY RACE. YOU'RE TRYING TO SNUFF US ALL OUT.
NONE OF YOU UNDERSTANDS THIS THING LIKE I DO. NONE OF YOU KNOWS THIS GIRL LIKE ME.
THIS WAS ALL MEANT TO HAPPEN.
HOPE AND THE PHOENIX ARE MEANT TO BE TOGETHER...

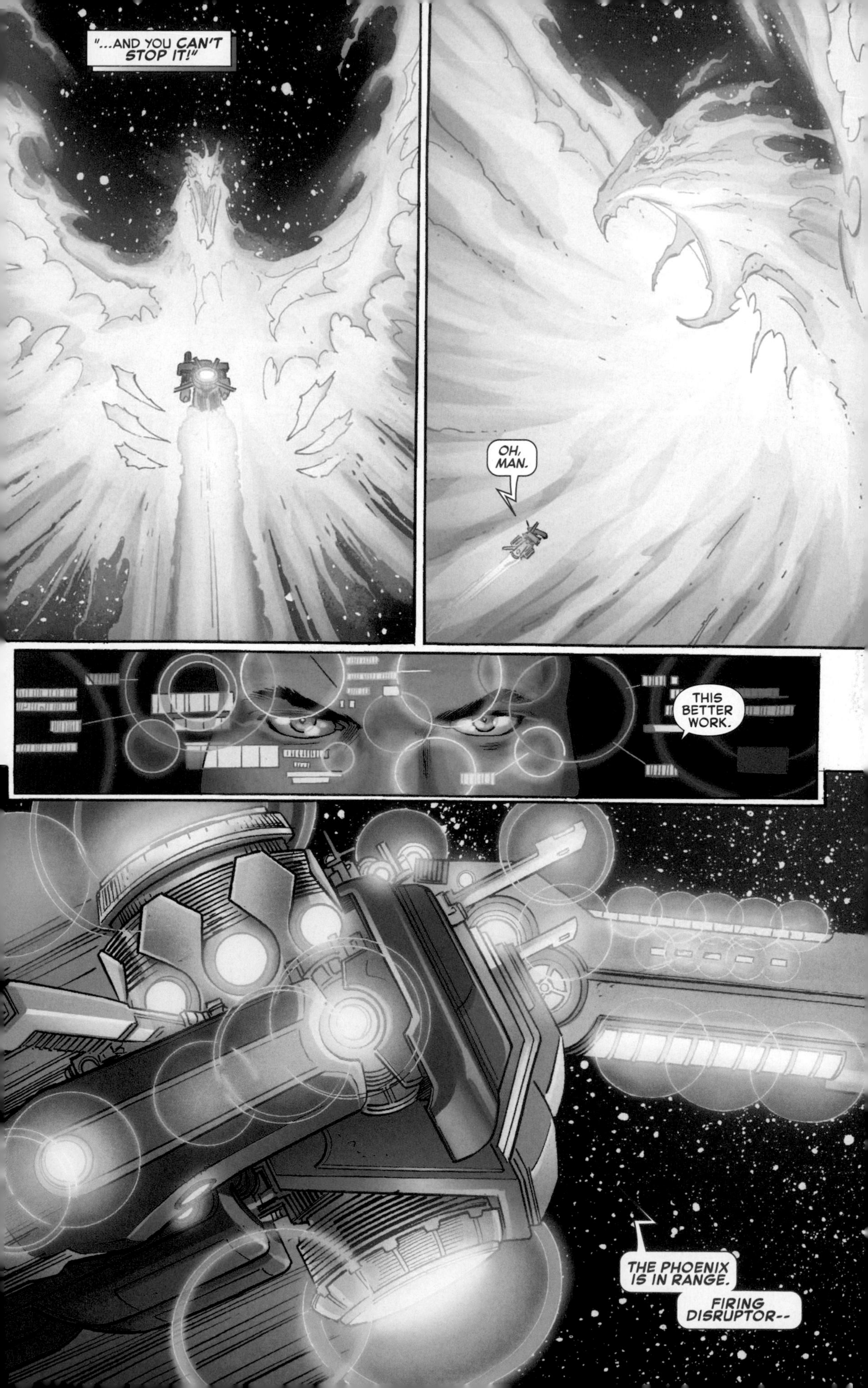
"...AND YOU CAN'T STOP IT!"
OH, MAN.
THIS BETTER WORK.
THE PHOENIX IS IN RANGE.
FIRING DISRUPTOR--

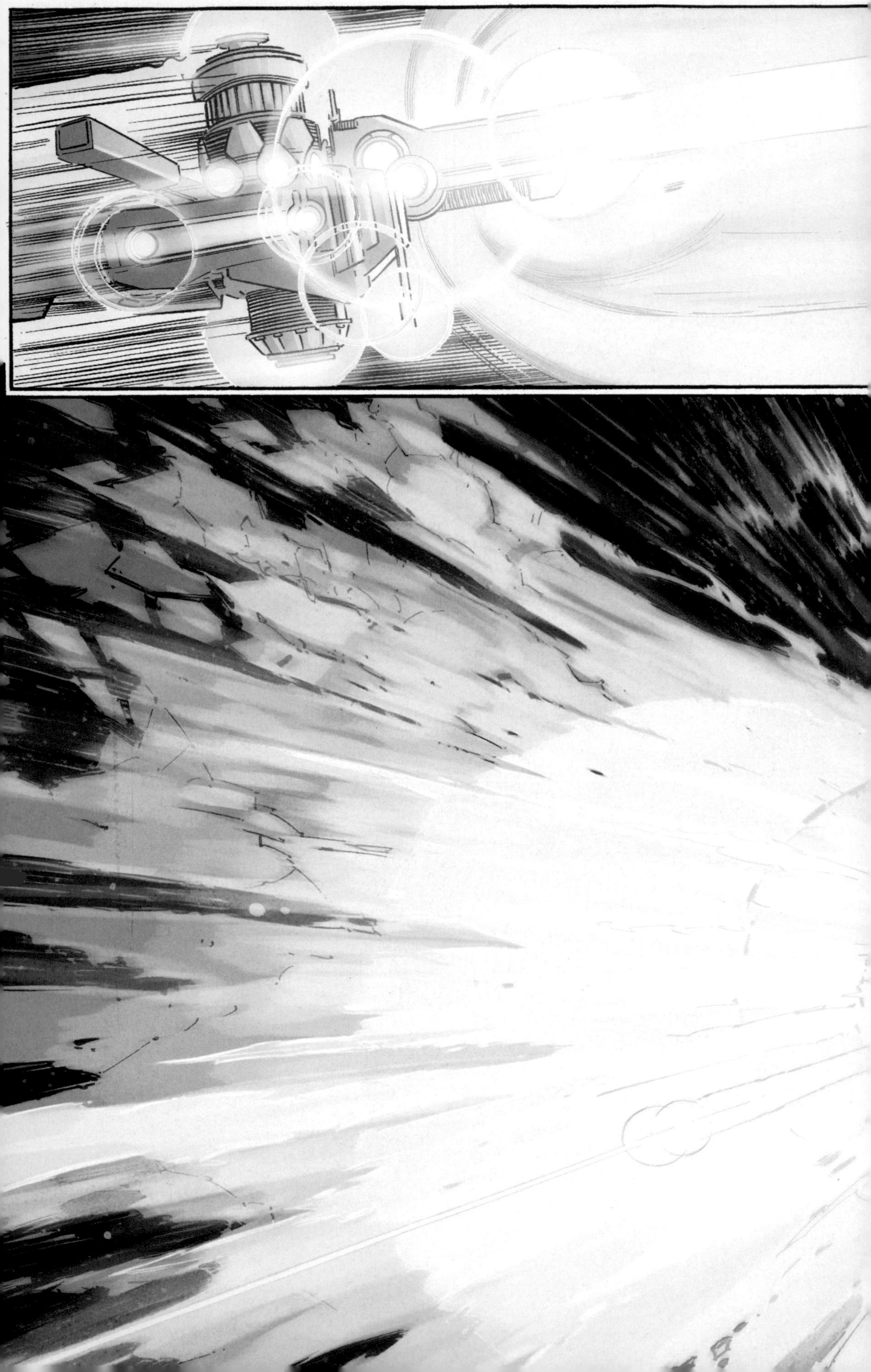

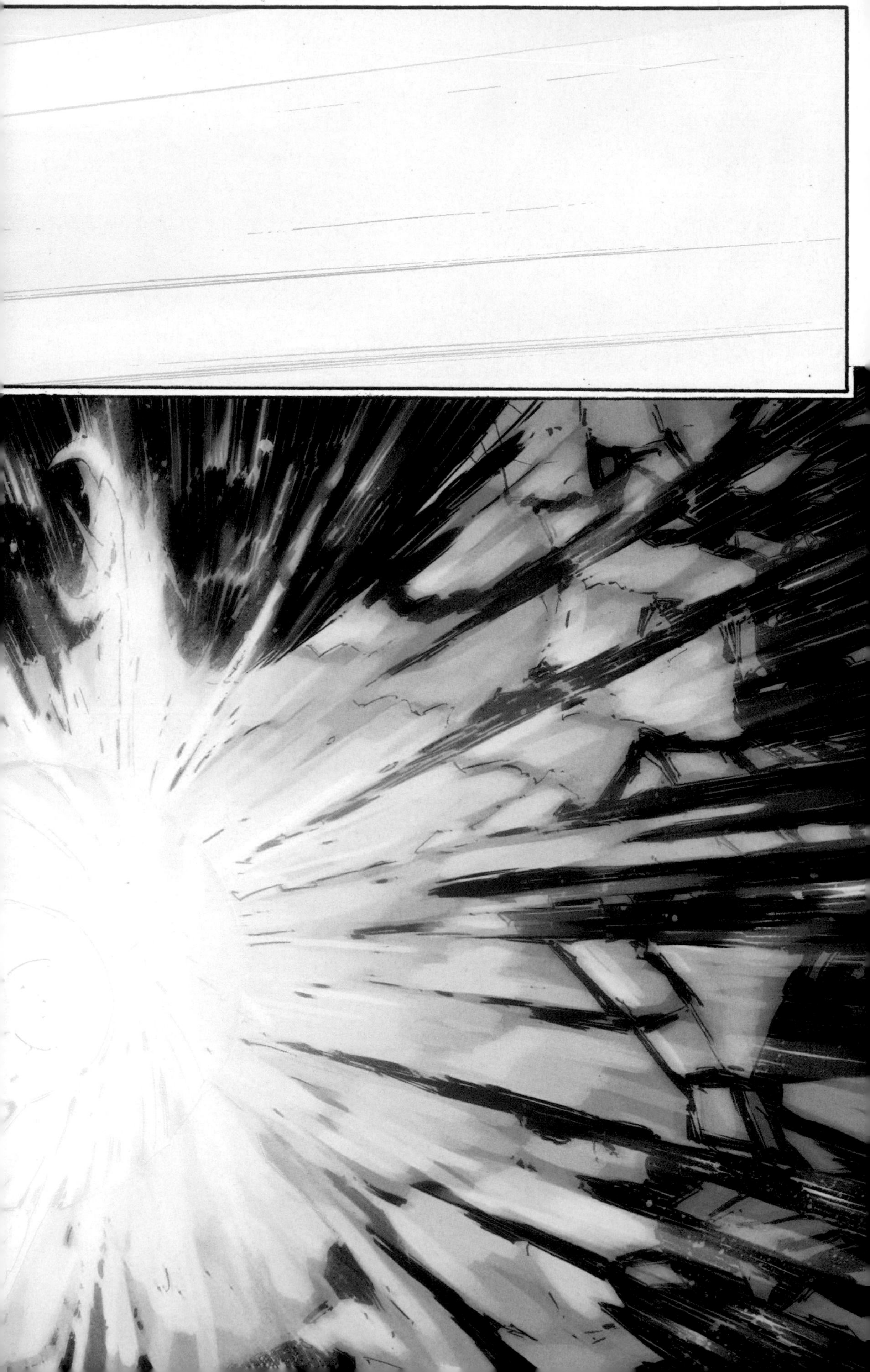

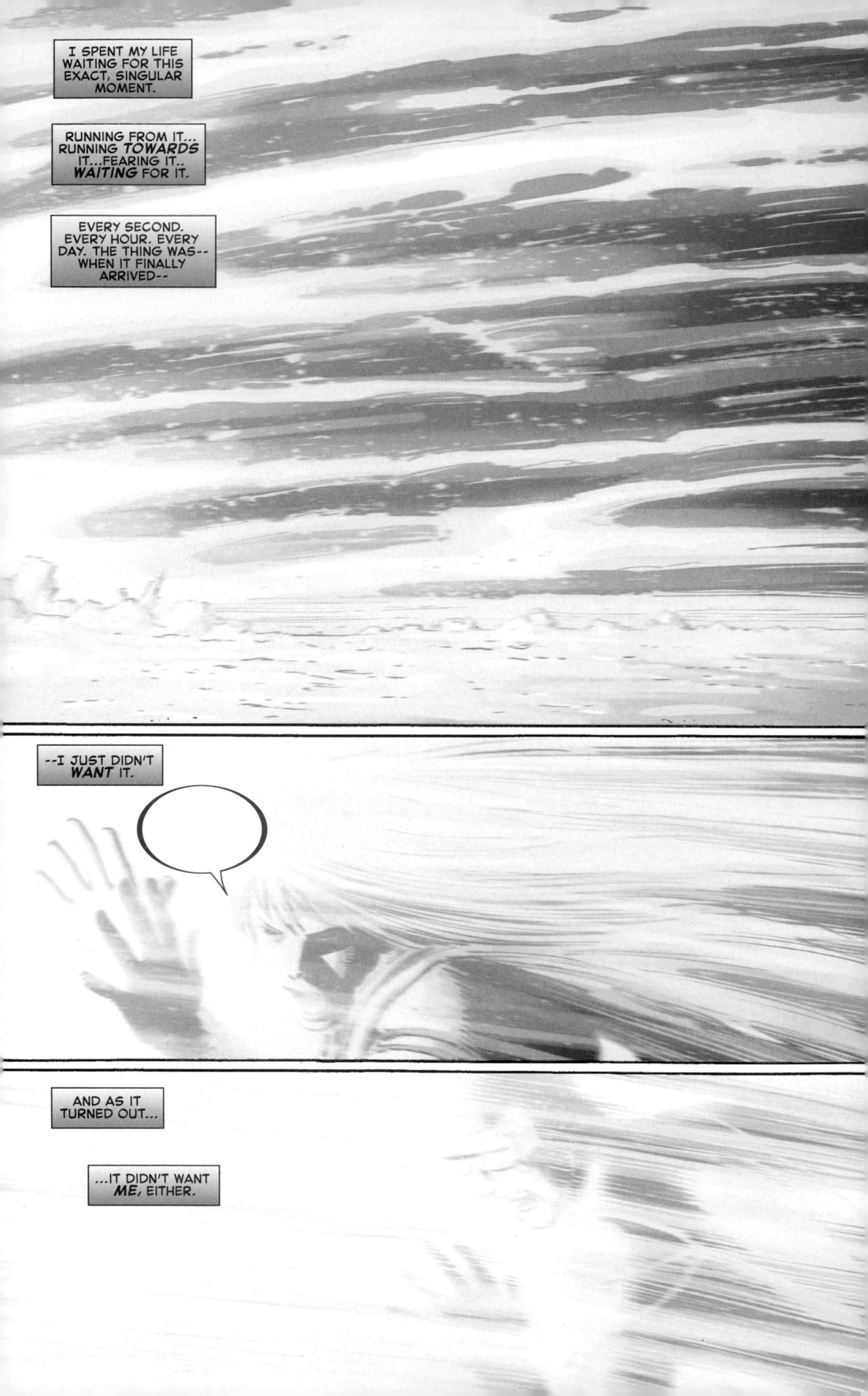
I SPENT MY LIFE WAITING FOR THIS EXACT, SINGULAR MOMENT.
RUNNING FROM IT... RUNNING *TOWARDS* IT...FEARING IT.. *WAITING* FOR IT.
EVERY SECOND. EVERY HOUR. EVERY DAY. THE THING WAS-- WHEN IT FINALLY ARRIVED--
--I JUST DIDN'T *WANT* IT.
AND AS IT TURNED OUT...
...IT DIDN'T WANT *ME,* EITHER.

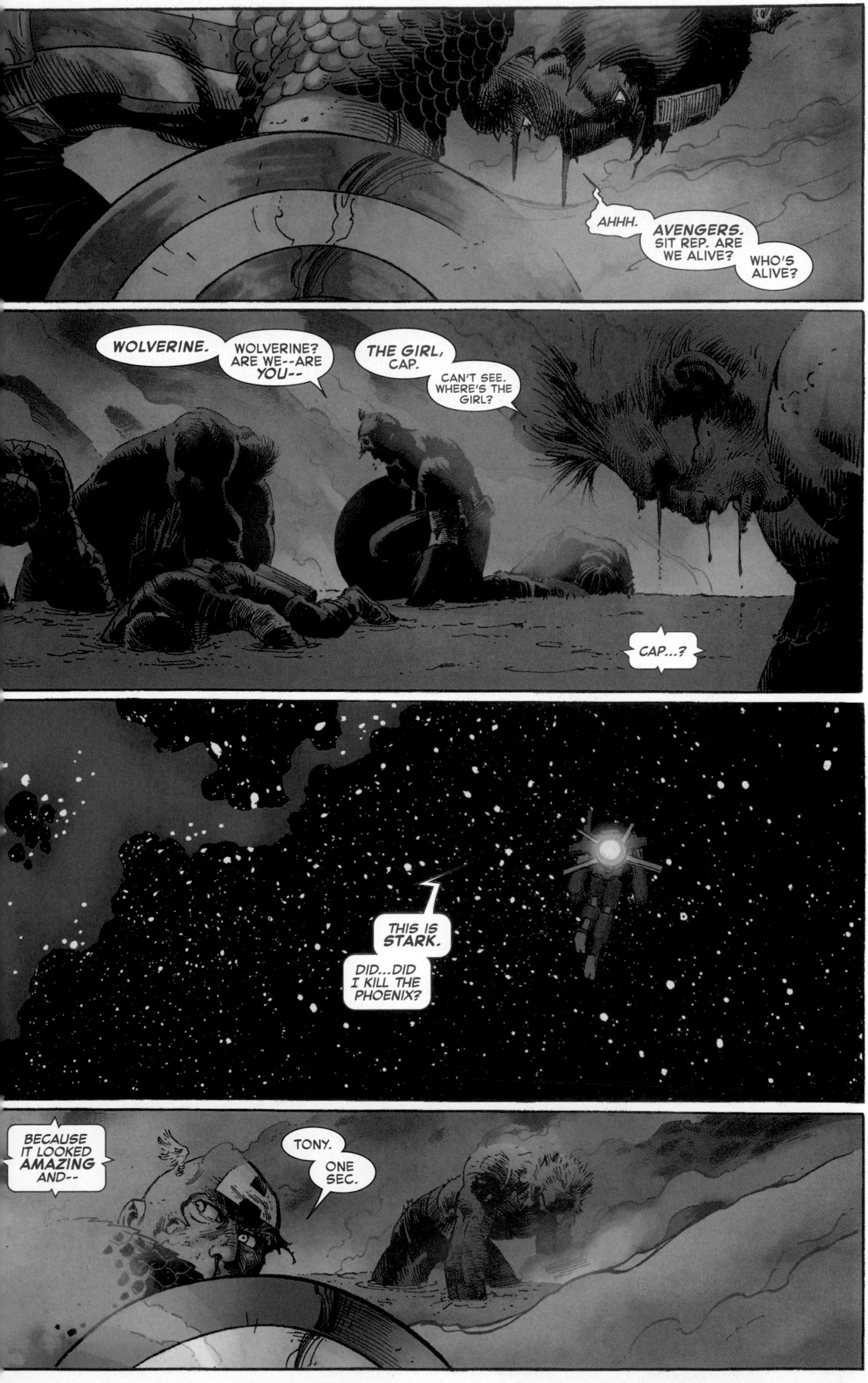
AHHH.
AVENGERS. SIT REP. ARE WE ALIVE?
WHO'S ALIVE?
WOLVERINE.
WOLVERINE? ARE WE--ARE YOU--
THE GIRL, CAP.
CAN'T SEE. WHERE'S THE GIRL?
CAP...?
THIS IS STARK.
DID...DID I KILL THE PHOENIX?
BECAUSE IT LOOKED AMAZING AND--
TONY.
ONE SEC.

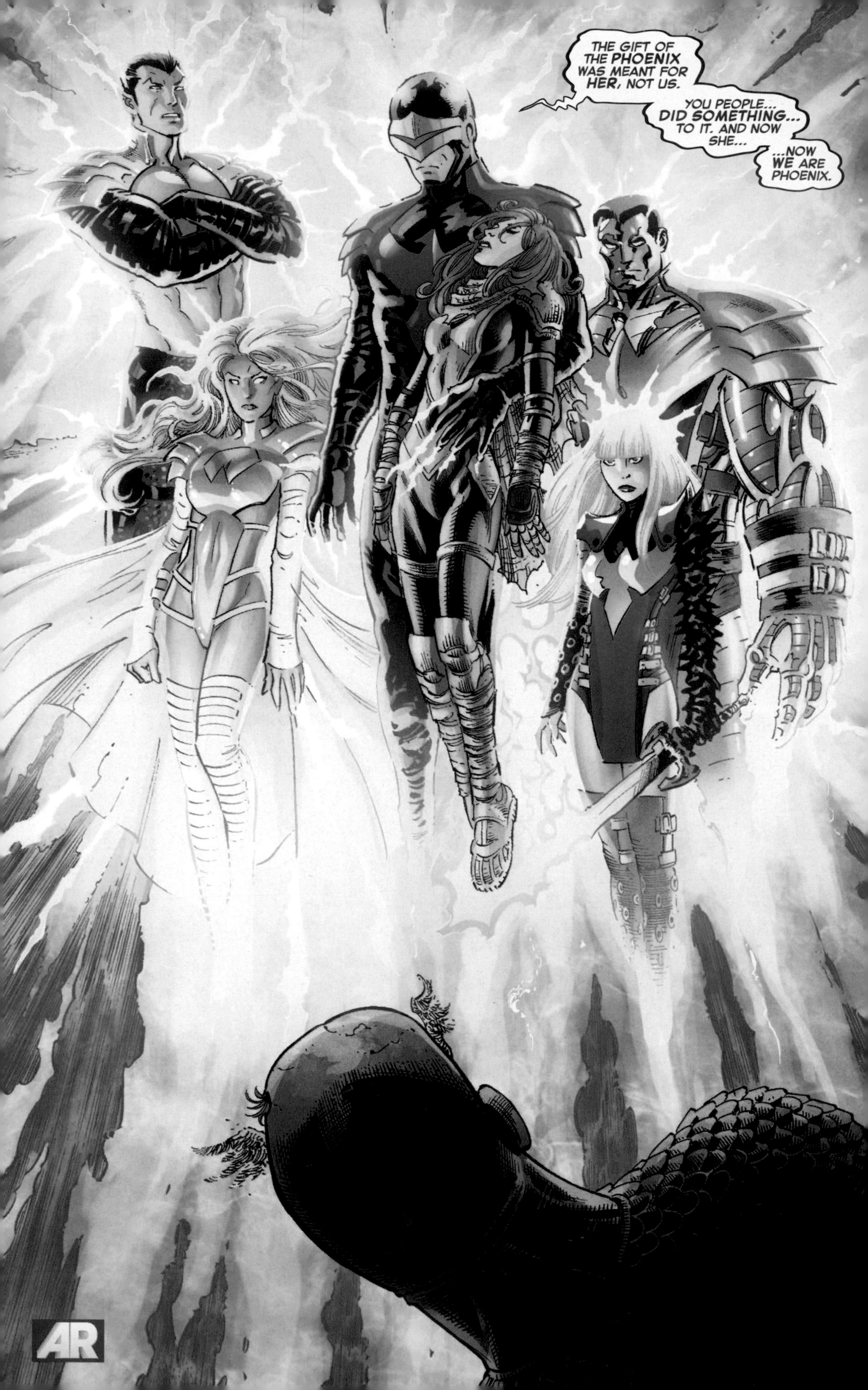
THE GIFT OF THE PHOENIX WAS MEANT FOR HER, NOT US.
YOU PEOPLE... DID SOMETHING... TO IT. AND NOW SHE...
...NOW WE ARE PHOENIX.

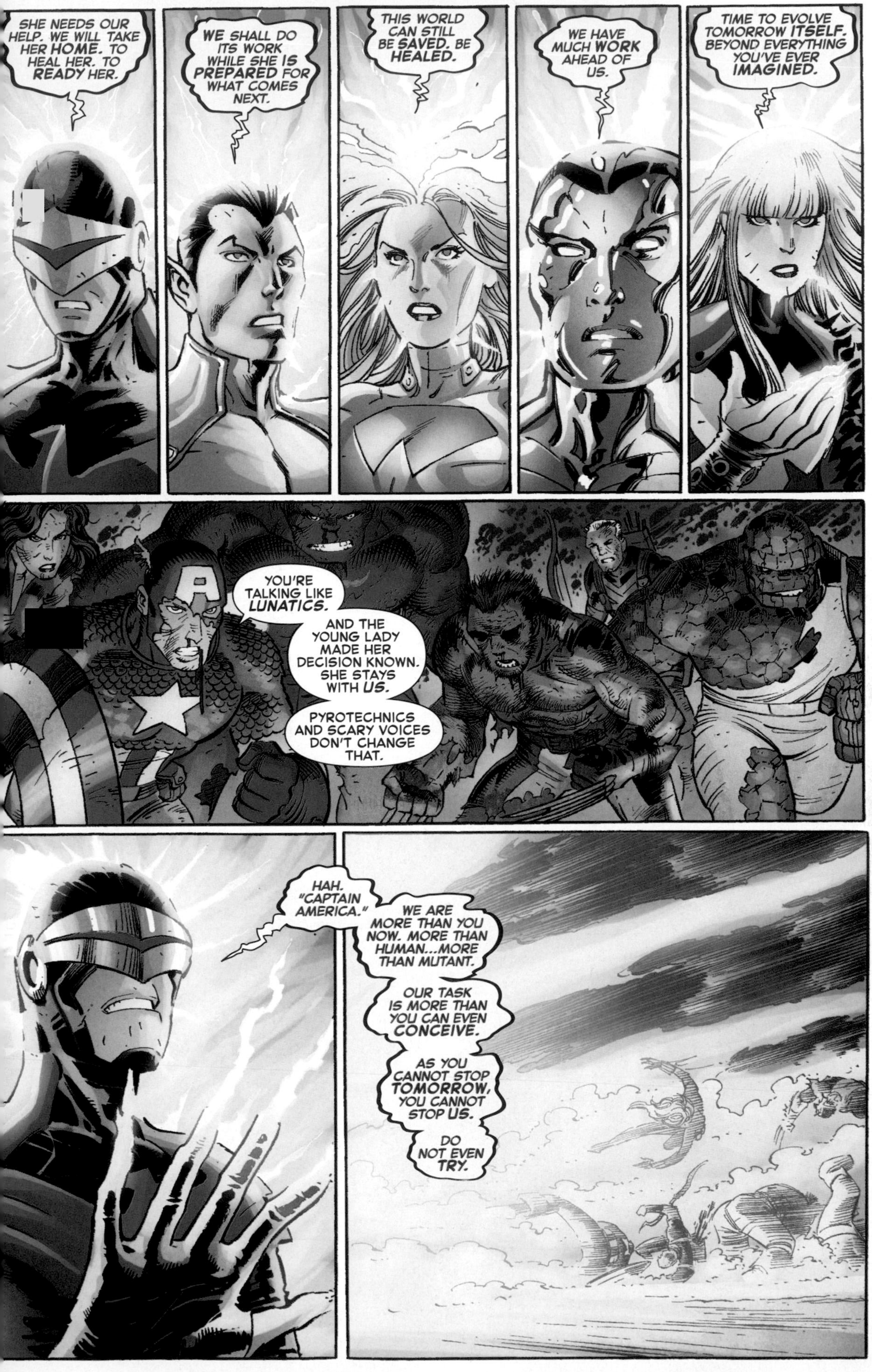
SHE NEEDS OUR HELP. WE WILL TAKE HER HOME. TO HEAL HER. TO READY HER.
WE SHALL DO ITS WORK WHILE SHE IS PREPARED FOR WHAT COMES NEXT.
THIS WORLD CAN STILL BE SAVED. BE HEALED.
WE HAVE MUCH WORK AHEAD OF US.
TIME TO EVOLVE TOMORROW ITSELF. BEYOND EVERYTHING YOU'VE EVER IMAGINED.
YOU'RE TALKING LIKE LUNATICS.
AND THE YOUNG LADY MADE HER DECISION KNOWN. SHE STAYS WITH US.
PYROTECHNICS AND SCARY VOICES DON'T CHANGE THAT.
HAH. "CAPTAIN AMERICA."
WE ARE MORE THAN YOU NOW. MORE THAN HUMAN...MORE THAN MUTANT.
OUR TASK IS MORE THAN YOU CAN EVEN CONCEIVE.
AS YOU CANNOT STOP TOMORROW, YOU CANNOT STOP US.
DO NOT EVEN TRY.

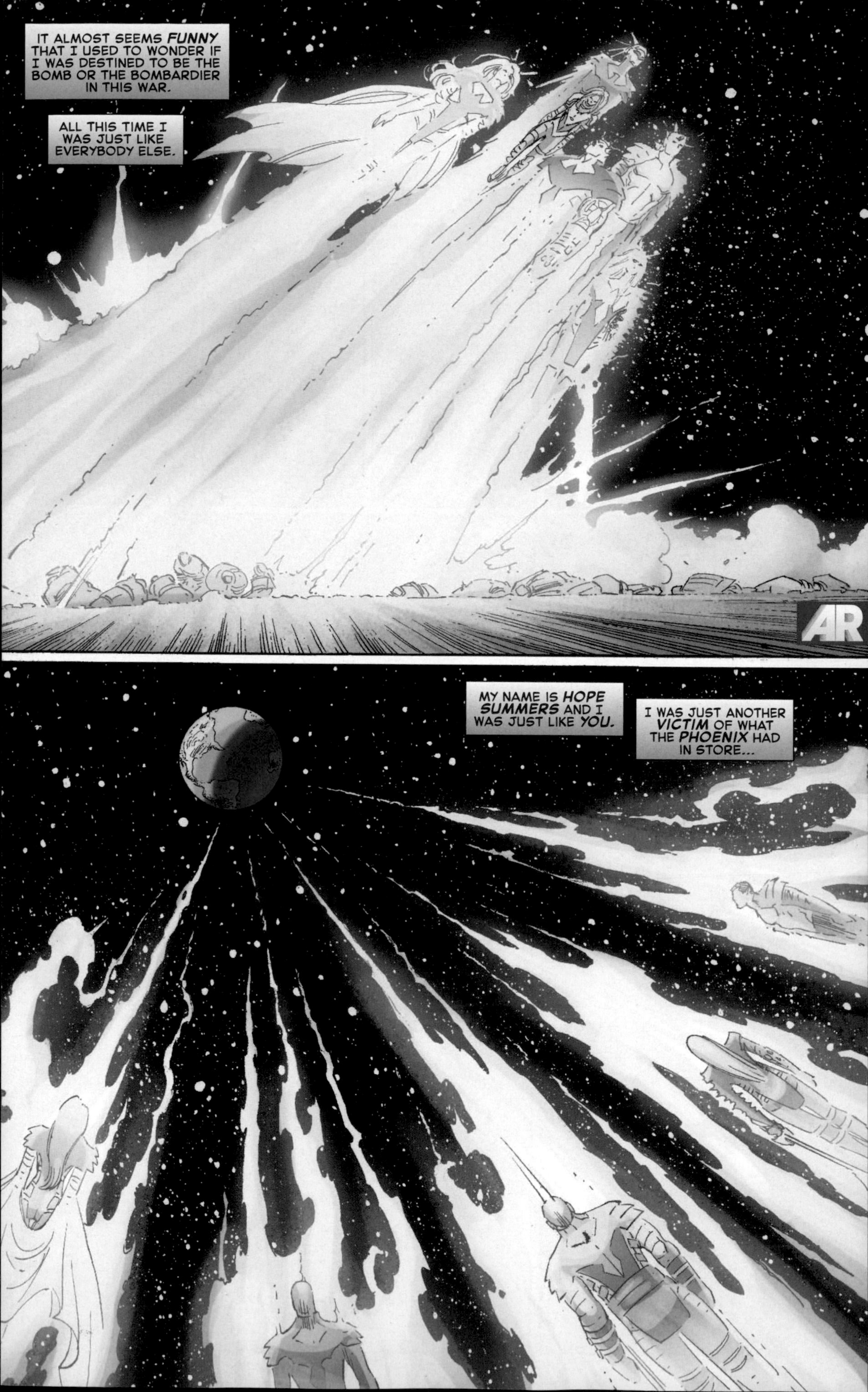
IT ALMOST SEEMS FUNNY THAT I USED TO WONDER IF I WAS DESTINED TO BE THE BOMB OR THE BOMBARDIER IN THIS WAR.
ALL THIS TIME I WAS JUST LIKE EVERYBODY ELSE.
MY NAME IS HOPE SUMMERS AND I WAS JUST LIKE YOU.
I WAS JUST ANOTHER VICTIM OF WHAT THE PHOENIX HAD IN STORE...

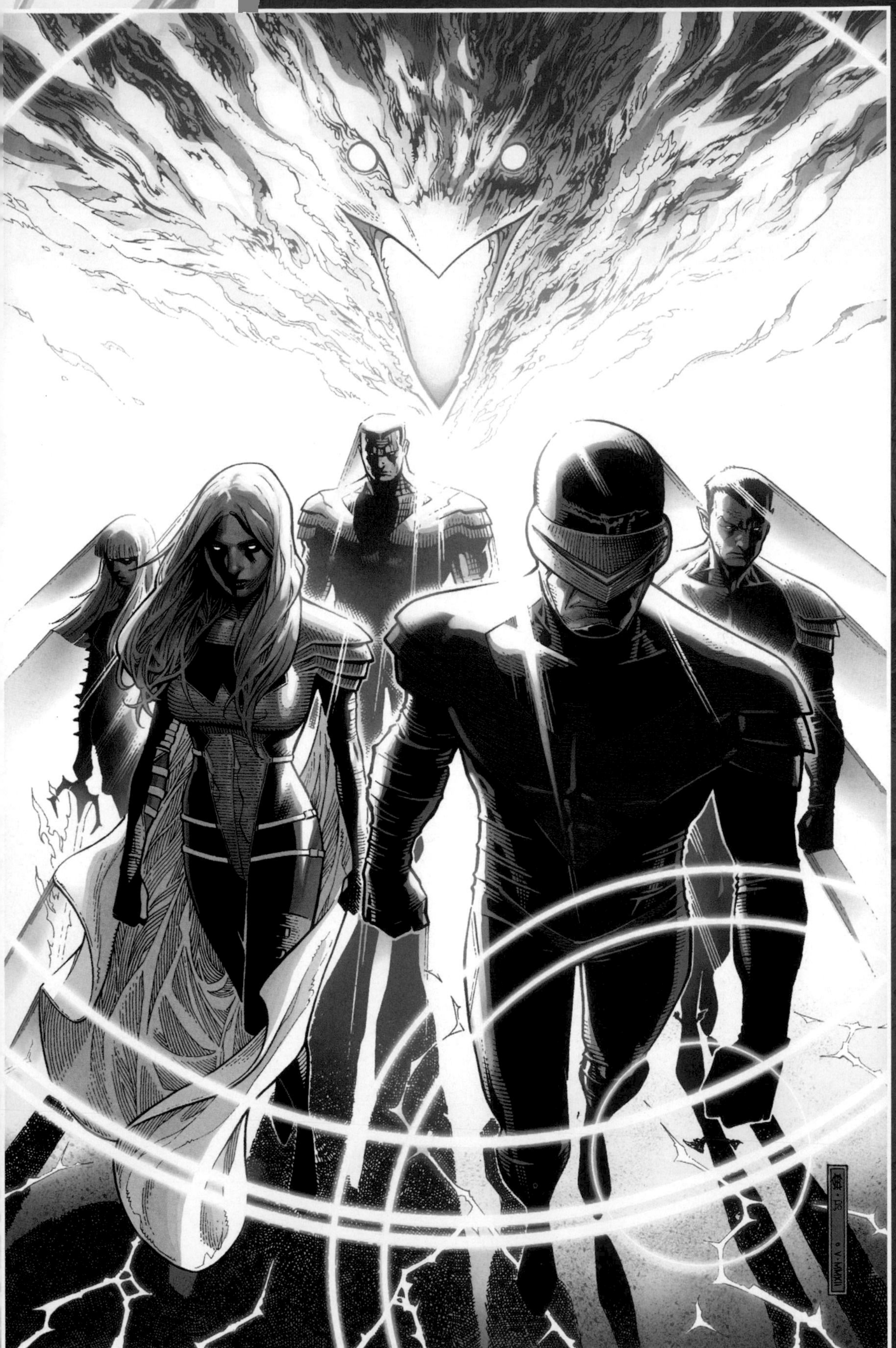

ROUND 6

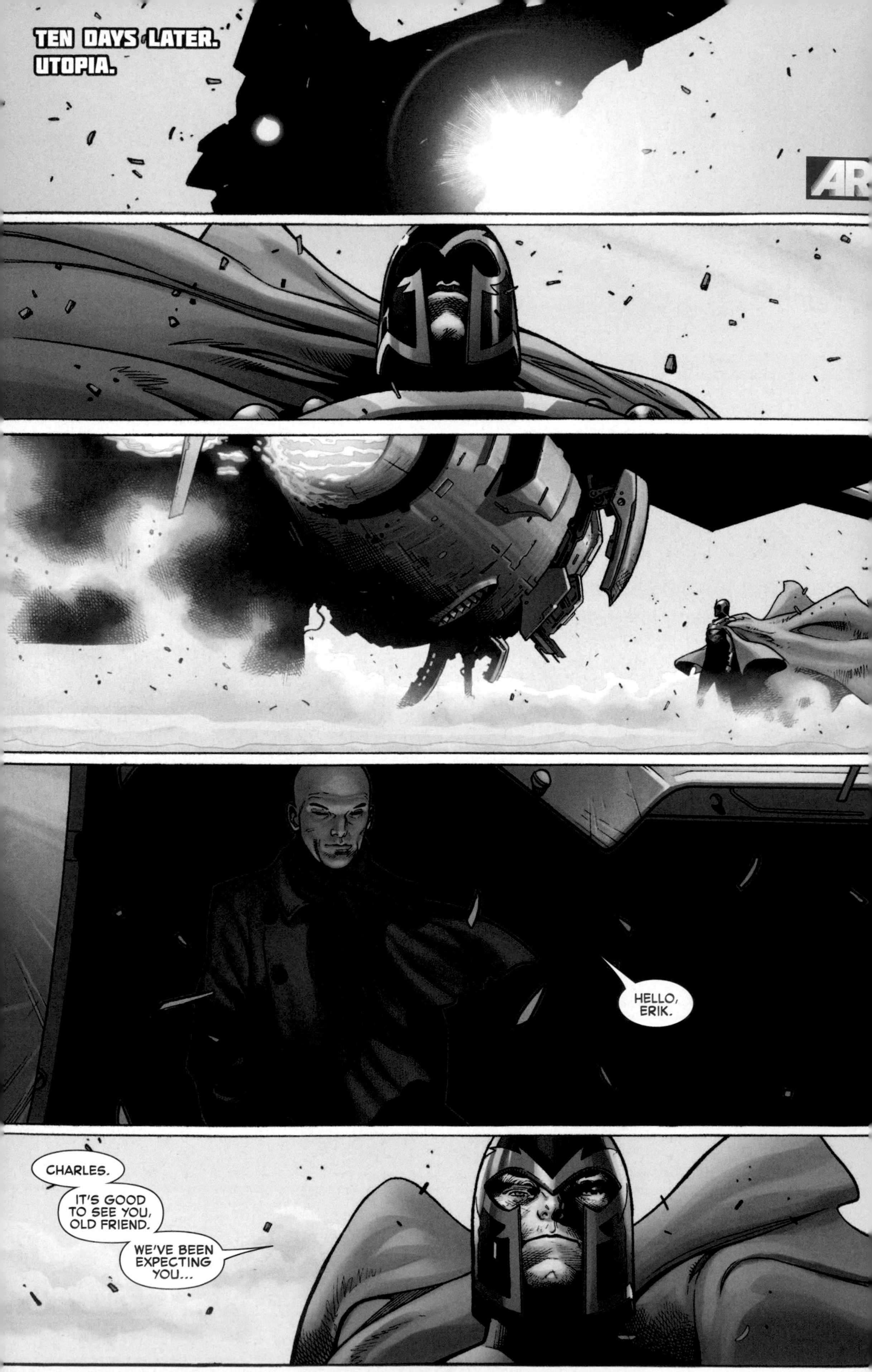
TEN DAYS LATER.
UTOPIA.
HELLO, ERIK.
CHARLES.
IT'S GOOD TO SEE YOU, OLD FRIEND.
WE'VE BEEN EXPECTING YOU...

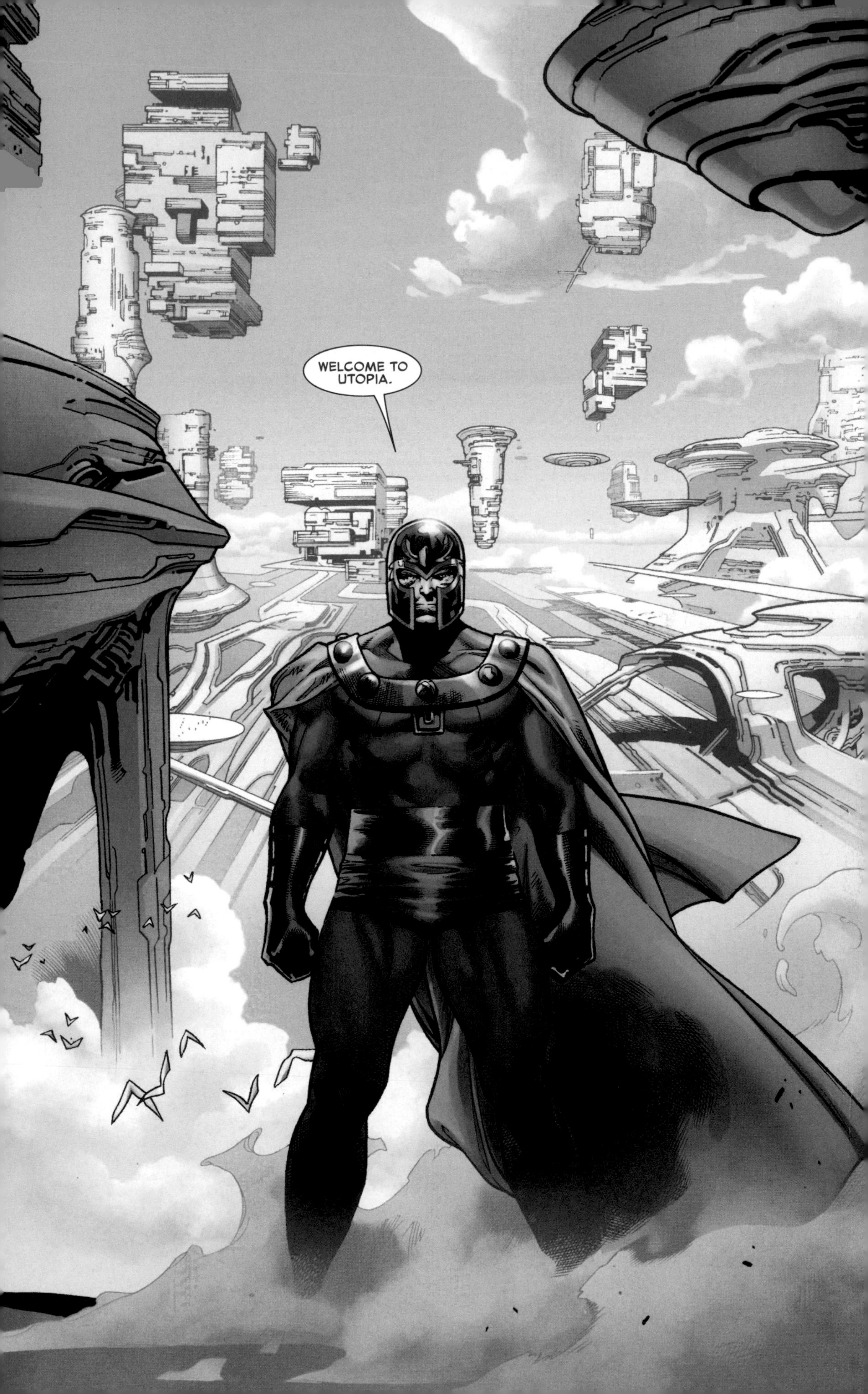
WELCOME TO UTOPIA.

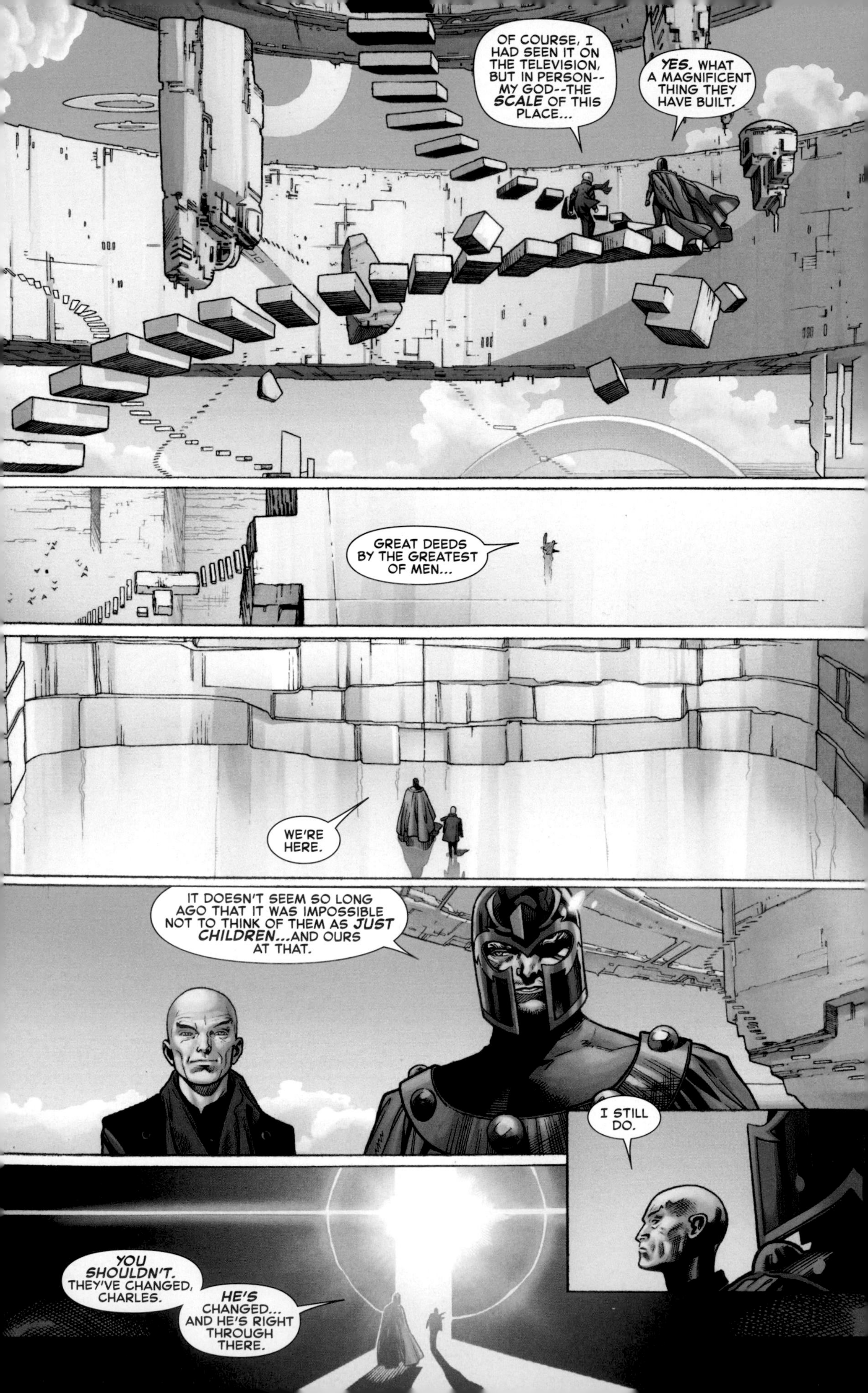
OF COURSE, I HAD SEEN IT ON THE TELEVISION, BUT IN PERSON-- MY GOD--THE SCALE OF THIS PLACE...
YES. WHAT A MAGNIFICENT THING THEY HAVE BUILT.
GREAT DEEDS BY THE GREATEST OF MEN...
WE'RE HERE.
IT DOESN'T SEEM SO LONG AGO THAT IT WAS IMPOSSIBLE NOT TO THINK OF THEM AS JUST CHILDREN...AND OURS AT THAT.
I STILL DO.
YOU SHOULDN'T. THEY'VE CHANGED, CHARLES.
HE'S CHANGED... AND HE'S RIGHT THROUGH THERE.

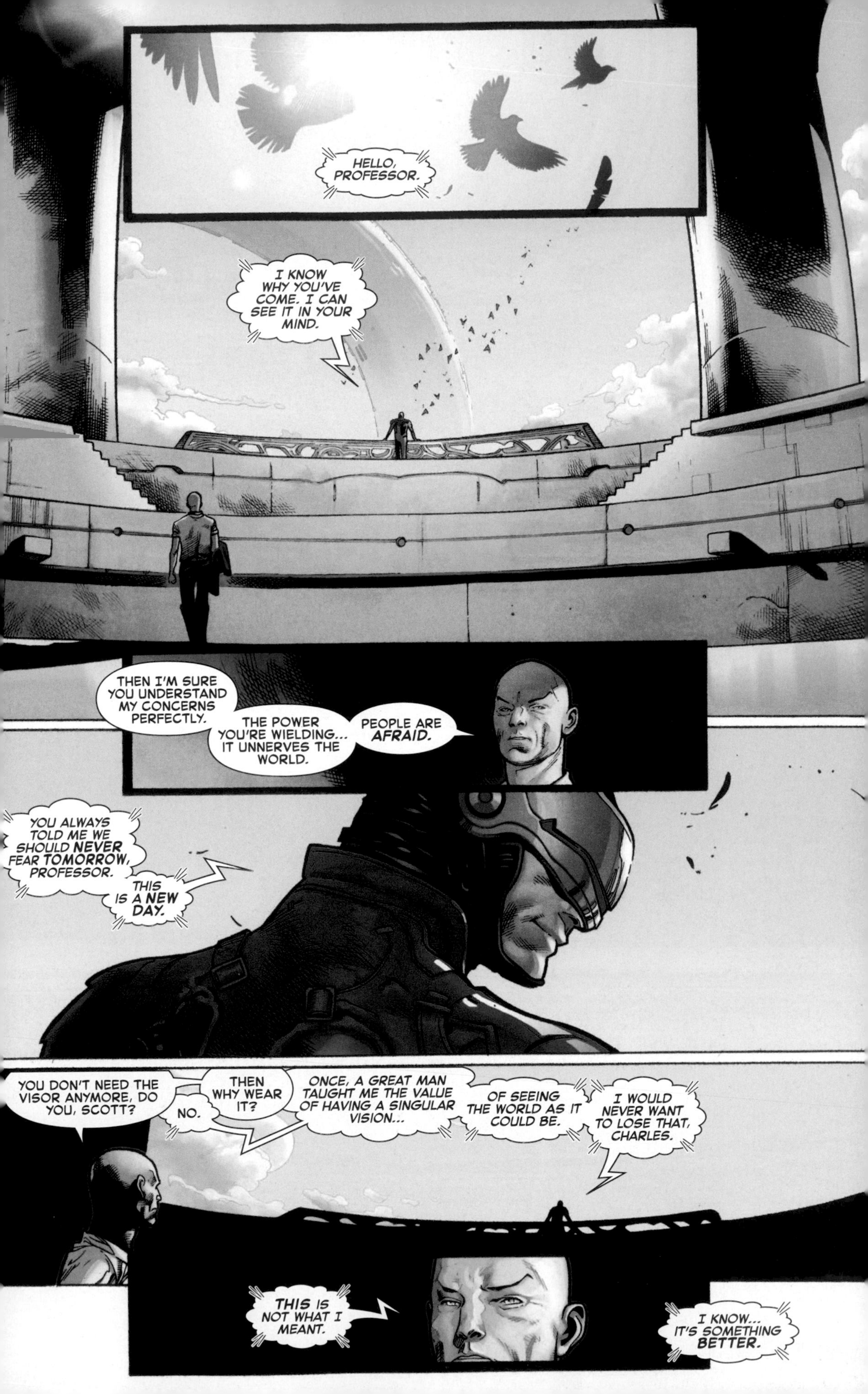
HELLO, PROFESSOR.
I KNOW WHY YOU'VE COME. I CAN SEE IT IN YOUR MIND.
THEN I'M SURE YOU UNDERSTAND MY CONCERNS PERFECTLY.
THE POWER YOU'RE WIELDING... IT UNNERVES THE WORLD.
PEOPLE ARE AFRAID.
YOU ALWAYS TOLD ME WE SHOULD NEVER FEAR TOMORROW, PROFESSOR.
THIS IS A NEW DAY.
YOU DON'T NEED THE VISOR ANYMORE, DO YOU, SCOTT?
NO.
THEN WHY WEAR IT?
ONCE, A GREAT MAN TAUGHT ME THE VALUE OF HAVING A SINGULAR VISION...
OF SEEING THE WORLD AS IT COULD BE.
I WOULD NEVER WANT TO LOSE THAT, CHARLES.
THIS IS NOT WHAT I MEANT.
I KNOW... IT'S SOMETHING BETTER.

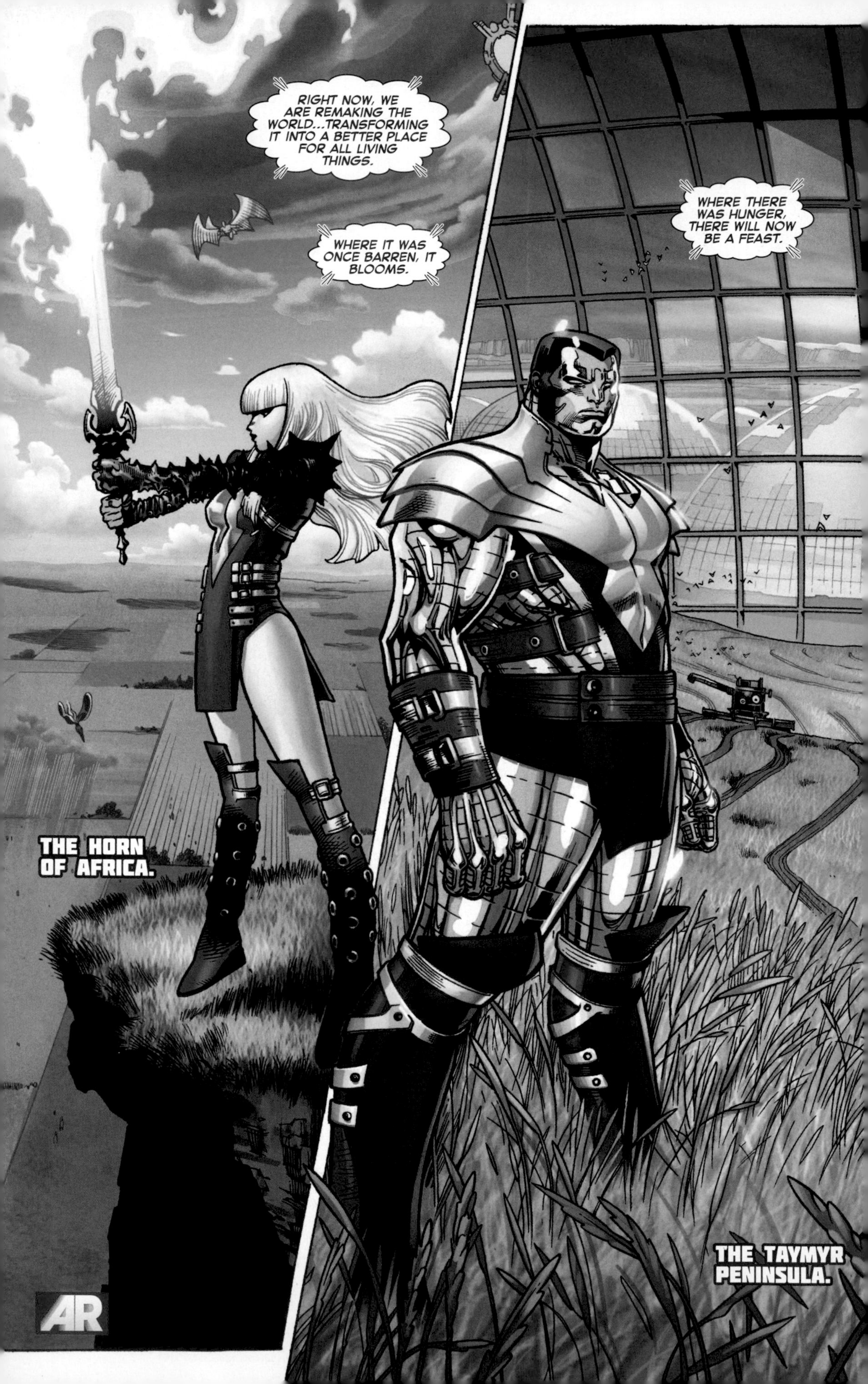
RIGHT NOW, WE ARE REMAKING THE WORLD...TRANSFORMING IT INTO A BETTER PLACE FOR ALL LIVING THINGS.
WHERE IT WAS ONCE BARREN, IT BLOOMS.
WHERE THERE WAS HUNGER, THERE WILL NOW BE A FEAST.
THE HORN OF AFRICA.
THE TAYMYR PENINSULA.
AR

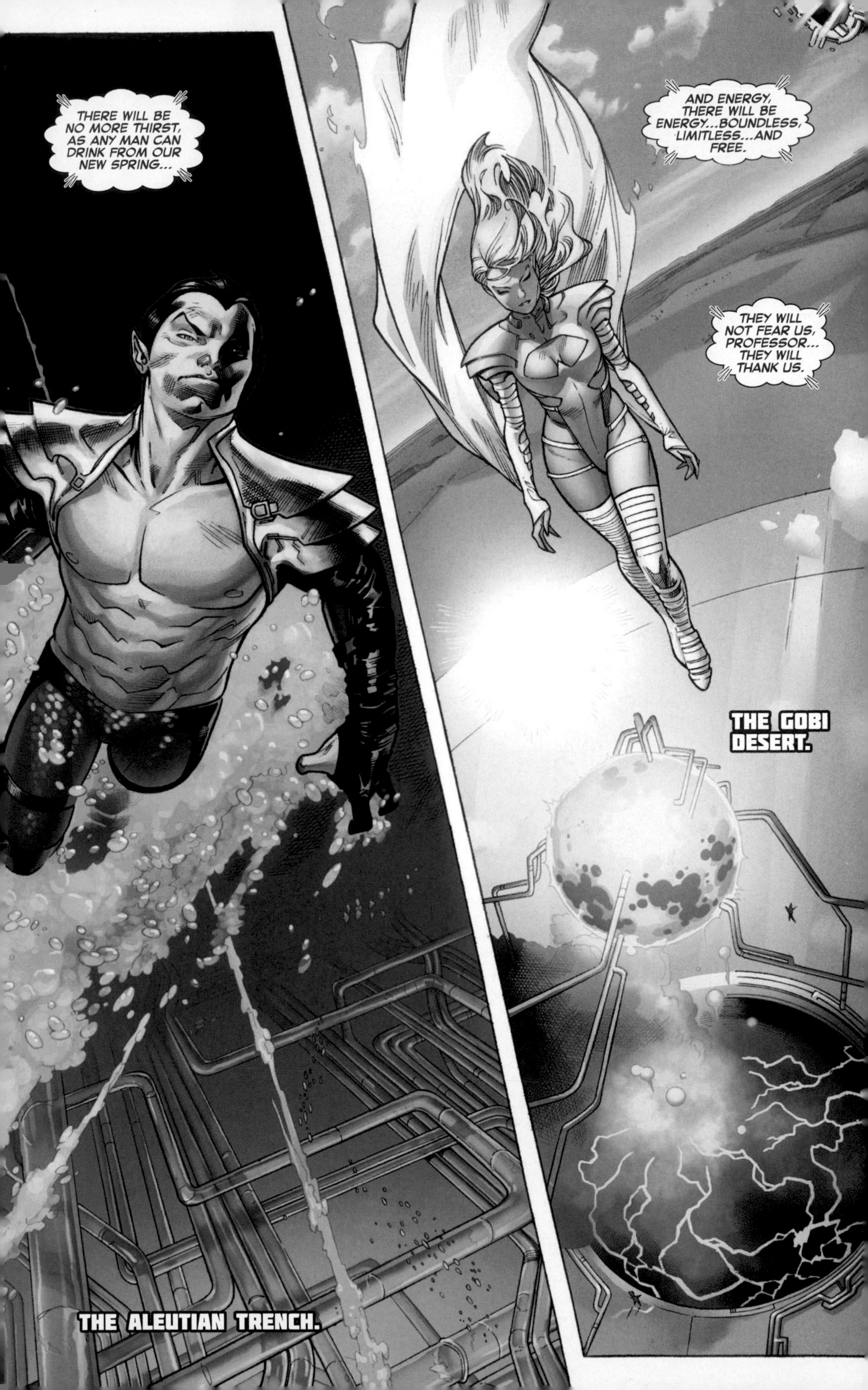
THERE WILL BE NO MORE THIRST, AS ANY MAN CAN DRINK FROM OUR NEW SPRING...
AND ENERGY, THERE WILL BE ENERGY...BOUNDLESS, LIMITLESS...AND FREE.
THEY WILL NOT FEAR US, PROFESSOR... THEY WILL THANK US.
THE GOBI DESERT.
THE ALEUTIAN TRENCH.

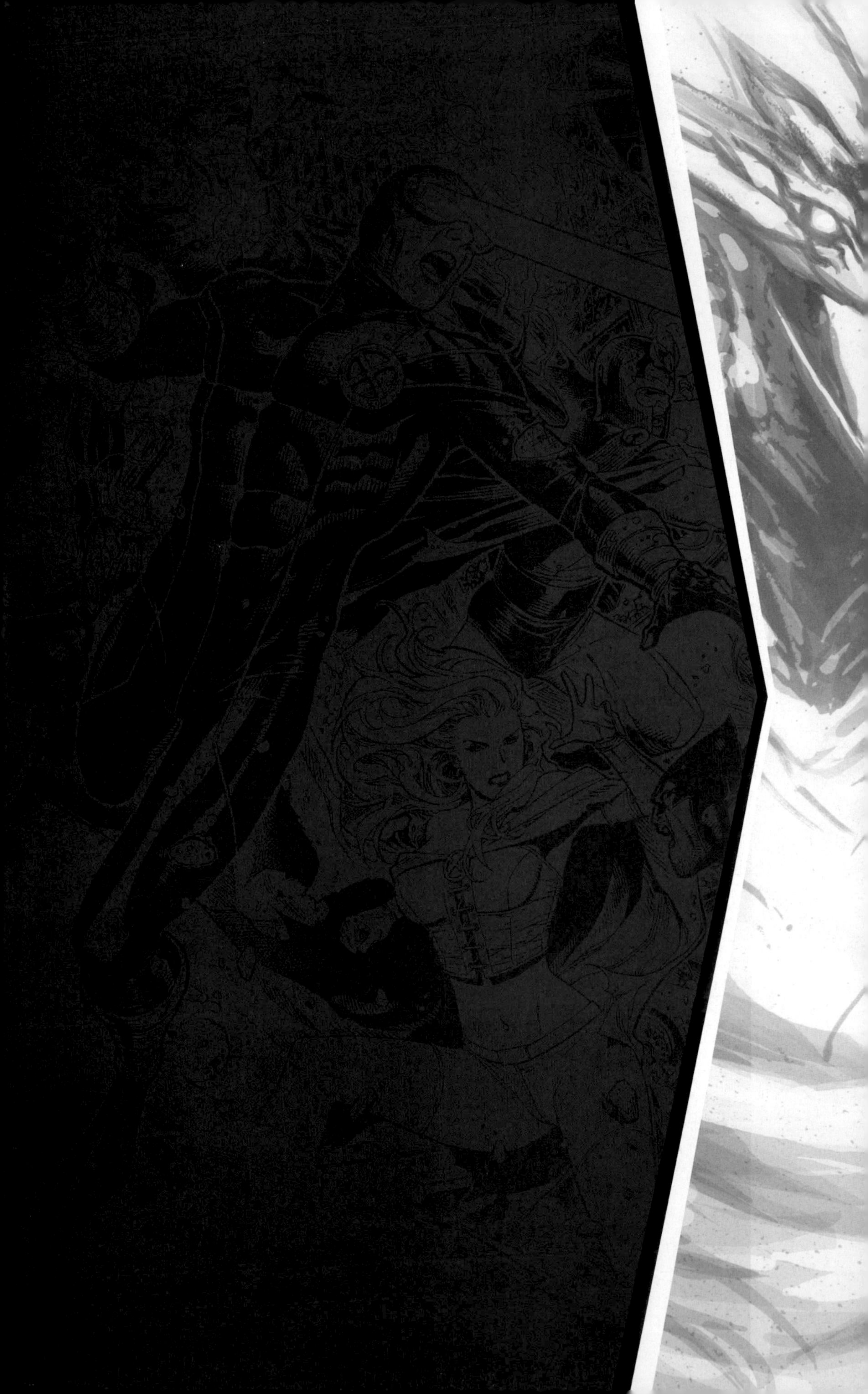

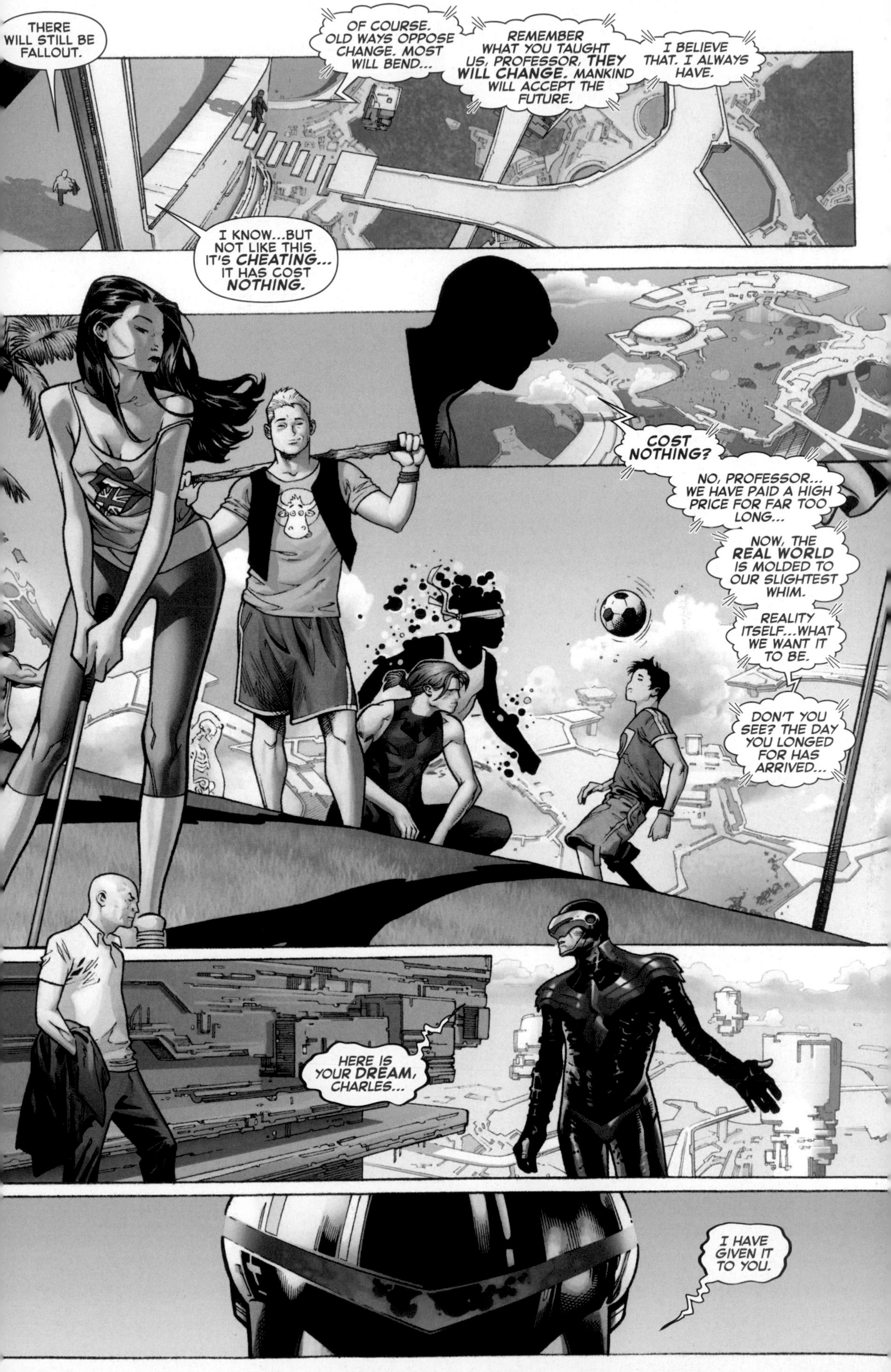
THERE WILL STILL BE FALLOUT.
OF COURSE. OLD WAYS OPPOSE CHANGE. MOST WILL BEND...
REMEMBER WHAT YOU TAUGHT US, PROFESSOR. THEY WILL CHANGE. MANKIND WILL ACCEPT THE FUTURE.
I BELIEVE THAT. I ALWAYS HAVE.
I KNOW...BUT NOT LIKE THIS. IT'S CHEATING... IT HAS COST NOTHING.
COST NOTHING?
NO, PROFESSOR... WE HAVE PAID A HIGH PRICE FOR FAR TOO LONG...
NOW, THE REAL WORLD IS MOLDED TO OUR SLIGHTEST WHIM.
REALITY ITSELF...WHAT WE WANT IT TO BE.
DON'T YOU SEE? THE DAY YOU LONGED FOR HAS ARRIVED...
HERE IS YOUR DREAM, CHARLES...
I HAVE GIVEN IT TO YOU.

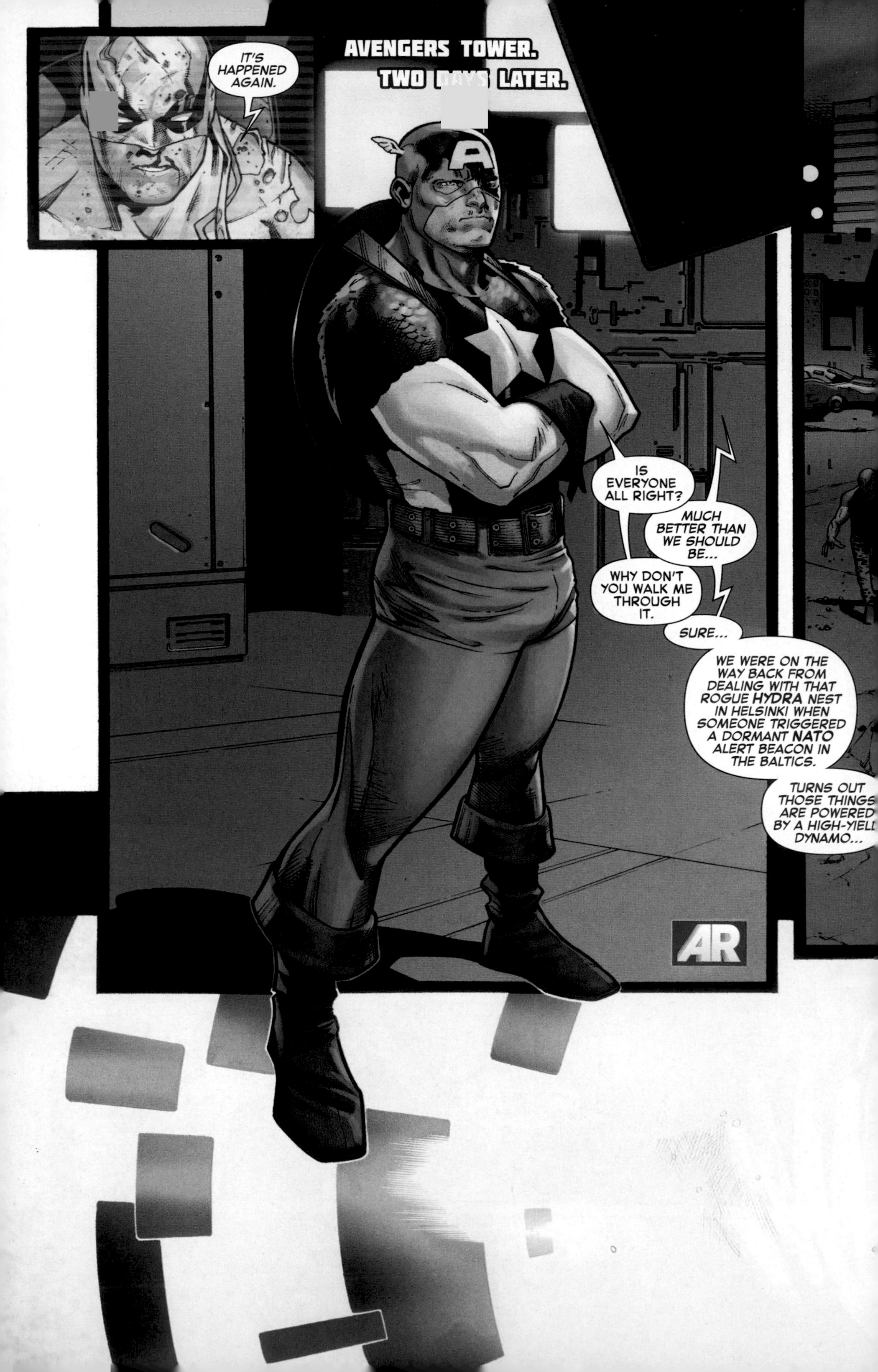

IT'S HAPPENED AGAIN.
AVENGERS TOWER.
TWO DAYS LATER.
IS EVERYONE ALL RIGHT?
MUCH BETTER THAN WE SHOULD BE...
WHY DON'T YOU WALK ME THROUGH IT.
SURE...
WE WERE ON THE WAY BACK FROM DEALING WITH THAT ROGUE HYDRA NEST IN HELSINKI WHEN SOMEONE TRIGGERED A DORMANT NATO ALERT BEACON IN THE BALTICS.
TURNS OUT THOSE THINGS ARE POWERED BY A HIGH-YIELL DYNAMO...

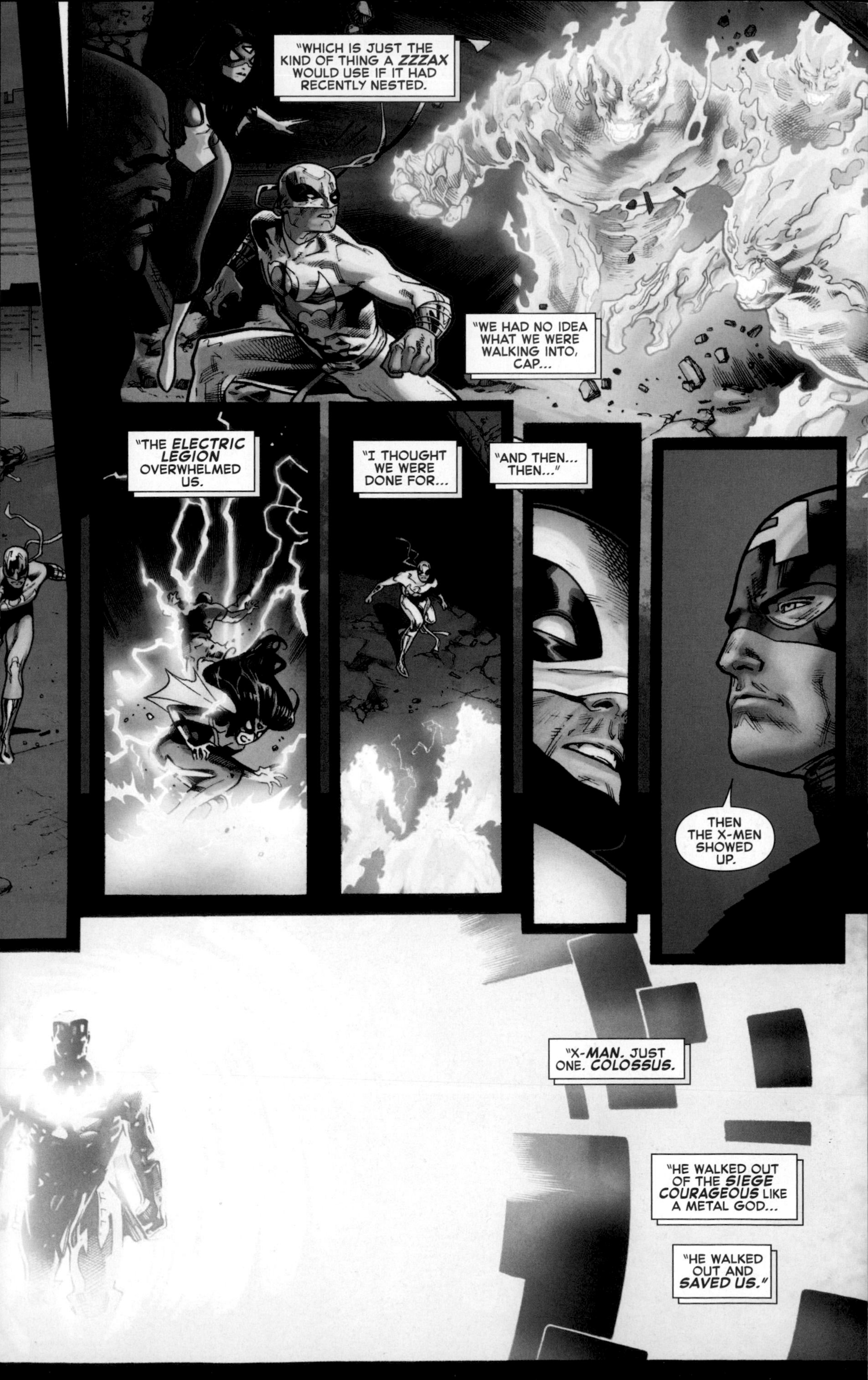
"WHICH IS JUST THE KIND OF THING A ZZZAX WOULD USE IF IT HAD RECENTLY NESTED.
"WE HAD NO IDEA WHAT WE WERE WALKING INTO, CAP...
"THE ELECTRIC LEGION OVERWHELMED US.
"I THOUGHT WE WERE DONE FOR...
"AND THEN... THEN..."
THEN THE X-MEN SHOWED UP.
"X-MAN. JUST ONE. COLOSSUS.
"HE WALKED OUT OF THE SIEGE COURAGEOUS LIKE A METAL GOD...
"HE WALKED OUT AND SAVED US."

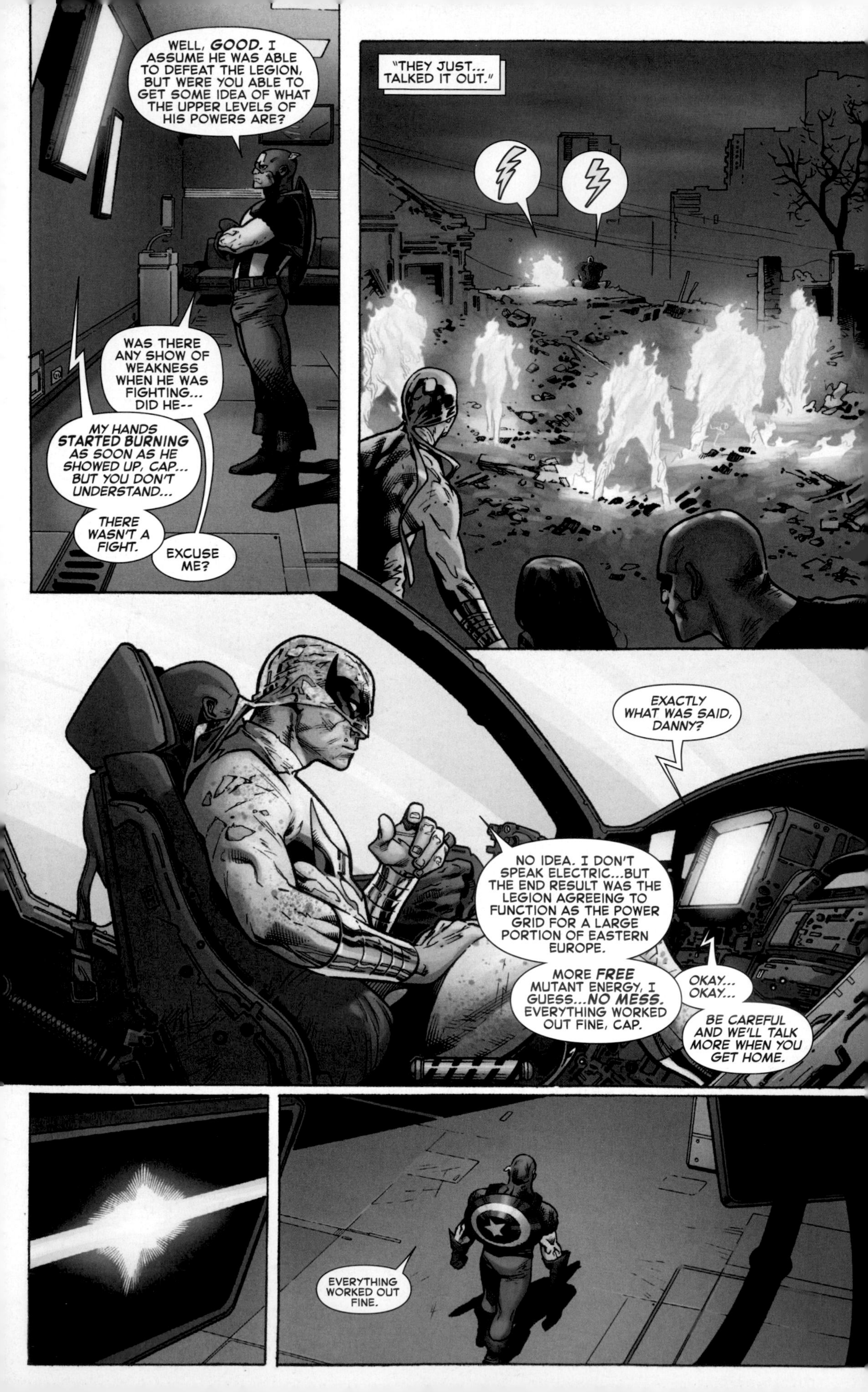
WELL, GOOD. I ASSUME HE WAS ABLE TO DEFEAT THE LEGION, BUT WERE YOU ABLE TO GET SOME IDEA OF WHAT THE UPPER LEVELS OF HIS POWERS ARE?
"THEY JUST... TALKED IT OUT."
WAS THERE ANY SHOW OF WEAKNESS WHEN HE WAS FIGHTING... DID HE--
MY HANDS STARTED BURNING AS SOON AS HE SHOWED UP, CAP... BUT YOU DON'T UNDERSTAND...
THERE WASN'T A FIGHT.
EXCUSE ME?
EXACTLY WHAT WAS SAID, DANNY?
NO IDEA. I DON'T SPEAK ELECTRIC...BUT THE END RESULT WAS THE LEGION AGREEING TO FUNCTION AS THE POWER GRID FOR A LARGE PORTION OF EASTERN EUROPE.
MORE FREE MUTANT ENERGY, I GUESS...NO MESS. EVERYTHING WORKED OUT FINE, CAP.
OKAY... OKAY...
BE CAREFUL AND WE'LL TALK MORE WHEN YOU GET HOME.
EVERYTHING WORKED OUT FINE.

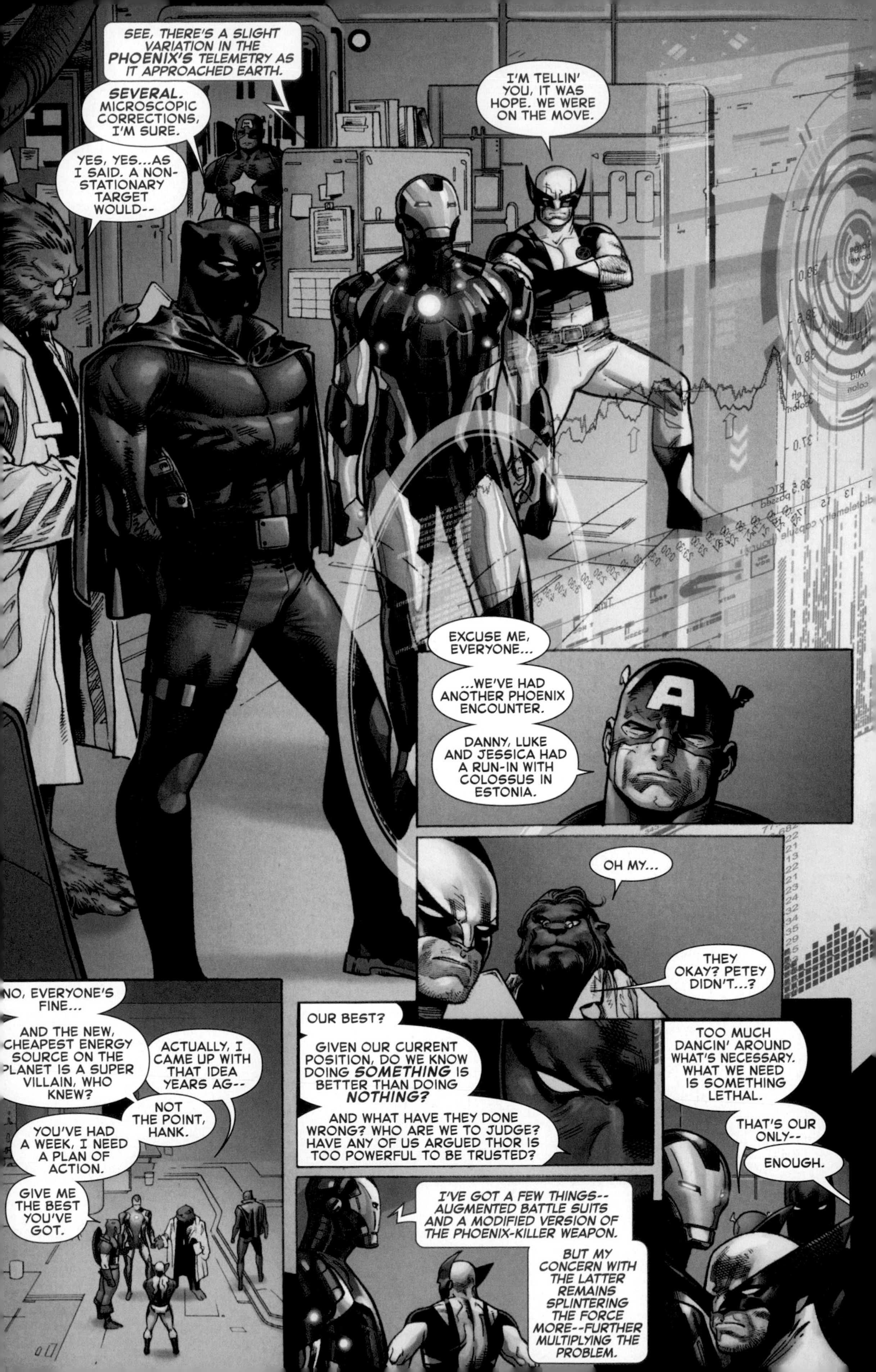

SEE, THERE'S A SLIGHT VARIATION IN THE PHOENIX'S TELEMETRY AS IT APPROACHED EARTH.
SEVERAL. MICROSCOPIC CORRECTIONS, I'M SURE.
YES, YES...AS I SAID. A NON-STATIONARY TARGET WOULD--
I'M TELLIN' YOU, IT WAS HOPE. WE WERE ON THE MOVE.
EXCUSE ME, EVERYONE...
...WE'VE HAD ANOTHER PHOENIX ENCOUNTER.
DANNY, LUKE AND JESSICA HAD A RUN-IN WITH COLOSSUS IN ESTONIA.
OH MY...
THEY OKAY? PETEY DIDN'T...?
NO, EVERYONE'S FINE...
AND THE NEW, CHEAPEST ENERGY SOURCE ON THE PLANET IS A SUPER VILLAIN, WHO KNEW?
ACTUALLY, I CAME UP WITH THAT IDEA YEARS AG--
NOT THE POINT, HANK.
YOU'VE HAD A WEEK, I NEED A PLAN OF ACTION.
GIVE ME THE BEST YOU'VE GOT.
OUR BEST?
GIVEN OUR CURRENT POSITION, DO WE KNOW DOING SOMETHING IS BETTER THAN DOING NOTHING?
AND WHAT HAVE THEY DONE WRONG? WHO ARE WE TO JUDGE? HAVE ANY OF US ARGUED THOR IS TOO POWERFUL TO BE TRUSTED?
TOO MUCH DANCIN' AROUND WHAT'S NECESSARY. WHAT WE NEED IS SOMETHING LETHAL.
THAT'S OUR ONLY--
ENOUGH.
I'VE GOT A FEW THINGS-- AUGMENTED BATTLE SUITS AND A MODIFIED VERSION OF THE PHOENIX-KILLER WEAPON.
BUT MY CONCERN WITH THE LATTER REMAINS SPLINTERING THE FORCE MORE--FURTHER MULTIPLYING THE PROBLEM.

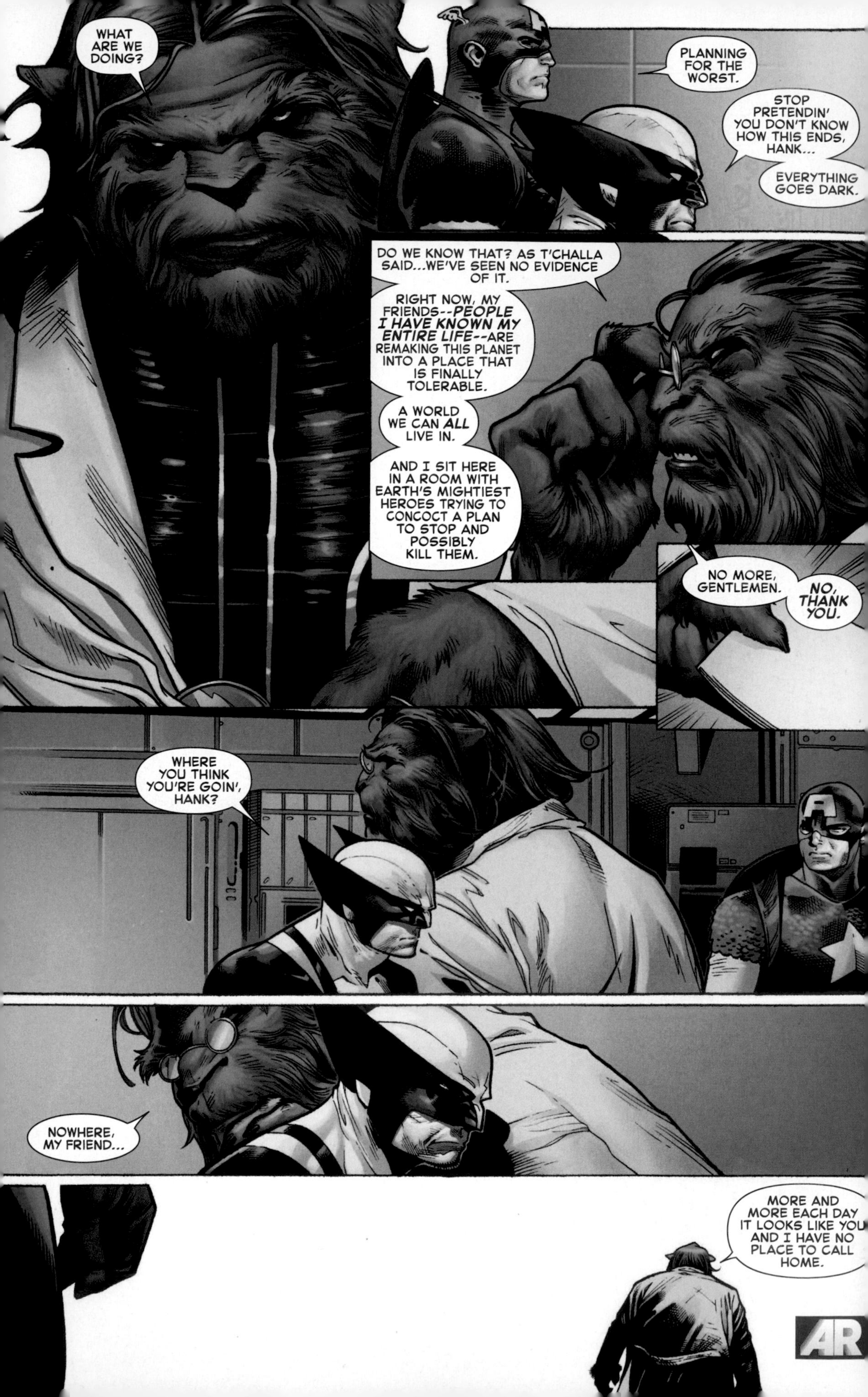
WHAT ARE WE DOING?
PLANNING FOR THE WORST.
STOP PRETENDIN' YOU DON'T KNOW HOW THIS ENDS, HANK...
EVERYTHING GOES DARK.
DO WE KNOW THAT? AS T'CHALLA SAID...WE'VE SEEN NO EVIDENCE OF IT.
RIGHT NOW, MY FRIENDS--PEOPLE I HAVE KNOWN MY ENTIRE LIFE--ARE REMAKING THIS PLANET INTO A PLACE THAT IS FINALLY TOLERABLE.
A WORLD WE CAN ALL LIVE IN.
AND I SIT HERE IN A ROOM WITH EARTH'S MIGHTIEST HEROES TRYING TO CONCOCT A PLAN TO STOP AND POSSIBLY KILL THEM.
NO MORE, GENTLEMEN.
NO, THANK YOU.
WHERE YOU THINK YOU'RE GOIN', HANK?
NOWHERE, MY FRIEND...
MORE AND MORE EACH DAY IT LOOKS LIKE YOU AND I HAVE NO PLACE TO CALL HOME.
AR

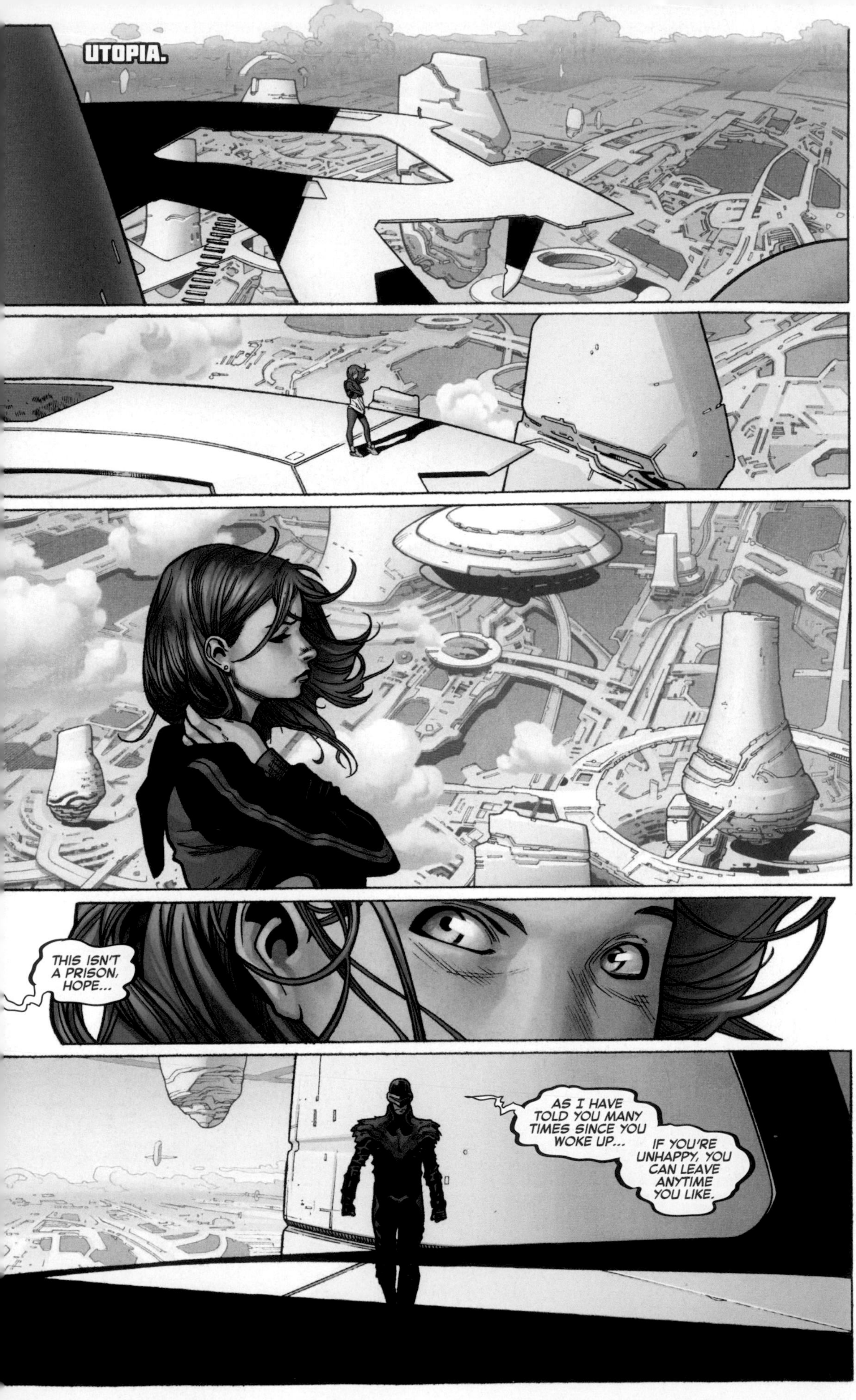
UTOPIA.
THIS ISN'T A PRISON, HOPE...
AS I HAVE TOLD YOU MANY TIMES SINCE YOU WOKE UP...
IF YOU'RE UNHAPPY, YOU CAN LEAVE ANYTIME YOU LIKE.

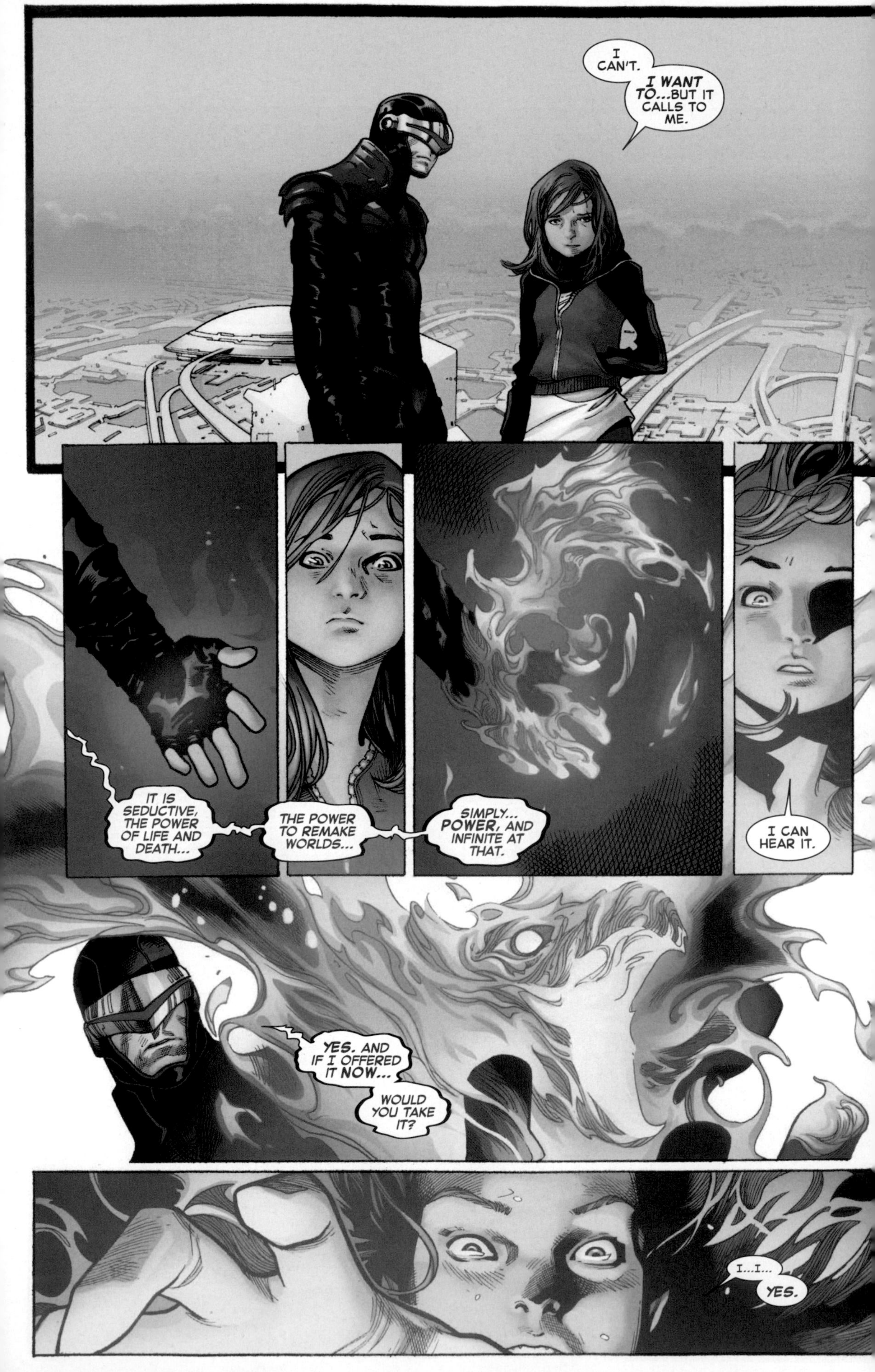
I CAN'T. I WANT TO...BUT IT CALLS TO ME.
IT IS SEDUCTIVE, THE POWER OF LIFE AND DEATH...
THE POWER TO REMAKE WORLDS...
SIMPLY... POWER, AND INFINITE AT THAT.
I CAN HEAR IT.
YES. AND IF I OFFERED IT NOW...
WOULD YOU TAKE IT?
I...I...
YES.

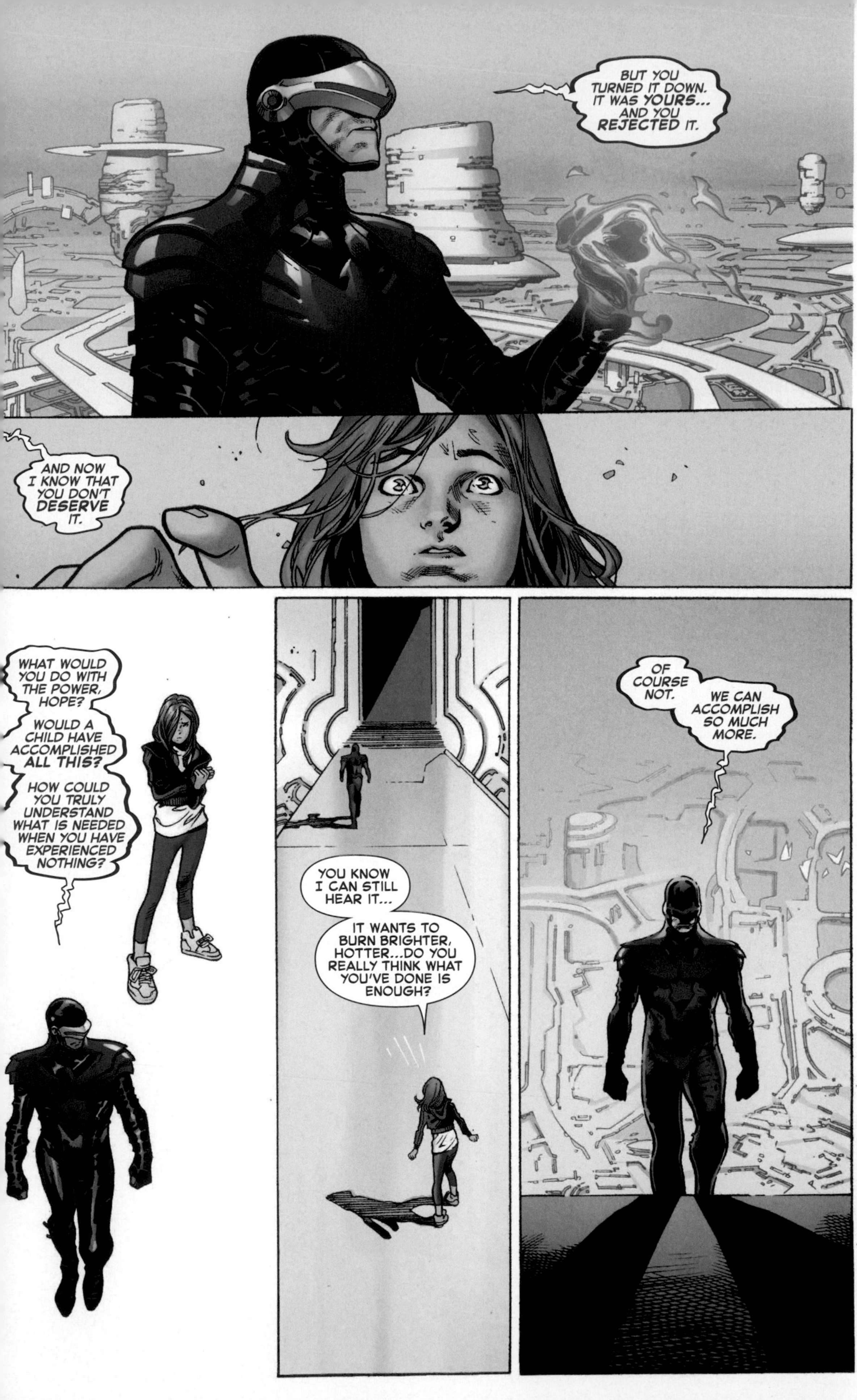
BUT YOU TURNED IT DOWN. IT WAS YOURS... AND YOU REJECTED IT.
AND NOW I KNOW THAT YOU DON'T DESERVE IT.
WHAT WOULD YOU DO WITH THE POWER, HOPE?
WOULD A CHILD HAVE ACCOMPLISHED ALL THIS?
HOW COULD YOU TRULY UNDERSTAND WHAT IS NEEDED WHEN YOU HAVE EXPERIENCED NOTHING?
YOU KNOW I CAN STILL HEAR IT...
IT WANTS TO BURN BRIGHTER, HOTTER...DO YOU REALLY THINK WHAT YOU'VE DONE IS ENOUGH?
OF COURSE NOT.
WE CAN ACCOMPLISH SO MUCH MORE.

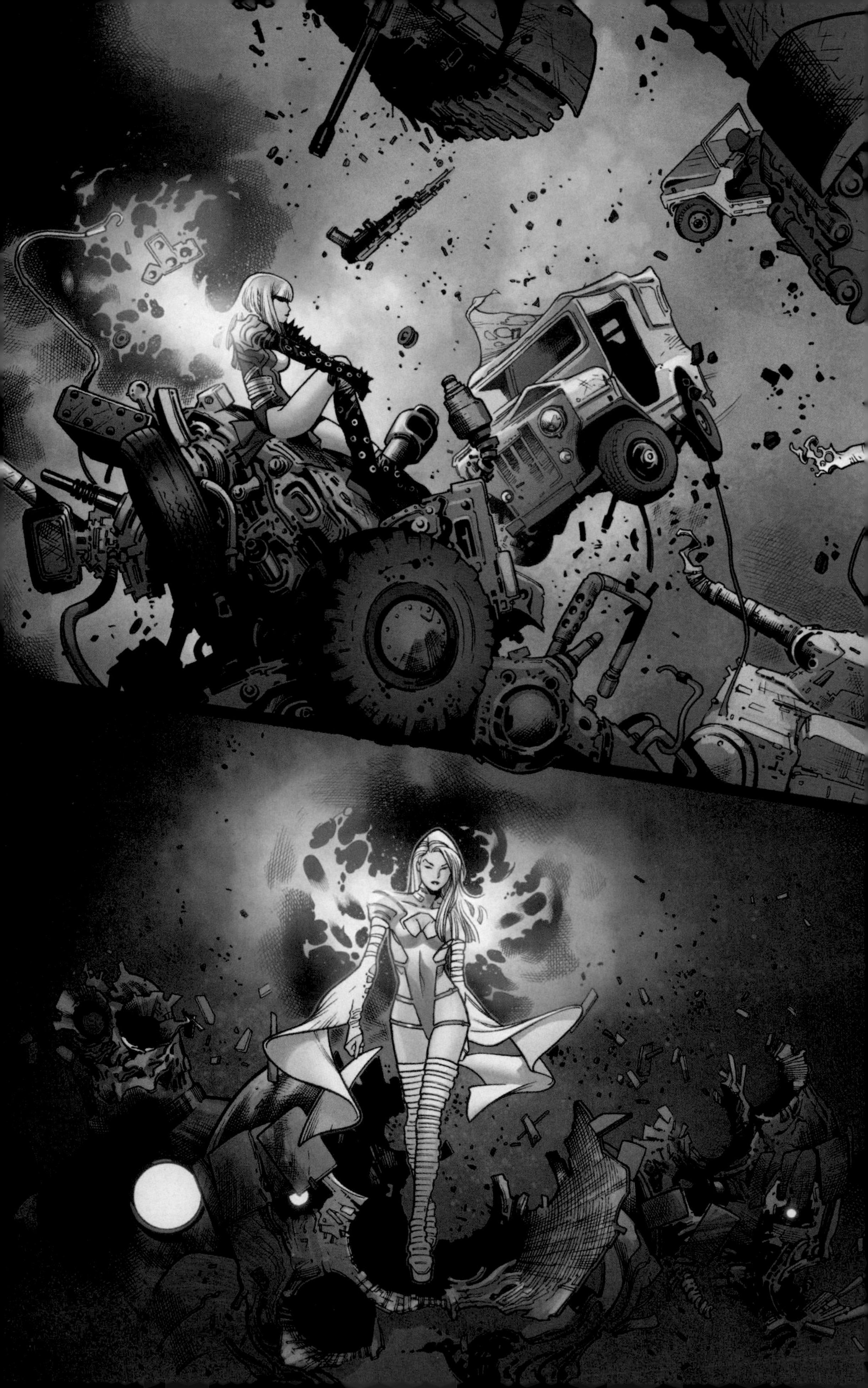

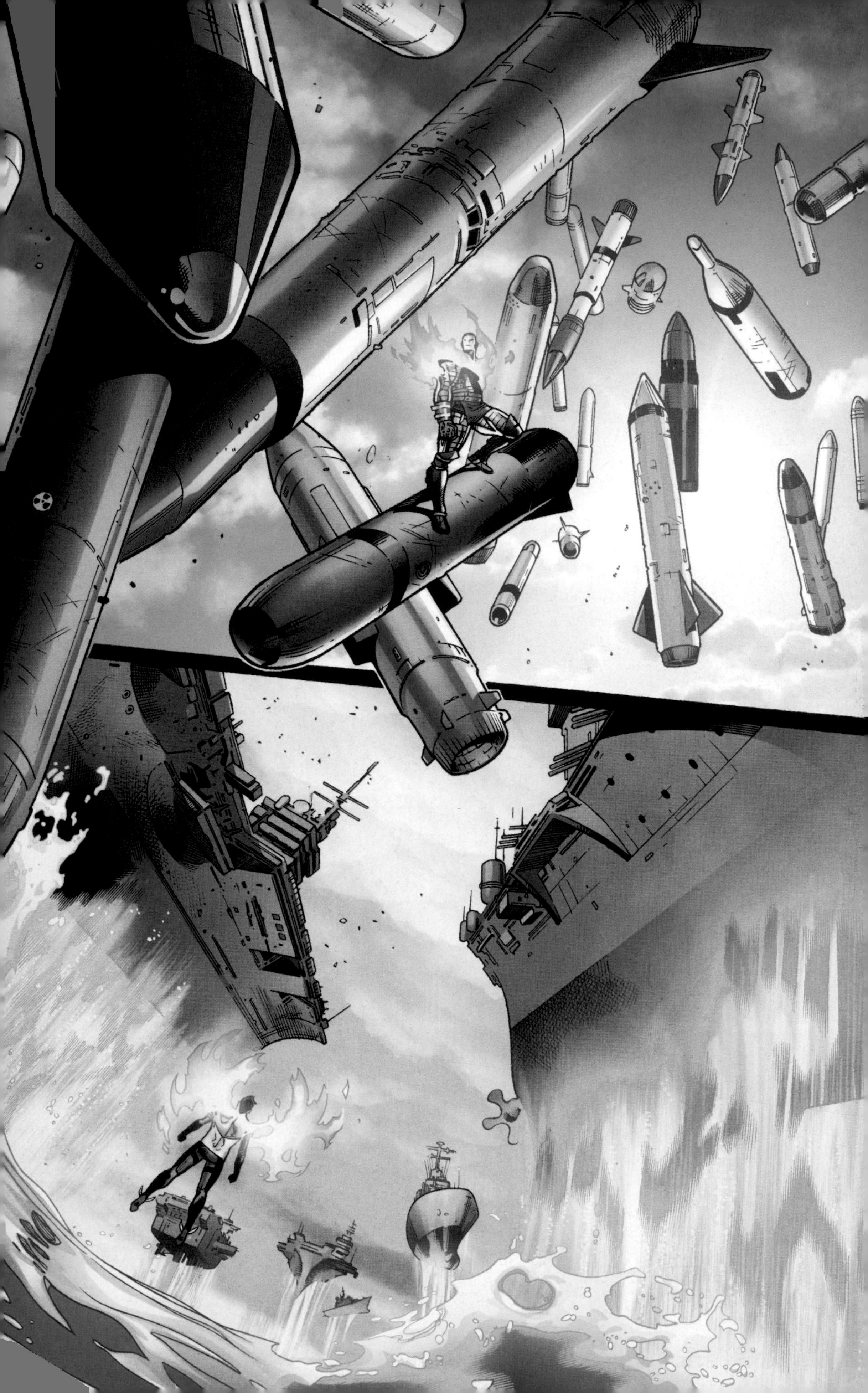

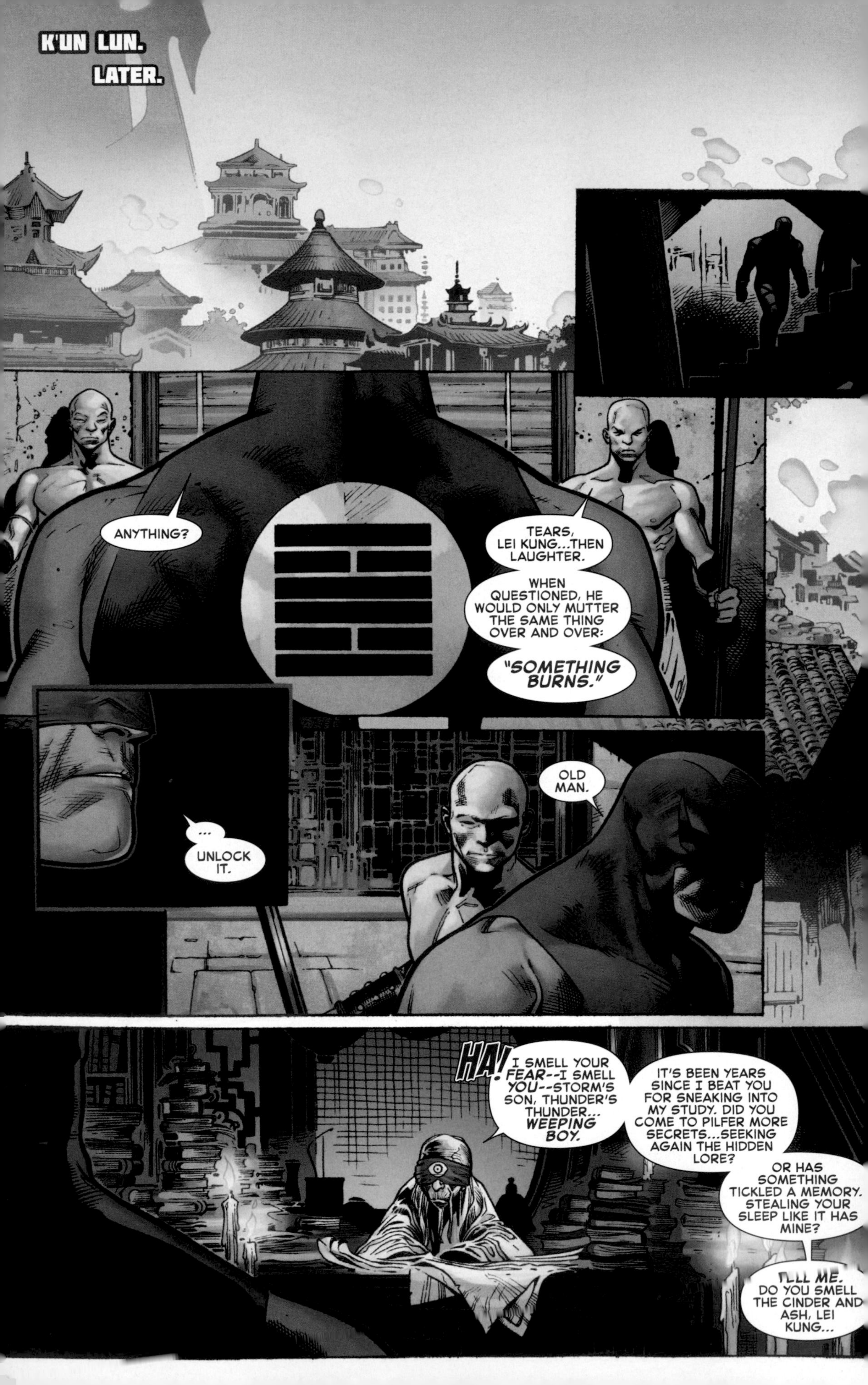
K'UN LUN.
LATER.
ANYTHING?
TEARS, LEI KUNG...THEN LAUGHTER.
WHEN QUESTIONED, HE WOULD ONLY MUTTER THE SAME THING OVER AND OVER:
"SOMETHING BURNS."
...
UNLOCK IT.
OLD MAN.
HA!
I SMELL YOUR FEAR--I SMELL YOU--STORM'S SON, THUNDER'S THUNDER... WEEPING BOY.
IT'S BEEN YEARS SINCE I BEAT YOU FOR SNEAKING INTO MY STUDY. DID YOU COME TO PILFER MORE SECRETS...SEEKING AGAIN THE HIDDEN LORE?
OR HAS SOMETHING TICKLED A MEMORY. STEALING YOUR SLEEP LIKE IT HAS MINE?
TELL ME. DO YOU SMELL THE CINDER AND ASH, LEI KUNG...

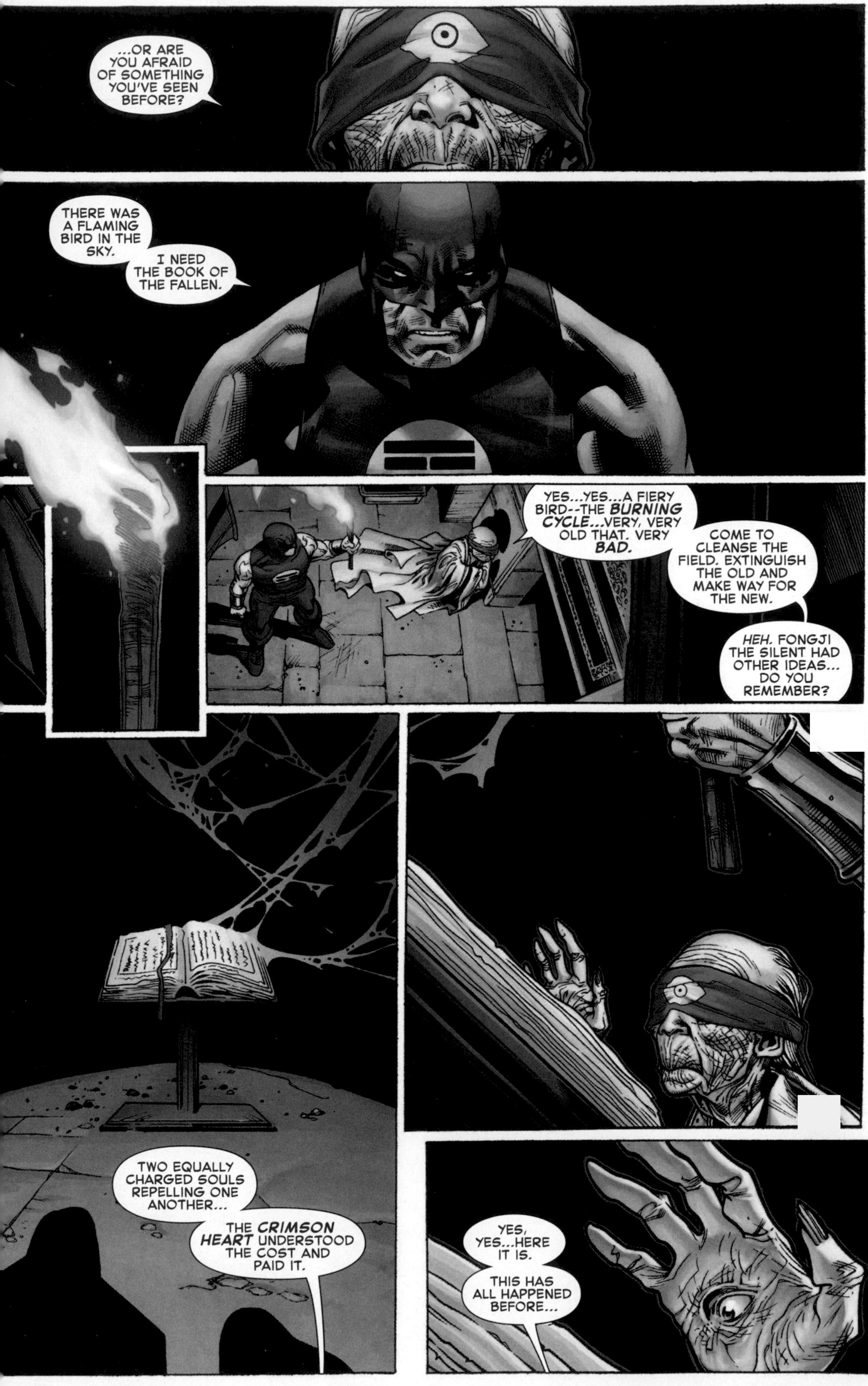
...OR ARE YOU AFRAID OF SOMETHING YOU'VE SEEN BEFORE?
THERE WAS A FLAMING BIRD IN THE SKY.
I NEED THE BOOK OF THE FALLEN.
YES...YES...A FIERY BIRD--THE BURNING CYCLE...VERY, VERY OLD THAT. VERY BAD.
COME TO CLEANSE THE FIELD. EXTINGUISH THE OLD AND MAKE WAY FOR THE NEW.
HEH. FONGJI THE SILENT HAD OTHER IDEAS... DO YOU REMEMBER?
TWO EQUALLY CHARGED SOULS REPELLING ONE ANOTHER...
THE CRIMSON HEART UNDERSTOOD THE COST AND PAID IT.
YES, YES...HERE IT IS.
THIS HAS ALL HAPPENED BEFORE...

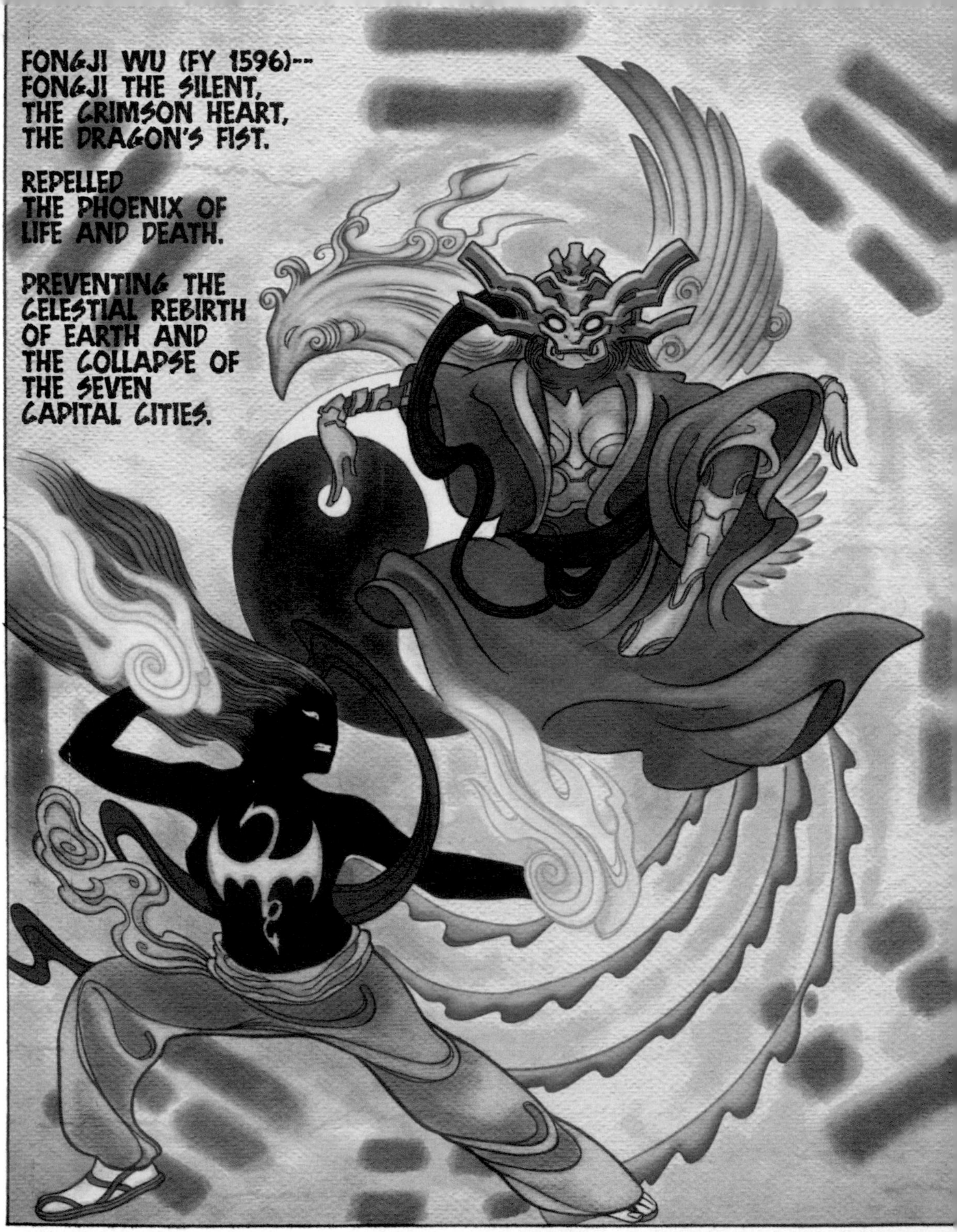
FONGJI WU (FY 1596)--
FONGJI THE SILENT, THE CRIMSON HEART, THE DRAGON'S FIST.
REPELLED THE PHOENIX OF LIFE AND DEATH.
PREVENTING THE CELESTIAL REBIRTH OF EARTH AND THE COLLAPSE OF THE SEVEN CAPITAL CITIES.

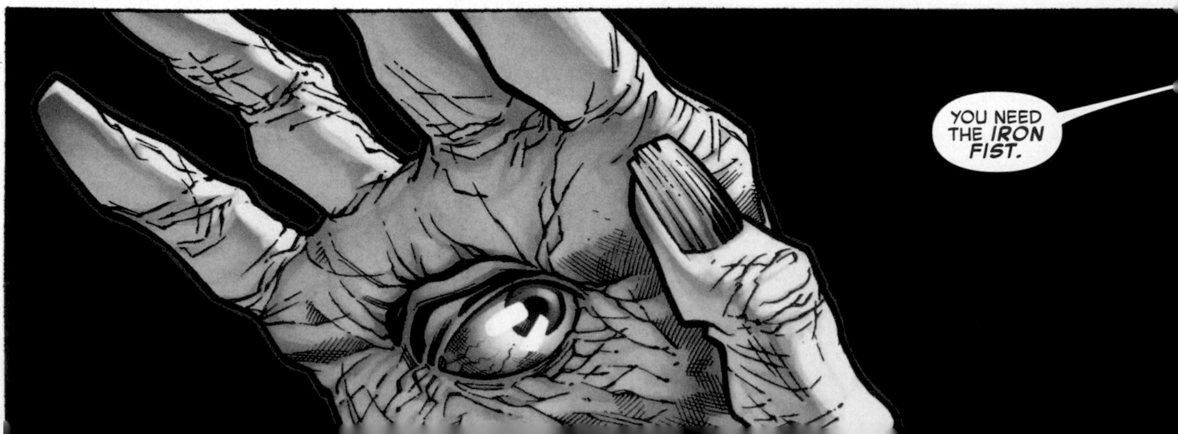
YOU NEED THE IRON FIST.

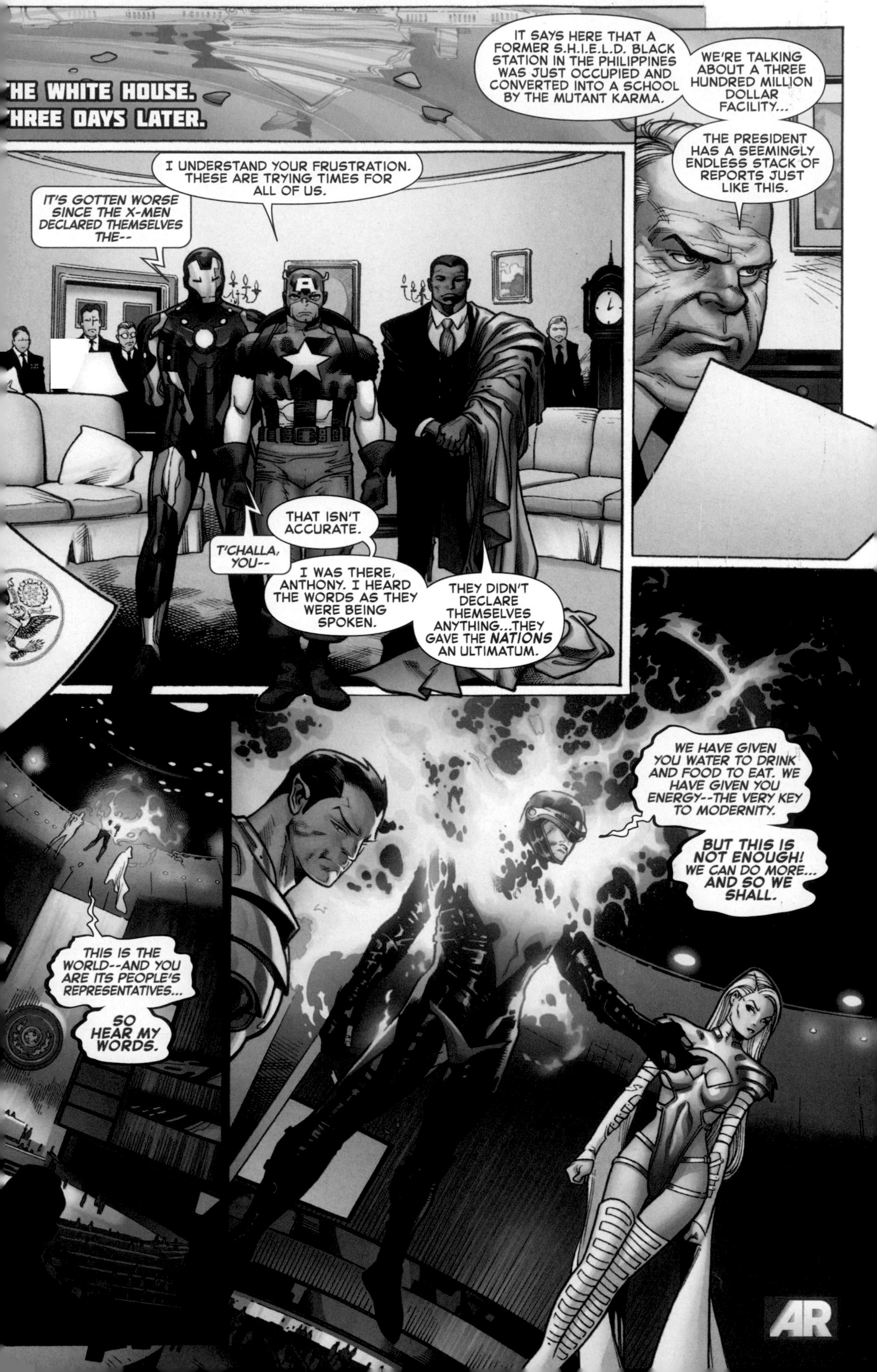
THE WHITE HOUSE. THREE DAYS LATER.
IT SAYS HERE THAT A FORMER S.H.I.E.L.D. BLACK STATION IN THE PHILIPPINES WAS JUST OCCUPIED AND CONVERTED INTO A SCHOOL BY THE MUTANT KARMA.
WE'RE TALKING ABOUT A THREE HUNDRED MILLION DOLLAR FACILITY...
THE PRESIDENT HAS A SEEMINGLY ENDLESS STACK OF REPORTS JUST LIKE THIS.
I UNDERSTAND YOUR FRUSTRATION. THESE ARE TRYING TIMES FOR ALL OF US.
IT'S GOTTEN WORSE SINCE THE X-MEN DECLARED THEMSELVES THE--
THAT ISN'T ACCURATE.
T'CHALLA, YOU--
I WAS THERE, ANTHONY. I HEARD THE WORDS AS THEY WERE BEING SPOKEN.
THEY DIDN'T DECLARE THEMSELVES ANYTHING...THEY GAVE THE NATIONS AN ULTIMATUM.
THIS IS THE WORLD--AND YOU ARE ITS PEOPLE'S REPRESENTATIVES...
SO HEAR MY WORDS.
WE HAVE GIVEN YOU WATER TO DRINK AND FOOD TO EAT. WE HAVE GIVEN YOU ENERGY--THE VERY KEY TO MODERNITY.
BUT THIS IS NOT ENOUGH! WE CAN DO MORE... AND SO WE SHALL.
AR

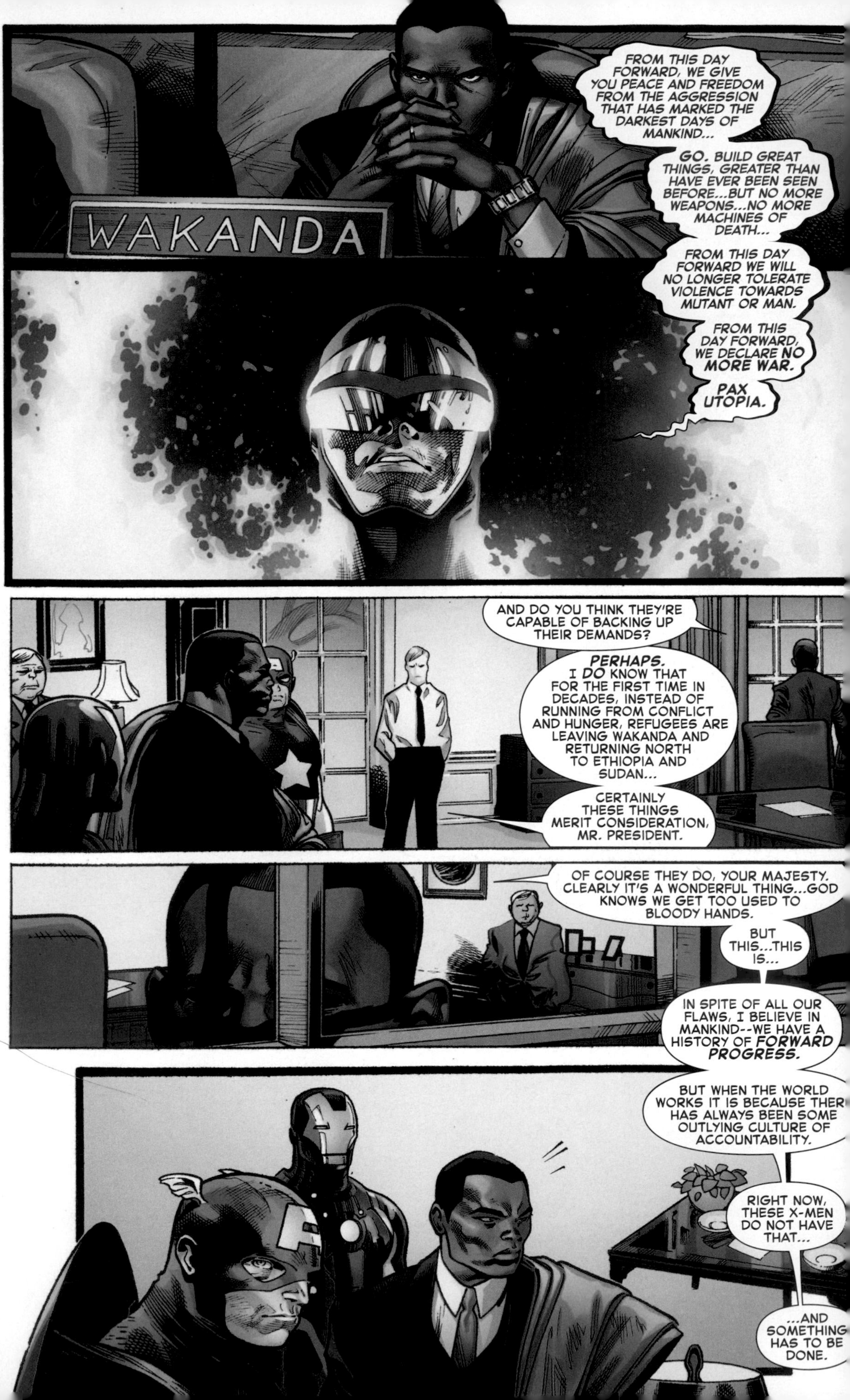
WAKANDA
FROM THIS DAY FORWARD, WE GIVE YOU PEACE AND FREEDOM FROM THE AGGRESSION THAT HAS MARKED THE DARKEST DAYS OF MANKIND...
GO. BUILD GREAT THINGS, GREATER THAN HAVE EVER BEEN SEEN BEFORE...BUT NO MORE WEAPONS...NO MORE MACHINES OF DEATH...
FROM THIS DAY FORWARD WE WILL NO LONGER TOLERATE VIOLENCE TOWARDS MUTANT OR MAN.
FROM THIS DAY FORWARD, WE DECLARE NO MORE WAR.
PAX UTOPIA.
AND DO YOU THINK THEY'RE CAPABLE OF BACKING UP THEIR DEMANDS?
PERHAPS. I DO KNOW THAT FOR THE FIRST TIME IN DECADES, INSTEAD OF RUNNING FROM CONFLICT AND HUNGER, REFUGEES ARE LEAVING WAKANDA AND RETURNING NORTH TO ETHIOPIA AND SUDAN...
CERTAINLY THESE THINGS MERIT CONSIDERATION, MR. PRESIDENT.
OF COURSE THEY DO, YOUR MAJESTY. CLEARLY IT'S A WONDERFUL THING...GOD KNOWS WE GET TOO USED TO BLOODY HANDS.
BUT THIS...THIS IS...
IN SPITE OF ALL OUR FLAWS, I BELIEVE IN MANKIND--WE HAVE A HISTORY OF FORWARD PROGRESS.
BUT WHEN THE WORLD WORKS IT IS BECAUSE THER HAS ALWAYS BEEN SOME OUTLYING CULTURE OF ACCOUNTABILITY.
RIGHT NOW, THESE X-MEN DO NOT HAVE THAT...
...AND SOMETHING HAS TO BE DONE.

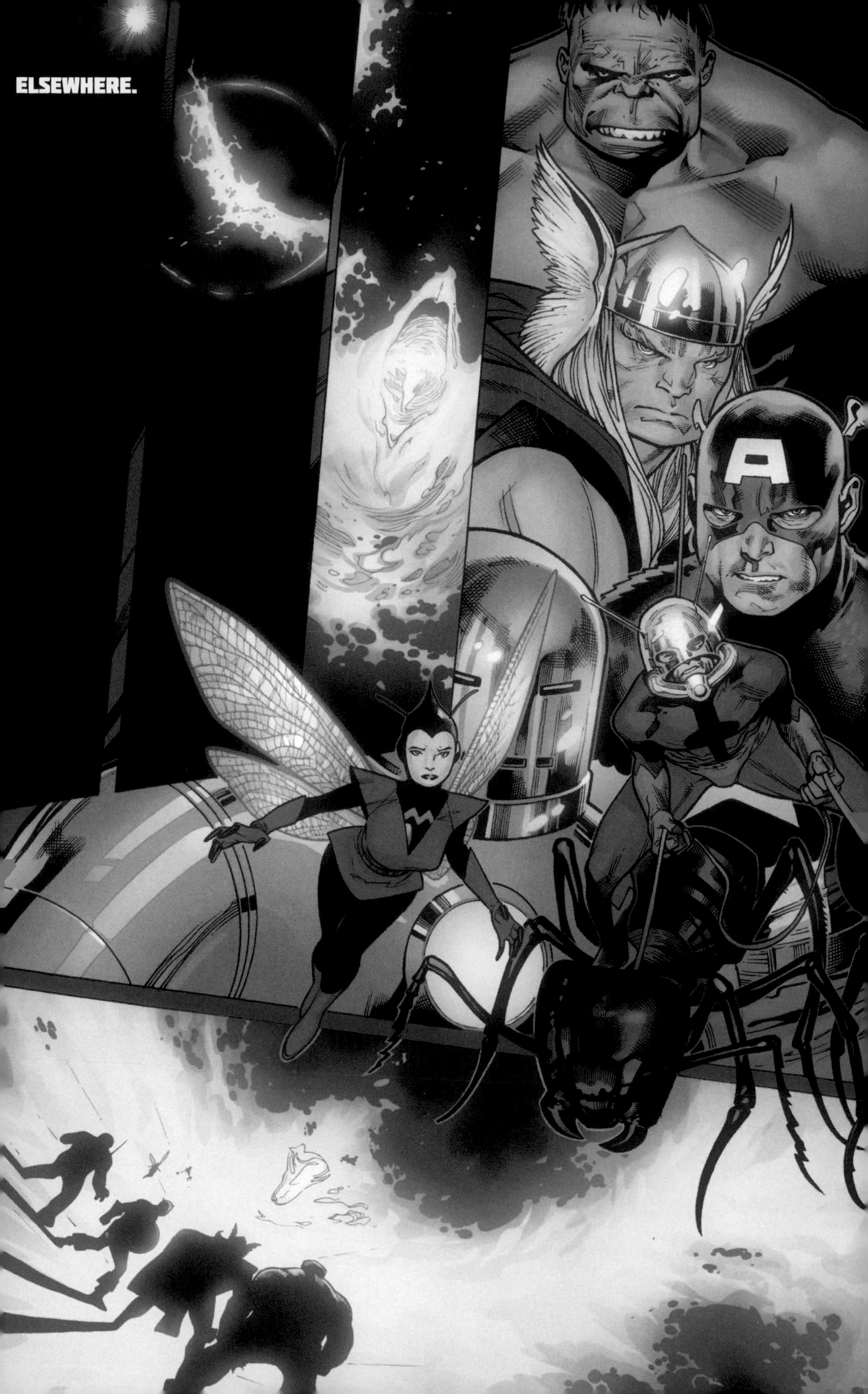
ELSEWHERE.

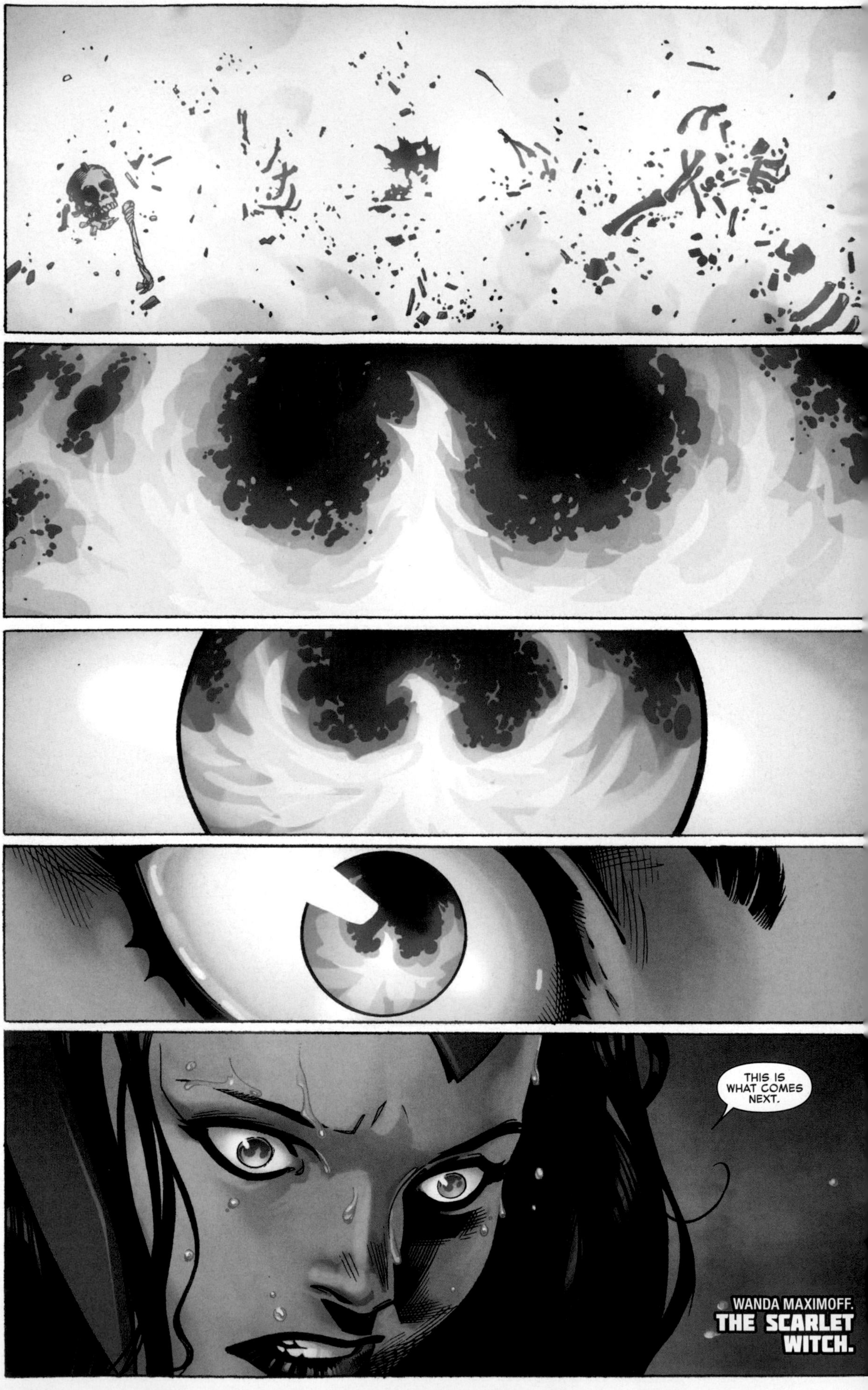
THIS IS WHAT COMES NEXT.
WANDA MAXIMOFF.
THE SCARLET WITCH.

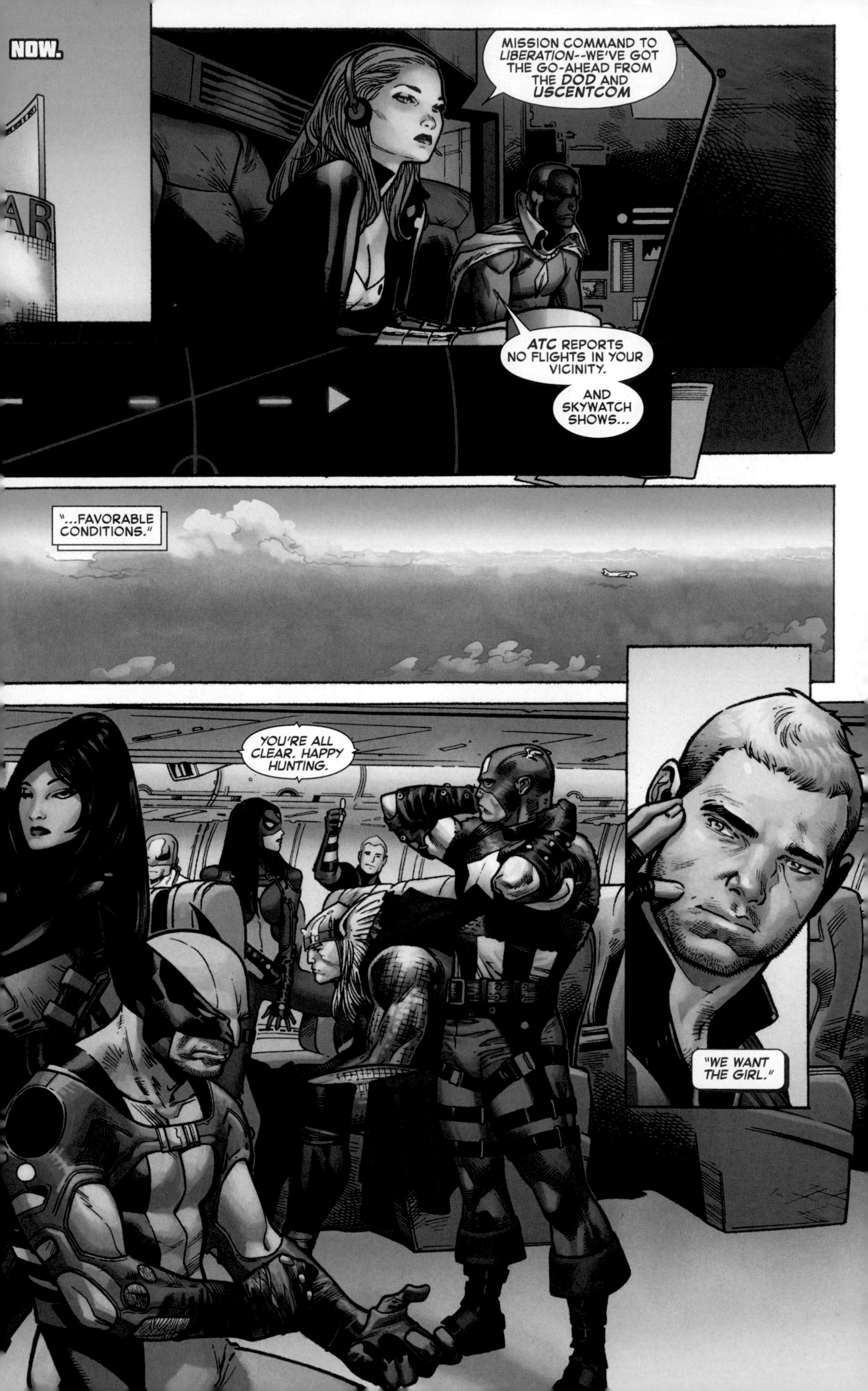
NOW.
MISSION COMMAND TO LIBERATION--WE'VE GOT THE GO-AHEAD FROM THE DOD AND USCENTCOM
ATC REPORTS NO FLIGHTS IN YOUR VICINITY.
AND SKYWATCH SHOWS...
"...FAVORABLE CONDITIONS."
YOU'RE ALL CLEAR. HAPPY HUNTING.
"WE WANT THE GIRL."

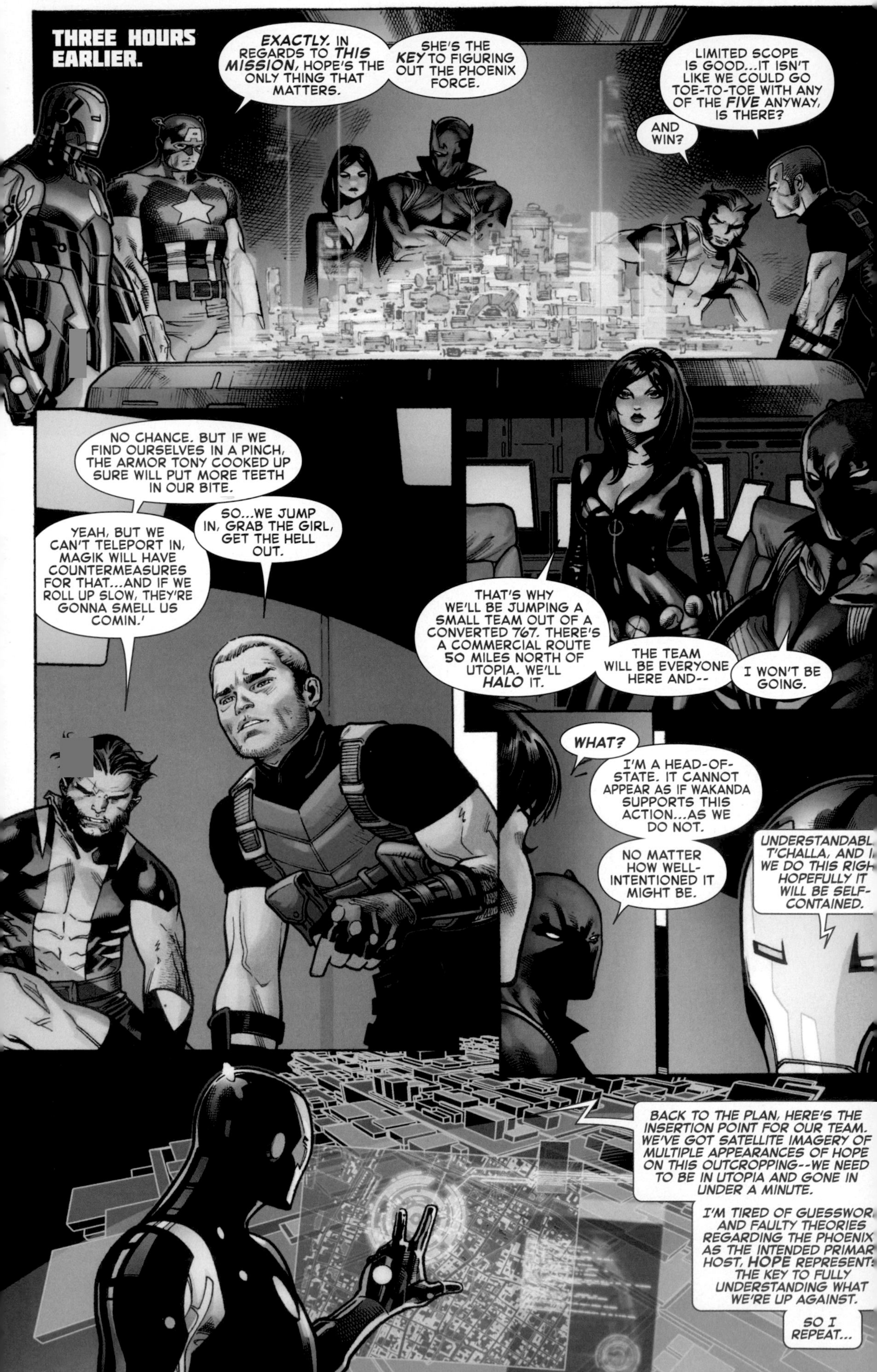
THREE HOURS EARLIER.
EXACTLY. IN REGARDS TO THIS MISSION, HOPE'S THE ONLY THING THAT MATTERS.
SHE'S THE KEY TO FIGURING OUT THE PHOENIX FORCE.
LIMITED SCOPE IS GOOD...IT ISN'T LIKE WE COULD GO TOE-TO-TOE WITH ANY OF THE FIVE ANYWAY, IS THERE?
AND WIN?
NO CHANCE. BUT IF WE FIND OURSELVES IN A PINCH, THE ARMOR TONY COOKED UP SURE WILL PUT MORE TEETH IN OUR BITE.
SO...WE JUMP IN, GRAB THE GIRL, GET THE HELL OUT.
YEAH, BUT WE CAN'T TELEPORT IN, MAGIK WILL HAVE COUNTERMEASURES FOR THAT...AND IF WE ROLL UP SLOW, THEY'RE GONNA SMELL US COMIN.'
THAT'S WHY WE'LL BE JUMPING A SMALL TEAM OUT OF A CONVERTED 767. THERE'S A COMMERCIAL ROUTE 50 MILES NORTH OF UTOPIA. WE'LL HALO IT.
THE TEAM WILL BE EVERYONE HERE AND--
I WON'T BE GOING.
WHAT?
I'M A HEAD-OF-STATE. IT CANNOT APPEAR AS IF WAKANDA SUPPORTS THIS ACTION...AS WE DO NOT.
NO MATTER HOW WELL-INTENTIONED IT MIGHT BE.
UNDERSTANDABL T'CHALLA, AND I WE DO THIS RIGH HOPEFULLY IT WILL BE SELF-CONTAINED.
BACK TO THE PLAN, HERE'S THE INSERTION POINT FOR OUR TEAM. WE'VE GOT SATELLITE IMAGERY OF MULTIPLE APPEARANCES OF HOPE ON THIS OUTCROPPING--WE NEED TO BE IN UTOPIA AND GONE IN UNDER A MINUTE.
I'M TIRED OF GUESSWOR AND FAULTY THEORIES REGARDING THE PHOENIX AS THE INTENDED PRIMAR HOST, HOPE REPRESENT THE KEY TO FULLY UNDERSTANDING WHAT WE'RE UP AGAINST.
SO I REPEAT...

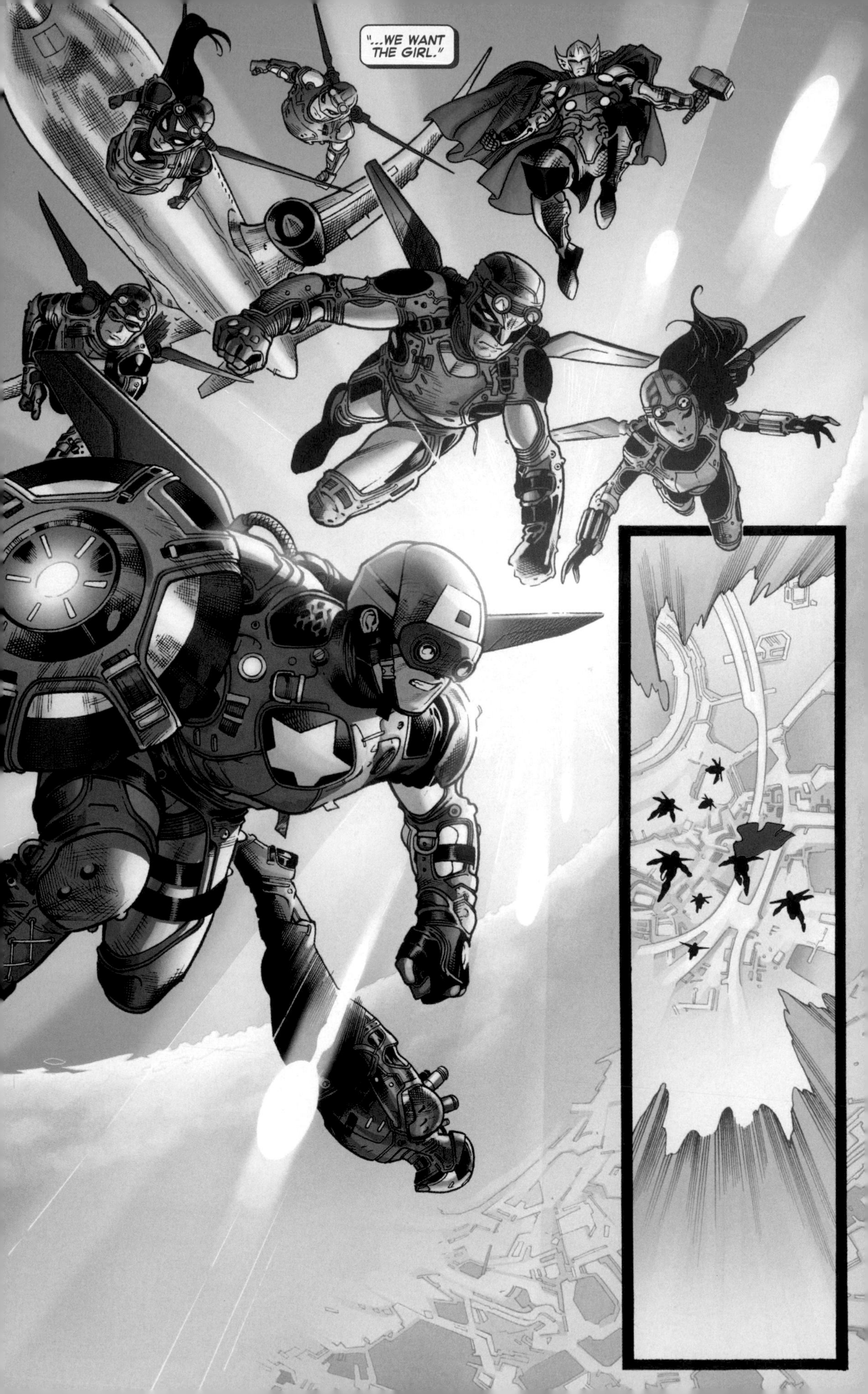
"...WE WANT THE GIRL."

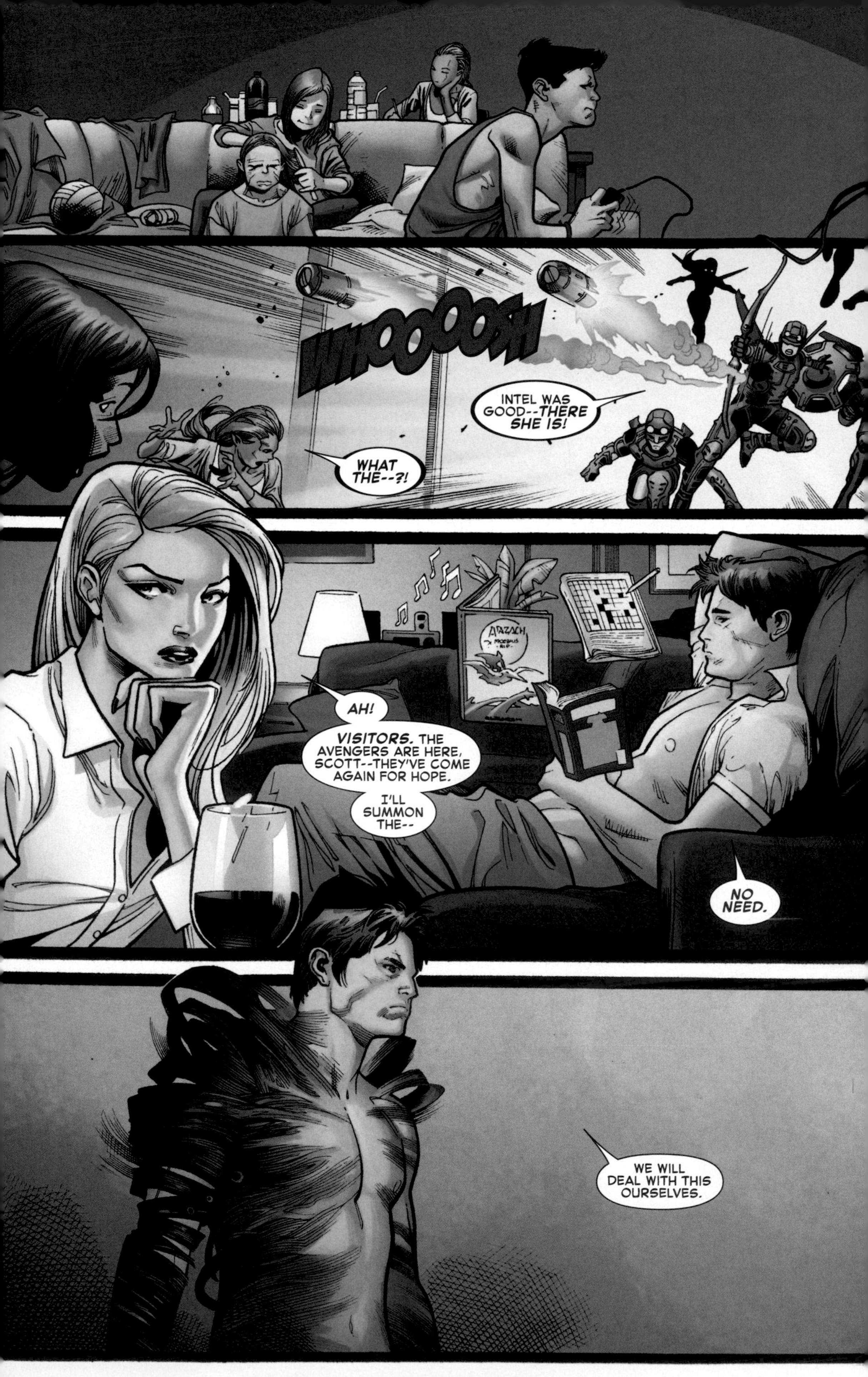
WHOOOOOSH
WHAT THE--?!
INTEL WAS GOOD--THERE SHE IS!
AH!
VISITORS. THE AVENGERS ARE HERE, SCOTT--THEY'VE COME AGAIN FOR HOPE.
I'LL SUMMON THE--
NO NEED.
WE WILL DEAL WITH THIS OURSELVES.

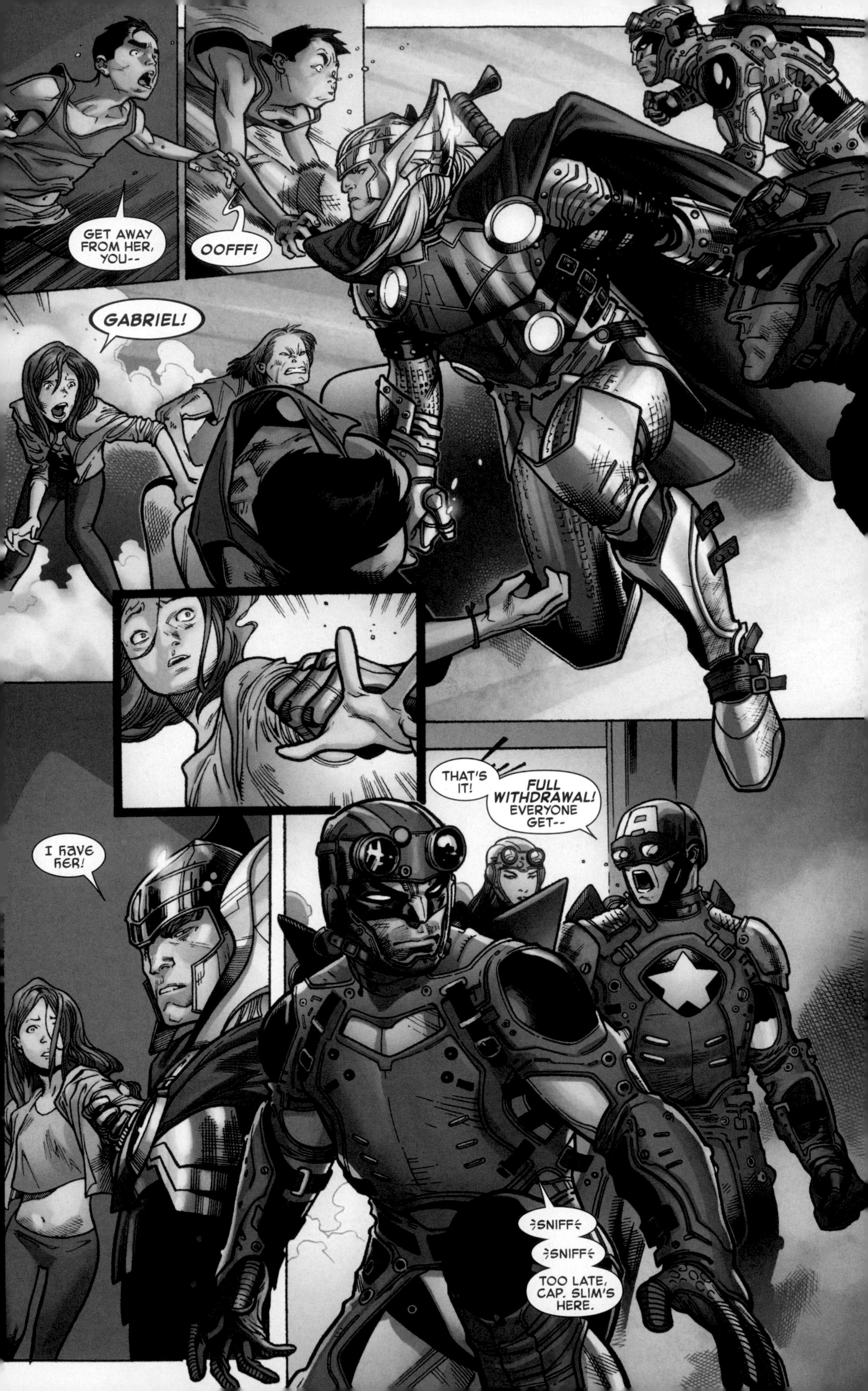
GET AWAY FROM HER, YOU--
OOFFF!
GABRIEL!
I HAVE HER!
THAT'S IT!
FULL WITHDRAWAL! EVERYONE GET--
SNIFF
SNIFF
TOO LATE, CAP. SLIM'S HERE.

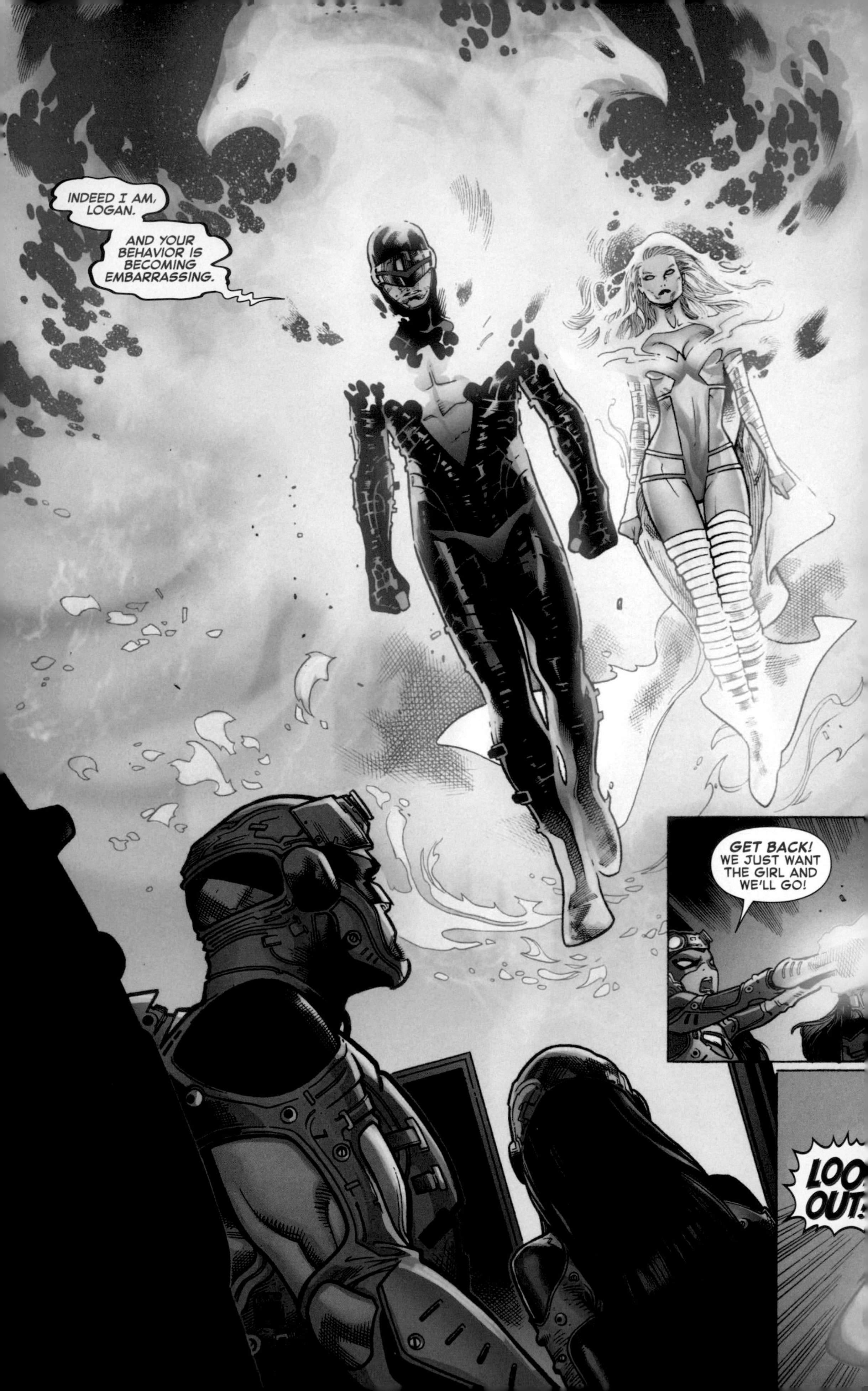
INDEED I AM, LOGAN.
AND YOUR BEHAVIOR IS BECOMING EMBARRASSING.
GET BACK! WE JUST WANT THE GIRL AND WE'LL GO!

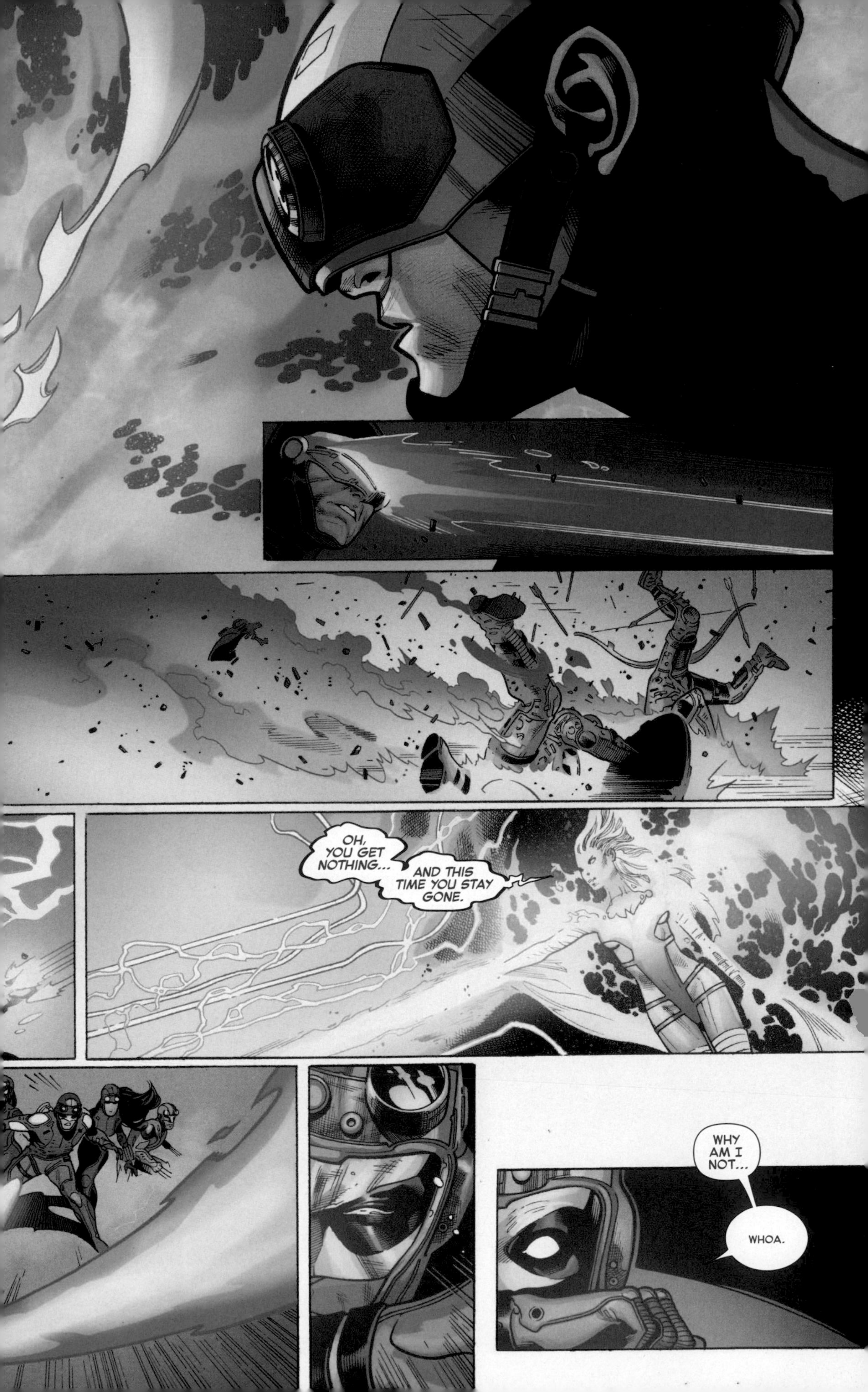
OH, YOU GET NOTHING...
AND THIS TIME YOU STAY GONE.
WHY AM I NOT...
WHOA.

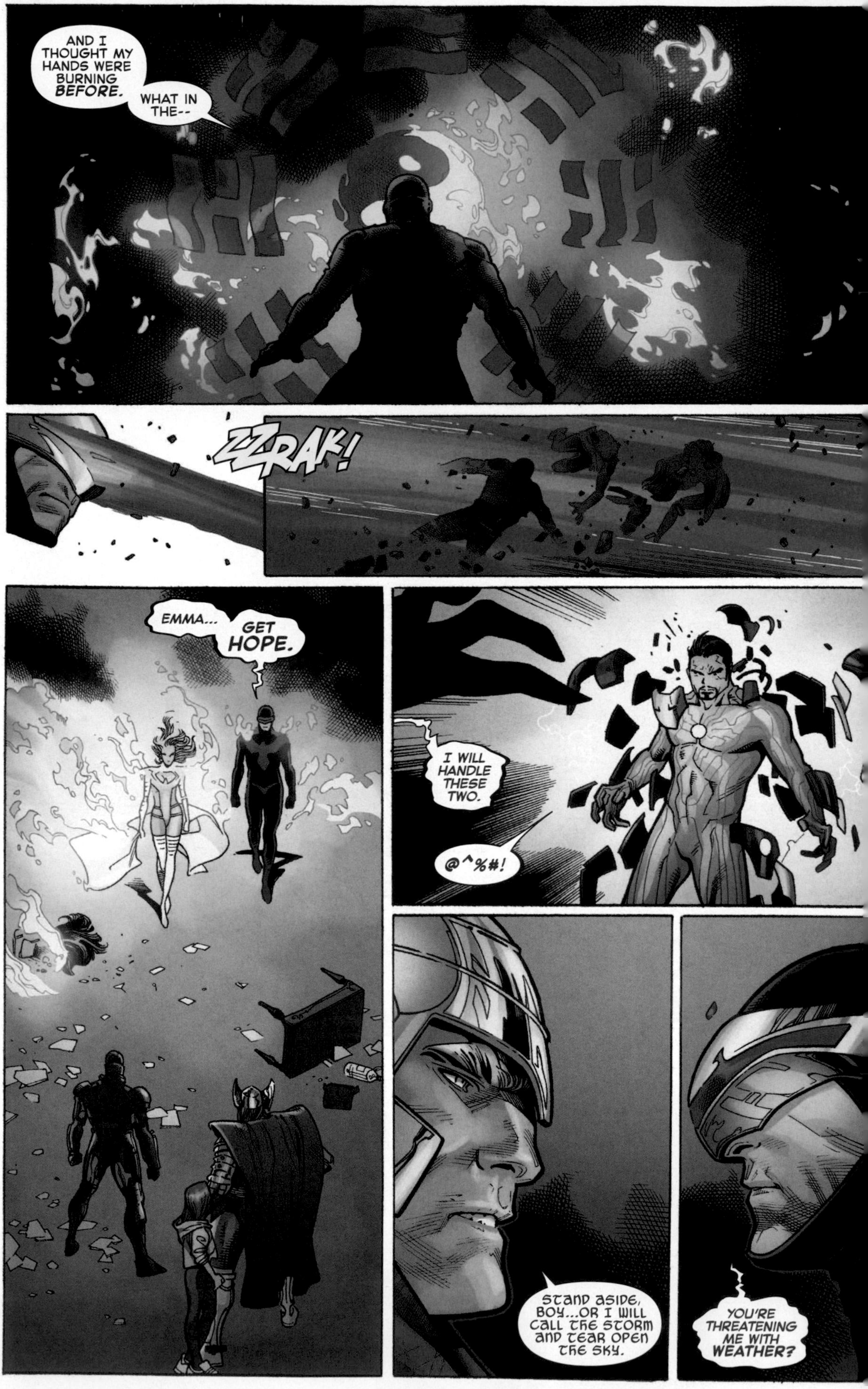
AND I THOUGHT MY HANDS WERE BURNING BEFORE.
WHAT IN THE--
ZZRAK!
EMMA... GET HOPE.
I WILL HANDLE THESE TWO.
@^%#!
STAND ASIDE, BOY...OR I WILL CALL THE STORM AND TEAR OPEN THE SKY.
YOU'RE THREATENING ME WITH WEATHER?

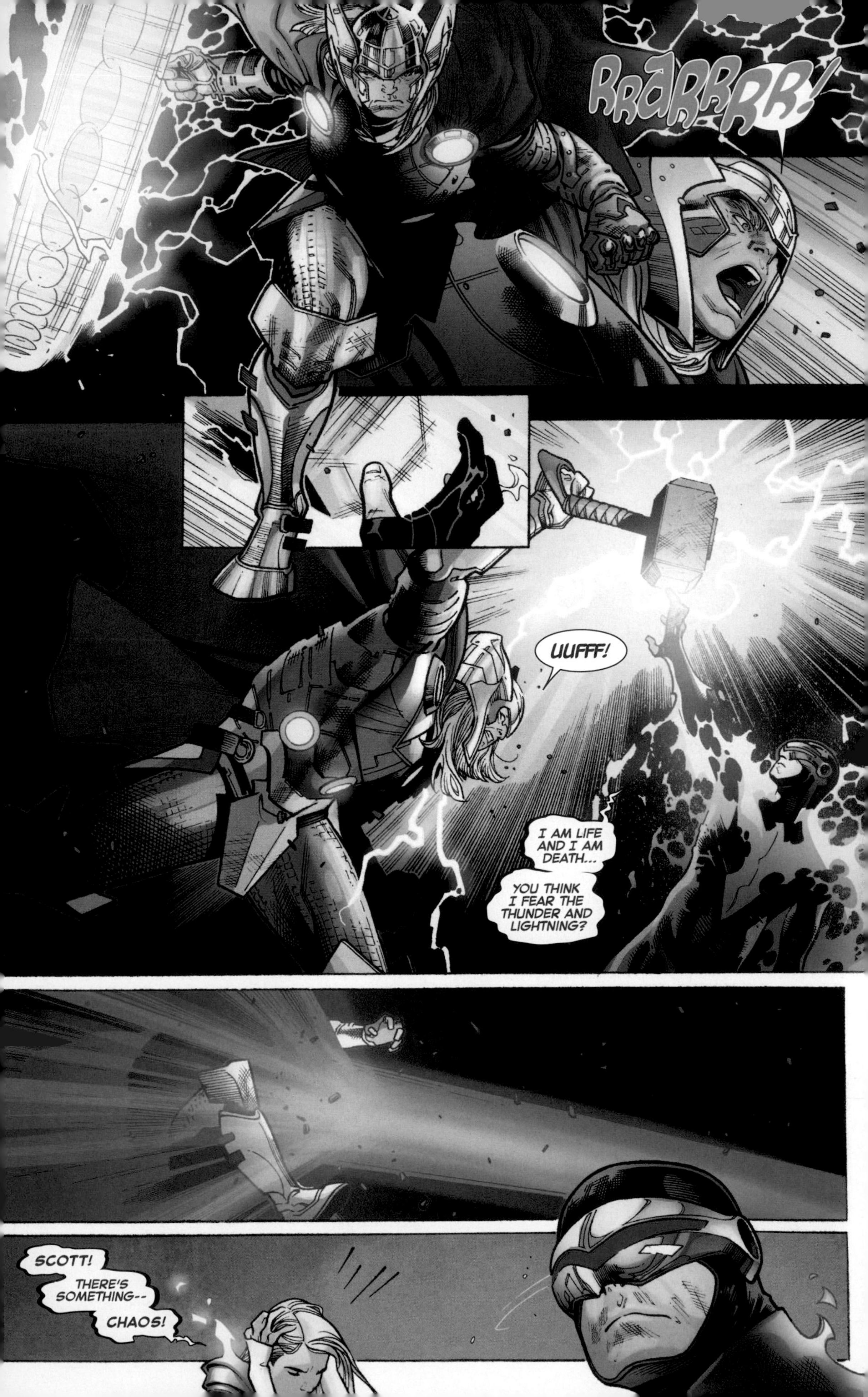

RRARRRR!
UUFFF!
I AM LIFE AND I AM DEATH...
YOU THINK I FEAR THE THUNDER AND LIGHTNING?
SCOTT!
THERE'S SOMETHING--
CHAOS!

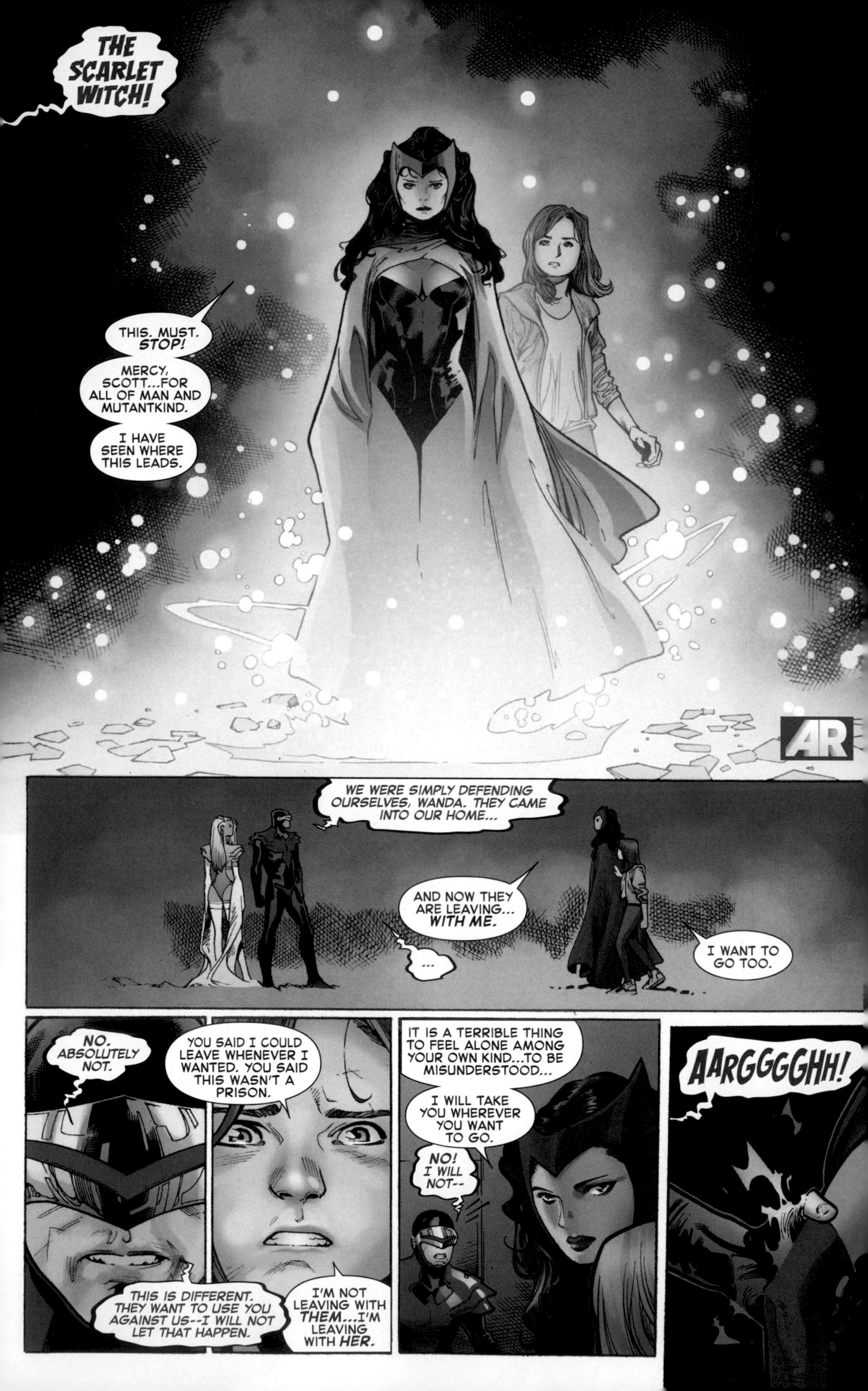
THE SCARLET WITCH!
THIS. MUST. STOP!
MERCY, SCOTT...FOR ALL OF MAN AND MUTANTKIND.
I HAVE SEEN WHERE THIS LEADS.
AR
WE WERE SIMPLY DEFENDING OURSELVES, WANDA. THEY CAME INTO OUR HOME...
AND NOW THEY ARE LEAVING... WITH ME.
...
I WANT TO GO TOO.
NO. ABSOLUTELY NOT.
YOU SAID I COULD LEAVE WHENEVER I WANTED. YOU SAID THIS WASN'T A PRISON.
THIS IS DIFFERENT. THEY WANT TO USE YOU AGAINST US--I WILL NOT LET THAT HAPPEN.
I'M NOT LEAVING WITH THEM...I'M LEAVING WITH HER.
IT IS A TERRIBLE THING TO FEEL ALONE AMONG YOUR OWN KIND...TO BE MISUNDERSTOOD...
I WILL TAKE YOU WHEREVER YOU WANT TO GO.
NO! I WILL NOT--
AARGGGGHH!

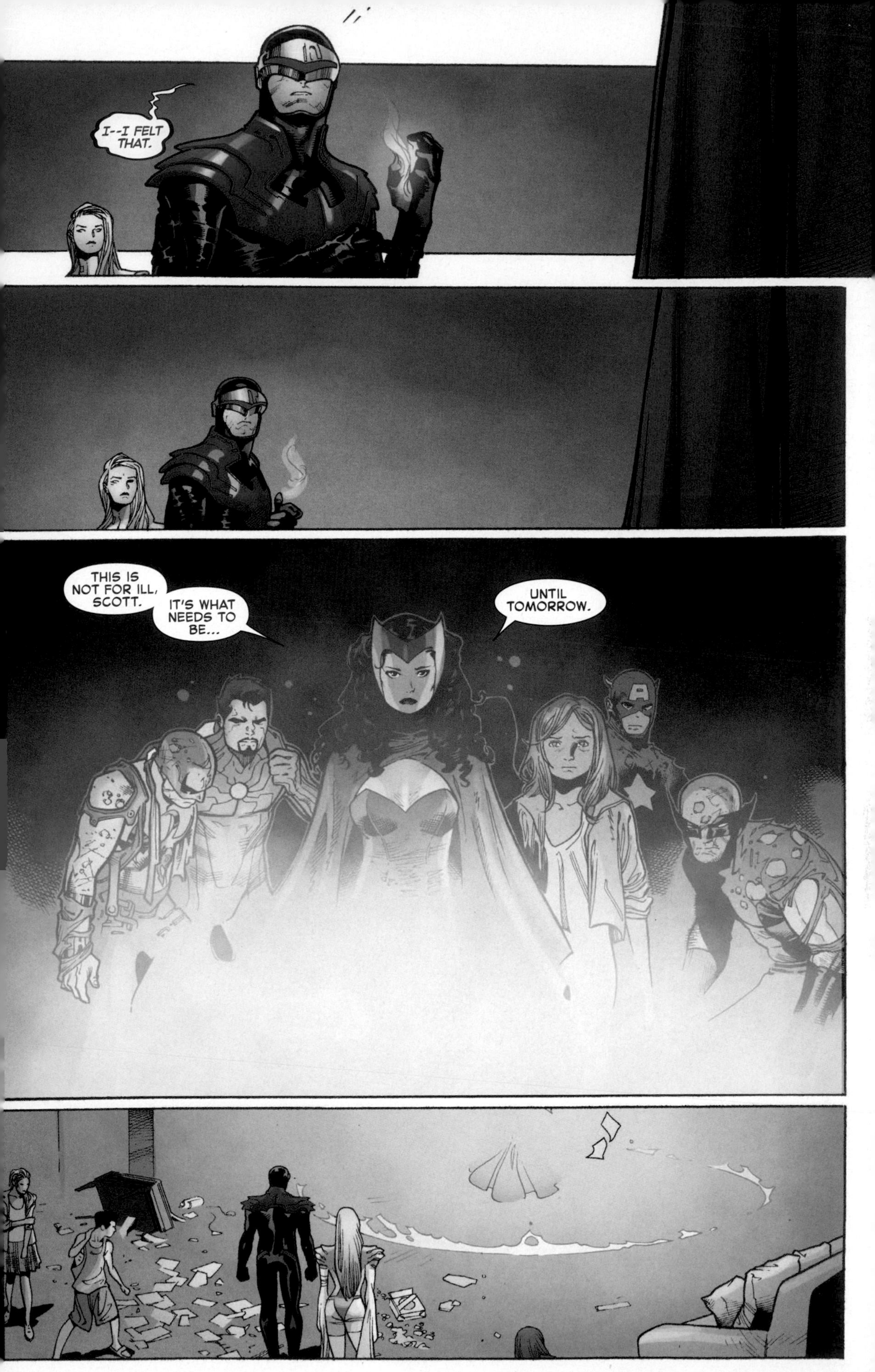

I--I FELT THAT.
THIS IS NOT FOR ILL, SCOTT.
IT'S WHAT NEEDS TO BE...
UNTIL TOMORROW.

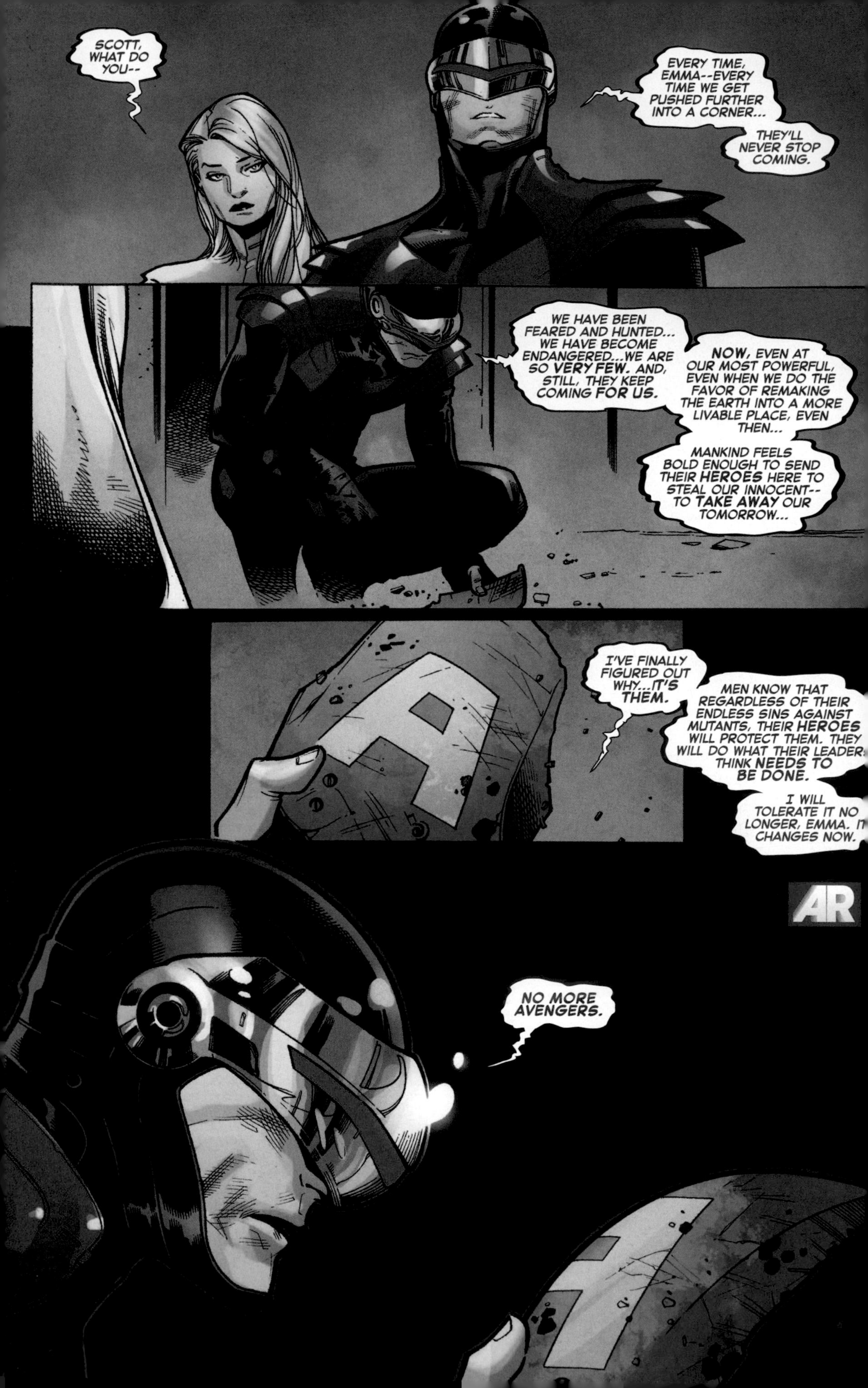
SCOTT, WHAT DO YOU--
EVERY TIME, EMMA--EVERY TIME WE GET PUSHED FURTHER INTO A CORNER...
THEY'LL NEVER STOP COMING.
WE HAVE BEEN FEARED AND HUNTED... WE HAVE BECOME ENDANGERED...WE ARE SO VERY FEW. AND, STILL, THEY KEEP COMING FOR US.
NOW, EVEN AT OUR MOST POWERFUL, EVEN WHEN WE DO THE FAVOR OF REMAKING THE EARTH INTO A MORE LIVABLE PLACE, EVEN THEN...
MANKIND FEELS BOLD ENOUGH TO SEND THEIR HEROES HERE TO STEAL OUR INNOCENT-- TO TAKE AWAY OUR TOMORROW...
I'VE FINALLY FIGURED OUT WHY...IT'S THEM.
MEN KNOW THAT REGARDLESS OF THEIR ENDLESS SINS AGAINST MUTANTS, THEIR HEROES WILL PROTECT THEM. THEY WILL DO WHAT THEIR LEADERS THINK NEEDS TO BE DONE.
I WILL TOLERATE IT NO LONGER, EMMA. IT CHANGES NOW.
NO MORE AVENGERS.

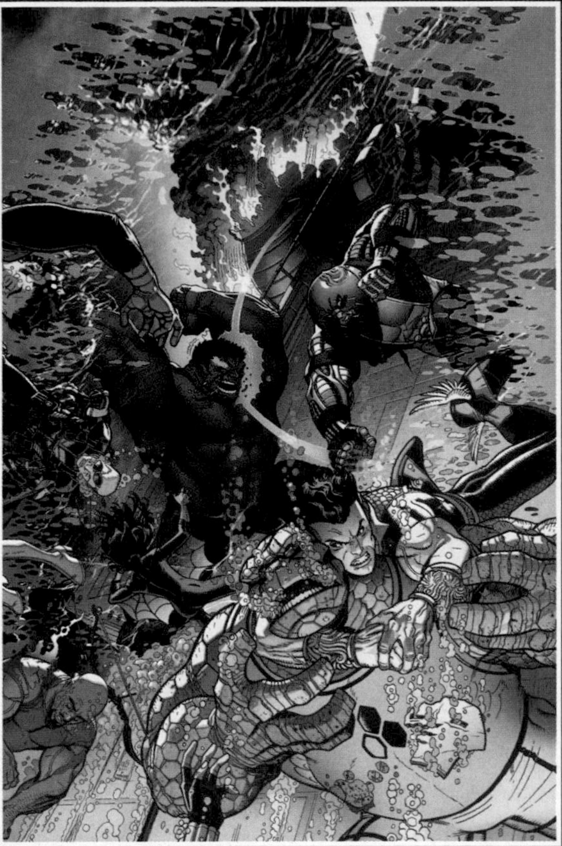

AVX #2 VARIANT
BY **NICK BRADSHAW & MARTE GRACIA**

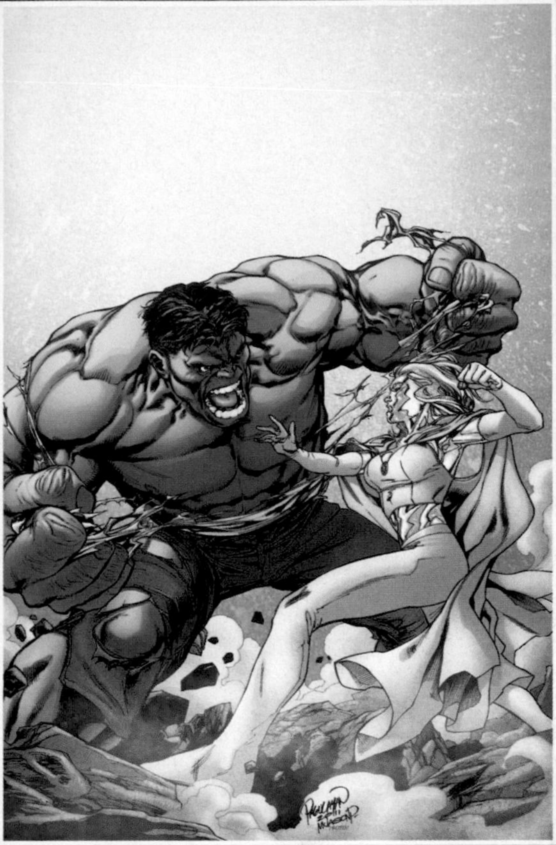

AVX #2 VARIANT
BY **CARLO PAGULAYAN, JASON PAZ & CHRIS SOTOMAYOR**

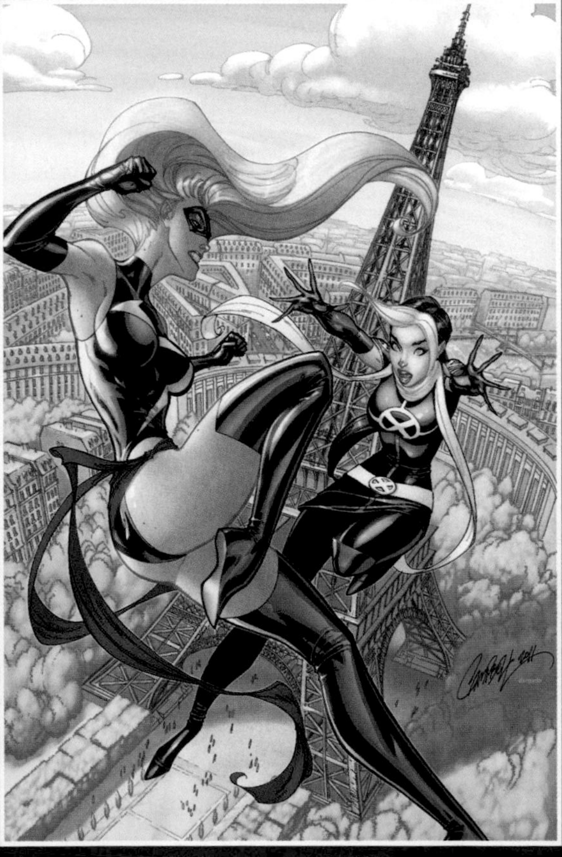

AVX #3 VARIANT
BY **J. SCOTT CAMPBELL & EDGAR DELGADO**

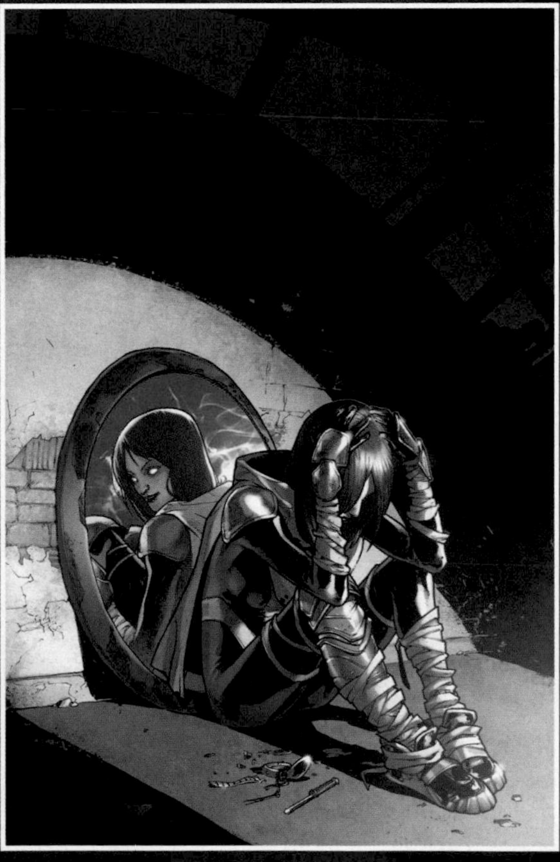

AVX #3 VARIANT
BY **SARA PICHELLI & JUSTIN PONSOR**

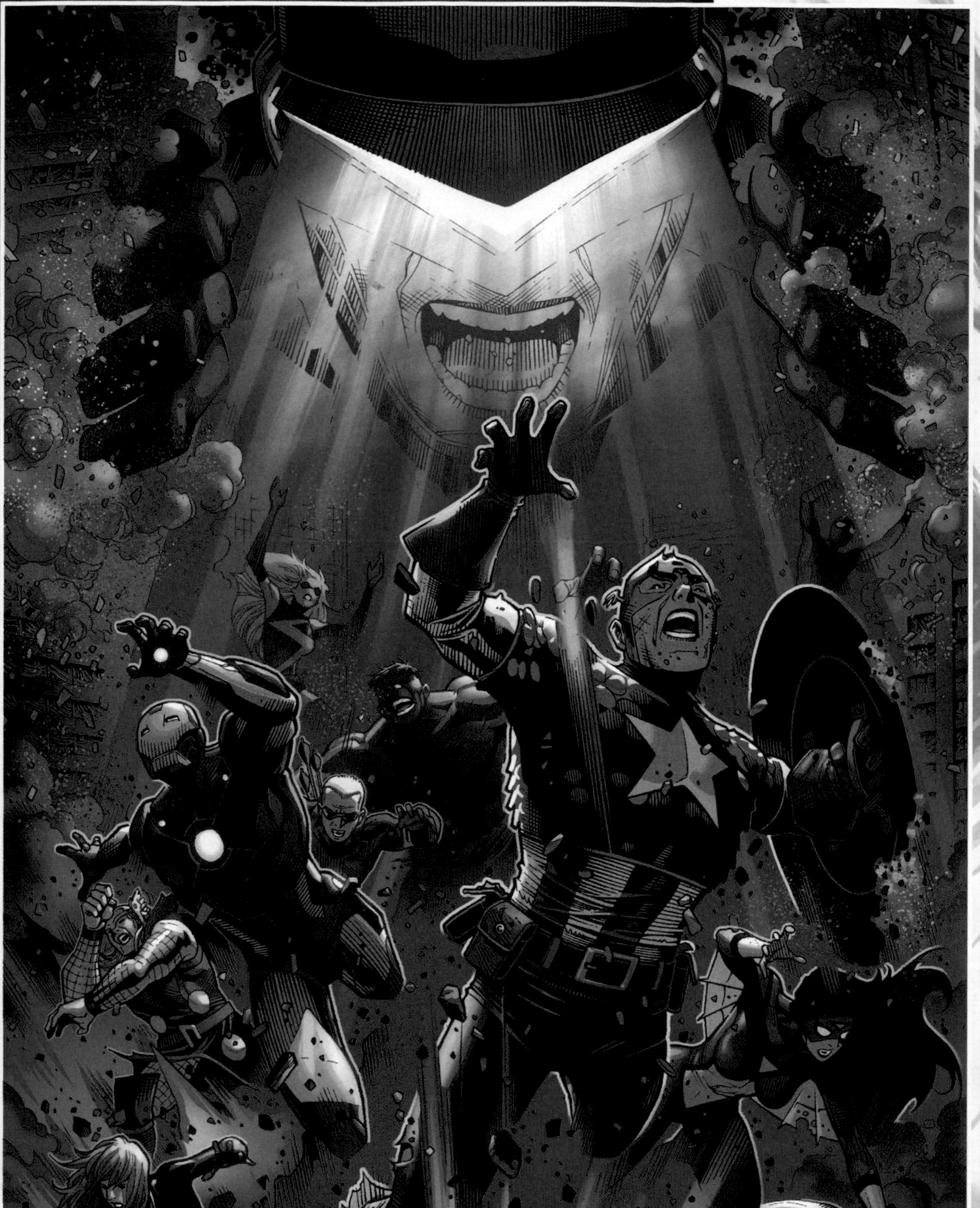

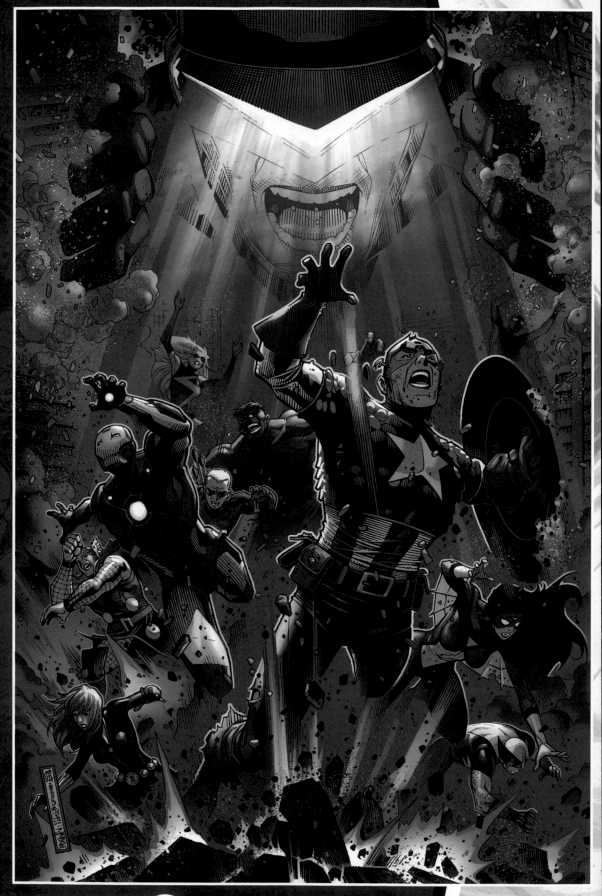

ROUND 7

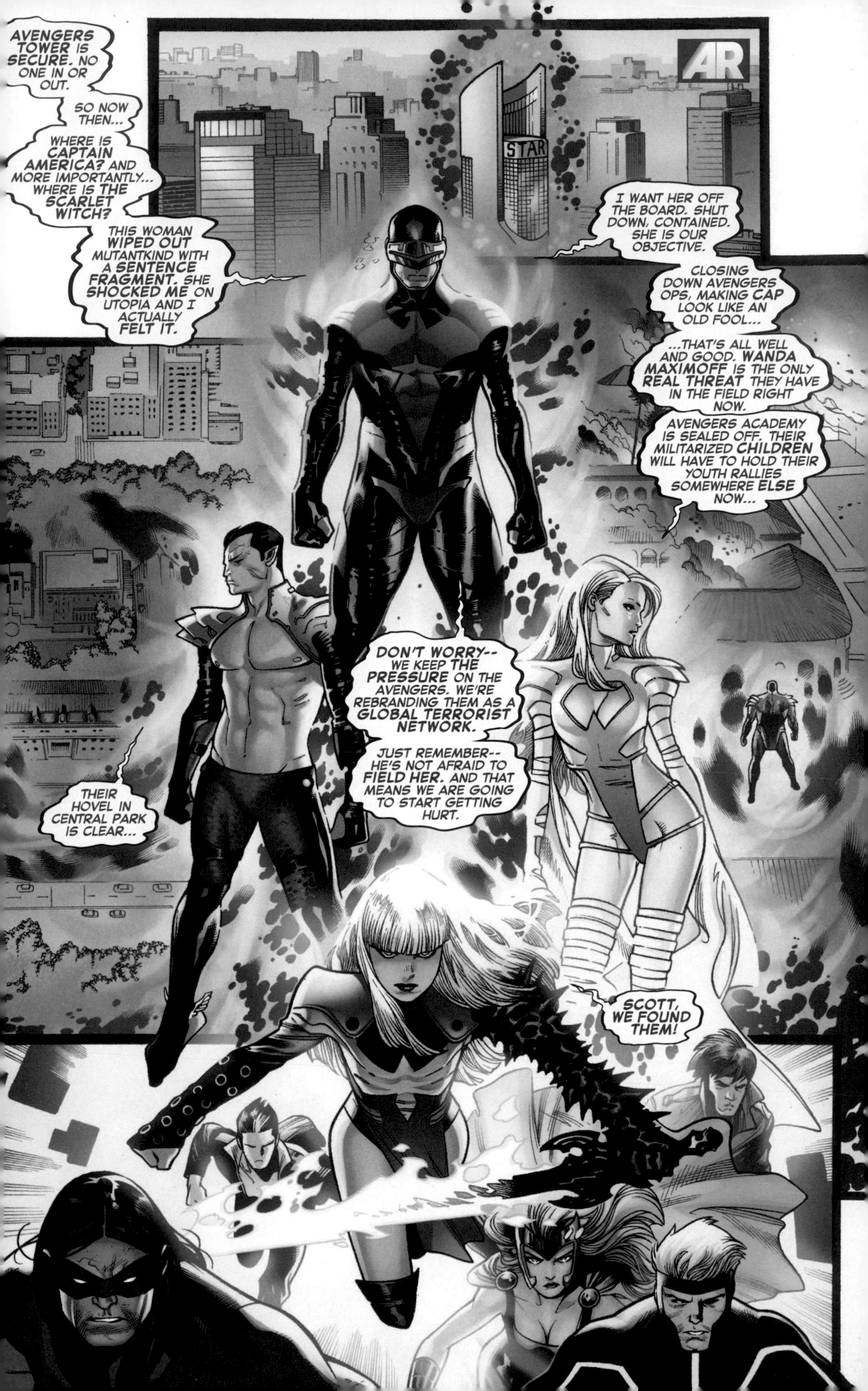
AR
AVENGERS TOWER IS SECURE. NO ONE IN OR OUT.
SO NOW THEN...
WHERE IS CAPTAIN AMERICA? AND MORE IMPORTANTLY... WHERE IS THE SCARLET WITCH?
THIS WOMAN WIPED OUT MUTANTKIND WITH A SENTENCE FRAGMENT. SHE SHOCKED ME ON UTOPIA AND I ACTUALLY FELT IT.
STAR
I WANT HER OFF THE BOARD. SHUT DOWN, CONTAINED. SHE IS OUR OBJECTIVE.
CLOSING DOWN AVENGERS OPS, MAKING CAP LOOK LIKE AN OLD FOOL...
...THAT'S ALL WELL AND GOOD. WANDA MAXIMOFF IS THE ONLY REAL THREAT THEY HAVE IN THE FIELD RIGHT NOW.
AVENGERS ACADEMY IS SEALED OFF. THEIR MILITARIZED CHILDREN WILL HAVE TO HOLD THEIR YOUTH RALLIES SOMEWHERE ELSE NOW...
DON'T WORRY-- WE KEEP THE PRESSURE ON THE AVENGERS. WE'RE REBRANDING THEM AS A GLOBAL TERRORIST NETWORK.
JUST REMEMBER-- HE'S NOT AFRAID TO FIELD HER. AND THAT MEANS WE ARE GOING TO START GETTING HURT.
THEIR HOVEL IN CENTRAL PARK IS CLEAR...
SCOTT, WE FOUND THEM!

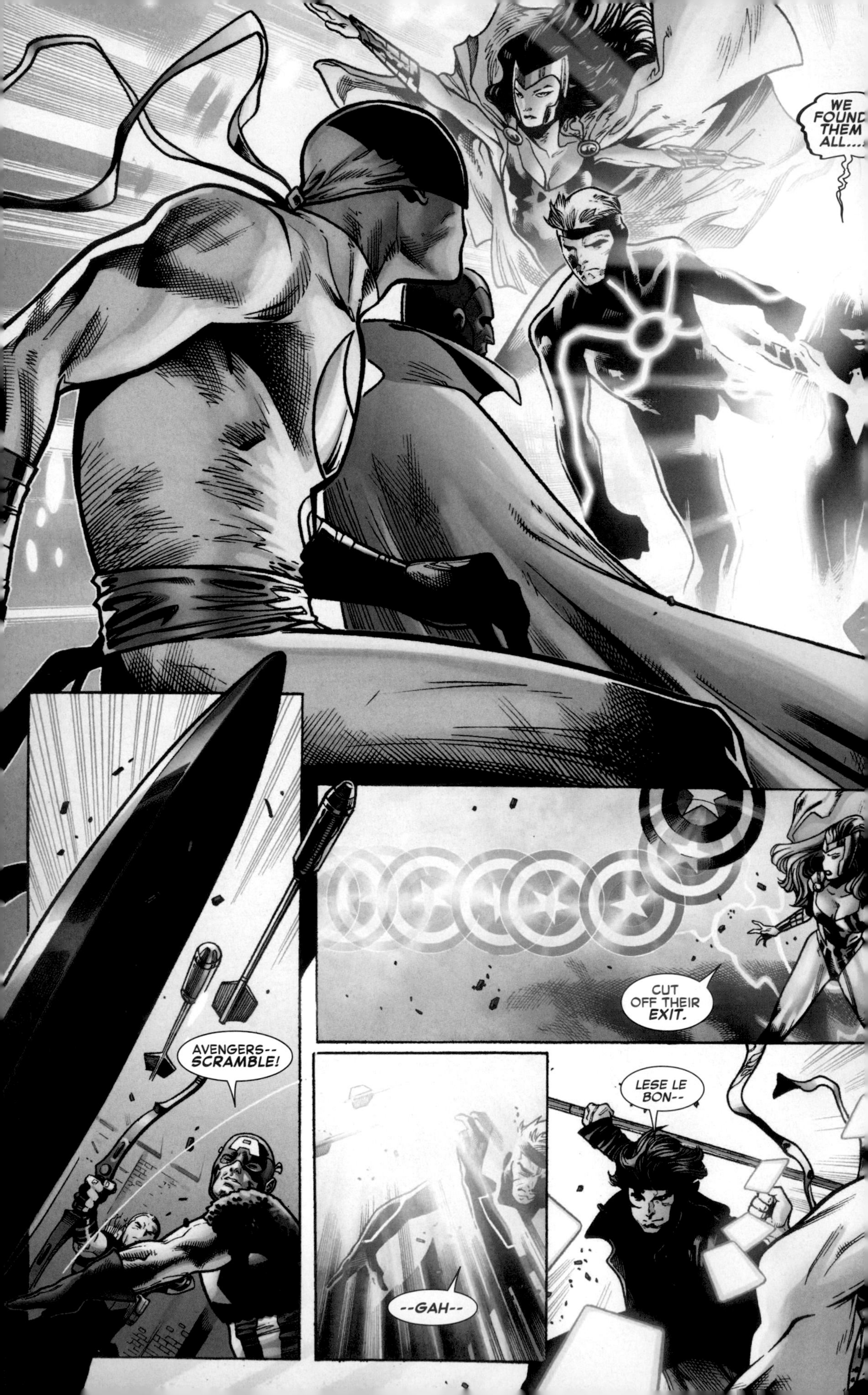
WE FOUND THEM ALL....
CUT OFF THEIR EXIT.
AVENGERS-- SCRAMBLE!
--GAH--
LESE LE BON--

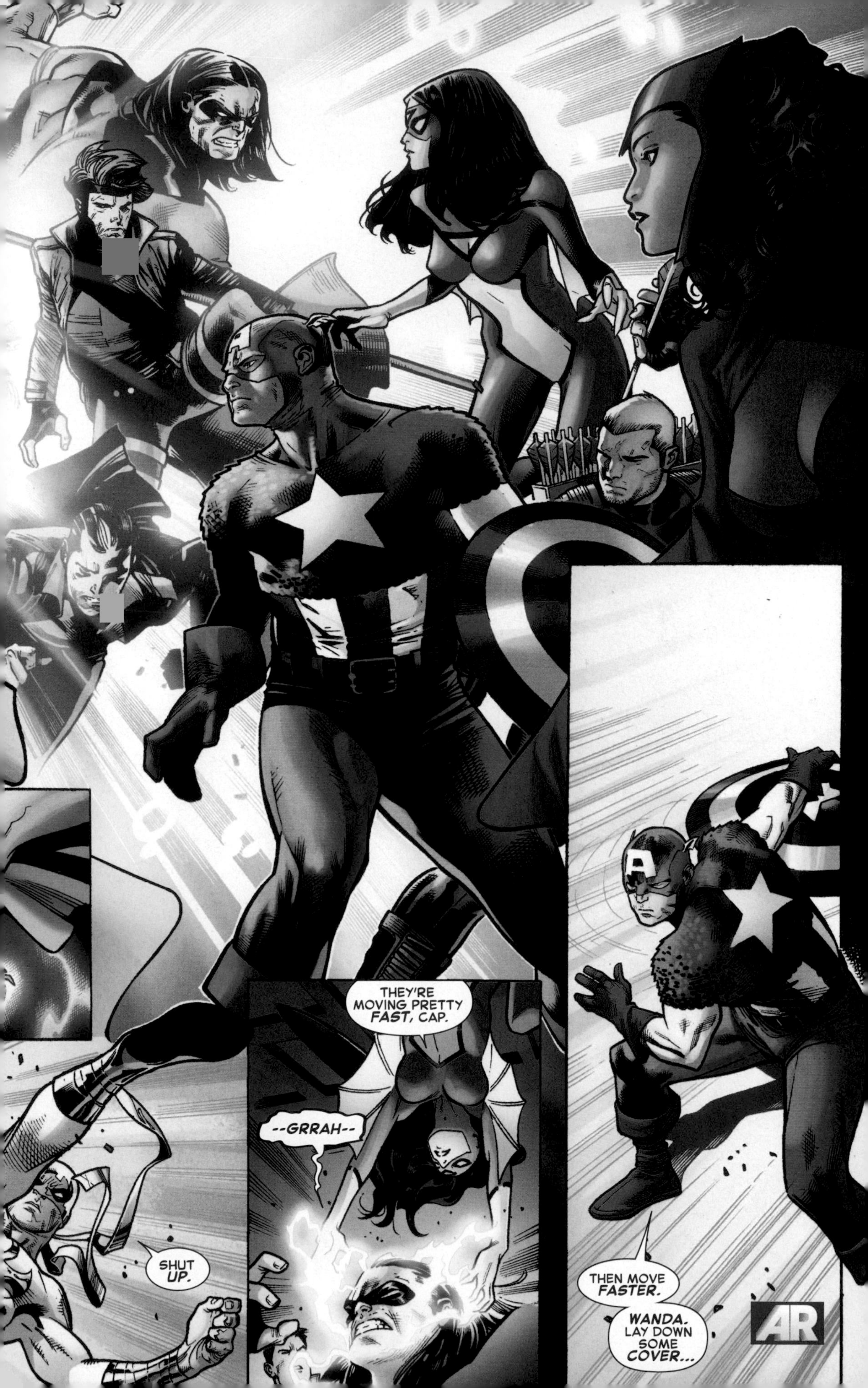
THEY'RE MOVING PRETTY FAST, CAP.
--GRRAH--
SHUT UP.
THEN MOVE FASTER.
WANDA. LAY DOWN SOME COVER...

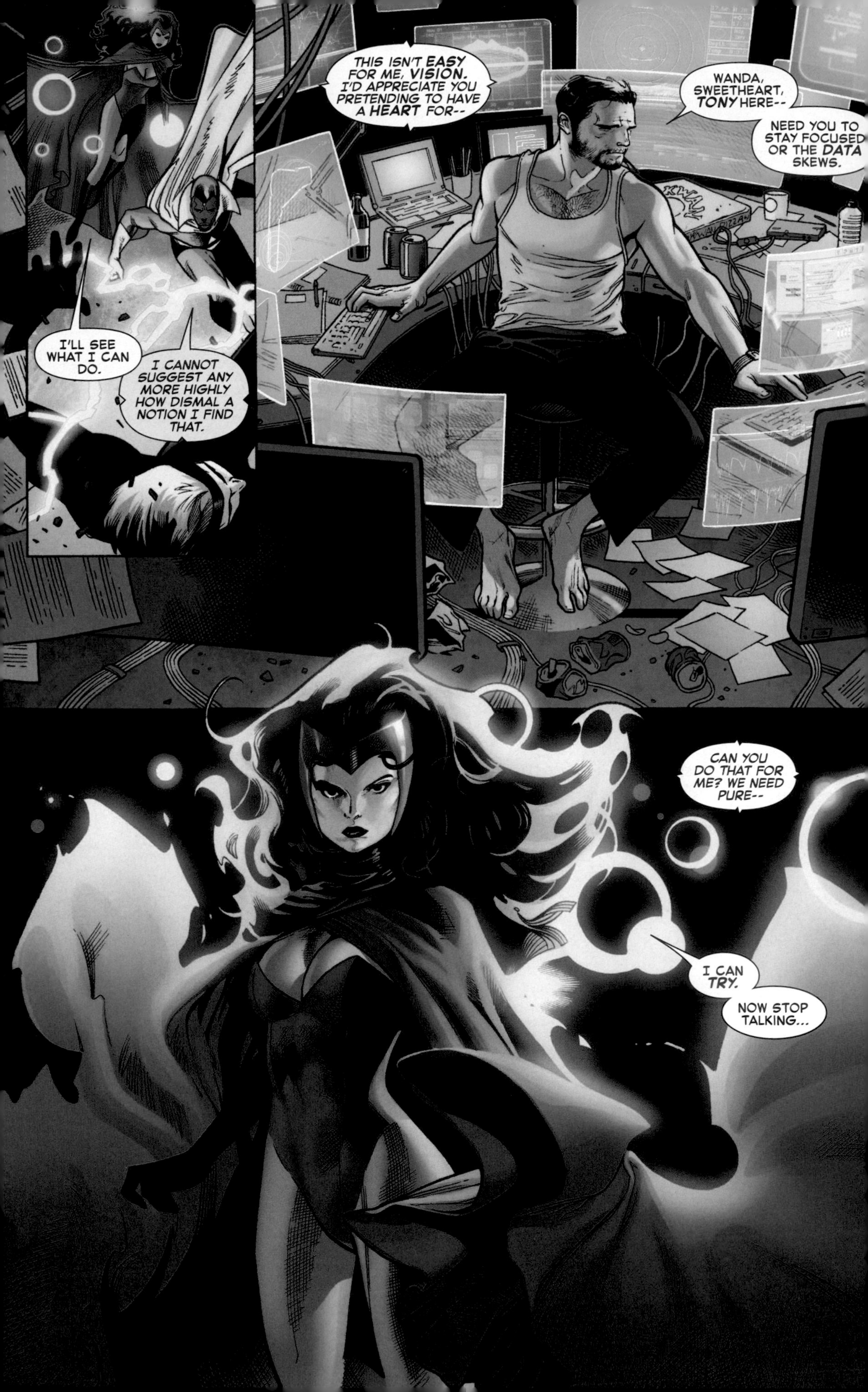
THIS ISN'T EASY FOR ME, VISION. I'D APPRECIATE YOU PRETENDING TO HAVE A HEART FOR--
WANDA, SWEETHEART, TONY HERE--
NEED YOU TO STAY FOCUSED OR THE DATA SKEWS.
I'LL SEE WHAT I CAN DO.
I CANNOT SUGGEST ANY MORE HIGHLY HOW DISMAL A NOTION I FIND THAT.
CAN YOU DO THAT FOR ME? WE NEED PURE--
I CAN TRY.
NOW STOP TALKING...

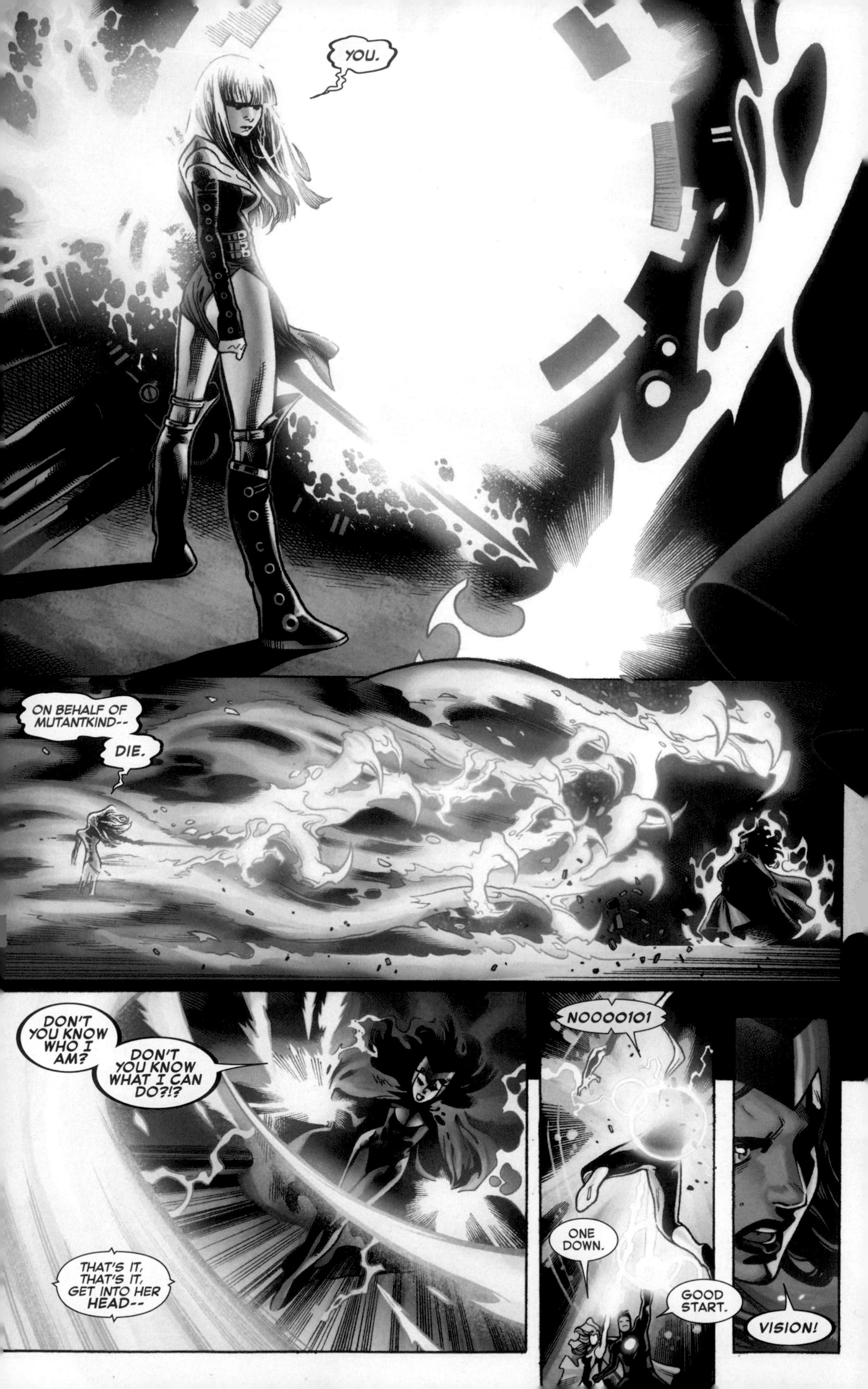
YOU.
ON BEHALF OF MUTANTKIND--
DIE.
DON'T YOU KNOW WHO I AM?
DON'T YOU KNOW WHAT I CAN DO?!?
THAT'S IT, THAT'S IT, GET INTO HER HEAD--
NOOOO101
ONE DOWN.
GOOD START.
VISION!

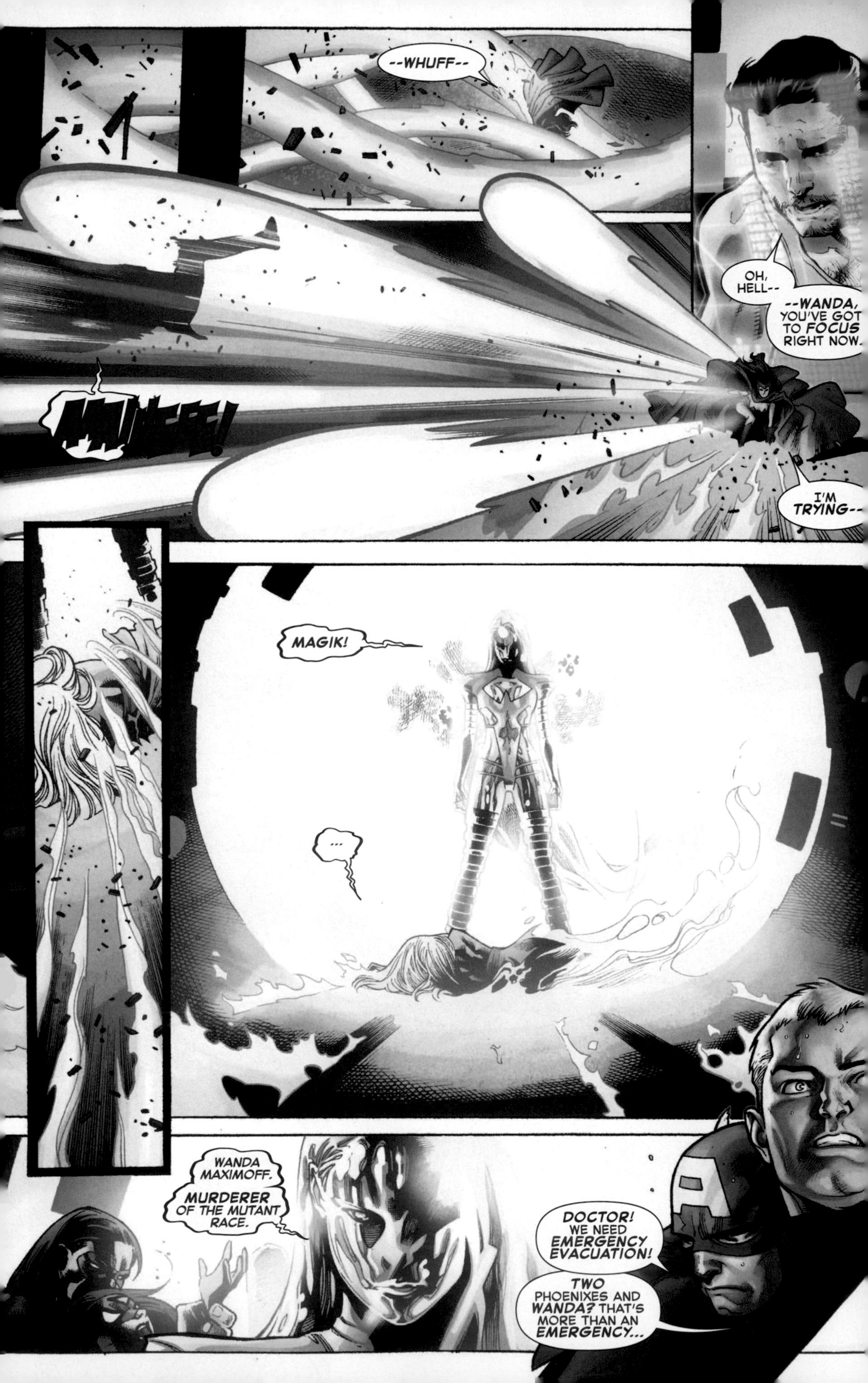
--WHUFF--
OH, HELL--
--WANDA, YOU'VE GOT TO FOCUS RIGHT NOW.
I'M TRYING--
MAGIK!
...
WANDA MAXIMOFF.
MURDERER OF THE MUTANT RACE.
DOCTOR! WE NEED EMERGENCY EVACUATION!
TWO PHOENIXES AND WANDA? THAT'S MORE THAN AN EMERGENCY...

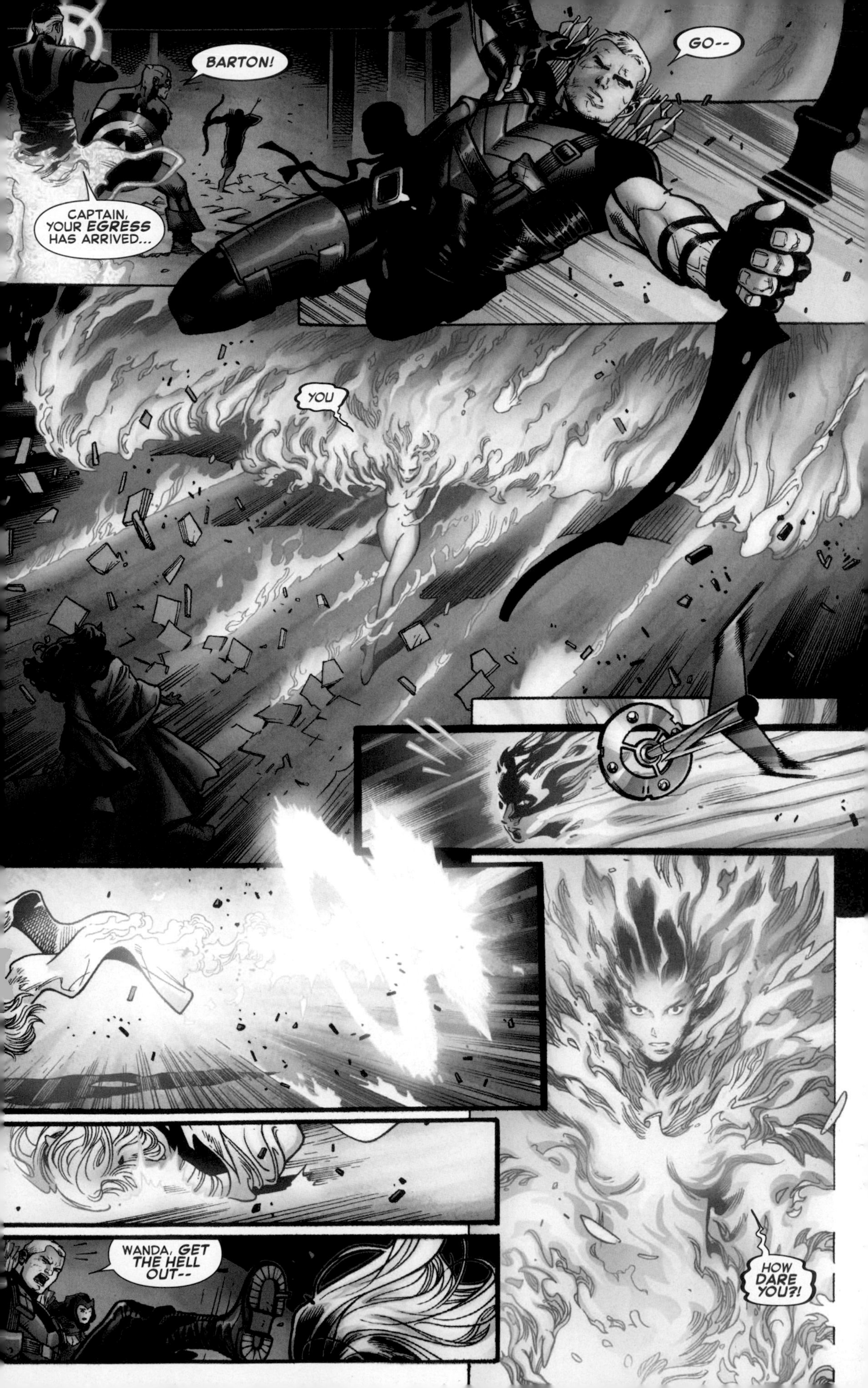
BARTON!
GO--
CAPTAIN, YOUR EGRESS HAS ARRIVED...
YOU
WANDA, GET THE HELL OUT--
HOW DARE YOU?!

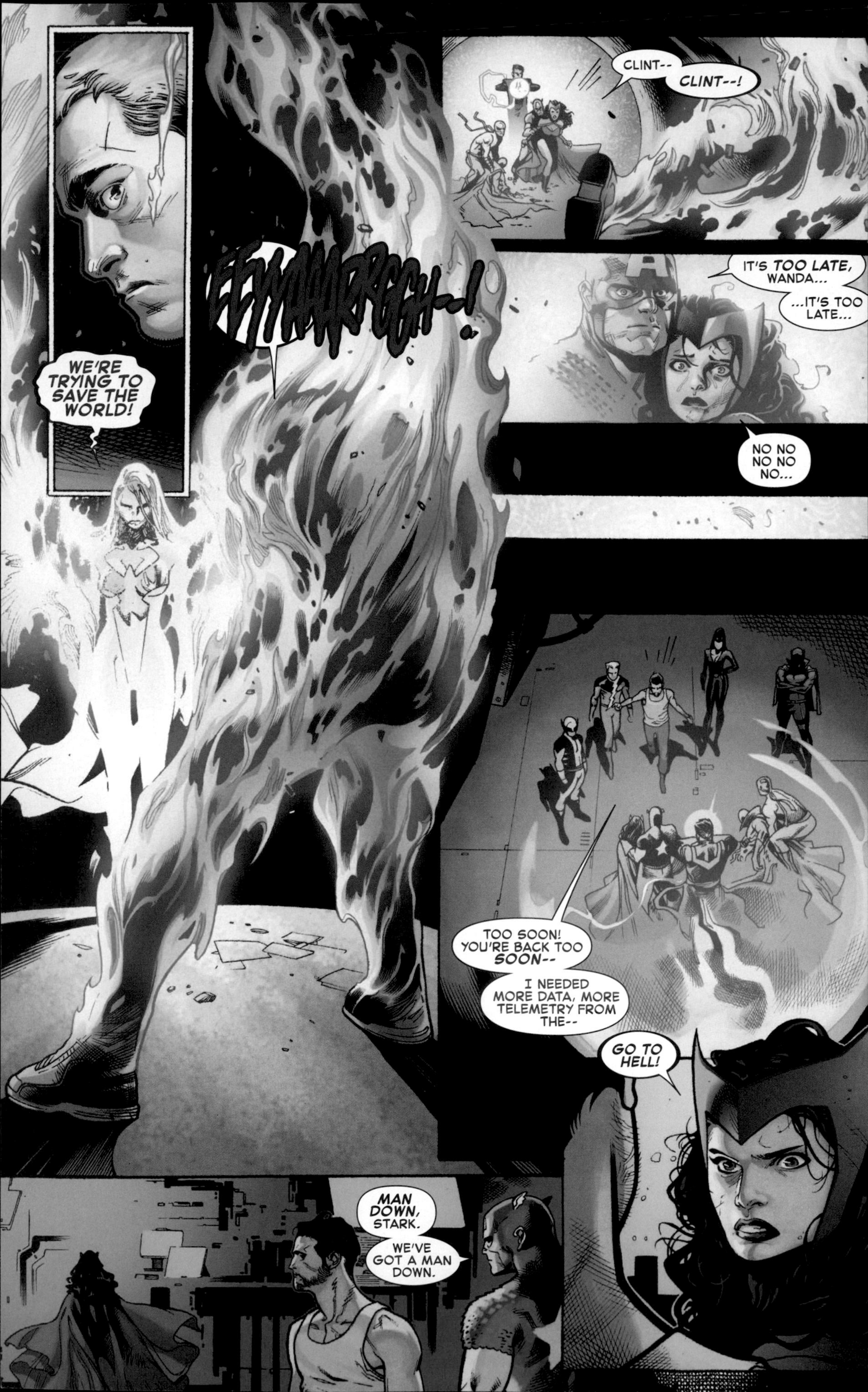
WE'RE TRYING TO SAVE THE WORLD!
EEYYAAARRGH--!
CLINT--
CLINT--!
IT'S TOO LATE, WANDA...
...IT'S TOO LATE...
NO NO NO NO NO...
TOO SOON! YOU'RE BACK TOO SOON--
I NEEDED MORE DATA, MORE TELEMETRY FROM THE--
GO TO HELL!
MAN DOWN, STARK.
WE'VE GOT A MAN DOWN.

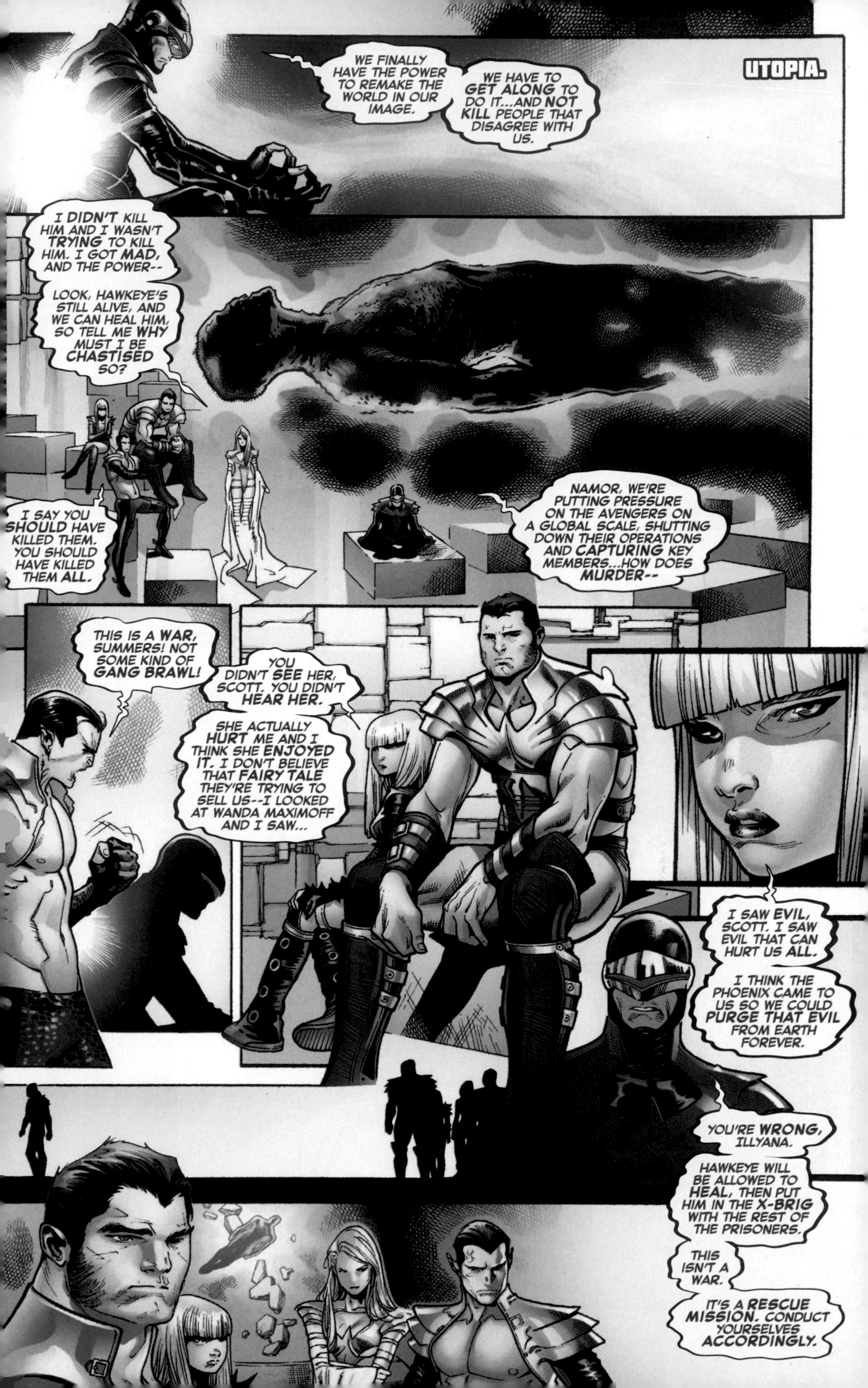
UTOPIA.
WE FINALLY HAVE THE POWER TO REMAKE THE WORLD IN OUR IMAGE.
WE HAVE TO GET ALONG TO DO IT...AND NOT KILL PEOPLE THAT DISAGREE WITH US.
I DIDN'T KILL HIM AND I WASN'T TRYING TO KILL HIM. I GOT MAD, AND THE POWER--
LOOK, HAWKEYE'S STILL ALIVE, AND WE CAN HEAL HIM, SO TELL ME WHY MUST I BE CHASTISED SO?
I SAY YOU SHOULD HAVE KILLED THEM. YOU SHOULD HAVE KILLED THEM ALL.
NAMOR, WE'RE PUTTING PRESSURE ON THE AVENGERS ON A GLOBAL SCALE, SHUTTING DOWN THEIR OPERATIONS AND CAPTURING KEY MEMBERS...HOW DOES MURDER--
THIS IS A WAR, SUMMERS! NOT SOME KIND OF GANG BRAWL!
YOU DIDN'T SEE HER, SCOTT. YOU DIDN'T HEAR HER.
SHE ACTUALLY HURT ME AND I THINK SHE ENJOYED IT. I DON'T BELIEVE THAT FAIRY TALE THEY'RE TRYING TO SELL US--I LOOKED AT WANDA MAXIMOFF AND I SAW...
I SAW EVIL, SCOTT. I SAW EVIL THAT CAN HURT US ALL.
I THINK THE PHOENIX CAME TO US SO WE COULD PURGE THAT EVIL FROM EARTH FOREVER.
YOU'RE WRONG, ILLYANA.
HAWKEYE WILL BE ALLOWED TO HEAL, THEN PUT HIM IN THE X-BRIG WITH THE REST OF THE PRISONERS.
THIS ISN'T A WAR.
IT'S A RESCUE MISSION. CONDUCT YOURSELVES ACCORDINGLY.

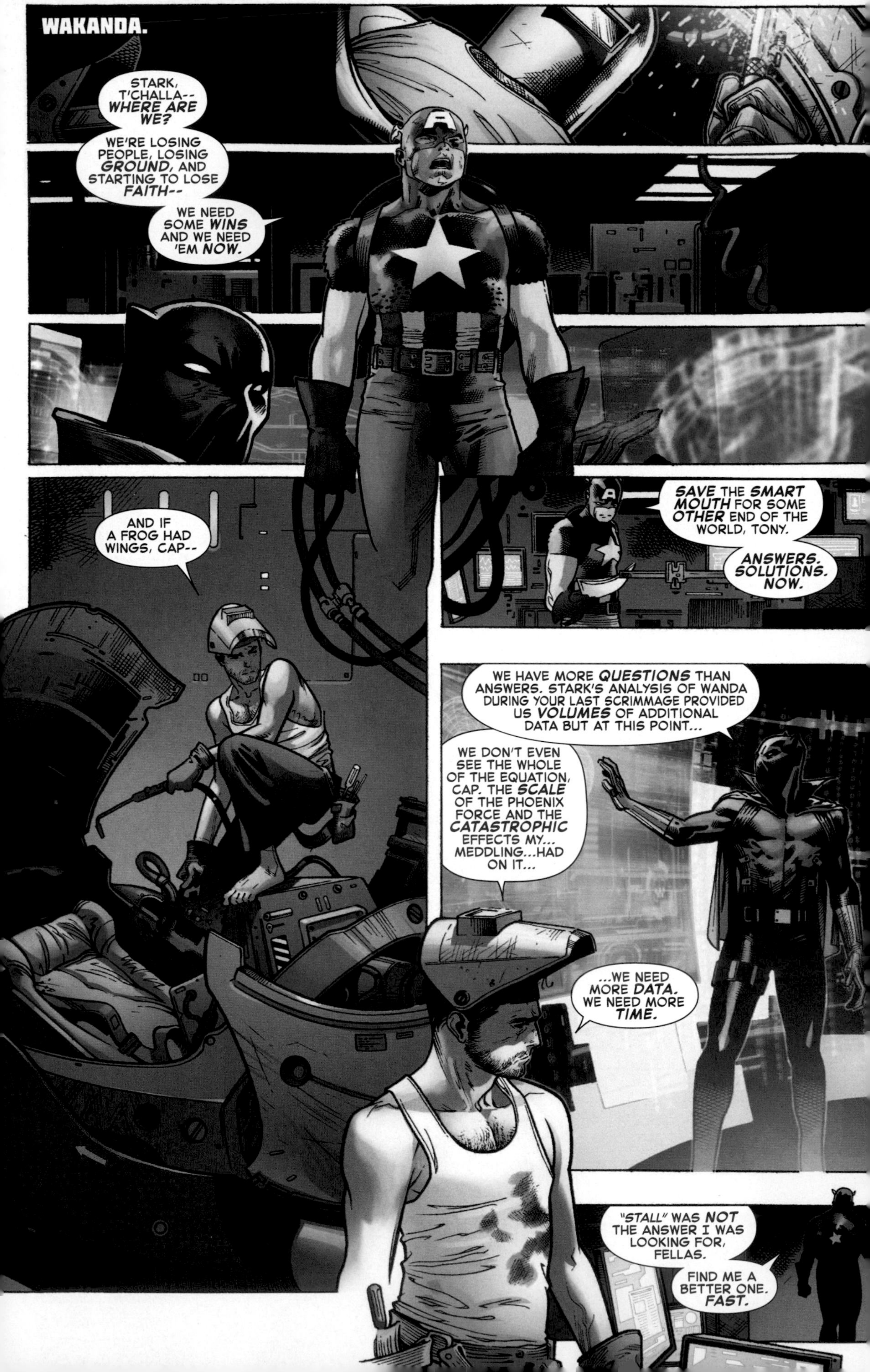
WAKANDA.
STARK, T'CHALLA-- WHERE ARE WE?
WE'RE LOSING PEOPLE, LOSING GROUND, AND STARTING TO LOSE FAITH--
WE NEED SOME WINS AND WE NEED 'EM NOW.
AND IF A FROG HAD WINGS, CAP--
SAVE THE SMART MOUTH FOR SOME OTHER END OF THE WORLD, TONY.
ANSWERS. SOLUTIONS. NOW.
WE HAVE MORE QUESTIONS THAN ANSWERS. STARK'S ANALYSIS OF WANDA DURING YOUR LAST SCRIMMAGE PROVIDED US VOLUMES OF ADDITIONAL DATA BUT AT THIS POINT...
WE DON'T EVEN SEE THE WHOLE OF THE EQUATION, CAP. THE SCALE OF THE PHOENIX FORCE AND THE CATASTROPHIC EFFECTS MY... MEDDLING...HAD ON IT...
...WE NEED MORE DATA. WE NEED MORE TIME.
"STALL" WAS NOT THE ANSWER I WAS LOOKING FOR, FELLAS.
FIND ME A BETTER ONE. FAST.

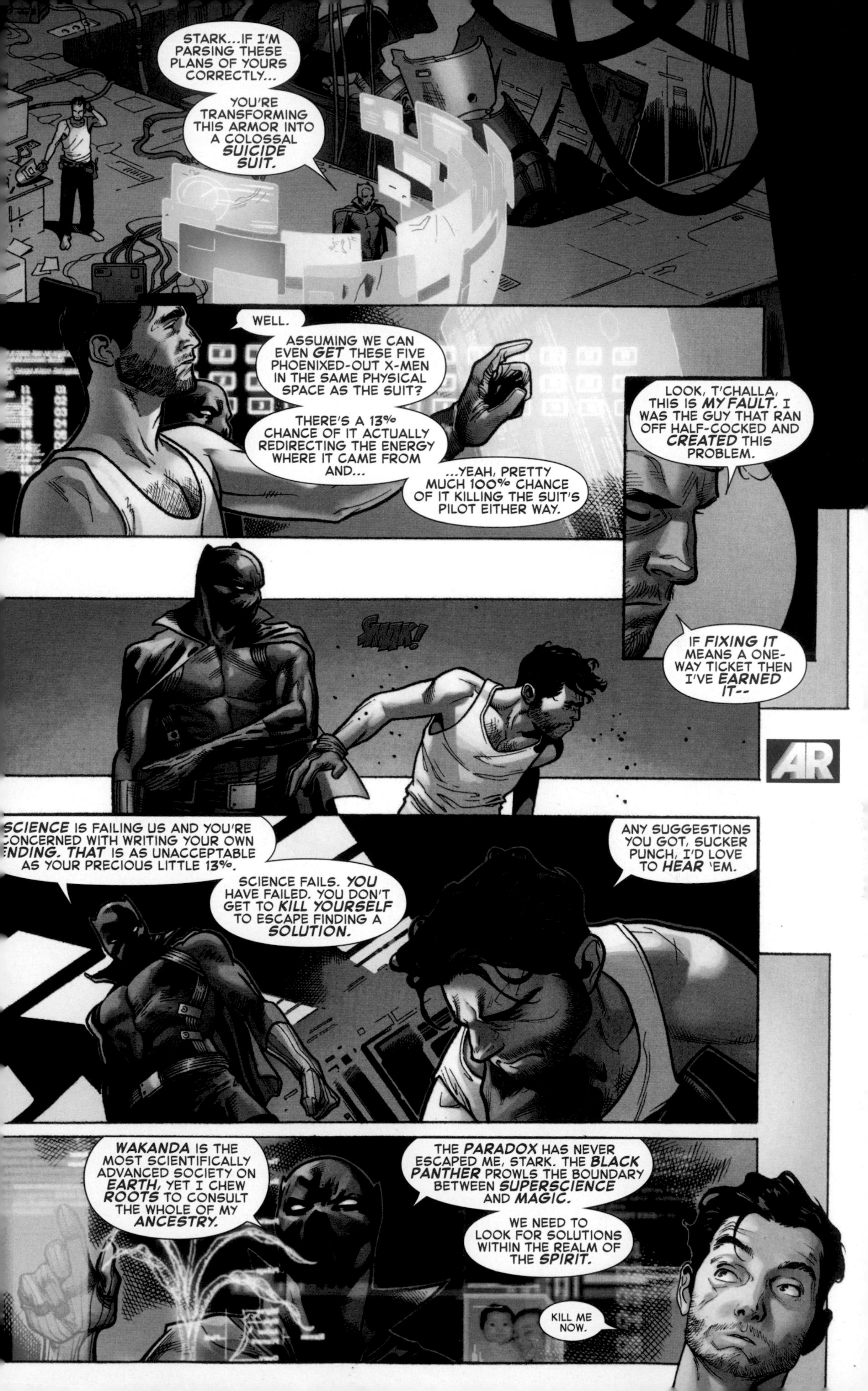
STARK...IF I'M PARSING THESE PLANS OF YOURS CORRECTLY...
YOU'RE TRANSFORMING THIS ARMOR INTO A COLOSSAL SUICIDE SUIT.
WELL.
ASSUMING WE CAN EVEN GET THESE FIVE PHOENIXED-OUT X-MEN IN THE SAME PHYSICAL SPACE AS THE SUIT?
THERE'S A 13% CHANCE OF IT ACTUALLY REDIRECTING THE ENERGY WHERE IT CAME FROM AND...
...YEAH, PRETTY MUCH 100% CHANCE OF IT KILLING THE SUIT'S PILOT EITHER WAY.
LOOK, T'CHALLA, THIS IS MY FAULT. I WAS THE GUY THAT RAN OFF HALF-COCKED AND CREATED THIS PROBLEM.
IF FIXING IT MEANS A ONE-WAY TICKET THEN I'VE EARNED IT--
SHAK!
AR
SCIENCE IS FAILING US AND YOU'RE CONCERNED WITH WRITING YOUR OWN ENDING. THAT IS AS UNACCEPTABLE AS YOUR PRECIOUS LITTLE 13%.
SCIENCE FAILS. YOU HAVE FAILED. YOU DON'T GET TO KILL YOURSELF TO ESCAPE FINDING A SOLUTION.
ANY SUGGESTIONS YOU GOT, SUCKER PUNCH, I'D LOVE TO HEAR 'EM.
WAKANDA IS THE MOST SCIENTIFICALLY ADVANCED SOCIETY ON EARTH, YET I CHEW ROOTS TO CONSULT THE WHOLE OF MY ANCESTRY.
THE PARADOX HAS NEVER ESCAPED ME, STARK. THE BLACK PANTHER PROWLS THE BOUNDARY BETWEEN SUPERSCIENCE AND MAGIC.
WE NEED TO LOOK FOR SOLUTIONS WITHIN THE REALM OF THE SPIRIT.
KILL ME NOW.

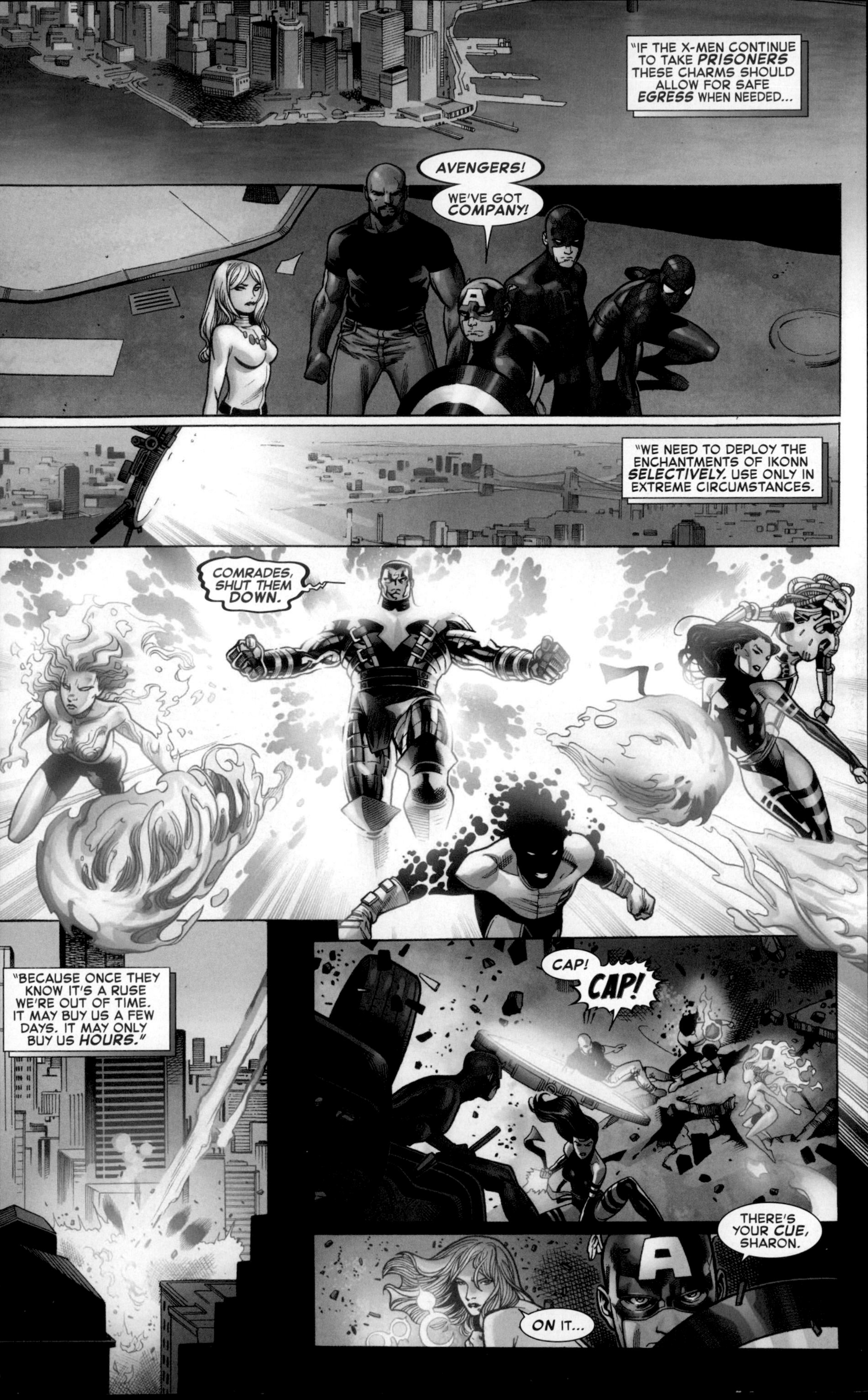
"IF THE X-MEN CONTINUE TO TAKE PRISONERS THESE CHARMS SHOULD ALLOW FOR SAFE EGRESS WHEN NEEDED...
AVENGERS!
WE'VE GOT COMPANY!
"WE NEED TO DEPLOY THE ENCHANTMENTS OF IKONN SELECTIVELY. USE ONLY IN EXTREME CIRCUMSTANCES.
COMRADES, SHUT THEM DOWN.
"BECAUSE ONCE THEY KNOW IT'S A RUSE WE'RE OUT OF TIME. IT MAY BUY US A FEW DAYS. IT MAY ONLY BUY US HOURS."
CAP!
CAP!
THERE'S YOUR CUE, SHARON.
ON IT...

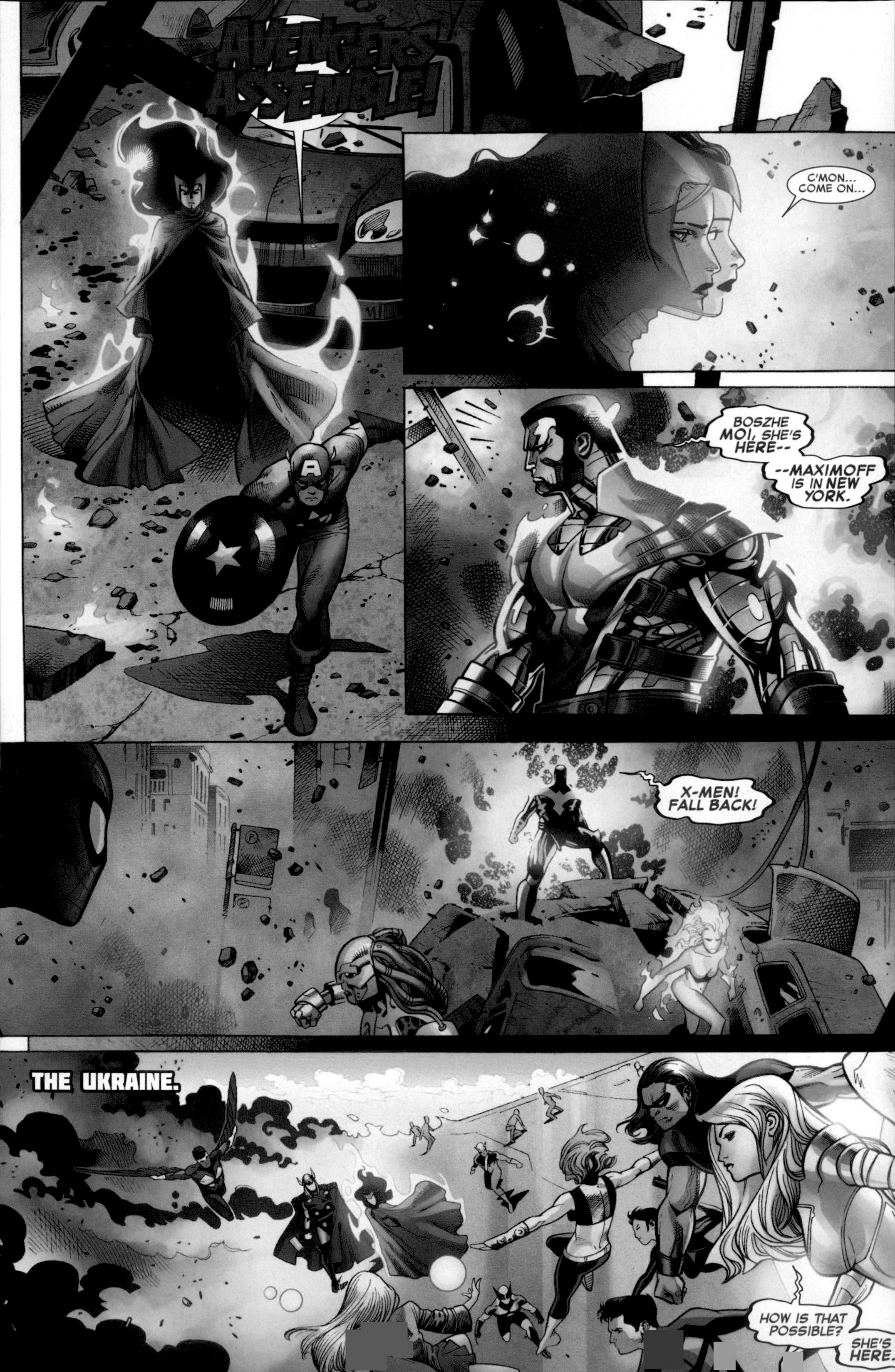
AVENGERS ASSEMBLE!
C'MON... COME ON...
BOSZHE MOI, SHE'S HERE--
--MAXIMOFF IS IN NEW YORK.
X-MEN! FALL BACK!
THE UKRAINE.
HOW IS THAT POSSIBLE?
SHE'S HERE.

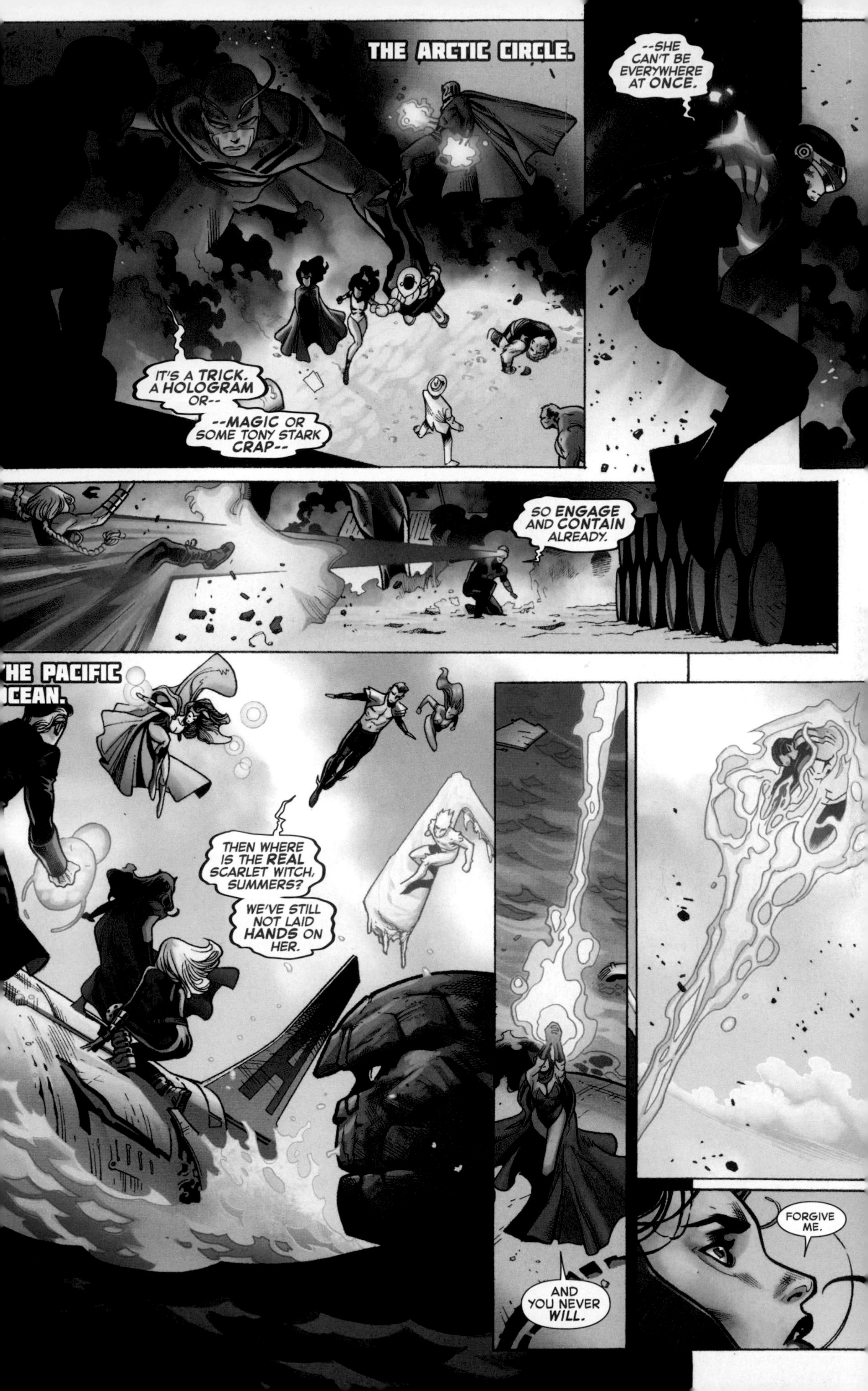
THE ARCTIC CIRCLE.
--SHE CAN'T BE EVERYWHERE AT ONCE.
IT'S A TRICK. A HOLOGRAM OR--
--MAGIC OR SOME TONY STARK CRAP--
SO ENGAGE AND CONTAIN ALREADY.
THE PACIFIC OCEAN.
THEN WHERE IS THE REAL SCARLET WITCH, SUMMERS?
WE'VE STILL NOT LAID HANDS ON HER.
AND YOU NEVER WILL.
FORGIVE ME.

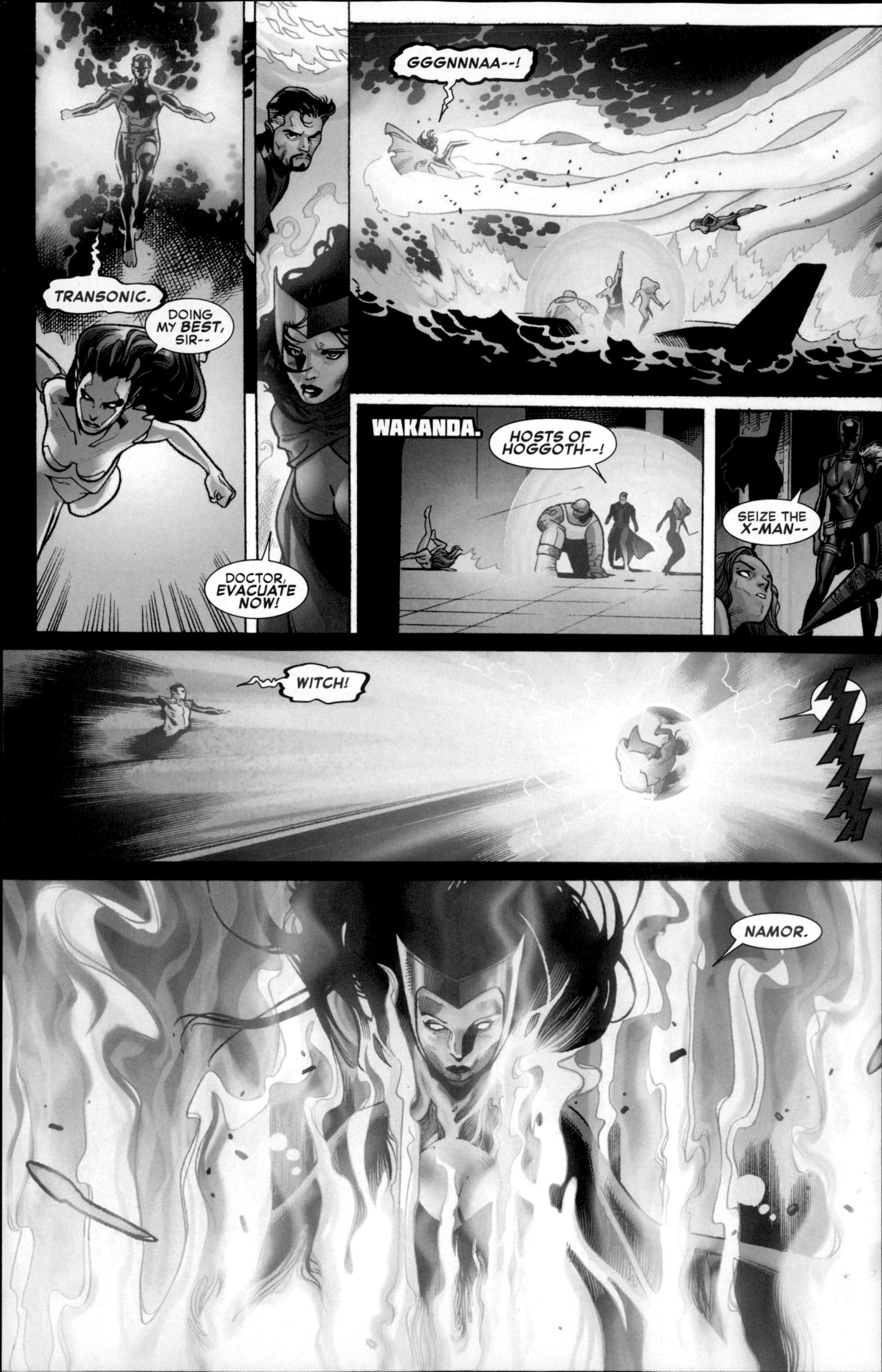
TRANSONIC.
DOING MY BEST, SIR--
DOCTOR, EVACUATE NOW!
GGGNNNAA--!
WAKANDA.
HOSTS OF HOGGOTH--!
SEIZE THE X-MAN--
WITCH!
NAMOR.

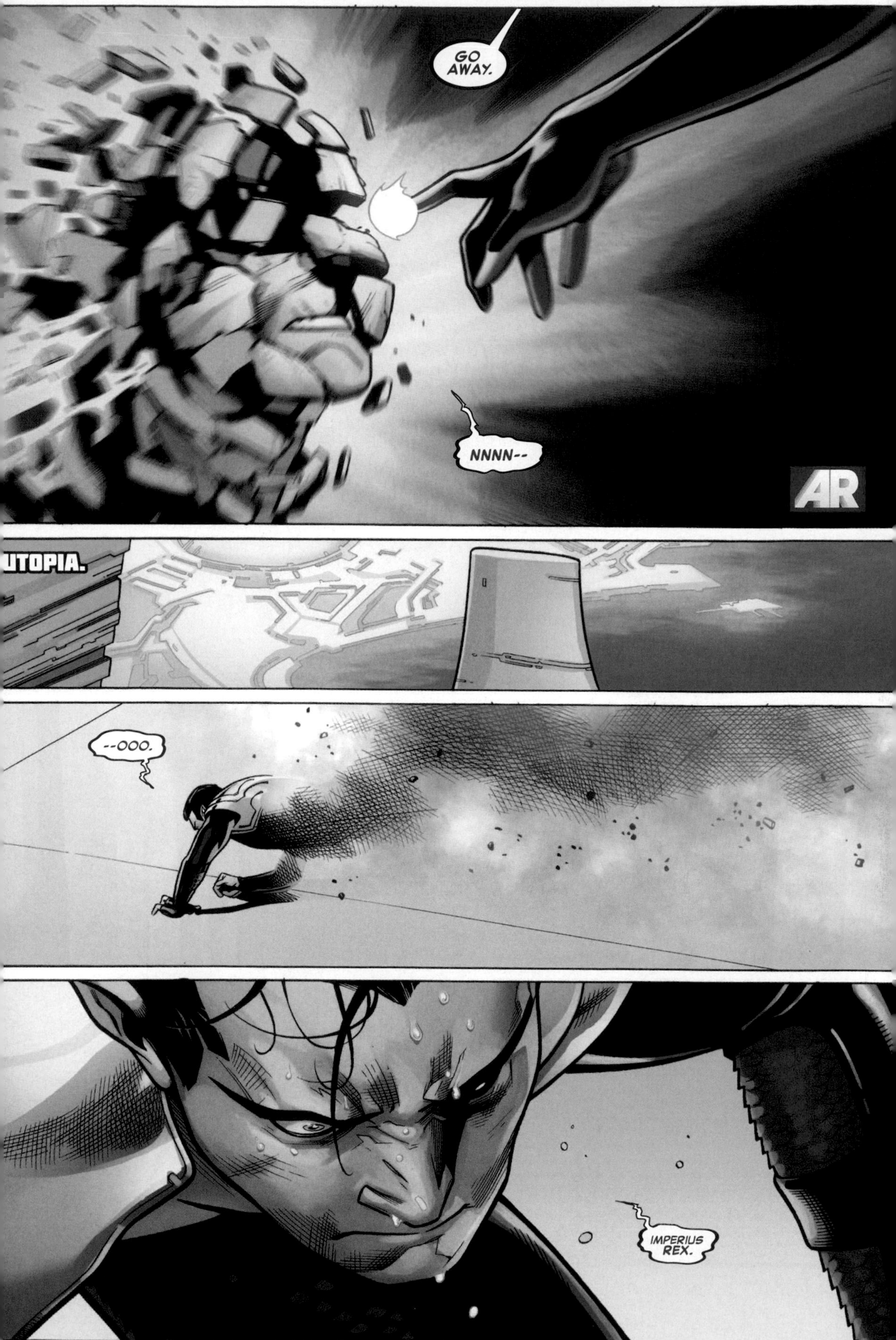
GO AWAY.
NNNN--
AR
UTOPIA.
--OOO.
IMPERIUS REX.

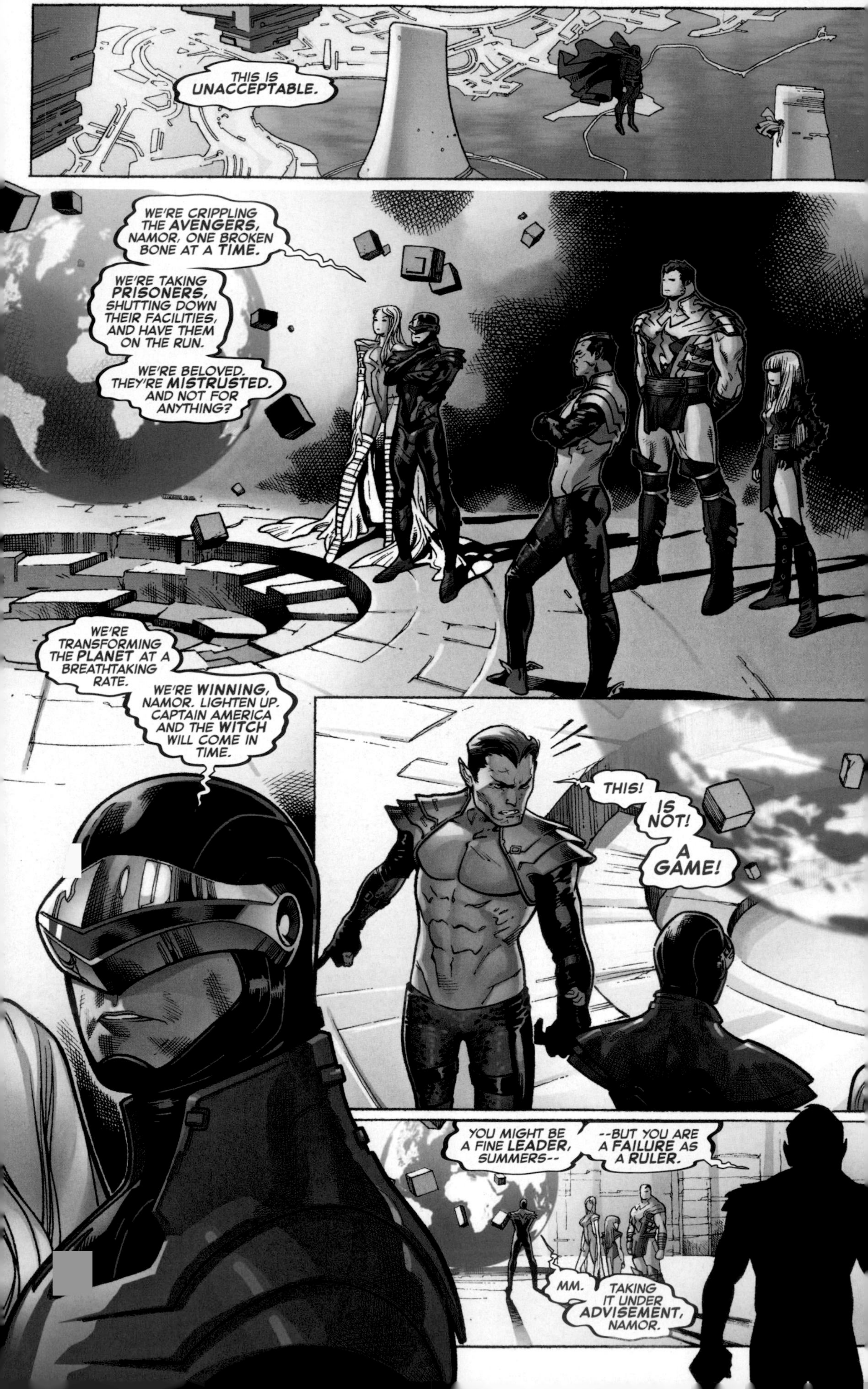
THIS IS UNACCEPTABLE.
WE'RE CRIPPLING THE AVENGERS, NAMOR, ONE BROKEN BONE AT A TIME.
WE'RE TAKING PRISONERS, SHUTTING DOWN THEIR FACILITIES, AND HAVE THEM ON THE RUN.
WE'RE BELOVED. THEY'RE MISTRUSTED. AND NOT FOR ANYTHING?
WE'RE TRANSFORMING THE PLANET AT A BREATHTAKING RATE.
WE'RE WINNING, NAMOR. LIGHTEN UP. CAPTAIN AMERICA AND THE WITCH WILL COME IN TIME.
THIS!
IS NOT!
A GAME!
YOU MIGHT BE A FINE LEADER, SUMMERS--
--BUT YOU ARE A FAILURE AS A RULER.
MM.
TAKING IT UNDER ADVISEMENT, NAMOR.

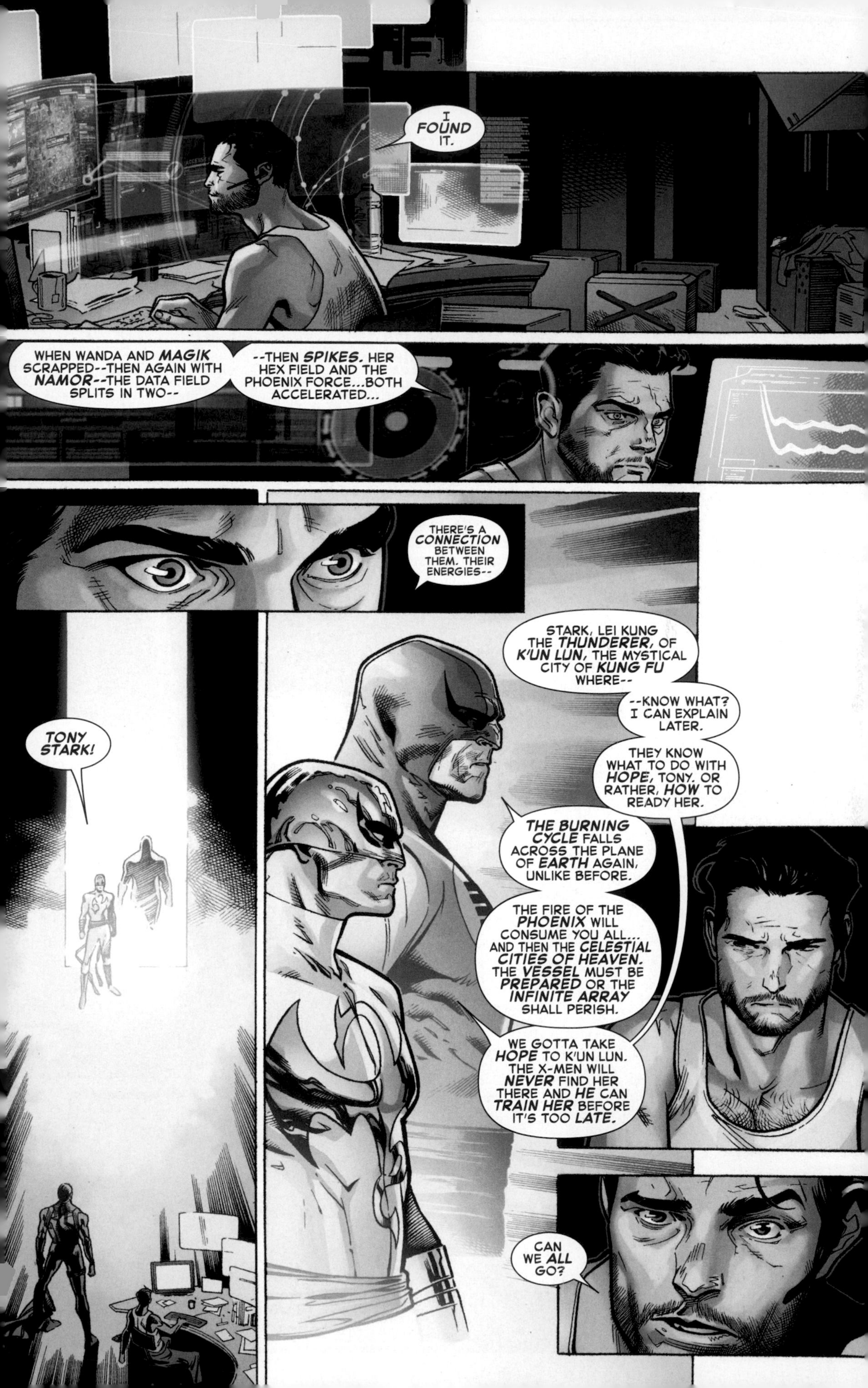
I FOUND IT.
WHEN WANDA AND MAGIK SCRAPPED--THEN AGAIN WITH NAMOR--THE DATA FIELD SPLITS IN TWO--
--THEN SPIKES. HER HEX FIELD AND THE PHOENIX FORCE...BOTH ACCELERATED...
THERE'S A CONNECTION BETWEEN THEM. THEIR ENERGIES--
TONY STARK!
STARK, LEI KUNG THE THUNDERER, OF K'UN LUN, THE MYSTICAL CITY OF KUNG FU WHERE--
--KNOW WHAT? I CAN EXPLAIN LATER.
THEY KNOW WHAT TO DO WITH HOPE, TONY. OR RATHER, HOW TO READY HER.
THE BURNING CYCLE FALLS ACROSS THE PLANE OF EARTH AGAIN, UNLIKE BEFORE.
THE FIRE OF THE PHOENIX WILL CONSUME YOU ALL... AND THEN THE CELESTIAL CITIES OF HEAVEN. THE VESSEL MUST BE PREPARED OR THE INFINITE ARRAY SHALL PERISH.
WE GOTTA TAKE HOPE TO K'UN LUN. THE X-MEN WILL NEVER FIND HER THERE AND HE CAN TRAIN HER BEFORE IT'S TOO LATE.
CAN WE ALL GO?

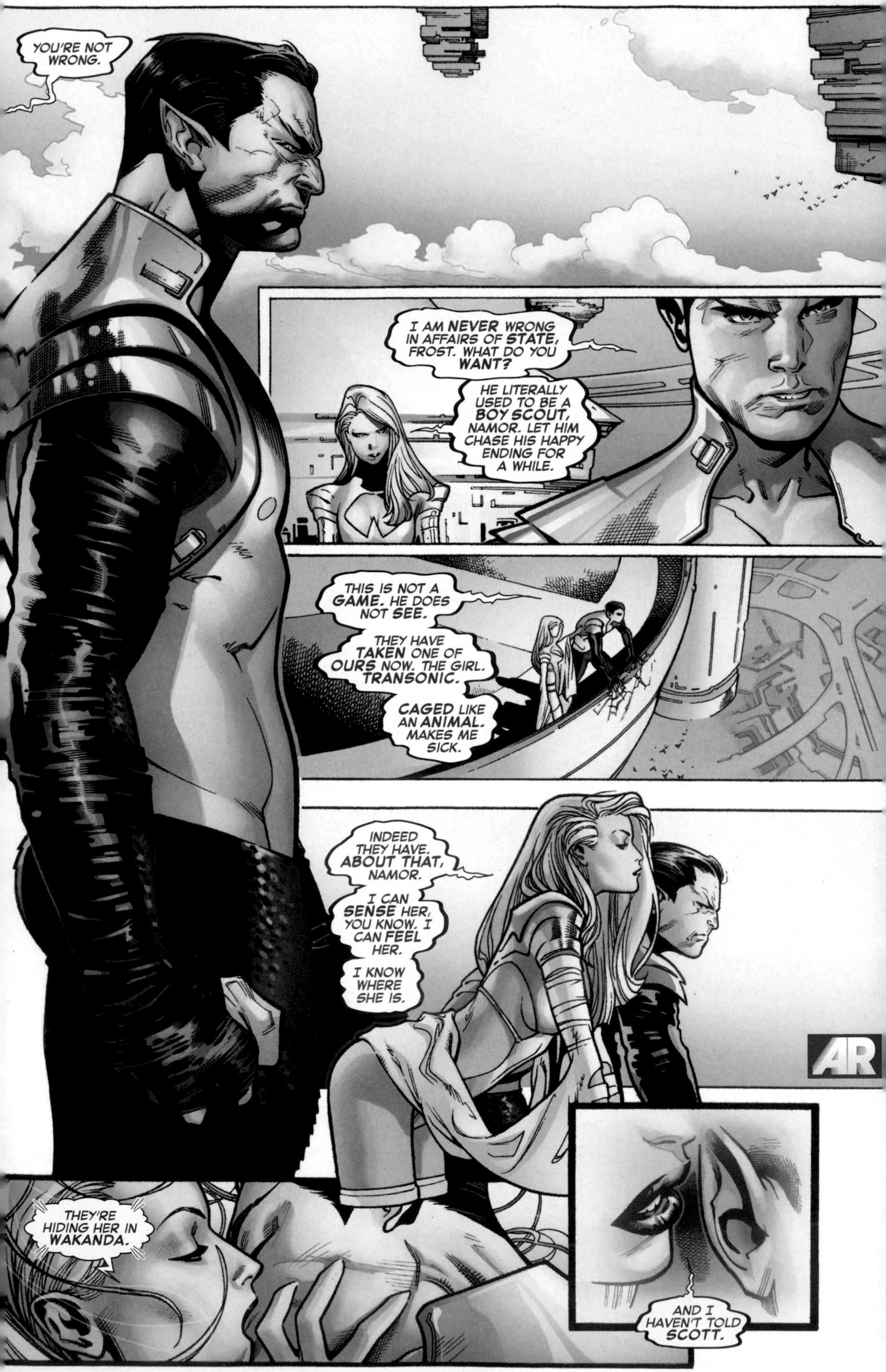
YOU'RE NOT WRONG.
I AM NEVER WRONG IN AFFAIRS OF STATE, FROST. WHAT DO YOU WANT?
HE LITERALLY USED TO BE A BOY SCOUT, NAMOR. LET HIM CHASE HIS HAPPY ENDING FOR A WHILE.
THIS IS NOT A GAME. HE DOES NOT SEE.
THEY HAVE TAKEN ONE OF OURS NOW. THE GIRL. TRANSONIC.
CAGED LIKE AN ANIMAL. MAKES ME SICK.
INDEED THEY HAVE. ABOUT THAT, NAMOR.
I CAN SENSE HER, YOU KNOW. I CAN FEEL HER.
I KNOW WHERE SHE IS.
AR
THEY'RE HIDING HER IN WAKANDA.
AND I HAVEN'T TOLD SCOTT.

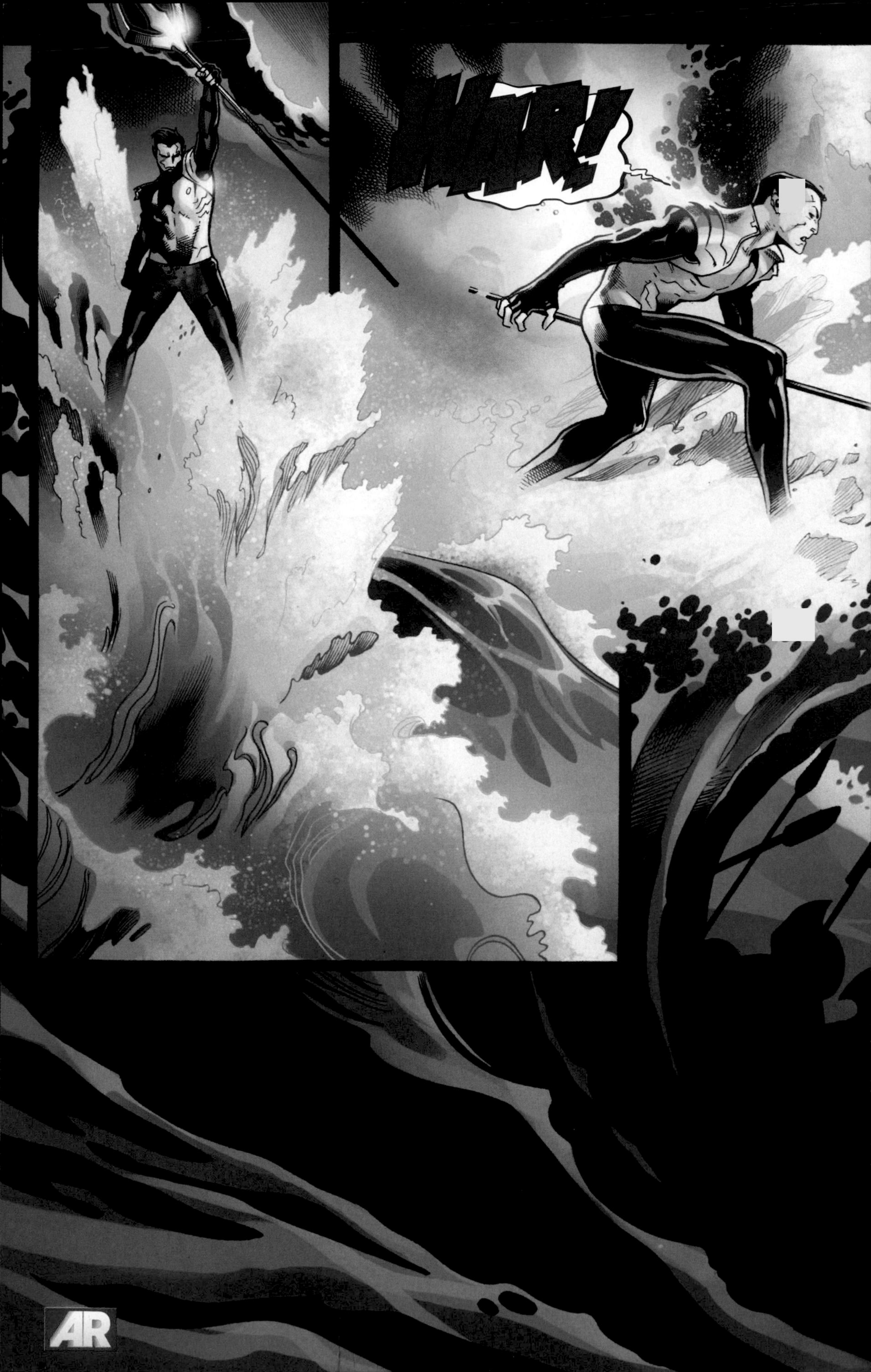

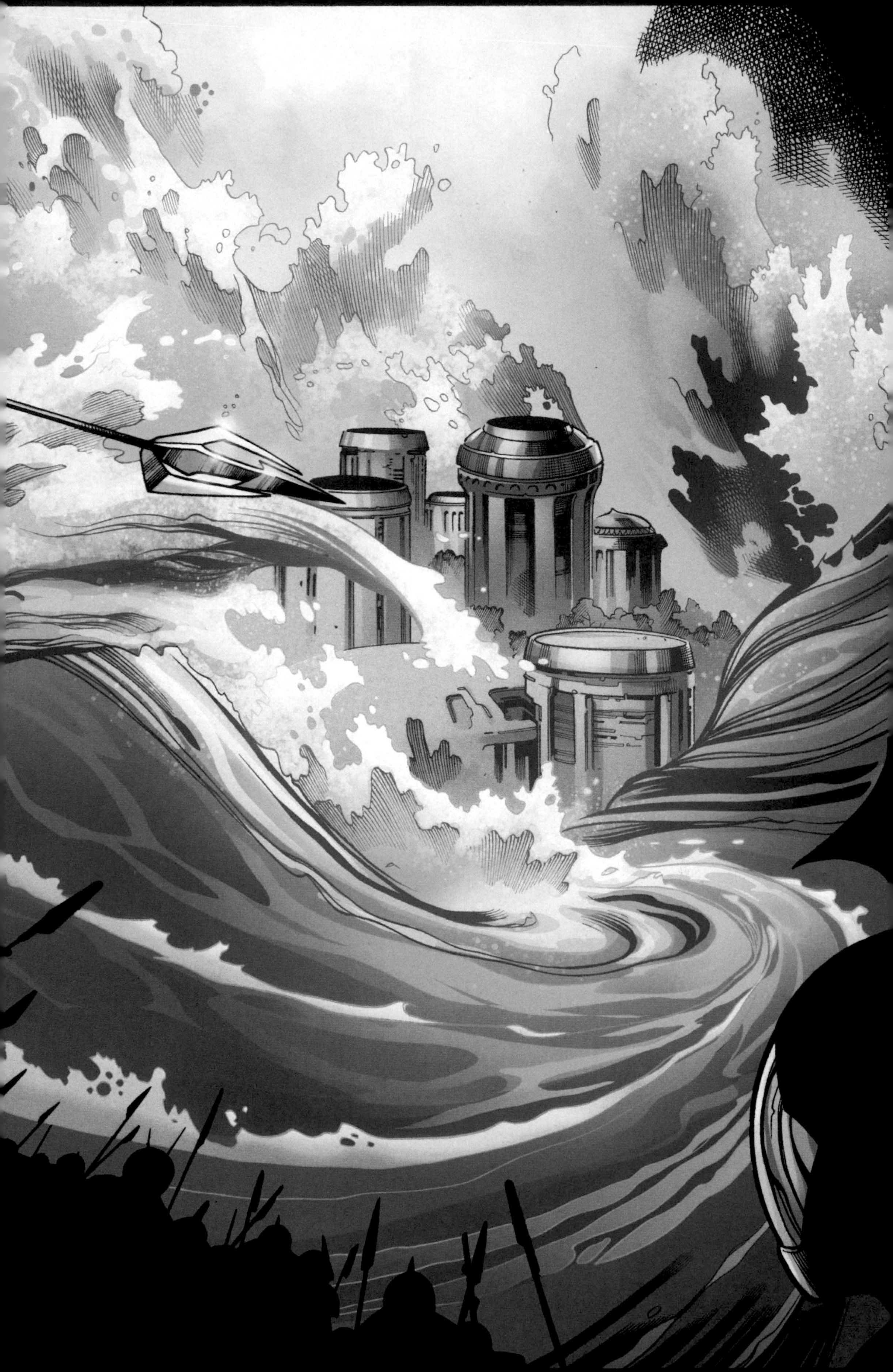

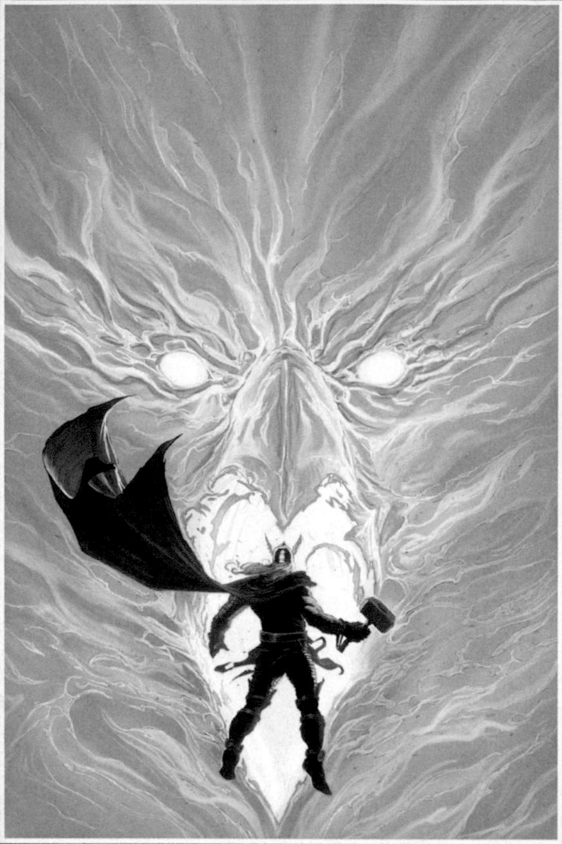

AVX #4 VARIANT
BY **JEROME OPEÑA & DEAN WHITE**

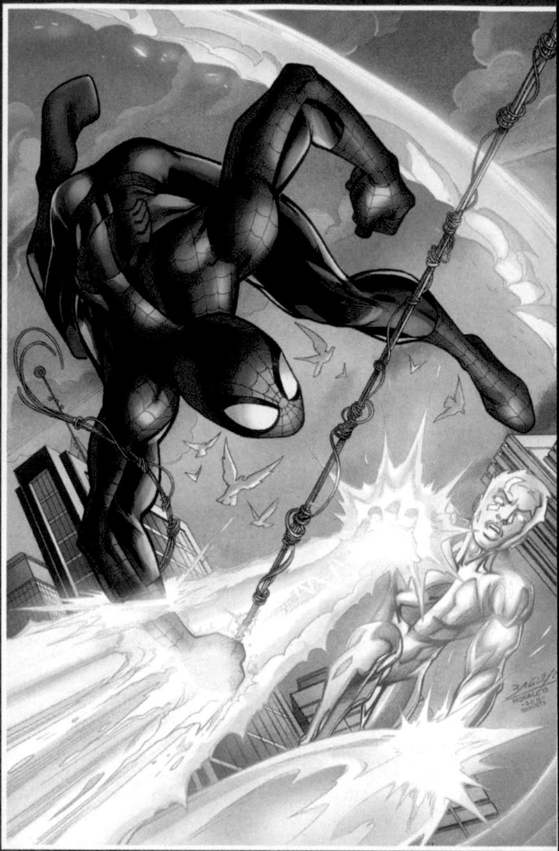

AVX #4 VARIANT
BY **MARK BAGLEY, MARK MORALES & PAUL MOUNTS**

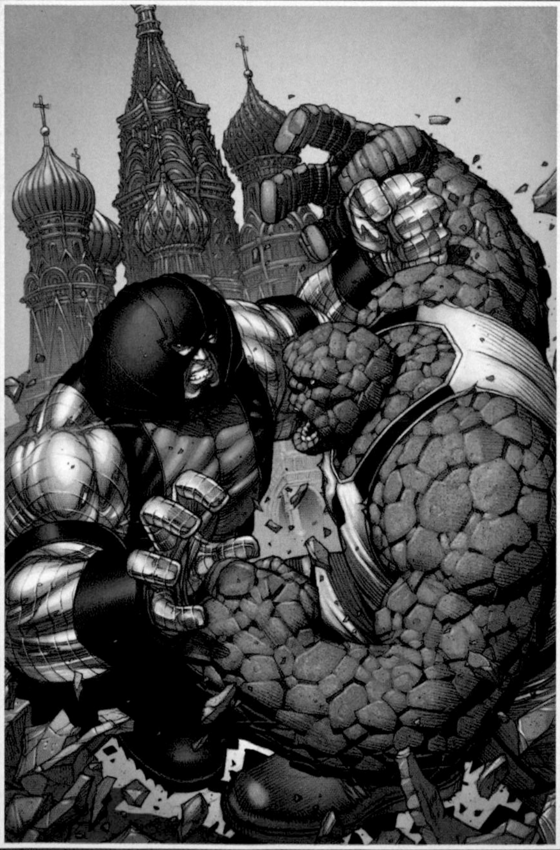

AVX #5 VARIANT
BY **DALE KEOWN & CHRIS SOTOMAYOR**

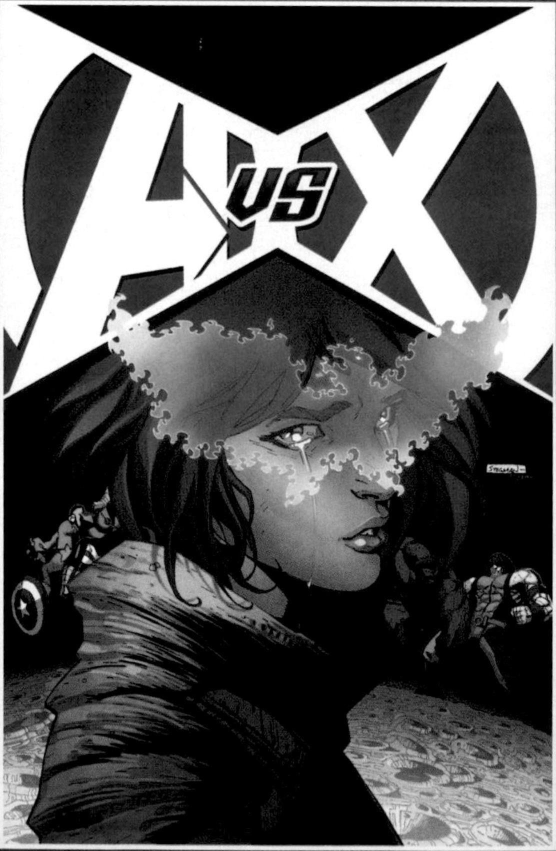
A VS X

AVX #5 VARIANT
BY **RYAN STEGMAN & MARTE GRACIA**

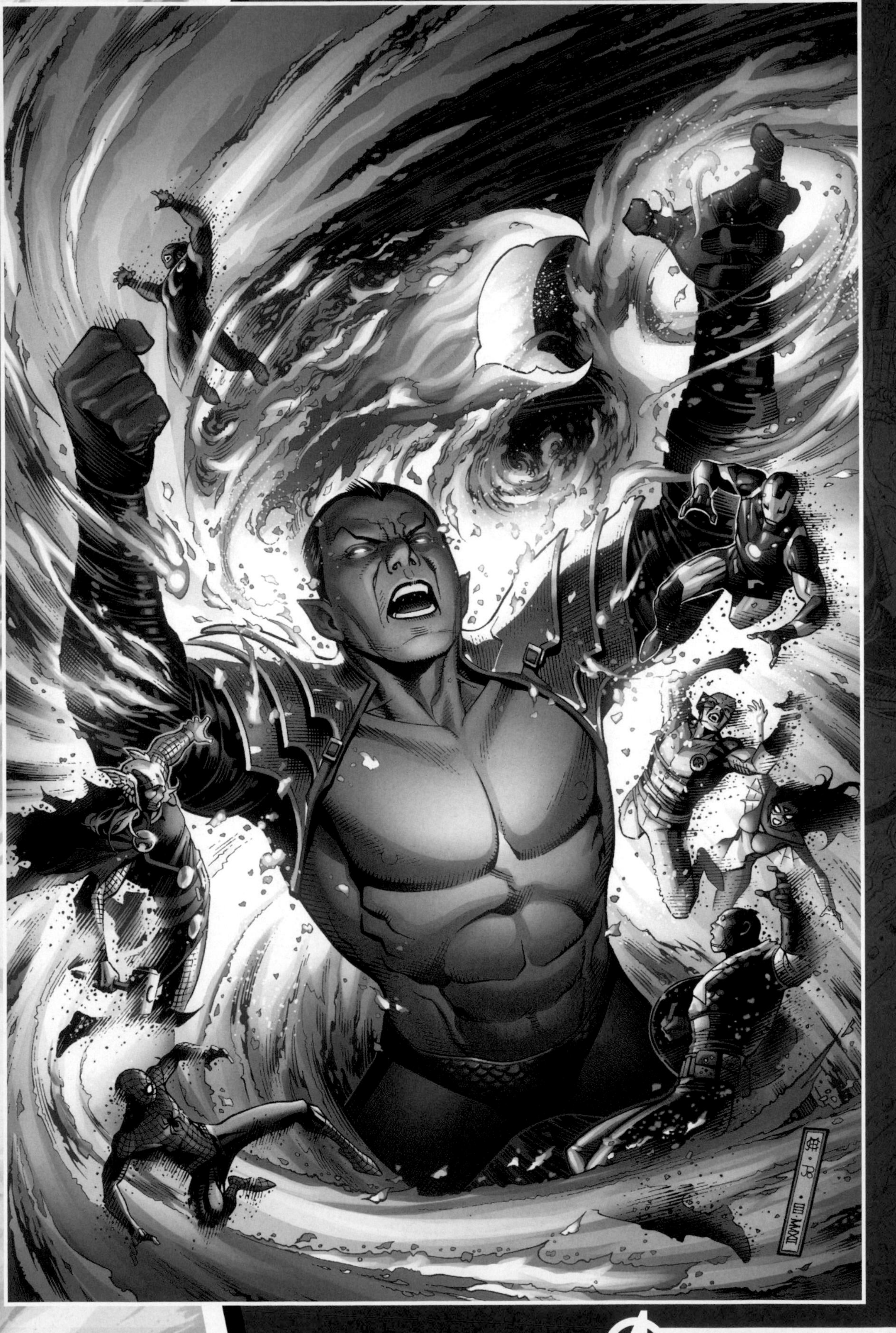

ROUND 8

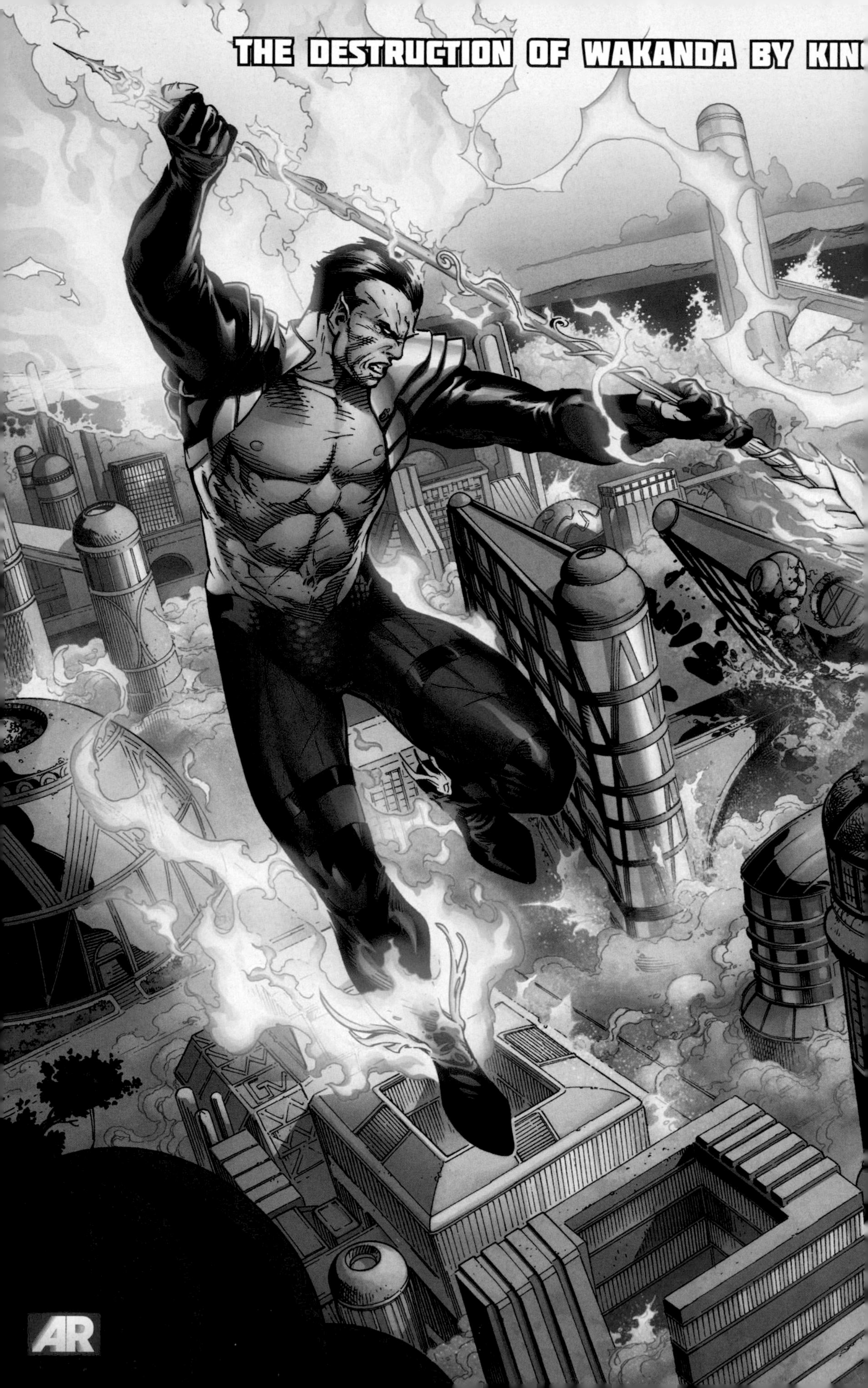
THE DESTRUCTION OF WAKANDA BY KIN

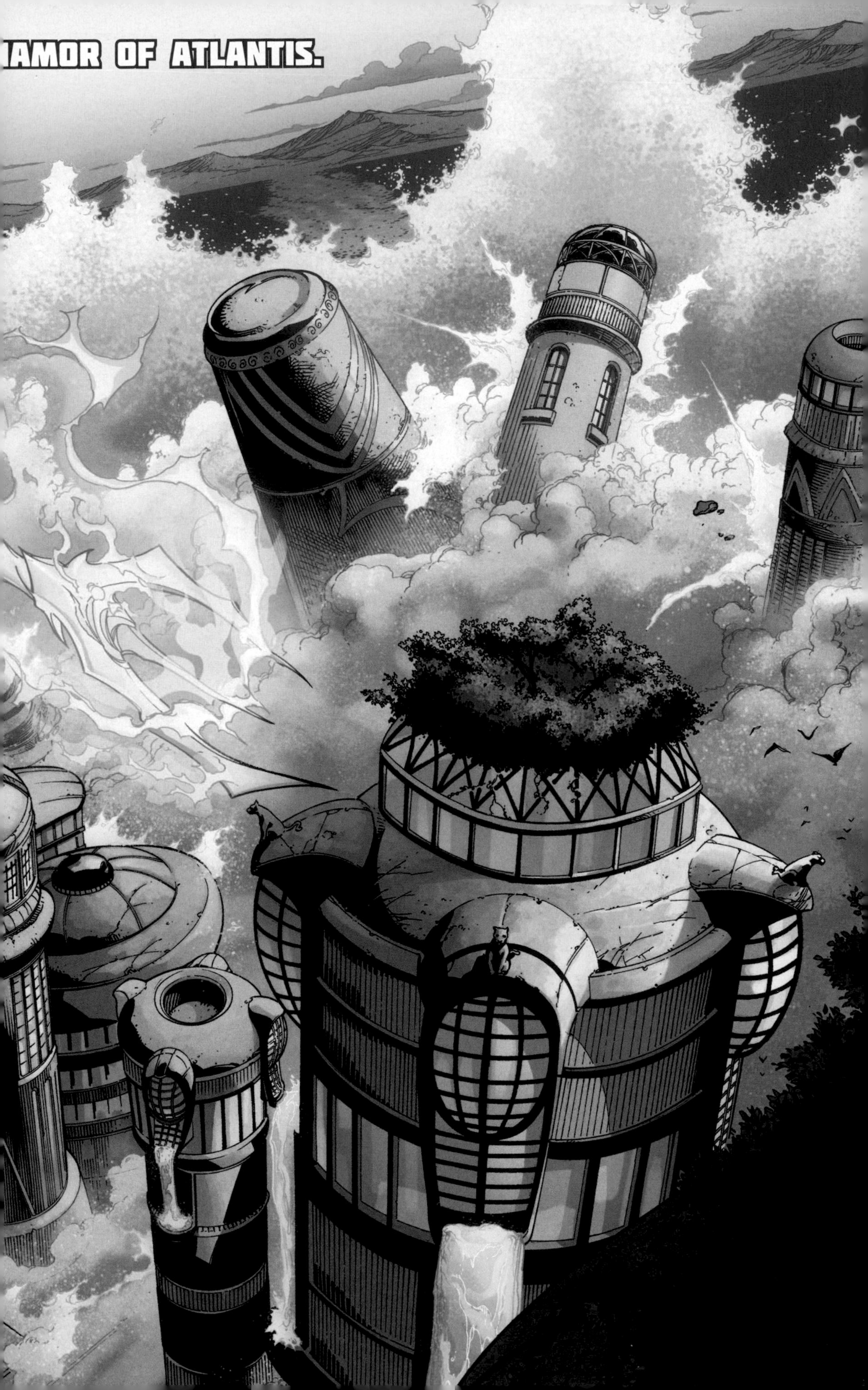
AMOR OF ATLANTIS.

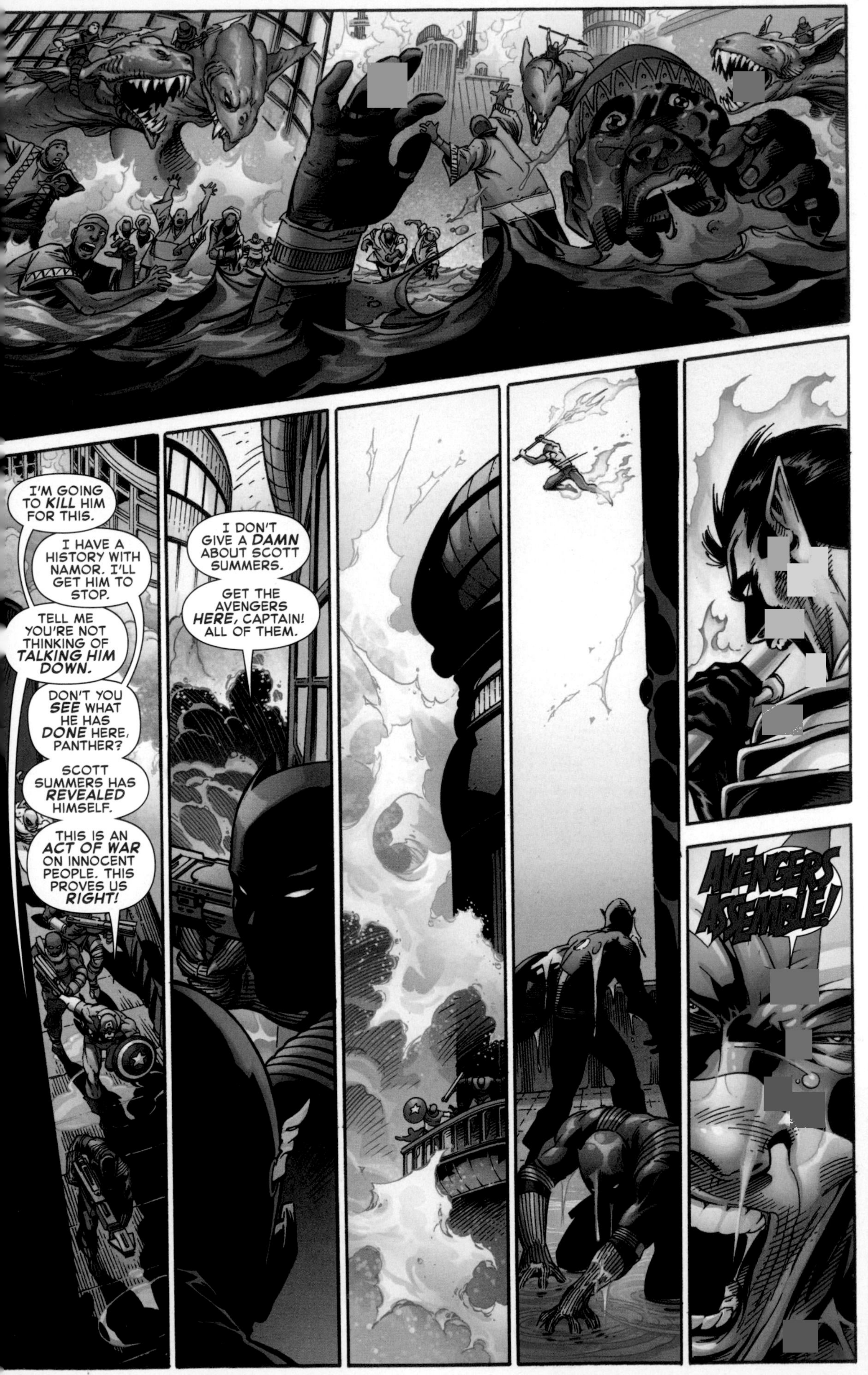
I'M GOING TO KILL HIM FOR THIS.
I HAVE A HISTORY WITH NAMOR. I'LL GET HIM TO STOP.
TELL ME YOU'RE NOT THINKING OF TALKING HIM DOWN.
DON'T YOU SEE WHAT HE HAS DONE HERE, PANTHER?
SCOTT SUMMERS HAS REVEALED HIMSELF.
THIS IS AN ACT OF WAR ON INNOCENT PEOPLE. THIS PROVES US RIGHT!
I DON'T GIVE A DAMN ABOUT SCOTT SUMMERS.
GET THE AVENGERS HERE, CAPTAIN! ALL OF THEM.
AVENGERS ASSEMBLE!

WOW.

YUP.

K'UN-LUN.

THE CITY WHERE KUNG FU WAS BORN.

HEADS UP!

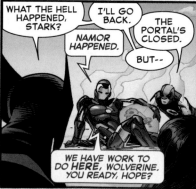

WHAT THE HELL HAPPENED, STARK?

NAMOR HAPPENED.

I'LL GO BACK.

THE PORTAL'S CLOSED.

BUT--

WE HAVE WORK TO DO *HERE*, WOLVERINE. YOU READY, HOPE?

SURE.

READY FOR WHAT EXACTLY?

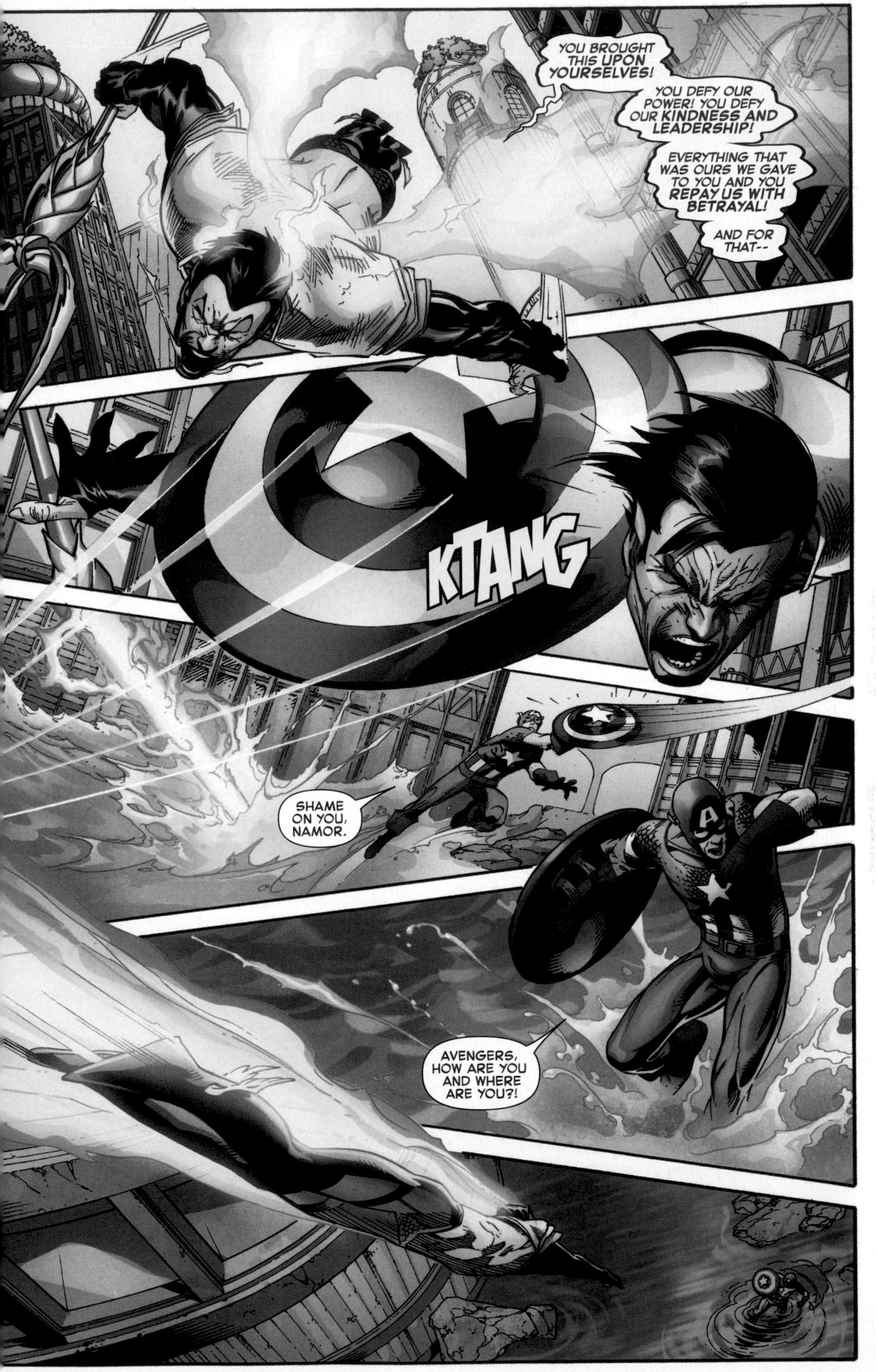
YOU BROUGHT THIS UPON YOURSELVES!
YOU DEFY OUR POWER! YOU DEFY OUR KINDNESS AND LEADERSHIP!
EVERYTHING THAT WAS OURS WE GAVE TO YOU AND YOU REPAY US WITH BETRAYAL!
AND FOR THAT--
KTANG
SHAME ON YOU, NAMOR.
AVENGERS, HOW ARE YOU AND WHERE ARE YOU?!

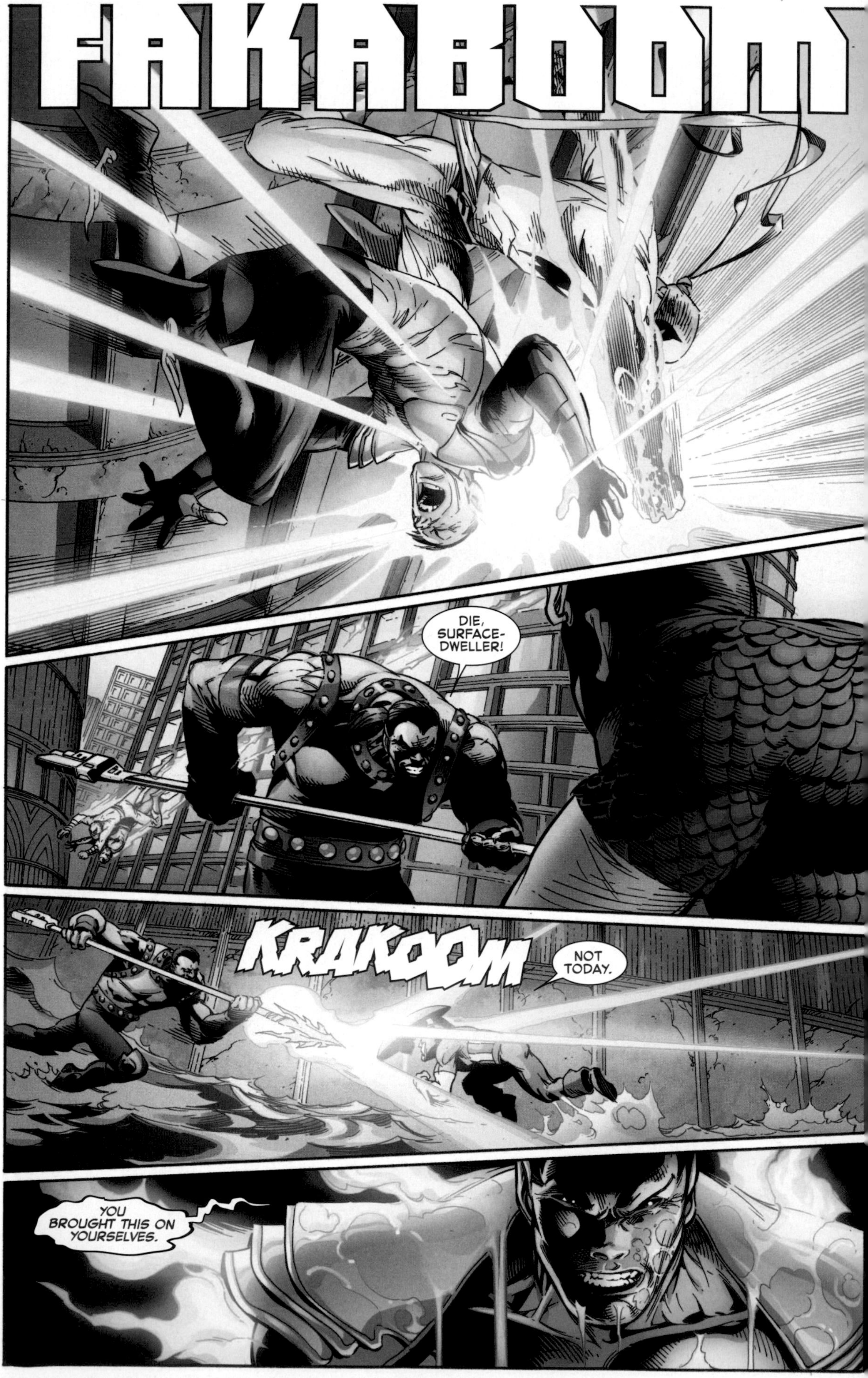
FAKABOOM
DIE, SURFACE-DWELLER!
KRAKOOM
NOT TODAY.
YOU BROUGHT THIS ON YOURSELVES.

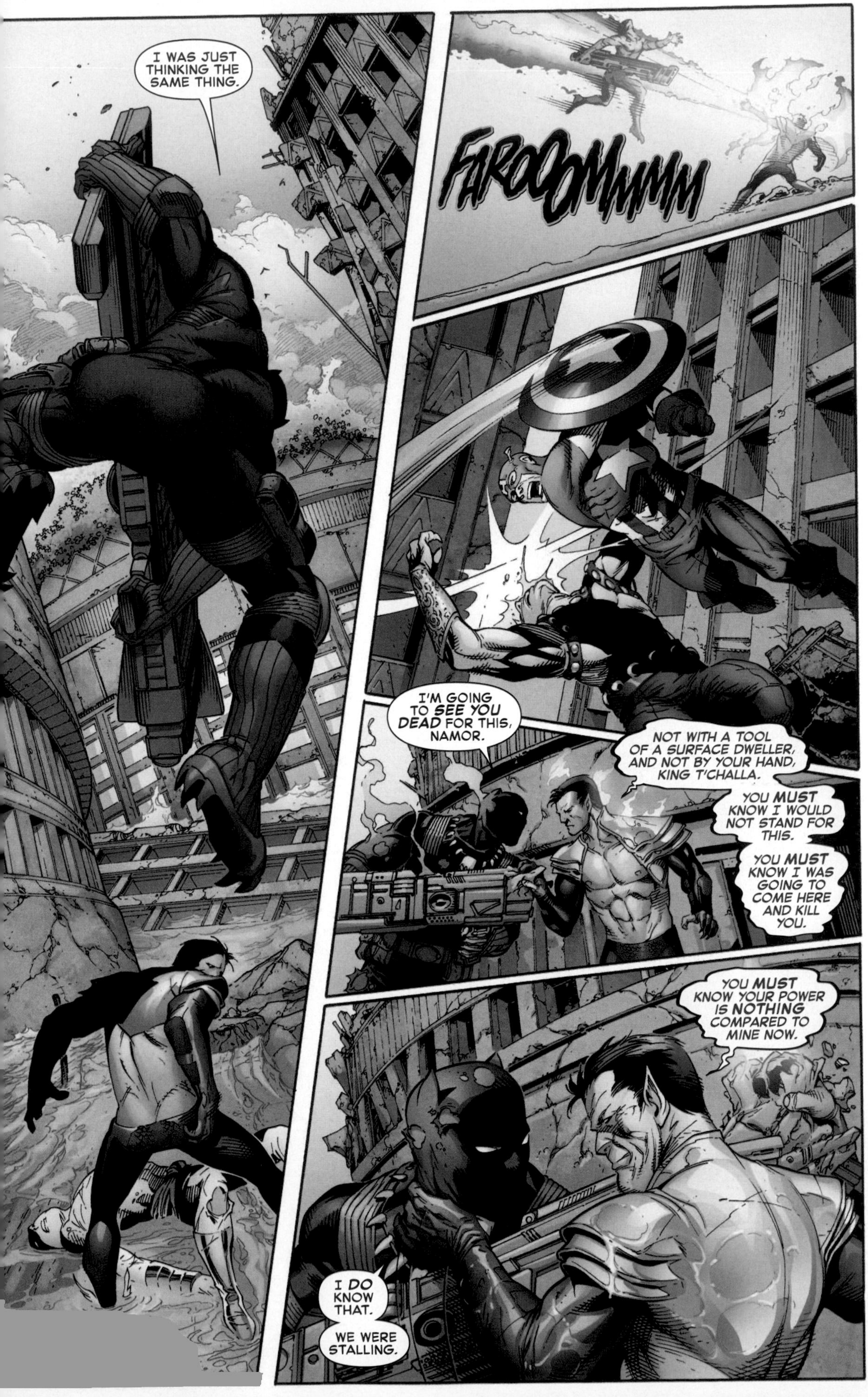
I WAS JUST THINKING THE SAME THING.
FAROOOMMMM
I'M GOING TO SEE YOU DEAD FOR THIS, NAMOR.
NOT WITH A TOOL OF A SURFACE DWELLER, AND NOT BY YOUR HAND, KING T'CHALLA.
YOU MUST KNOW I WOULD NOT STAND FOR THIS.
YOU MUST KNOW I WAS GOING TO COME HERE AND KILL YOU.
YOU MUST KNOW YOUR POWER IS NOTHING COMPARED TO MINE NOW.
I DO KNOW THAT.
WE WERE STALLING.

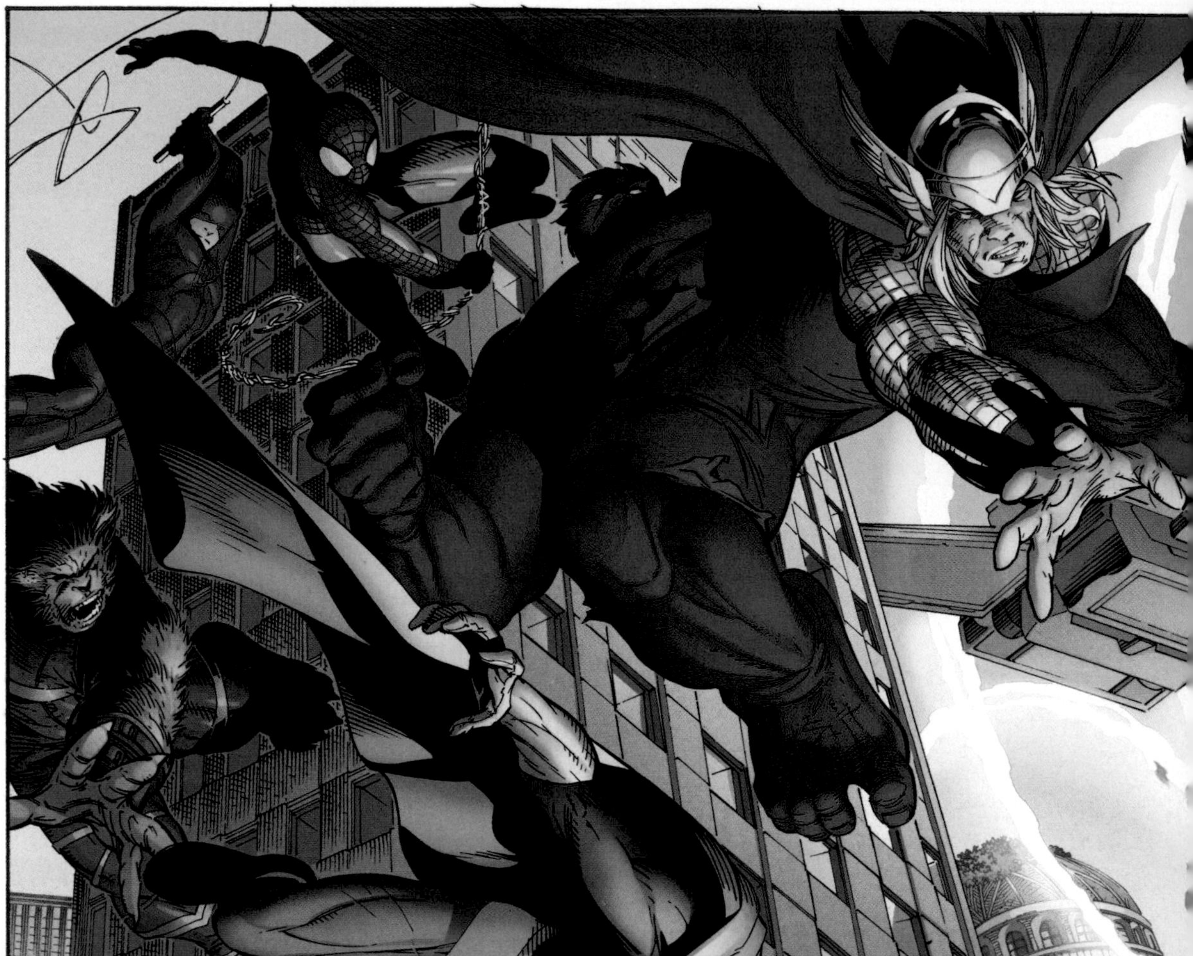
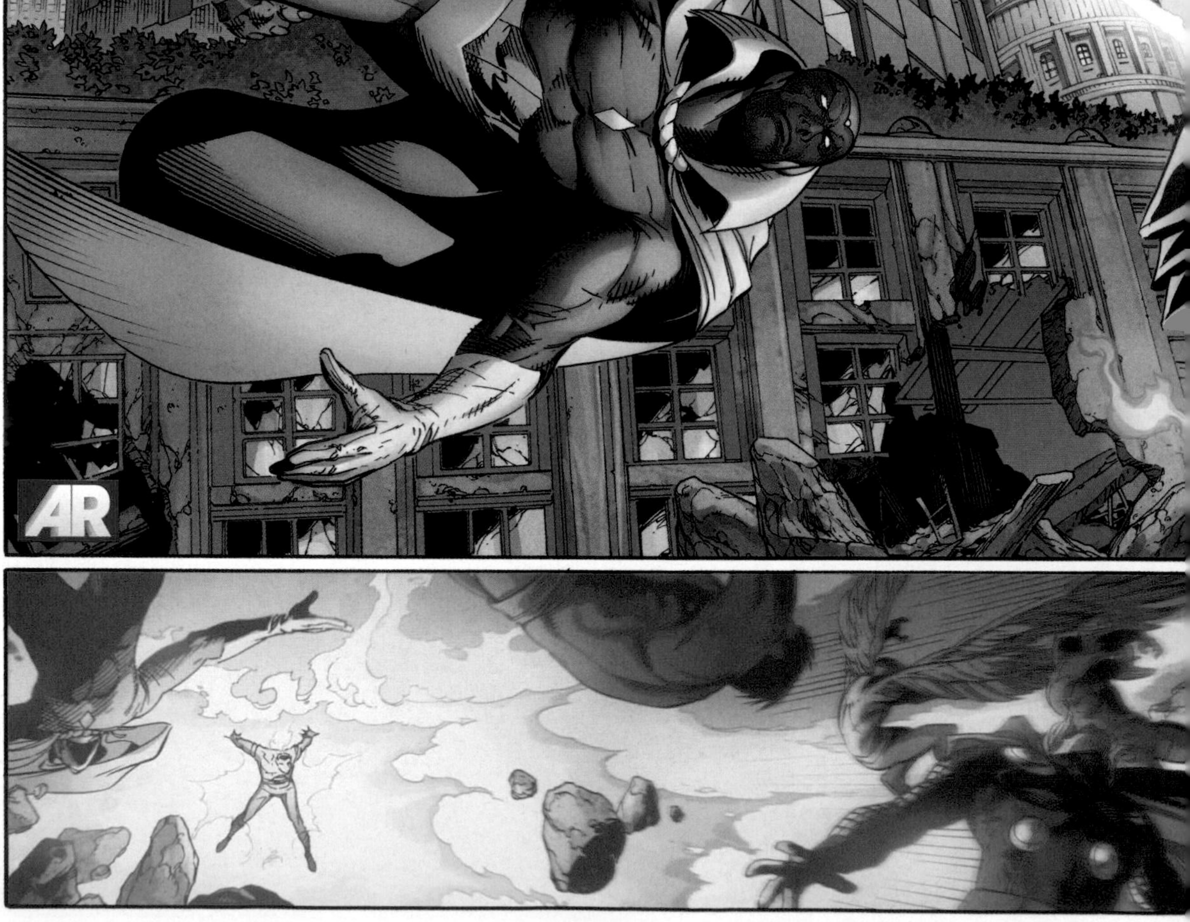

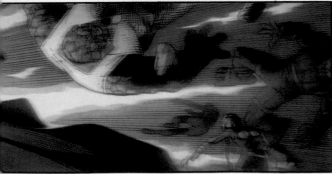

IMPERIUS REX!

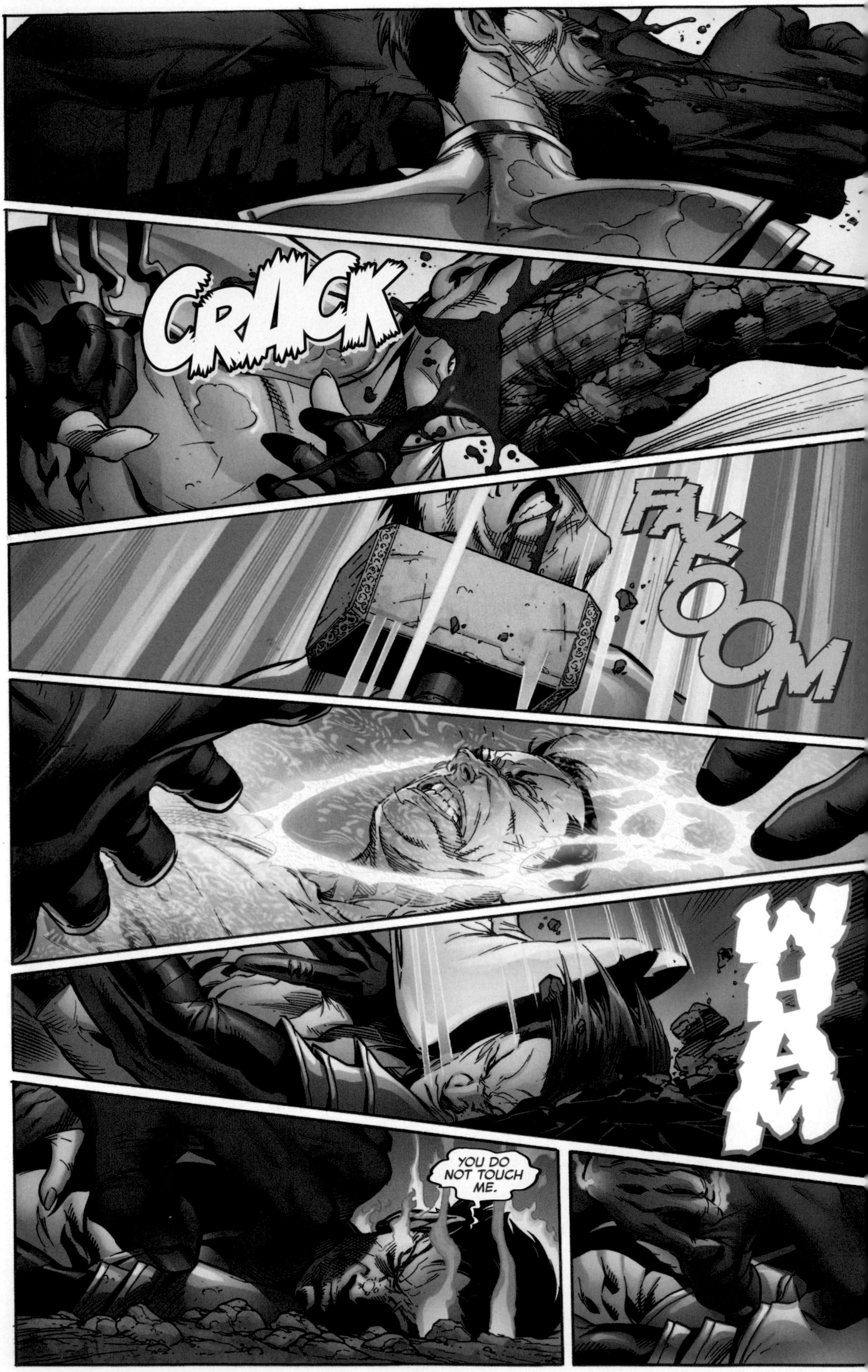
WHACK
CRACK
FAKOOM
WHAM
YOU DO NOT TOUCH ME.

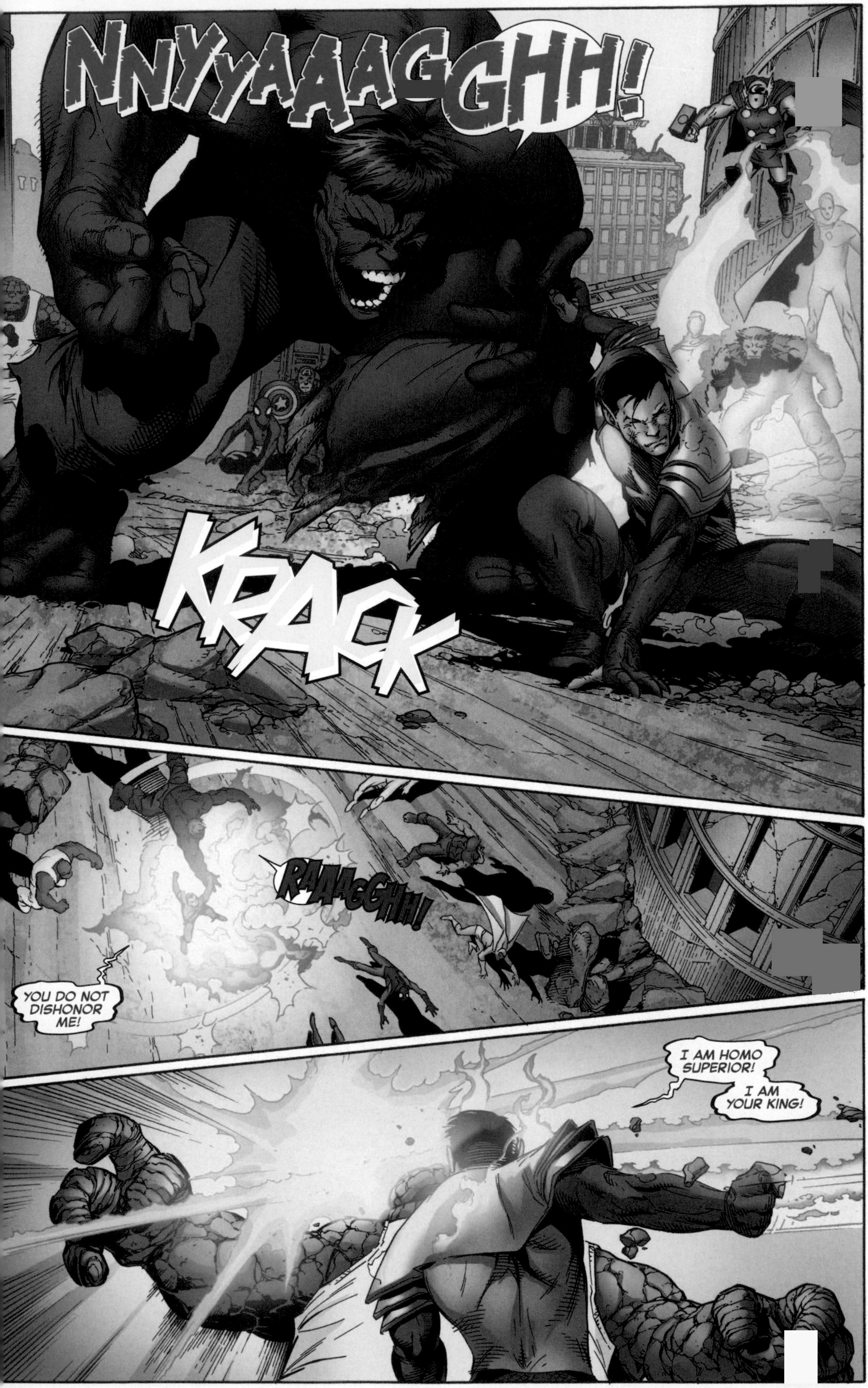
NNYYAAA[redacted]GHH!
KRACK
RAAAGGHH!
YOU DO NOT DISHONOR ME!
I AM HOMO SUPERIOR!
I AM YOUR KING!

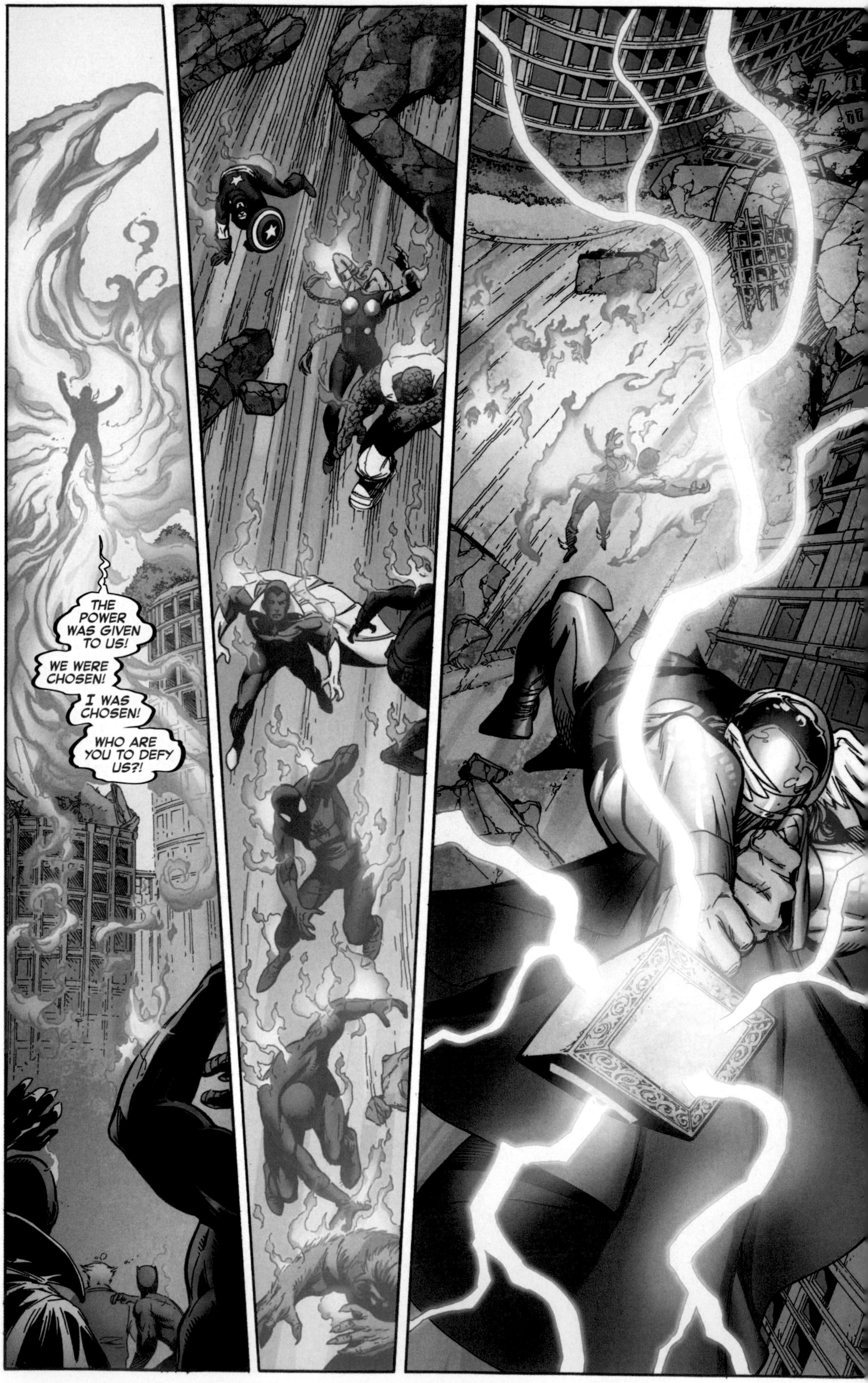
THE POWER WAS GIVEN TO US!
WE WERE CHOSEN!
I WAS CHOSEN!
WHO ARE YOU TO DEFY US?!

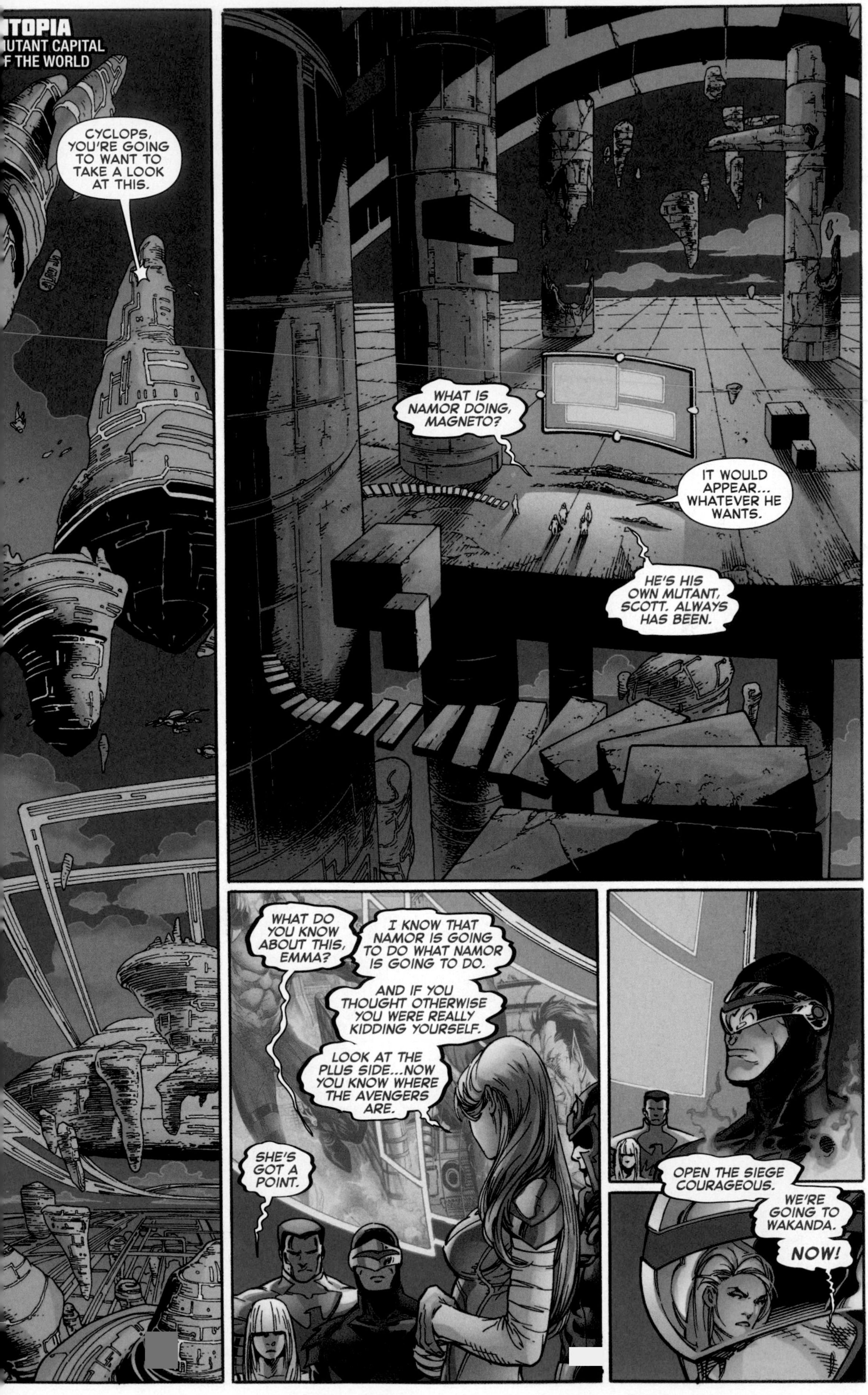
TOPIA
UTANT CAPITAL
F THE WORLD
CYCLOPS, YOU'RE GOING TO WANT TO TAKE A LOOK AT THIS.
WHAT IS NAMOR DOING, MAGNETO?
IT WOULD APPEAR... WHATEVER HE WANTS.
HE'S HIS OWN MUTANT, SCOTT. ALWAYS HAS BEEN.
WHAT DO YOU KNOW ABOUT THIS, EMMA?
I KNOW THAT NAMOR IS GOING TO DO WHAT NAMOR IS GOING TO DO.
AND IF YOU THOUGHT OTHERWISE YOU WERE REALLY KIDDING YOURSELF.
LOOK AT THE PLUS SIDE...NOW YOU KNOW WHERE THE AVENGERS ARE.
SHE'S GOT A POINT.
OPEN THE SIEGE COURAGEOUS.
WE'RE GOING TO WAKANDA.
NOW!

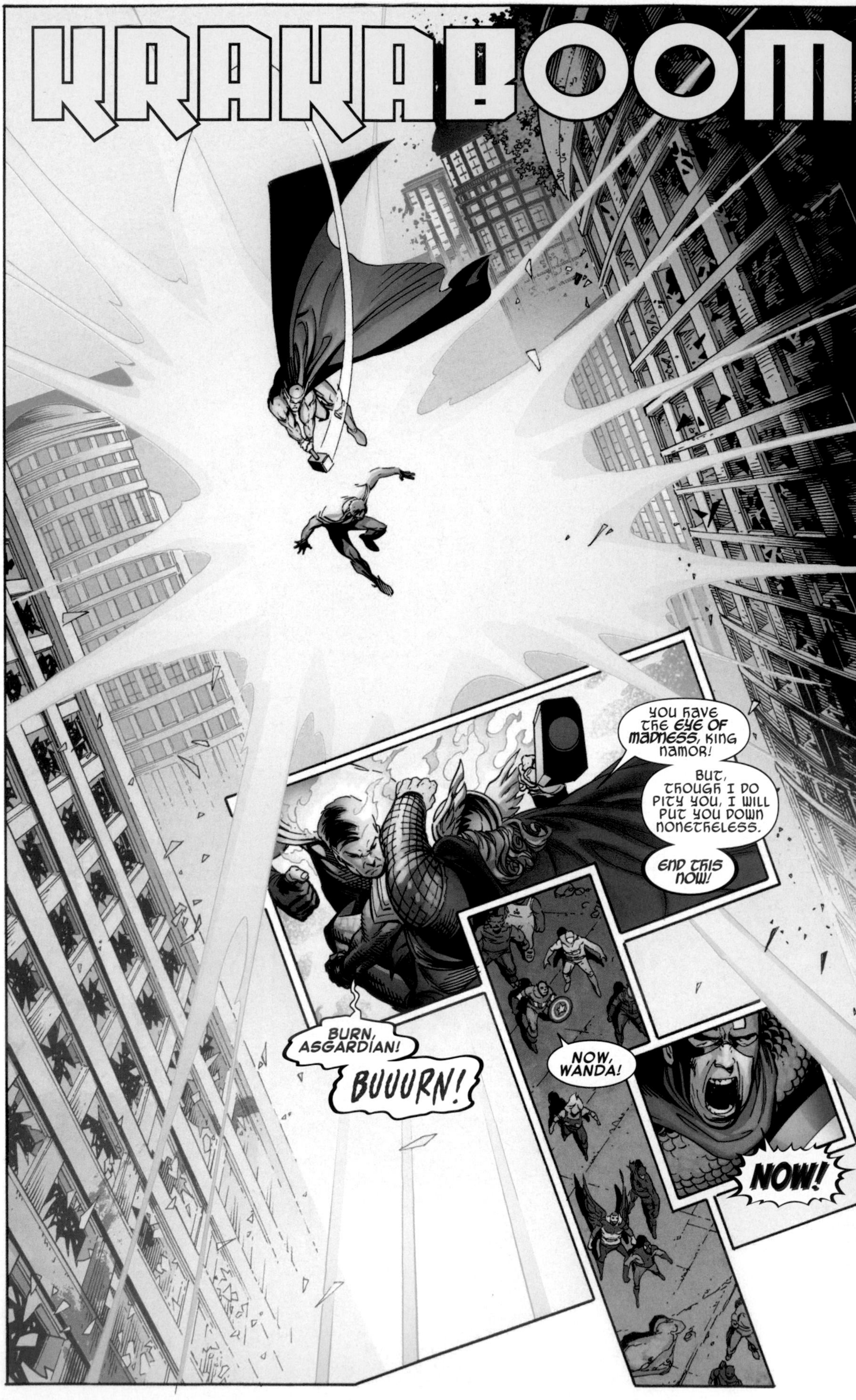
KRAKABOOM
YOU HAVE THE EYE OF MADNESS, KING NAMOR!
BUT, THOUGH I DO PITY YOU, I WILL PUT YOU DOWN NONETHELESS.
END THIS NOW!
BURN, ASGARDIAN!
BUUURN!
NOW, WANDA!
NOW!

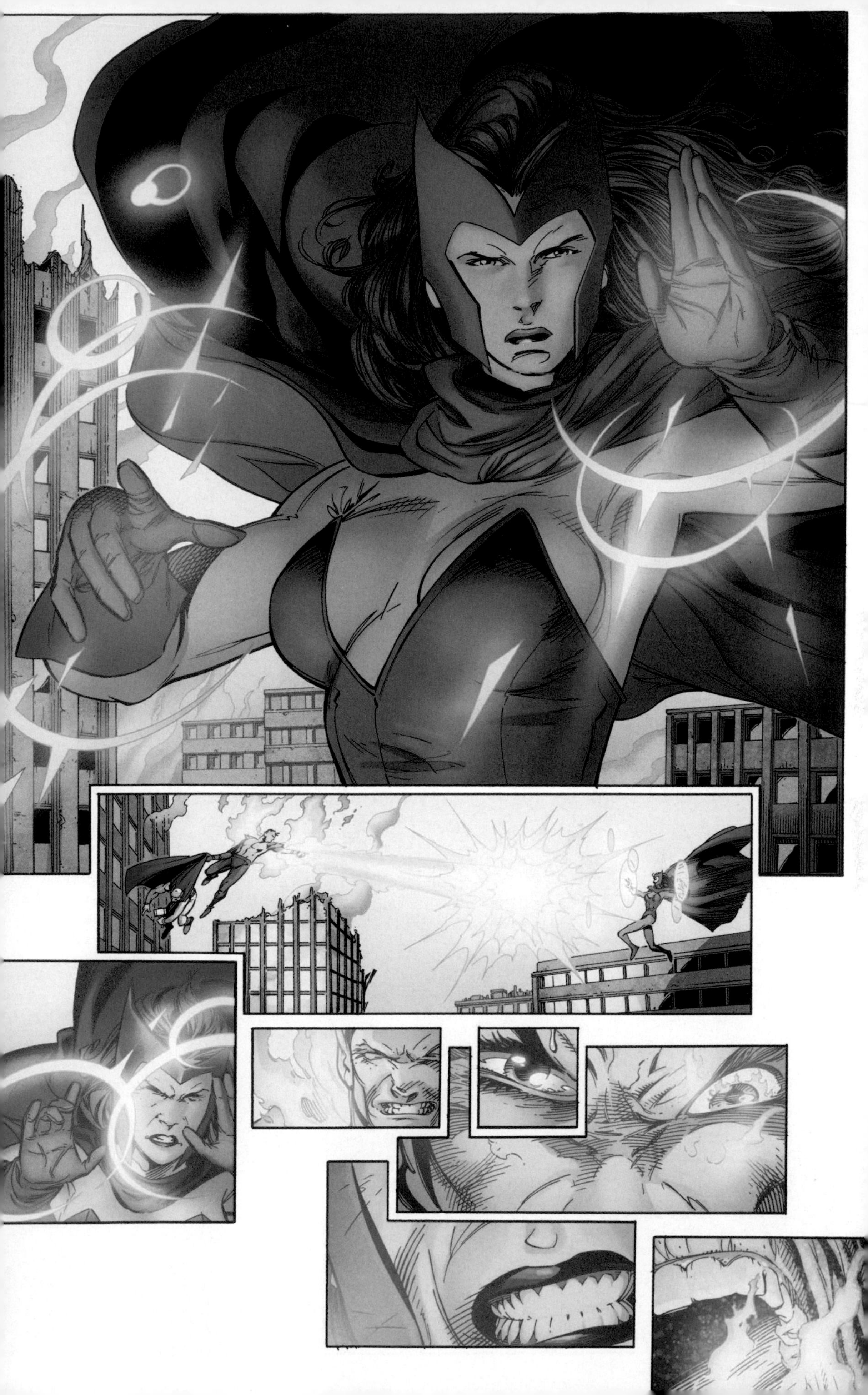

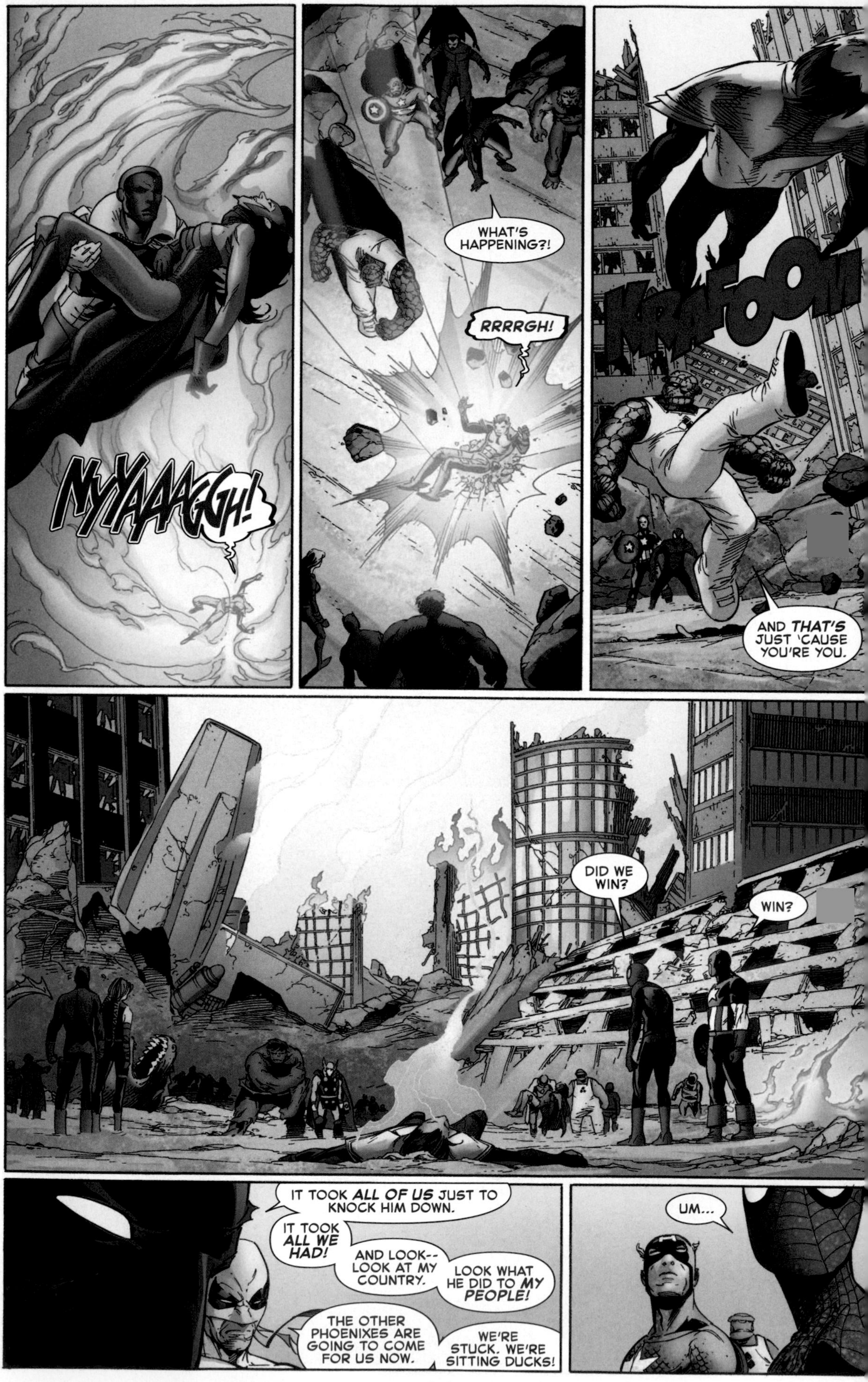
NYYAAAGGH!
WHAT'S HAPPENING?!
RRRRGH!
KRAFOOM
AND THAT'S JUST 'CAUSE YOU'RE YOU.
DID WE WIN?
WIN?
IT TOOK ALL OF US JUST TO KNOCK HIM DOWN.
IT TOOK ALL WE HAD!
AND LOOK-- LOOK AT MY COUNTRY.
LOOK WHAT HE DID TO MY PEOPLE!
THE OTHER PHOENIXES ARE GOING TO COME FOR US NOW.
WE'RE STUCK. WE'RE SITTING DUCKS!
UM...

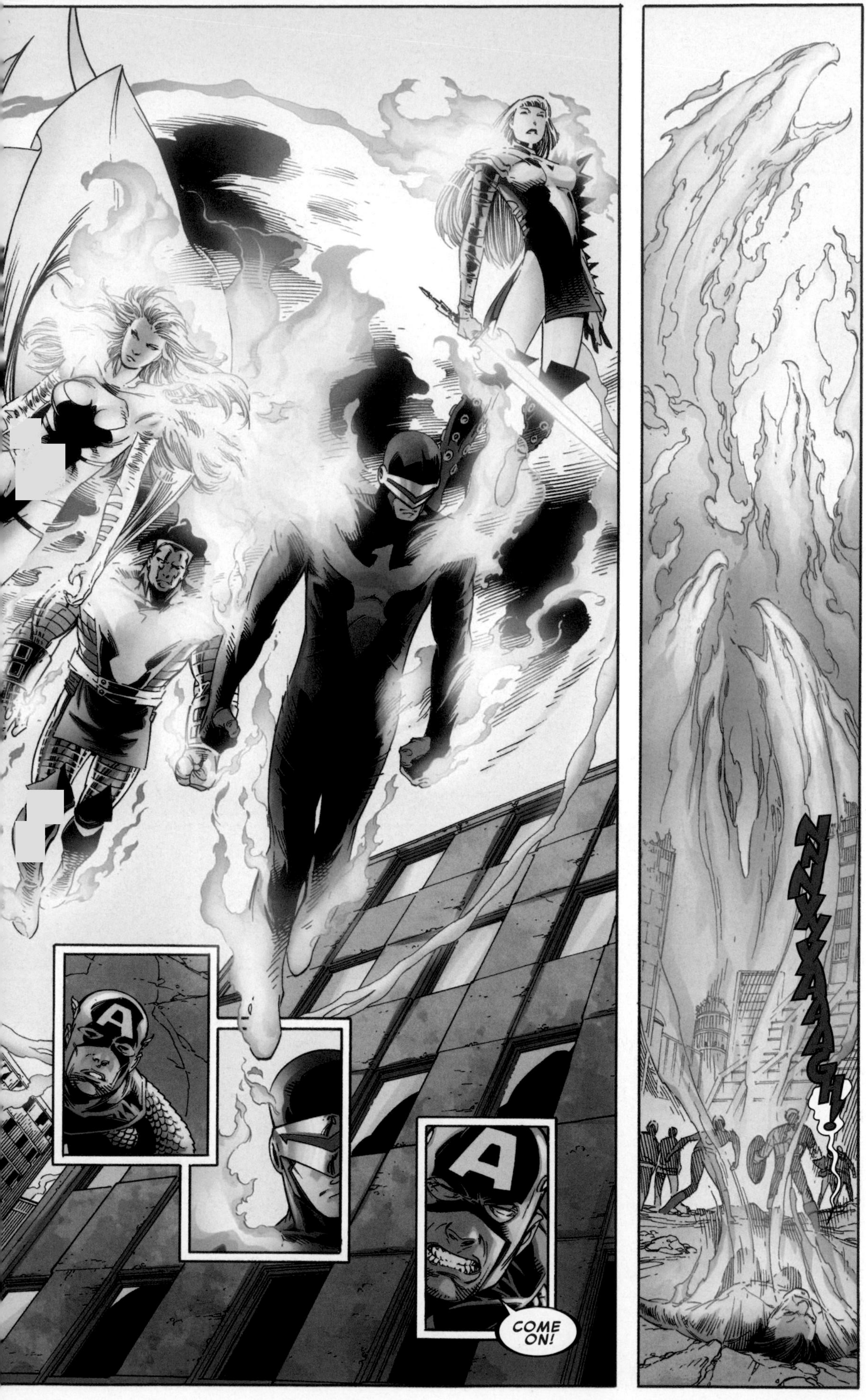
COME ON!
NNYYAAGH!

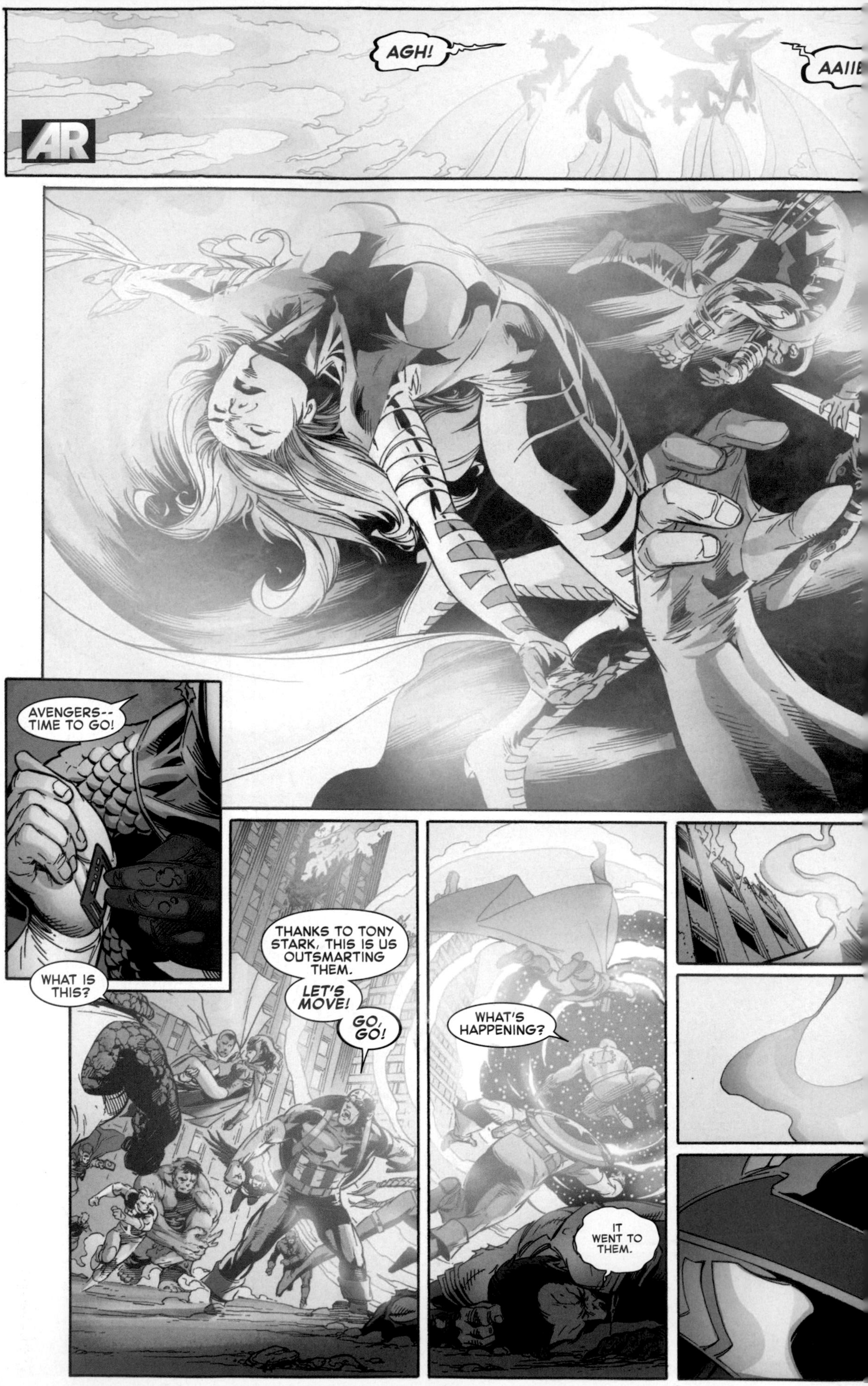
AGH!
AAIIE
AVENGERS-- TIME TO GO!
WHAT IS THIS?
THANKS TO TONY STARK, THIS IS US OUTSMARTING THEM.
LET'S MOVE!
GO, GO!
WHAT'S HAPPENING?
IT WENT TO THEM.

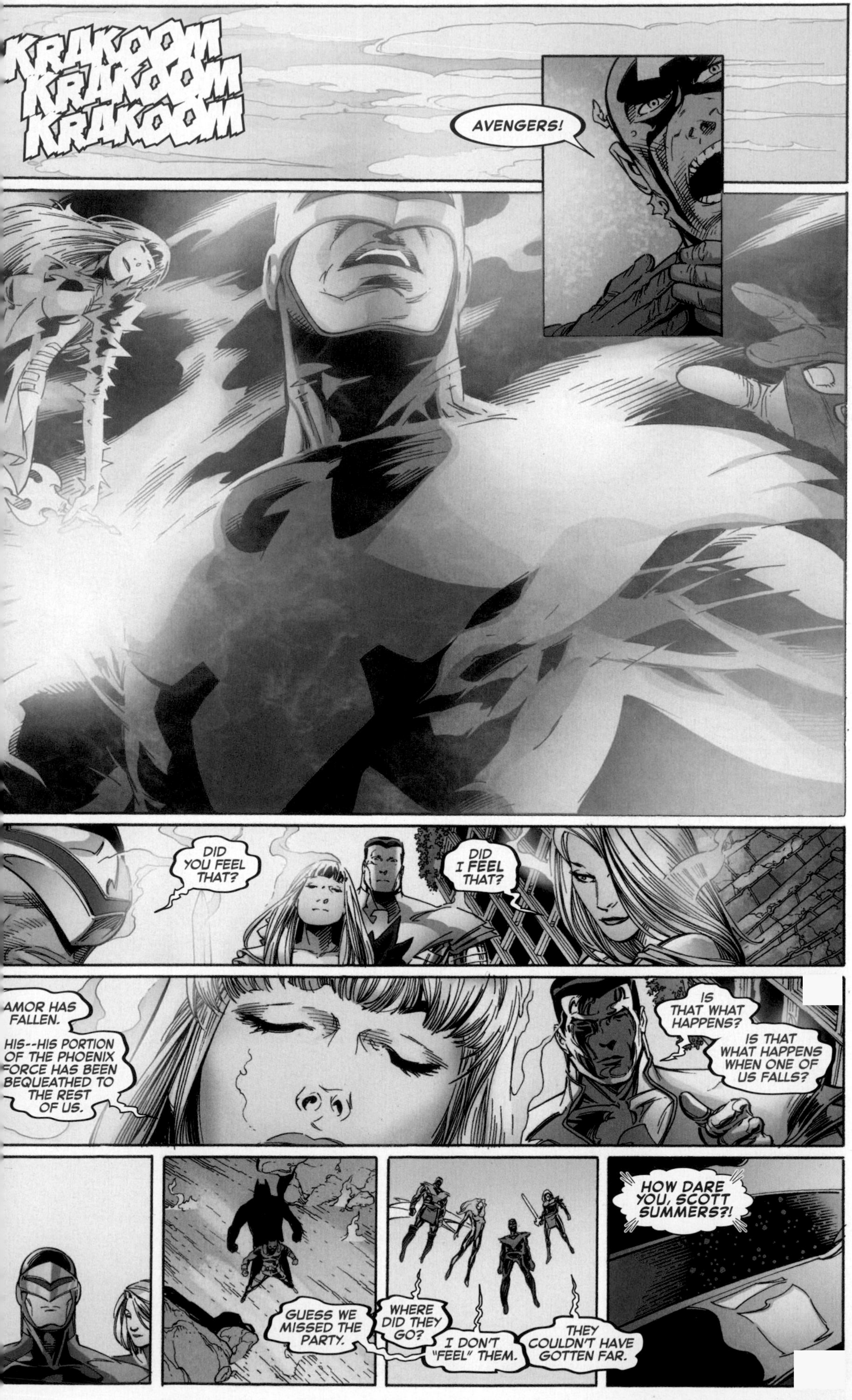
KRAKOOM
KRAKOOM
KRAKOOM
AVENGERS!
DID YOU FEEL THAT?
DID I FEEL THAT?
AMOR HAS FALLEN.
HIS--HIS PORTION OF THE PHOENIX FORCE HAS BEEN BEQUEATHED TO THE REST OF US.
IS THAT WHAT HAPPENS?
IS THAT WHAT HAPPENS WHEN ONE OF US FALLS?
GUESS WE MISSED THE PARTY.
WHERE DID THEY GO?
I DON'T "FEEL" THEM.
THEY COULDN'T HAVE GOTTEN FAR.
HOW DARE YOU, SCOTT SUMMERS?!

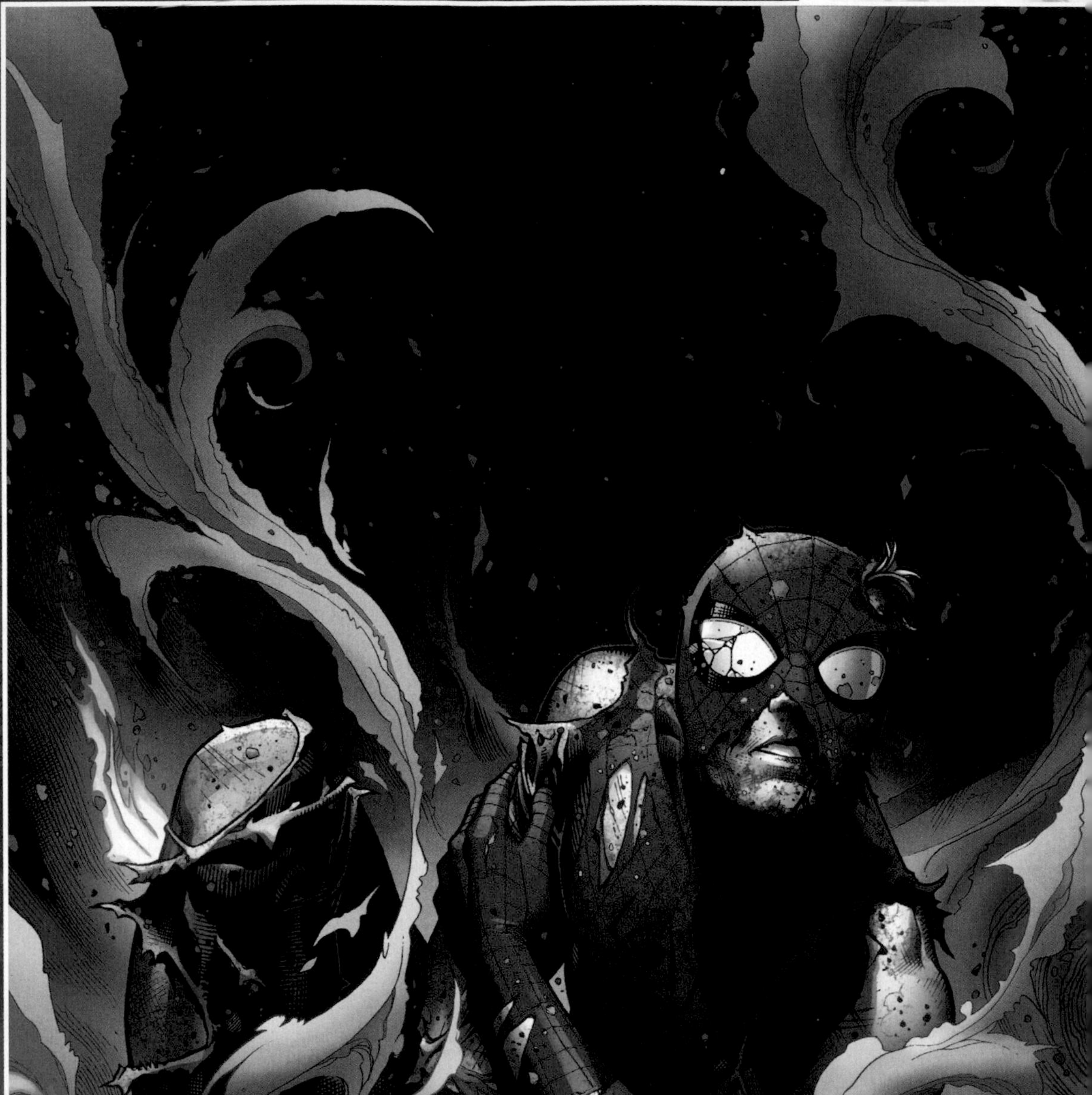

ROUND 9

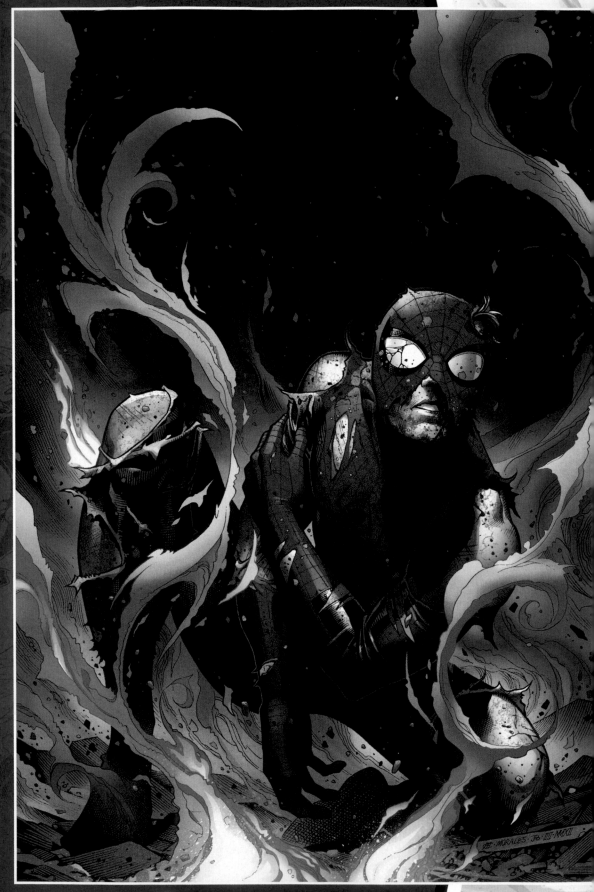

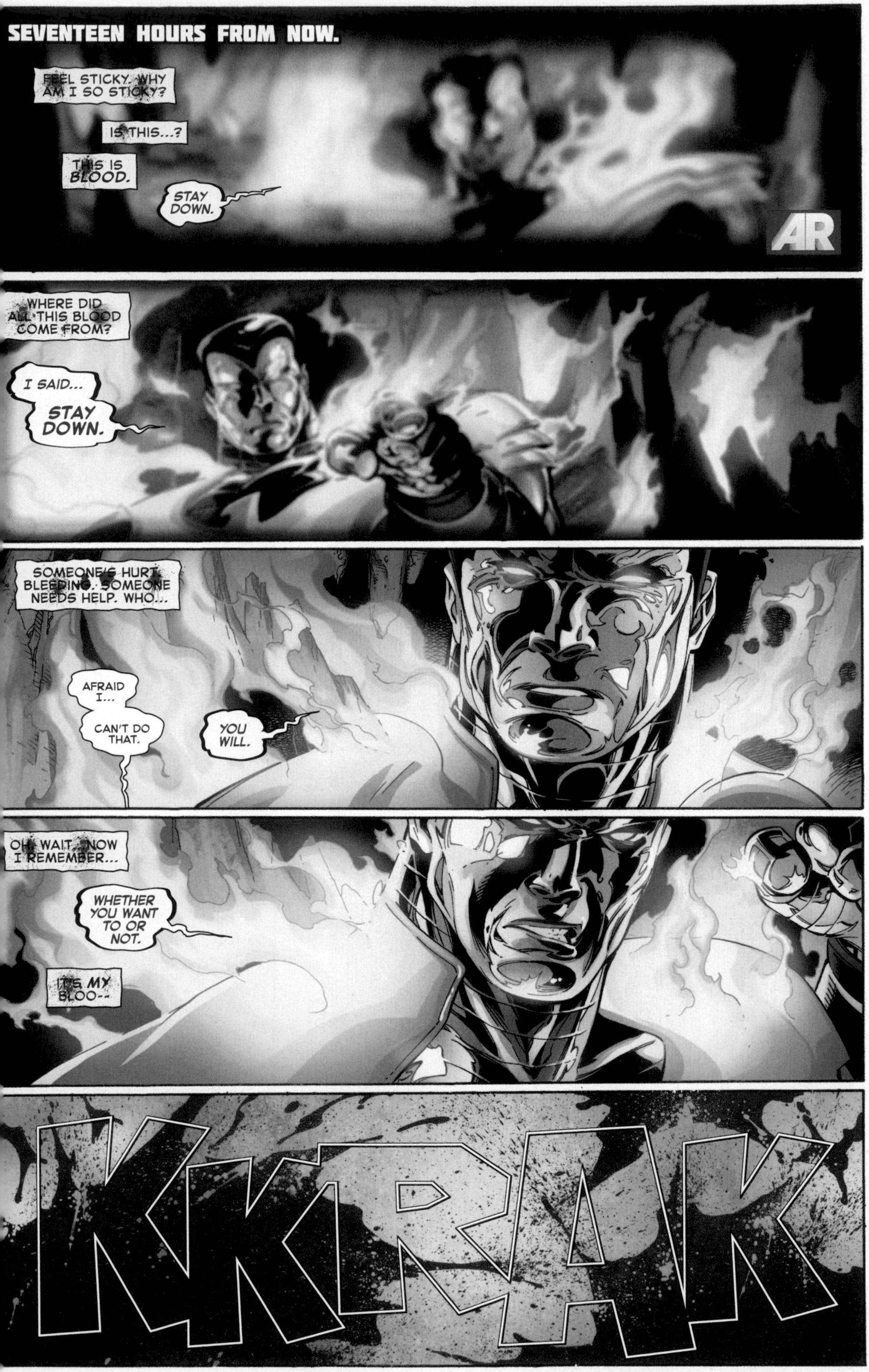
SEVENTEEN HOURS FROM NOW.
FEEL STICKY. WHY AM I SO STICKY?
IS THIS...?
THIS IS BLOOD.
STAY DOWN.
AR
WHERE DID ALL THIS BLOOD COME FROM?
I SAID... STAY DOWN.
SOMEONE'S HURT. BLEEDING. SOMEONE NEEDS HELP. WHO...
AFRAID I...
CAN'T DO THAT.
YOU WILL.
OH, WAIT. NOW I REMEMBER...
WHETHER YOU WANT TO OR NOT.
IT'S MY BLOO--
KKRAK

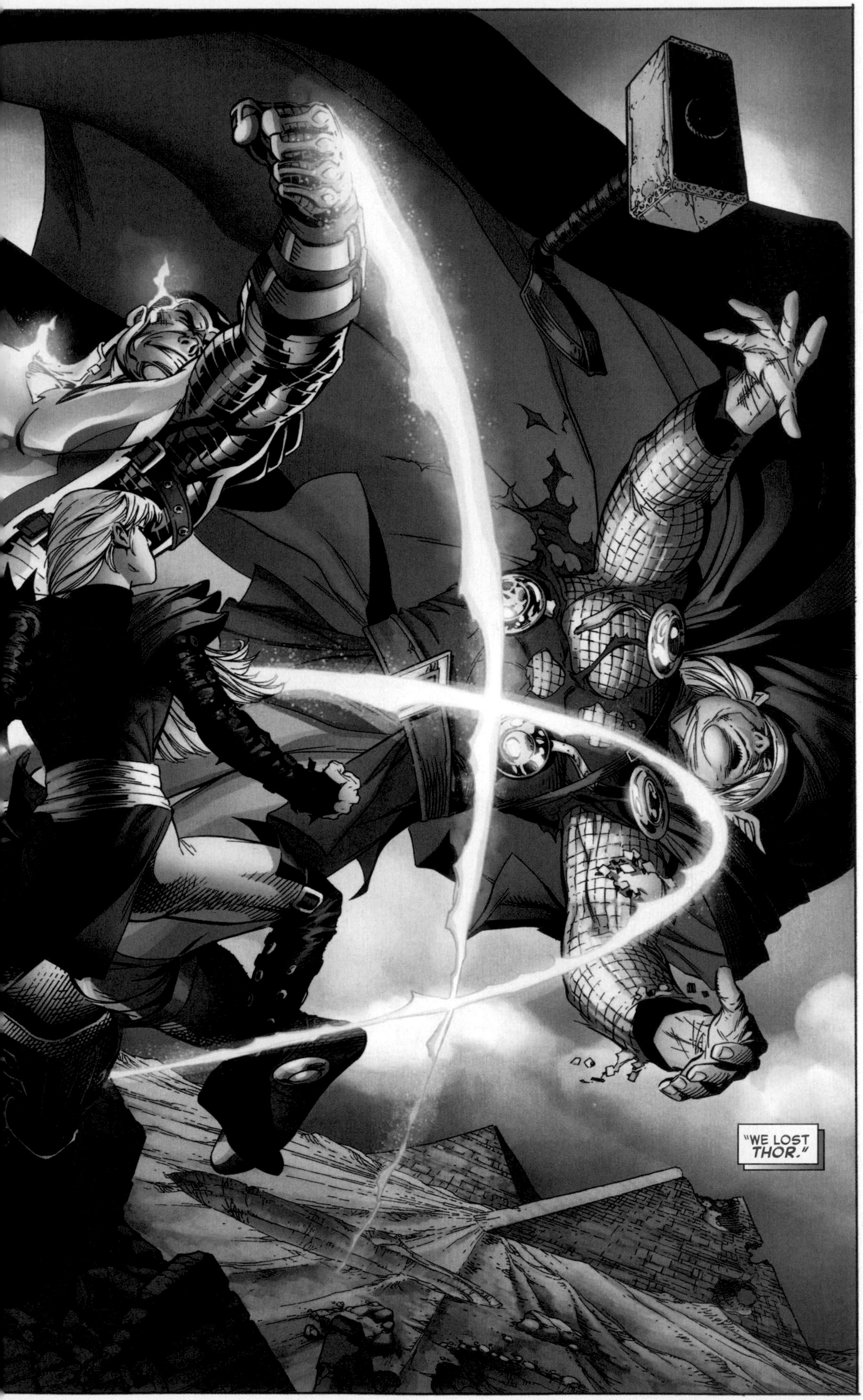
"WE LOST THOR."

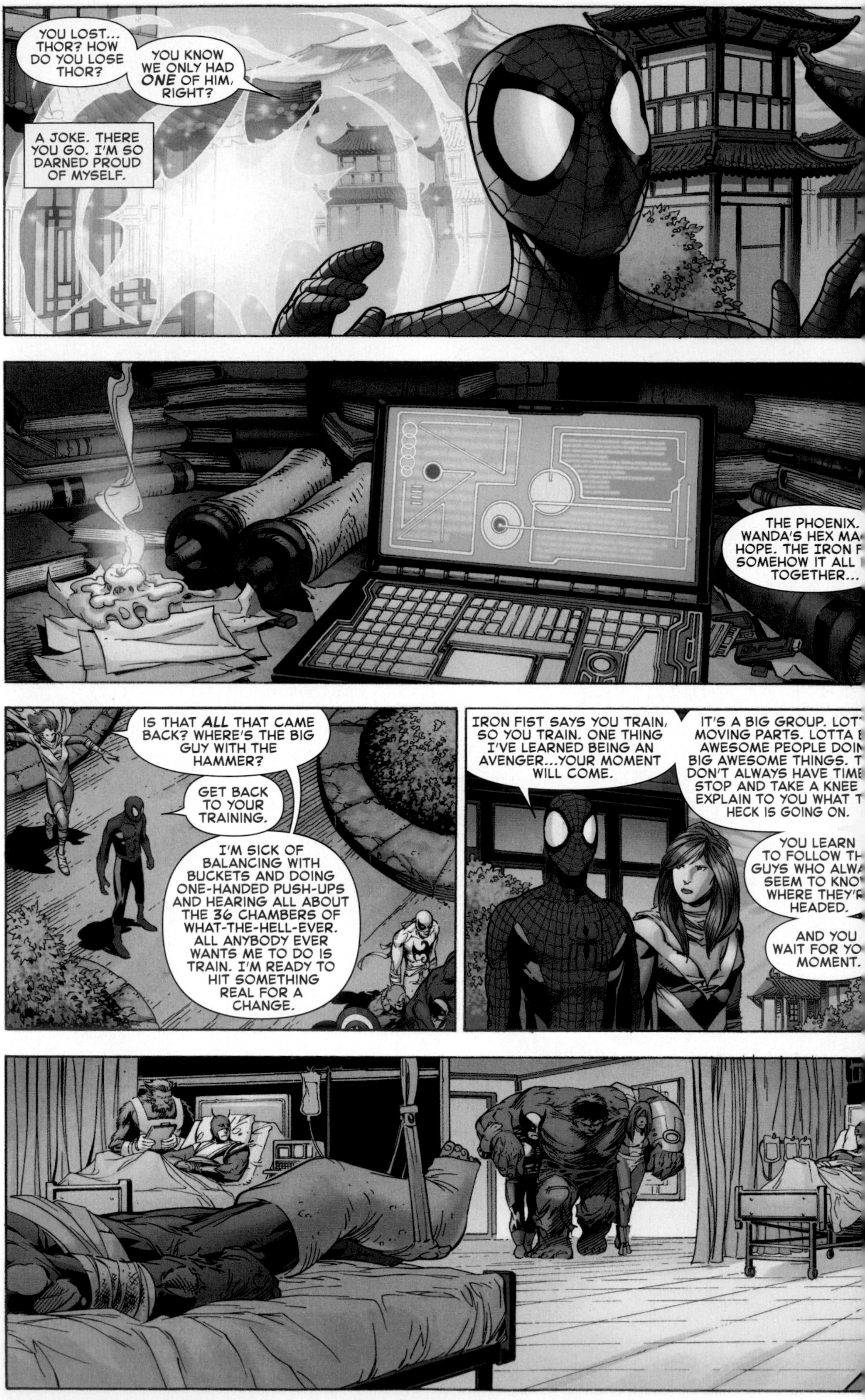
YOU LOST... THOR? HOW DO YOU LOSE THOR?
YOU KNOW WE ONLY HAD ONE OF HIM, RIGHT?
A JOKE. THERE YOU GO. I'M SO DARNED PROUD OF MYSELF.
THE PHOENIX. WANDA'S HEX MA HOPE. THE IRON F SOMEHOW IT ALL TOGETHER...
IS THAT ALL THAT CAME BACK? WHERE'S THE BIG GUY WITH THE HAMMER?
GET BACK TO YOUR TRAINING.
I'M SICK OF BALANCING WITH BUCKETS AND DOING ONE-HANDED PUSH-UPS AND HEARING ALL ABOUT THE 36 CHAMBERS OF WHAT-THE-HELL-EVER. ALL ANYBODY EVER WANTS ME TO DO IS TRAIN. I'M READY TO HIT SOMETHING REAL FOR A CHANGE.
IRON FIST SAYS YOU TRAIN, SO YOU TRAIN. ONE THING I'VE LEARNED BEING AN AVENGER...YOUR MOMENT WILL COME.
IT'S A BIG GROUP. LOTT MOVING PARTS. LOTTA AWESOME PEOPLE DOIN BIG AWESOME THINGS. T DON'T ALWAYS HAVE TIME STOP AND TAKE A KNEE EXPLAIN TO YOU WHAT T HECK IS GOING ON.
YOU LEARN TO FOLLOW TH GUYS WHO ALWA SEEM TO KNO WHERE THEY'R HEADED.
AND YOU WAIT FOR YO MOMENT.

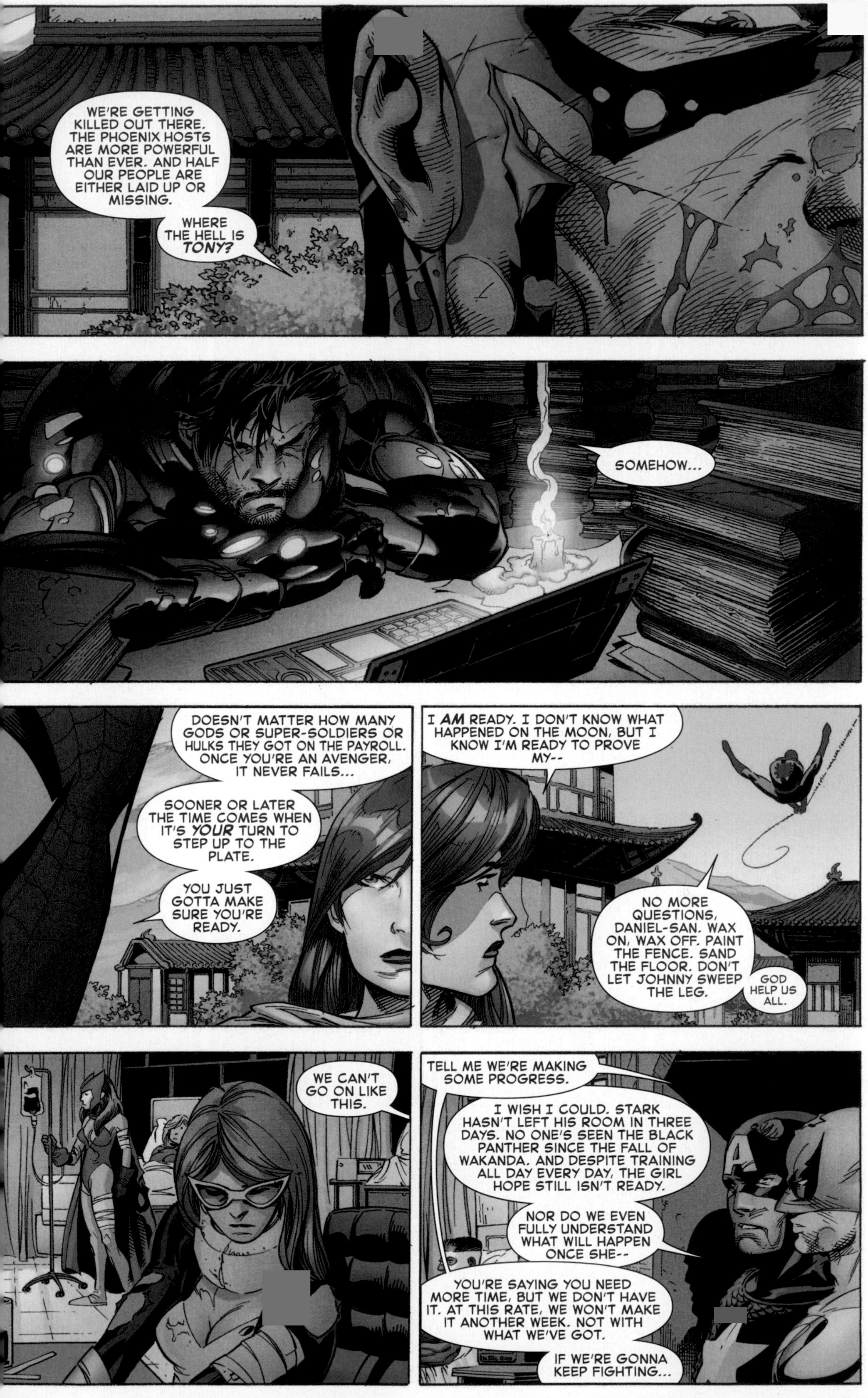
WE'RE GETTING KILLED OUT THERE. THE PHOENIX HOSTS ARE MORE POWERFUL THAN EVER. AND HALF OUR PEOPLE ARE EITHER LAID UP OR MISSING.
WHERE THE HELL IS TONY?
SOMEHOW...
DOESN'T MATTER HOW MANY GODS OR SUPER-SOLDIERS OR HULKS THEY GOT ON THE PAYROLL. ONCE YOU'RE AN AVENGER, IT NEVER FAILS...
SOONER OR LATER THE TIME COMES WHEN IT'S YOUR TURN TO STEP UP TO THE PLATE.
YOU JUST GOTTA MAKE SURE YOU'RE READY.
I AM READY. I DON'T KNOW WHAT HAPPENED ON THE MOON, BUT I KNOW I'M READY TO PROVE MY--
NO MORE QUESTIONS, DANIEL-SAN. WAX ON, WAX OFF. PAINT THE FENCE. SAND THE FLOOR. DON'T LET JOHNNY SWEEP THE LEG.
GOD HELP US ALL.
WE CAN'T GO ON LIKE THIS.
TELL ME WE'RE MAKING SOME PROGRESS.
I WISH I COULD. STARK HASN'T LEFT HIS ROOM IN THREE DAYS. NO ONE'S SEEN THE BLACK PANTHER SINCE THE FALL OF WAKANDA. AND DESPITE TRAINING ALL DAY EVERY DAY, THE GIRL HOPE STILL ISN'T READY.
NOR DO WE EVEN FULLY UNDERSTAND WHAT WILL HAPPEN ONCE SHE--
YOU'RE SAYING YOU NEED MORE TIME, BUT WE DON'T HAVE IT. AT THIS RATE, WE WON'T MAKE IT ANOTHER WEEK. NOT WITH WHAT WE'VE GOT.
IF WE'RE GONNA KEEP FIGHTING...

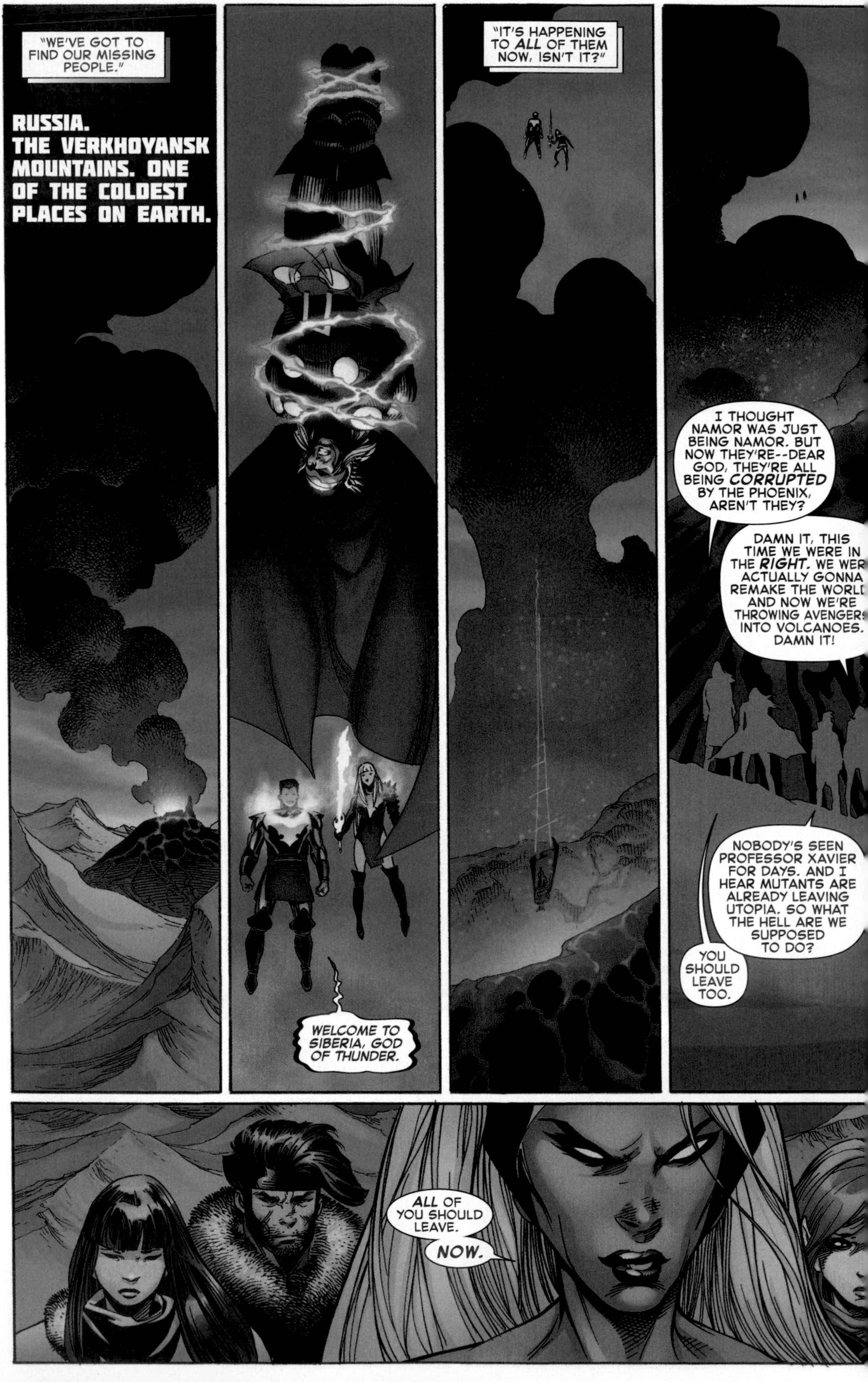

"WE'VE GOT TO FIND OUR MISSING PEOPLE."
RUSSIA. THE VERKHOYANSK MOUNTAINS. ONE OF THE COLDEST PLACES ON EARTH.
WELCOME TO SIBERIA, GOD OF THUNDER.
"IT'S HAPPENING TO ALL OF THEM NOW, ISN'T IT?"
I THOUGHT NAMOR WAS JUST BEING NAMOR. BUT NOW THEY'RE--DEAR GOD, THEY'RE ALL BEING CORRUPTED BY THE PHOENIX, AREN'T THEY?
DAMN IT, THIS TIME WE WERE IN THE RIGHT. WE WER ACTUALLY GONNA REMAKE THE WORL AND NOW WE'RE THROWING AVENGER INTO VOLCANOES. DAMN IT!
NOBODY'S SEEN PROFESSOR XAVIER FOR DAYS. AND I HEAR MUTANTS ARE ALREADY LEAVING UTOPIA. SO WHAT THE HELL ARE WE SUPPOSED TO DO?
YOU SHOULD LEAVE TOO.
ALL OF YOU SHOULD LEAVE.
NOW.

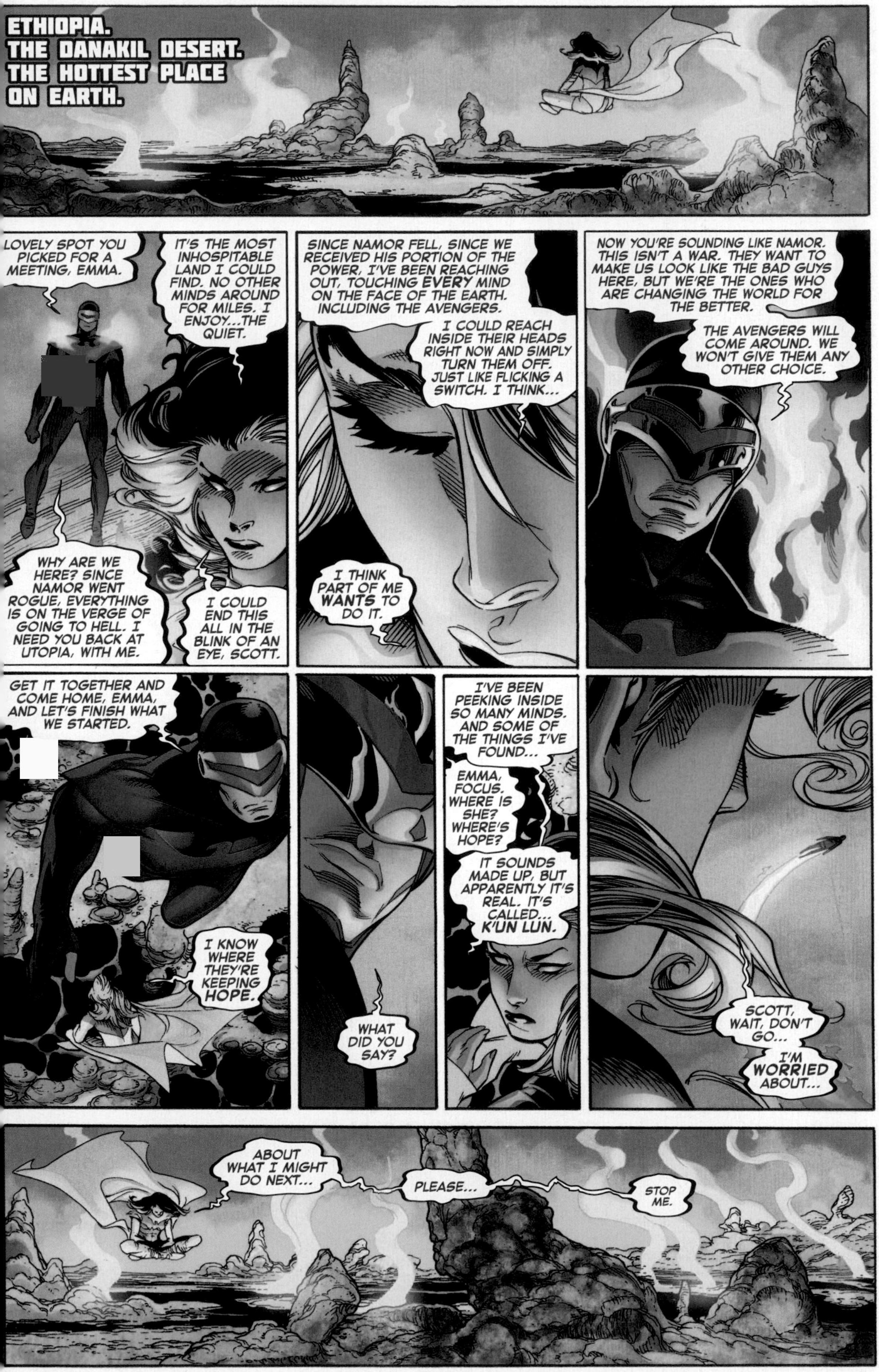
ETHIOPIA. THE DANAKIL DESERT. THE HOTTEST PLACE ON EARTH.
LOVELY SPOT YOU PICKED FOR A MEETING, EMMA.
IT'S THE MOST INHOSPITABLE LAND I COULD FIND. NO OTHER MINDS AROUND FOR MILES. I ENJOY...THE QUIET.
WHY ARE WE HERE? SINCE NAMOR WENT ROGUE, EVERYTHING IS ON THE VERGE OF GOING TO HELL. I NEED YOU BACK AT UTOPIA, WITH ME.
I COULD END THIS ALL IN THE BLINK OF AN EYE, SCOTT.
SINCE NAMOR FELL, SINCE WE RECEIVED HIS PORTION OF THE POWER, I'VE BEEN REACHING OUT, TOUCHING EVERY MIND ON THE FACE OF THE EARTH. INCLUDING THE AVENGERS.
I COULD REACH INSIDE THEIR HEADS RIGHT NOW AND SIMPLY TURN THEM OFF. JUST LIKE FLICKING A SWITCH. I THINK...
I THINK PART OF ME WANTS TO DO IT.
NOW YOU'RE SOUNDING LIKE NAMOR. THIS ISN'T A WAR. THEY WANT TO MAKE US LOOK LIKE THE BAD GUYS HERE, BUT WE'RE THE ONES WHO ARE CHANGING THE WORLD FOR THE BETTER.
THE AVENGERS WILL COME AROUND. WE WON'T GIVE THEM ANY OTHER CHOICE.
GET IT TOGETHER AND COME HOME, EMMA, AND LET'S FINISH WHAT WE STARTED.
I KNOW WHERE THEY'RE KEEPING HOPE.
WHAT DID YOU SAY?
I'VE BEEN PEEKING INSIDE SO MANY MINDS. AND SOME OF THE THINGS I'VE FOUND...
EMMA, FOCUS. WHERE IS SHE? WHERE'S HOPE?
IT SOUNDS MADE UP, BUT APPARENTLY IT'S REAL. IT'S CALLED... K'UN LUN.
SCOTT, WAIT, DON'T GO...
I'M WORRIED ABOUT...
ABOUT WHAT I MIGHT DO NEXT...
PLEASE...
STOP ME.

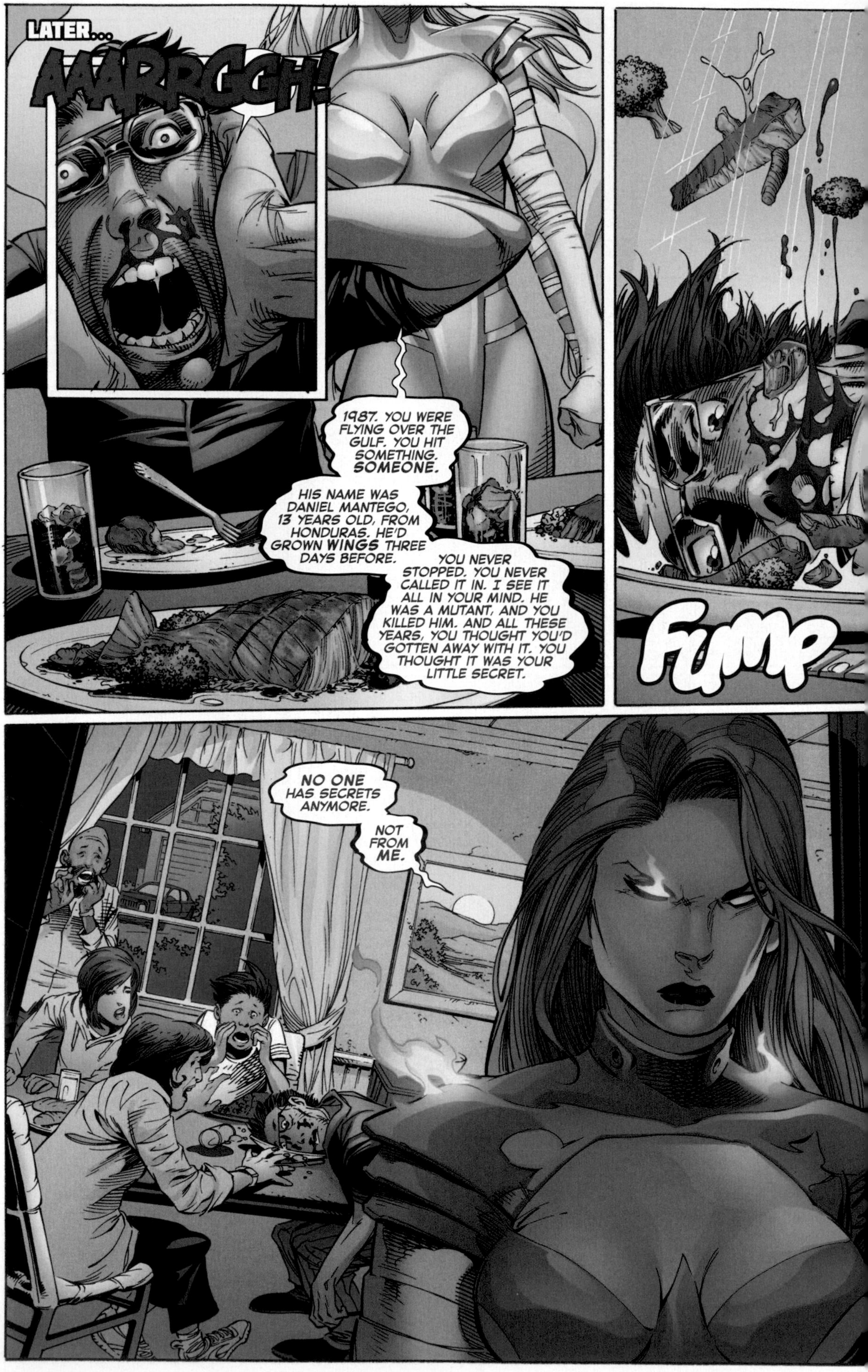
LATER...
AAARRGGH!
1987. YOU WERE FLYING OVER THE GULF. YOU HIT SOMETHING. SOMEONE.
HIS NAME WAS DANIEL MANTEGO, 13 YEARS OLD, FROM HONDURAS. HE'D GROWN WINGS THREE DAYS BEFORE.
YOU NEVER STOPPED. YOU NEVER CALLED IT IN. I SEE IT ALL IN YOUR MIND. HE WAS A MUTANT, AND YOU KILLED HIM. AND ALL THESE YEARS, YOU THOUGHT YOU'D GOTTEN AWAY WITH IT. YOU THOUGHT IT WAS YOUR LITTLE SECRET.
FUMP
NO ONE HAS SECRETS ANYMORE.
NOT FROM ME.

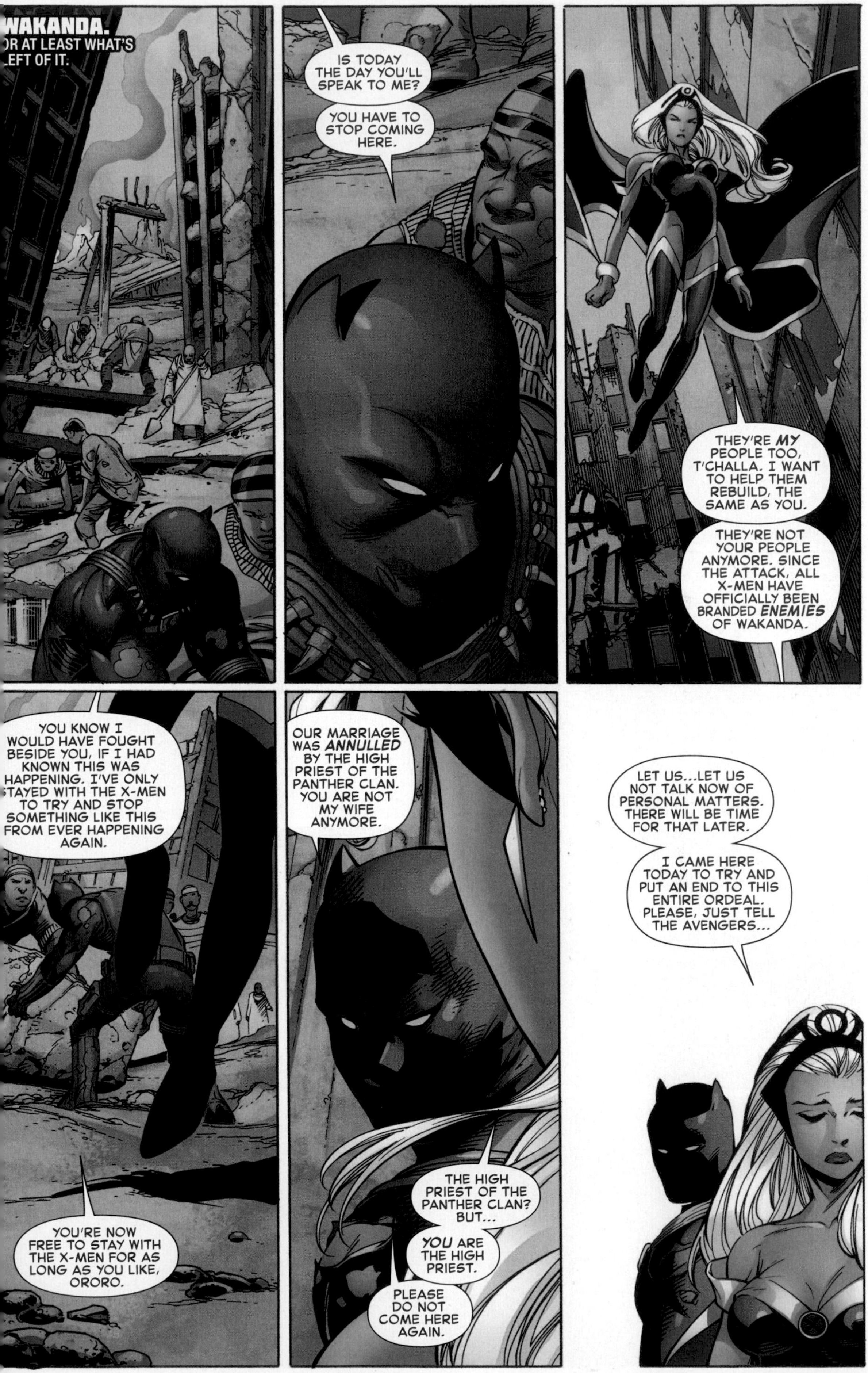
WAKANDA.
OR AT LEAST WHAT'S LEFT OF IT.
IS TODAY THE DAY YOU'LL SPEAK TO ME?
YOU HAVE TO STOP COMING HERE.
THEY'RE MY PEOPLE TOO, T'CHALLA. I WANT TO HELP THEM REBUILD, THE SAME AS YOU.
THEY'RE NOT YOUR PEOPLE ANYMORE. SINCE THE ATTACK, ALL X-MEN HAVE OFFICIALLY BEEN BRANDED ENEMIES OF WAKANDA.
YOU KNOW I WOULD HAVE FOUGHT BESIDE YOU, IF I HAD KNOWN THIS WAS HAPPENING. I'VE ONLY STAYED WITH THE X-MEN TO TRY AND STOP SOMETHING LIKE THIS FROM EVER HAPPENING AGAIN.
YOU'RE NOW FREE TO STAY WITH THE X-MEN FOR AS LONG AS YOU LIKE, ORORO.
OUR MARRIAGE WAS ANNULLED BY THE HIGH PRIEST OF THE PANTHER CLAN. YOU ARE NOT MY WIFE ANYMORE.
THE HIGH PRIEST OF THE PANTHER CLAN? BUT...
YOU ARE THE HIGH PRIEST.
PLEASE DO NOT COME HERE AGAIN.
LET US...LET US NOT TALK NOW OF PERSONAL MATTERS. THERE WILL BE TIME FOR THAT LATER.
I CAME HERE TODAY TO TRY AND PUT AN END TO THIS ENTIRE ORDEAL. PLEASE, JUST TELL THE AVENGERS...

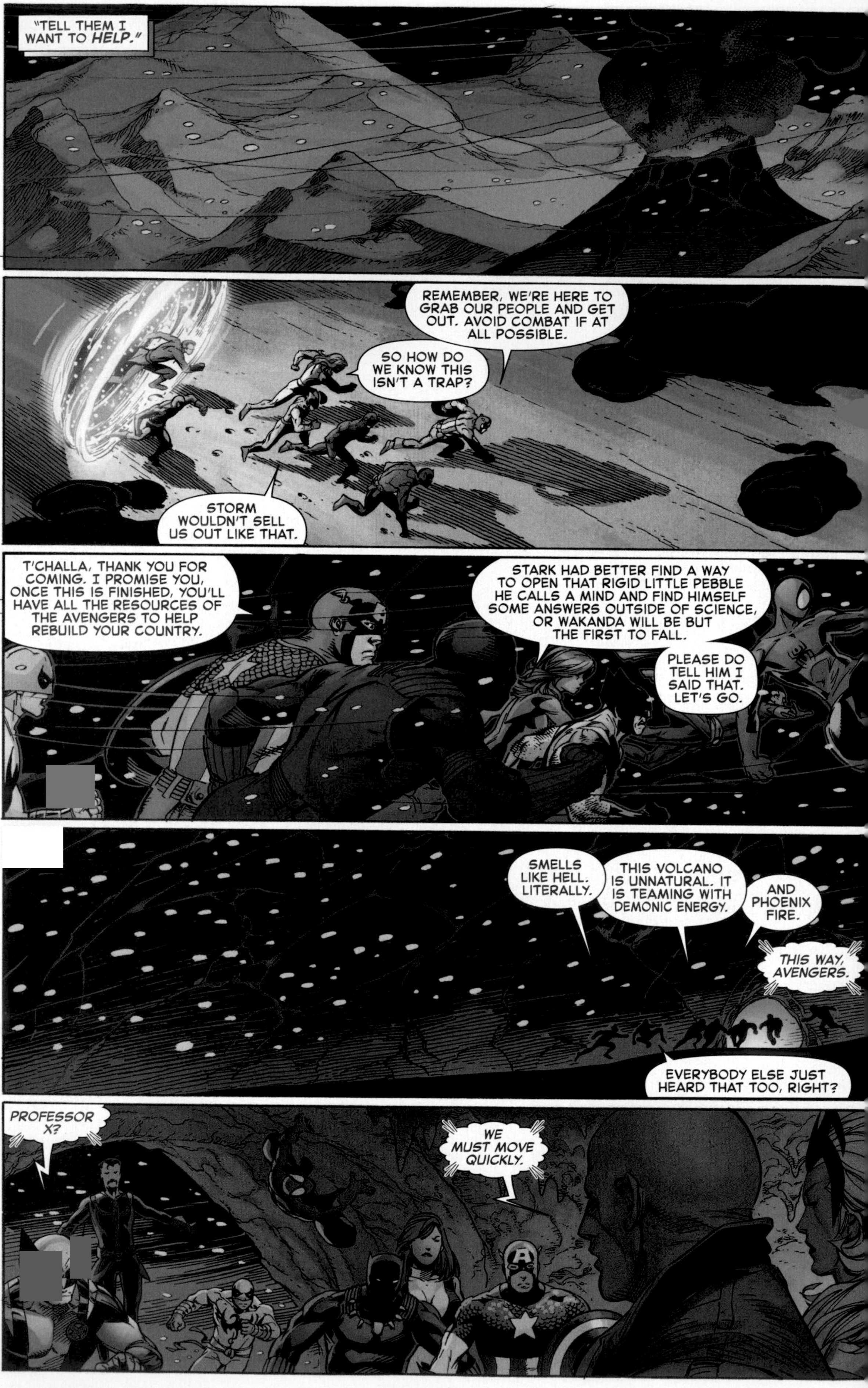
"TELL THEM I WANT TO *HELP.*"
REMEMBER, WE'RE HERE TO GRAB OUR PEOPLE AND GET OUT. AVOID COMBAT IF AT ALL POSSIBLE.
SO HOW DO WE KNOW THIS ISN'T A TRAP?
STORM WOULDN'T SELL US OUT LIKE THAT.
T'CHALLA, THANK YOU FOR COMING. I PROMISE YOU, ONCE THIS IS FINISHED, YOU'LL HAVE ALL THE RESOURCES OF THE AVENGERS TO HELP REBUILD YOUR COUNTRY.
STARK HAD BETTER FIND A WAY TO OPEN THAT RIGID LITTLE PEBBLE HE CALLS A MIND AND FIND HIMSELF SOME ANSWERS OUTSIDE OF SCIENCE, OR WAKANDA WILL BE BUT THE FIRST TO FALL.
PLEASE DO TELL HIM I SAID THAT. LET'S GO.
SMELLS LIKE HELL. LITERALLY.
THIS VOLCANO IS UNNATURAL. IT IS TEAMING WITH DEMONIC ENERGY.
AND PHOENIX FIRE.
THIS WAY, AVENGERS.
EVERYBODY ELSE JUST HEARD THAT TOO, RIGHT?
PROFESSOR X?
WE MUST MOVE QUICKLY.

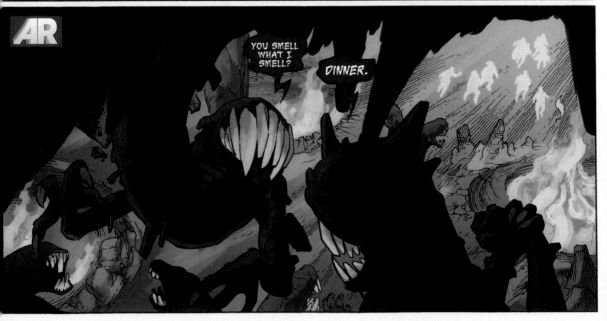

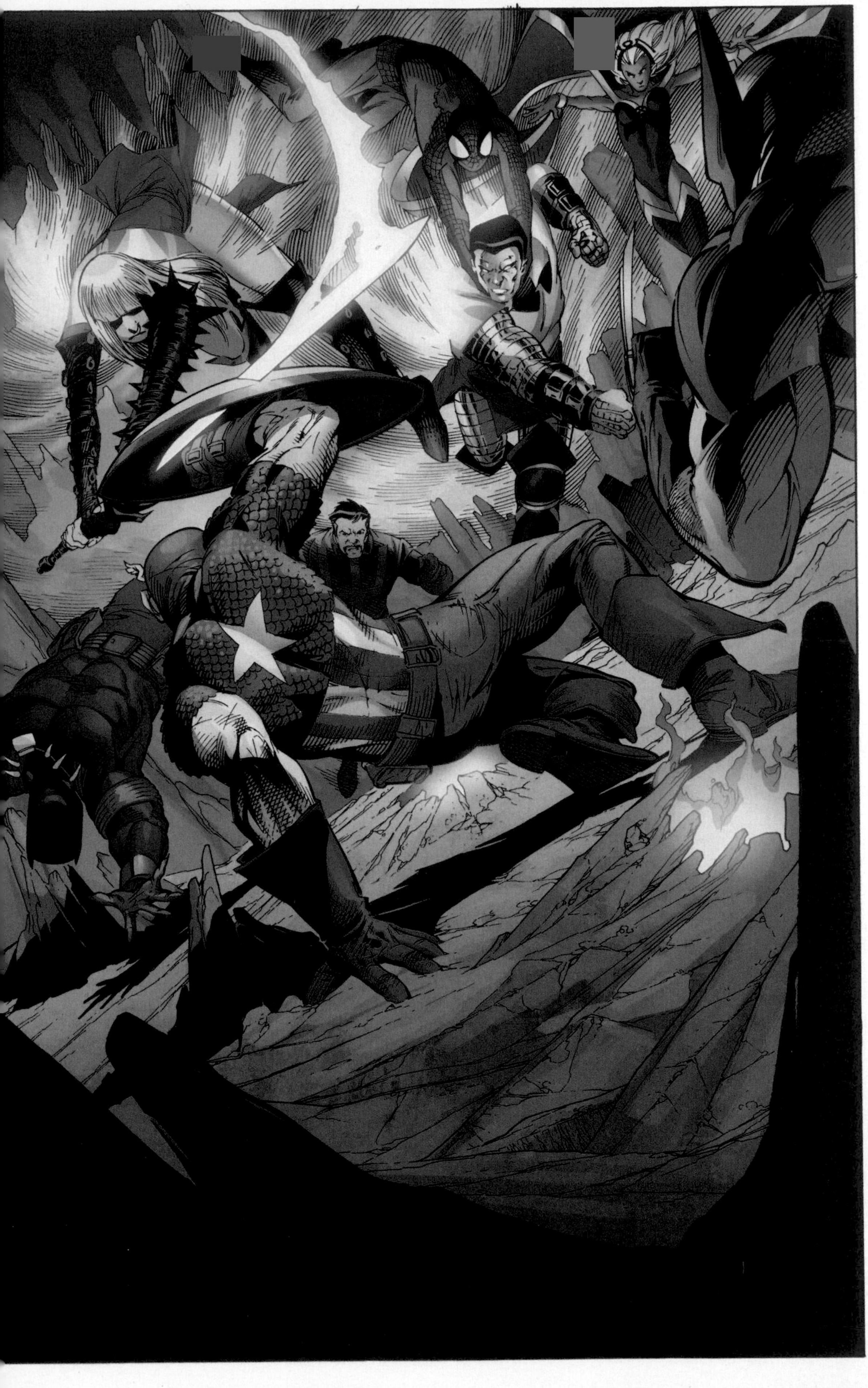

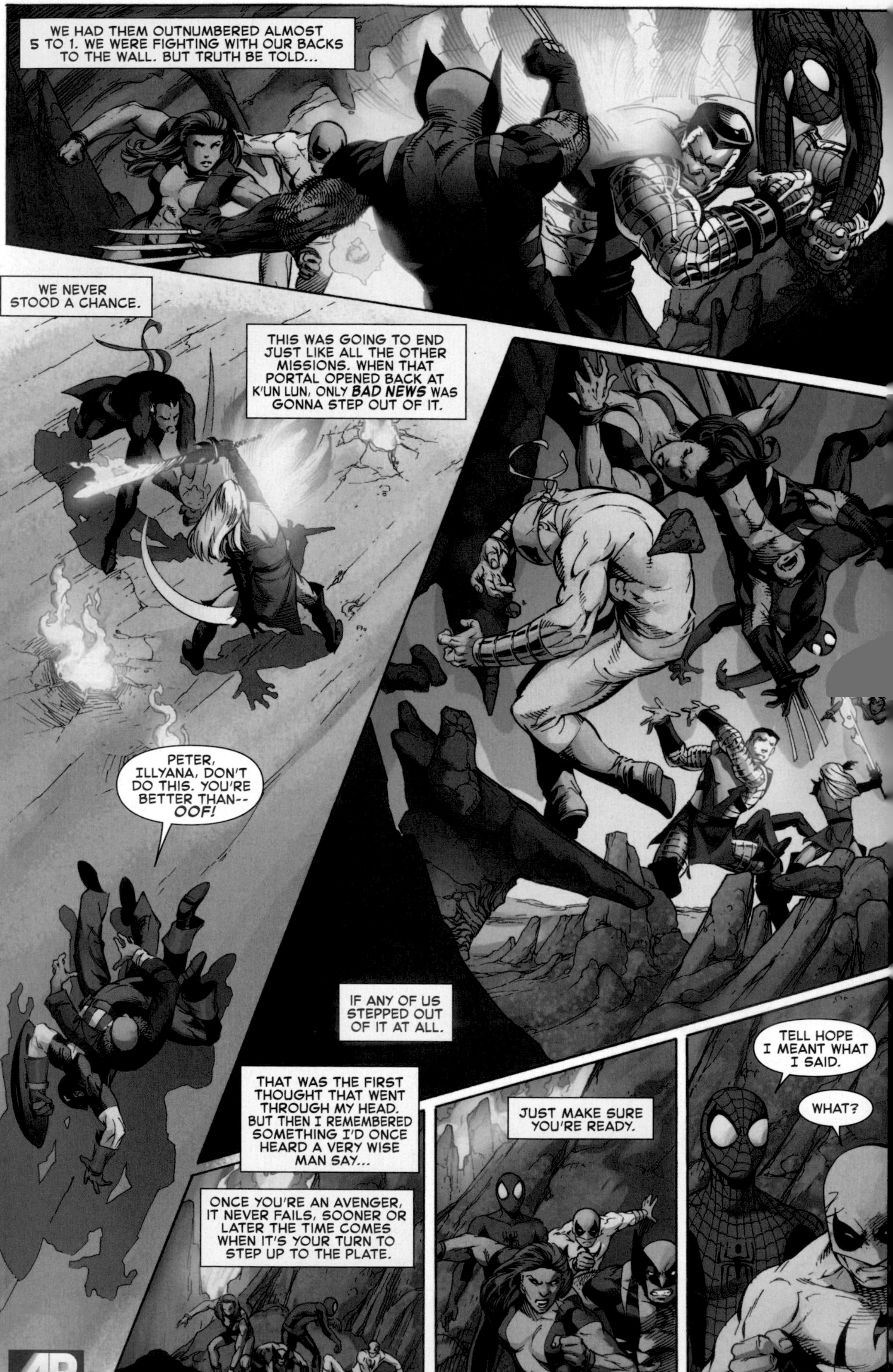
WE HAD THEM OUTNUMBERED ALMOST 5 TO 1. WE WERE FIGHTING WITH OUR BACKS TO THE WALL. BUT TRUTH BE TOLD...
WE NEVER STOOD A CHANCE.
THIS WAS GOING TO END JUST LIKE ALL THE OTHER MISSIONS. WHEN THAT PORTAL OPENED BACK AT K'UN LUN, ONLY BAD NEWS WAS GONNA STEP OUT OF IT.
PETER, ILLYANA, DON'T DO THIS. YOU'RE BETTER THAN-- OOF!
IF ANY OF US STEPPED OUT OF IT AT ALL.
THAT WAS THE FIRST THOUGHT THAT WENT THROUGH MY HEAD. BUT THEN I REMEMBERED SOMETHING I'D ONCE HEARD A VERY WISE MAN SAY...
ONCE YOU'RE AN AVENGER, IT NEVER FAILS, SOONER OR LATER THE TIME COMES WHEN IT'S YOUR TURN TO STEP UP TO THE PLATE.
JUST MAKE SURE YOU'RE READY.
TELL HOPE I MEANT WHAT I SAID.
WHAT?
AR

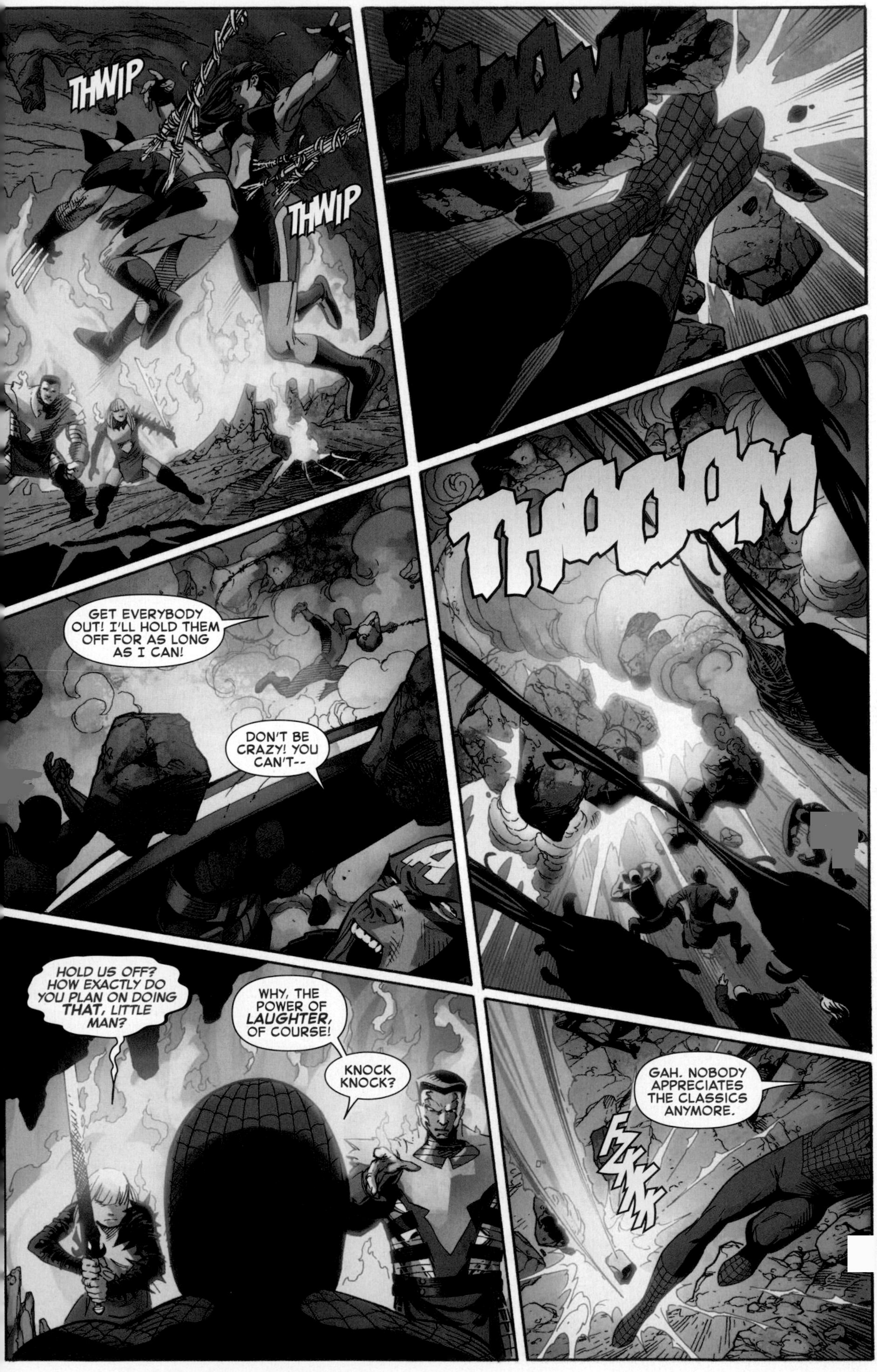
THWIP
THWIP
KROOOM
GET EVERYBODY OUT! I'LL HOLD THEM OFF FOR AS LONG AS I CAN!
DON'T BE CRAZY! YOU CAN'T--
THOOOM
HOLD US OFF? HOW EXACTLY DO YOU PLAN ON DOING THAT, LITTLE MAN?
WHY, THE POWER OF LAUGHTER, OF COURSE!
KNOCK KNOCK?
GAH. NOBODY APPRECIATES THE CLASSICS ANYMORE.

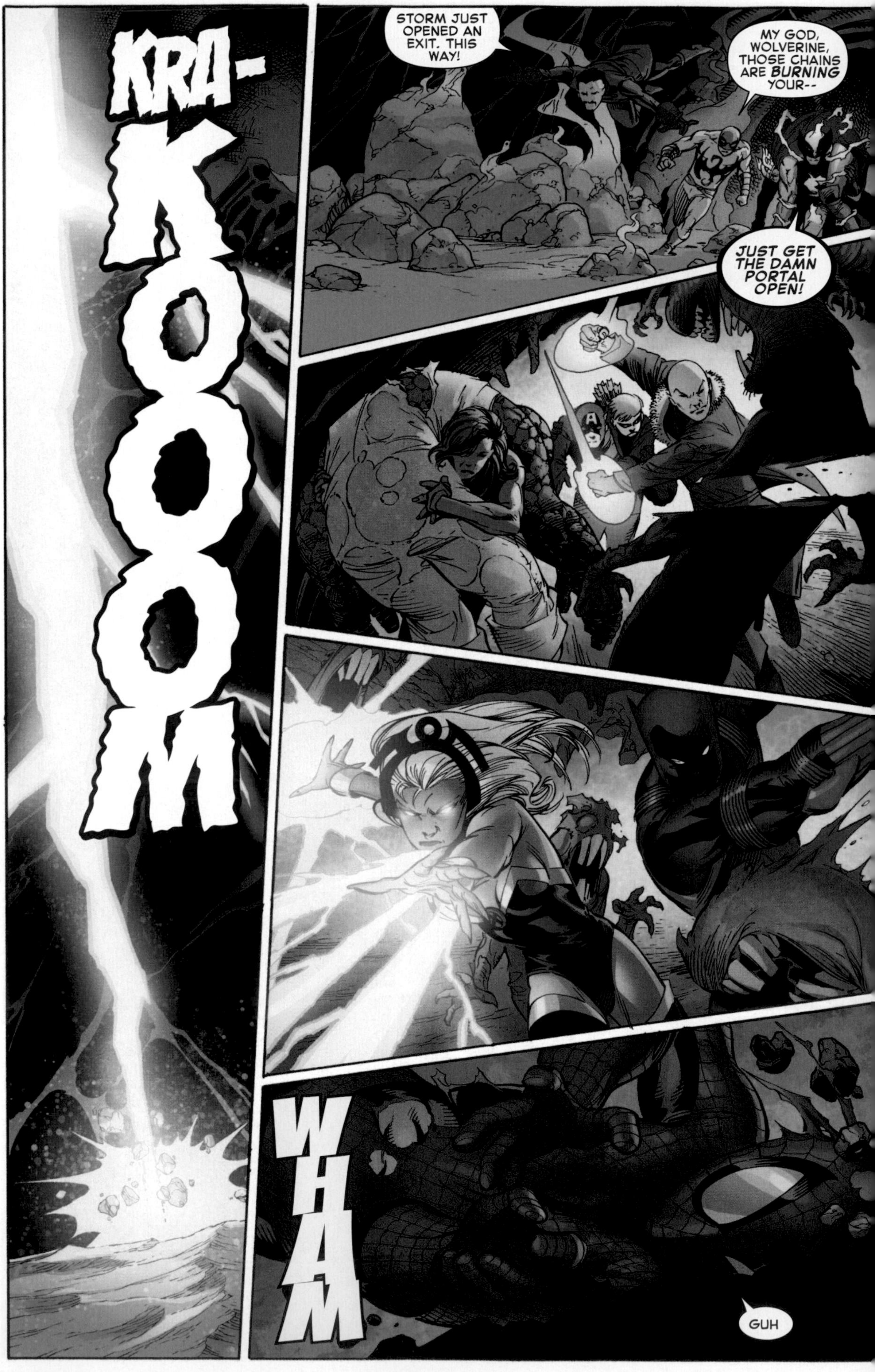
KRA-KOOOM
STORM JUST OPENED AN EXIT. THIS WAY!
MY GOD, WOLVERINE, THOSE CHAINS ARE BURNING YOUR--
JUST GET THE DAMN PORTAL OPEN!
WHAM
GUH

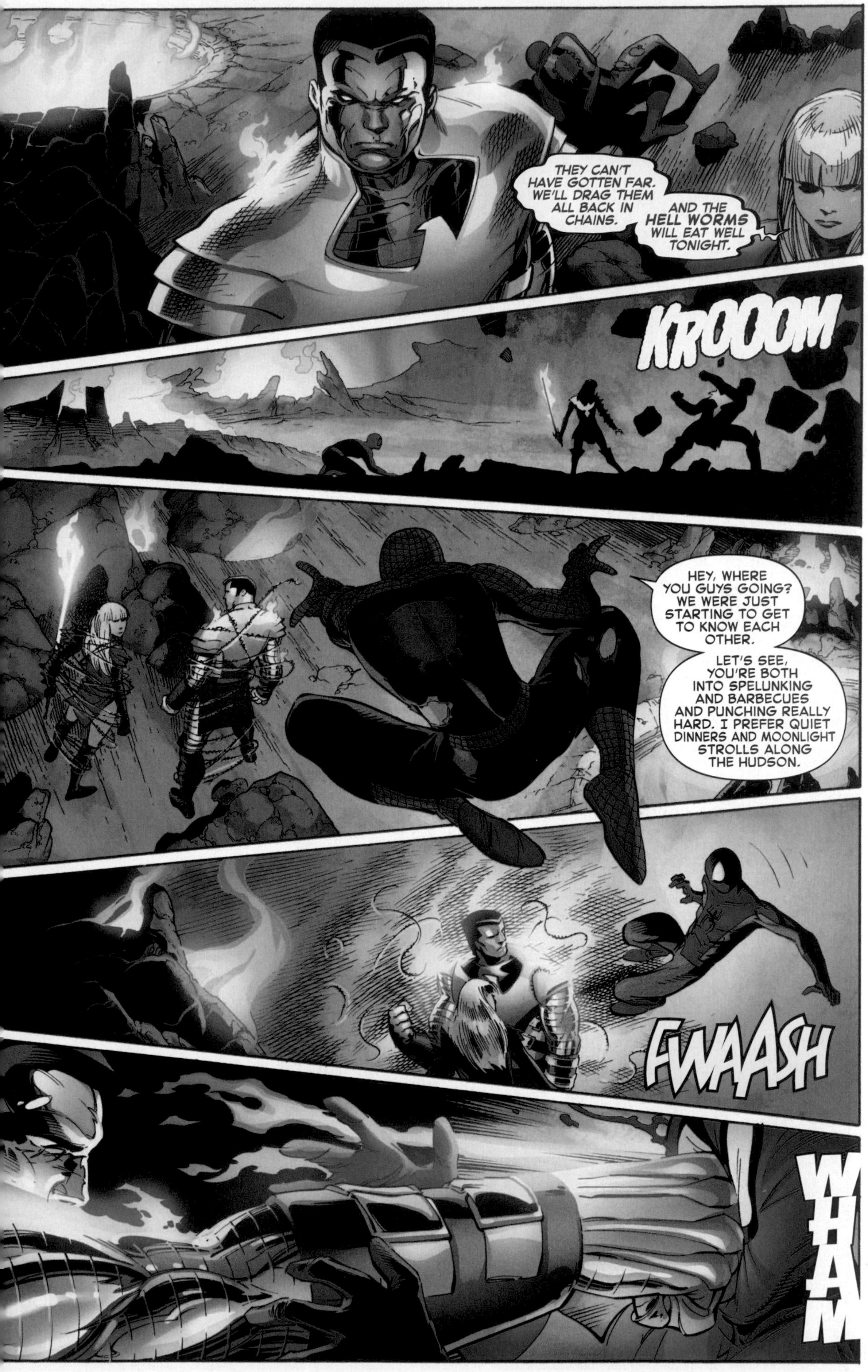
THEY CAN'T HAVE GOTTEN FAR. WE'LL DRAG THEM ALL BACK IN CHAINS.
AND THE HELL WORMS WILL EAT WELL TONIGHT.
KROOOM
HEY, WHERE YOU GUYS GOING? WE WERE JUST STARTING TO GET TO KNOW EACH OTHER.
LET'S SEE, YOU'RE BOTH INTO SPELUNKING AND BARBECUES AND PUNCHING REALLY HARD. I PREFER QUIET DINNERS AND MOONLIGHT STROLLS ALONG THE HUDSON.
FWAASH
WHAM

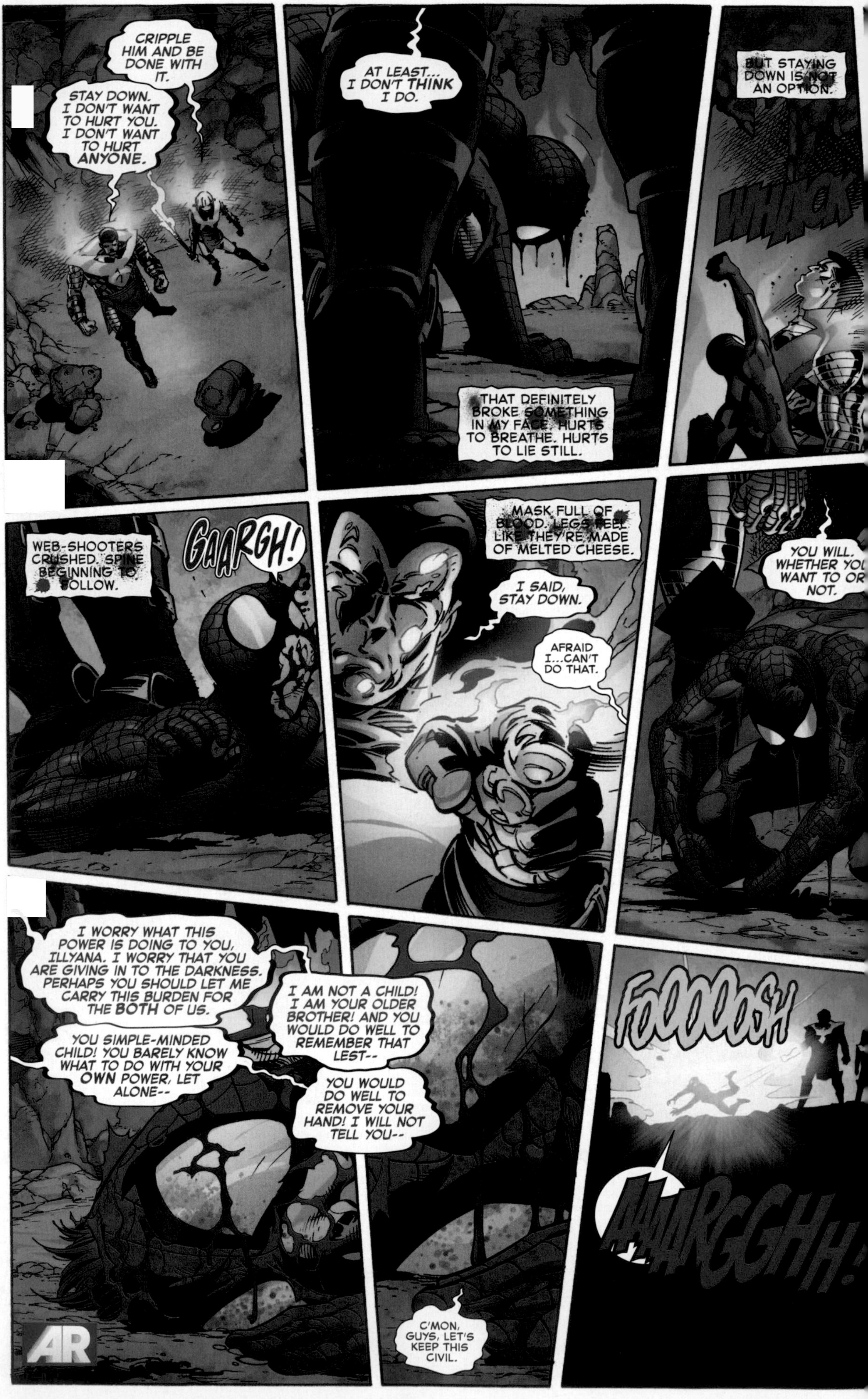
CRIPPLE HIM AND BE DONE WITH IT.
STAY DOWN. I DON'T WANT TO HURT YOU. I DON'T WANT TO HURT ANYONE.
AT LEAST... I DON'T THINK I DO.
THAT DEFINITELY BROKE SOMETHING IN MY FACE. HURTS TO BREATHE. HURTS TO LIE STILL.
BUT STAYING DOWN IS NOT AN OPTION.
WHACK
WEB-SHOOTERS CRUSHED. SPINE BEGINNING TO FOLLOW.
GAARGH!
MASK FULL OF BLOOD. LEGS FEEL LIKE THEY'RE MADE OF MELTED CHEESE.
I SAID, STAY DOWN.
AFRAID I...CAN'T DO THAT.
YOU WILL. WHETHER YO WANT TO OR NOT.
I WORRY WHAT THIS POWER IS DOING TO YOU, ILLYANA. I WORRY THAT YOU ARE GIVING IN TO THE DARKNESS. PERHAPS YOU SHOULD LET ME CARRY THIS BURDEN FOR THE BOTH OF US.
YOU SIMPLE-MINDED CHILD! YOU BARELY KNOW WHAT TO DO WITH YOUR OWN POWER, LET ALONE--
I AM NOT A CHILD! I AM YOUR OLDER BROTHER! AND YOU WOULD DO WELL TO REMEMBER THAT LEST--
YOU WOULD DO WELL TO REMOVE YOUR HAND! I WILL NOT TELL YOU--
C'MON, GUYS, LET'S KEEP THIS CIVIL.
FOOOOOSH
AAAARGGHH

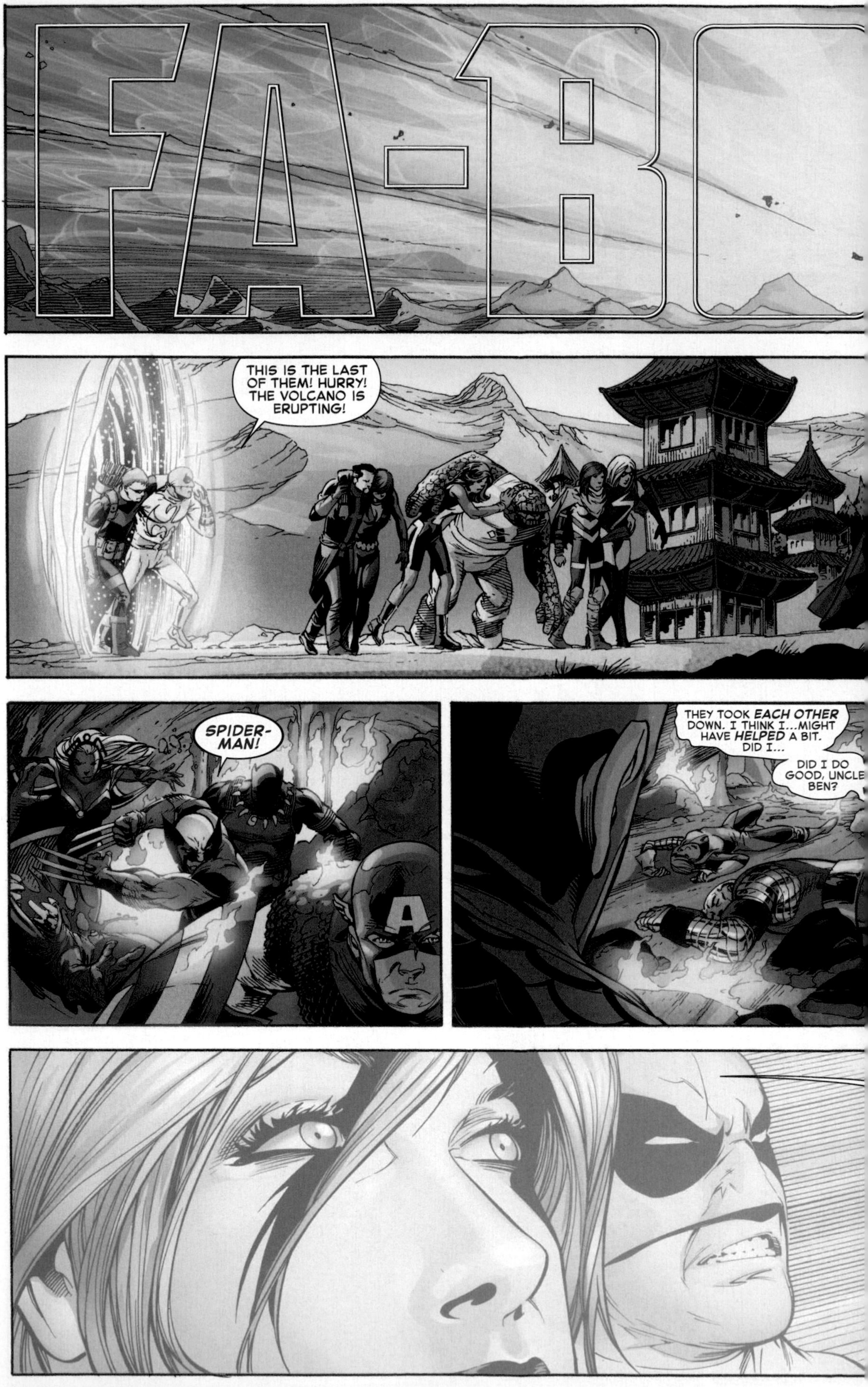
FA-BC
THIS IS THE LAST OF THEM! HURRY! THE VOLCANO IS ERUPTING!
SPIDER-MAN!
THEY TOOK EACH OTHER DOWN. I THINK I...MIGHT HAVE HELPED A BIT. DID I...
DID I DO GOOD, UNCLE BEN?

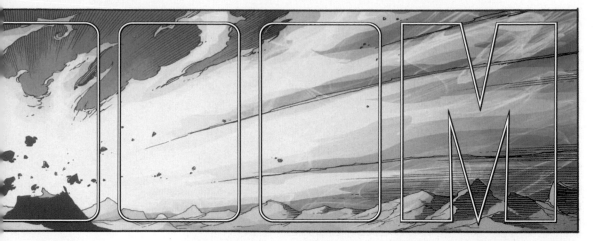

BUT WAIT... WHERE'S... WHERE'S SPIDER-MAN?

I'M JUST GONNA COLLAPSE INTO A PILE OF GOO NOW, IF THAT'S ALL RIGHT.

IF THEY'RE *BOTH* DOWN, THAT MEANS THEIR POWER JUST WENT...

YES. YES, IT DID.

WHAT IN THE WORLD IS THAT?

THAT IS WHAT IT LOOKS LIKE WHEN SOMEONE TEARS THEIR WAY THROUGH DIMENSIONS. I AM SORRY, HOPE. I TRULY AM.

SORRY, WHAT DO YOU...OH GOD...

I AM SORRY WE WILL NEVER GET TO FINISH YOUR TRAINING.

HOPE!

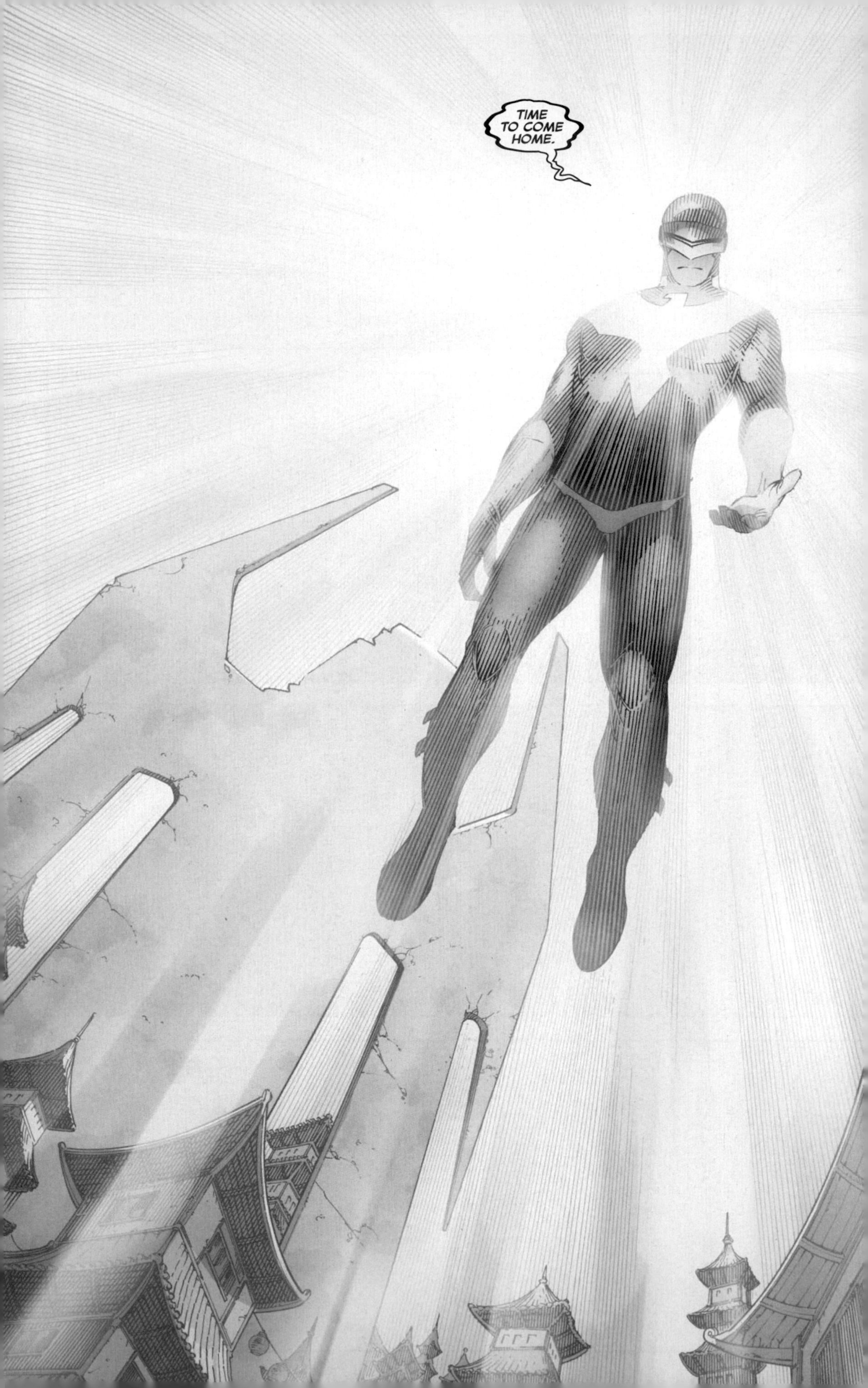
TIME TO COME HOME.

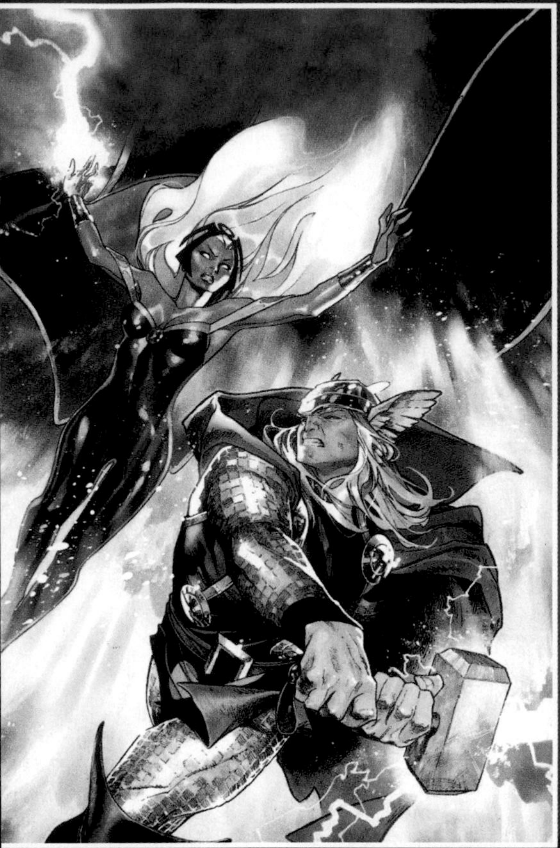

AVX #6 VARIANT
BY **OLIVIER COIPEL**

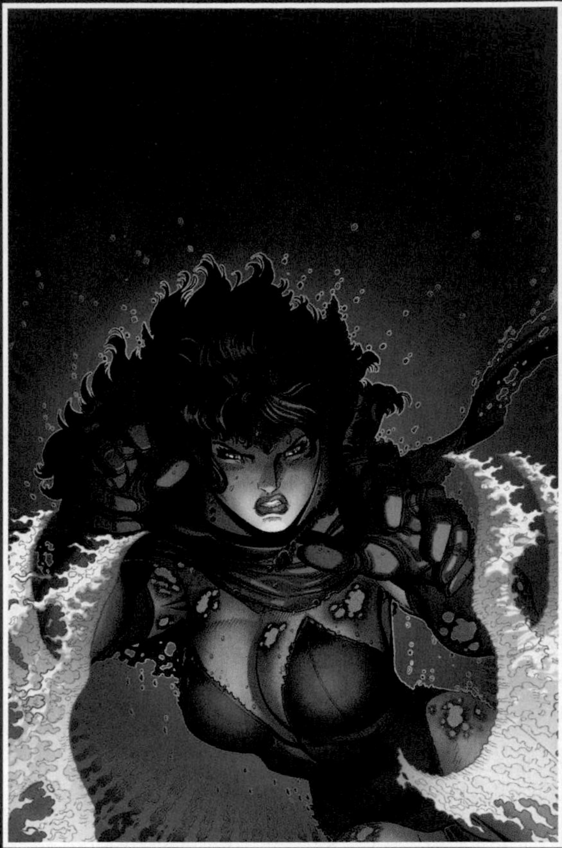

AVX #6 VARIANT
BY **NICK BRADSHAW & MARTE GRACIA**

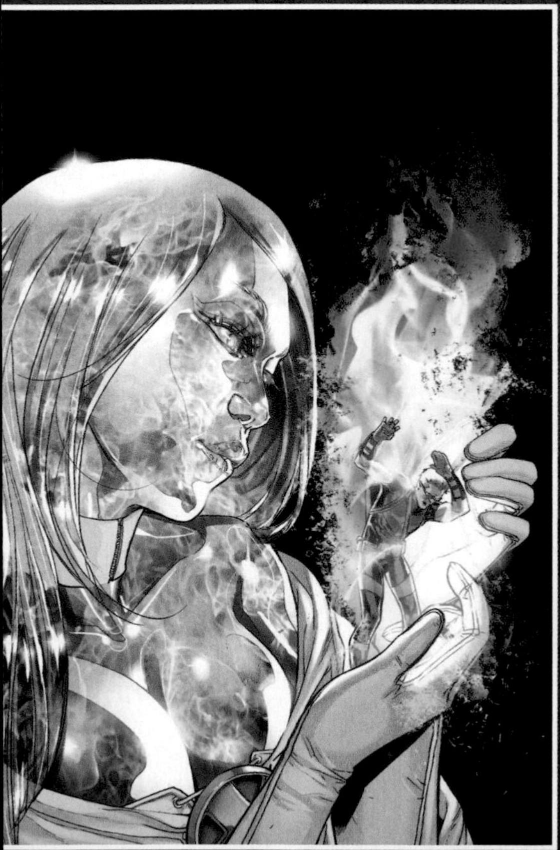

AVX #7 VARIANT
BY **SARA PICHELLI & JUSTIN PONSOR**

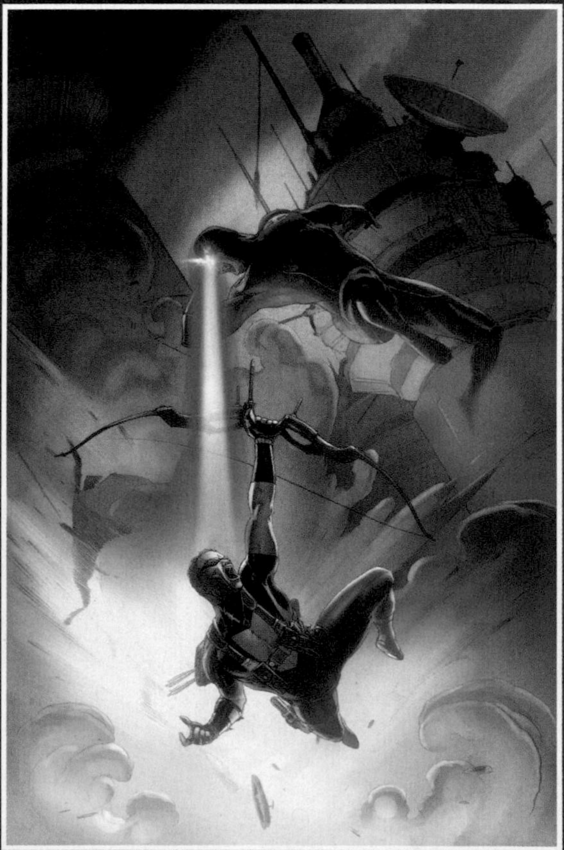

AVX #7 VARIANT
BY **ESAD RIBIC**

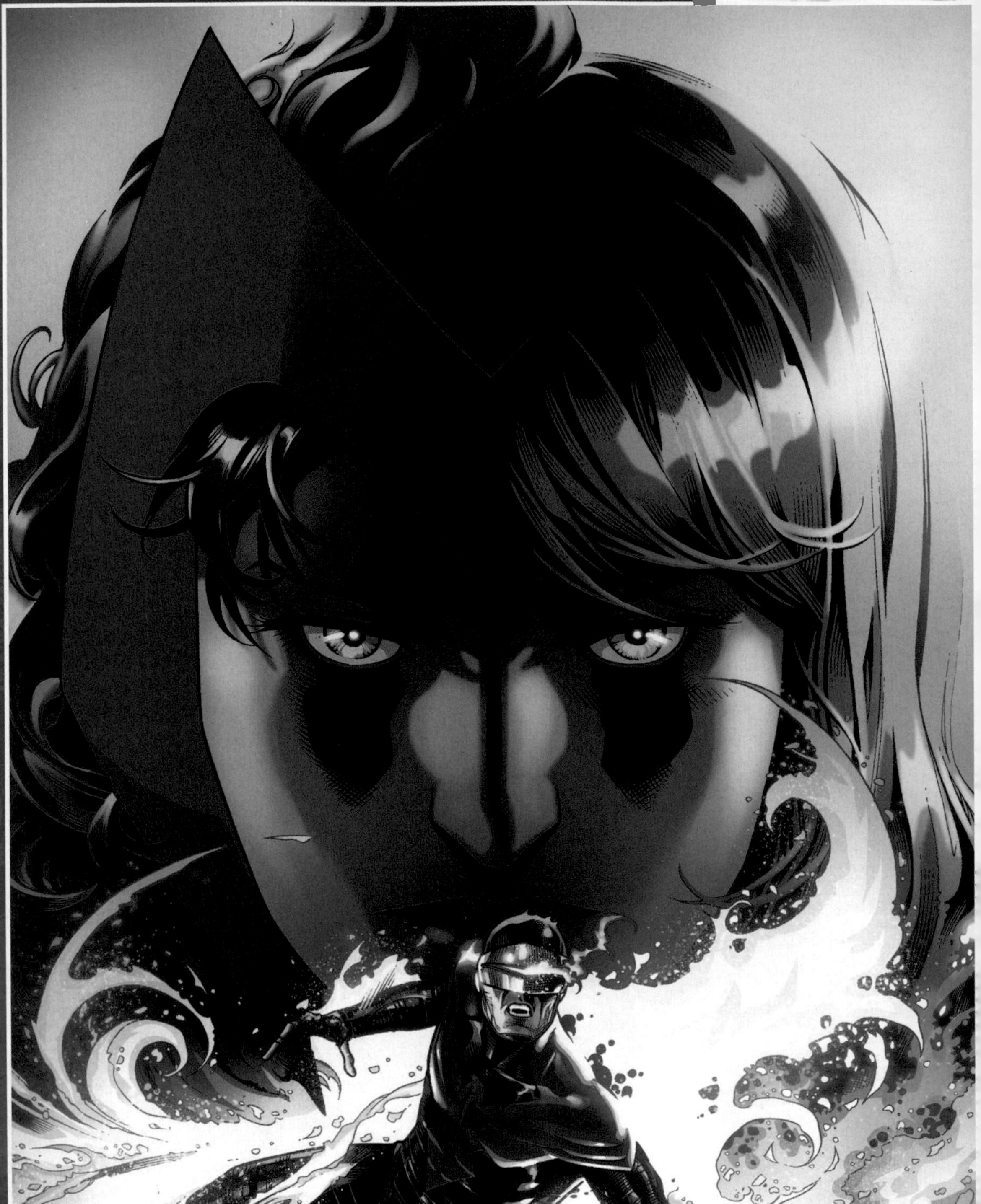

ROUND 10

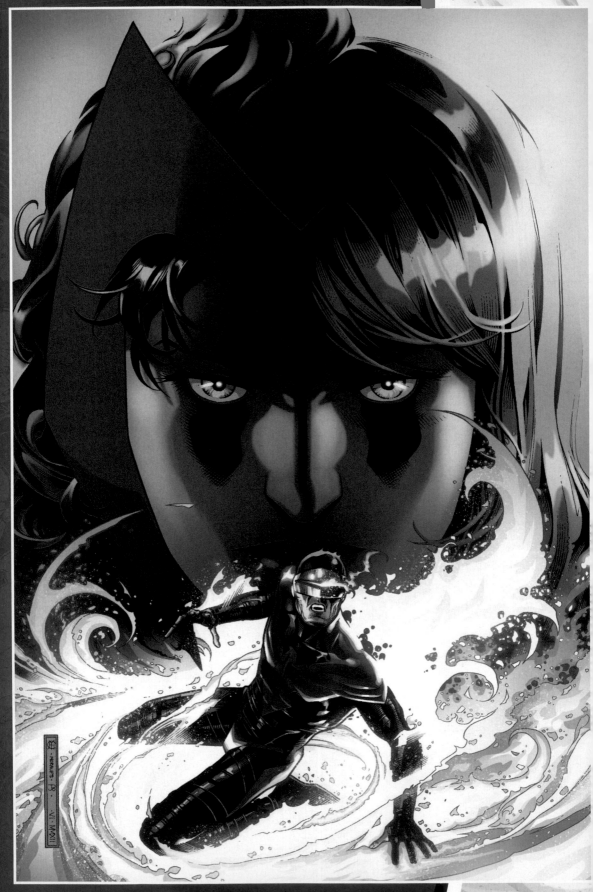

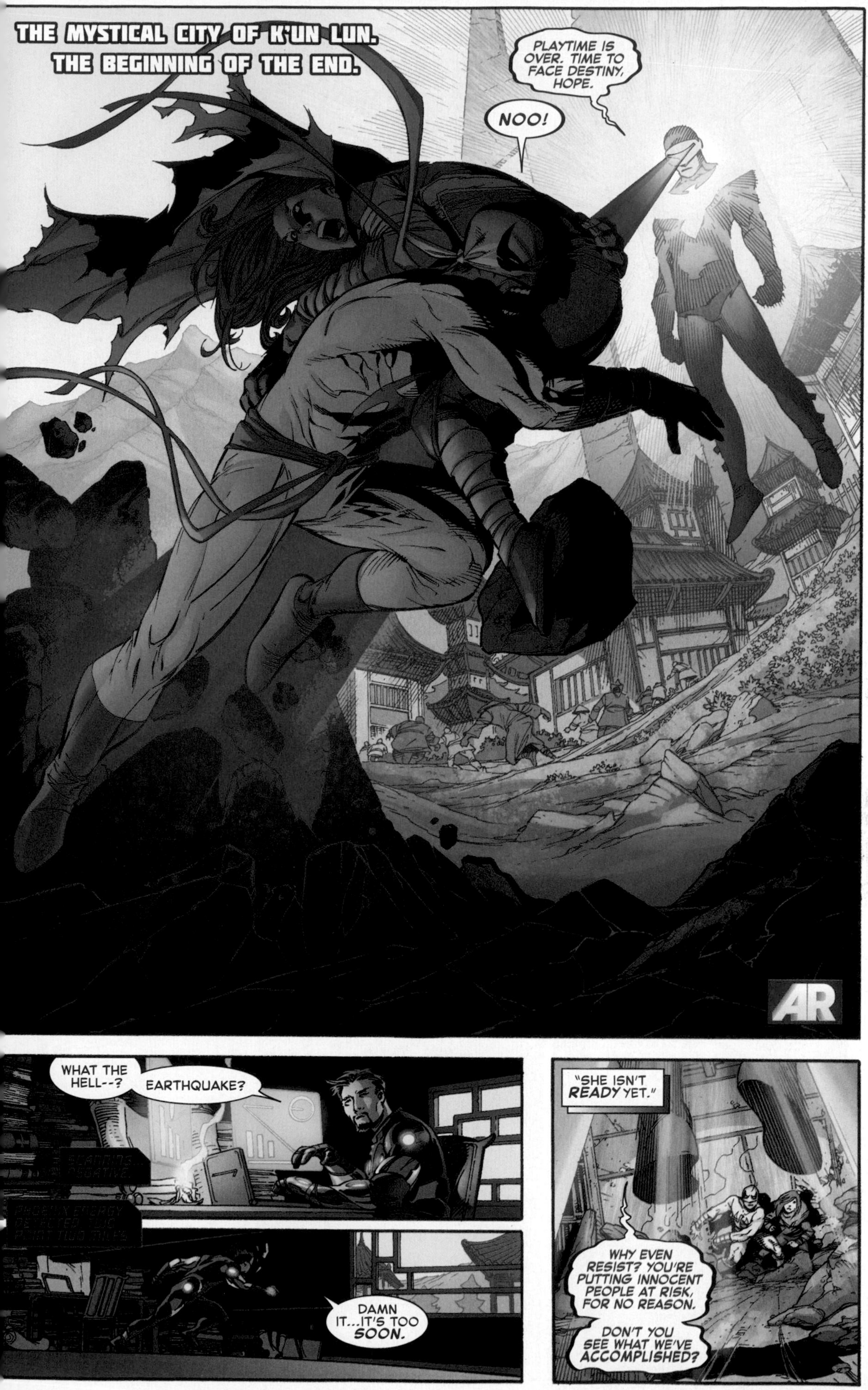
THE MYSTICAL CITY OF K'UN LUN.
THE BEGINNING OF THE END.
PLAYTIME IS OVER. TIME TO FACE DESTINY, HOPE.
NOO!
WHAT THE HELL--?
EARTHQUAKE?
DAMN IT...IT'S TOO SOON.
"SHE ISN'T READY YET."
WHY EVEN RESIST? YOU'RE PUTTING INNOCENT PEOPLE AT RISK, FOR NO REASON.
DON'T YOU SEE WHAT WE'VE ACCOMPLISHED?

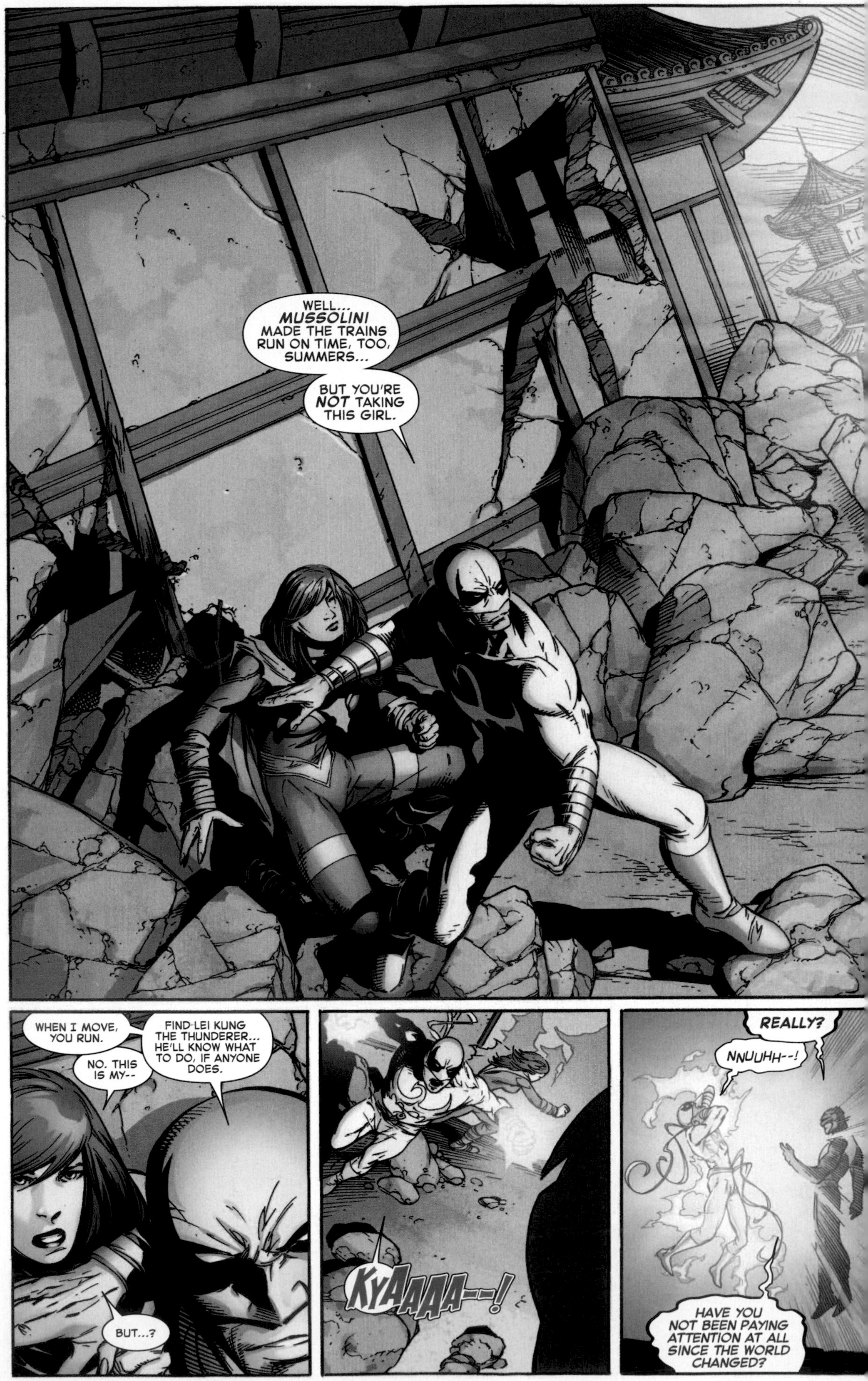
WELL... MUSSOLINI MADE THE TRAINS RUN ON TIME, TOO, SUMMERS...
BUT YOU'RE NOT TAKING THIS GIRL.
WHEN I MOVE, YOU RUN.
NO. THIS IS MY--
FIND LEI KUNG THE THUNDERER... HE'LL KNOW WHAT TO DO, IF ANYONE DOES.
BUT...?
KYAAAA--!
REALLY?
NNUUHH--!
HAVE YOU NOT BEEN PAYING ATTENTION AT ALL SINCE THE WORLD CHANGED?

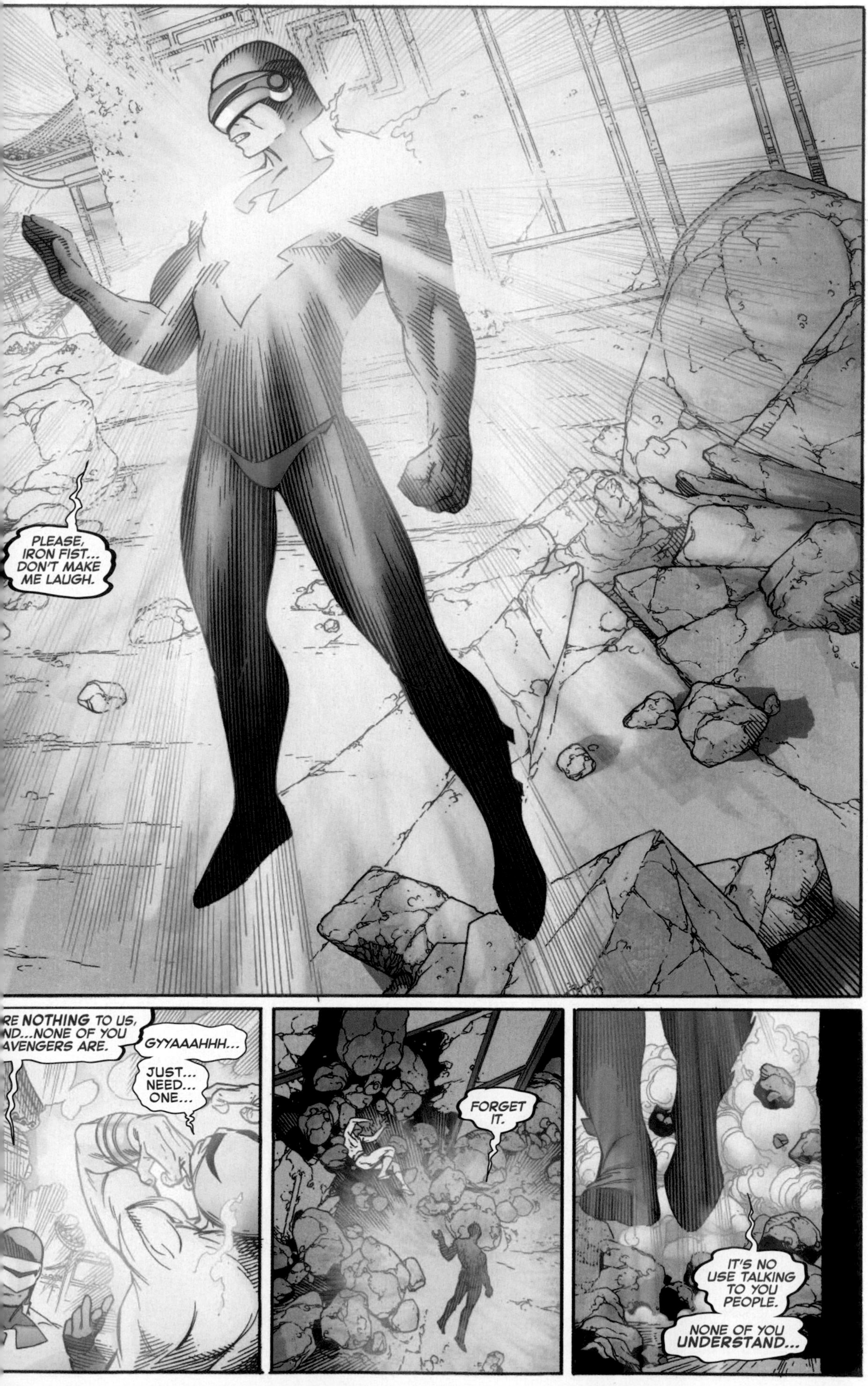

PLEASE, IRON FIST... DON'T MAKE ME LAUGH.
RE NOTHING TO US, ND...NONE OF YOU AVENGERS ARE.
GYYAAAHHH...
JUST... NEED... ONE...
FORGET IT.
IT'S NO USE TALKING TO YOU PEOPLE.
NONE OF YOU UNDERSTAND...

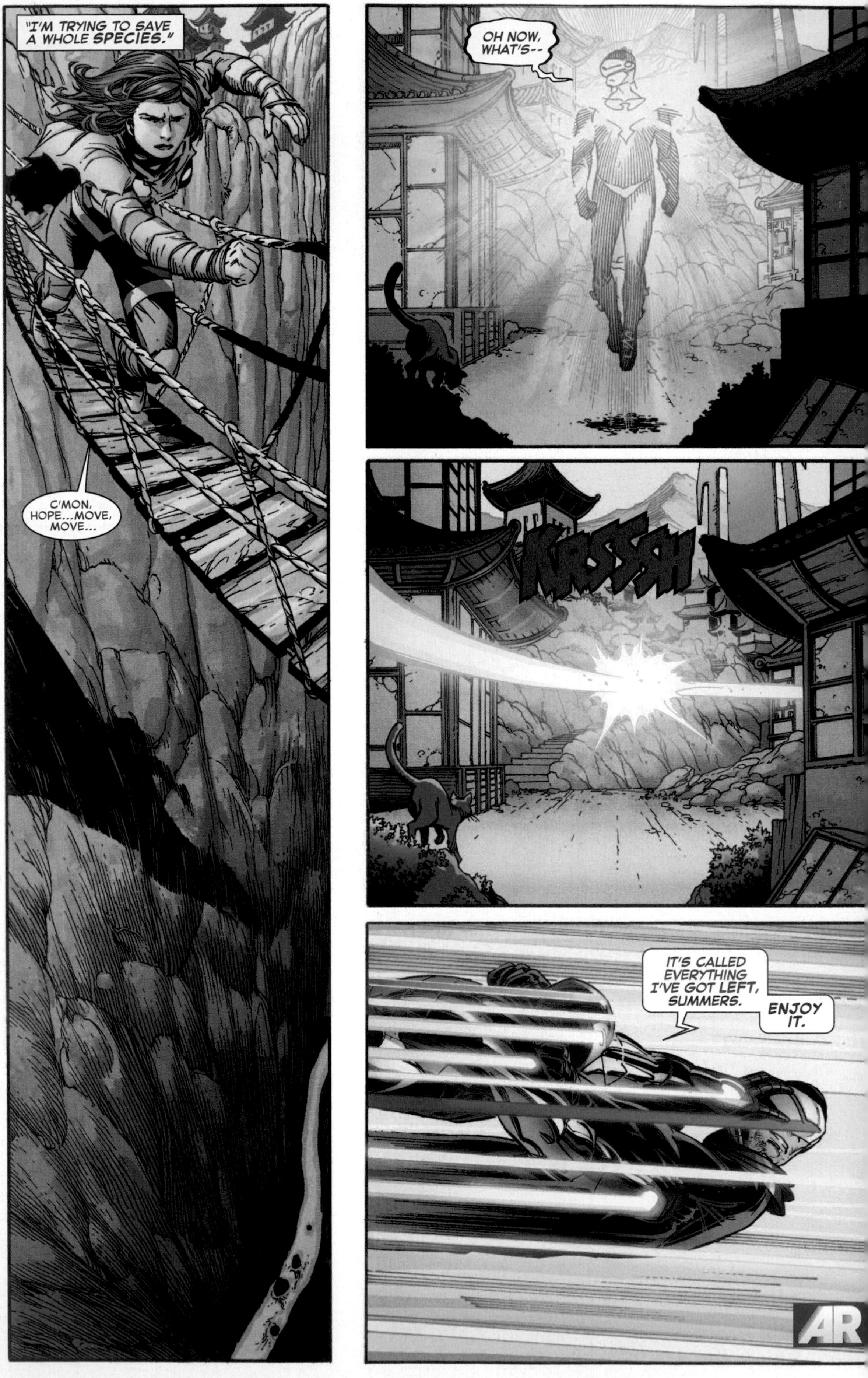
"I'M TRYING TO SAVE A WHOLE SPECIES."
C'MON, HOPE...MOVE, MOVE...
OH NOW, WHAT'S--
KRSSSH
IT'S CALLED EVERYTHING I'VE GOT LEFT, SUMMERS.
ENJOY IT.

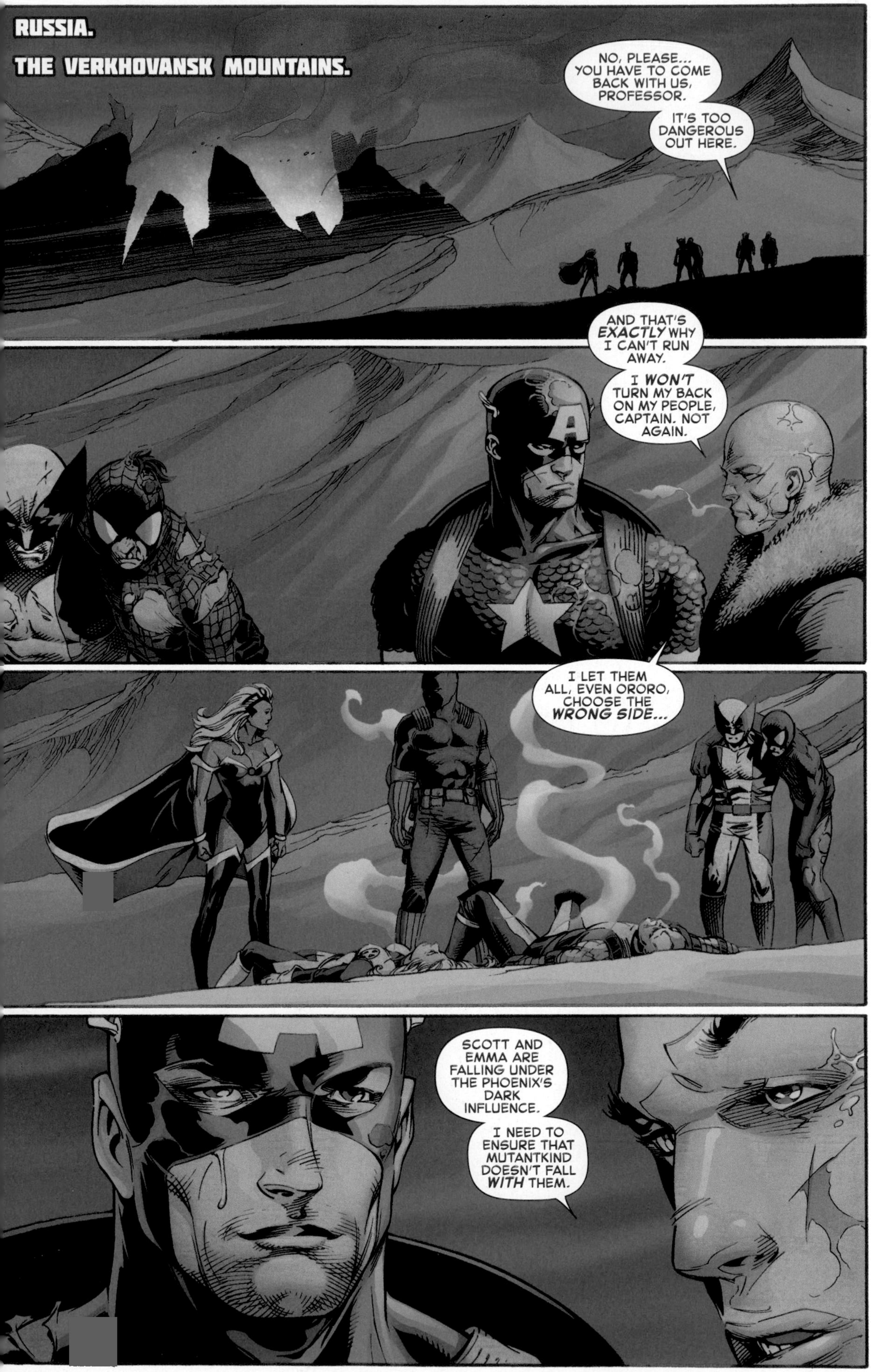
RUSSIA.
THE VERKHOVANSK MOUNTAINS.
NO, PLEASE... YOU HAVE TO COME BACK WITH US, PROFESSOR.
IT'S TOO DANGEROUS OUT HERE.
AND THAT'S EXACTLY WHY I CAN'T RUN AWAY.
I WON'T TURN MY BACK ON MY PEOPLE, CAPTAIN. NOT AGAIN.
I LET THEM ALL, EVEN ORORO, CHOOSE THE WRONG SIDE...
SCOTT AND EMMA ARE FALLING UNDER THE PHOENIX'S DARK INFLUENCE.
I NEED TO ENSURE THAT MUTANTKIND DOESN'T FALL WITH THEM.

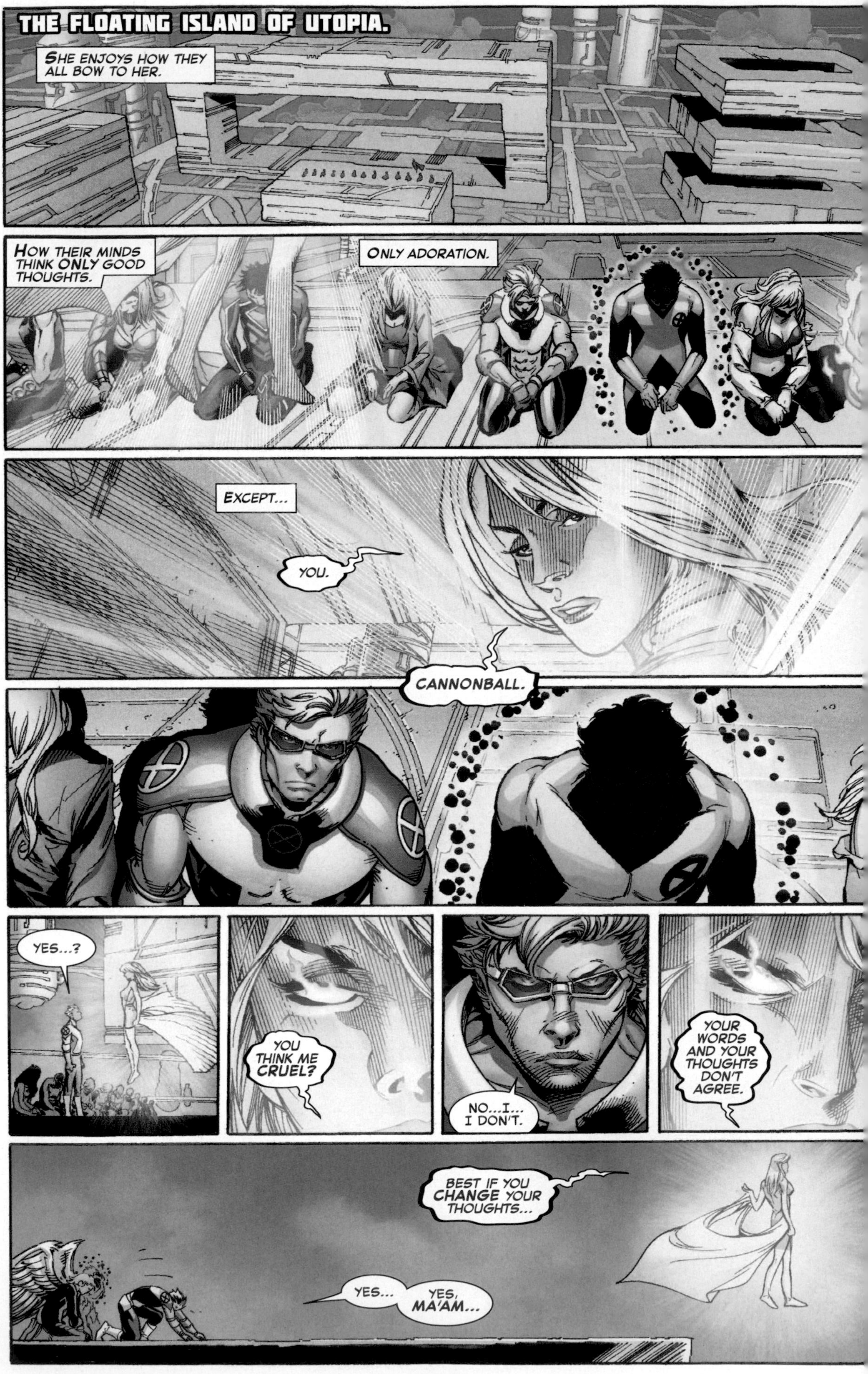
THE FLOATING ISLAND OF UTOPIA.
SHE ENJOYS HOW THEY ALL BOW TO HER.
HOW THEIR MINDS THINK ONLY GOOD THOUGHTS.
ONLY ADORATION.
EXCEPT...
YOU.
CANNONBALL.
YES...?
YOU THINK ME CRUEL?
NO...I... I DON'T.
YOUR WORDS AND YOUR THOUGHTS DON'T AGREE.
BEST IF YOU CHANGE YOUR THOUGHTS...
YES...
YES, MA'AM...

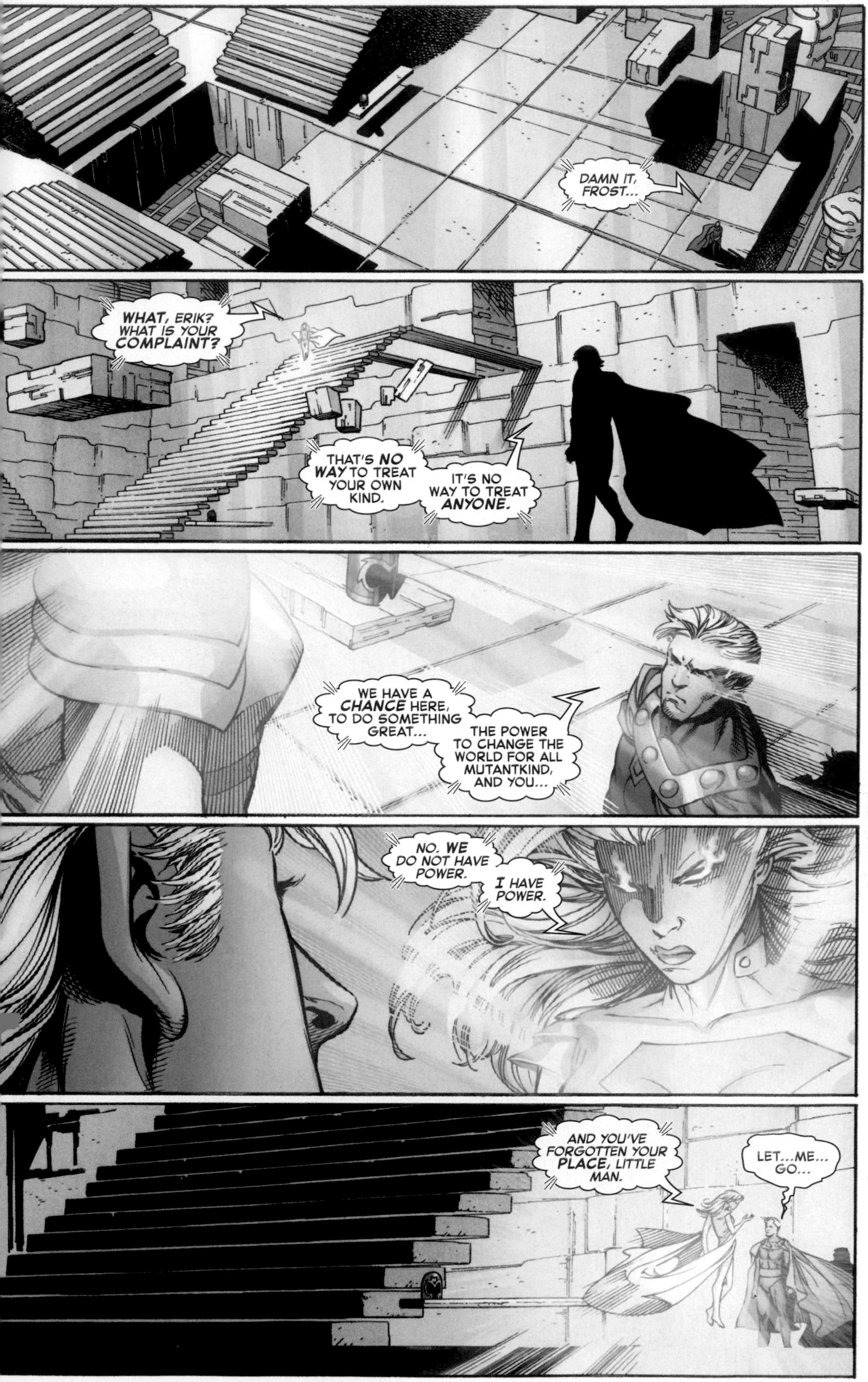
DAMN IT, FROST...
WHAT, ERIK? WHAT IS YOUR COMPLAINT?
THAT'S NO WAY TO TREAT YOUR OWN KIND.
IT'S NO WAY TO TREAT ANYONE.
WE HAVE A CHANCE HERE, TO DO SOMETHING GREAT...
THE POWER TO CHANGE THE WORLD FOR ALL MUTANTKIND, AND YOU...
NO. WE DO NOT HAVE POWER.
I HAVE POWER.
AND YOU'VE FORGOTTEN YOUR PLACE, LITTLE MAN.
LET...ME... GO...

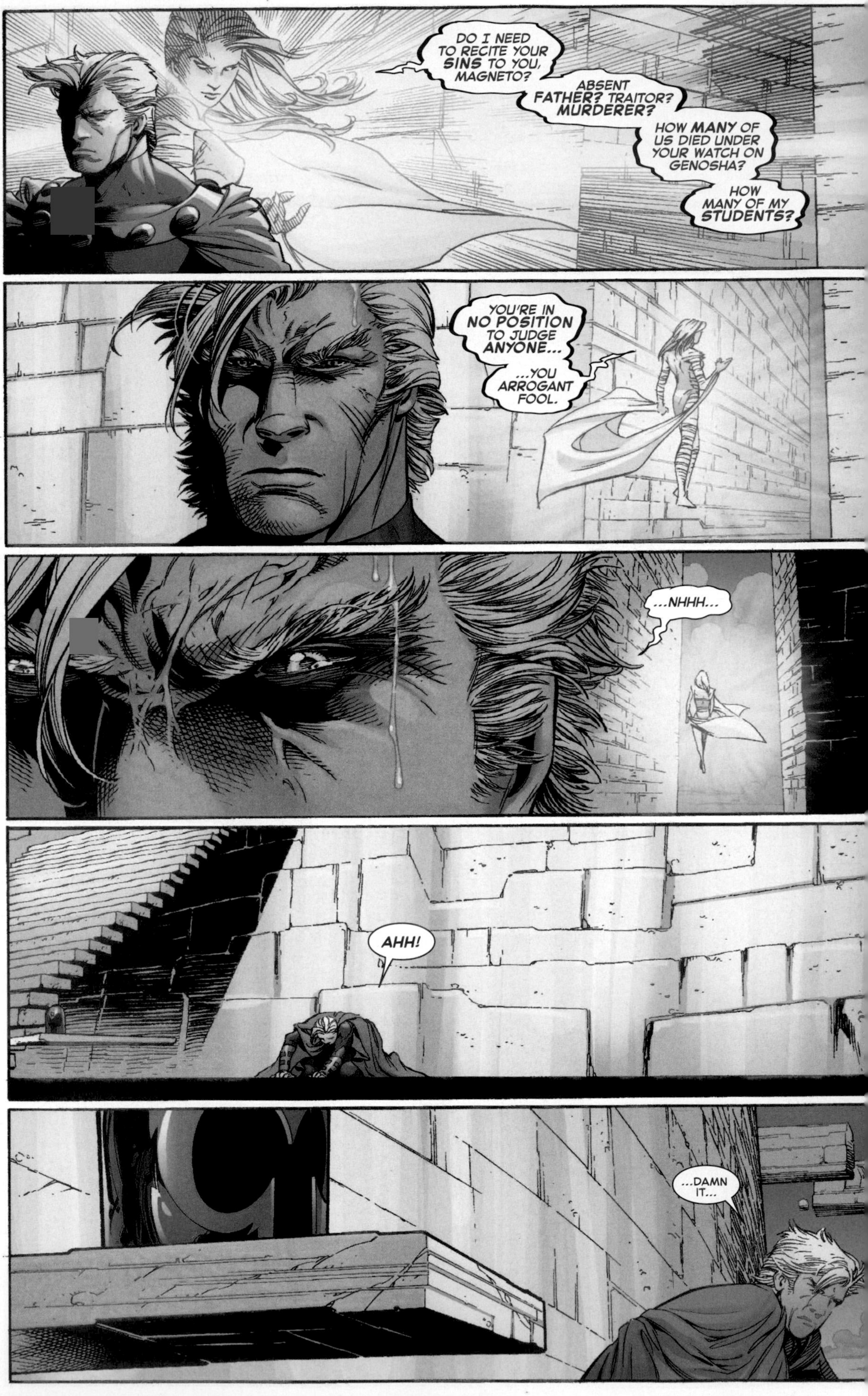
DO I NEED TO RECITE YOUR SINS TO YOU, MAGNETO?
ABSENT FATHER? TRAITOR? MURDERER?
HOW MANY OF US DIED UNDER YOUR WATCH ON GENOSHA?
HOW MANY OF MY STUDENTS?
YOU'RE IN NO POSITION TO JUDGE ANYONE...
...YOU ARROGANT FOOL.
...NHHH...
AHH!
...DAMN IT...

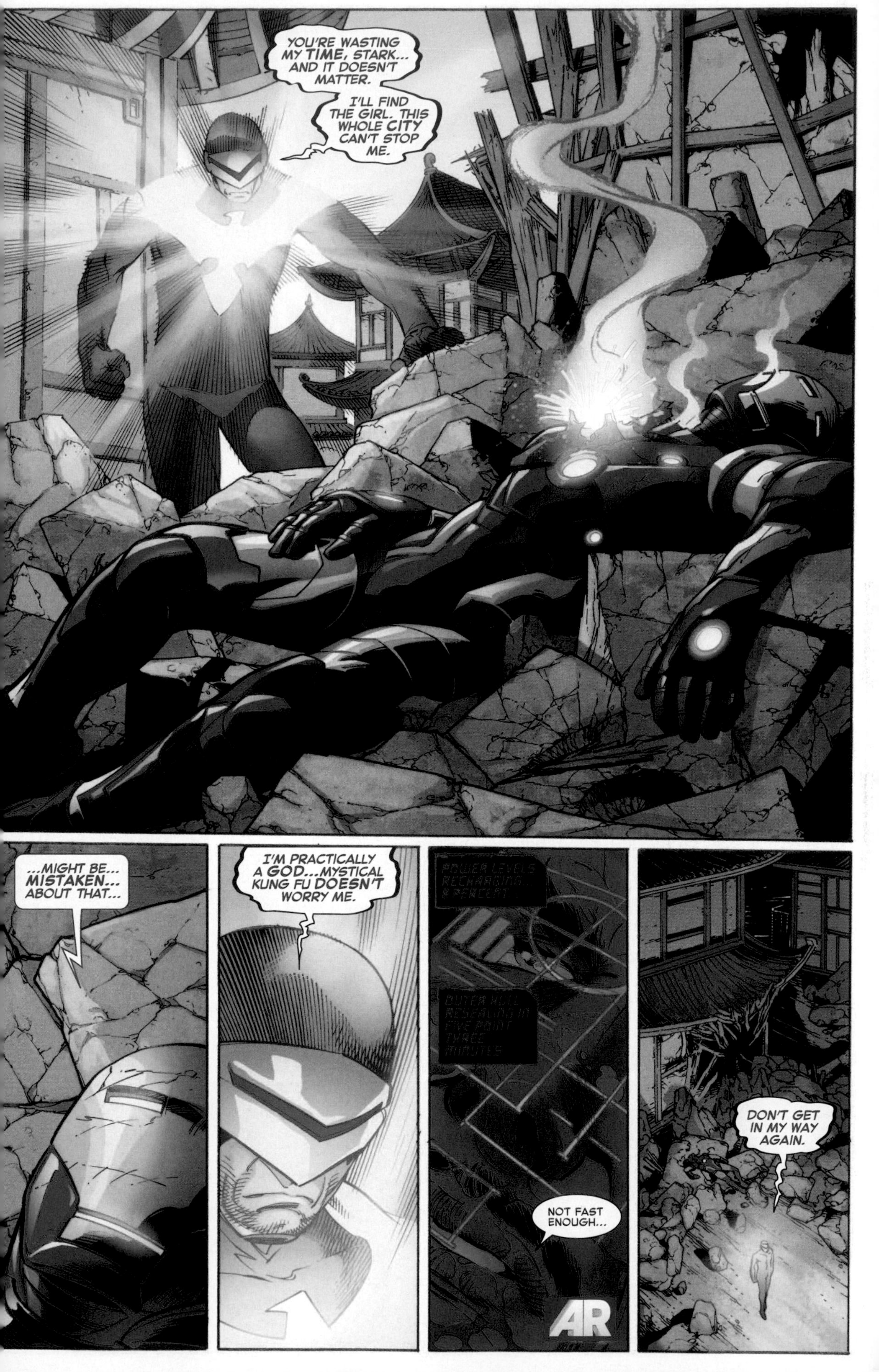
YOU'RE WASTING MY TIME, STARK... AND IT DOESN'T MATTER.
I'LL FIND THE GIRL. THIS WHOLE CITY CAN'T STOP ME.
...MIGHT BE... MISTAKEN... ABOUT THAT...
I'M PRACTICALLY A GOD...MYSTICAL KUNG FU DOESN'T WORRY ME.
POWER LEVELS RECHARGING... 8 PERCENT
OUTER HULL RESEALING IN FIVE POINT THREE MINUTES
NOT FAST ENOUGH...
AR
DON'T GET IN MY WAY AGAIN.

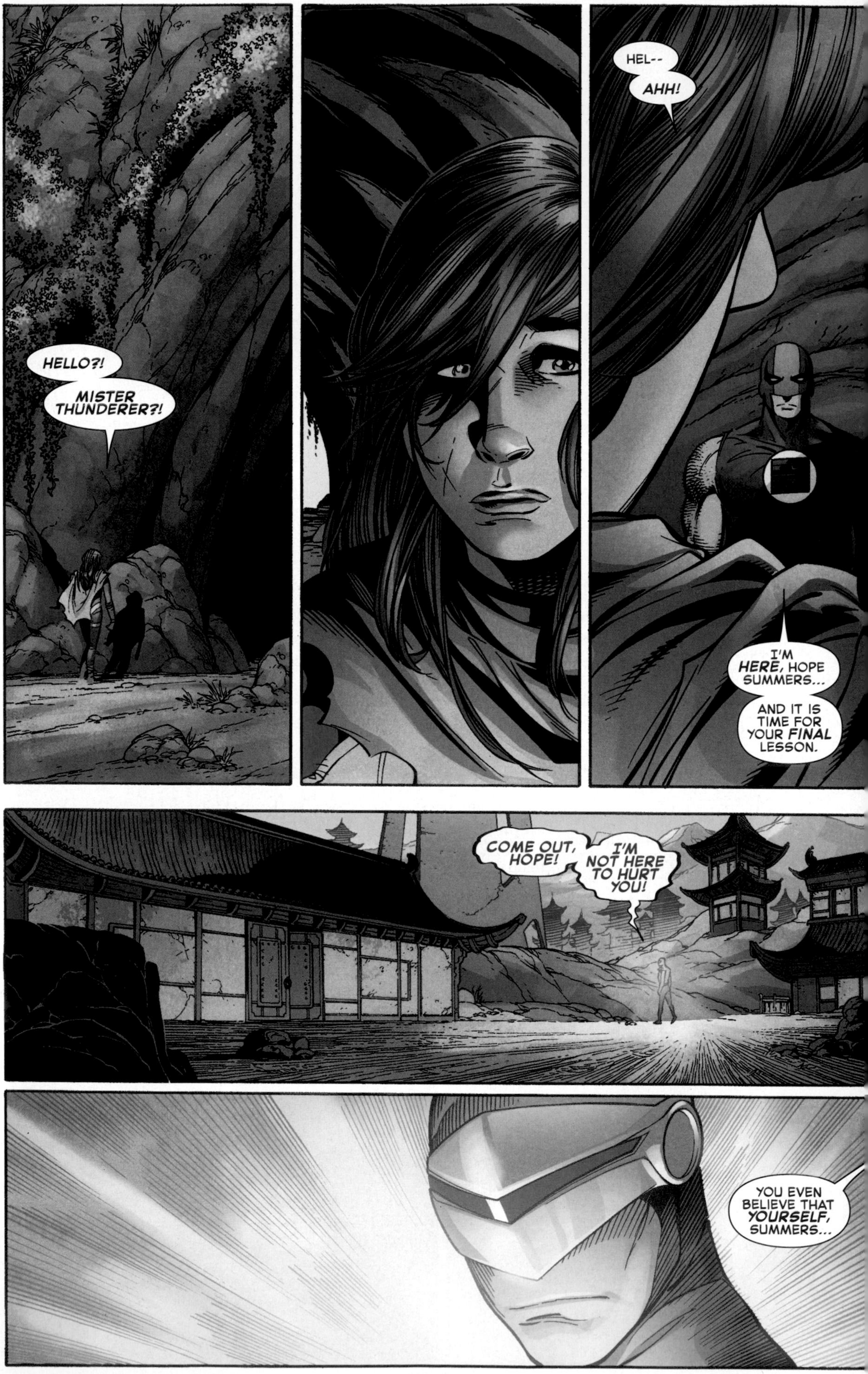
HELLO?!
MISTER THUNDERER?!
HEL--
AHH!
I'M HERE, HOPE SUMMERS...
AND IT IS TIME FOR YOUR FINAL LESSON.
COME OUT, HOPE!
I'M NOT HERE TO HURT YOU!
YOU EVEN BELIEVE THAT YOURSELF, SUMMERS...

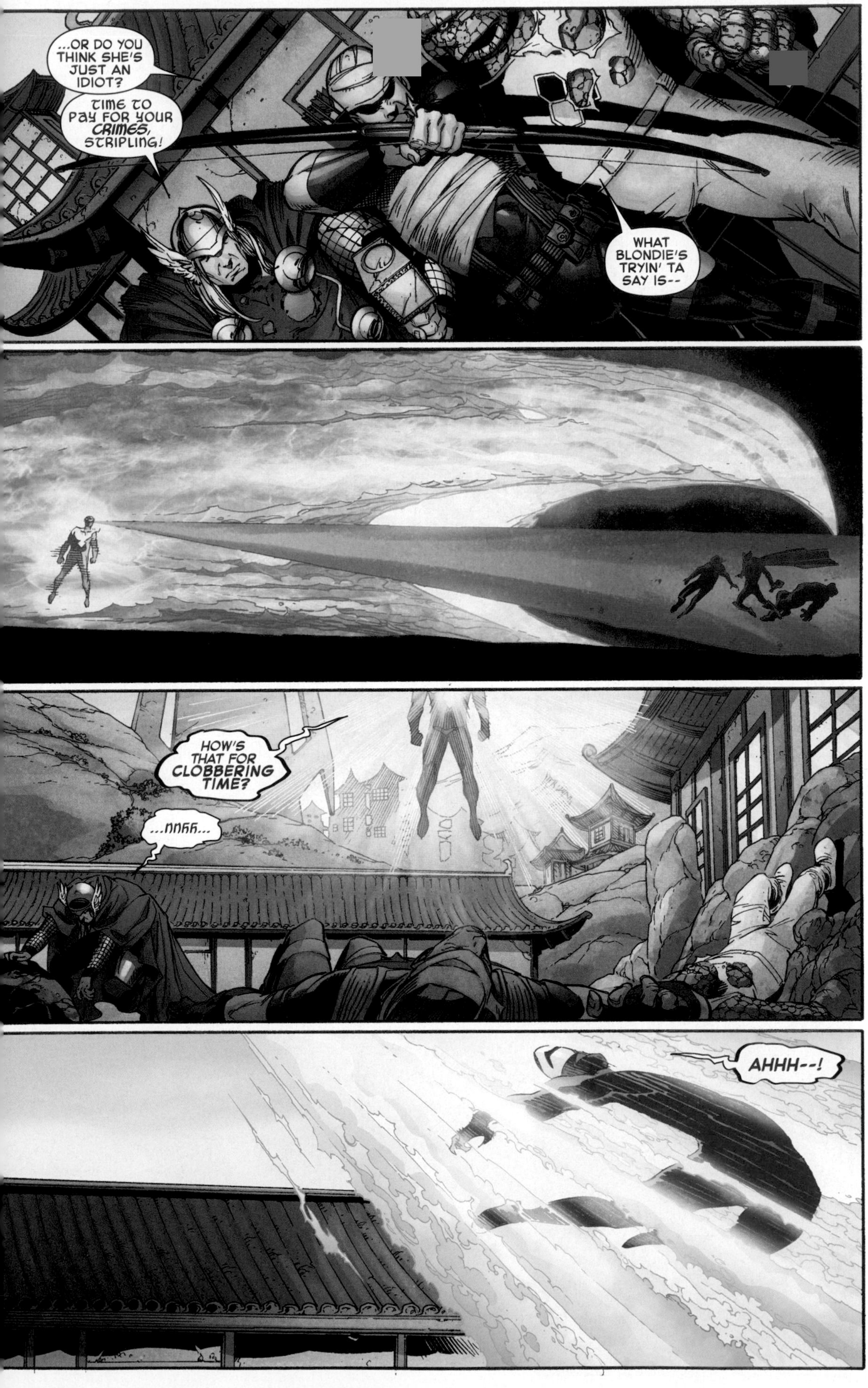
...OR DO YOU THINK SHE'S JUST AN IDIOT?
TIME TO PAY FOR YOUR CRIMES, STRIPLING!
WHAT BLONDIE'S TRYIN' TA SAY IS--
HOW'S THAT FOR CLOBBERING TIME?
...NNHH...
AHHH--!

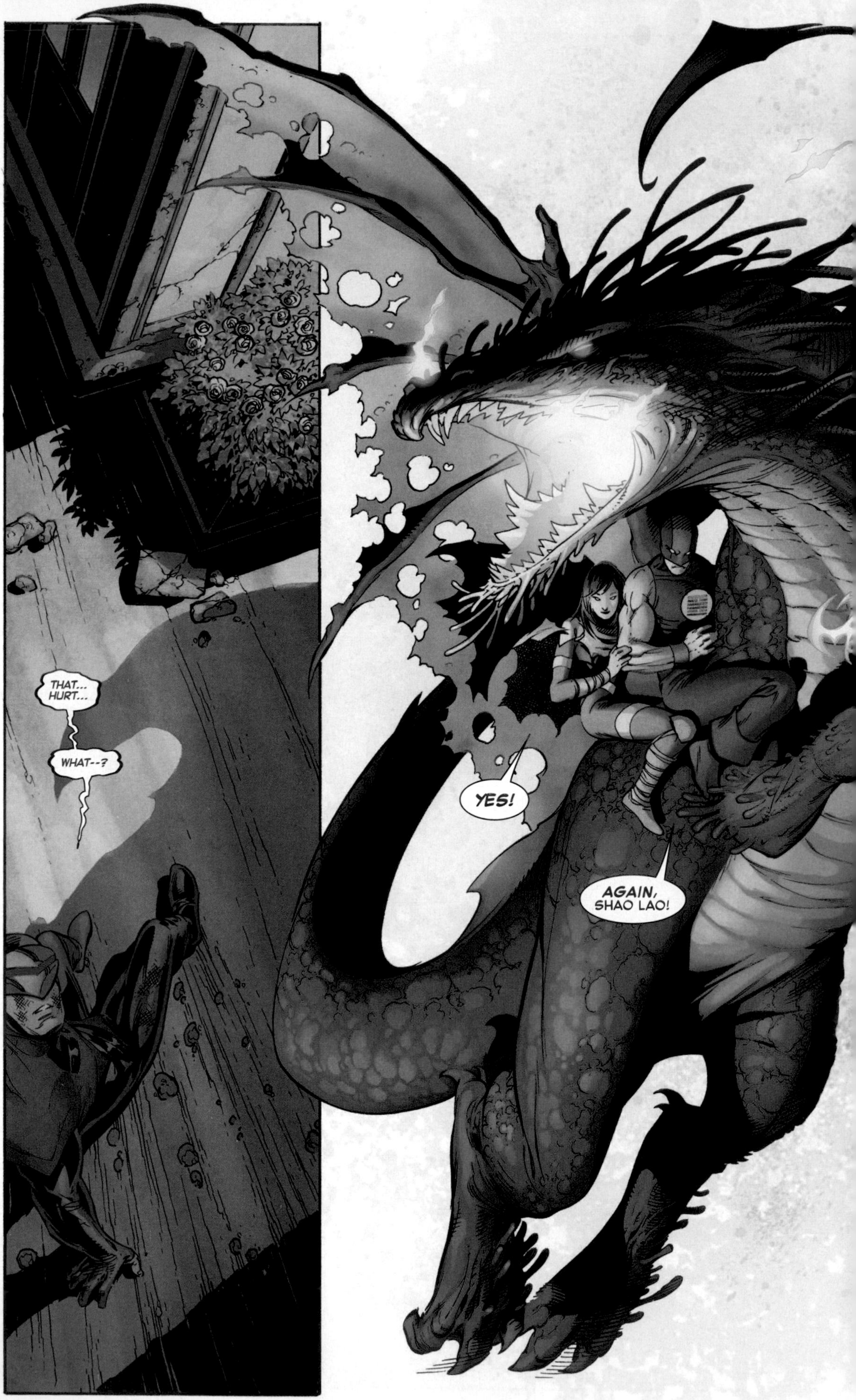
THAT... HURT...
WHAT--?
YES!
AGAIN, SHAO LAO!

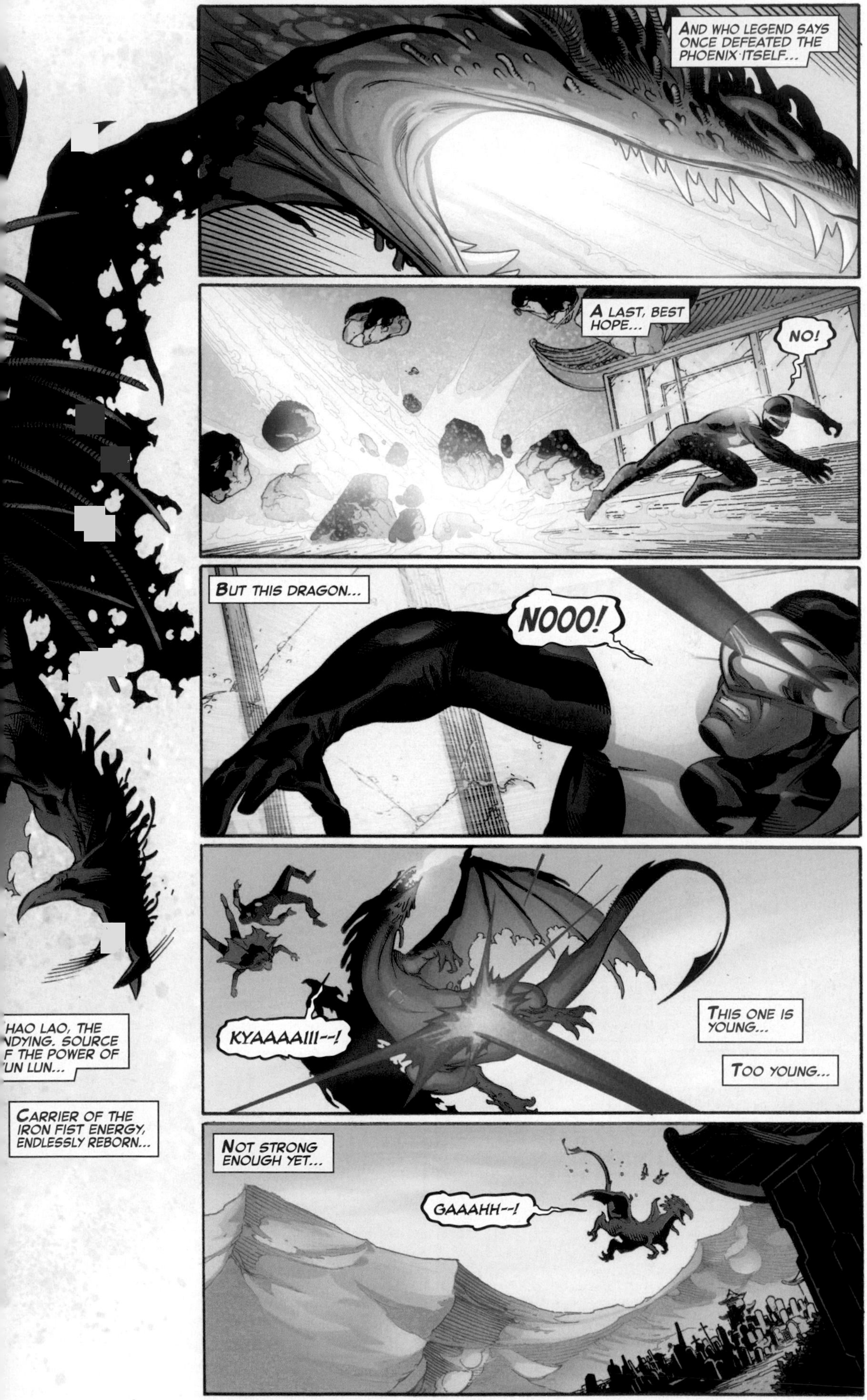
HAO LAO, THE NDYING. SOURCE F THE POWER OF UN LUN...
CARRIER OF THE IRON FIST ENERGY, ENDLESSLY REBORN...
AND WHO LEGEND SAYS ONCE DEFEATED THE PHOENIX ITSELF...
A LAST, BEST HOPE...
NO!
BUT THIS DRAGON...
NOOO!
KYAAAAIII--!
THIS ONE IS YOUNG...
TOO YOUNG...
NOT STRONG ENOUGH YET...
GAAAHH--!

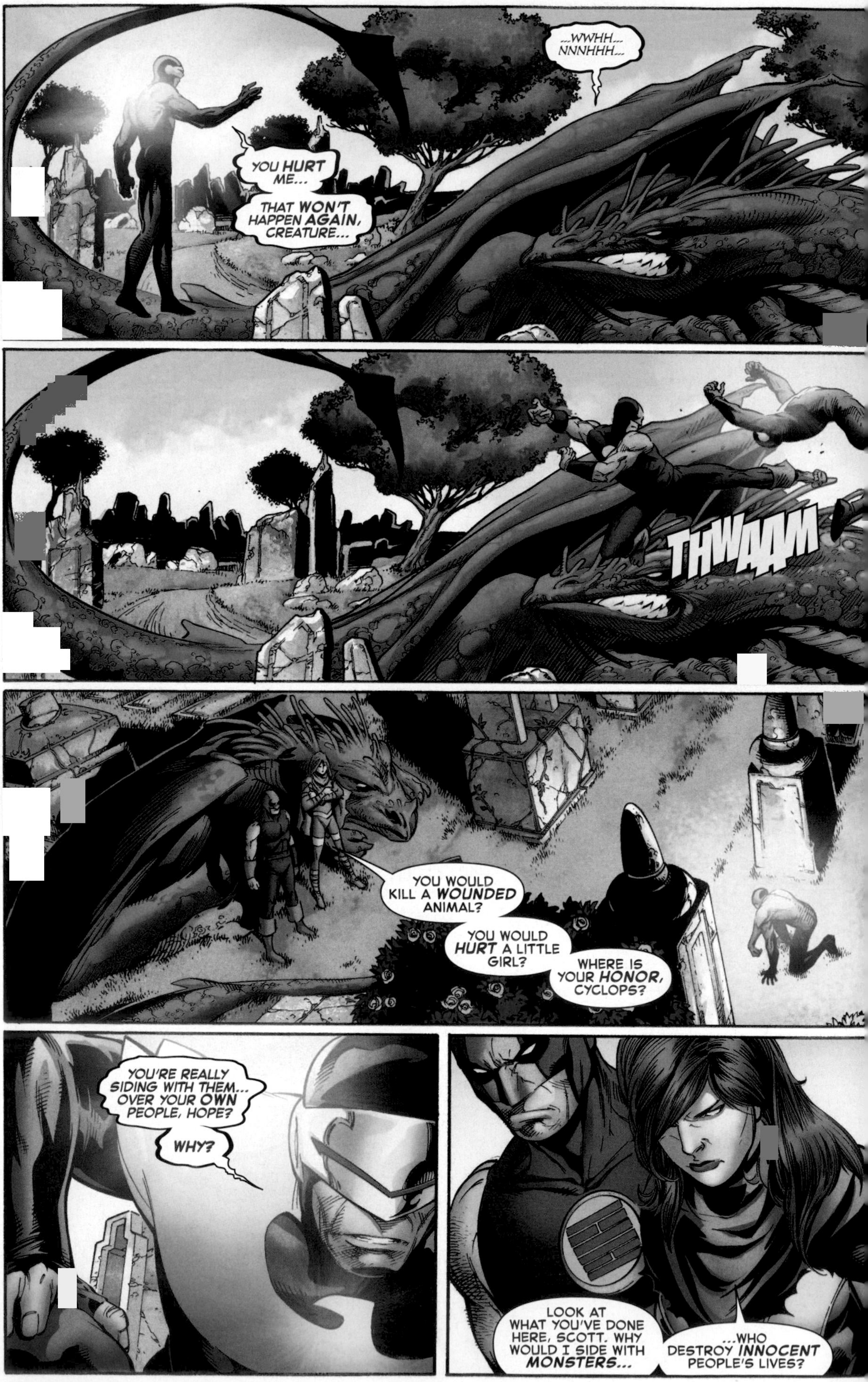
...WWHH... NNNHHH...
YOU HURT ME...
THAT WON'T HAPPEN AGAIN, CREATURE...
THWAAM
YOU WOULD KILL A WOUNDED ANIMAL?
YOU WOULD HURT A LITTLE GIRL?
WHERE IS YOUR HONOR, CYCLOPS?
YOU'RE REALLY SIDING WITH THEM... OVER YOUR OWN PEOPLE, HOPE?
WHY?
LOOK AT WHAT YOU'VE DONE HERE, SCOTT. WHY WOULD I SIDE WITH MONSTERS...
...WHO DESTROY INNOCENT PEOPLE'S LIVES?

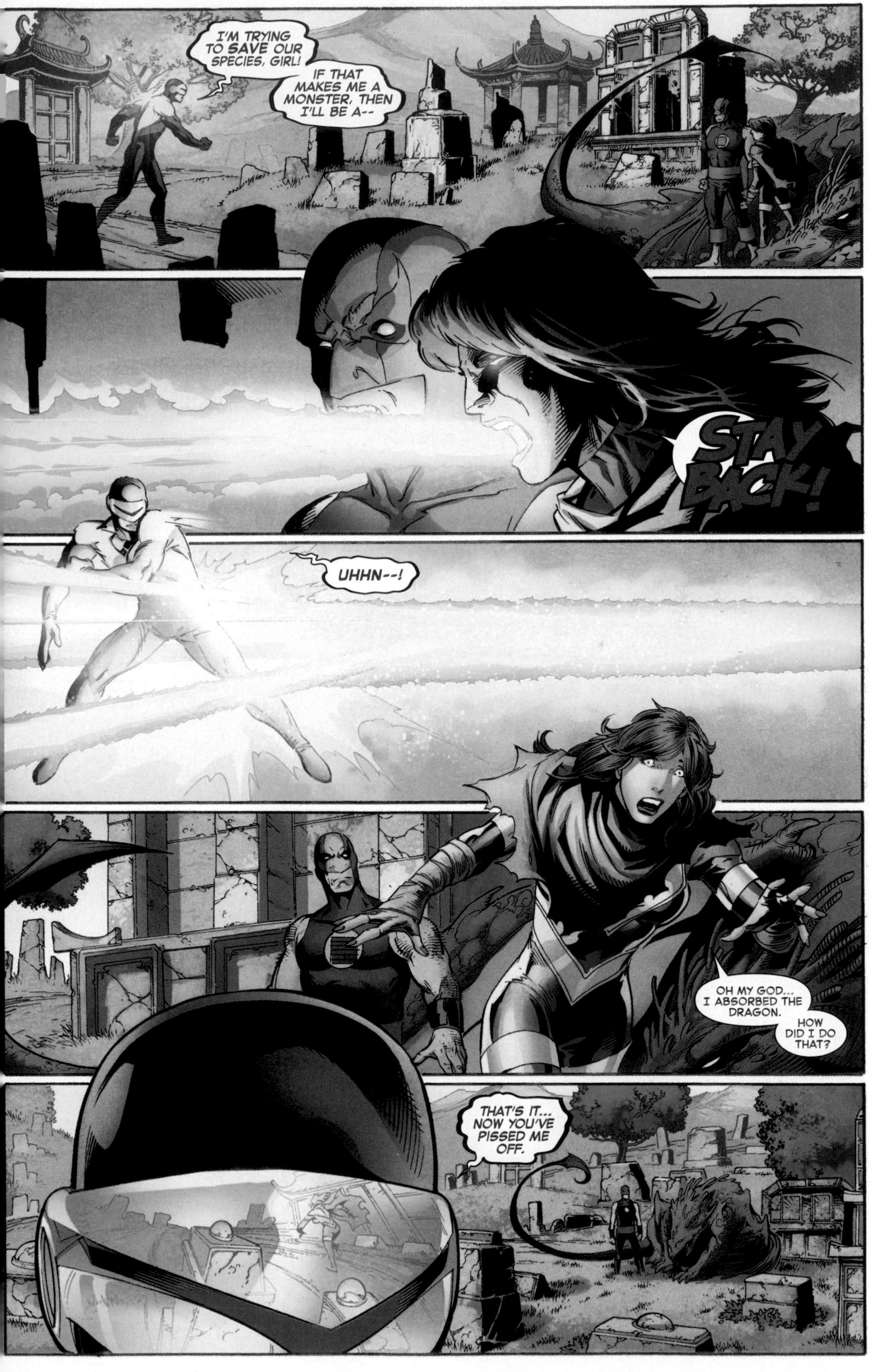
I'M TRYING TO SAVE OUR SPECIES, GIRL!
IF THAT MAKES ME A MONSTER, THEN I'LL BE A--
STAY BACK!
UHHN--!
OH MY GOD... I ABSORBED THE DRAGON.
HOW DID I DO THAT?
THAT'S IT... NOW YOU'VE PISSED ME OFF.

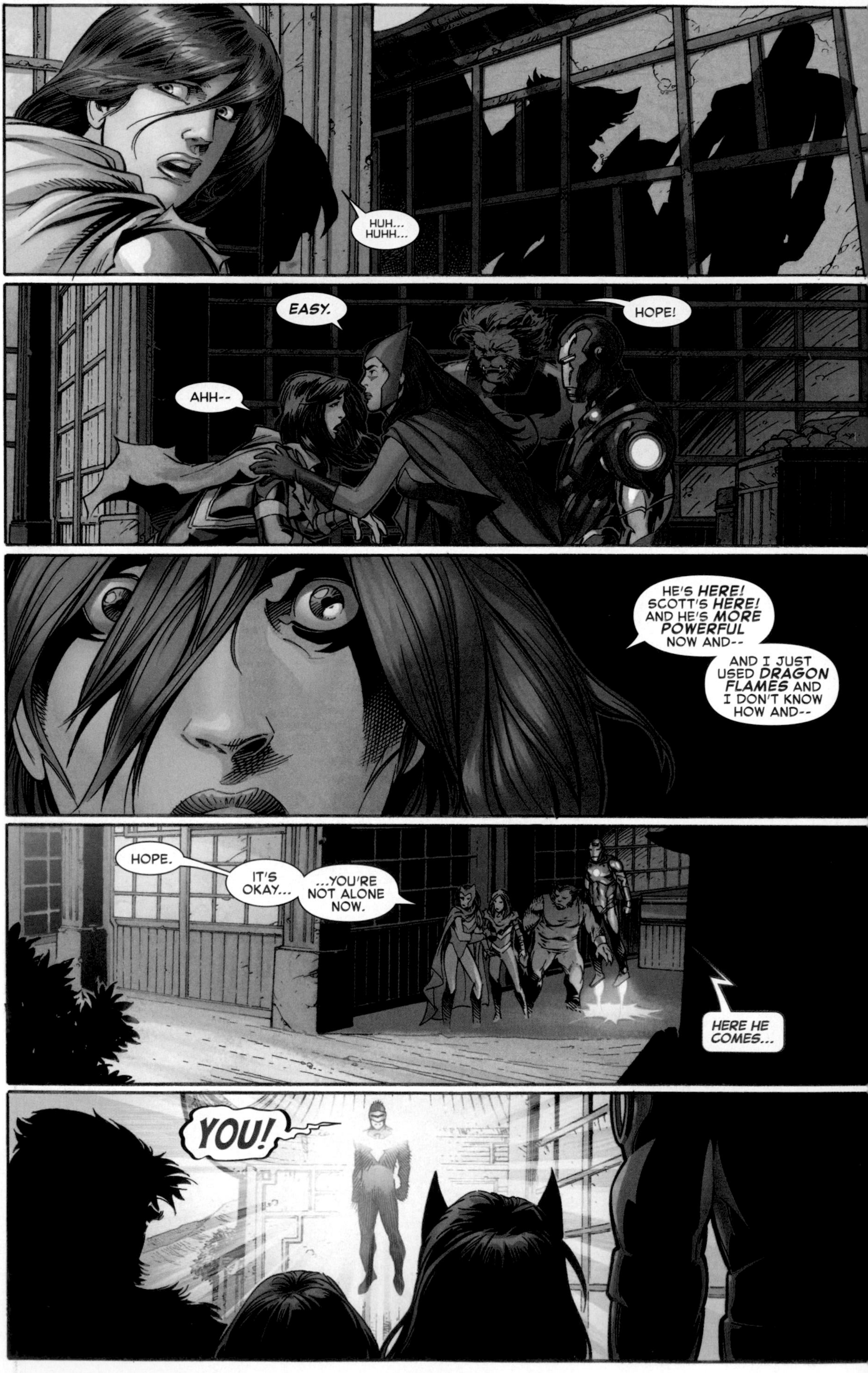
HUH... HUHH...
EASY.
HOPE!
AHH--
HE'S HERE! SCOTT'S HERE! AND HE'S MORE POWERFUL NOW AND--
AND I JUST USED DRAGON FLAMES AND I DON'T KNOW HOW AND--
HOPE.
IT'S OKAY...
...YOU'RE NOT ALONE NOW.
HERE HE COMES...
YOU!

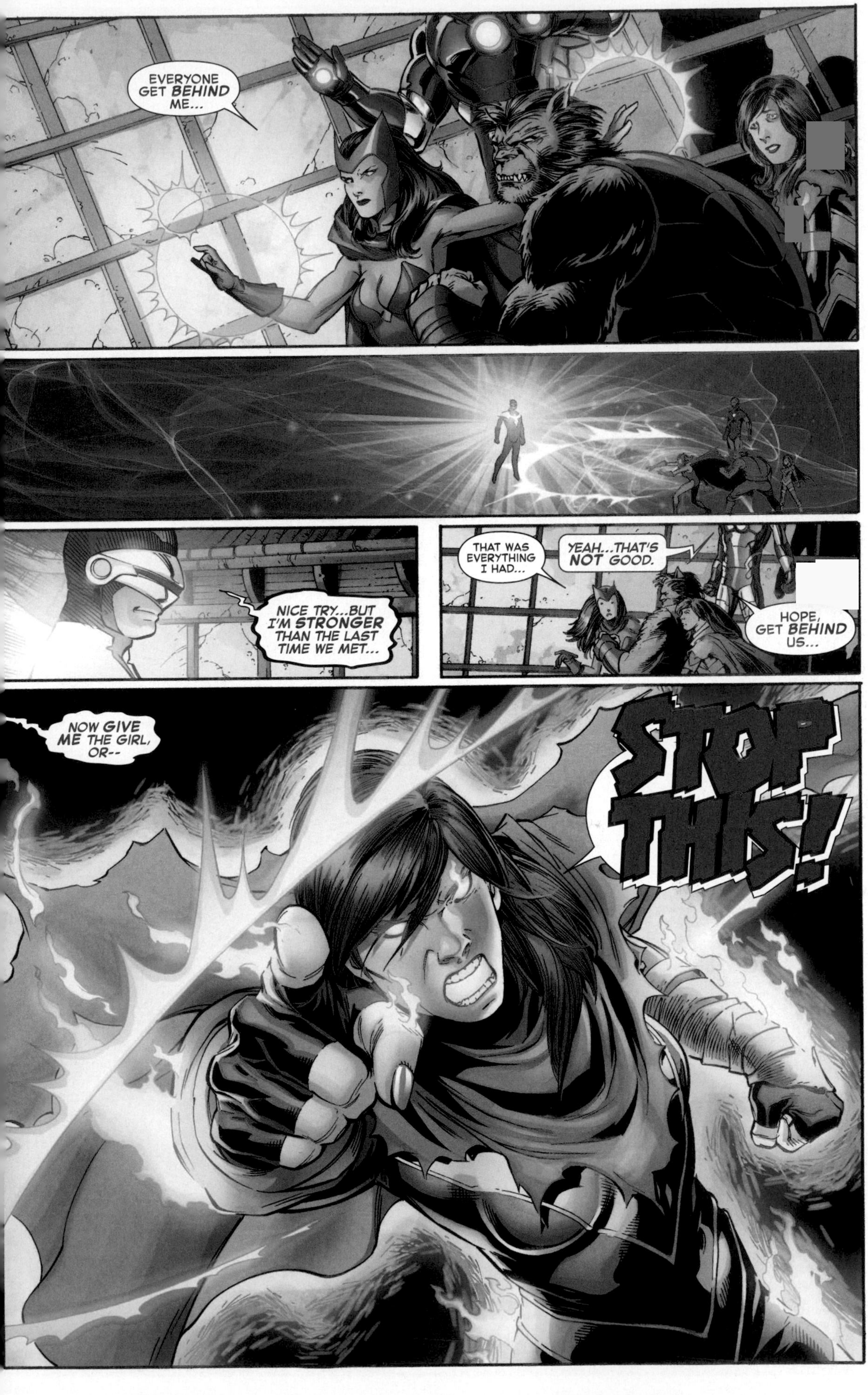
EVERYONE GET BEHIND ME...
NICE TRY...BUT I'M STRONGER THAN THE LAST TIME WE MET...
THAT WAS EVERYTHING I HAD...
YEAH...THAT'S NOT GOOD.
HOPE, GET BEHIND US...
NOW GIVE ME THE GIRL, OR--
STOP THIS!

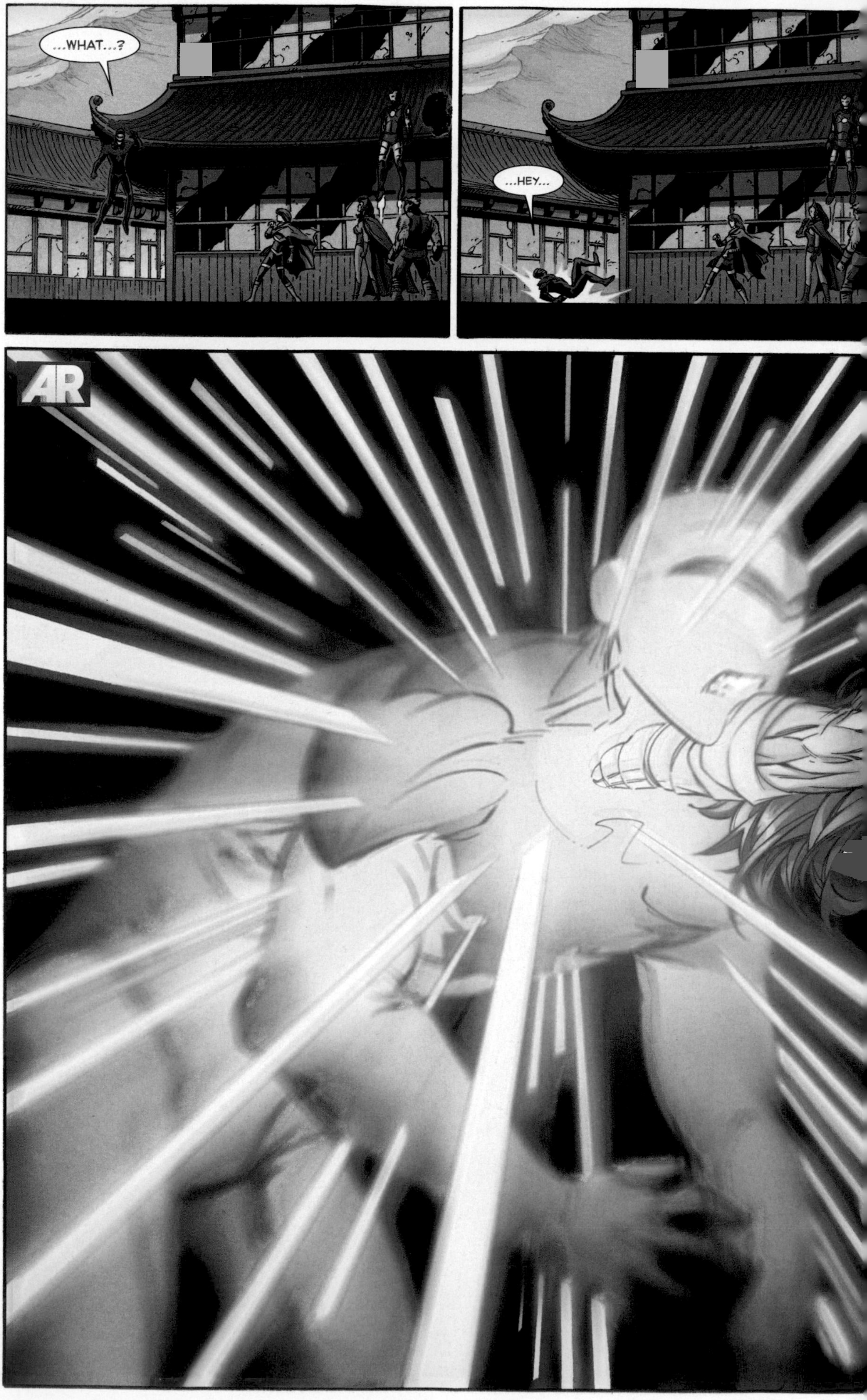
...WHAT...?
...HEY...

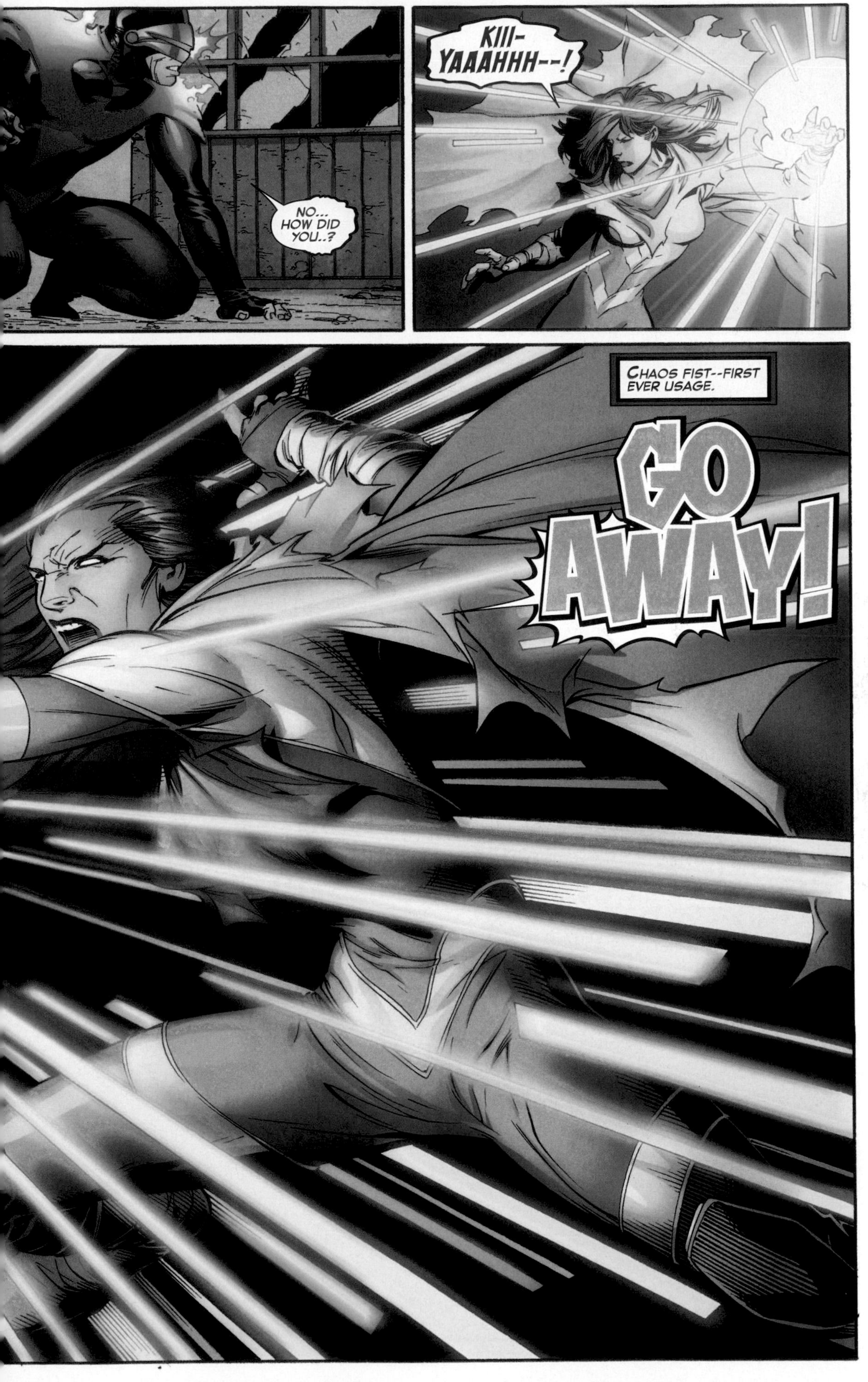
NO... HOW DID YOU..?
KIII- YAAAHHH--!
CHAOS FIST--FIRST EVER USAGE.
GO AWAY!

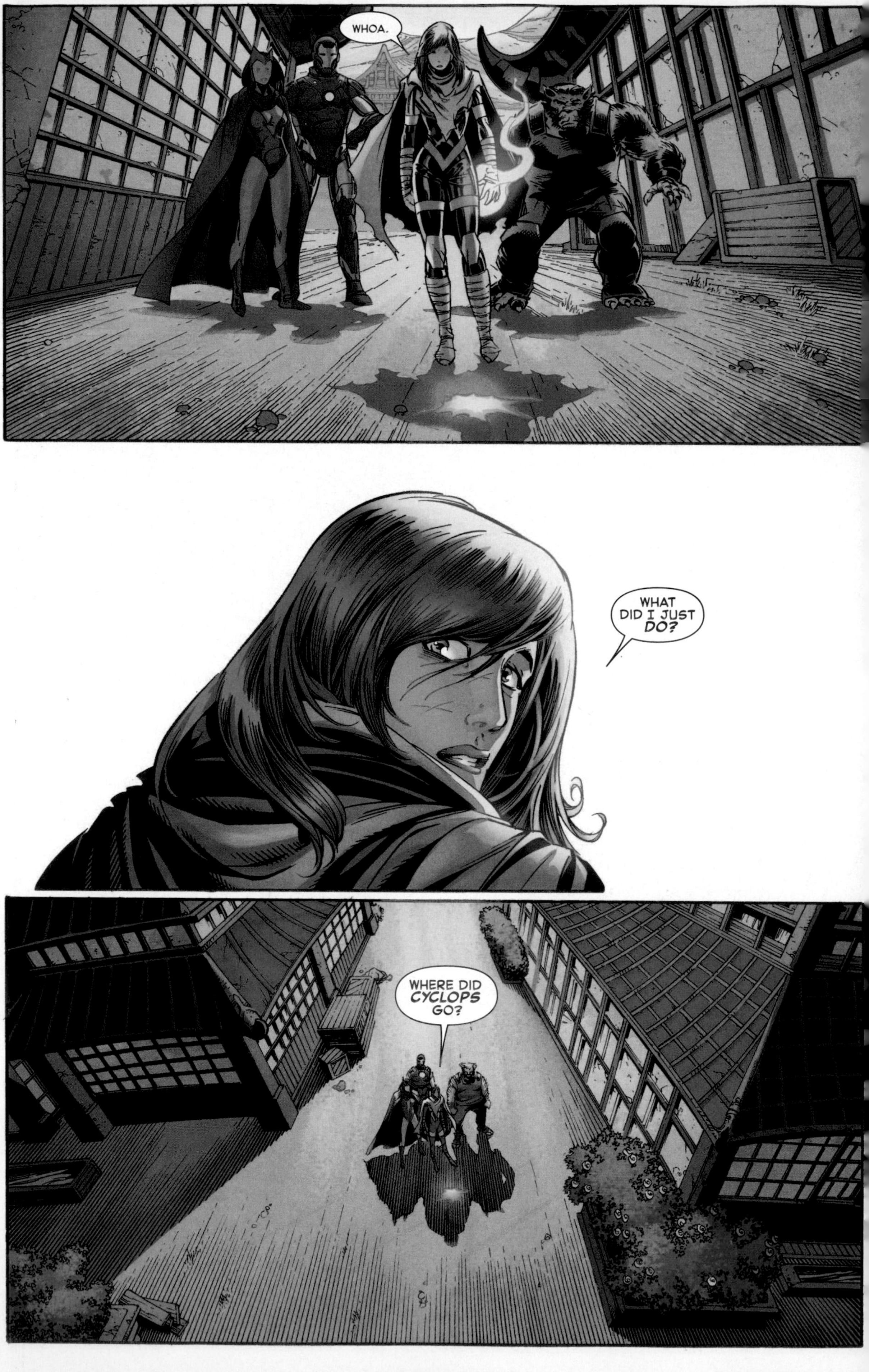
WHOA.
WHAT DID I JUST DO?
WHERE DID CYCLOPS GO?

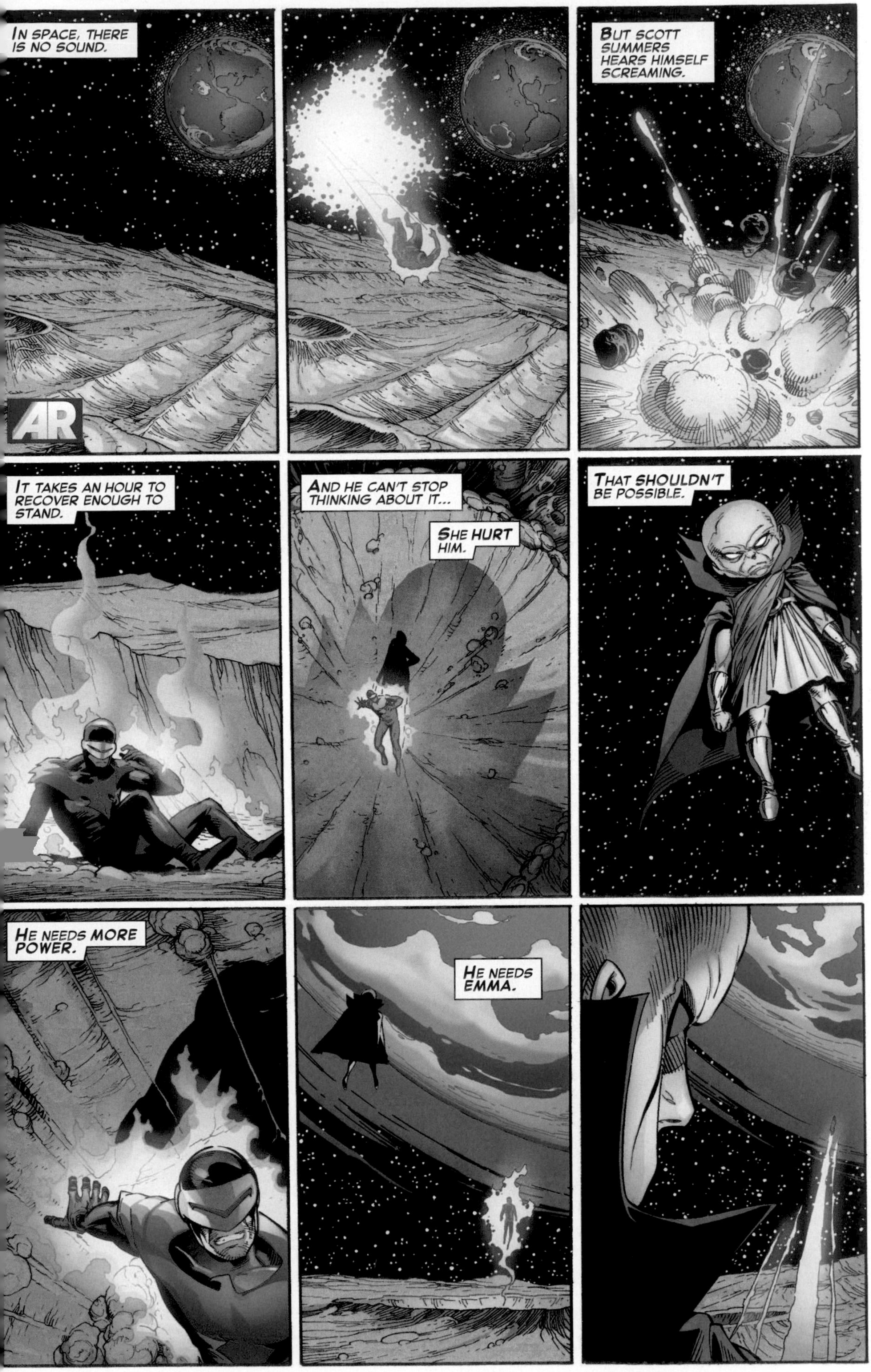
IN SPACE, THERE IS NO SOUND.
BUT SCOTT SUMMERS HEARS HIMSELF SCREAMING.
IT TAKES AN HOUR TO RECOVER ENOUGH TO STAND.
AND HE CAN'T STOP THINKING ABOUT IT...
SHE HURT HIM.
THAT SHOULDN'T BE POSSIBLE.
HE NEEDS MORE POWER.
HE NEEDS EMMA.

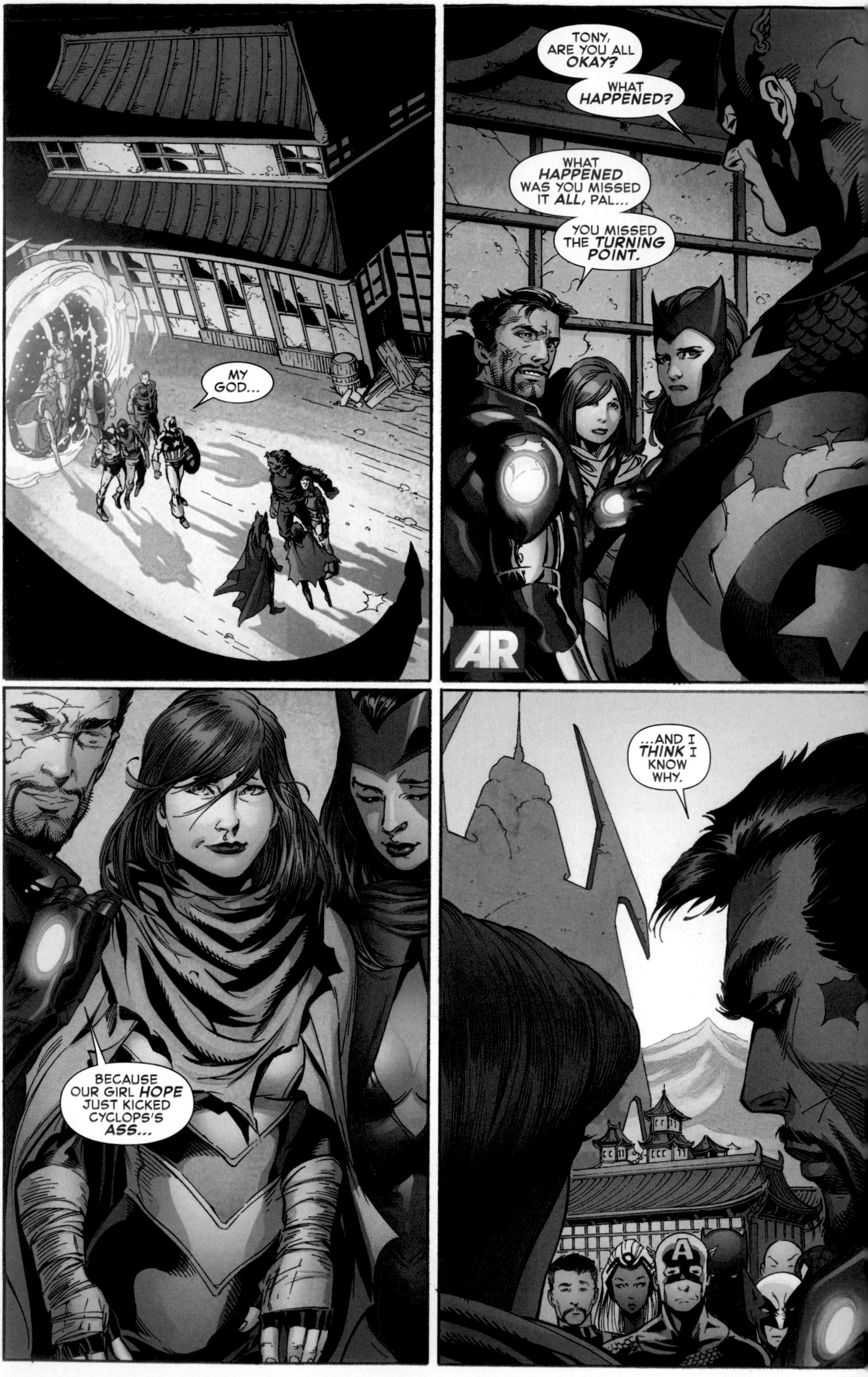
MY GOD...
TONY, ARE YOU ALL OKAY?
WHAT HAPPENED?
WHAT HAPPENED WAS YOU MISSED IT ALL, PAL...
YOU MISSED THE TURNING POINT.
BECAUSE OUR GIRL HOPE JUST KICKED CYCLOPS'S ASS...
...AND I THINK I KNOW WHY.

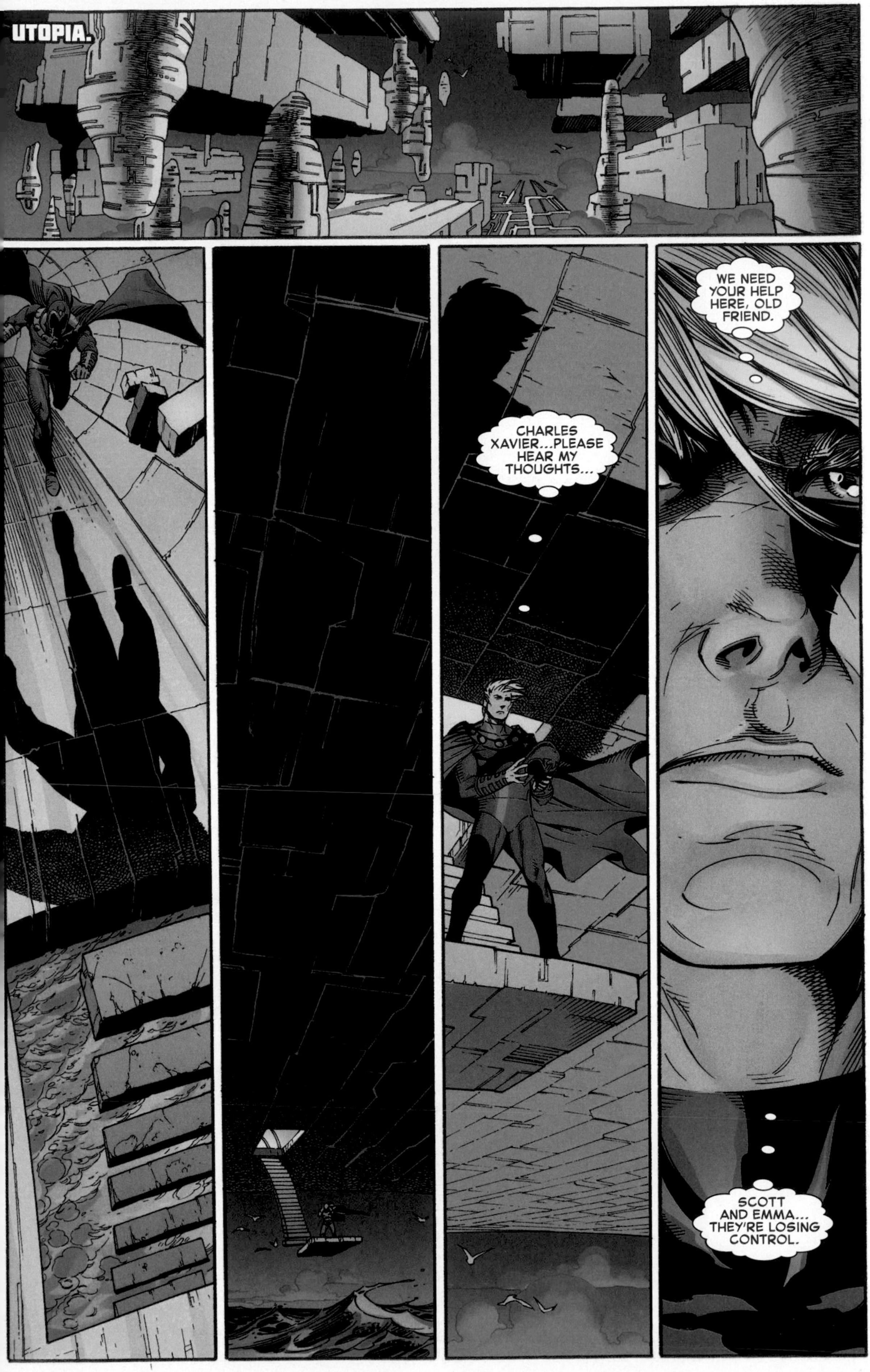
UTOPIA.
CHARLES XAVIER...PLEASE HEAR MY THOUGHTS...
WE NEED YOUR HELP HERE, OLD FRIEND.
SCOTT AND EMMA... THEY'RE LOSING CONTROL.

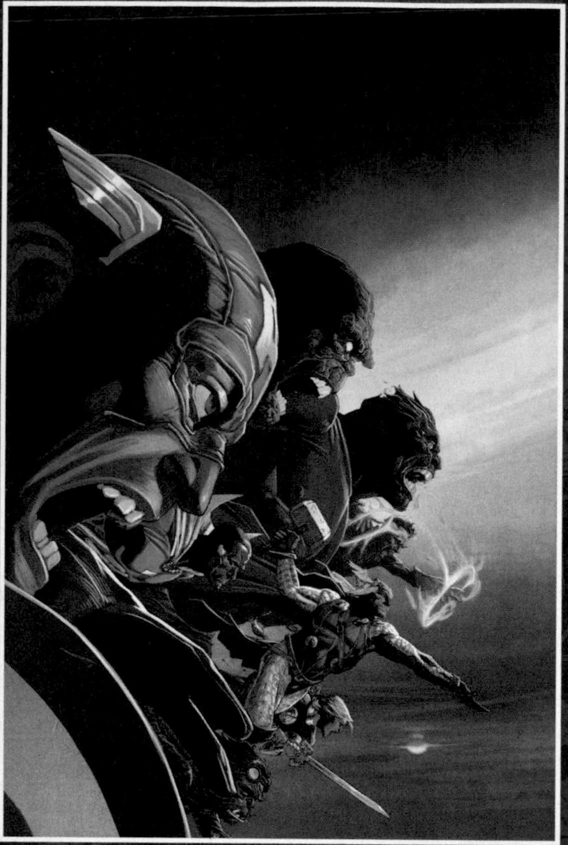

AVX #8 VARIANT
BY JEROME OPEÑA & DEAN WHITE

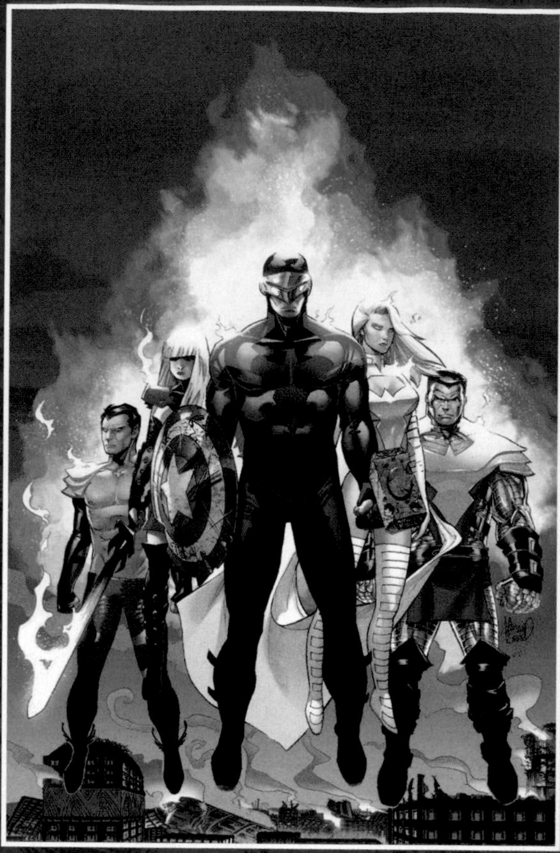

AVX #8 VARIANT
BY ADAM KUBERT & JUSTIN PONSOR

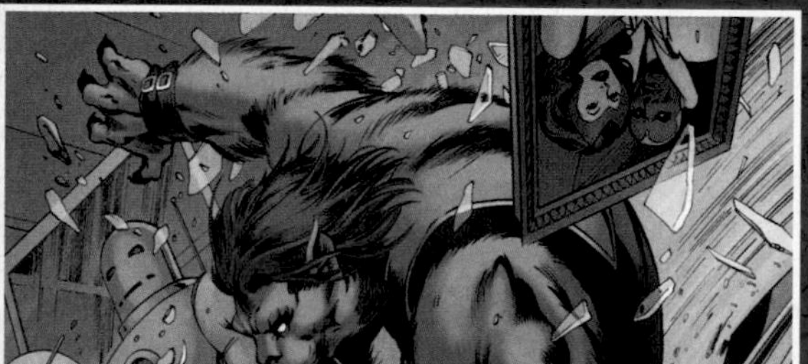

AVX #8 VARIANT
BY ALAN DAVIS, MARK FARMER & VAL STAPLES

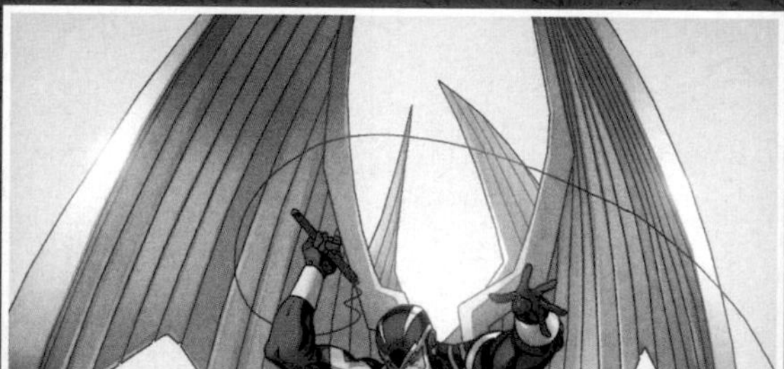

AVX #9 VARIANT
BY SALVADOR LARROCA & JASON KEITH

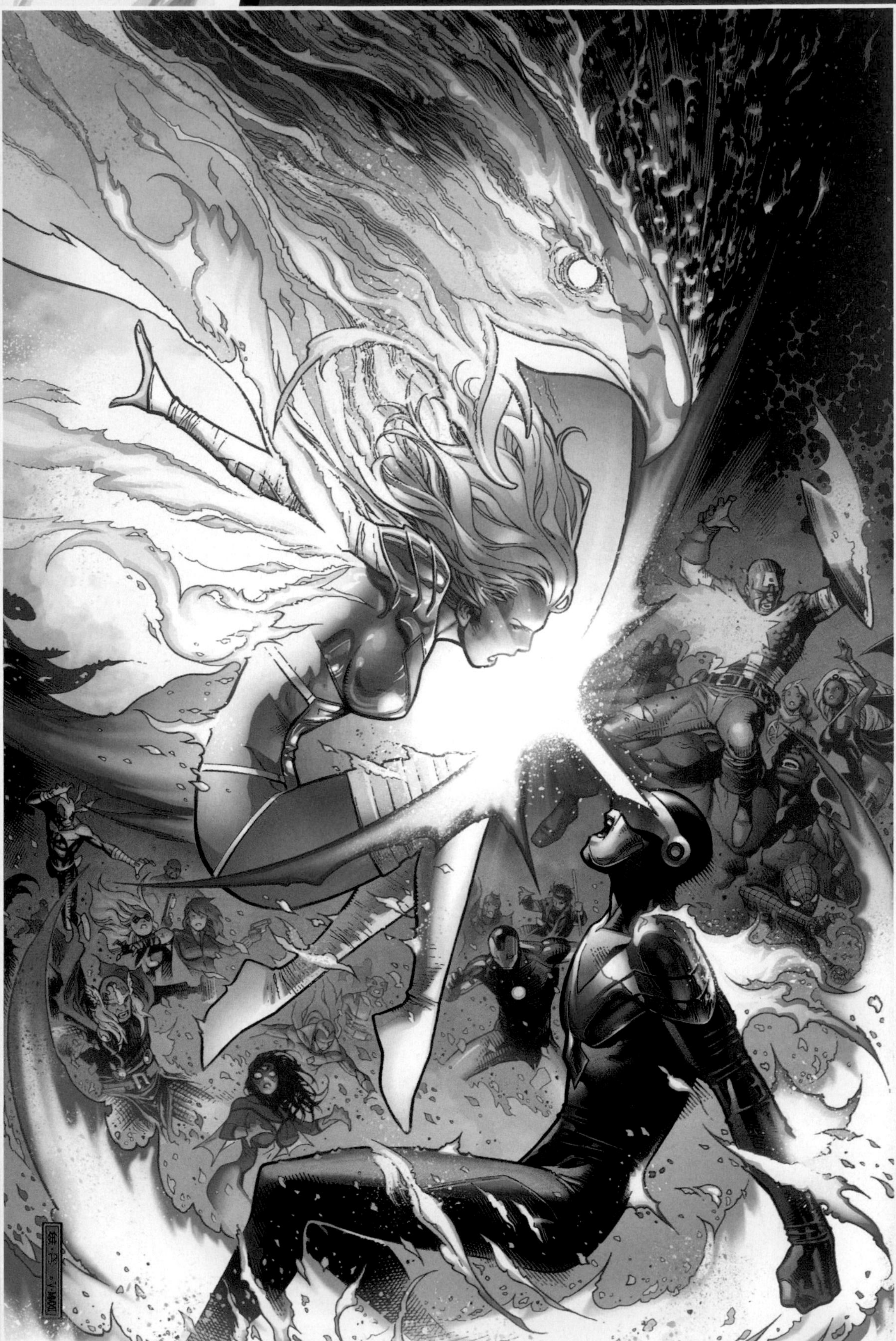

ROUND 11

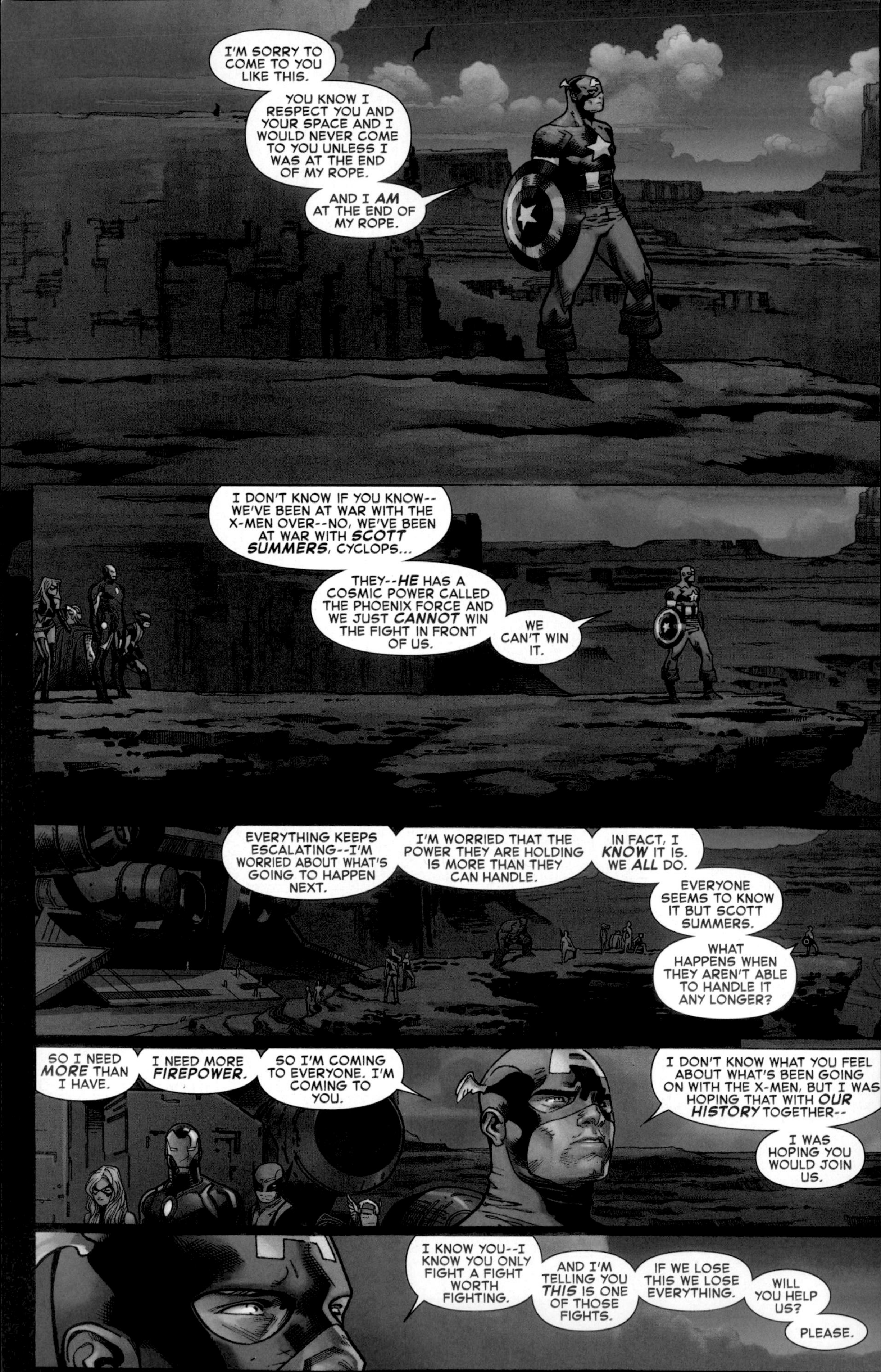
I'M SORRY TO COME TO YOU LIKE THIS.
YOU KNOW I RESPECT YOU AND YOUR SPACE AND I WOULD NEVER COME TO YOU UNLESS I WAS AT THE END OF MY ROPE.
AND I AM AT THE END OF MY ROPE.
I DON'T KNOW IF YOU KNOW-- WE'VE BEEN AT WAR WITH THE X-MEN OVER--NO, WE'VE BEEN AT WAR WITH SCOTT SUMMERS, CYCLOPS...
THEY--HE HAS A COSMIC POWER CALLED THE PHOENIX FORCE AND WE JUST CANNOT WIN THE FIGHT IN FRONT OF US.
WE CAN'T WIN IT.
EVERYTHING KEEPS ESCALATING--I'M WORRIED ABOUT WHAT'S GOING TO HAPPEN NEXT.
I'M WORRIED THAT THE POWER THEY ARE HOLDING IS MORE THAN THEY CAN HANDLE.
IN FACT, I KNOW IT IS. WE ALL DO.
EVERYONE SEEMS TO KNOW IT BUT SCOTT SUMMERS.
WHAT HAPPENS WHEN THEY AREN'T ABLE TO HANDLE IT ANY LONGER?
SO I NEED MORE THAN I HAVE.
I NEED MORE FIREPOWER.
SO I'M COMING TO EVERYONE. I'M COMING TO YOU.
I DON'T KNOW WHAT YOU FEEL ABOUT WHAT'S BEEN GOING ON WITH THE X-MEN, BUT I WAS HOPING THAT WITH OUR HISTORY TOGETHER--
I WAS HOPING YOU WOULD JOIN US.
I KNOW YOU--I KNOW YOU ONLY FIGHT A FIGHT WORTH FIGHTING.
AND I'M TELLING YOU THIS IS ONE OF THOSE FIGHTS.
IF WE LOSE THIS WE LOSE EVERYTHING.
WILL YOU HELP US?
PLEASE.

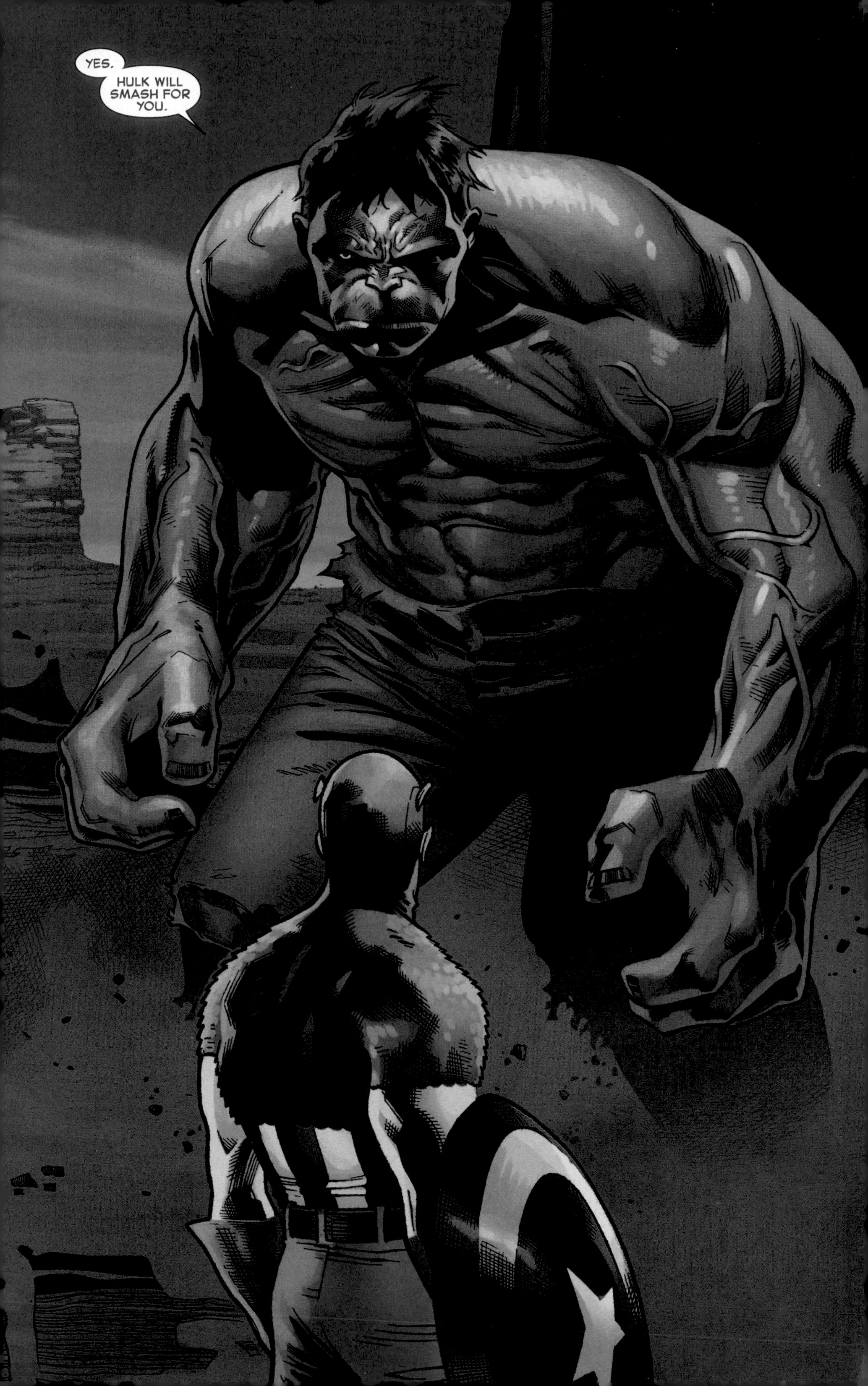
YES.
HULK WILL SMASH FOR YOU.

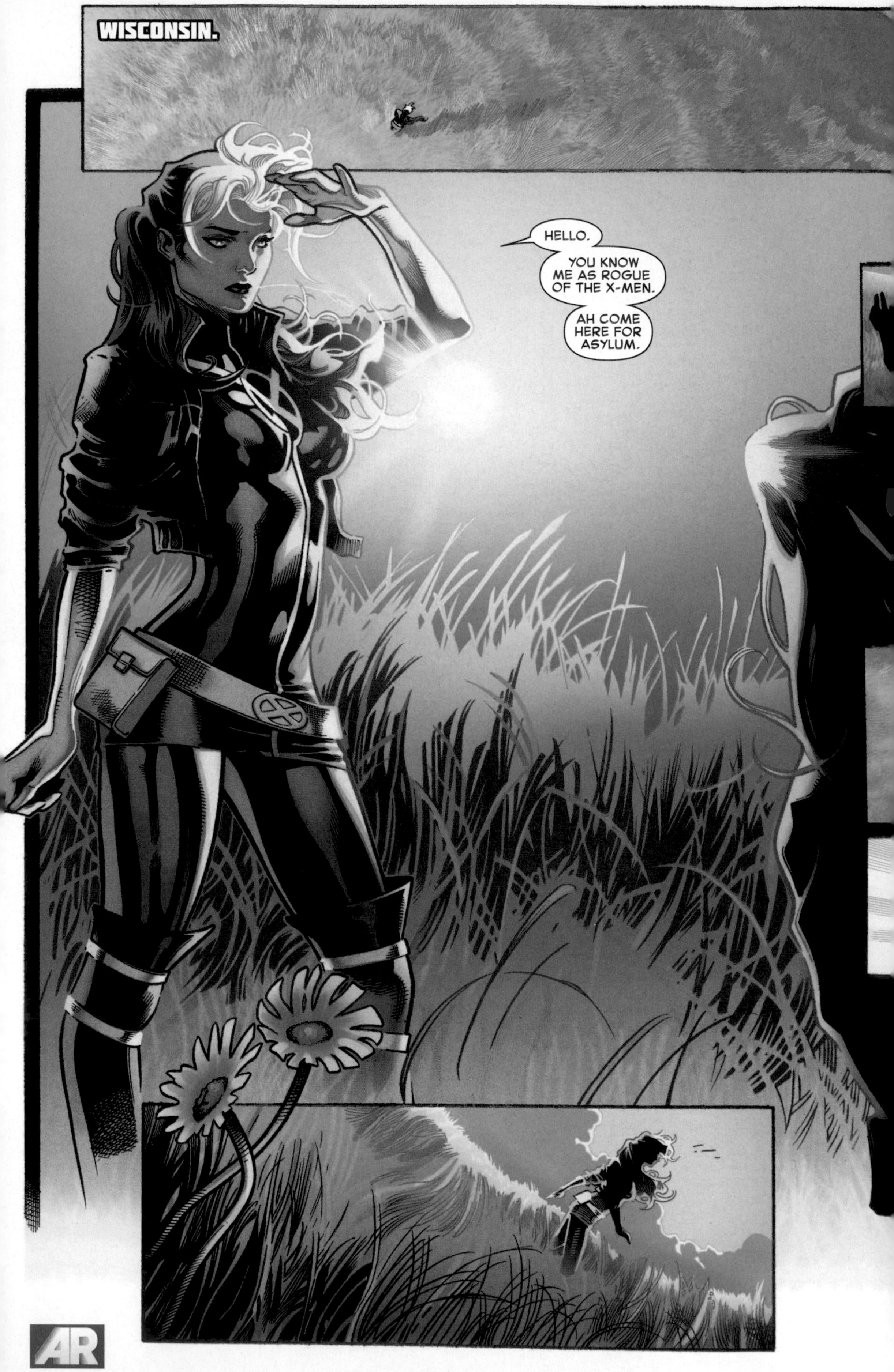
WISCONSIN.
HELLO.
YOU KNOW ME AS ROGUE OF THE X-MEN.
AH COME HERE FOR ASYLUM.

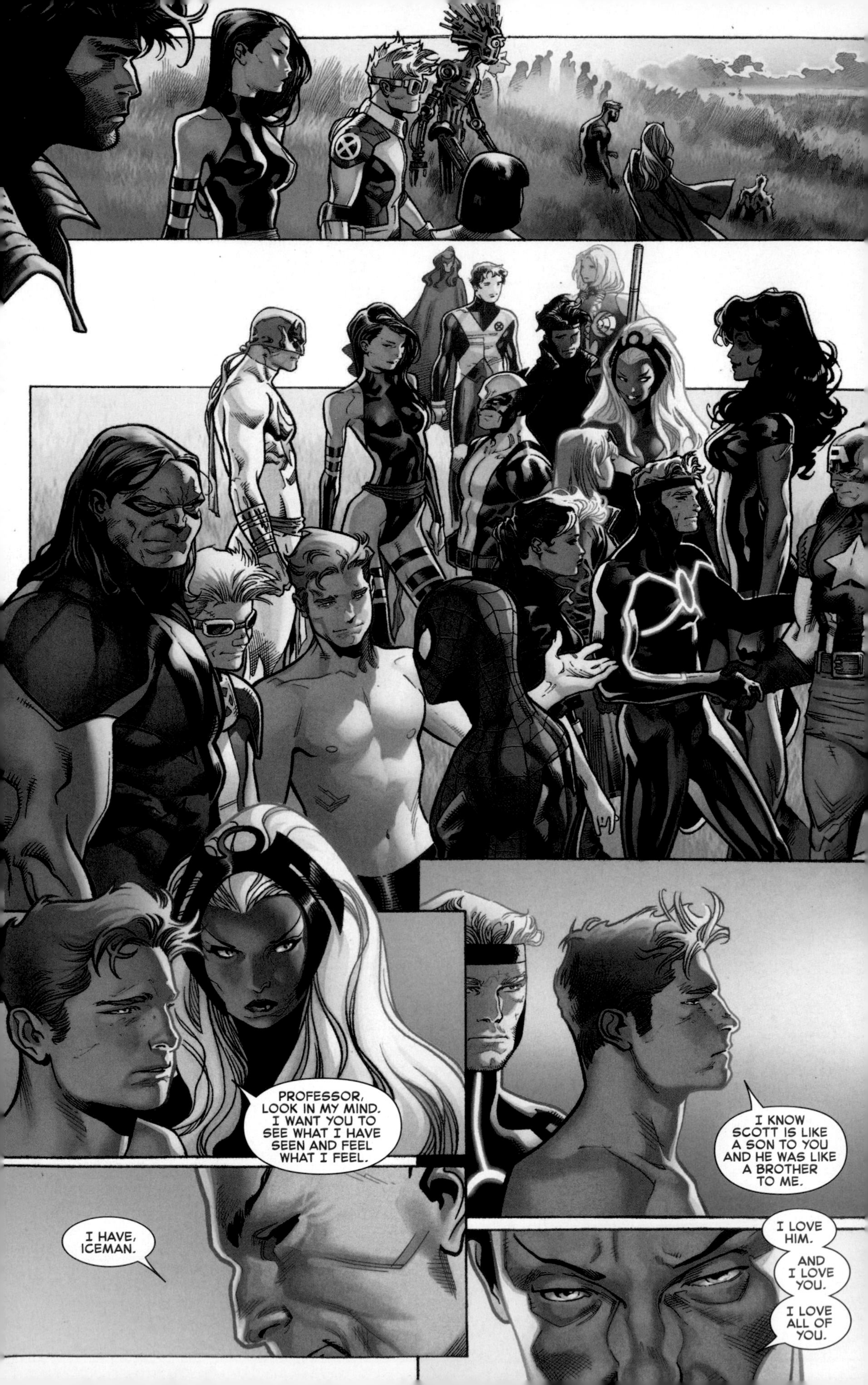
PROFESSOR, LOOK IN MY MIND. I WANT YOU TO SEE WHAT I HAVE SEEN AND FEEL WHAT I FEEL.
I KNOW SCOTT IS LIKE A SON TO YOU AND HE WAS LIKE A BROTHER TO ME.
I HAVE, ICEMAN.
I LOVE HIM.
AND I LOVE YOU.
I LOVE ALL OF YOU.

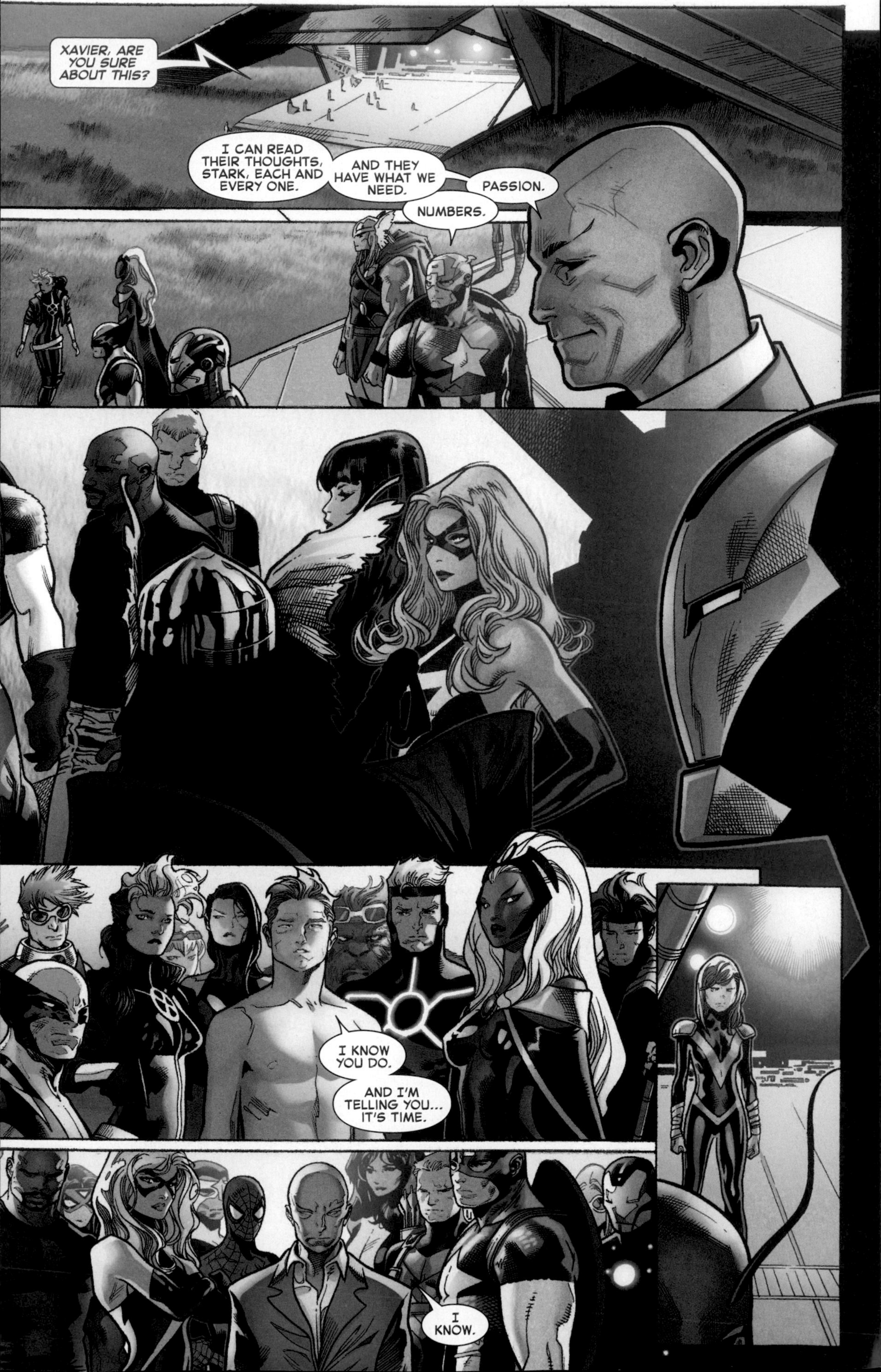
XAVIER, ARE YOU SURE ABOUT THIS?
I CAN READ THEIR THOUGHTS, STARK, EACH AND EVERY ONE.
AND THEY HAVE WHAT WE NEED.
PASSION.
NUMBERS.
I KNOW YOU DO.
AND I'M TELLING YOU... IT'S TIME.
I KNOW.

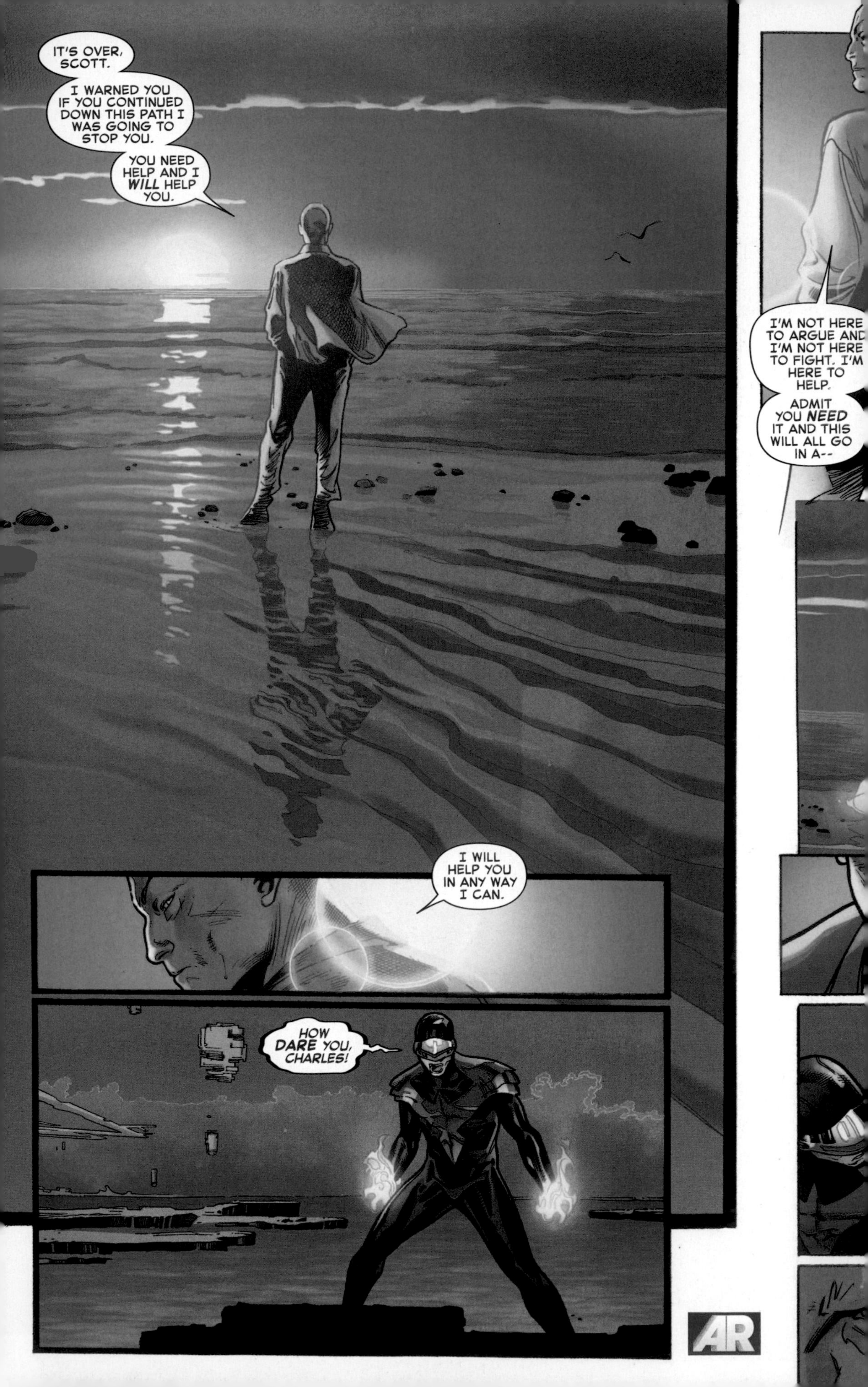
IT'S OVER, SCOTT.
I WARNED YOU IF YOU CONTINUED DOWN THIS PATH I WAS GOING TO STOP YOU.
YOU NEED HELP AND I WILL HELP YOU.
I WILL HELP YOU IN ANY WAY I CAN.
HOW DARE YOU, CHARLES!
I'M NOT HERE TO ARGUE AND I'M NOT HERE TO FIGHT. I'M HERE TO HELP.
ADMIT YOU NEED IT AND THIS WILL ALL GO IN A--

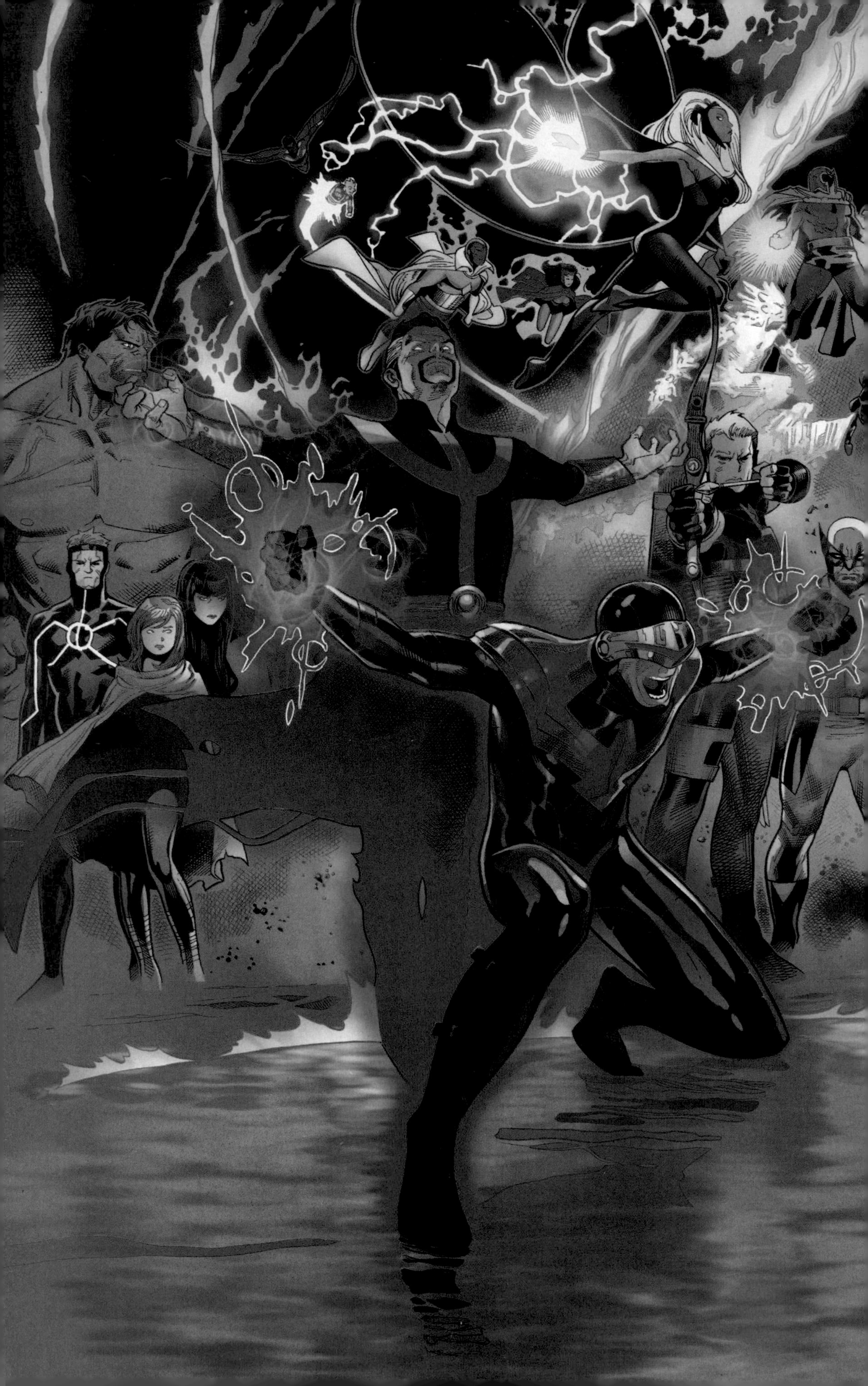

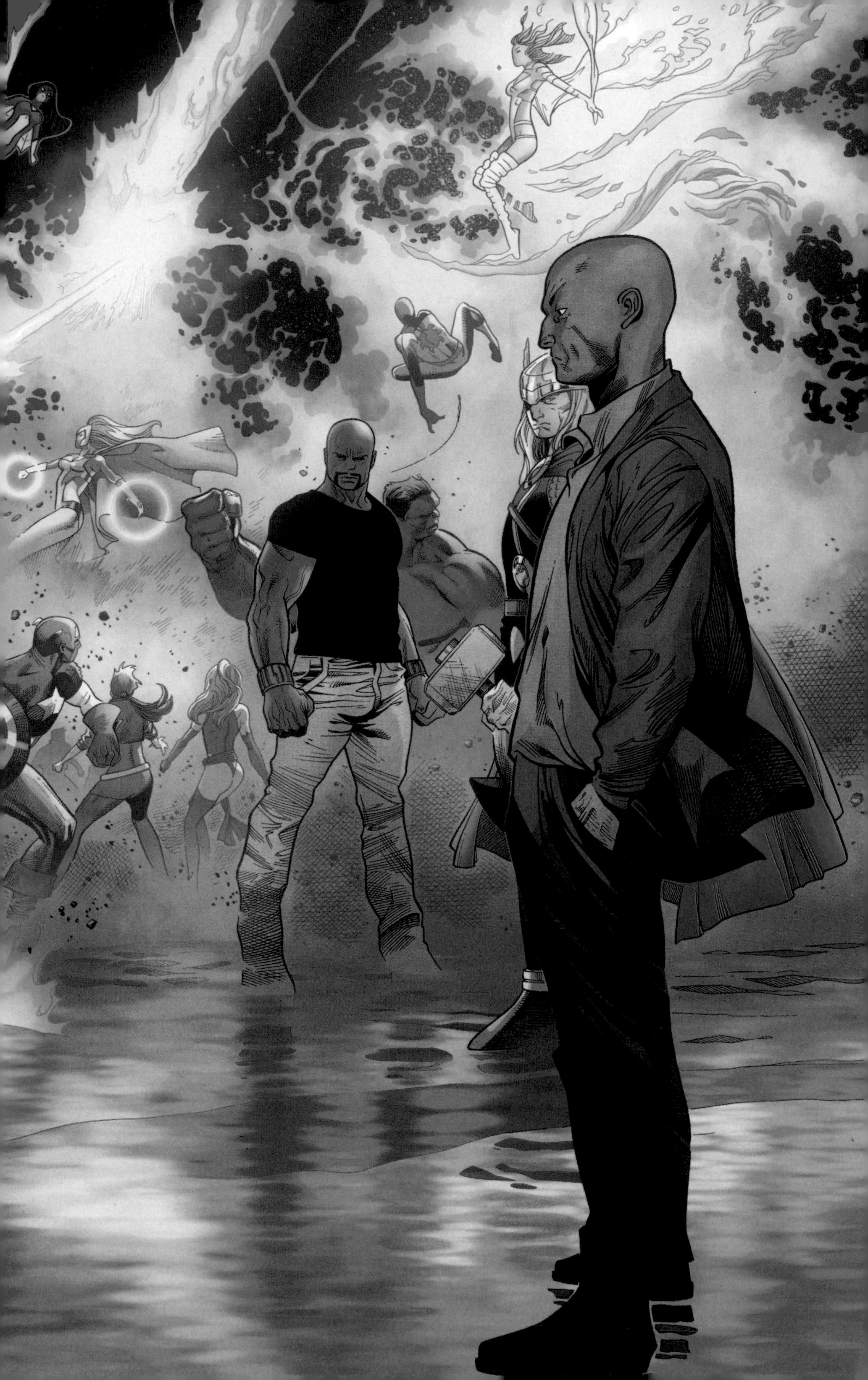

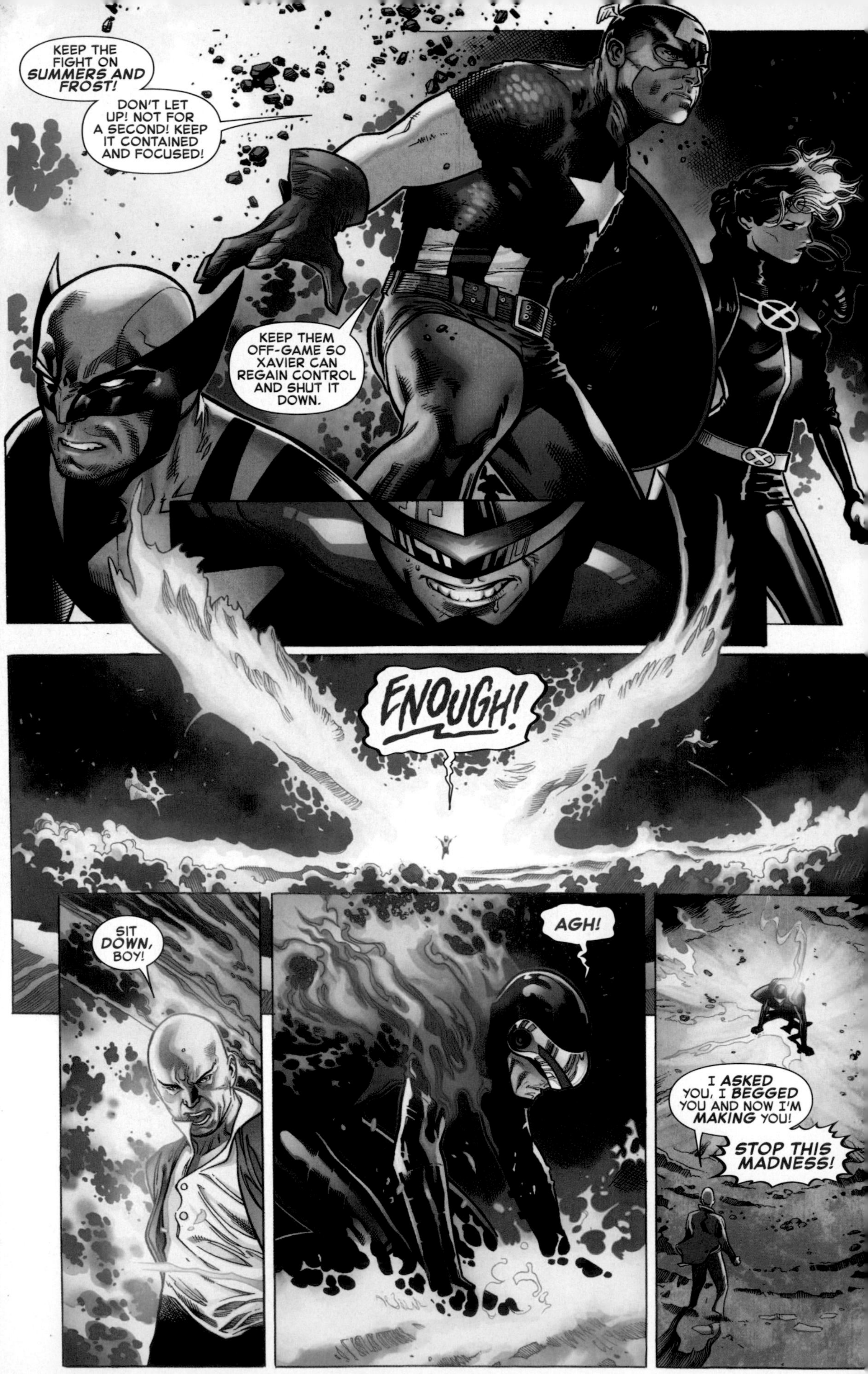
KEEP THE FIGHT ON SUMMERS AND FROST!
DON'T LET UP! NOT FOR A SECOND! KEEP IT CONTAINED AND FOCUSED!
KEEP THEM OFF-GAME SO XAVIER CAN REGAIN CONTROL AND SHUT IT DOWN.
ENOUGH!
SIT DOWN, BOY!
AGH!
I ASKED YOU, I BEGGED YOU AND NOW I'M MAKING YOU!
STOP THIS MADNESS!

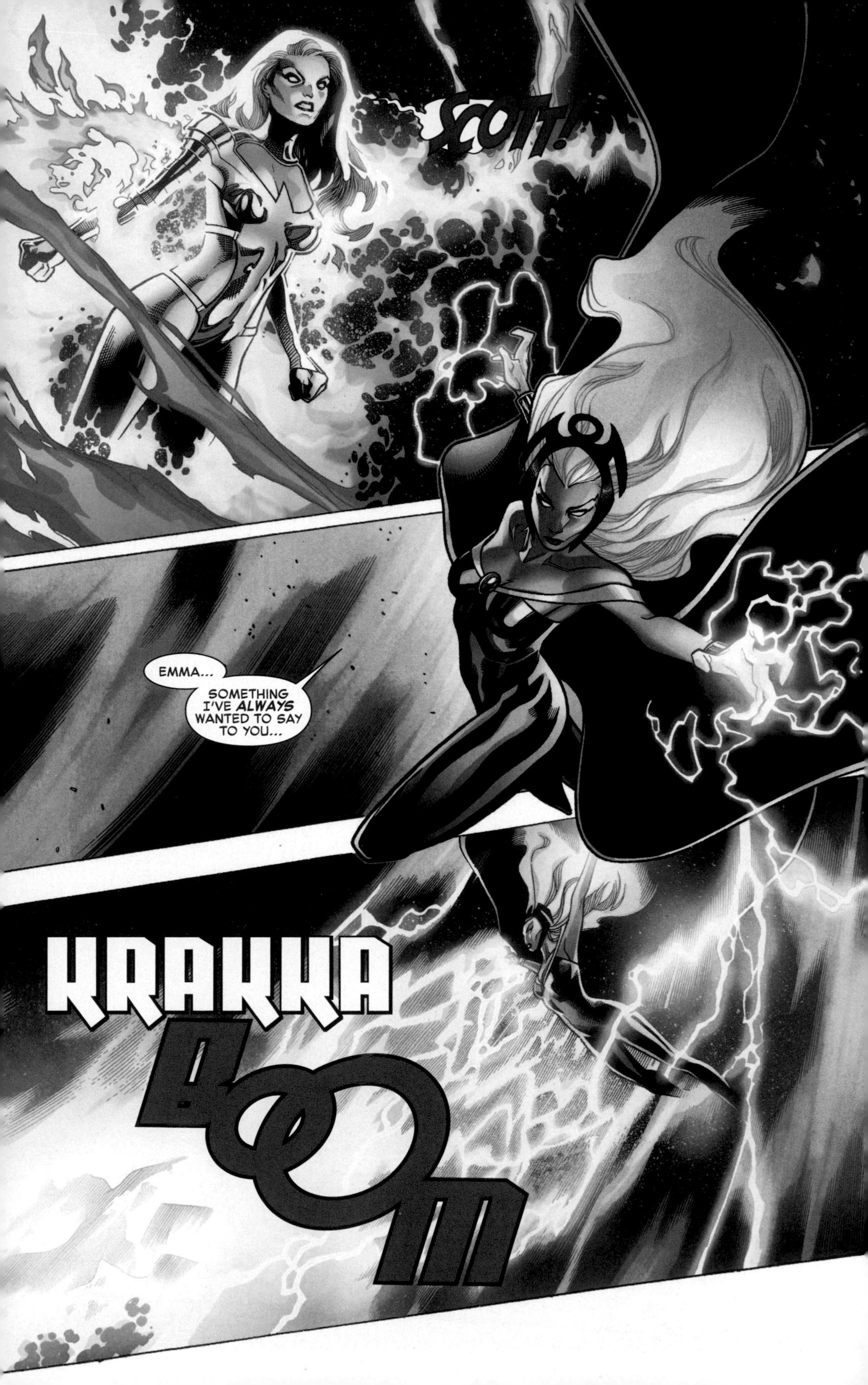
SCOTT!
EMMA...
SOMETHING I'VE ALWAYS WANTED TO SAY TO YOU...
KRAKKA
BOOM

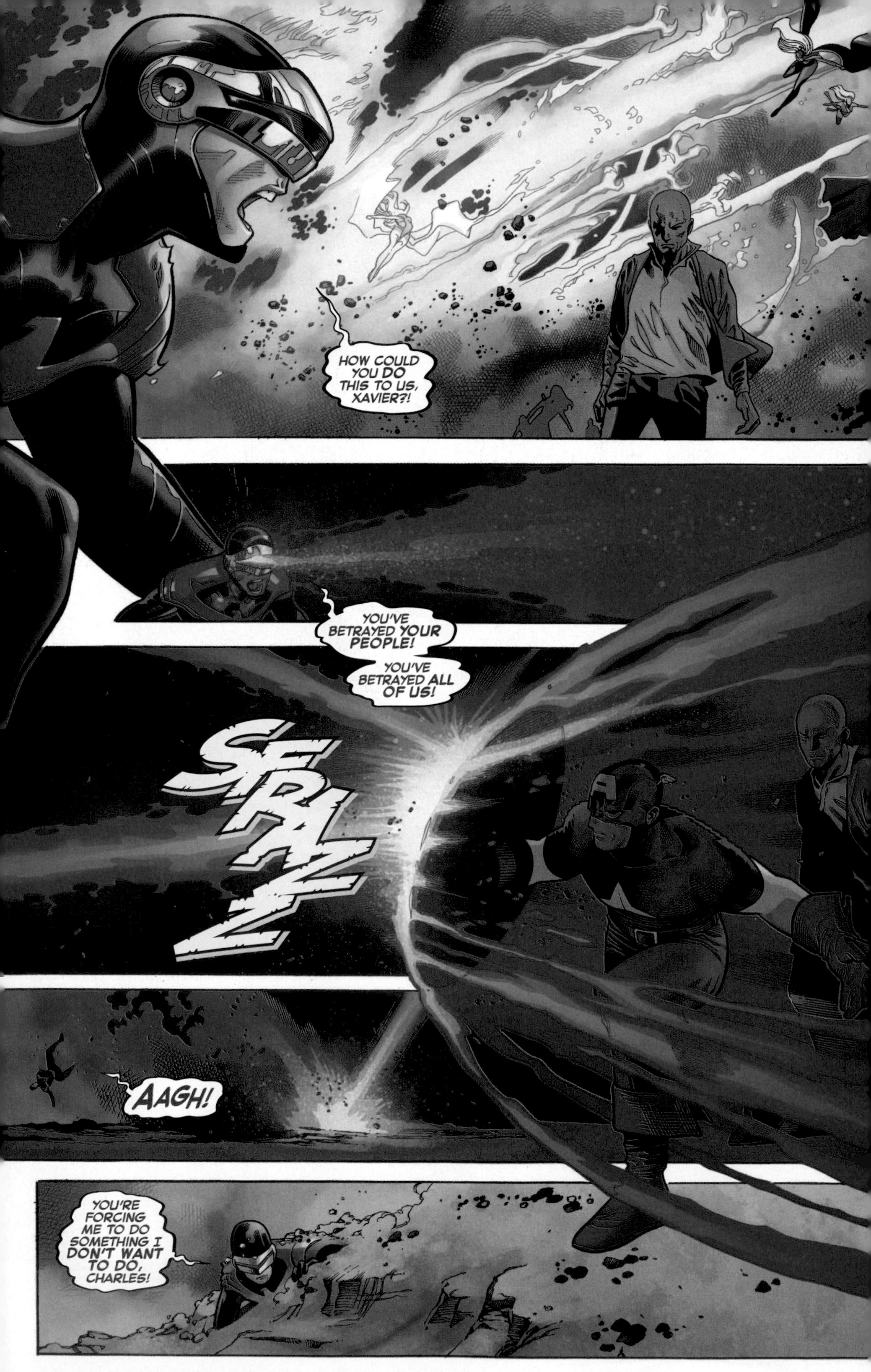
HOW COULD YOU DO THIS TO US, XAVIER?!
YOU'VE BETRAYED YOUR PEOPLE!
YOU'VE BETRAYED ALL OF US!
SFZZZ
AAGH!
YOU'RE FORCING ME TO DO SOMETHING I DON'T WANT TO DO, CHARLES!

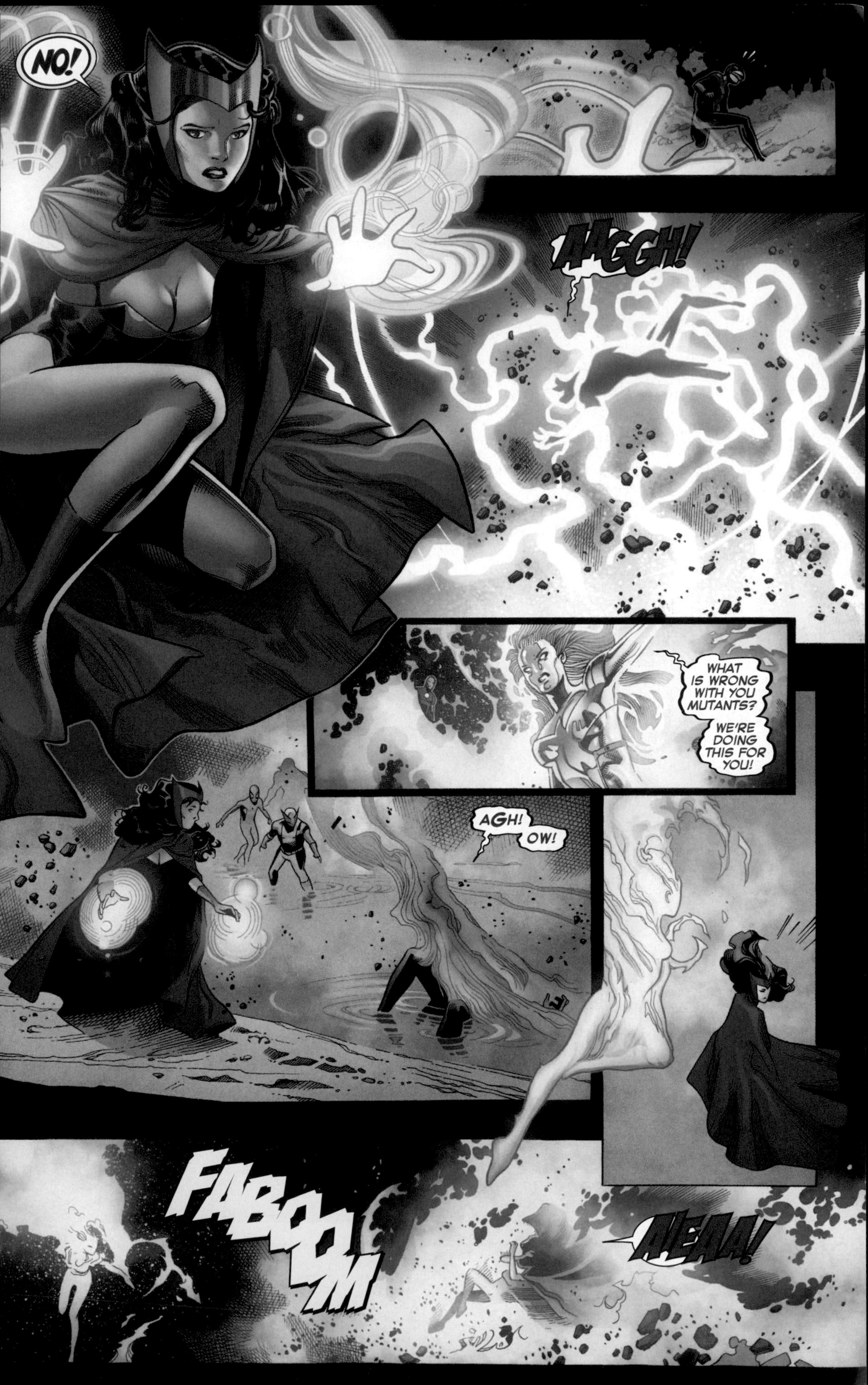
NO!
AAGGH!
WHAT IS WRONG WITH YOU MUTANTS?
WE'RE DOING THIS FOR YOU!
AGH!
OW!
FABOOM
AIEAA!

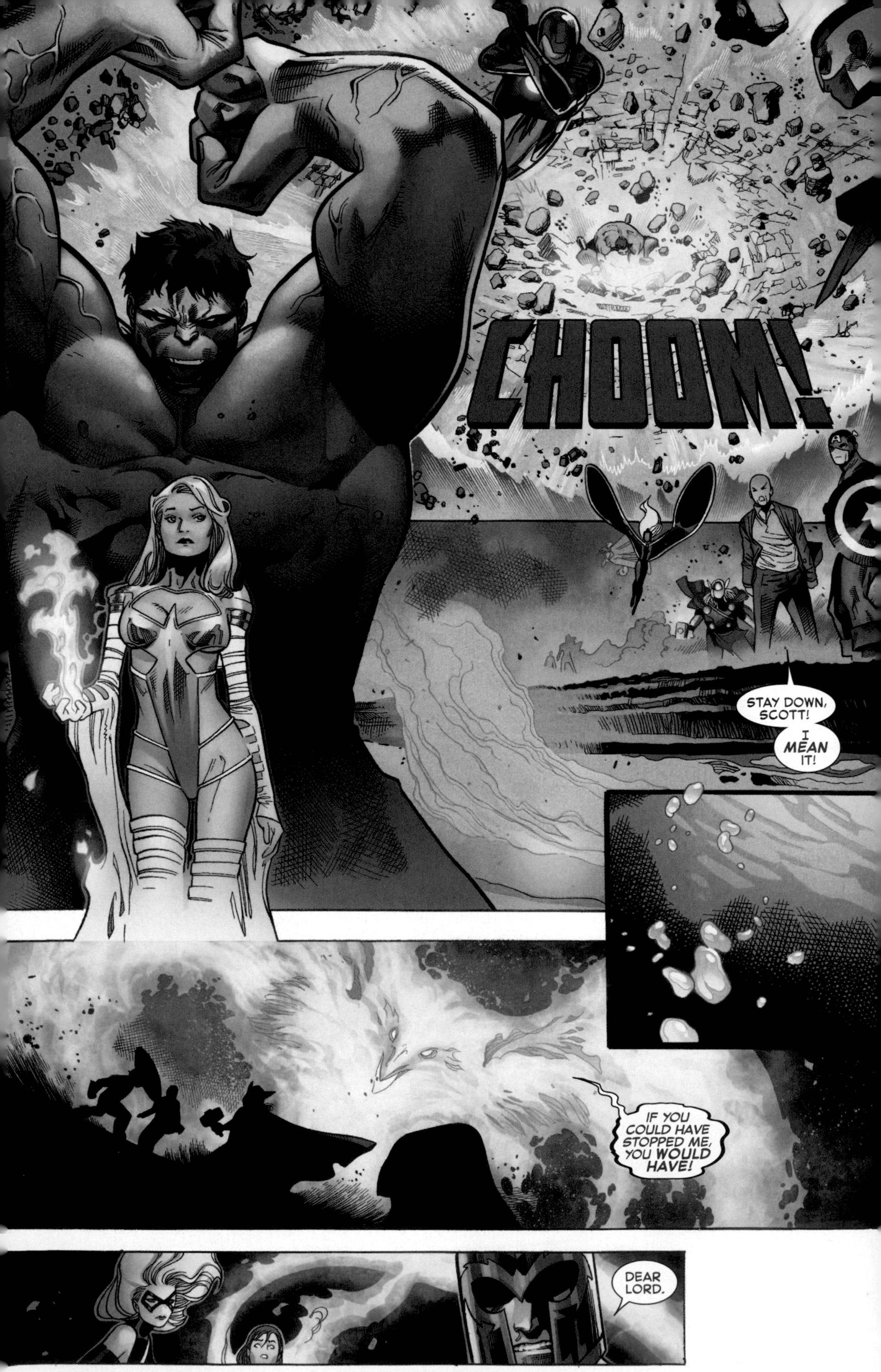
CHOOM!
STAY DOWN, SCOTT!
I MEAN IT!
IF YOU COULD HAVE STOPPED ME, YOU WOULD HAVE!
DEAR LORD.

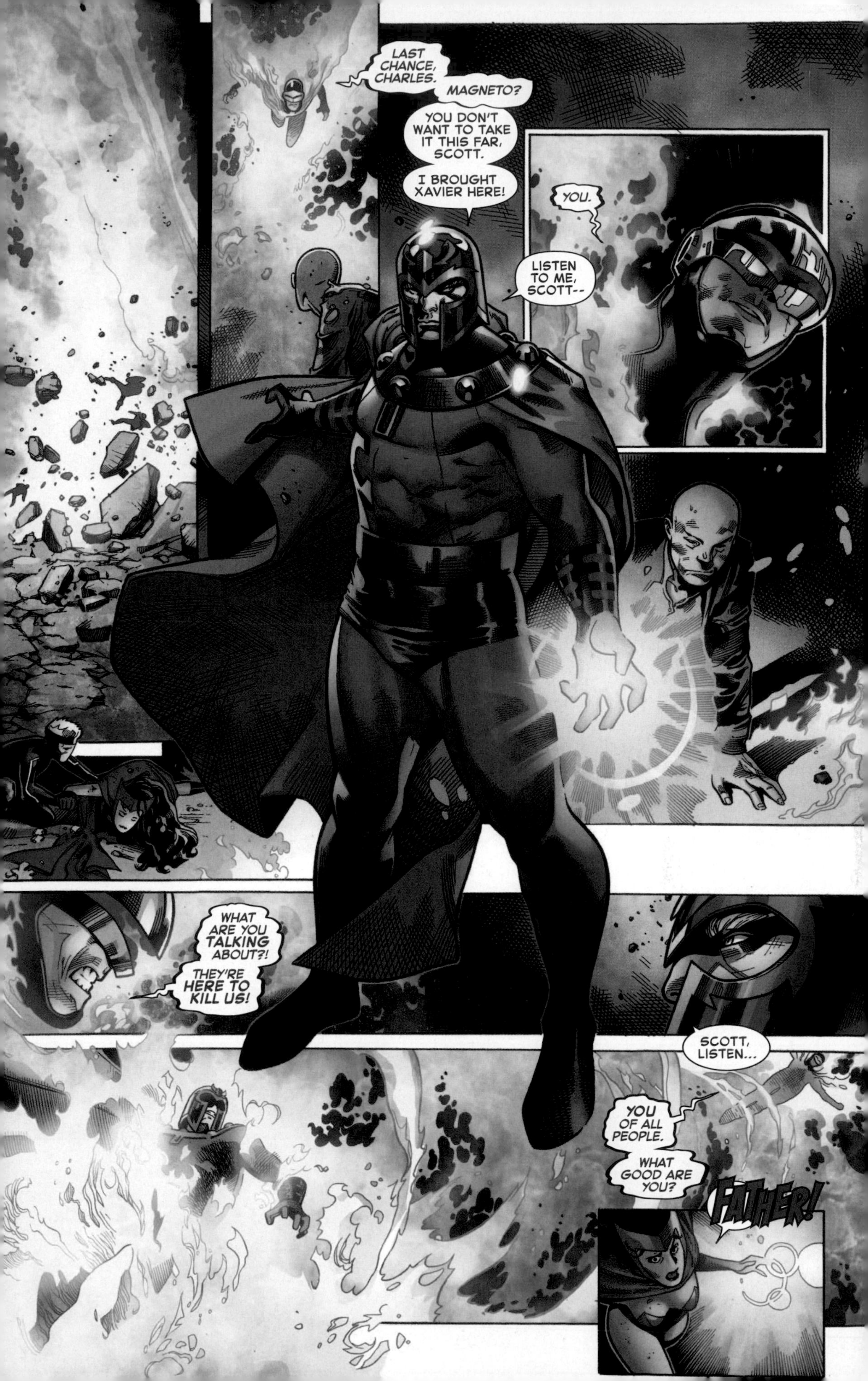
LAST CHANCE, CHARLES.
MAGNETO?
YOU DON'T WANT TO TAKE IT THIS FAR, SCOTT.
I BROUGHT XAVIER HERE!
YOU.
LISTEN TO ME, SCOTT--
WHAT ARE YOU TALKING ABOUT?!
THEY'RE HERE TO KILL US!
SCOTT, LISTEN...
YOU OF ALL PEOPLE.
WHAT GOOD ARE YOU?
FATHER!

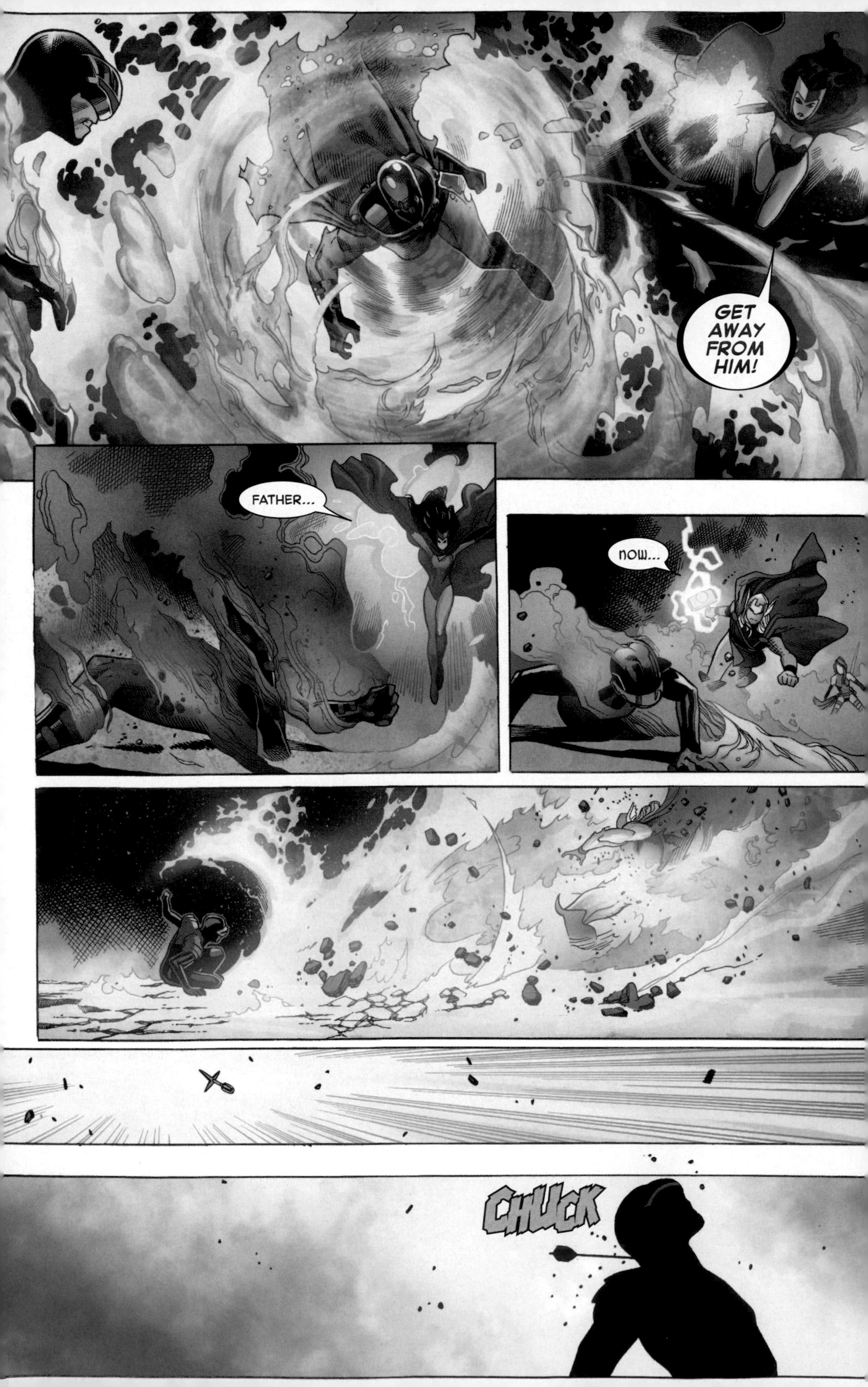
GET AWAY FROM HIM!
FATHER...
NOW...
CHUCK

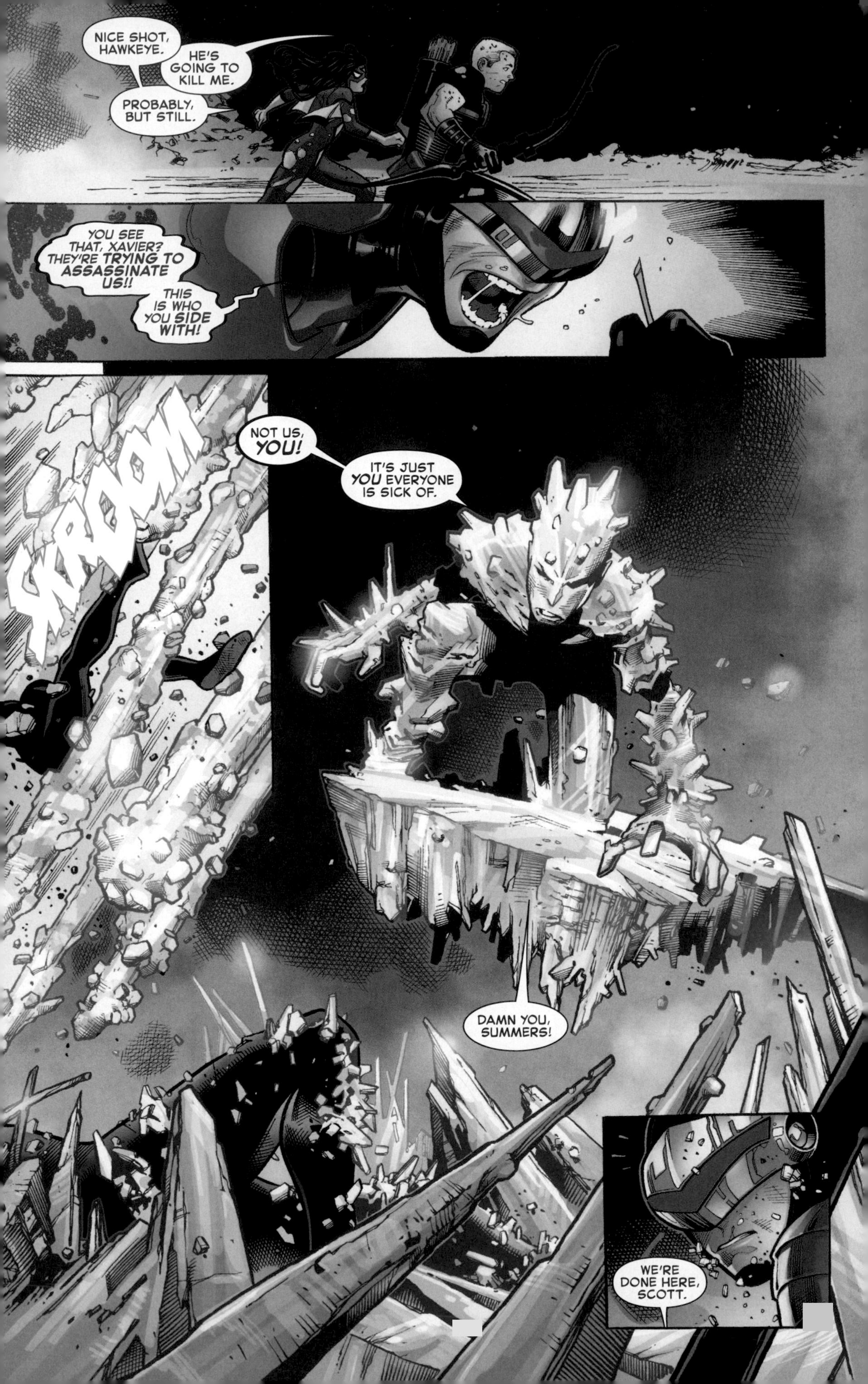
NICE SHOT, HAWKEYE.
HE'S GOING TO KILL ME.
PROBABLY, BUT STILL.
YOU SEE THAT, XAVIER? THEY'RE TRYING TO ASSASSINATE US!!
THIS IS WHO YOU SIDE WITH!
SKROOM
NOT US, YOU!
IT'S JUST YOU EVERYONE IS SICK OF.
DAMN YOU, SUMMERS!
WE'RE DONE HERE, SCOTT.

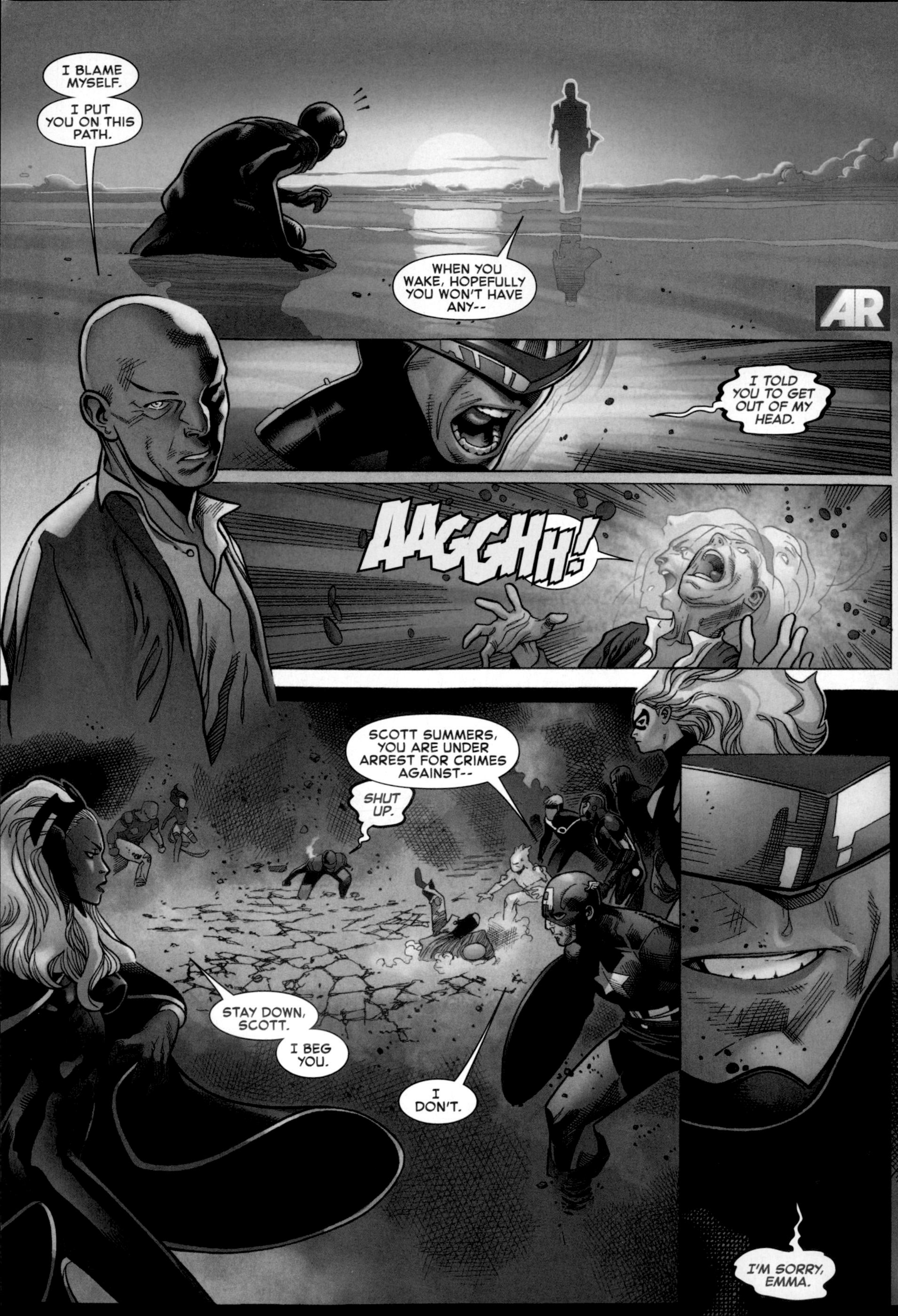

I BLAME MYSELF.
I PUT YOU ON THIS PATH.
WHEN YOU WAKE, HOPEFULLY YOU WON'T HAVE ANY--
AR
I TOLD YOU TO GET OUT OF MY HEAD.
AAGGHH!
SCOTT SUMMERS, YOU ARE UNDER ARREST FOR CRIMES AGAINST--
SHUT UP.
STAY DOWN, SCOTT.
I BEG YOU.
I DON'T.
I'M SORRY, EMMA.

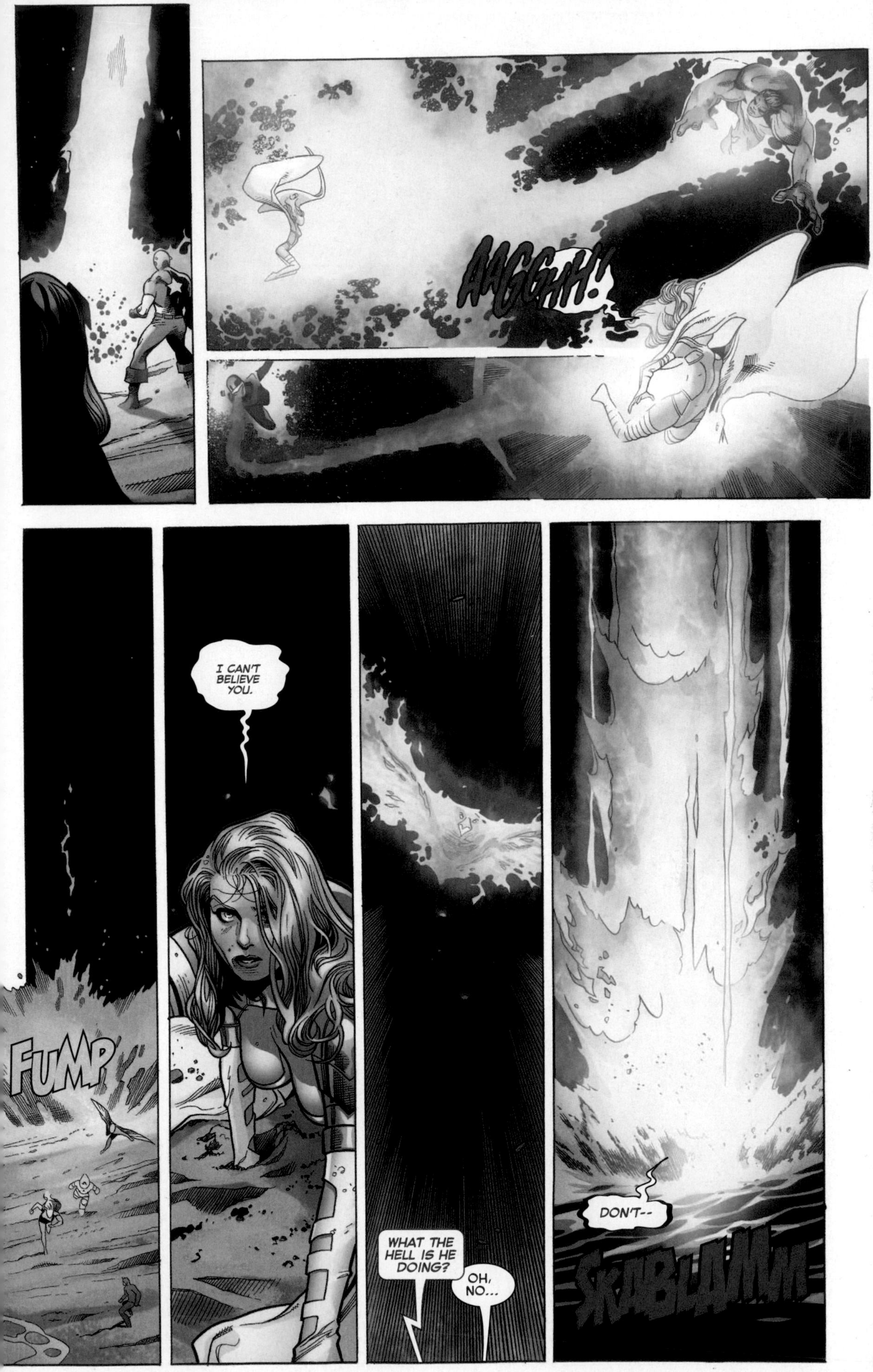
AAGGHH!
FUMP
I CAN'T BELIEVE YOU.
WHAT THE HELL IS HE DOING?
OH, NO...
DON'T--
SKABLAMM

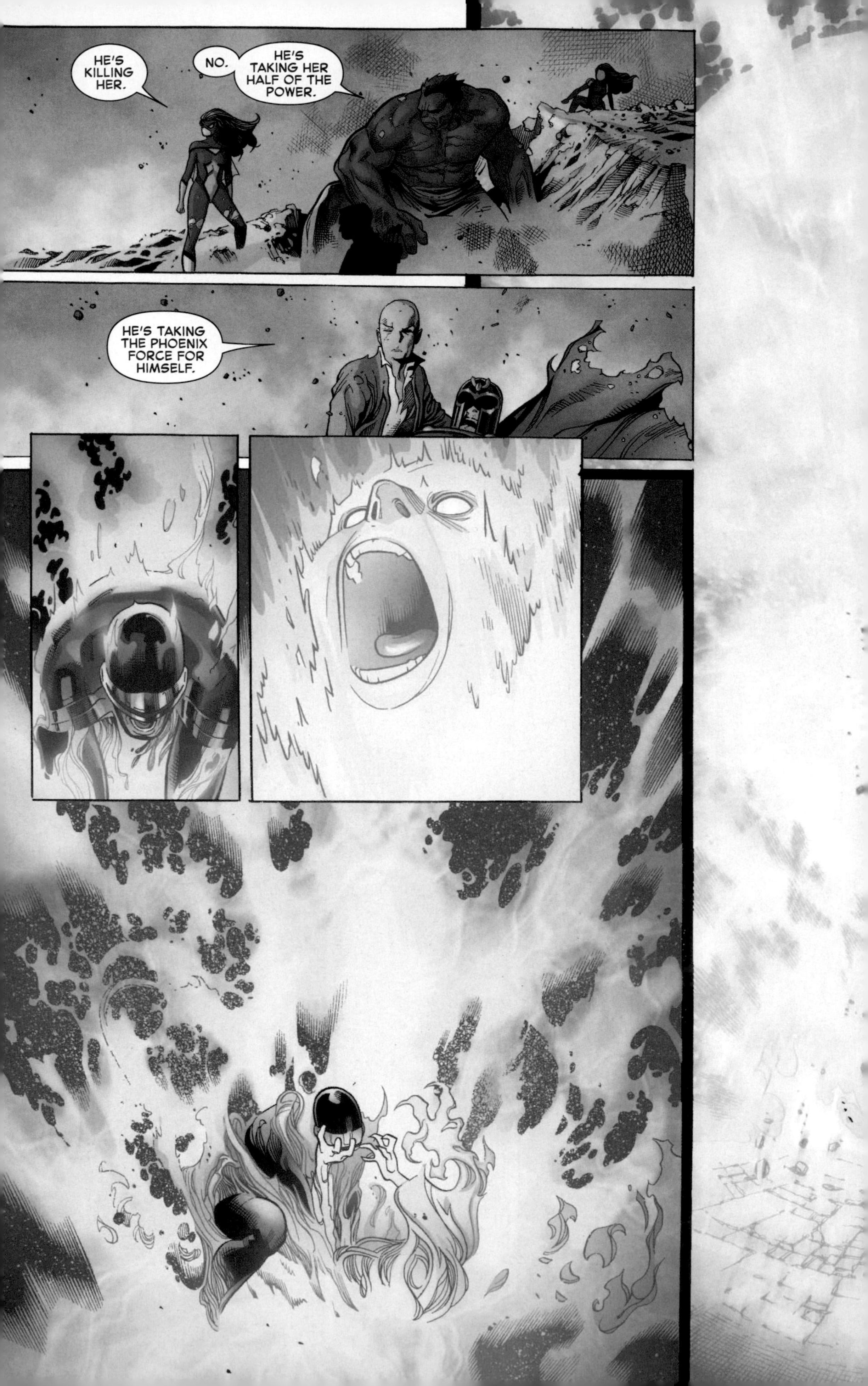
HE'S KILLING HER.
NO.
HE'S TAKING HER HALF OF THE POWER.
HE'S TAKING THE PHOENIX FORCE FOR HIMSELF.

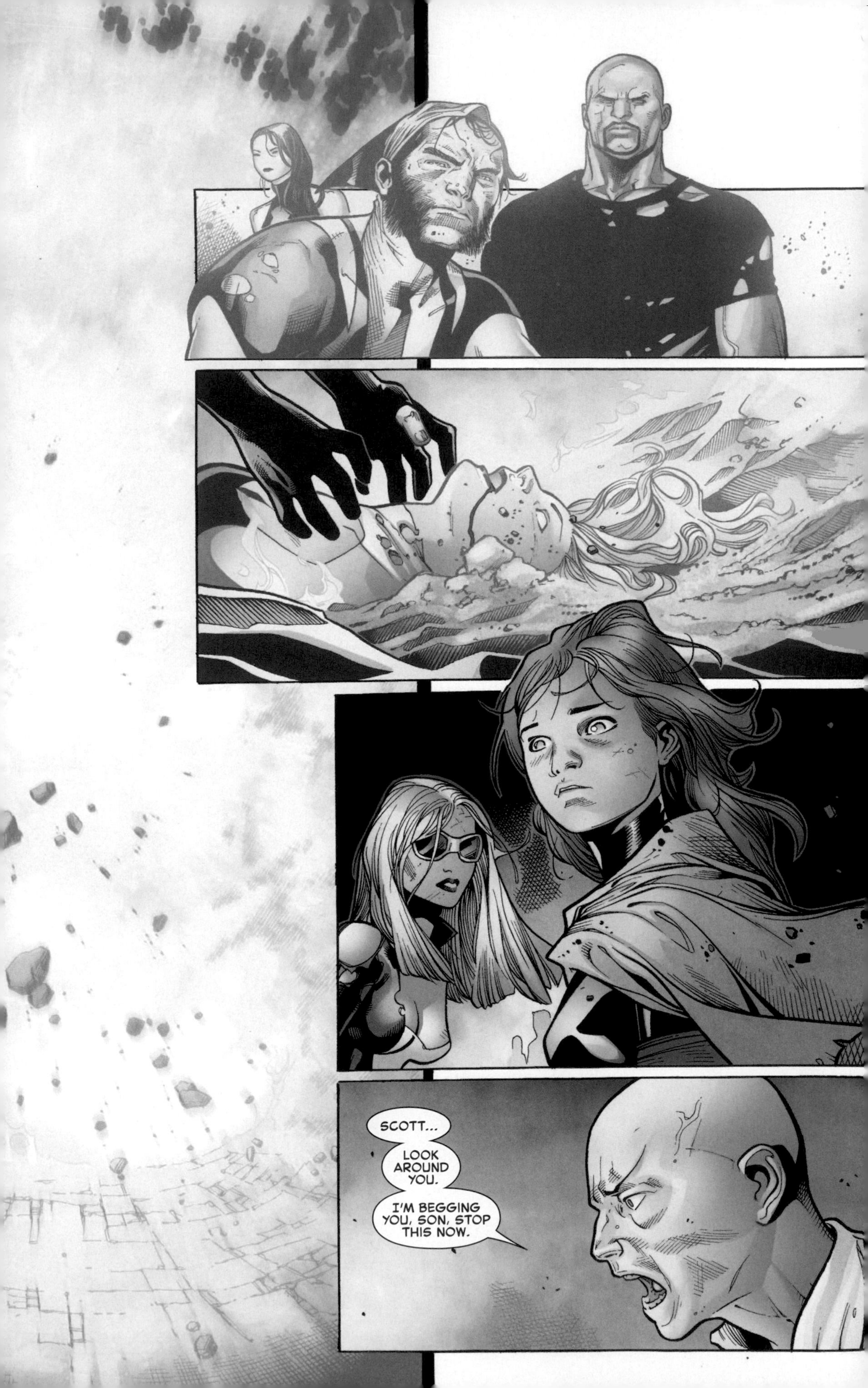
SCOTT...
LOOK AROUND YOU.
I'M BEGGING YOU, SON, STOP THIS NOW.

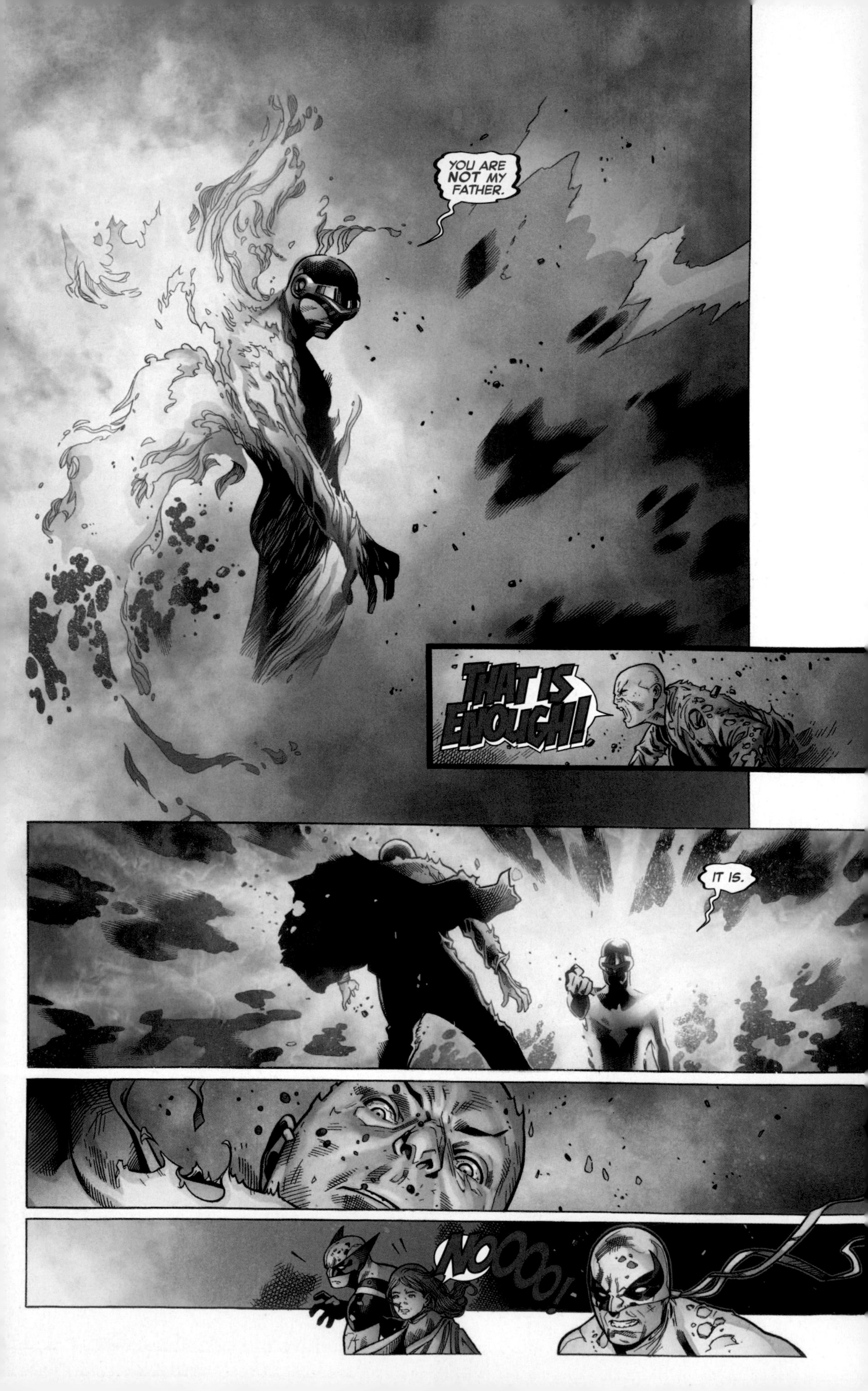
YOU ARE NOT MY FATHER.
THAT IS ENOUGH!
IT IS.
NOOOO!

AR

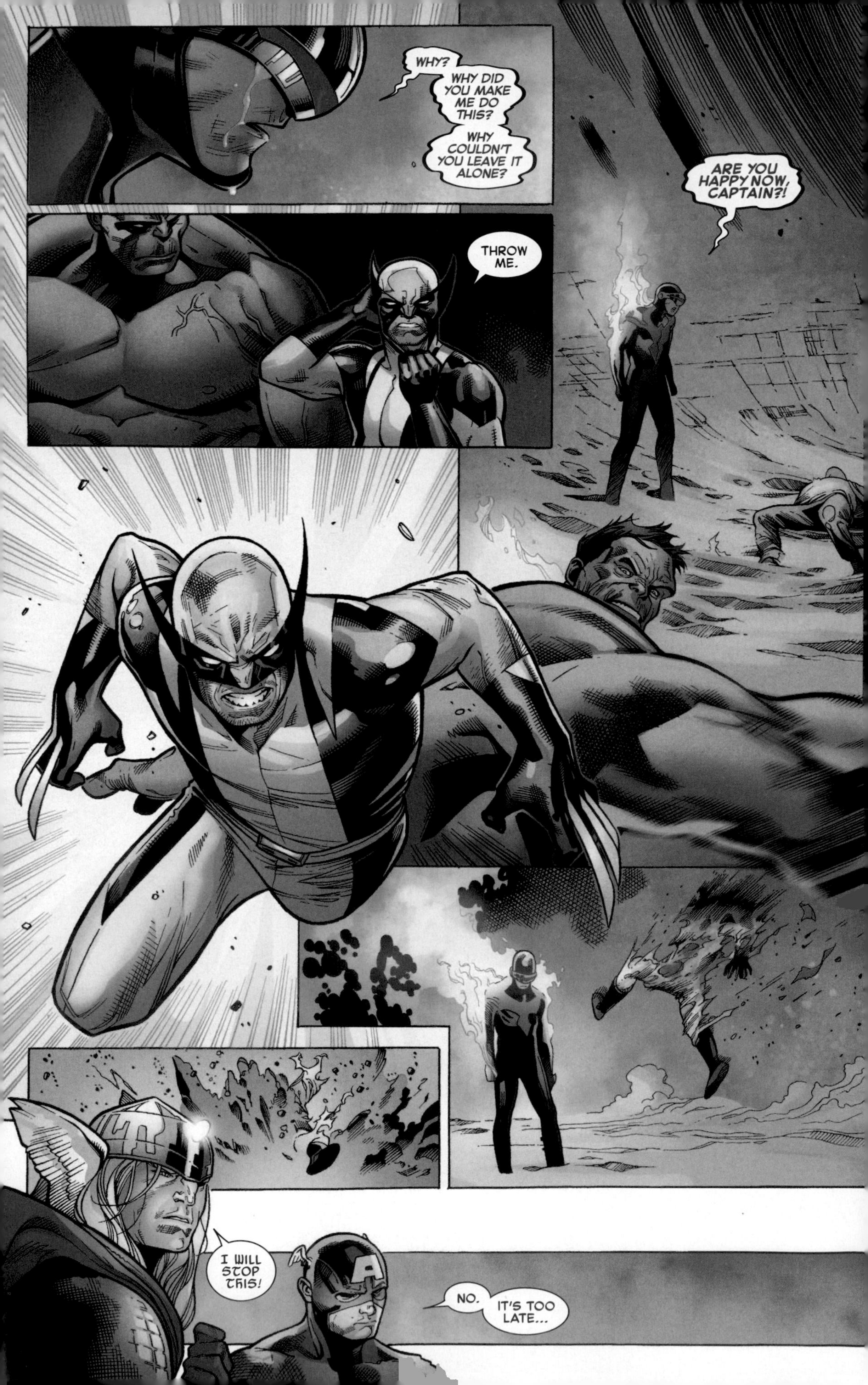
WHY?
WHY DID YOU MAKE ME DO THIS?
WHY COULDN'T YOU LEAVE IT ALONE?
ARE YOU HAPPY NOW, CAPTAIN?!
THROW ME.
I WILL STOP THIS!
NO.
IT'S TOO LATE...

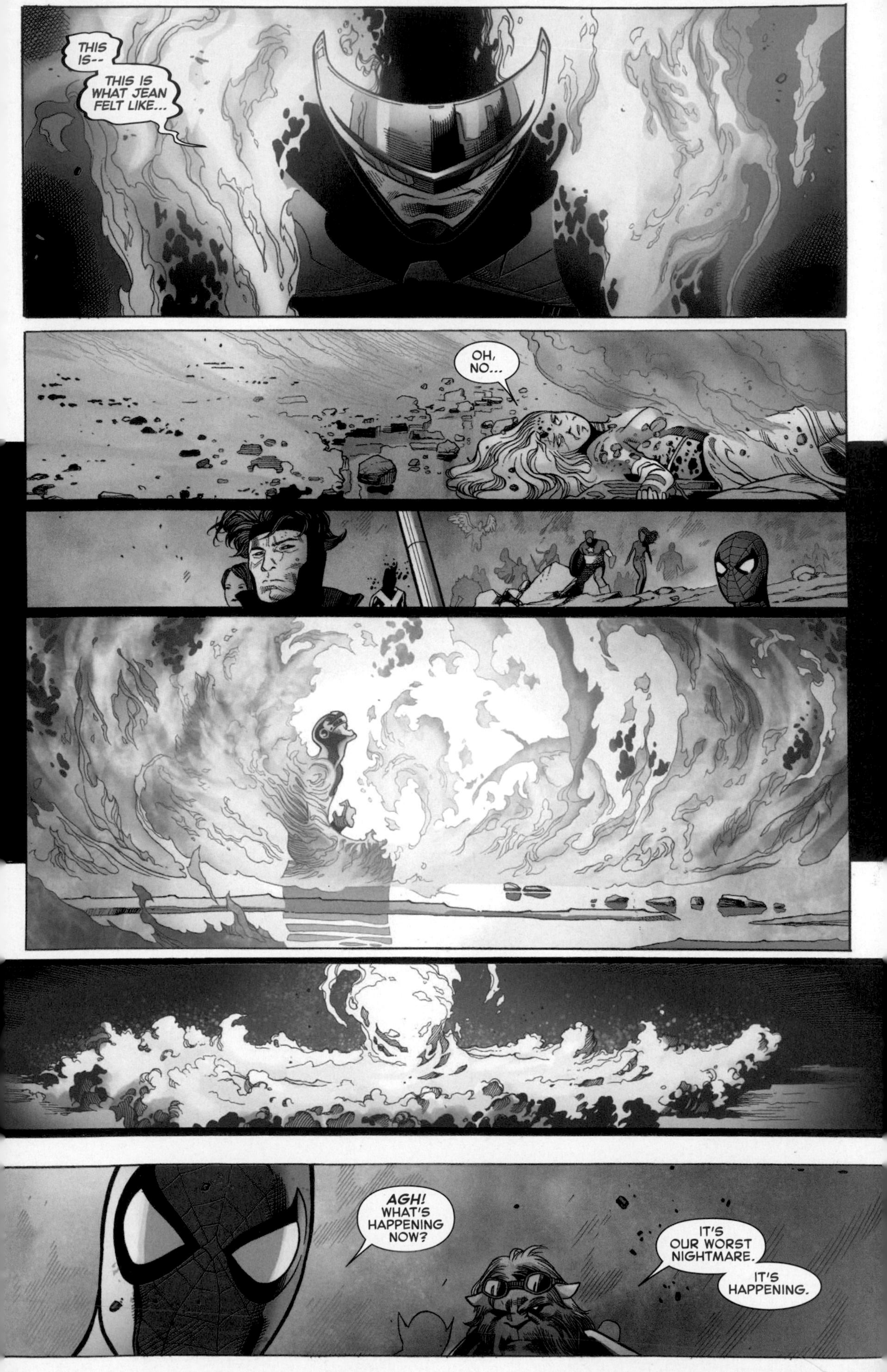
THIS IS--
THIS IS WHAT JEAN FELT LIKE...
OH, NO...
AGH! WHAT'S HAPPENING NOW?
IT'S OUR WORST NIGHTMARE.
IT'S HAPPENING.

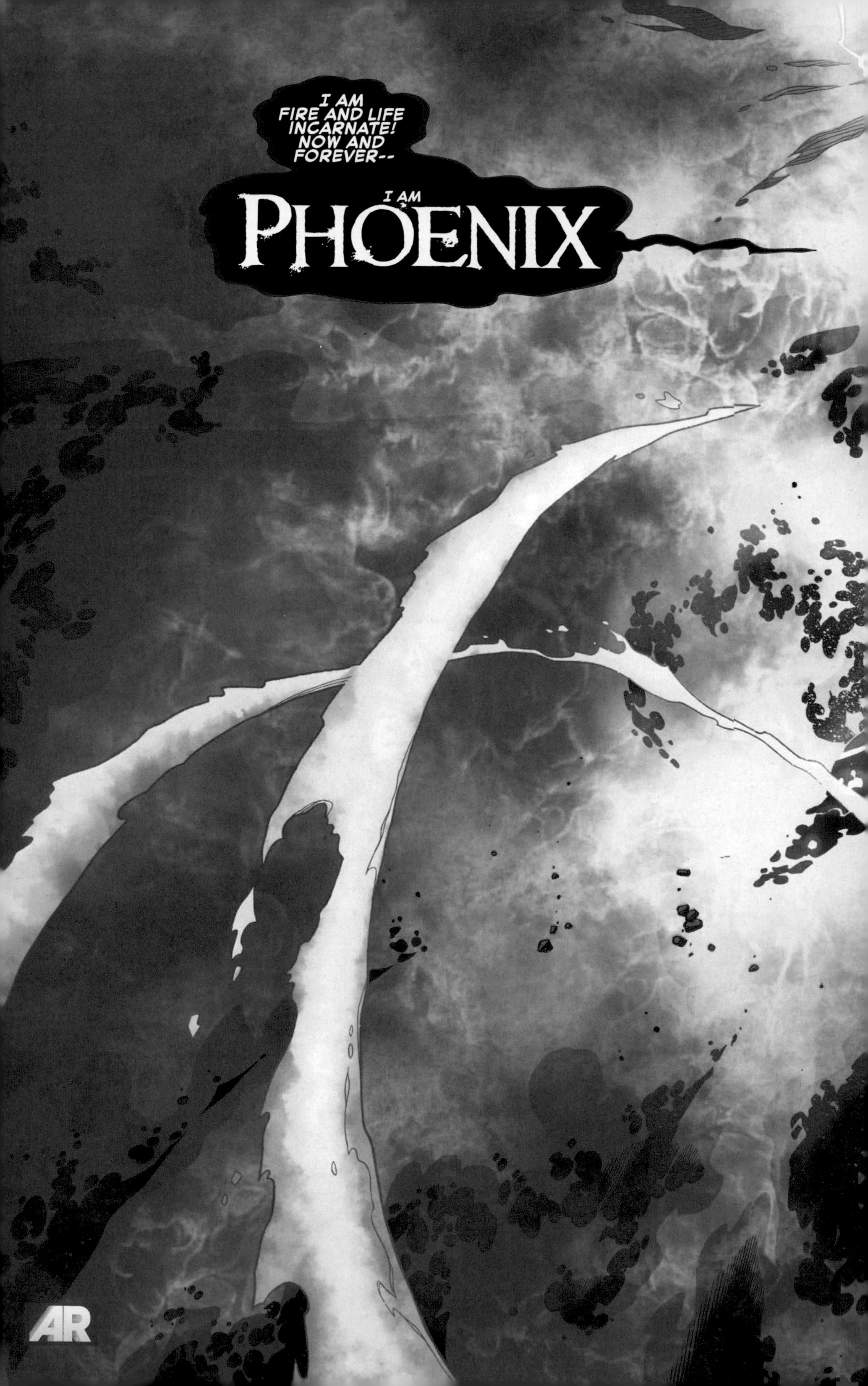
I AM FIRE AND LIFE INCARNATE! NOW AND FOREVER--
I AM PHOENIX

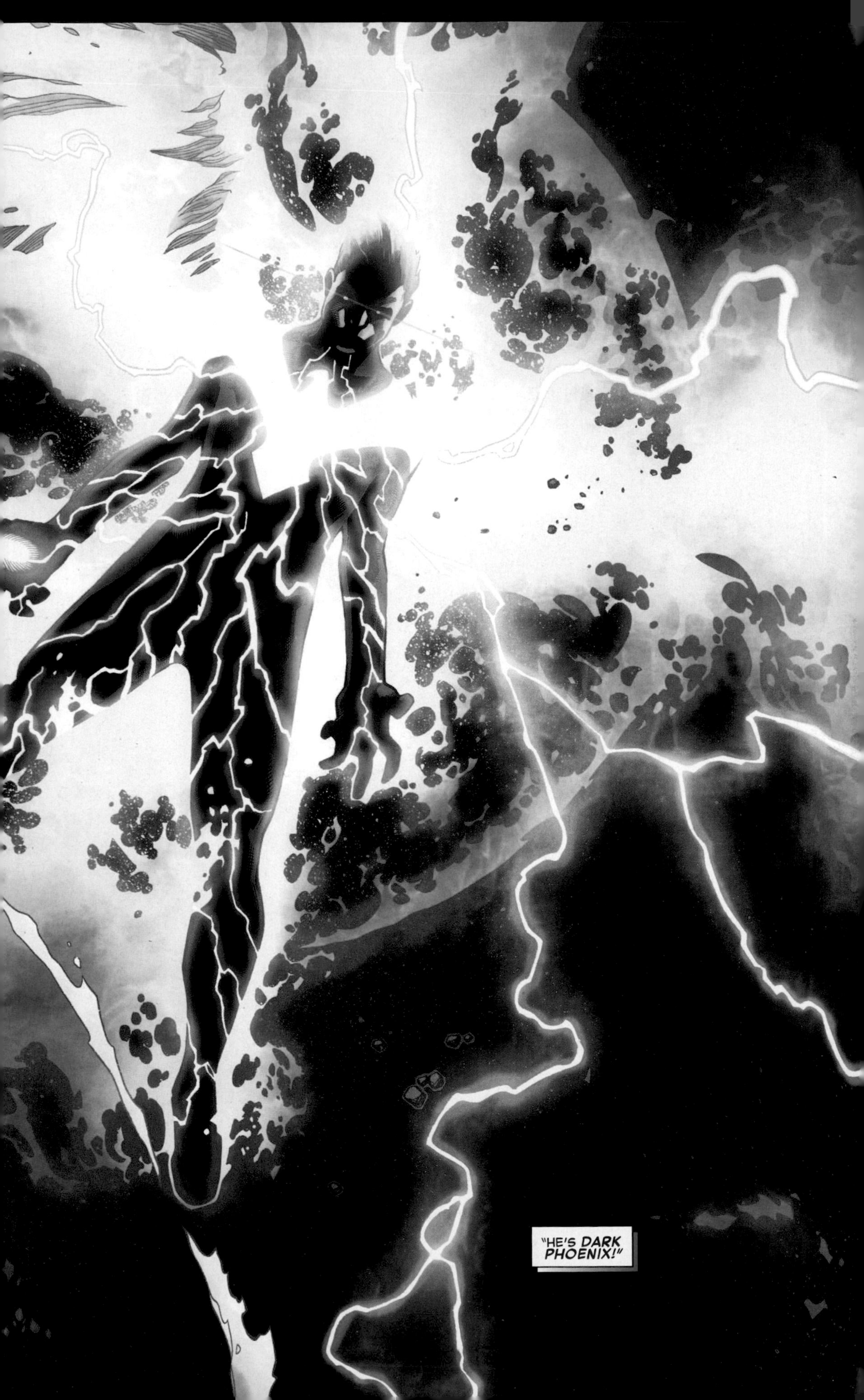
"HE'S DARK PHOENIX!"

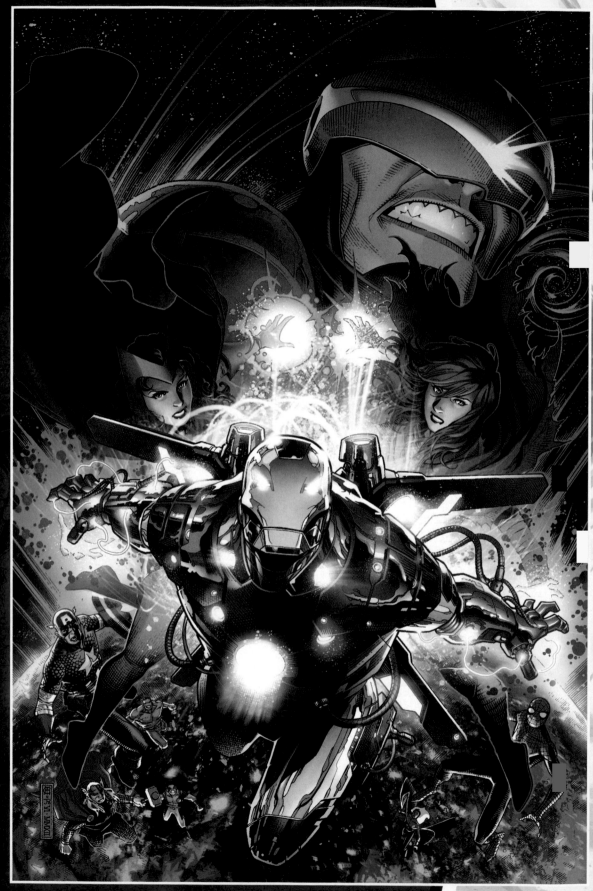

ROUND 12

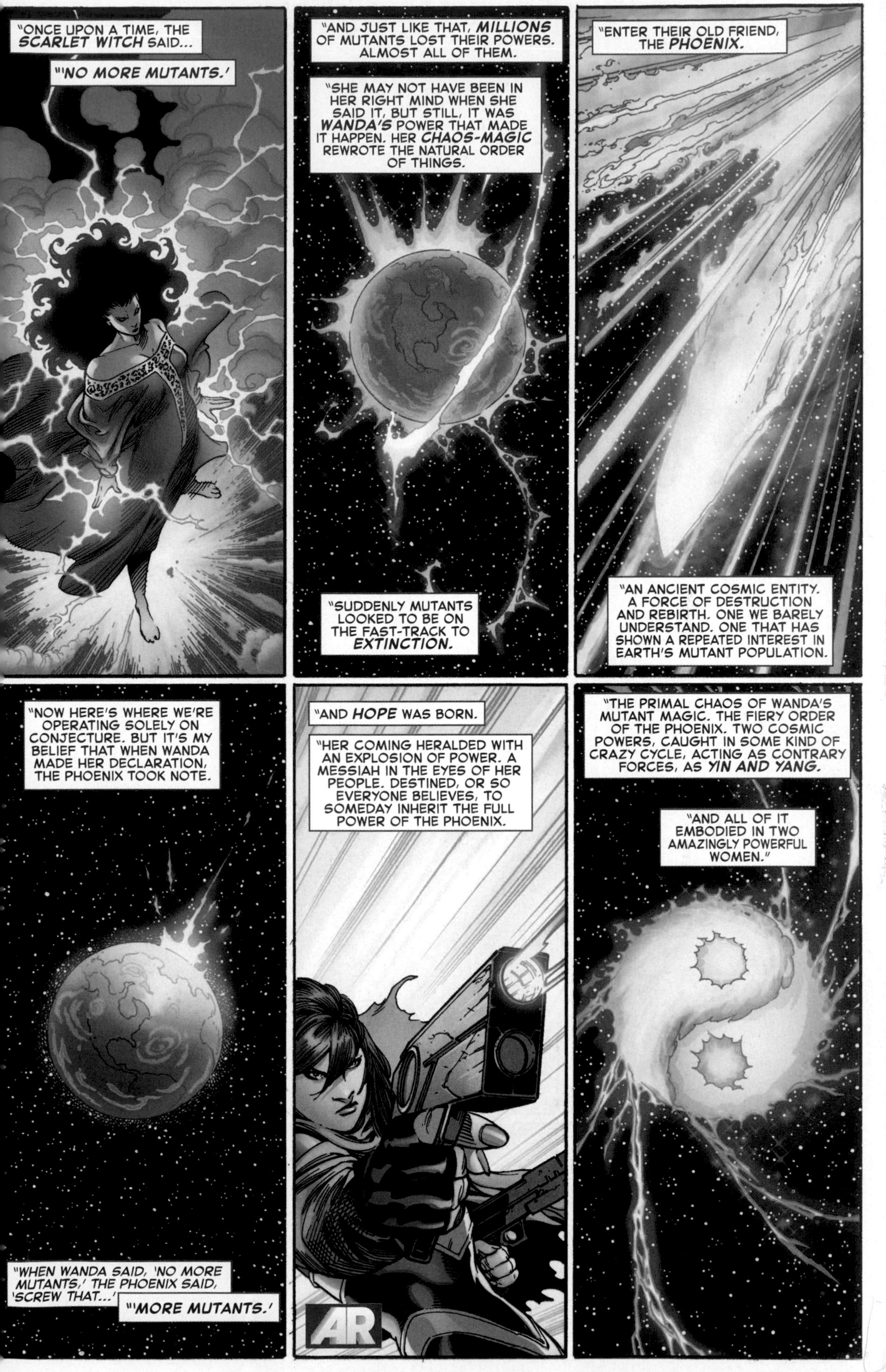
"ONCE UPON A TIME, THE SCARLET WITCH SAID...
"'NO MORE MUTANTS.'
"AND JUST LIKE THAT, MILLIONS OF MUTANTS LOST THEIR POWERS. ALMOST ALL OF THEM.
"SHE MAY NOT HAVE BEEN IN HER RIGHT MIND WHEN SHE SAID IT, BUT STILL, IT WAS WANDA'S POWER THAT MADE IT HAPPEN. HER CHAOS-MAGIC REWROTE THE NATURAL ORDER OF THINGS.
"SUDDENLY MUTANTS LOOKED TO BE ON THE FAST-TRACK TO EXTINCTION.
"ENTER THEIR OLD FRIEND, THE PHOENIX.
"AN ANCIENT COSMIC ENTITY. A FORCE OF DESTRUCTION AND REBIRTH. ONE WE BARELY UNDERSTAND. ONE THAT HAS SHOWN A REPEATED INTEREST IN EARTH'S MUTANT POPULATION.
"NOW HERE'S WHERE WE'RE OPERATING SOLELY ON CONJECTURE. BUT IT'S MY BELIEF THAT WHEN WANDA MADE HER DECLARATION, THE PHOENIX TOOK NOTE.
"WHEN WANDA SAID, 'NO MORE MUTANTS,' THE PHOENIX SAID, 'SCREW THAT...'
"'MORE MUTANTS.'
"AND HOPE WAS BORN.
"HER COMING HERALDED WITH AN EXPLOSION OF POWER. A MESSIAH IN THE EYES OF HER PEOPLE. DESTINED, OR SO EVERYONE BELIEVES, TO SOMEDAY INHERIT THE FULL POWER OF THE PHOENIX.
AR
"THE PRIMAL CHAOS OF WANDA'S MUTANT MAGIC. THE FIERY ORDER OF THE PHOENIX. TWO COSMIC POWERS, CAUGHT IN SOME KIND OF CRAZY CYCLE, ACTING AS CONTRARY FORCES, AS YIN AND YANG.
"AND ALL OF IT EMBODIED IN TWO AMAZINGLY POWERFUL WOMEN."

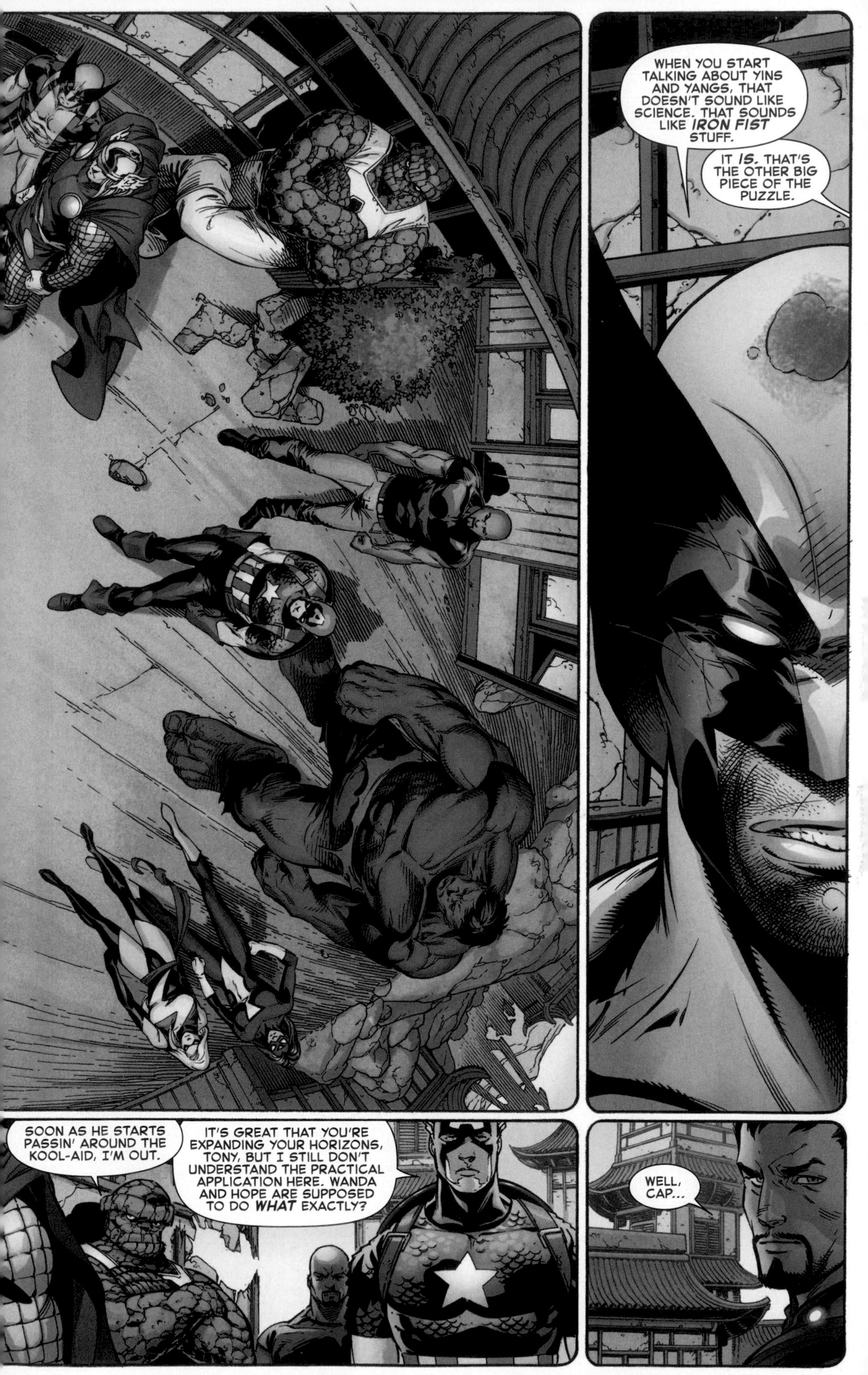
WHEN YOU START TALKING ABOUT YINS AND YANGS, THAT DOESN'T SOUND LIKE SCIENCE. THAT SOUNDS LIKE IRON FIST STUFF.
IT IS. THAT'S THE OTHER BIG PIECE OF THE PUZZLE.
SOON AS HE STARTS PASSIN' AROUND THE KOOL-AID, I'M OUT.
IT'S GREAT THAT YOU'RE EXPANDING YOUR HORIZONS, TONY, BUT I STILL DON'T UNDERSTAND THE PRACTICAL APPLICATION HERE. WANDA AND HOPE ARE SUPPOSED TO DO WHAT EXACTLY?
WELL, CAP...

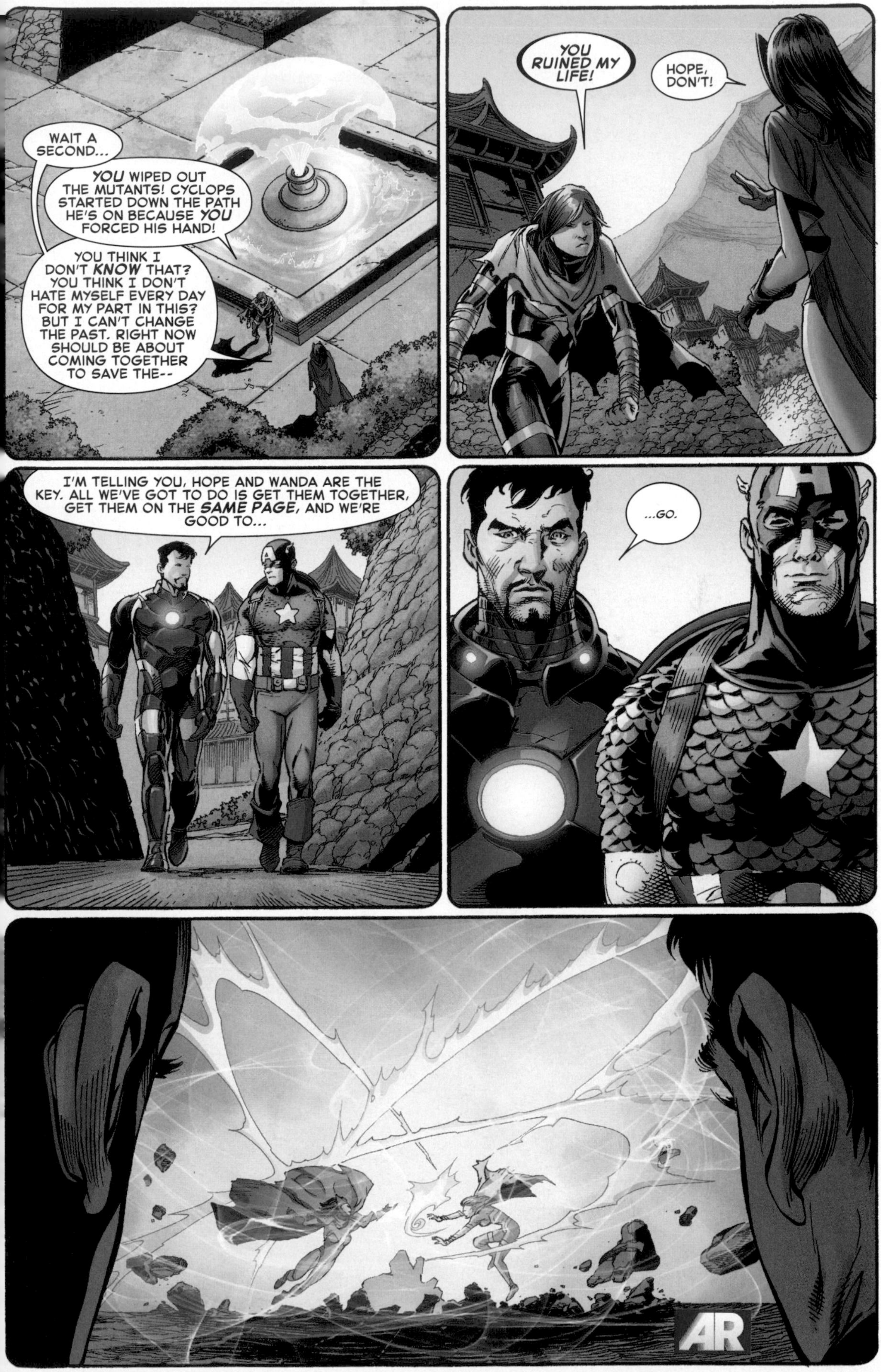
WAIT A SECOND...
YOU WIPED OUT THE MUTANTS! CYCLOPS STARTED DOWN THE PATH HE'S ON BECAUSE YOU FORCED HIS HAND!
YOU THINK I DON'T KNOW THAT? YOU THINK I DON'T HATE MYSELF EVERY DAY FOR MY PART IN THIS? BUT I CAN'T CHANGE THE PAST. RIGHT NOW SHOULD BE ABOUT COMING TOGETHER TO SAVE THE--
YOU RUINED MY LIFE!
HOPE, DON'T!
I'M TELLING YOU, HOPE AND WANDA ARE THE KEY. ALL WE'VE GOT TO DO IS GET THEM TOGETHER, GET THEM ON THE SAME PAGE, AND WE'RE GOOD TO...
...GO.
AR

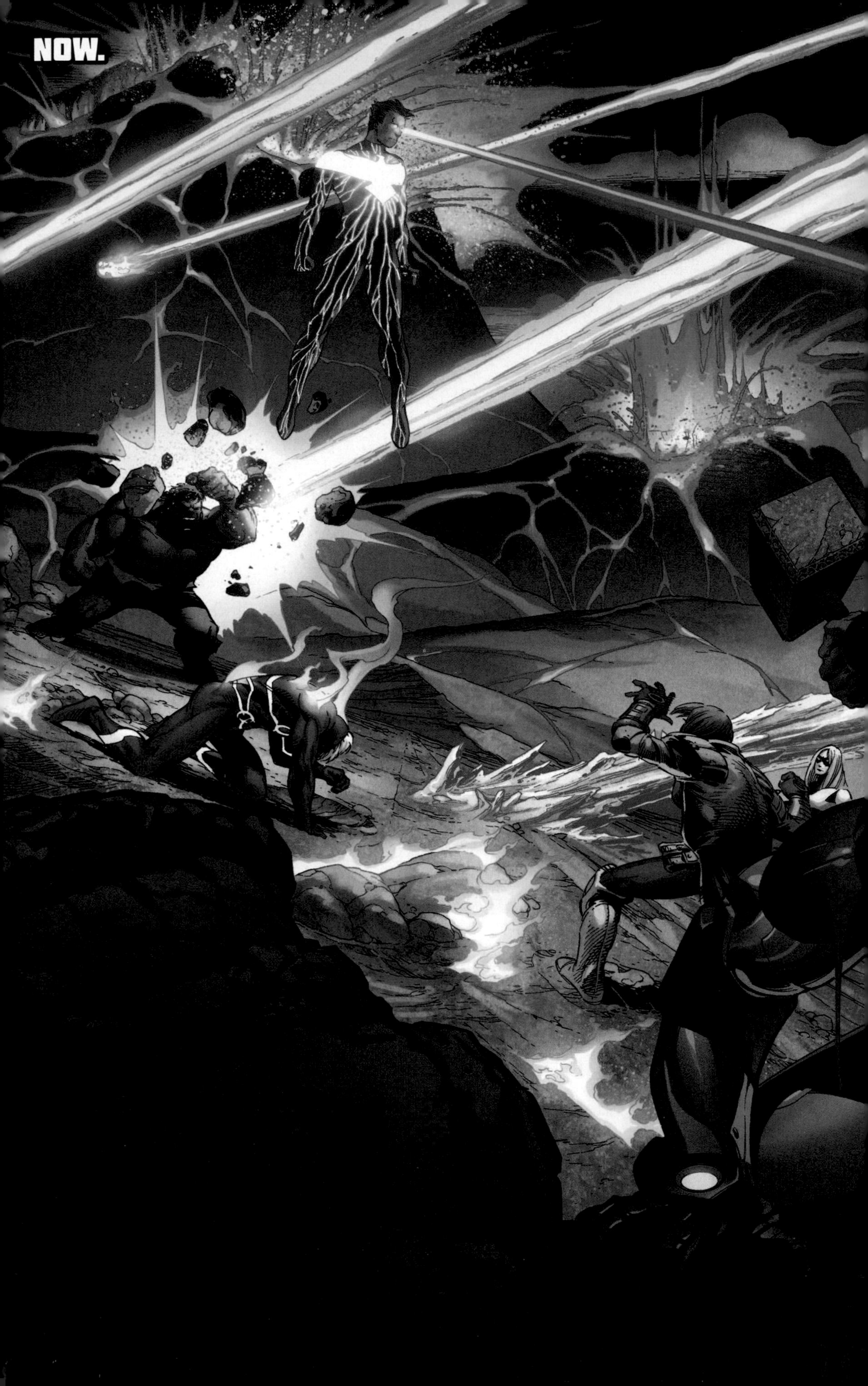
NOW.

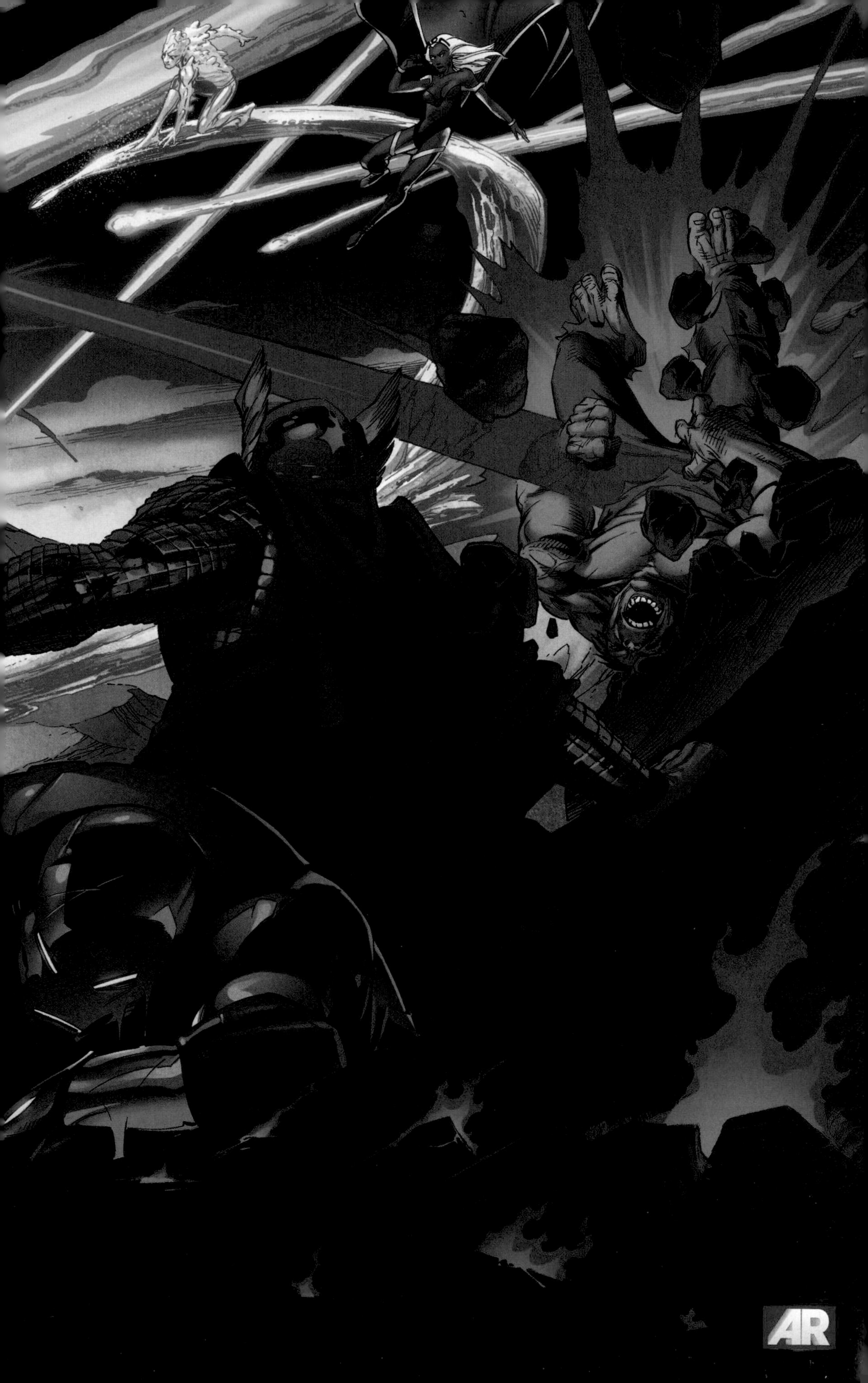

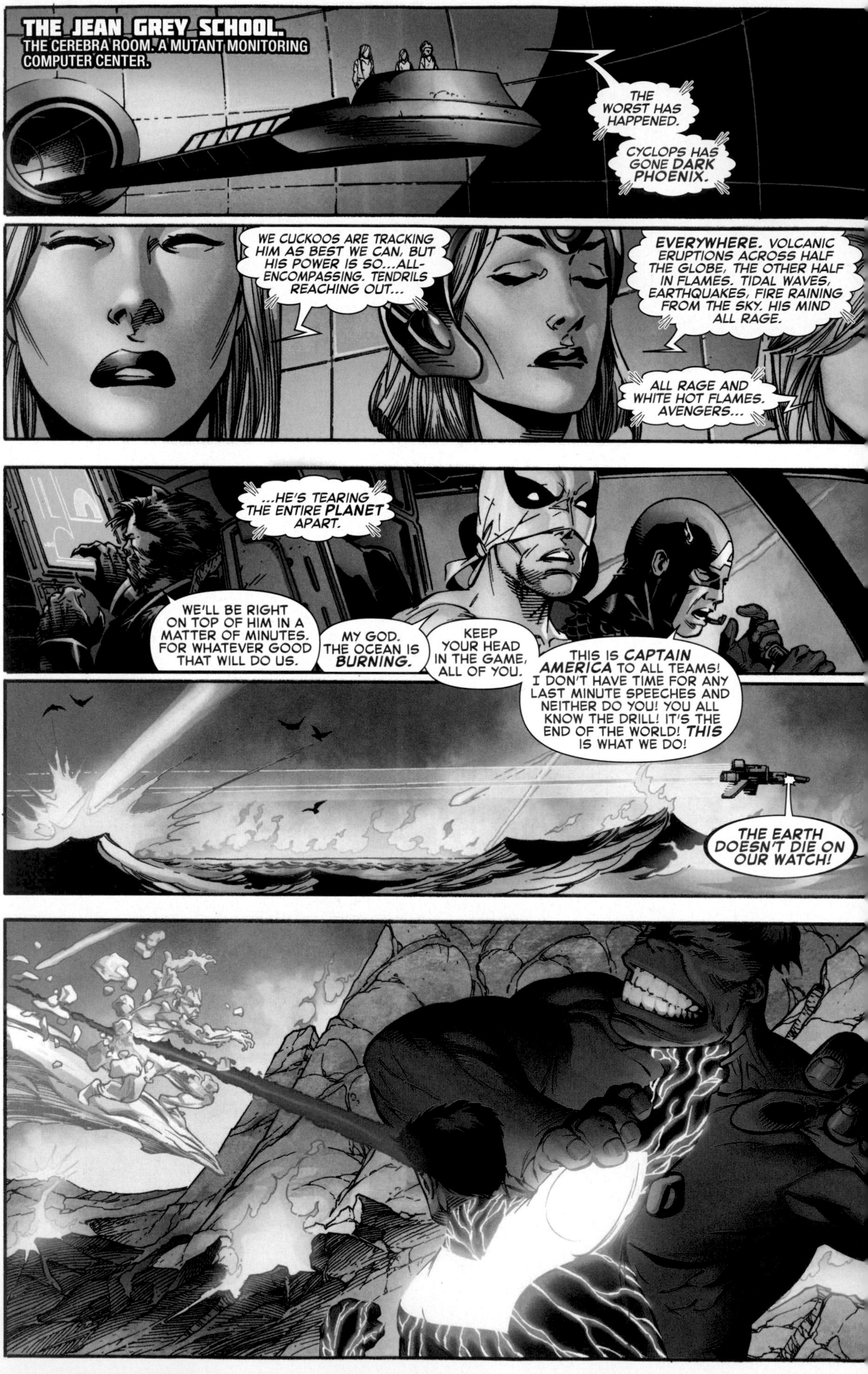
THE JEAN GREY SCHOOL.
THE CEREBRA ROOM. A MUTANT MONITORING COMPUTER CENTER.
THE WORST HAS HAPPENED.
CYCLOPS HAS GONE DARK PHOENIX.
WE CUCKOOS ARE TRACKING HIM AS BEST WE CAN, BUT HIS POWER IS SO...ALL-ENCOMPASSING. TENDRILS REACHING OUT...
EVERYWHERE. VOLCANIC ERUPTIONS ACROSS HALF THE GLOBE, THE OTHER HALF IN FLAMES. TIDAL WAVES, EARTHQUAKES, FIRE RAINING FROM THE SKY. HIS MIND ALL RAGE.
ALL RAGE AND WHITE HOT FLAMES. AVENGERS...
...HE'S TEARING THE ENTIRE PLANET APART.
WE'LL BE RIGHT ON TOP OF HIM IN A MATTER OF MINUTES. FOR WHATEVER GOOD THAT WILL DO US.
MY GOD. THE OCEAN IS BURNING.
KEEP YOUR HEAD IN THE GAME, ALL OF YOU.
THIS IS CAPTAIN AMERICA TO ALL TEAMS! I DON'T HAVE TIME FOR ANY LAST MINUTE SPEECHES AND NEITHER DO YOU! YOU ALL KNOW THE DRILL! IT'S THE END OF THE WORLD! THIS IS WHAT WE DO!
THE EARTH DOESN'T DIE ON OUR WATCH!

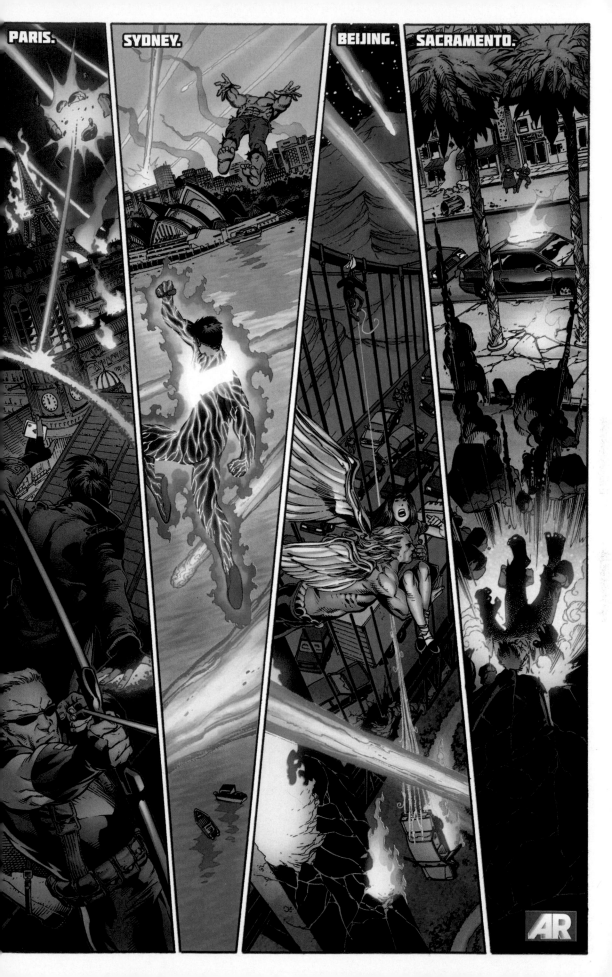

PARIS.

SYDNEY.

BEIJING.

SACRAMENTO.

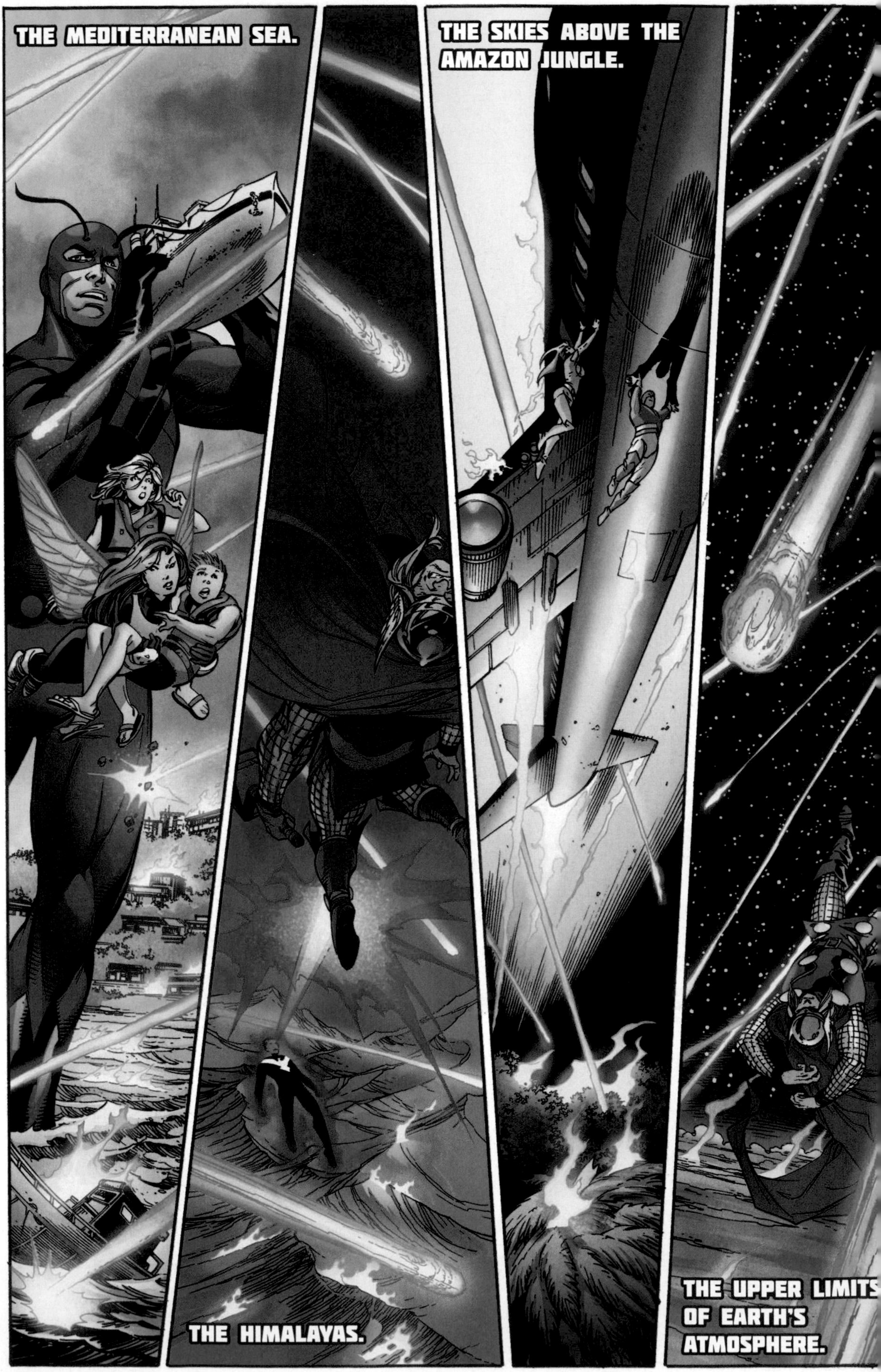
THE MEDITERRANEAN SEA.
THE HIMALAYAS.
THE SKIES ABOVE THE AMAZON JUNGLE.
THE UPPER LIMITS OF EARTH'S ATMOSPHERE.

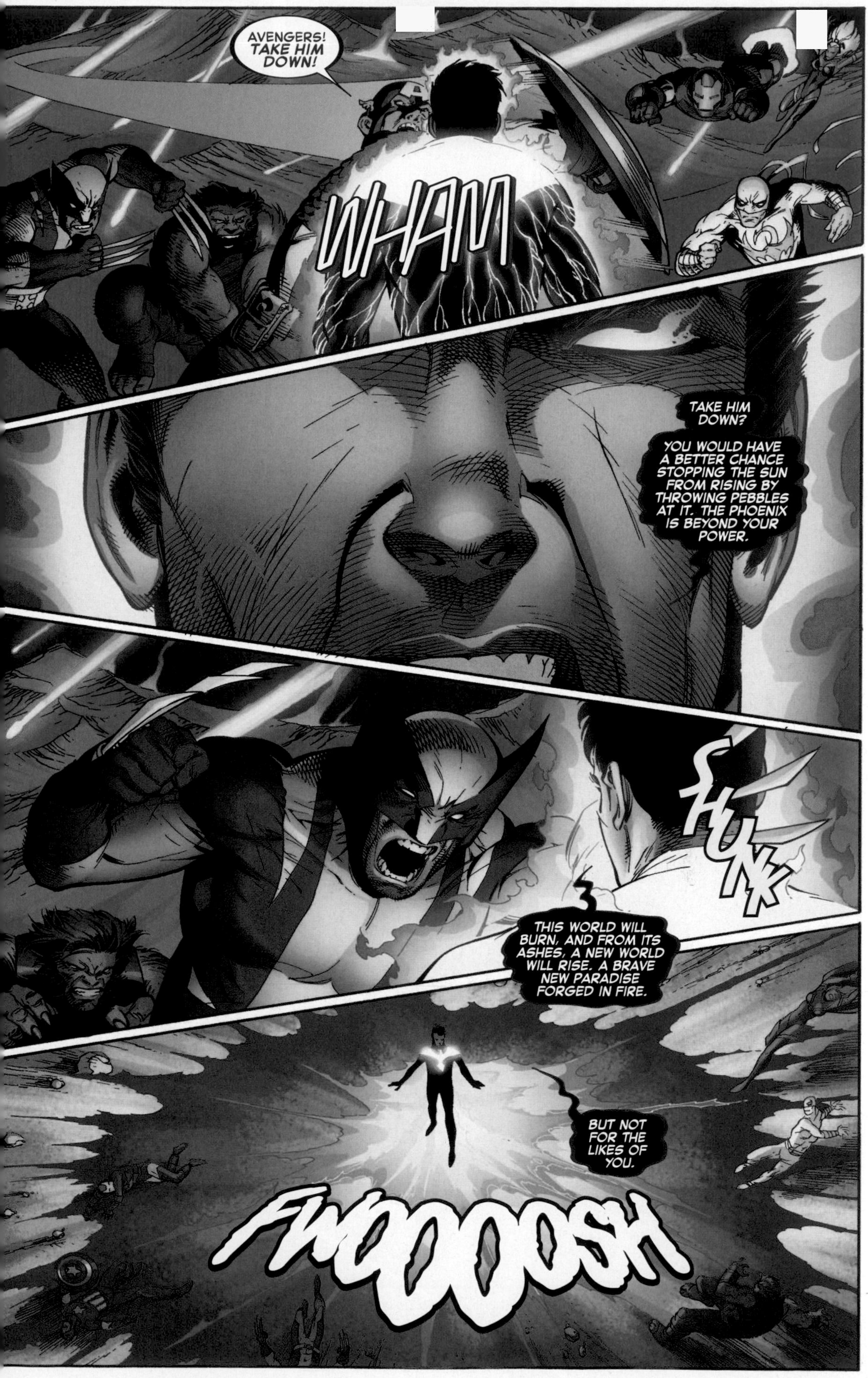
AVENGERS! TAKE HIM DOWN!
WHAM
TAKE HIM DOWN?
YOU WOULD HAVE A BETTER CHANCE STOPPING THE SUN FROM RISING BY THROWING PEBBLES AT IT. THE PHOENIX IS BEYOND YOUR POWER.
SHUNK
THIS WORLD WILL BURN, AND FROM ITS ASHES, A NEW WORLD WILL RISE. A BRAVE NEW PARADISE FORGED IN FIRE.
BUT NOT FOR THE LIKES OF YOU.
FWOOOOSH

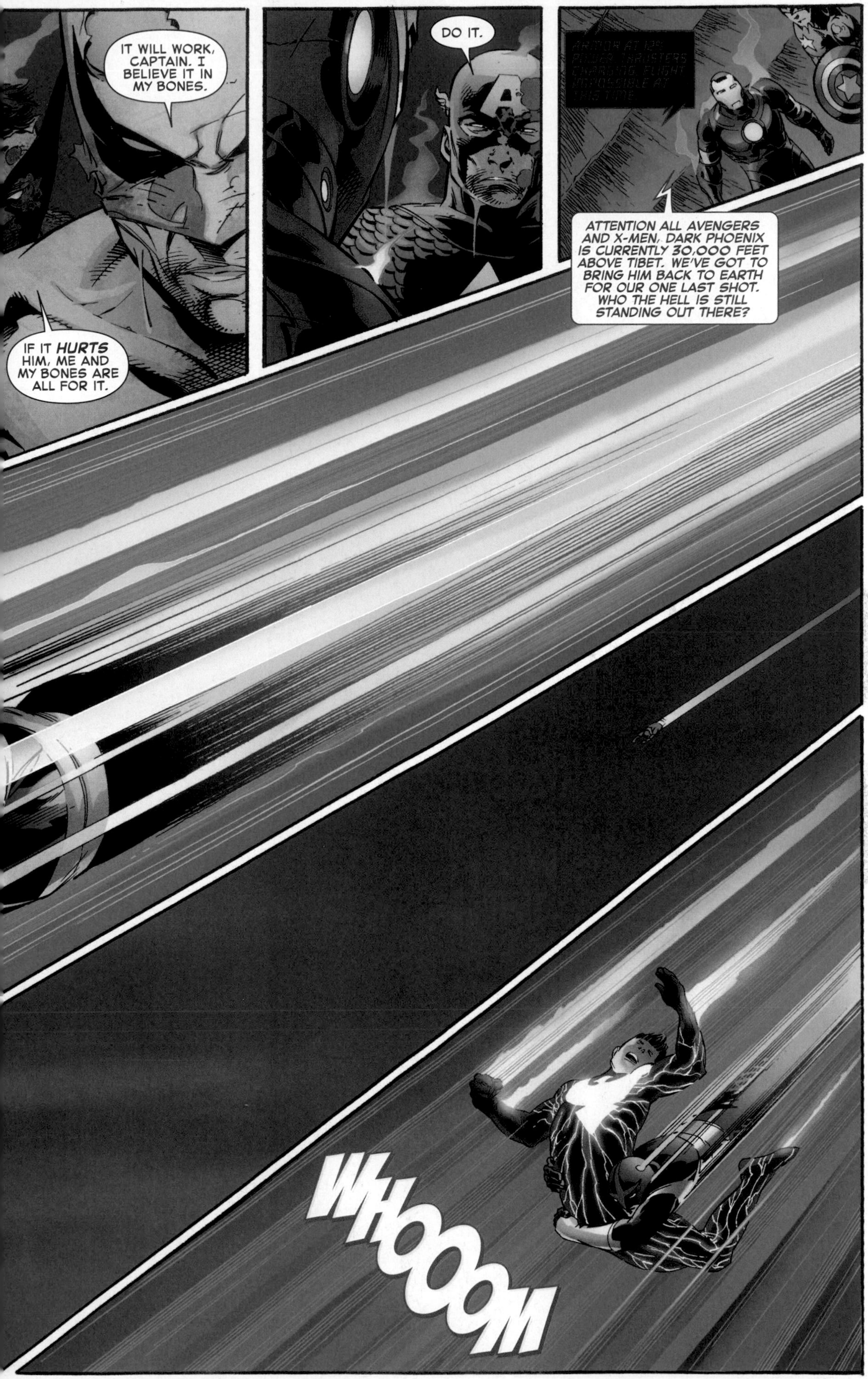
IT WILL WORK, CAPTAIN. I BELIEVE IT IN MY BONES.
IF IT *HURTS* HIM, ME AND MY BONES ARE ALL FOR IT.
DO IT.
ARMOR AT 12%. POWER THRUSTERS CHARGING. FLIGHT IMPOSSIBLE AT THIS TIME.
ATTENTION ALL AVENGERS AND X-MEN. DARK PHOENIX IS CURRENTLY 30,000 FEET ABOVE TIBET. WE'VE GOT TO BRING HIM BACK TO EARTH FOR OUR ONE LAST SHOT. WHO THE HELL IS STILL STANDING OUT THERE?
WHOOOM

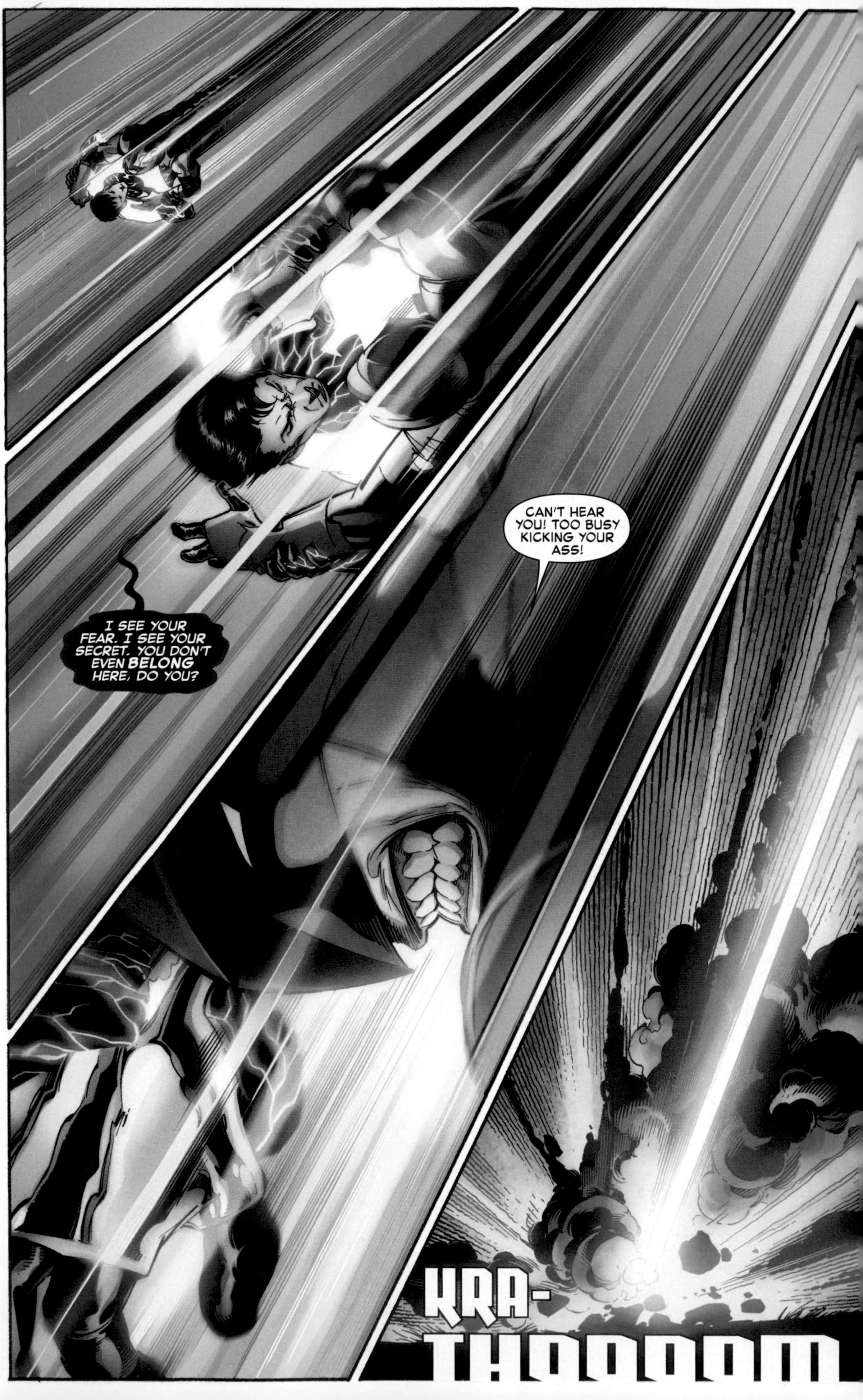
I SEE YOUR FEAR. I SEE YOUR SECRET. YOU DON'T EVEN BELONG HERE, DO YOU?
CAN'T HEAR YOU! TOO BUSY KICKING YOUR ASS!
KRA-THOOOOM

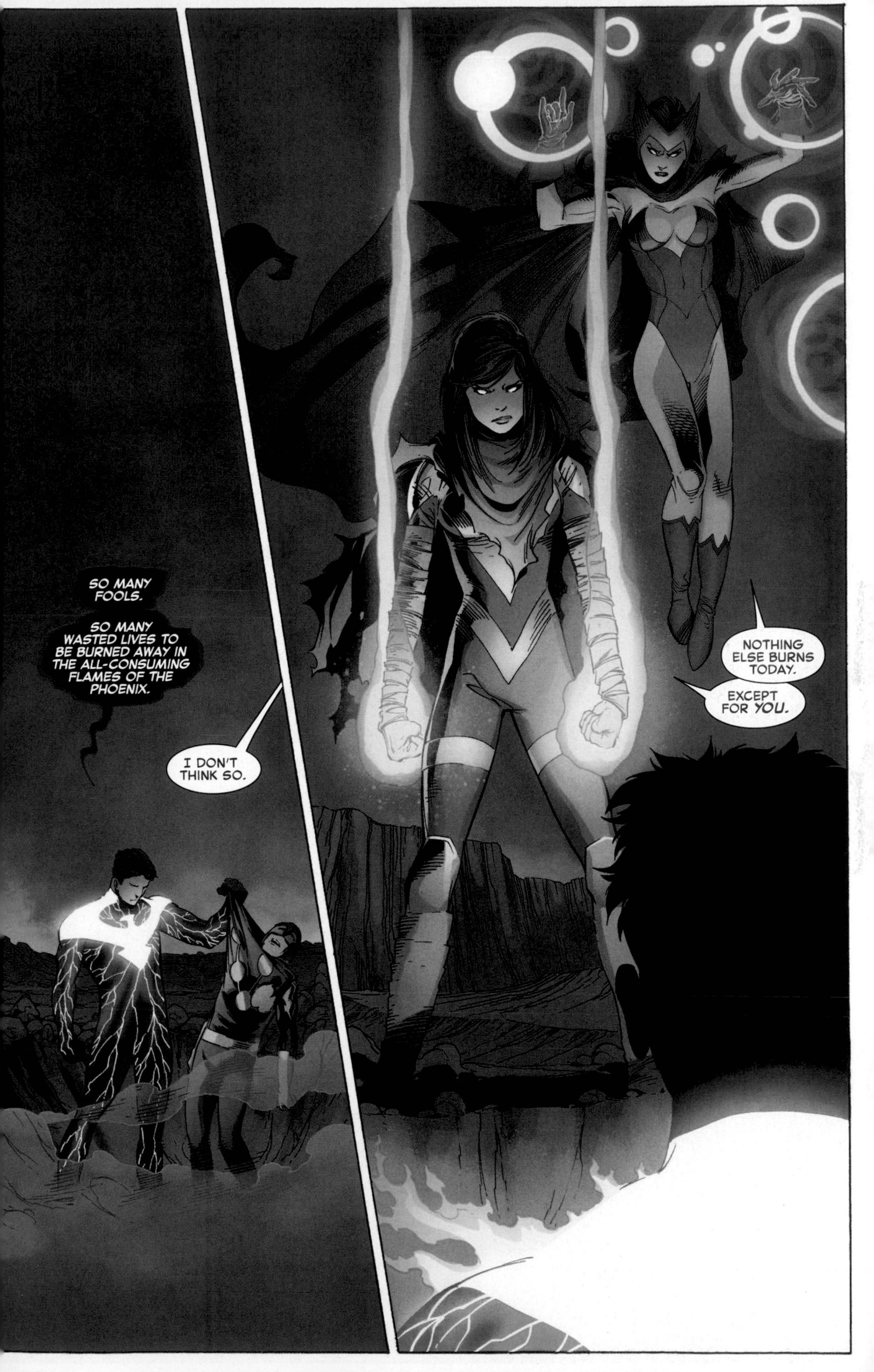
SO MANY FOOLS.
SO MANY WASTED LIVES TO BE BURNED AWAY IN THE ALL-CONSUMING FLAMES OF THE PHOENIX.
I DON'T THINK SO.
NOTHING ELSE BURNS TODAY.
EXCEPT FOR *YOU*.

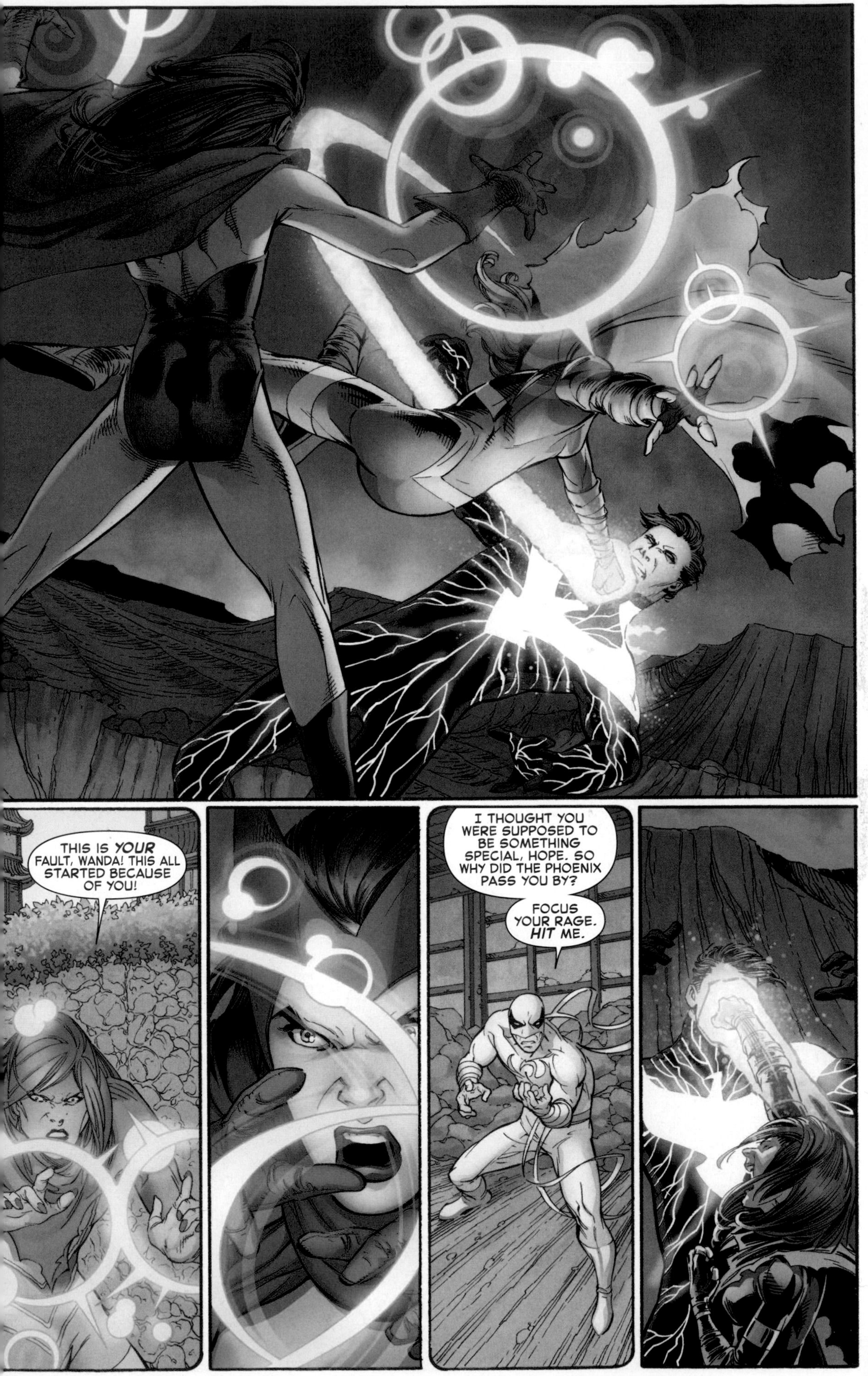
THIS IS *YOUR* FAULT, WANDA! THIS ALL STARTED BECAUSE OF YOU!
I THOUGHT YOU WERE SUPPOSED TO BE SOMETHING SPECIAL, HOPE. SO WHY DID THE PHOENIX PASS YOU BY?
FOCUS YOUR RAGE. *HIT* ME.

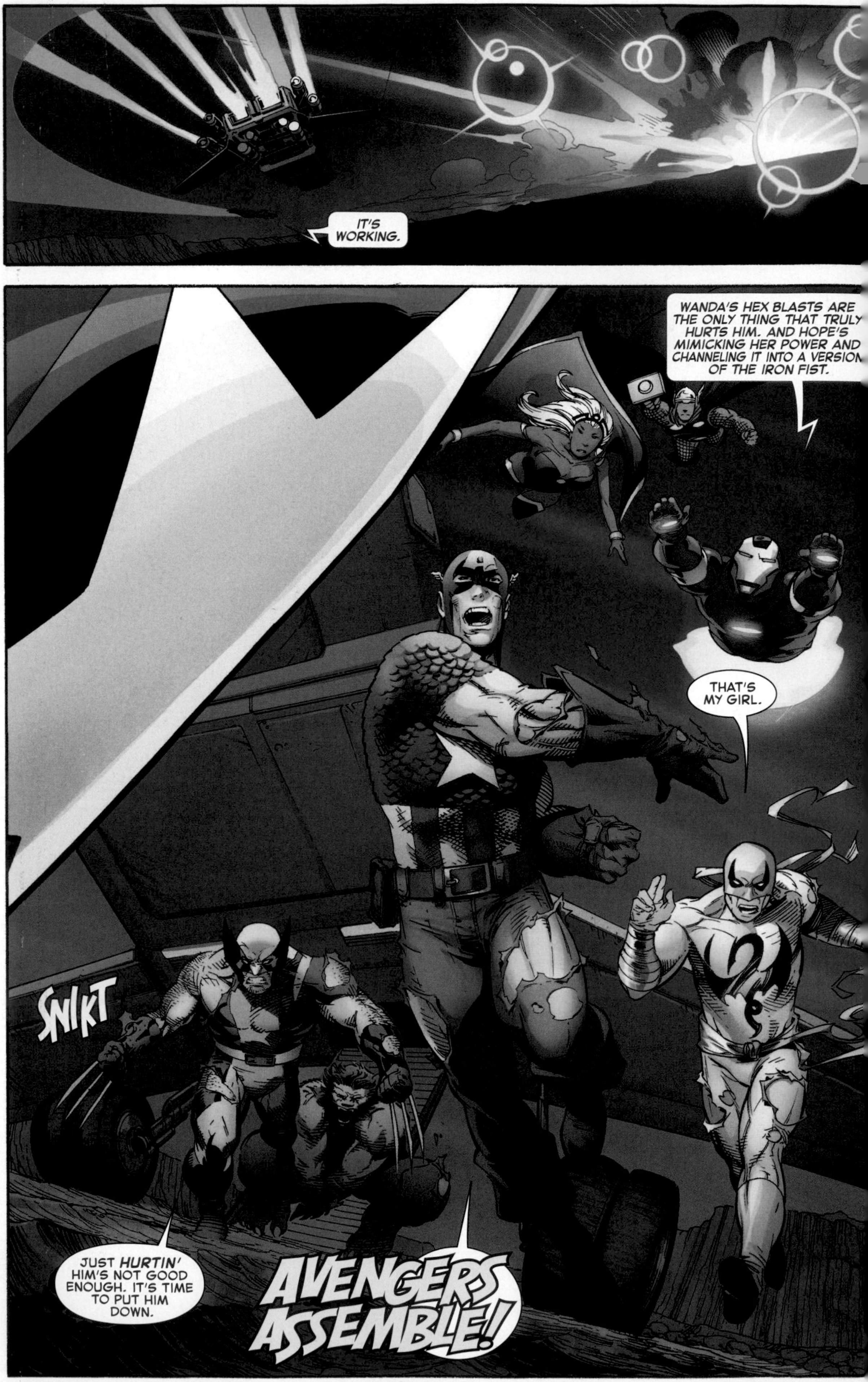
IT'S WORKING.
WANDA'S HEX BLASTS ARE THE ONLY THING THAT TRULY HURTS HIM. AND HOPE'S MIMICKING HER POWER AND CHANNELING IT INTO A VERSION OF THE IRON FIST.
THAT'S MY GIRL.
SNIKT
JUST HURTIN' HIM'S NOT GOOD ENOUGH. IT'S TIME TO PUT HIM DOWN.
AVENGERS ASSEMBLE!!

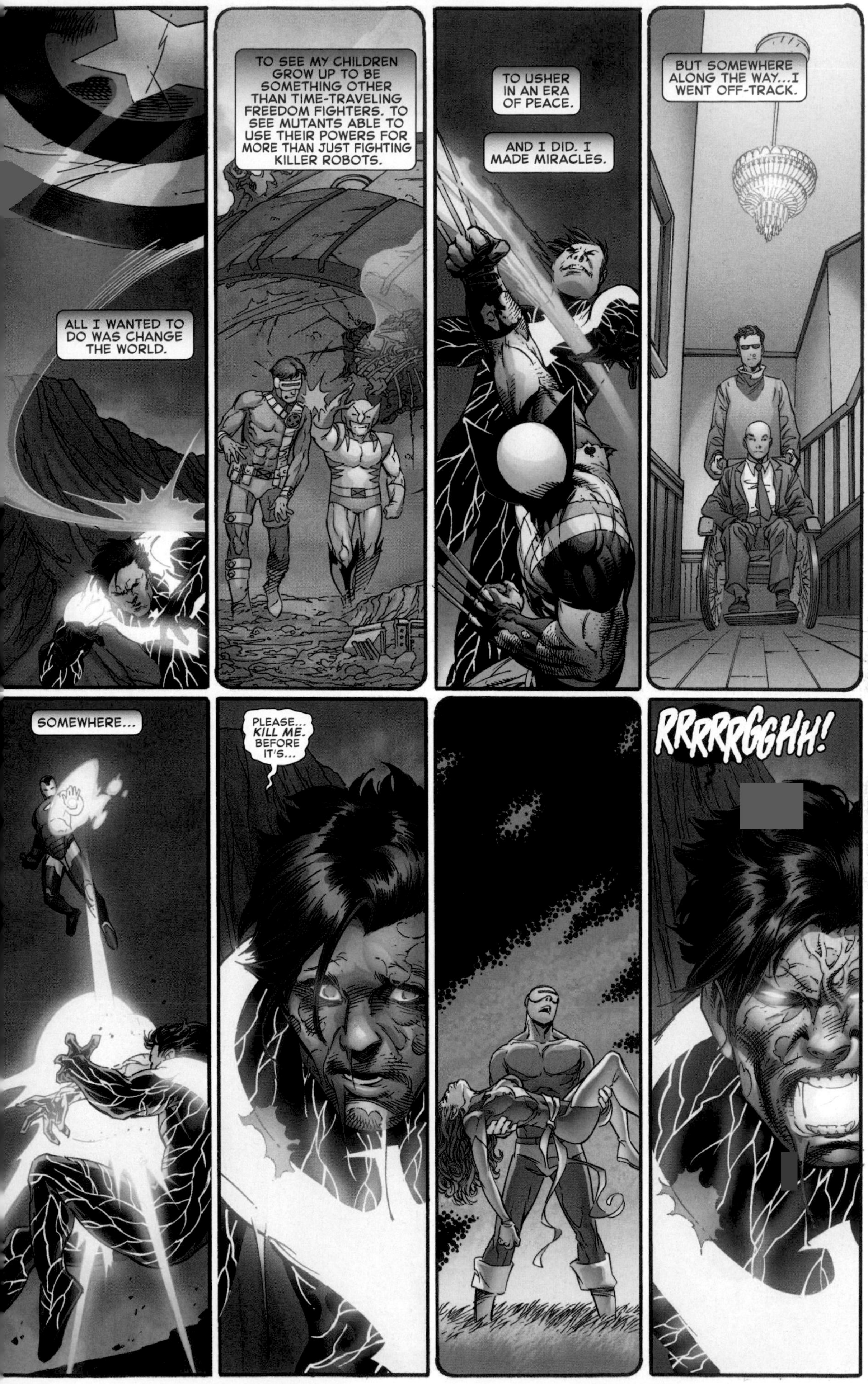
ALL I WANTED TO DO WAS CHANGE THE WORLD.
TO SEE MY CHILDREN GROW UP TO BE SOMETHING OTHER THAN TIME-TRAVELING FREEDOM FIGHTERS. TO SEE MUTANTS ABLE TO USE THEIR POWERS FOR MORE THAN JUST FIGHTING KILLER ROBOTS.
TO USHER IN AN ERA OF PEACE.
AND I DID. I MADE MIRACLES.
BUT SOMEWHERE ALONG THE WAY...I WENT OFF-TRACK.
SOMEWHERE...
PLEASE... *KILL ME.* BEFORE IT'S...
RRRRRGGHH!

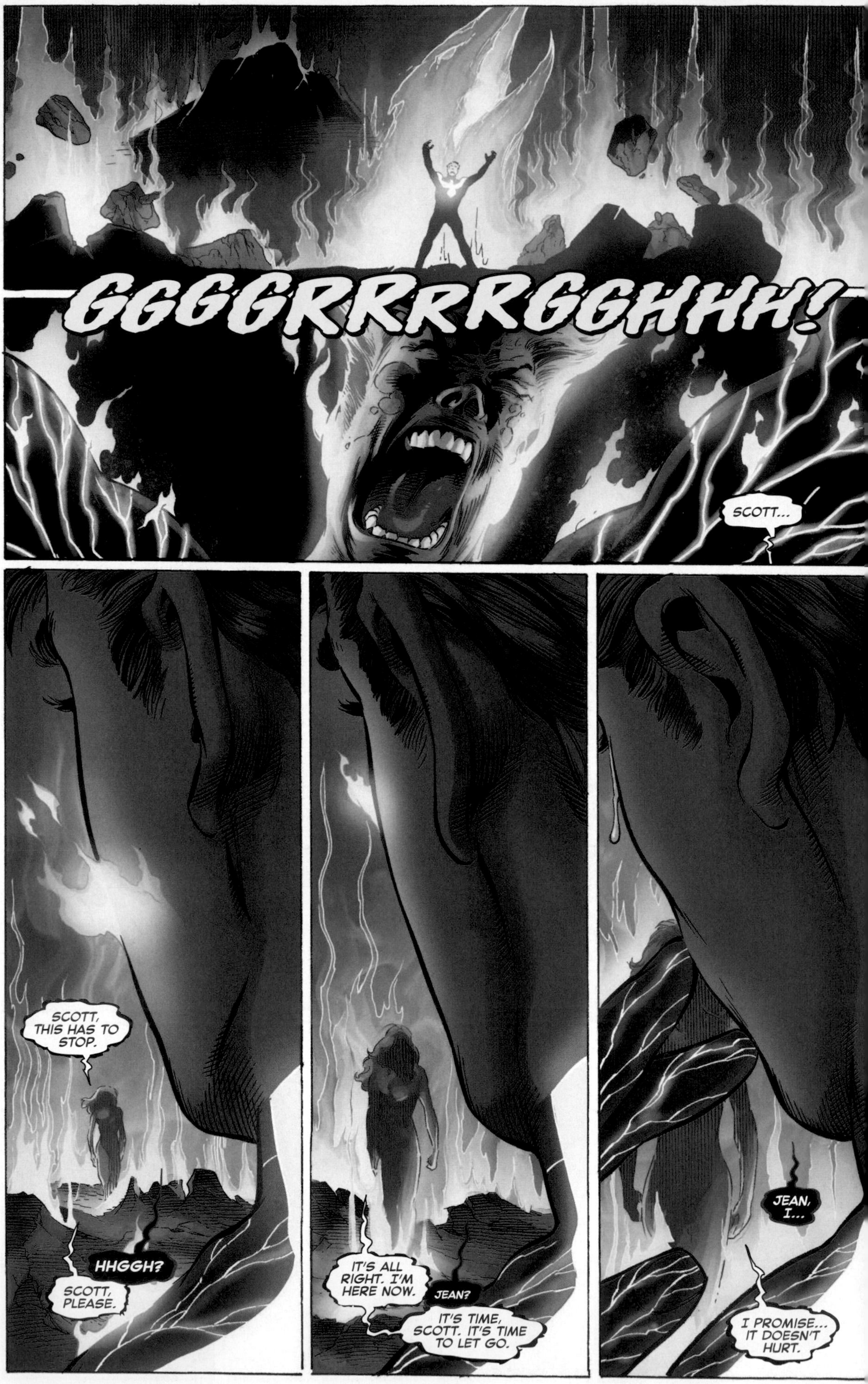
GGGGRRRRGGHHH!
SCOTT...
SCOTT, THIS HAS TO STOP.
HHGGH?
SCOTT, PLEASE.
IT'S ALL RIGHT. I'M HERE NOW.
JEAN?
IT'S TIME, SCOTT. IT'S TIME TO LET GO.
JEAN, I...
I PROMISE... IT DOESN'T HURT.

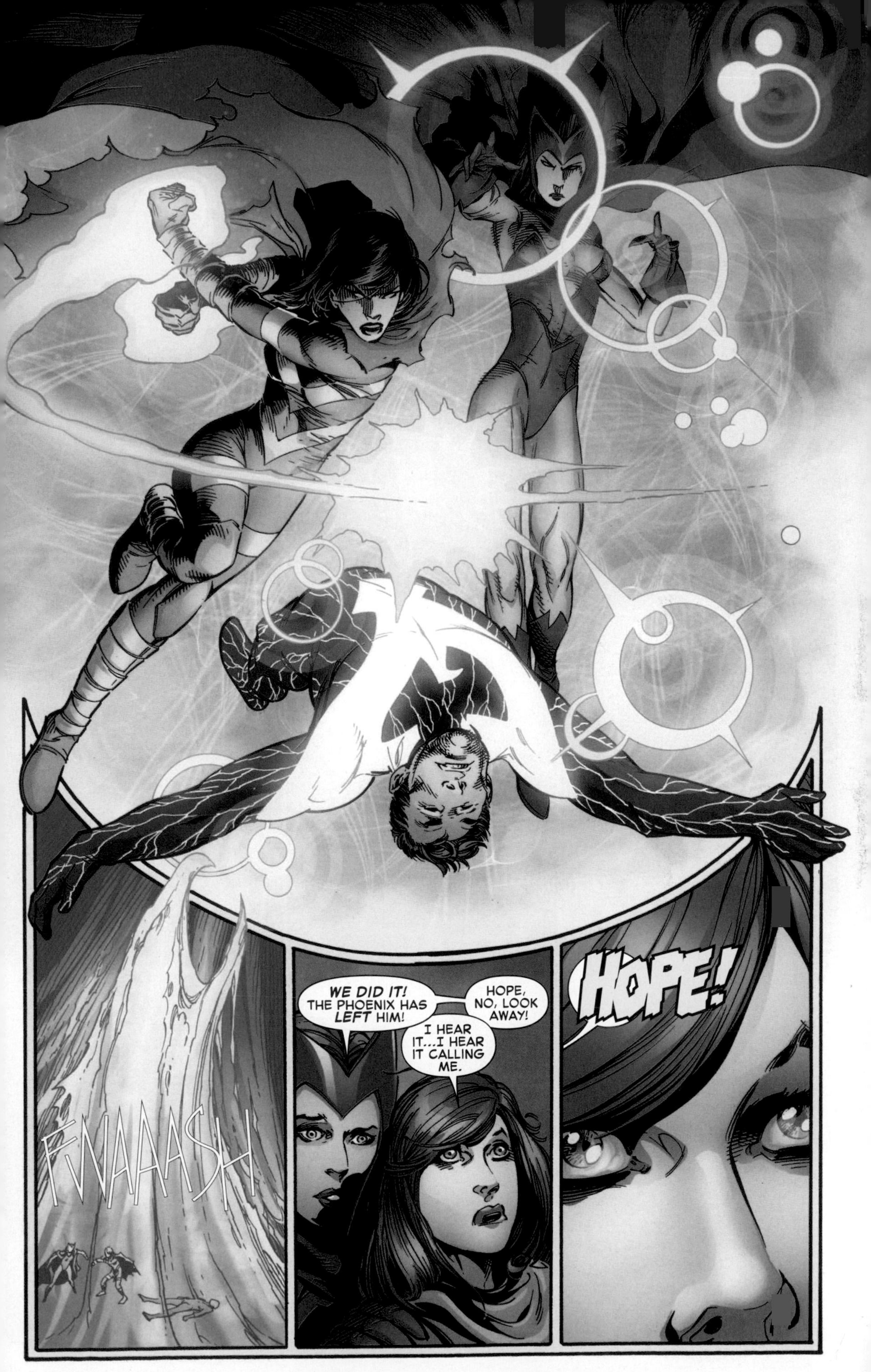
FWAAASH
WE DID IT! THE PHOENIX HAS LEFT HIM!
HOPE, NO, LOOK AWAY!
I HEAR IT...I HEAR IT CALLING ME.
HOPE!

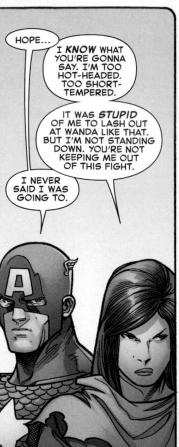

HOPE...

I *KNOW* WHAT YOU'RE GONNA SAY. I'M TOO HOT-HEADED. TOO SHORT-TEMPERED.

IT WAS *STUPID* OF ME TO LASH OUT AT WANDA LIKE THAT. BUT I'M NOT STANDING DOWN. YOU'RE NOT KEEPING ME OUT OF THIS FIGHT.

I NEVER SAID I WAS GOING TO.

YOU THINK I HAVEN'T BEEN *WATCHING* YOU THIS ENTIRE TIME? I'VE SEEN YOU TRAIN. I KNOW HOW YOU HANDLED YOURSELF WHEN CYCLOPS ATTACKED K'UN LUN.

YES, YOU'RE FIERY, BUT YOU'VE EARNED THE RIGHT TO STAND WITH THE AVENGERS, TO LEAD YOUR PEOPLE INTO BATTLE.

NO, MY QUESTION IS ABOUT WHAT COMES *AFTER*.

SAY WE TAKE DOWN THE PHOENIX X-MEN. THAT POWER HAS TO GO SOMEWHERE, RIGHT? STARK TELLS ME IT CAN'T BE CONTAINED, EXCEPT IN A *HOST*.

ALL THIS STARTED BECAUSE WE WERE TOLD IT WAS COMING FOR *YOU*. WELL, WHAT IF IT STILL IS?

I SENT GOOD PEOPLE INTO BATTLE TO FIGHT TO *PREVENT* THAT VERY THING FROM HAPPENING. ARE YOU TELLING ME NOW I SHOULD SEND THEM BACK, TO FIGHT TO MAKE SURE IT *DOES*? TO RISK EVERYTHING TO MAKE YOU THE PHOENIX?

I'M NOT TELLING YOU TO SEND ANYONE ANYWHERE. JUST DON'T TRY AND STOP ME.

YOU BELIEVE IN YOURSELF. THAT MUCH IS OBVIOUS. I GUESS MY ULTIMATE QUESTION IS...

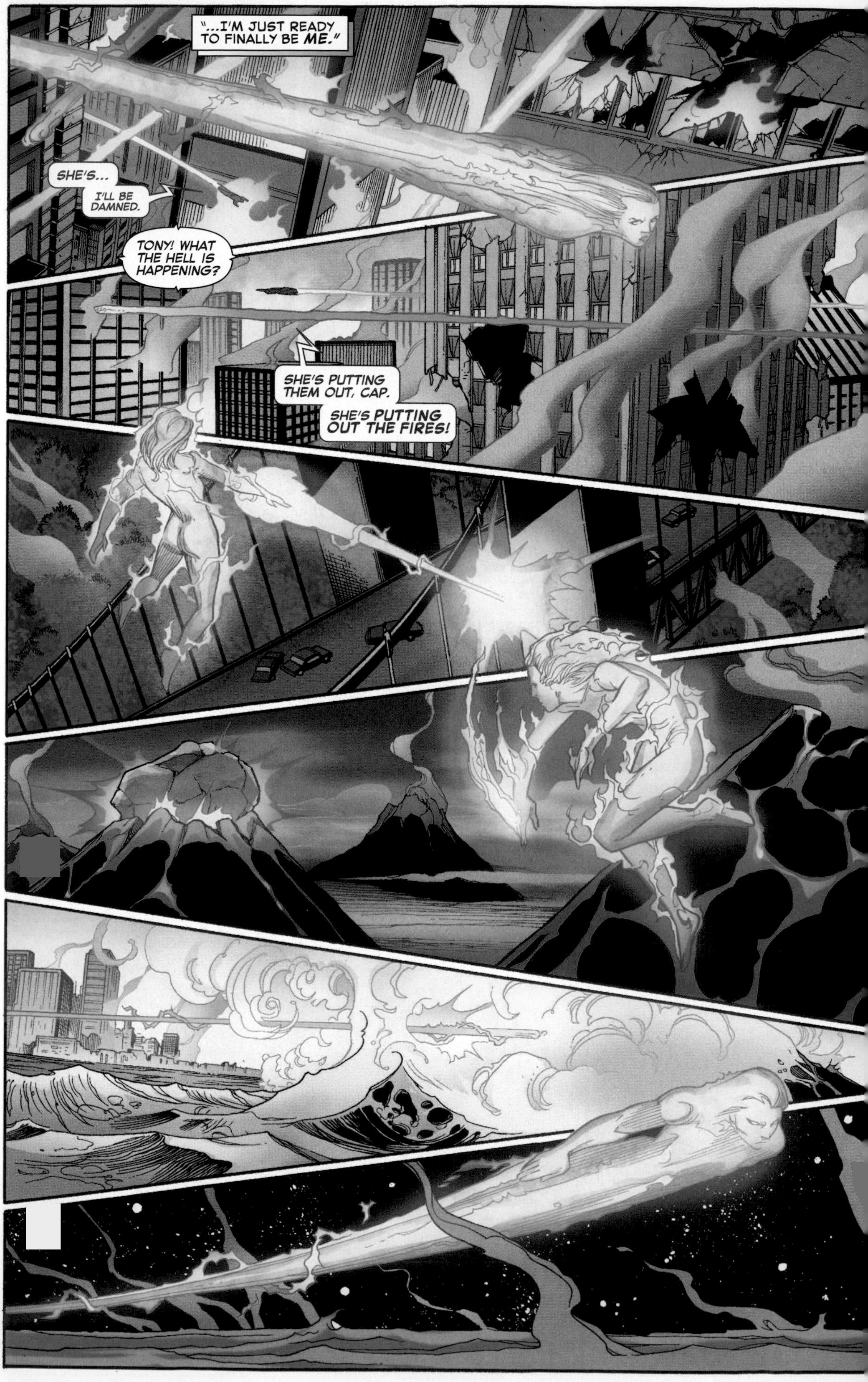
"...I'M JUST READY TO FINALLY BE ME."
SHE'S...
I'LL BE DAMNED.
TONY! WHAT THE HELL IS HAPPENING?
SHE'S PUTTING THEM OUT, CAP.
SHE'S PUTTING OUT THE FIRES!

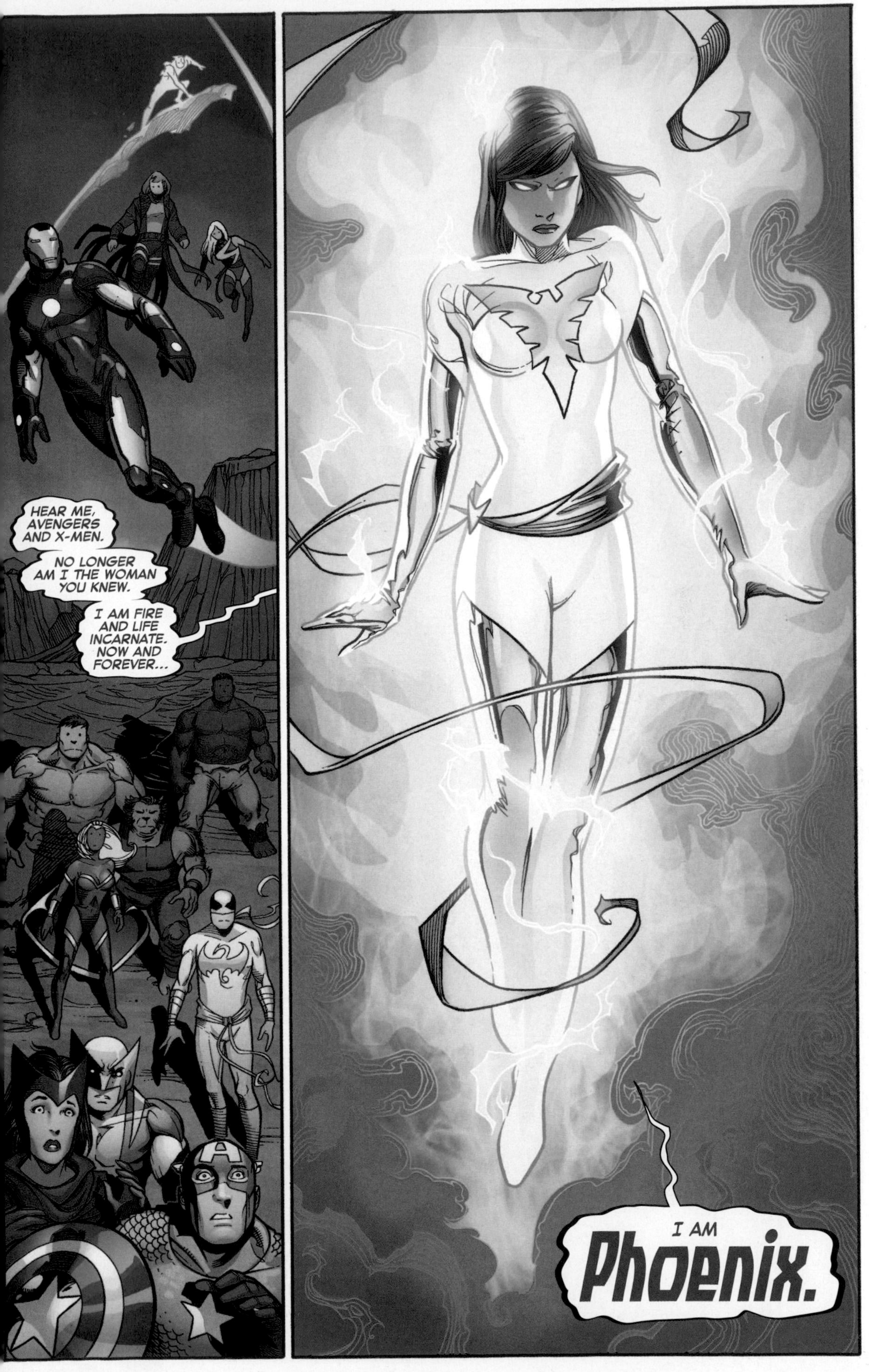
HEAR ME, AVENGERS AND X-MEN.
NO LONGER AM I THE WOMAN YOU KNEW.
I AM FIRE AND LIFE INCARNATE. NOW AND FOREVER...
I AM Phoenix.

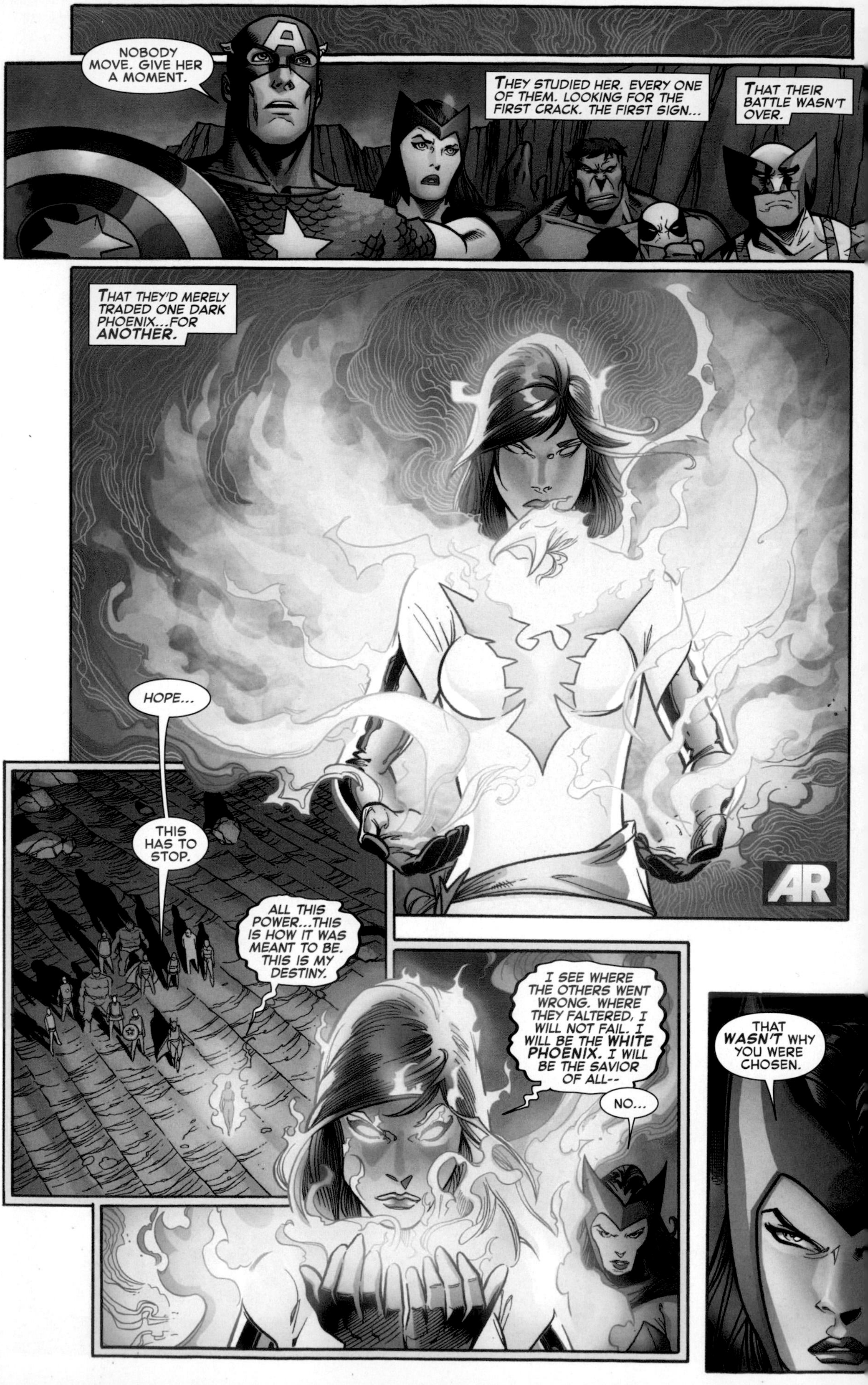
NOBODY MOVE. GIVE HER A MOMENT.
THEY STUDIED HER. EVERY ONE OF THEM. LOOKING FOR THE FIRST CRACK. THE FIRST SIGN...
THAT THEIR BATTLE WASN'T OVER.
THAT THEY'D MERELY TRADED ONE DARK PHOENIX...FOR ANOTHER.
HOPE...
THIS HAS TO STOP.
AR
ALL THIS POWER...THIS IS HOW IT WAS MEANT TO BE. THIS IS MY DESTINY.
I SEE WHERE THE OTHERS WENT WRONG. WHERE THEY FALTERED, I WILL NOT FAIL. I WILL BE THE WHITE PHOENIX. I WILL BE THE SAVIOR OF ALL--
NO...
THAT WASN'T WHY YOU WERE CHOSEN.

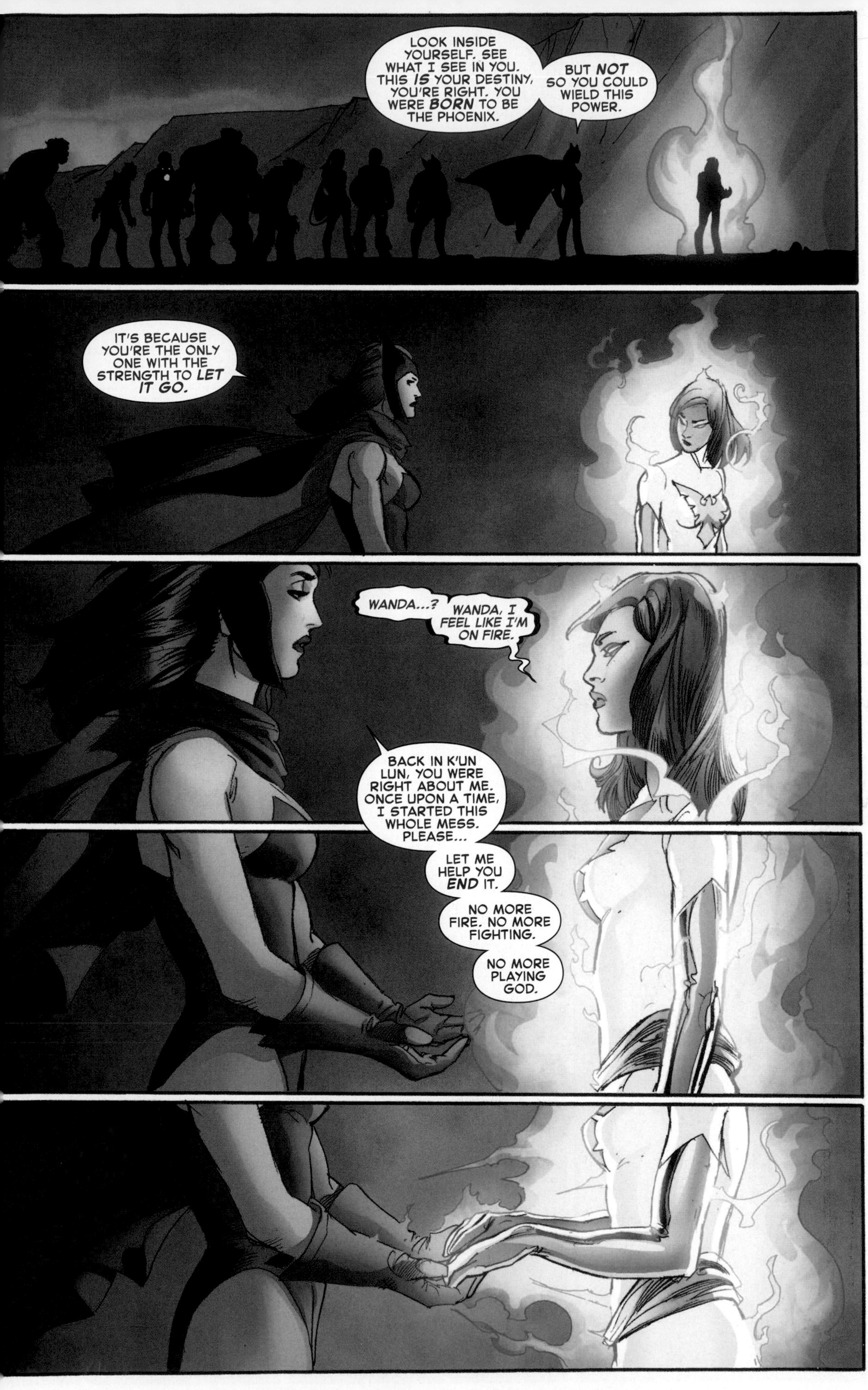
LOOK INSIDE YOURSELF. SEE WHAT I SEE IN YOU. THIS *IS* YOUR DESTINY, YOU'RE RIGHT. YOU WERE *BORN* TO BE THE PHOENIX.
BUT *NOT* SO YOU COULD WIELD THIS POWER.
IT'S BECAUSE YOU'RE THE ONLY ONE WITH THE STRENGTH TO *LET IT GO.*
WANDA...?
WANDA, I FEEL LIKE I'M ON FIRE.
BACK IN K'UN LUN, YOU WERE RIGHT ABOUT ME. ONCE UPON A TIME, I STARTED THIS WHOLE MESS. PLEASE...
LET ME HELP YOU *END* IT.
NO MORE FIRE. NO MORE FIGHTING.
NO MORE PLAYING GOD.

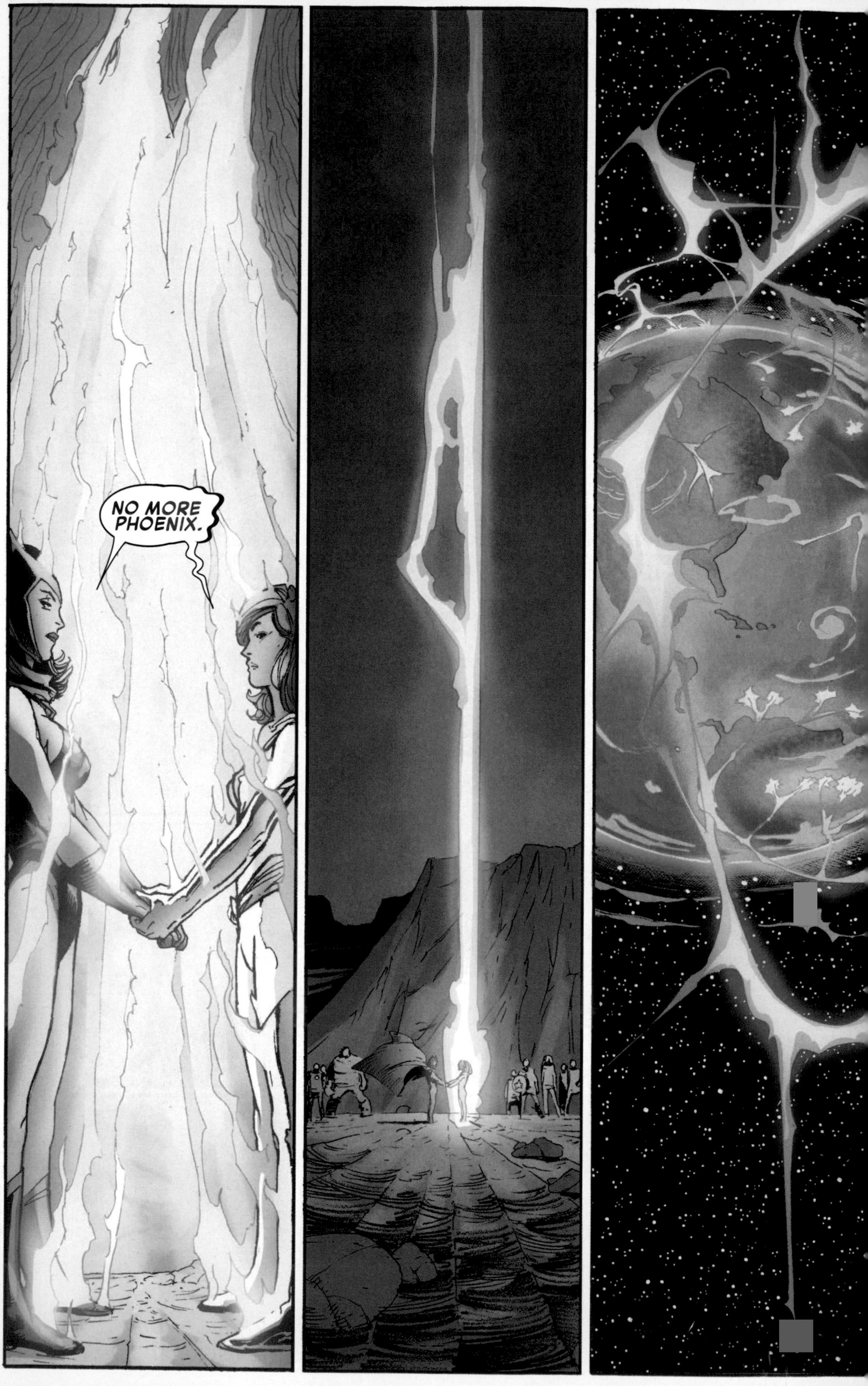
NO MORE PHOENIX.

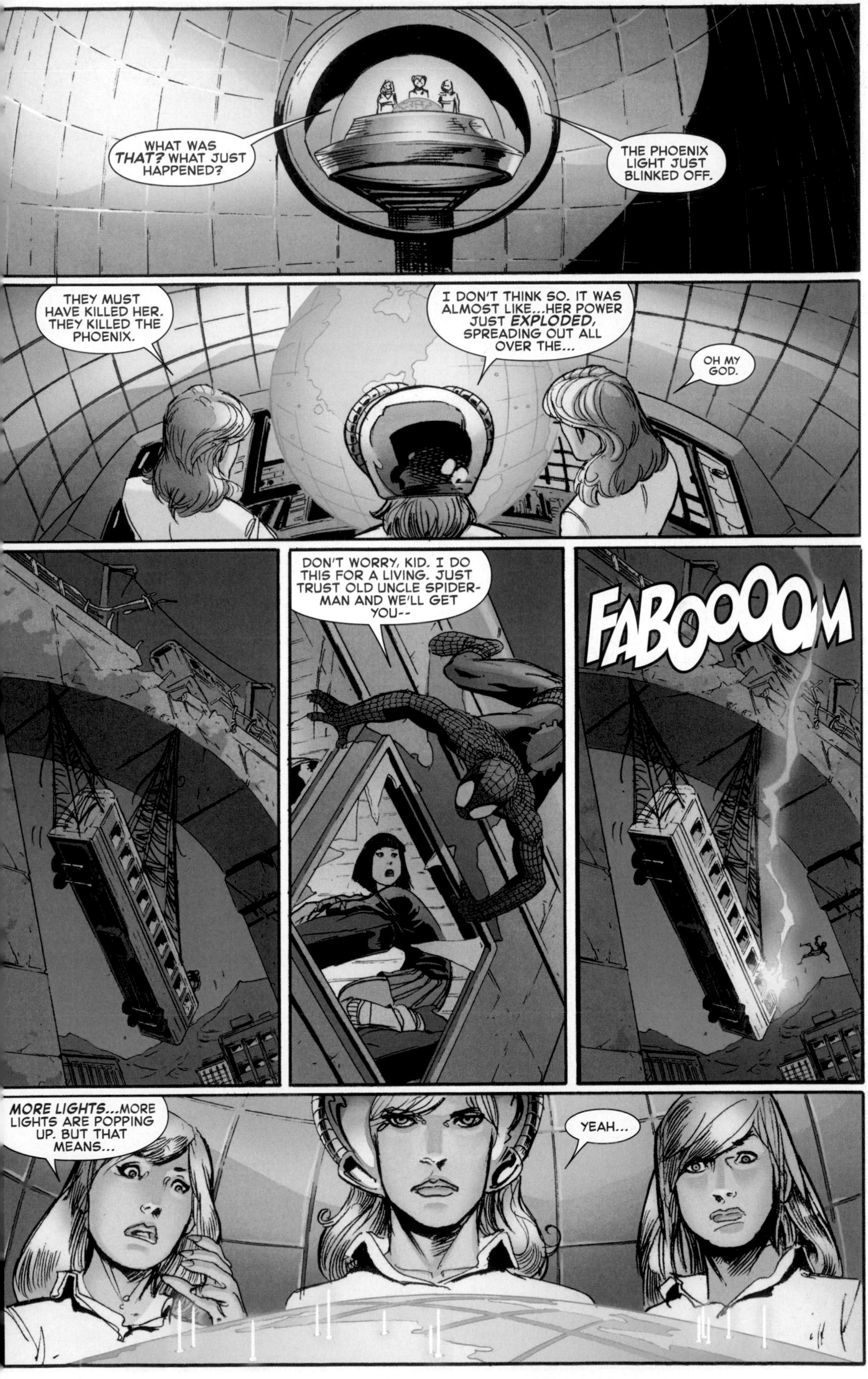
WHAT WAS THAT? WHAT JUST HAPPENED?
THE PHOENIX LIGHT JUST BLINKED OFF.
THEY MUST HAVE KILLED HER. THEY KILLED THE PHOENIX.
I DON'T THINK SO. IT WAS ALMOST LIKE...HER POWER JUST EXPLODED, SPREADING OUT ALL OVER THE...
OH MY GOD.
DON'T WORRY, KID. I DO THIS FOR A LIVING. JUST TRUST OLD UNCLE SPIDER-MAN AND WE'LL GET YOU--
FABOOOOOM
MORE LIGHTS...MORE LIGHTS ARE POPPING UP. BUT THAT MEANS...
YEAH...

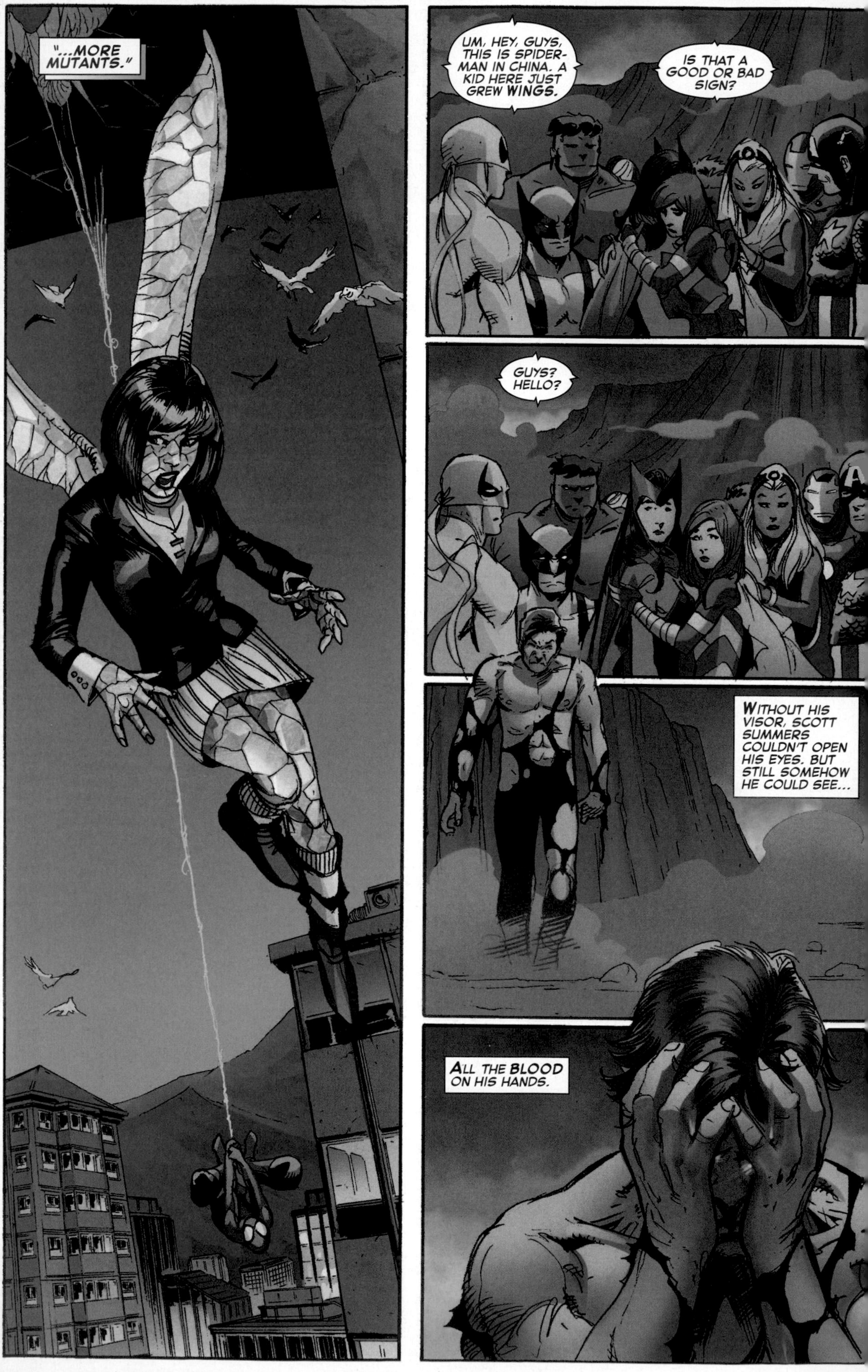
"...MORE MUTANTS."
UM, HEY, GUYS, THIS IS SPIDER-MAN IN CHINA. A KID HERE JUST GREW WINGS.
IS THAT A GOOD OR BAD SIGN?
GUYS? HELLO?
WITHOUT HIS VISOR, SCOTT SUMMERS COULDN'T OPEN HIS EYES. BUT STILL SOMEHOW HE COULD SEE...
ALL THE BLOOD ON HIS HANDS.

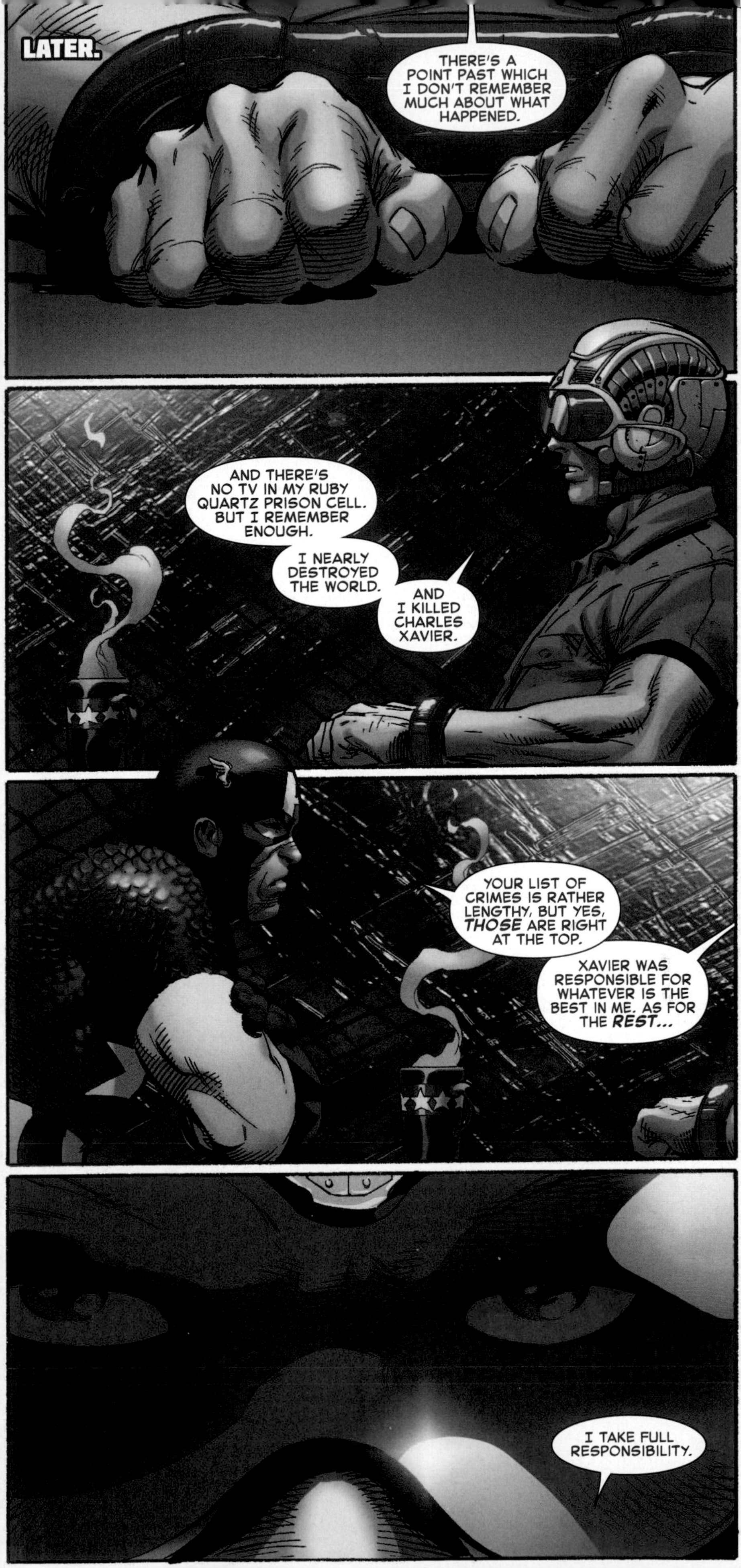
LATER.
THERE'S A POINT PAST WHICH I DON'T REMEMBER MUCH ABOUT WHAT HAPPENED.
AND THERE'S NO TV IN MY RUBY QUARTZ PRISON CELL. BUT I REMEMBER ENOUGH.
I NEARLY DESTROYED THE WORLD.
AND I KILLED CHARLES XAVIER.
YOUR LIST OF CRIMES IS RATHER LENGTHY, BUT YES, *THOSE* ARE RIGHT AT THE TOP.
XAVIER WAS RESPONSIBLE FOR WHATEVER IS THE BEST IN ME. AS FOR THE *REST*...
I TAKE FULL RESPONSIBILITY.

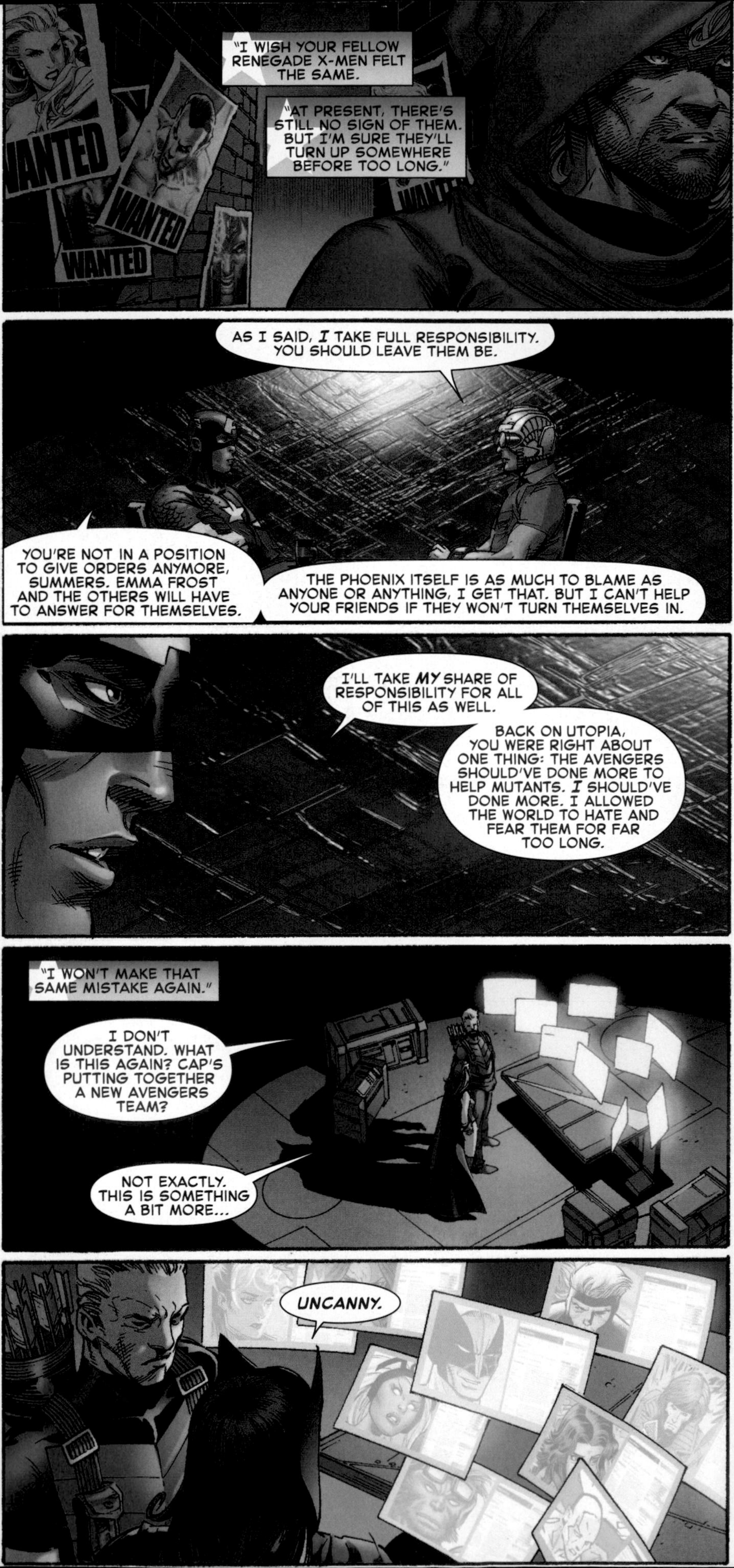

"I WISH YOUR FELLOW RENEGADE X-MEN FELT THE SAME.
"AT PRESENT, THERE'S STILL NO SIGN OF THEM. BUT I'M SURE THEY'LL TURN UP SOMEWHERE BEFORE TOO LONG."
WANTED
WANTED
WANTED
AS I SAID, *I* TAKE FULL RESPONSIBILITY. YOU SHOULD LEAVE THEM BE.
YOU'RE NOT IN A POSITION TO GIVE ORDERS ANYMORE, SUMMERS. EMMA FROST AND THE OTHERS WILL HAVE TO ANSWER FOR THEMSELVES.
THE PHOENIX ITSELF IS AS MUCH TO BLAME AS ANYONE OR ANYTHING, I GET THAT. BUT I CAN'T HELP YOUR FRIENDS IF THEY WON'T TURN THEMSELVES IN.
I'LL TAKE *MY* SHARE OF RESPONSIBILITY FOR ALL OF THIS AS WELL.
BACK ON UTOPIA, YOU WERE RIGHT ABOUT ONE THING: THE AVENGERS SHOULD'VE DONE MORE TO HELP MUTANTS. *I* SHOULD'VE DONE MORE. I ALLOWED THE WORLD TO HATE AND FEAR THEM FOR FAR TOO LONG.
"I WON'T MAKE THAT SAME MISTAKE AGAIN."
I DON'T UNDERSTAND. WHAT IS THIS AGAIN? CAP'S PUTTING TOGETHER A NEW AVENGERS TEAM?
NOT EXACTLY. THIS IS SOMETHING A BIT MORE...
UNCANNY.

WELL THEN, I GUESS THIS BEGINS A *NEW AGE* FOR THE AVENGERS AND X-MEN BOTH.

DON'T YOU DARE! DON'T YOU DARE TRY AND TURN THIS INTO A *WIN!*

YOU WAGED A WAR THAT SET FRIEND AGAINST FRIEND! YOU PLAYED RUSSIAN ROULETTE WITH THE *PLANET!*

"YOU LEFT WOUNDS THAT WILL TAKE YEARS TO HEAL, IF THEY EVER HEAL AT ALL."

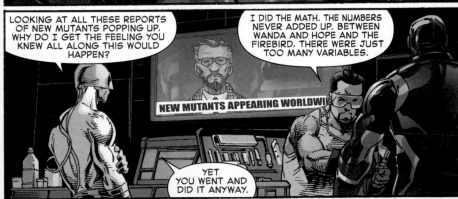

AND YOU KILLED ONE OF THE FINEST MEN I'VE EVER KNOWN.

IF YOU CONSIDER THAT A *WIN...*

I *PITY* YOU. I REALLY DO.

LOOKING AT ALL THESE REPORTS OF NEW MUTANTS POPPING UP, WHY DO I GET THE FEELING YOU KNEW ALL ALONG THIS WOULD HAPPEN?

I DID THE MATH. THE NUMBERS NEVER ADDED UP. BETWEEN WANDA AND HOPE AND THE FIREBIRD, THERE WERE JUST TOO MANY VARIABLES.

NEW MUTANTS APPEARING WORLDWI

YET YOU WENT AND DID IT ANYWAY.

THERE'S STILL A CHANCE I COULD BE INSANE. IF I WAS INSANE, YOU'D TELL ME, RIGHT?

ANTS APPEARING WO

TONY STARK, MAN OF FAITH. WILL WONDERS NEVER CEASE?

NOT IF I CAN HELP IT.

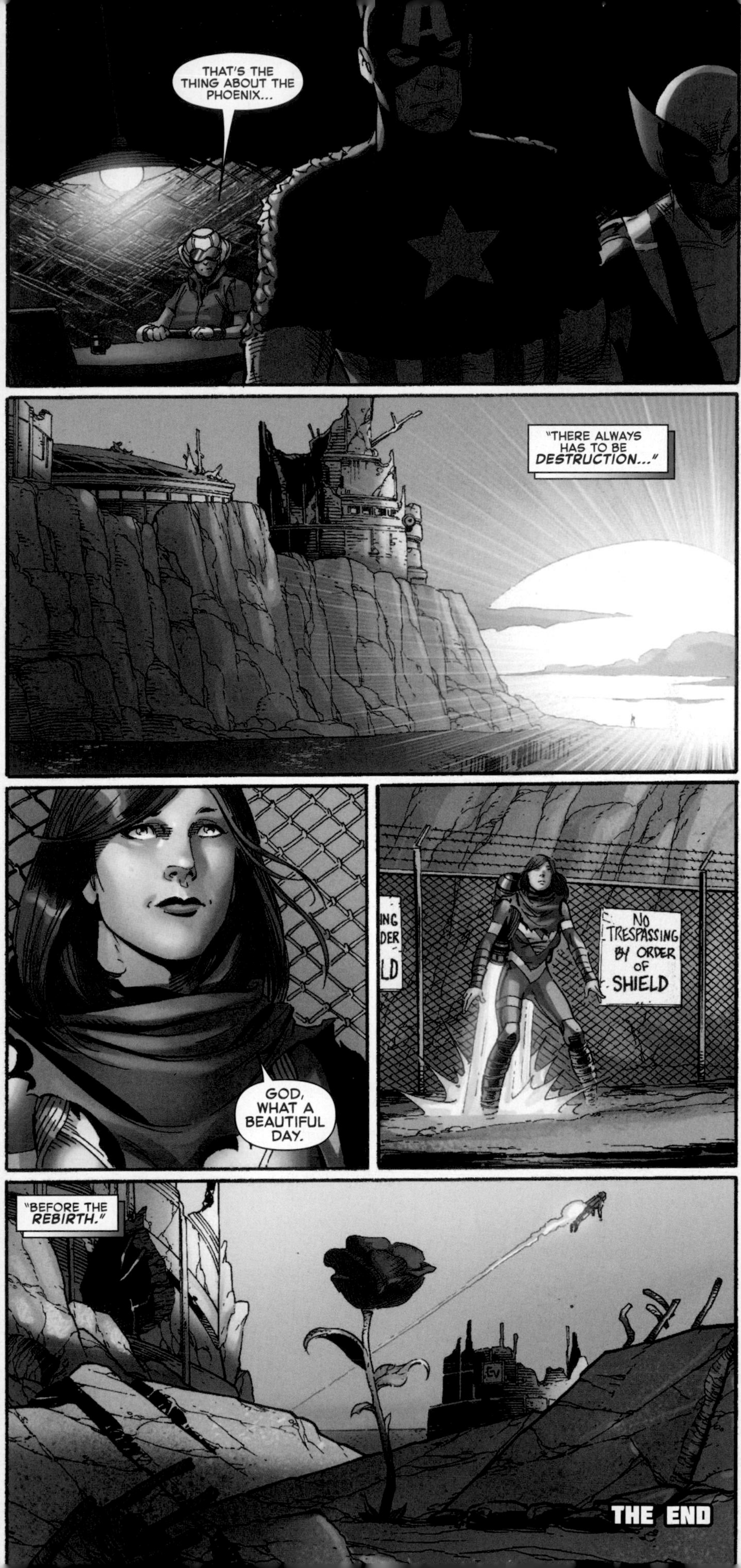
THAT'S THE THING ABOUT THE PHOENIX...
"THERE ALWAYS HAS TO BE DESTRUCTION..."
GOD, WHAT A BEAUTIFUL DAY.
NO TRESPASSING BY ORDER OF SHIELD
"BEFORE THE REBIRTH."
THE END

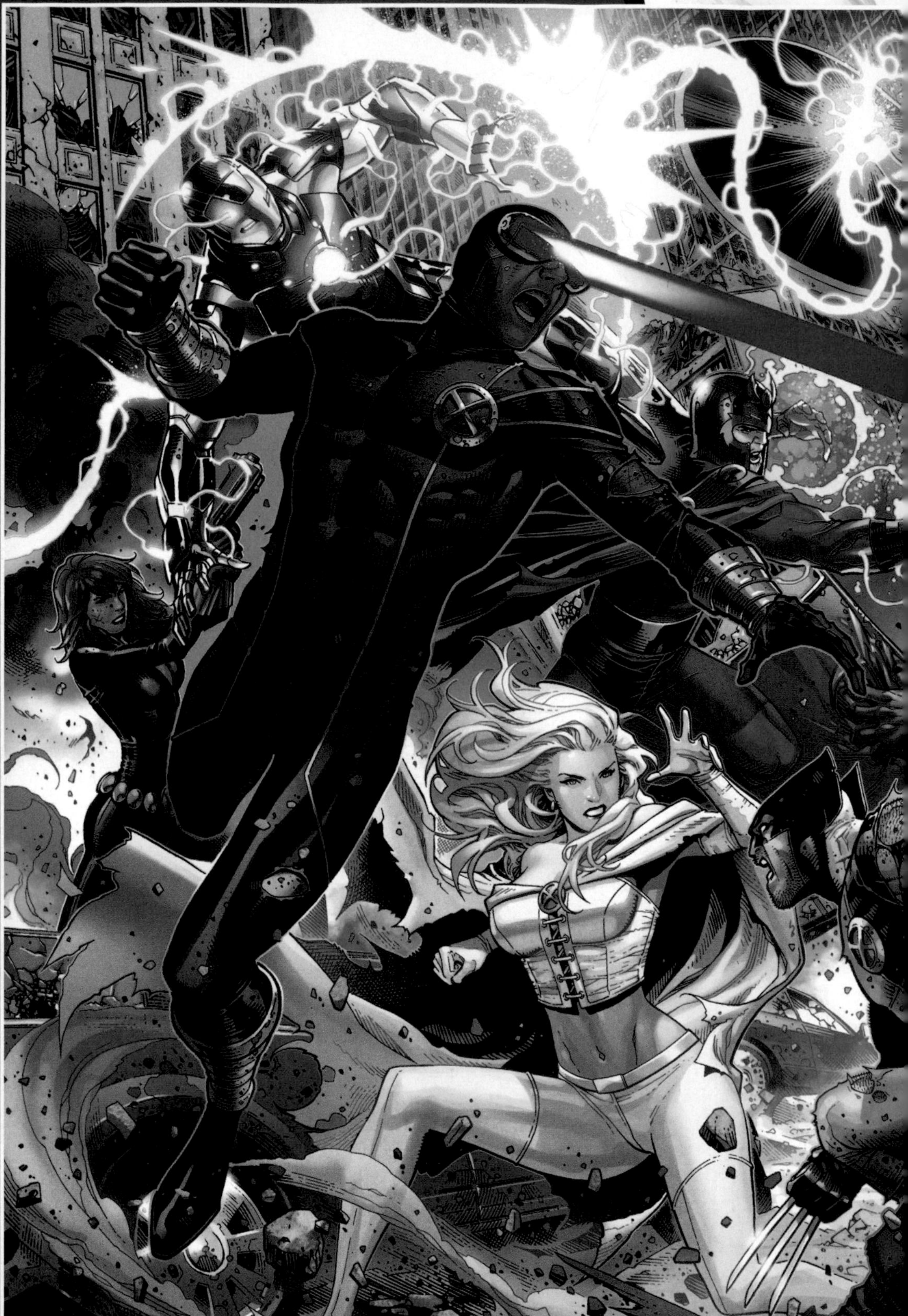

AVX #0 VARIANT

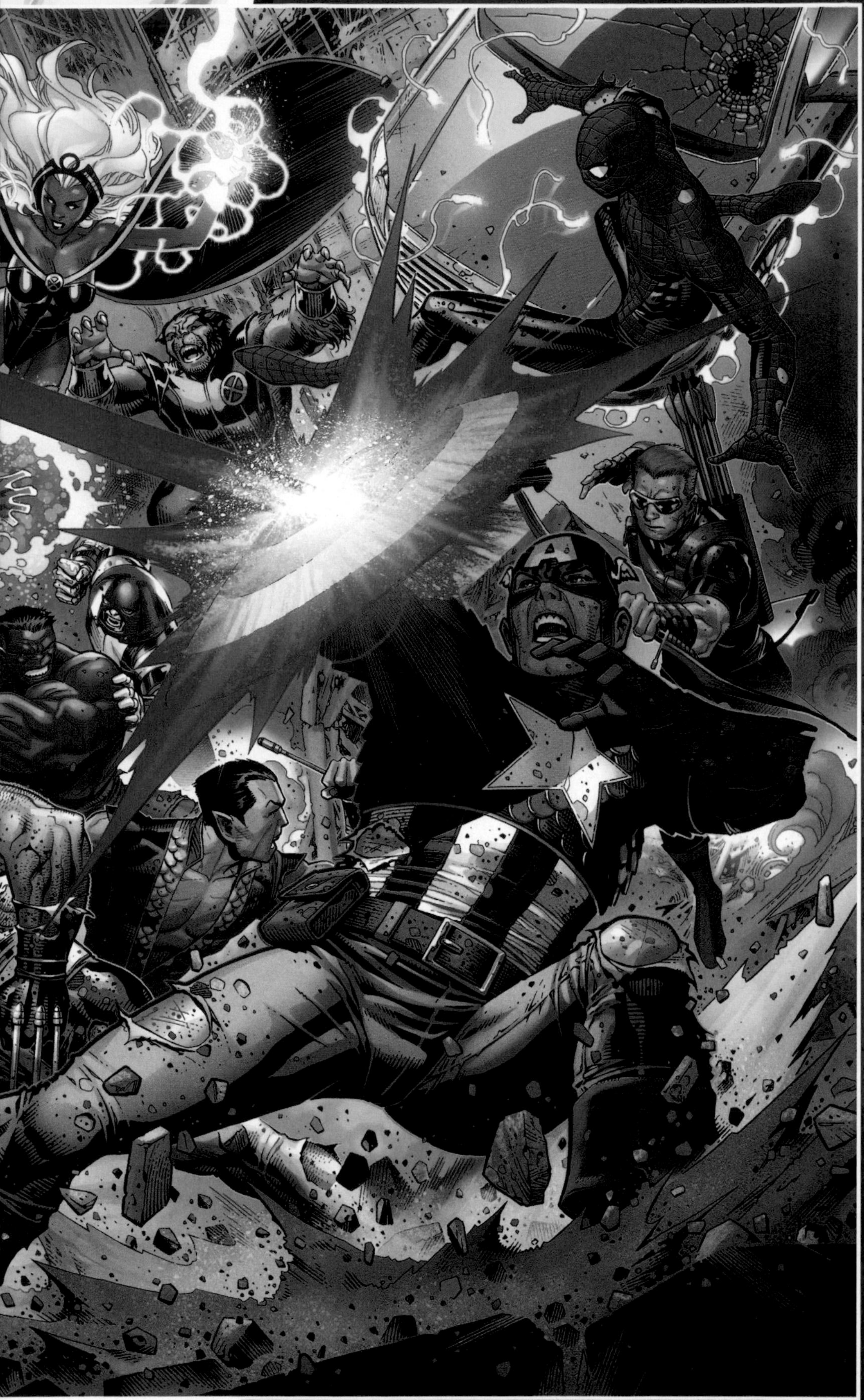

BY JIM CHEUNG & JUSTIN PONSOR

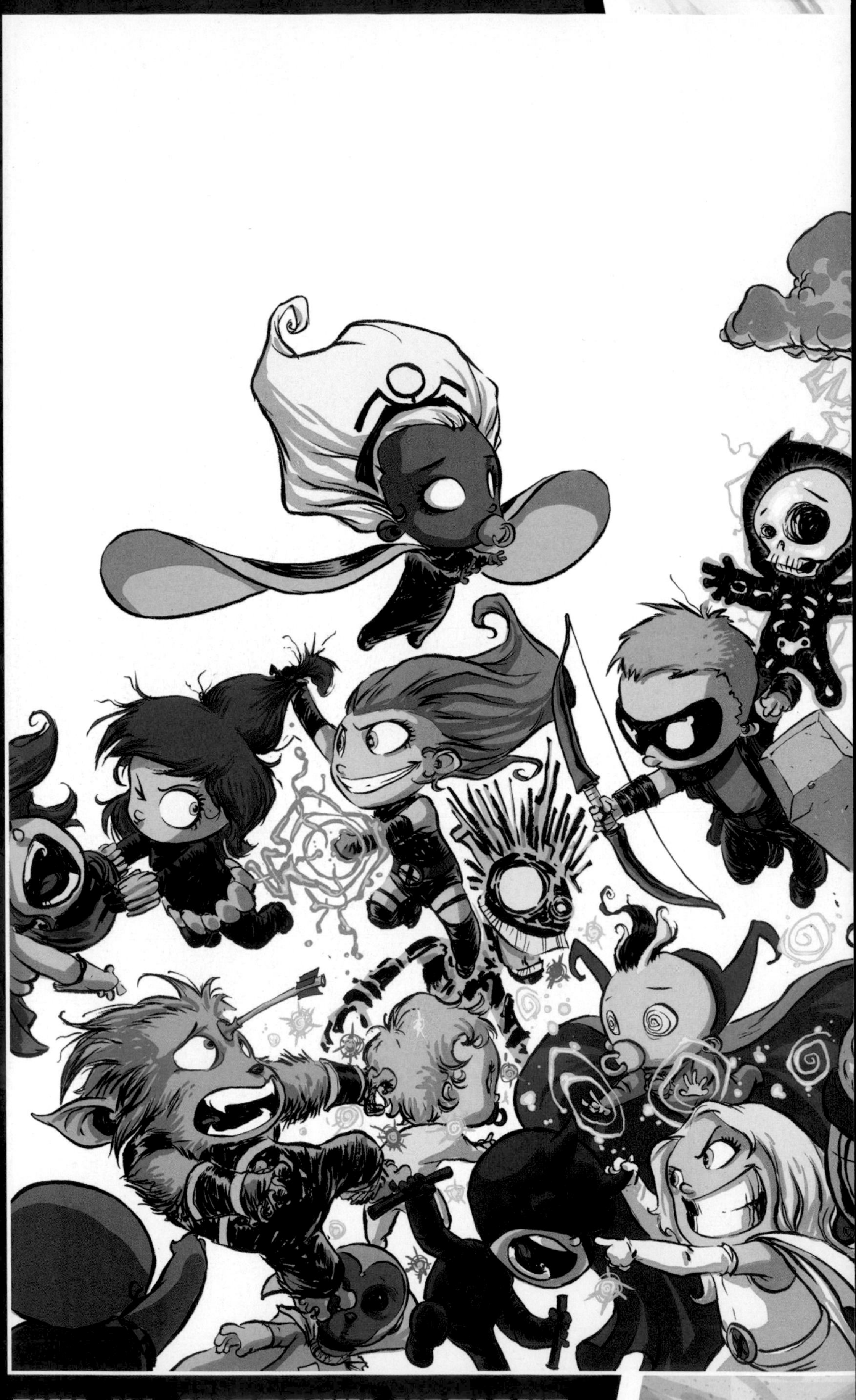

AVX #1 MIDTOWN VARIANT

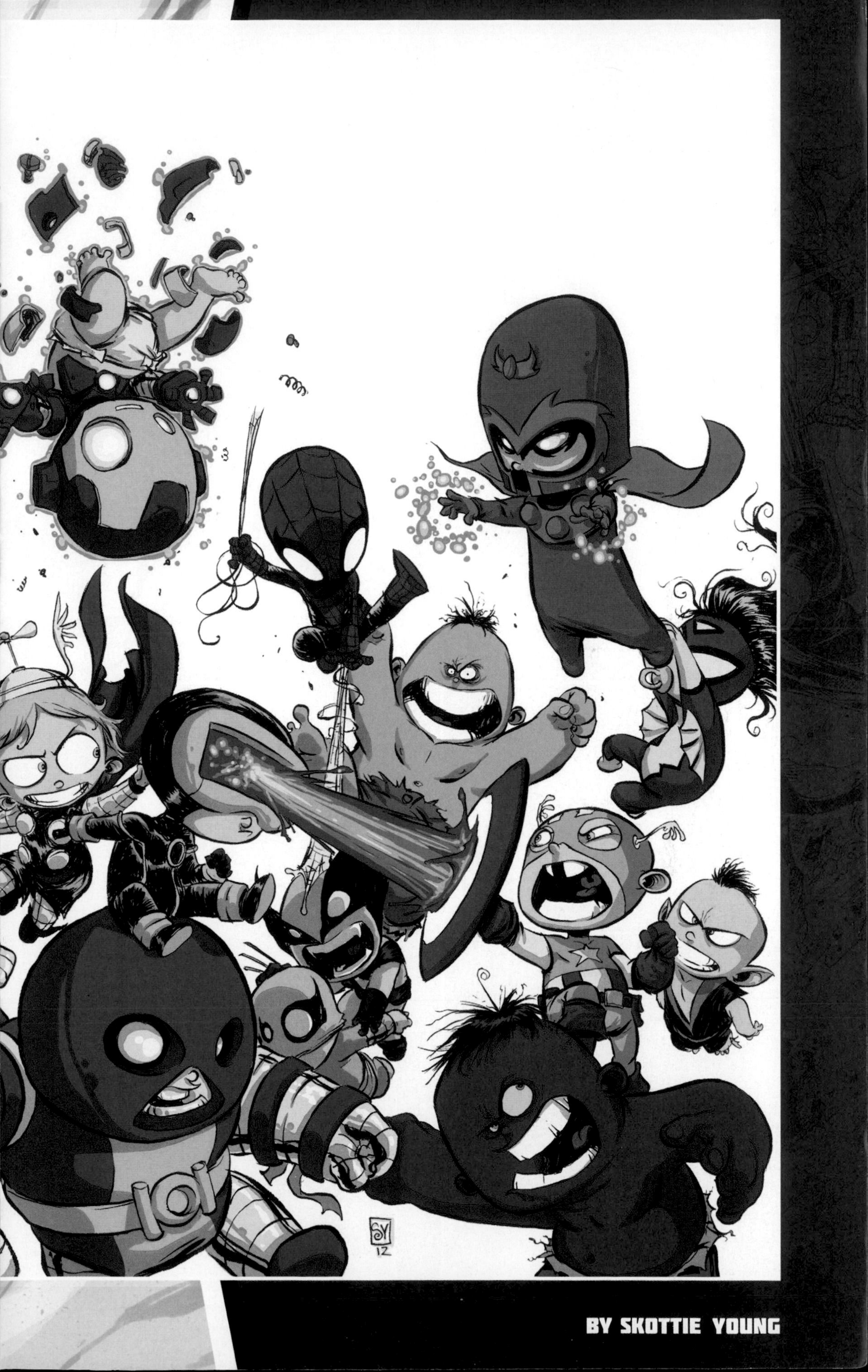

BY SKOTTIE YOUNG

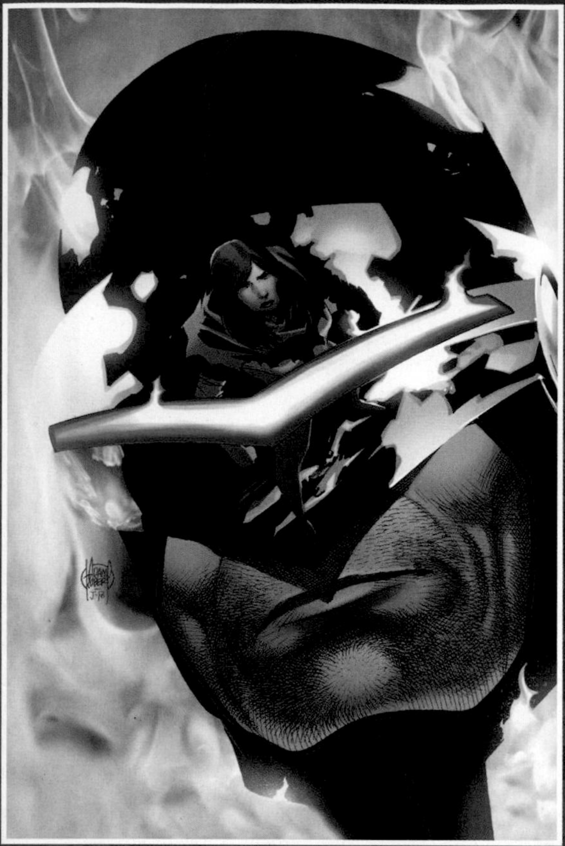

AVX #9 VARIANT
BY **ADAM KUBERT & JUSTIN PONSOR**

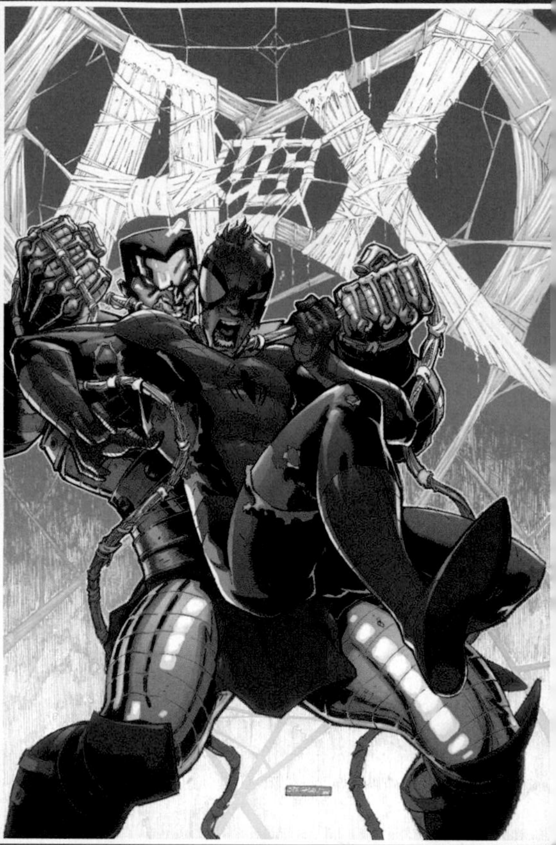

AVX #9 VARIANT
BY **RYAN STEGMAN & MATT WILSON**

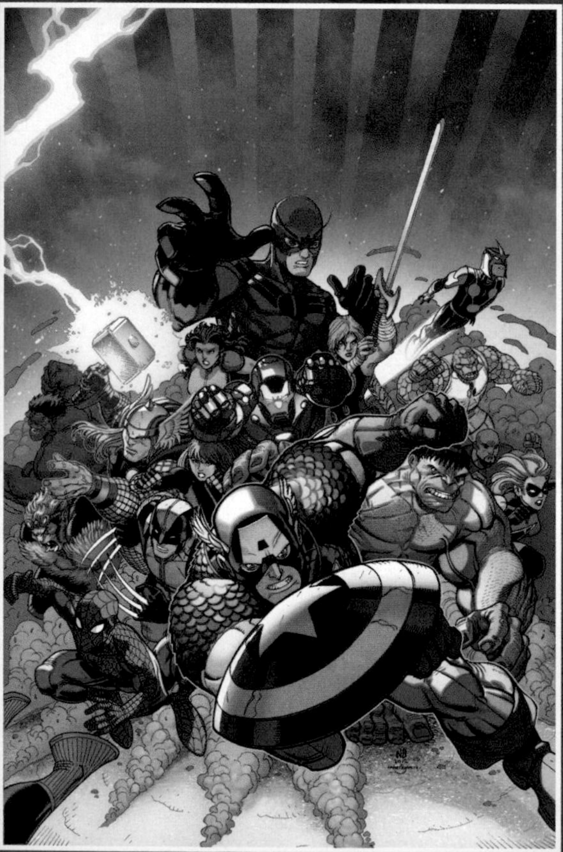

AVX #10 VARIANT
BY **NICK BRADSHAW & MARTE GRACIA**

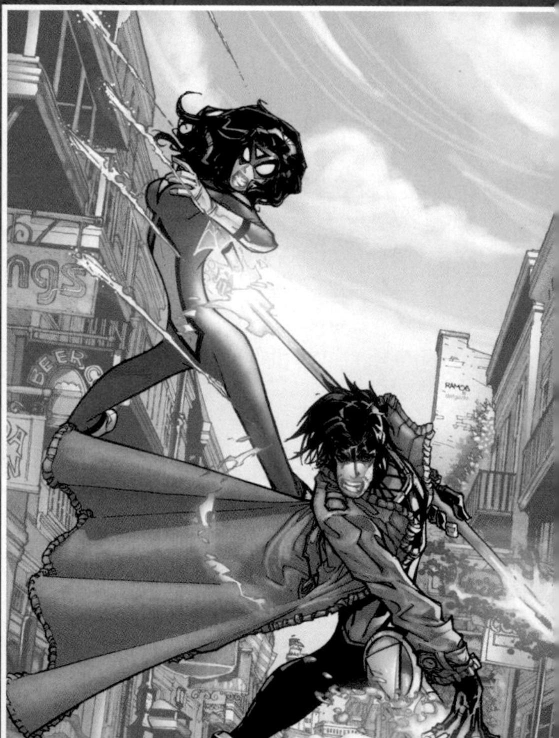

AVX #10 VARIANT
BY **HUMBERTO RAMOS & EDGAR DELGADO**

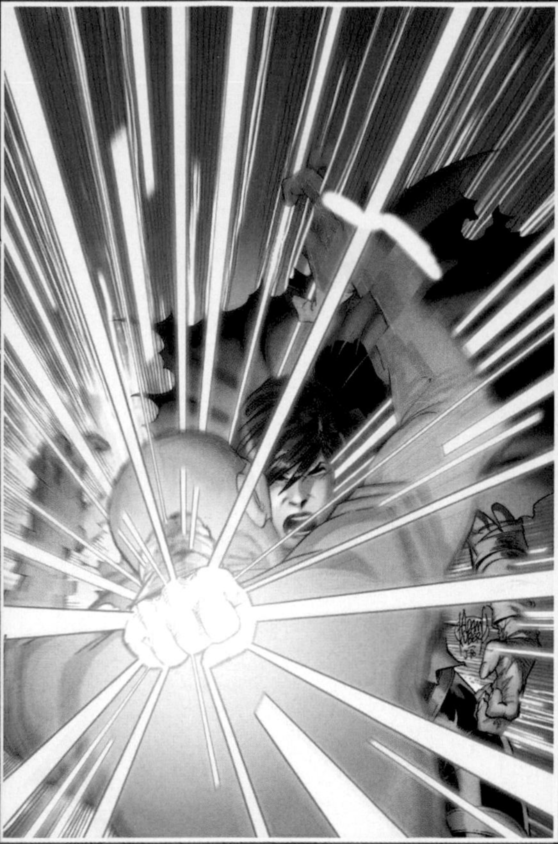

AVX #10 VARIANT
BY ADAM KUBERT & JUSTIN PONSOR

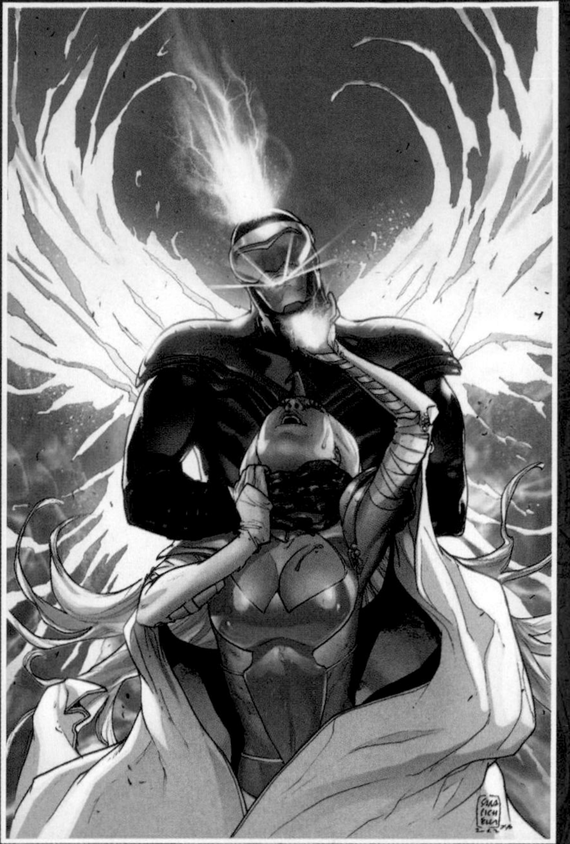

AVX #11 VARIANT
BY SARA PICHELLI & JUSTIN PONSOR

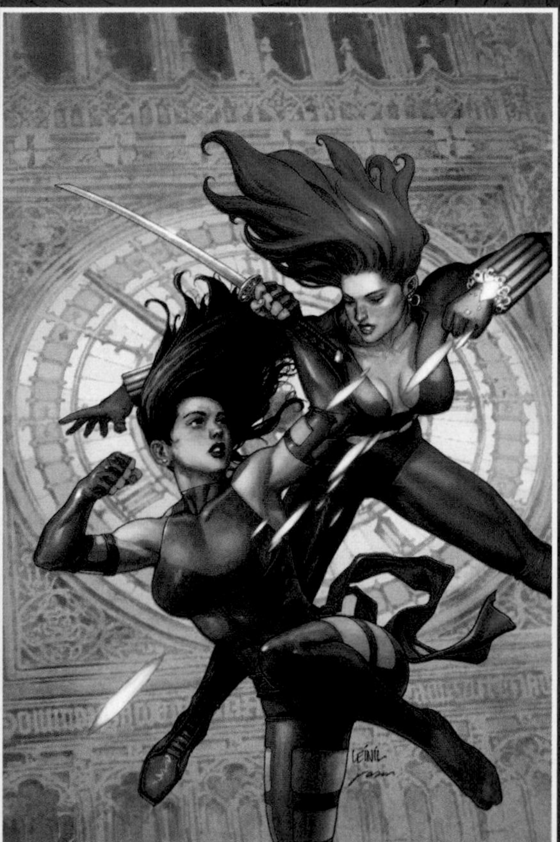

AVX #11 VARIANT
BY LEINIL YU & JASON KEITH

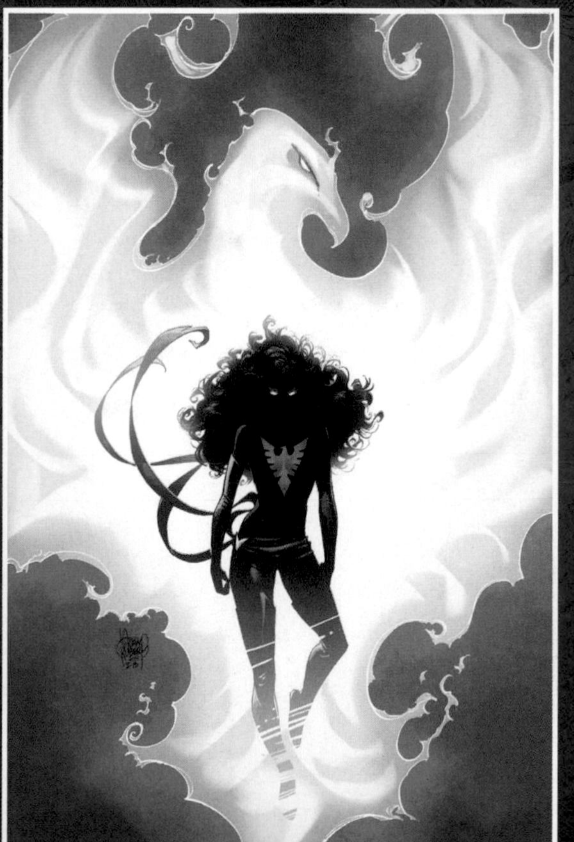

AVX #12 VARIANT
BY ADAM KUBERT & JUSTIN PONSOR

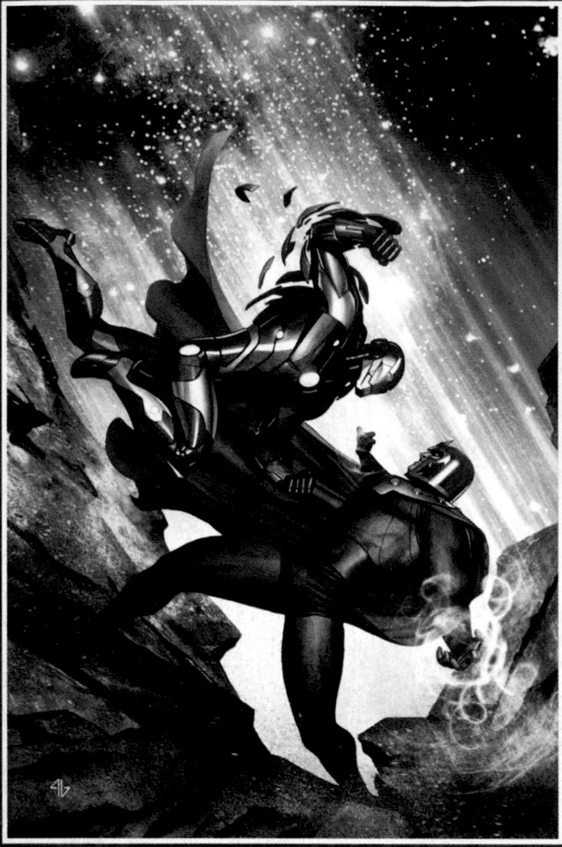

AVX #12 VARIANT
BY **ADI GRANOV**

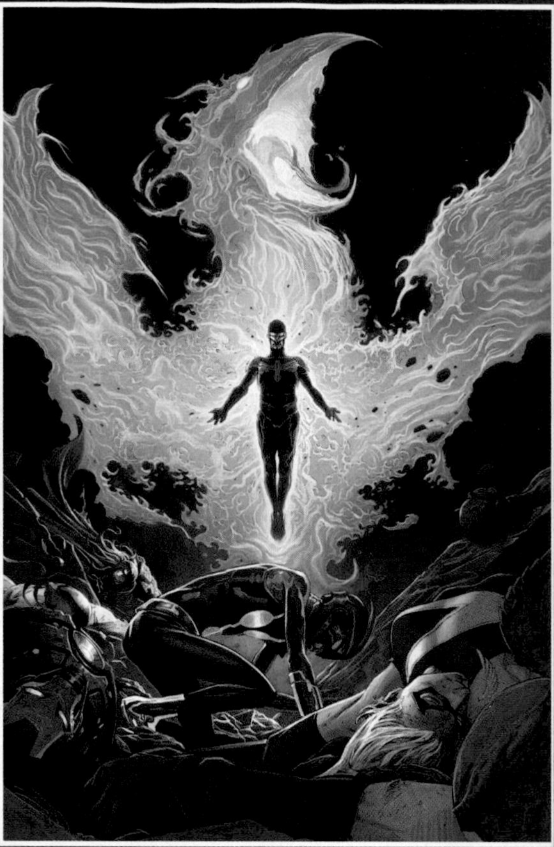

AVX #12 VARIANT
BY **JEROME OPEÑA & DEAN WHITE**

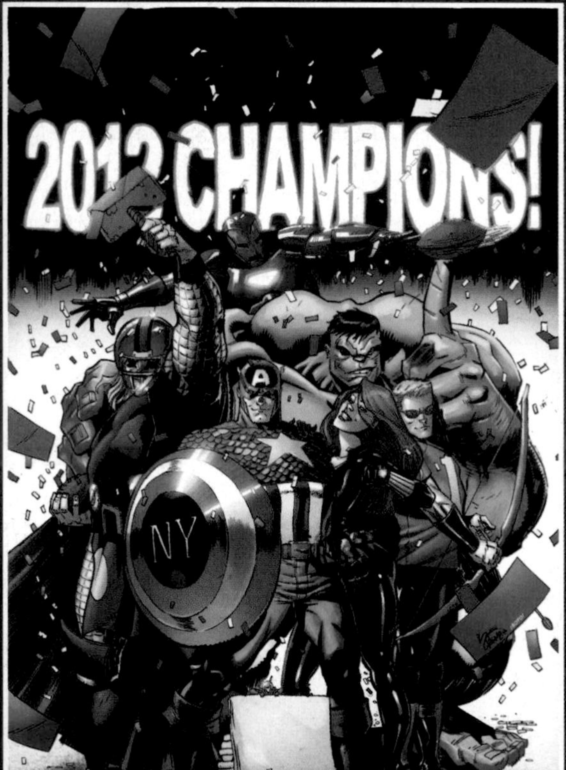
2012 CHAMPIONS!
NY

AVX #12 AVENGERS VARIANT
BY **RYAN STEGMAN & CHRIS SOTOMAYOR**

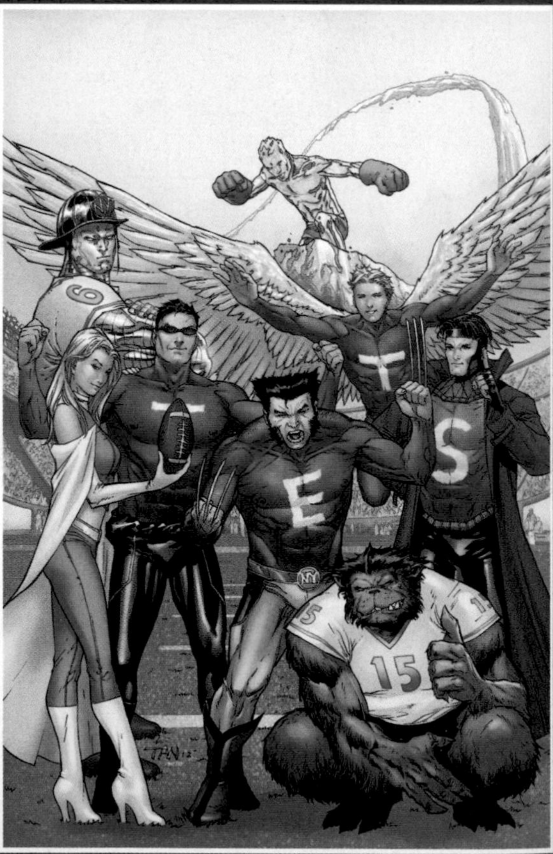

AVX #12 X-MEN VARIANT
BY **BILLY TAN & CHRIS SOTOMAYOR**

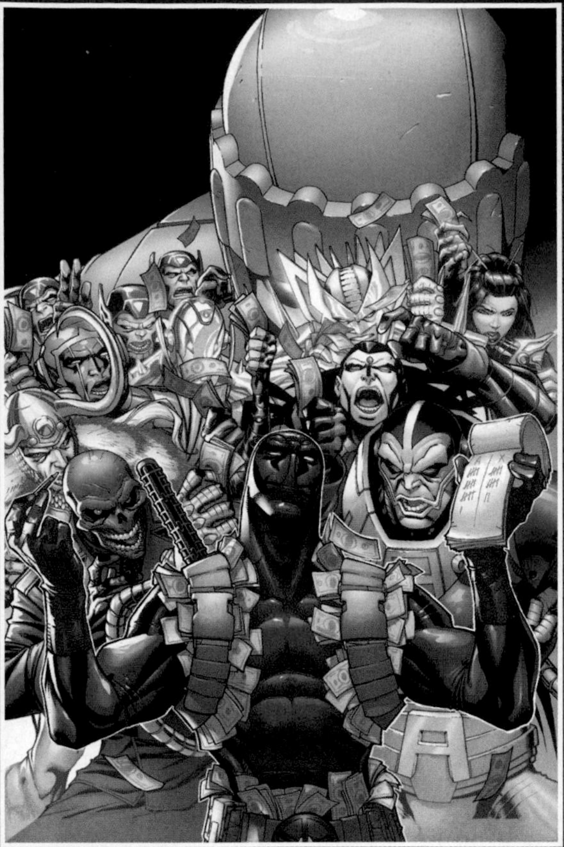

AVX #1 HASTINGS VARIANT
BY CARLO BARBERI & EDGAR DELGADO

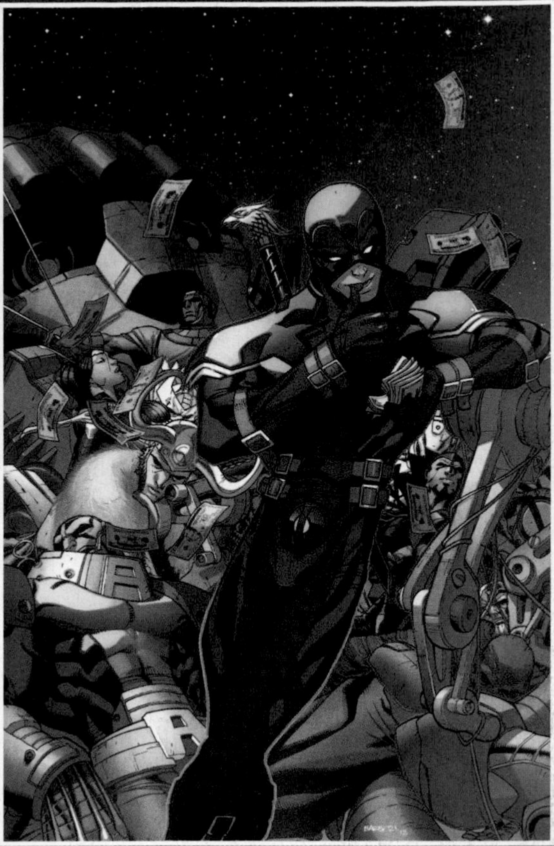

AVX #12 HASTINGS VARIANT
BY CARLO BARBERI & MARTE GRACIA

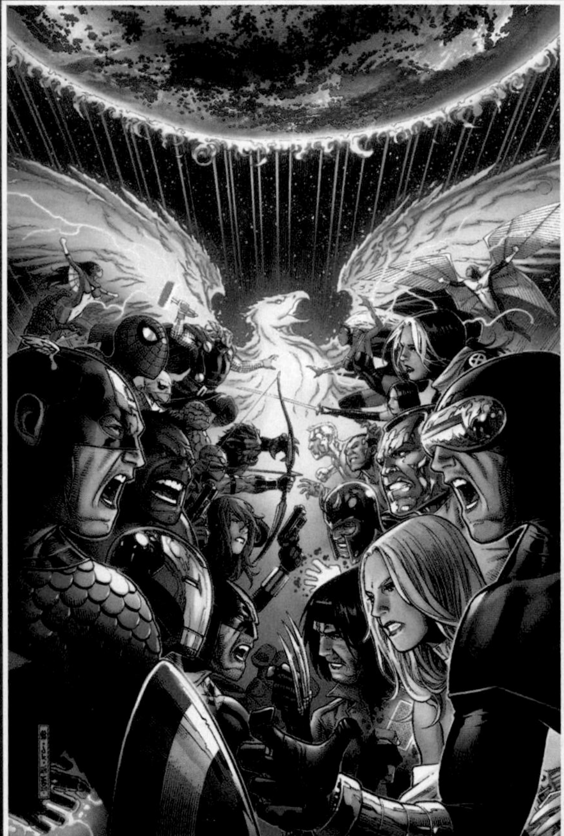

AVX HARDCOVER COVER
BY JIM CHEUNG & JUSTIN PONSOR

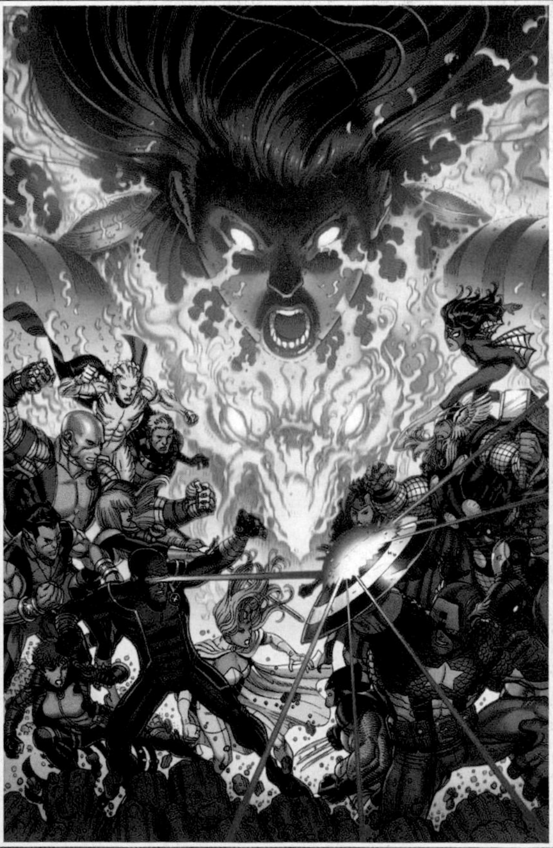

AVX HARDCOVER VARIANT COVER
BY NICK BRADSHAW & JASON KEITH

NOTICE THE AR ICON DURING AVENGERS VS. X-MEN?

THE FREE NEW *MARVEL AUGMENTED REALITY APP* ENHANCES AND CHANGES THE WAY YOU EXPERIENCE COMICS!

To access the Marvel Augmented Reality App...

MARVEL AR

- **Download the app for free via marvel.com/ARapp**
- **Launch the app on your camera-enabled Apple iOS® or Android™ device***
- **Hold your mobile device's camera over any cover or panel with the AR graphic.**
- **Sit back and see the future of comics in action!**

FEATURING:

ACTION-PACKED TRAILERS, VISUAL CHARACTER BIOS, CREATOR VIDEO COMMENTARIES *AND MUCH MORE!*

MARVEL
AR
AUGMENTED REALITY
POWERED BY Aurasma
AR

*Available on most camera-enabled Apple iC
and Android™ devices. Content subject
change and availabil

WHAT ARE YOU WAITING FOR?
GET STARTED NOW!

www.marvel.com/ARapp

MARVEL AR

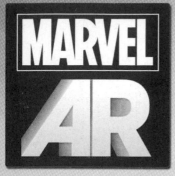

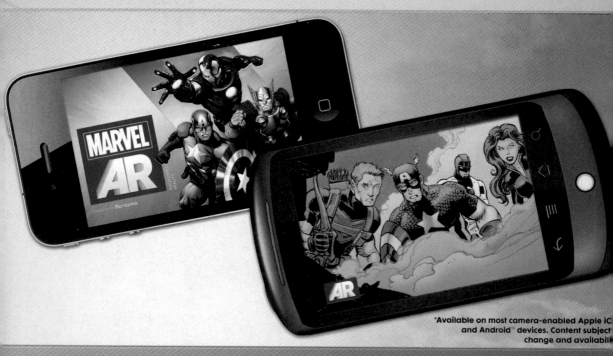

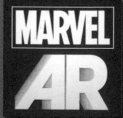